Turkey
Guide

Travel Guides to Planet Earth!

OPEN ROAD TRAVEL GUIDES SHOW YOU
HOW TO BE A TRAVELER – NOT A TOURIST!

Whether you're going abroad or planning a trip in the United States, take Open Road along on your journey. Our books have been praised by **Travel & Leisure, The Los Angeles Times, Newsday, Booklist, US News & World Report, Endless Vacation, American Bookseller, Coast to Coast,** *and many other magazines and newspapers!*

Don't just see the world – experience it with Open Road!

About the Authors

Adam Peck and Manja Sachet first traveled to Turkey in 1992. Since that time, they have lived in, worked in, gotten engaged in, and fallen in love with Turkey. Today, the authors are married and live in Seattle, Washington with their son.

Open Road -
Travel Guides to Planet Earth!

Open Road Publishing has guide books to exciting, fun destinations on four continents. As veteran travelers, our goal is to bring you the best travel guides available anywhere!

No small task, but here's what we offer:

• All Open Road travel guides are written by authors with a distinct, opinionated point of view – not some sterile committee or team of writers. Our authors are experts in the areas covered and are polished writers.

• Our guides are geared to people who want to make their own travel choices. We'll show you how to discover the real destination – not just see some place from a tour bus window.

• We're strong on the basics, but we also provide terrific choices for those looking to get off the beaten path and experience the country or city – not just see it or pass through it.

• We give you the best, but we also tell you about the worst and what to avoid. Nobody should waste their time and money on their hard-earned vacation because of bad or inadequate travel advice.

• Our guides assume nothing. We tell you everything you need to know to have the trip of a lifetime – presented in a fun, literate, nononsense style.

• And, above all, we welcome your input, ideas, and suggestions to help us put out the best travel guides possible.

Turkey
Guide

Travel Guides to Planet Earth!

Adam Peck & Manja Sachet

open road publishing

Open Road Publishing

We offer travel guides to American and foreign locales. Our books tell it like it is, often with an opinionated edge, and our experienced authors always give you all the information you need to have the trip of a lifetime. Write for your free catalog of all our titles.

Open Road Publishing
P.O. Box 284, Cold Spring Harbor, NY 11724
E-mail: Jopenroad@aol.com

3rd Edition

To Willi and Manja Geier, Waldo and Eleanor MacKenzie, and Helen Sachet.

The authors have made every effort to be as accurate as possible, but neither they nor the publisher assume responsibility for the services provided by any business listed in this guide; for any errors or omissions; or any loss, damage, or disruptions in your travels for any reason.

Turkey Guide

contents

15. The Black Sea Coast   387

16. The East   431

17. Eastern Mediterranean Coast   442

Sidebars

Sidebars

Acknowledgments

We recall standing at the Pyramids years ago, a guide book in hand, and feeling adrift without historical context. We were elated to be there, but the guide book did little to put Cheops and Chephren in context, did little to say who the pharoahs were or why the pyramids were built. Open Road books hunt up excellent accommodations, restaurants, and background information as a matter of course; our personal inspiration for writing this book was to give the visitor perspective on the ancient wonders of Turkey and its long journey to becoming a vital modern republic. Credit for our success is shared by many; blame for any shortcomings is certainly ours.

Thanks, first, to Alice Johnson, who made all of this possible. Our publisher Jon Stein has honed our work through three editions. Nalan Yıldız at the Turkish Embassy in Washington D.C., like Sami Orcun before her, proved a great resource, as have the people manning the Tourism Information offices throughout Turkey.

We thank friends and readers for their invaluable insight and assistance. This includes Martha Dale, Richard Mooney, Jim and Lesley Mooney, Steve and Bridget Zaro, Dave Johnson, Alice Johnson, Cara Jacobson, Erin Keown, Kim Bernhardt, Gökhan Karakuş, Funda Çilga, Mehmet Turan, Ayşin and Işik Uman, Alp Berker, Cem Çelebiler, Kevin and Caroline Pedigo, Dominic Sachet, Jenny Peck, Natasha Curry, and Sebastian Peck (for his patience with the flight).

In Turkey, the line between a professional and a personal relationship is, quite sensibly, blurred. This book wouldn't have been possible, or fun, without the assistance of Aydin Guney with Argeus, Ufuk Güven and Phillip Buckley with Bougainvillea Travel, Mustafa and Mutlu Caner with the Mutlu Kaptan, Saim at Imperial Tourism, Mehmet Uçar at Ipek Yolu, Zafer and Selmin Başak at Antik Tiyatro, Nilgun Kaytancı at Nilya, O!nder and Selma Elitez at Turk Ev, and the indestructible Renault Clio.

Once again, thanks to Professor Christian Jeppeson, who, in a single aside, threw light on traveling in Turkey. When a truck began suddenly dumping a ton and a half of gravel at an indiscriminate spot at his archaeological dig site he groaned and rolled his eyes. "Is that bad?" we asked. "Not bad," he said, "Unexpected.")

We hope this book is adequate thanks for the many hotel and restaurant managers, museum directors, fellow travelers, and even traffic cops who have made Turkey such a pleasure for us.

Finally, thanks to our parents Karen, Jim, Heidi, and Paul, and to Katie, Sinan and Sunaliza.

Chapter 1

People who choose to visit Turkey usually have three things in mind: an interest in witnessing firsthand a culture that is unfamiliar, a desire to see one of the great legacies of ruins in the world, and a hope of relaxing along one of the most breathtaking coastlines anywhere.

This guide is dedicated to achieving these aims. We have traveled and lived in Turkey since 1992, sifting through hotels, restaurants, and ruins of Turkey with a single criterion: do we feel lucky to be there? In most of the places we list the answer is an emphatic "yes."

Turkey has accommodation ranging from elite five star resorts to cheap breezeblock hotels, but our emphasis has always been on the increasing number of affordable, lovely pensions and bed and breakfasts. In these pages you have your pick of bungalows in orange groves, rooms carved out of stone, restored Ottoman mansions, and squat, whitewashed houses crouched above the Aegean. Within İstanbul itself you'll find artful, thoughtfully designed accommodations in many price ranges: even in this metropolis you can get a decent double for $14, $2,000, or, more to our liking, $60-$80.

To complement these accommodations, we've picked through the restaurants of Turkey and listed our favorites. Dining here is a great pleasure, whether your taste runs to simple Mediterranean fare or sophisticated dishes devised in the kitchens of the sultans.

With gorgeous little inns and restaurants as an incentive to keep the pace "yavaş, yavaş" (slow, slow), we guide you to the ruins, great and small, popular and remote. Ruins are interesting for their own sake, but we have plumbed myths and history to help you understand who lived here and what these stone ghost towns once were. We understand the temptation to speed through Turkey and visit the marquee ruins, but we firmly advise finding time to stay put awhile. You won't miss anything; to those who are aghast that you didn't see Troy, say, you'll be as aghast that they missed Arycanda, Aphrodisias, the Island of the Amazons, or the view from the deck of your wooden sailing ship. It's our opinion that two extra days at Cappadocia or Üçağız are worth much more than two hours of racing through Pergamon.

This book, the result of thousands of years of research and scholarship, only scratches the surface. On your way to any of the great historic sites mentioned in these pages you can take a left, then a right and find a tomb or a fortress that no one has written about, of which few people even know the name. We've tried to distill the best the country has to offer, but with any luck you'll leave here in respectful disagreement. Turkey is a place to be explored.

Chapter 2

Overview

If you are ever going to visit Turkey, do it now. There are a few heavily-touristed places where the golden age has come and gone (Marmaris, Kuşadası, and Kemer recommend themselves), but the vast majority of the country is a delight. There are several reasons why.

The people: Turkey has a solid standard of living and a relatively robust economy. Turks tend to be cautious around travelers, but only out of politeness. If you smile or, better yet, attempt some small talk in Turkish, most will open up in eagerly. Whether in cities or towns, people tend to be honest, friendly, and hard-working. There is a strong ethic of hospitality, so much so that it can be unsettling to an American or Canadian little used to invitations to dine or visit. Throughout the country, your worst enemy will be your own conditioned wariness.

The sites: The most impressive ruins in ancient Greece aren't in Greece, they're in Turkey, and they're only a small part of the historic wealth scattered throughout the country. Lest you think it unfair that the Turks are in possession of Hellenistic ruins, it's the latest round in territorial tit-for-tat that dates back to prehistory. Consider that in the 10th century B.C. the 'Greeks,' such as they were, seized lands that included the walled Hittite cities in the interior and the legendary site of Troy at the mouth of the Hellespont. The country is an improbable thicket of mountaintop fortresses from the Byzantine and Ottoman empires, of temples and citadels built by peoples and empires of which you've likely never heard. The legacy of the

A Wealth of History

For many, the great appeal of Turkey is its stunning historic legacy. Aristotle taught here. Alexander fought here. Julius Caesar left here saying "Veni, Vidi, Vici." Native sons Homer and Herodotus gave us accounts of the Trojan War and the Persian invasions of Greece. What will amaze you is that all of this post-dates the settlement of Çatal Hüyük by at least 6,000 years. The history of this land is thick, layer upon layer, a sticky, delectable, impossible thing, like a 70-foot tall baklava.

people here is complemented by arresting landscapes, whether the blue-green water of the Mediterranean or the subterranean artistry of Cappadocia.

The alternatives: What is there to do? Cruise the Turkish coast in a twin-masted 60-foot gulet, scale mountainsides to investigate Lycian rock-cut tombs, discover churches carved out of the stone walls of Ihlara Valley, ski at Bolu, go rafting on the Köprüçay or Çoruh, copy out as-yet-undeciphered Lycian carvings, go birding, scuba-dive above sunken amphorae at Kaş, lounge on the fine white sand of Patara beach, pub crawl in Kuşadası, study the evolution of monumental architecture, and visit the living flames of the Chimaera.

The cost: Turkey is inexpensive by American – let alone European – standards. Getting there is not cheap, but once there internal plane flights between any two points in western Turkey cost no more than $80. An overnight bus from the north to the south costs about $25. Many of the finest hotels – even in relatively expensive İstanbul – are in the $80 range, and, as you'd expect, pensions are just a fraction of that.

Food & Drink

Turkish cuisine is a delicious melange. Mediterranean staples such as tomatoes, garlic, onions and olive oil are combined with recipes that Turkish nomads transported west in their migration from the Mongolian steppe.

There is a vitality and richness to good Turkish cooking that betrays its long history, and its long migration. You're likely to recognize traces of Indian, Greek, and even Chinese cuisine in the meals set forth before you. Successive empires and kingdoms have done away with the expendable and adopted the best of what had gone before; the result is a hybrid cuisine that is rich and impressive.

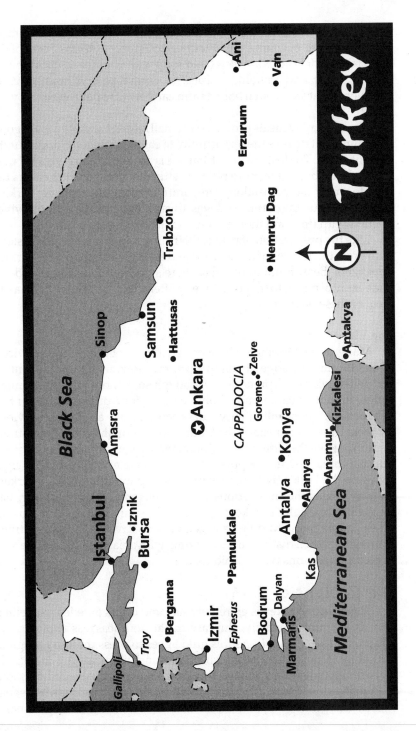

A few of the staples of a Turkish kitchen that you will almost certainly try are, of course, the *köfte* (meatballs) and *şiş kebaps*. Some of the more refined delicacies are *cacık* (cold soup with yogurt and cucumbers), *mantı* (yogurt and ravioli), *su börek* (a cheese pastry), and *güveç* (a succulent meat stew, often boiled in an earthenware pot and sealed with bread).

The workaday meals produced in small *kebapcis* and *köftecis* are good and filling, but do take the opportunity to eat well when the opportunity presents itself. The test of Turkish cuisine is not in the "hazır yemek" (fast food) places, but in the more refined settings where the kitchen has the time to make the painstaking preparation necessary for true Turkish cuisine. The cuisine of this land was always the preserve of housewives or chefs with time and money to spend; it remains so.

Like the preparation of meals, their consumption is best taken slow, with great thick slices of fresh bread and an emphasis on *meze* – Turkish appetizers. Bear in mind, too, that there's no need to rush beyond the wide array of mezes to the entree; we're often quite satisfied to make a full meal of these delicious appetizers.

The Vices

Many of the Ottoman elite were great fans of a few familiar vices, often blunting the edge of Koranic proscriptions with rather inventive and self-serving interpretations. Although some holy men condemned coffee, opium, tobacco and alcohol as the "four pillars of the tent of debauchery," most enlightened Turks chose to take an alternative view; for them these were instead the "four cushions on the sofa of pleasure."

Fitting that the latter view is dominant in Islam's model secular state. Turkish coffee remains popular and is available everywhere, and cigarettes are the Turk's signature vice. Opium's popularity (within Turkey, anyway) has gone into serious decline, but *rakı*, a late bloomer, has stepped in manfully to take its place. Rakı, similar to Greek ouzo and other liquors in the Middle East, is a licorice-flavored alcohol distilled from raisins, then distilled a second time with aniseed. In short, the sofa of pleasure remains well-cushioned.

The Regions of Turkey

The bulk of Turkey is extremely safe and offers excellent traveling. That is not, unfortunately, the case in the southeast, as explained in Chapter 4, *Land & People*. As this guide goes to press there is no sign of cessation of hostilities in the southeast and we echo the U.S. State Department's warning against traveling in a region plagued by more than a decade of bloody fighting between the Turks and Kurdish separatists. This guide covers the entire Turkish coast—the Black, Marmara,

Aegean, and Mediterranean seas—and the interior as far as Cappadocia. We offer a blueprint for travel further into the eastern and southeastern interior.

You'll find that this guide is arranged by regions. We start with the premise that you'll want to settle in for a few days at a time in various areas of the country, and we detail a route through the interior to Ankara and Cappadocia, which joins a loop clockwise around the Mediterranean and Aegean coastlines to Troy. The Black Sea is covered from west to east, leaving you the options of a Black Sea ferry, plane, or bus back toward İstanbul, and even an extended trip into the interior.

İstanbul

Turkey begins with İstanbul, a jarring and beautiful city where you're likely to disembark. İstanbul is epic, an historic place straddling Asia and Europe, Islam and Christianity, past and present. Reminders of Byzantine and Ottoman Empires that ruled here abound, mixed liberally with a brash, vital, seething city of 12 million. You can lose yourself in the warrens of the spice bazaar, take ferry cruises along the Bosphorous, see jazz shows in Taksim 'til dawn, hunt up carpets, kilims and beautiful old maps and prints; all of that, and never even enter the magnificent museums, palaces, and mosques that have given the city its renown.

İstanbul is unmanageably large, with the irritating habit of wandering off the edge of your map. Fortunately, visitors can concentrate on familiarizing themselves with a few fascinating areas such as **Sultanahmet** and **İstiklal Caddesi.**

The Interior

The interior of Turkey is home to the oldest traces of civilization (**Çatal Hüyük** near Konya, dating to 7,500 B.C.) the first civilization for which there are records (the **Hittites,** dating to ~2,000 B.C.-~1,270 B.C.), the home of young Abraham (**Harran,** 1921 B.C.), and much, much more. These sites, and others in the interior such as **Gordion** (the home of King Midas, 800 B.C.), are mute testimony to surprisingly sophisticated cultures that thrived near the headwaters of the Euphrates in those dim years before Western Civ lessons begin. Another of Turkey's most compelling places is **Cappadocia,** a plain of soft, undulating stone that conceals rock-cut churches, houses, and dozens of entire cities carved as deep as seven stories beneath the Earth.

The interior is served by **Ankara,** Turkey's capital. This is a surprisingly pretty city on the Anatolian Plateau, convenient to the oldest ruins in Turkey and an historic city in its own right. The city's fortress lends it a picturesque quality, while shrewd urban planning renders the town one of Turkey's most appealing. Other cities include the cluster at

Cappadocia, including **Ürgüp** and **Göreme**, and **Konya**, home of the whirling dervishes. Distances are long, but bus service is fairly comprehensive between most points, and roads are decent.

The Coast

The Turkish coast is immense, wrapping almost entirely around the country and including four different seas: the Black, the Marmara, the Aegean, and the Mediterranean. You will find Hellenistic ruins at even the most remote locations along this huge coastline, but the character of the ruins and towns varies widely (see *Planning Your Trip* chapter).

The Mediterranean

The **Mediterranean Coast** east of Antalya is interesting, but less alluring than the region from Antalya west. **Antalya**, roughly midway along the southern coast, has a top-notch cluster of appealing hotels and pensions and serves as a base for visits to several of Turkey's great Hellenistic ruins. A batch of holiday villages is located just west of Antalya, but beyond them the coast relaxes into a set of quieter, more beautiful coastal towns. This region, the **Lycian Coast**, is famed for its forbidding mountains and beautiful valleys, for its lovely beaches and picturesque ruins – such as those at **Olympos** and **Arycanda**. Most two week itineraries skip around this section of coast, opting to slip inland between Antalya and Ephesus; you might want to consider, instead, spending two weeks at the beaches, towns and ancient cities between **Antalya** and **Fethiye**.

The coast retains its remote character until **Marmaris**, although the Dalaman airport has led to the establishment of several large hotels at the western end of the Lycian coast. **Dalyan**, a city that hugs a beautiful, winding river below ancient **Caunos**, is of particular note.

The Aegean

The Mediterranean and **Aegean** meet at the tip of the Cnidos peninsula. Marmaris, the successor to the ancient city of Cnidos in the region and the southeastern-most city on the Aegean, is good to avoid; it is the worst sort of hyper-touristed beach town, a grimier, less-affluent version of Fort Lauderdale. The ruins of **Cnidos** far to the west are worth a visit, but quite inconvenient, requiring that you negotiate the harrowing mountain road between Marmaris and Datça. The road between Marmaris and Bodrum winds up to Muğla in the interior before continuing back down to the coast.

The steep, difficult coastline has proved an ideal setting for gulets, the two-masted wooden craft that ply these waters from April to October. Gulets can be booked for a week at a time out of several marinas, primarily those at Antalya, Fethiye, Marmaris, and Bodrum (where most of the ships are built). **Bodrum** is the next major city as you continue north, and is eminently preferable to Marmaris. Not only is the city on the site of one of the Seven Wonders of the World, it boasts the glorious Fortress of St. Peter, now an excellent museum, has excellent accomodations, and is quite near the recently completed Güllük International Airport.

The most famed of Turkey's ruins is **Ephesus**, further up the coast near Kuşadası. This was the second city of the Roman Empire, populated by an estimated 250,000 people, and the scale and grandeur of the city is almost shocking. There are good accommodations nearby, and Ephesus is just one of many fascinating ruins in the area. **Priene** and the tumbled **Oracle at Didyma** to the south are both compelling, as are **Pamukkale** and **Aphrodisias** inland, two of Turkey's most attractive sites.

Continuing north, Turkey's own second city, **İzmir**, stands on the site of the former **Smyrna**. İzmir has a pretty setting, but it has little place on a traveler's itinerary unless that itinerary involves business or transportation onward by train or airplane; the history of İzmir is fascinating, but little remains of its former glories. If you must stay nearby, better to settle in **Selçuk**, near Ephesus, or inland near **Sardis**, capital of Lydia and home to King Croesus in the sixth century B.C.

• The E-87 highway bears northeast through low rolling hills toward **Pergamon** and **Troy,** at various times the greatest cities in the northern Aegean, although the former, of which few have ever heard, is much more dramatic than the latter, of which we all have heard. Pergamon rose to great heights in the centuries before Christ, then atrophied during the late Roman period. Troy's fame, of course, derives from *The Iliad* of Homer. The jumble of ruins at Troy, however unremarkable it may now appear, is a worthy stop for anyone who has read the adventures of Hector, Achilles, and Odysseus. Not far south of Troy is **Assos**, once home to Aristotle, and now the site of an excellent set of waterfront pensions and hotels.

Troy stands at the mouth of the Dardanelle Straits, issuing forth from the **Sea of Marmara**. The **Gallipolli battlefields** are located across the straits to the north, connected to Thrace by a thin peninsula. The industrial city of Bandirma, on the southern shore of the Marmara, is at the railhead for İzmir and has ferry service direct to İstanbul.

Another of Turkey's great population centers, **Bursa**, is to the southeast, an hour inland of the Marmara coast. Bursa was one of the first Ottoman capitals, in the years when the former Byzantine hatchetmen began to emerge onto the global scene. Bursa still preserves touches of its Ottoman past in several excellent mosques and burial sites of early sultans. The city is also blessed with the curative geothermal waters welling up from the foothills of **Mt. Olympos**, atop which you will find **Uludağ** ski area.

The Black Sea

Just 18 kilometers northeast of İstanbul the Bosphorous opens into the Black Sea, the ancient Euxine Propontis. So-called because of its dark water and notorious storms, the Black Sea is not a staple of travel itineraries, and perhaps the better for it. Pensions and hotels are still available, of course, but the Black Sea coast is quieter, greener, and less well-traveled than the rest of the Turkish coast. The roads are good along the coast as far as Amasra, and the major bus lines resume service from Samsun eastward, many of them terminating at Trabzon.

Along the way, you find beautiful beaches, including those at **Amasra** and **Ünye**, strange, impressive ruins, and even an island that has

Do You Take Your Turkey with Disco?

If you're looking for a wild time, most large coastal towns have their share of large hotels and throbbing nightlife – but **Marmaris** on the Aegean coast must be considered (after İstanbul) the capital. Marmaris is packed with tourists in search of a good, loud time all day and night, a six-month long Spring Break Holiday for German, Russian and British tourists. The hotels of **Kemer** on the Mediterranean coast near Antalya also take their fun loud and aggressive, as, in truth, do many large hotels throughout the country. **Bodrum**, a city of which we're fond, strikes a careful balance with some famously loud nightspots and excellent little jazz bars, all of which are complemented by an excellent museum at the Castle of St. Peter and some pleasant, quiet accommodations.

If you're looking for a quieter time, you have the run of the country. **Olympos**, **Kekova/Üçağız**, and **Gelemiş/Patara** on the Lycian coast are especially fine, sedate spots in gorgeous settings. The Black Sea is home to several quiet spots such as **Ünye** and **Amasra**, and many small towns along the Aegean offer calm and coastal beauty. Good choices here include **Bozcaada Island** and some of the towns on the **Bodrum peninsula**. Small towns and cities throughout the interior are, as you might expect, quiet, probably more quiet than you want. Even the popular towns in the Cappadocia region are quite peaceful.

at various times been inhabited by **Amazons** and monks, now a free camping site just off the coast at Giresun.

Trabzon, once the capital of the Kingdom of Trebizond, is still decorated with the fallen walls of its palaces and several old churches and mosques. Inland of Trabzon, and in the interior stretching toward the Georgian and Iranian borders, are monasteries (such as the famous **Sumela Monastery**) and alpine meadows where travelers often choose to backpack or let the Çoruh River carry them by whitewater raft down toward the Black Sea.

Chapter 3

Even if you have two months, you don't have time to see everything in Turkey. It's a big country, rich with ruins and history—you need to decide what matters to you most. Below is a summary of conventional wisdom about itineraries, as well as our own opinions about what to see and how to see it.

In general, we suggest that you pick a spot and stay there for a little while. This isn't something you need a car to do (although it helps). Trust us: you can see just as many astounding things if you stay in one place for four days as you can by moving to a new hotel every night. It's a better way to become acquainted with the people who live in Turkey, and, besides, it's much more relaxing.

Of course, you don't want four days everywhere. Some towns are useful, not charming—these are suited for one night—Aphrodisias, Pamukkale, Hattuşas, Bursa, Konya, Izmir—you get the idea. Weave this pattern of "four day" destinations and overnight stops together, and you're on the way to a good itinerary.

We recommend the following locations on the quality of their accommodations and the number of incredible ruins, beaches, or natural wonders nearby.

Places to Spend Four Days

Your destination should depend on your interests, but, when asked, we recommend three days in İstanbul, three or four days in Cappadocia, and between four and seven days on a Blue Cruise along the western Mediterranean or southern Aegean coast.

İstanbul is a fixture of any trip to Turkey. Chances are you're flying and out of İstanbul, anyway, so take the opportunity to see the Byzantine-era Hagia Sophia, the Ottoman Topkapı Palace, the mosques, museums, bazaars, and stunning Bosphorus Strait that made this a more enduring Imperial capital than Rome.

Cappadocia, a region of central Anatolia, is renowned for the troglodytic dwellings of its inhabitants. The curving, heavily eroded landscape disguises an underground world of rock cut churches, monasteries and entire cities sunk hundreds of feet into the earth.

There's so much to do here, and it's such a relaxing place to be, that it may well absorb any slack in your travel plans.

Blue Cruises employ gulets (broad, single-masted wooden vessels once used for cargo) to explore the turquoise waters off the Turkish coast. You can charter a boat (including the captain and meals), or simply book a cabin—either way, you spend between four and seven days swimming, eating well, lounging on deck, sleeping on deck, and calling at picturesque coves and visiting the ruins that pepper the coast. This the finest way to see the coast, and it's surprisingly inexpensive.

Blue Cruise voyages depart from most marinas between Bodrum in the northwest and Antalya in the southeast.

Beyond that, we're not too bossy—here are some thoughts:

- One can make a strong argument that two or three days in **Selcuk** should be on your itinerary, for the sake of Ephesus, Priene, Didyma, and other ruins near Selcuk. You can even use Selcuk as your base for visiting Aphrodisias and/or Pamukkale—you'll find inexpensive daily tours from Selcuk throughout the summer, both guided and unguided.
- **Dalyan** is a slender wisp of a town along a river, just three miles upstream of Iztuzu Beach on the Mediterranean. The main avenue in town is Dalyan River itself, and you'll be ferried back and forth to the gorgeous sand beach at Iztuzu, the ruins at Caunos towering above town, and the hot springs and mud baths that percolate out of the earth.
- **Çiralı/Olympos** boasts a formidable combination: ruins, calm, a flaming geological puzzle, and miles of coarse sand beach. The picturesque ruins are those of Olympos, an ancient port town that climbs up into the valley behind the beach. A few kilometers away, the inextinguishable flames of the Chimera burn as they've burned for thousands of years. You can take this area in two flavors—the relaxed pace of hotels at Çiralı, or the cheap, rumbustious, sage-peddling mecca of Olympos.
- **Kalkan** is a beautiful little whitewashed fishing town perched above a small harbor on the Mediterranean. The town is convenient to ruined

Lycian cities of Xanthos, Letoon, Pınara and Tlos. It is, too, one-half hour from the endless white sand beach of Patara to the west or Kaş, the local hub of scuba diving, sailing, sea kayaking and dining (ah, Chez Evy), to the east.

• **Behramkale** is an escape, a tiny village built up around the ruins of Assos. A few beautiful stone houses on the hillside overlooking the Aegean have been converted into small hotels; they offer the opportunity you always wanted to eat well, walk ancient paths, read Aristotle (he once lived here), and breathe air that is famously good. The ruins of Troy are 1.5 hours north, you'll find beaches just to the east, and the waterfront far below is one of the best places in Turkey to enjoy mezes and rakı. It has a pleasantly soporific effect.

Transportation

While you're deciding how to get from place to place, consider all of the options. Rental cars are relatively expensive in Turkey, but they are a wonderful asset if you're interested in quick, easy access to ruins and beaches. A rental car can be used in concert with flights within the country. These flights are relatively inexpensive, and they're a good idea if you're short on time and covering large distances: direct flights to and from İstanbul and Ankara aren't difficult to arrange, but other flights, for instance from Antalya to Bodrum's Güllük Airport, are still uncommon. Check schedules online at Turkish Airlines' website, *www.turkishairlines.com*.

Meanwhile, another transportation option remains popular for both Turks and foreigners: bus travel. Buses are very good—far better than travelers from North America will be accustomed to—and they are inexpensive. It helps that western Turkey is magically arranged to have the diameter of an overnight bus ride. From any city on one side of the map to any city on the far side your ride is about 12 hours.

A fourth, often overlooked option is the train, which has a reputation for being slow and uncomfortable. The reputation is richly deserved, but there are exceptions; consider the slightly expensive sleeper trains between İstanbul and Pamukkale and between İstanbul and Ankara

İstanbul Itineraries

İstanbul has a lot to offer, a staggering array of things to do and see. Here are some suggested itineraries for vacations of between three days and one week. If you have longer, don't worry; you'll never run out of things to see.

These itineraries begin on the morning after you arrive.

THREE DAYS IN İSTANBUL

These agendas assume you're moving fast and not suffering unduly from jet lag. Most people can't (not to mention don't want to) see so much so fast. For that reason we recommend not adhering strictly to these agendas; when the mood strikes, buy a Herald Tribune and settle into a nice cafe or take a nap at the hotel. We get you through the day, but we leave dinner plans up to you: consult the *Where to Eat* section of our İstanbul chapter for further information.

Day 1 – Sultanahmet

Tour Topkapı Palace

Lunch at Konyalı restaurant on the grounds of Topkapı Palace (expensive, convenient), or the garden restaurant at Yeşil Ev just beyond the Hagia Sophia (expensive, good food), or Sultanahmet Koftecesi (along the tram tracks just uphill from the Hagia Sophia, inexpensive)

Visit the Hagia Sophia

Visit the Baths of Haseki Hürrem directly across from the Hagia Sophia, now a government carpet/kilim shop with fair, standard prices that give you a good idea what you should spend if you plan to make any purchases. You may even find what you're looking for here. (Unsolicited advice: sleep on it.)

Stroll along the Hippodrome

Visit the Islamic Art Museum

Coffee at the Islamic Art Museum

See the Blue Mosque

Visit the Mosaic Museum, behind the Blue Mosque

Return to the hotel, then dinner

Day 2 – Greater Sultanahmet

Follow Divan Yolu up to the entrance of the Grand Bazaar

Work your way along the upper side of the Bazaar to the Süleymaniye Mosque (helpful phrase: "Affedersiniz, Süleymaniye Camisi nerede?" - "Excuse me, where is the Süleymaniye Mosque?"). Grab a bite at Darüzziyafe across the street in the mosque complex if you're hungry (moderate)

Wind your way down towards the Spice Bazaar

Lunch at Pandeli in the Spice Bazaar (moderate-expensive), or pide or kebap on the street (inexpensive)

Visit the Yeni Cami, just outside the lower doors of the Spice Bazaar, then follow the course of the rail tracks back up past the Sirkeci railway station into Sultanahmet

Visit the Archaeological Museum complex on the Topkapı grounds, just inside the gate from Gülhane train stop. Tea or coffee at the Archaelogical Museum

Visit the Basilica Cistern
Return to the hotel, then dinner

Day 3 – The Bosphorous

Late start down to Eminönü for a regular Bosphorous ferry (10:35 and 13:35 departures)

Enjoy the cruise up the Bosphorous to Anadolu Kavağı

At Anadolu Kavağı visit the fortress and have lunch at the waterfront. Upon departure from Anadolu Kavağı (check schedule), the ferry crosses to Sariyer and continues down the strait; you can either cruise back to Eminönü or disembark at Sariyer, back on the European side.

At Sariyer visit the Sadberk Hanım museum.

Return down the Bosphorous by taxi (or by a public bus that lists "Rumeli Hisar") as far as Rumeli Hisar and visit the Ottoman fortress there.

Head down to Ortaköy for the afternoon, get coffee, relax, maybe look at some carpets and kilims

Consider having dinner at Körfez or at Sunset Marina

SEVEN DAYS IN İSTANBUL

Day 1 – Sultanahmet

Tour Topkapı Palace

Lunch at Topkapı's Konyalı restaurant (expensive, convenient), or the garden restaurant at Yeşil Ev just beyond the Hagia Sophia (expensive, better atmosphere and food), or Sultanahmet Koftecesi (along the tram tracks just uphill from the Hagia Sophia, inexpensive)

Stroll along the Hippodrome

Visit the Islamic Art Museum; Coffee at the museum

Visit the Blue Mosque

Visit the Mosaic Museum

Return to the hotel, then dinner

Day 2 – Greater Sultanahmet

Follow Divan Yolu up to the entrance of the Grand Bazaar

Work your way along the upper side of the Bazaar to the Süleymaniye Mosque. Grab a bite at Darüzziyafe across the street in the mosque complex if you're hungry (moderate)

Wind your way down towads the Spice Bazaar

Lunch at Pandeli in the Spice Bazaar (moderate-expensive), or pide or kebap on the street (inexpenive)

Visit the Yeni Cami, just outside the doors at the bottom of the Spice Market, then follow the course of the rail tracks back up past the Sirkeci railway station into Sultanahmet

Visit the Hagia Sophia
Visit the Basilica Cistern
Visit the Baths of Haseki Hürrem directly across from the Hagia Sophia, now a government carpet shop with fair prices that give you a good idea what you should spend if you plan to make any purchases.
Return to the hotel, then dinner.

Day 3 – The Bosphorous

Early start down to Eminönü for a Bosphorous ferry
Cruise the Bosphorous to either Sariyer or Anadolu Kavağı
At Anadolu Kavağı visit the fortress and have lunch at the waterfront. Upon departure from Anadolu Kavağı (check schedule), the ferry crosses to Sariyer and continues down the strait; you can either cruise back to Eminönü or disembark at Sariyer, back on the European side.
At Sariyer visit the Sadberk Hanım museum
Return down the Bosphorous by taxi (or by a public bus that lists "Rumeli Hisar") as far as Rumeli Hisar and visit the Ottoman fortress there.
Consider having dinner at Körfez or at Sunset Marina

Day 4 – The Land Walls (see "Along the Theodosian Land Walls")

Cab or train to Yedikule
Visit Yedikule, then walk along the outside of the walls to Silivri Kapı and turn Balıklı Church
Cab or dolmuş north along walls to the Church of Chora (Kariye Cami) inside Edirne Kapı
Visit the Church of Chora
Lunch nearby at Kariye Hotel's Asitane Restaurant
Taxi to Eyüp Cami
Stroll uphill through the cemetery to Pierre Loti's Cafe for coffee
Taxi, bus, or a long walk back to Sultanahmet via Eminönü
Return to the hotel, then dinner

Day 5 – İstiklal Caddesi

Walk across the Galata Bridge, take Tünel train to Galata
Stop in at Galata Tower, enjoy the view and have a cup of coffee
Stroll along İstiklal Caddesi, checking in at the bookstores and antique shops at the lower end of the street
Lunch at one of the many cafes and familiar fast food places along İstiklal
From Taksim Circle, taxi to the Askeri Müze (Military Museum)
Visit the upscale shops just beyond the Military Museum in the fashionable Nişantaşı district

Return to Taksim, return down İstiklal Caddesi
Dinner in the İstiklal area.

Day 6 – The Museums

Get a big breakfast and walk up to the Archaeological Museum Complex on the Topkapı grounds

Visit the Museum of the Ancient Orient, the Archaeological Museum and the Çinli Kösk.

Get lunch at one of the small gözleme and döner restaurants in Gülhane Park, just below the Archaelogical Museum complex, or return to Divan Yolu Caddesi and dine at Rumeli Cafe (moderate) or Sultanahmet Köftecesi (inexpensive).

Stroll through Gülhane Park, which continues out to the tip of the peninsula and the Column of the Goths. This area is rarely visited by tourists, and is a retreat for young Turkish couples and families

Return to the hotel, then dinner.

Day 7 – The Lower Bosphorous

Arrive early at Dolmabahçe Palace for a morning visit

Have coffee outside the Dolmabahçe Seraglio (harem)

Continue up the Bosphorous on foot to Beşiktaş for a visit at the Deniz Müzesi (Naval Museum) on the Beşiktaş waterfront

Walk up the Bosphorous, turning in at the Çirağan Palace for a walk along the palace grounds. Stop in at the patio bar for a drink

Continue walking to Ortaköy for an afternoon of shopping for evil eye bracelets, kilims, and sitting in a waterfront cafe writing postcards

Return to the hotel, then dinner

Historically Themed Sightseeing

Below we've grouped sights together by historical period.

Ottoman History
İstanbul
Bursa
Nicaea (İznik)
Konya

Ancient Anatolia
Cappadocia
Hattuşas
Nemrut Dağ
Troy

Ancient Greece
  Termessos
  Arykanda
  Olympos
  Dalyan (Caunos)
  Bodrum (Halicarnassus)
  Didyma/Priene/Miletus
  Ephesus
  Aphrodisias
  Bergama (Pergamon)

The Trail of Alexander
  Troy
  Assos (home of Alexander's tutor)
  Pergamon (home of Alexander's general)
  Sardis
  Ephesus (Resting place of the Virgin Mary)
  Miletus/Priene
  Bodrum

Christianity
  Cappadocia
  Ephesus
  İstanbul's Hagia Sophia and Church of the Chora
  Trabzon
  Antakya (Antioch)
  Bodrum (Castle of St. Peter/Knights of St. John)

l a n d & p e o p l e

Chapter 4

Land

Turkey straddles Europe and Asia, with İstanbul and a small section of the country jutting into Europe. The bulk of the country is in Asia, a giant rectangular peninsula that emerges from the east: Turkey has a convenient resemblance to your right hand, palm in, with İstanbul near the tip of your index finger. This "peninsula" is bounded by four separate seas: the **Black Sea** in the north, the small **Sea of Marmara** between the Bosphorous and Dardanelle straits, the **Aegean** in the west, and the **Mediterranean** in the south. All told Turkey is 780,500 square kilometers, larger than any country in Europe, and a little larger than Texas.

Turkey's great size and key location mean it has a lot of neighbors, which is not to say they are all a particularly close-knit community. Relations with Georgia, Azerbaijan, and Bulgaria are quite good, but relations between Turkey and her other neighbors (Armenia, Iran, Iraq, Greece and Syria) are always a little dicey.

Antagonism between **Armenia** and Turkey has a foundation that is 1,000 years old. Turkic tribes overran Armenia in the tenth century A.D. and destroyed their capital city of Ani before coursing west into Asia Minor. It is, however, more recent history that is at the heart of Armenian bitterness. Russia threw its support behind Armenians in Asia Minor at the turn of the century, sparking civil unrest that was intended to divide the weak Ottoman Empire. The Ottoman reaction was predictable and bloody, and a one-sided civil war — the Armenians use the word genocide — ensued, during which hundreds of thousands of Armenians in eastern Turkey were forcibly relocated to the south, where they were thought to pose less of a threat. Armenia was established in the wake of the Treaties of Sevres and reduced to its current size after Kemal Atatürk forced the Allies to ink new borders in the Treaty of Lausanne. Relations have been frosty ever since, although in recent years Armenia has been too preoccupied with Azerbaijan, another bitter Turkic rival, to goad its giant Turkish neighbor.

The most dangerous issues with **Iraq** and **Syria** to the south center on the ambitious, multi-billion dollar GAP Project in the Turkish southeast, which Iraq and Syria claim will jeopardize their water supply and the Turks claim will simply raise the standard of living in its most desolate region. The introduction of the GAP Project was followed closely by escalating Kurdish unrest, and this, Turks say, is the work of neighbors fearing a thriving economy on their borders. The Kurdish question has forced aside most discussion of the GAP Project, but the broad scope of this ongoing project should raise the standard of living in southeast Turkey, and may starve Kurdish separatists of the discontent they need. Meanwhile, the relationships with Iraq, Iran, and Syria are further complicated by Turkey's unique role as a secular Islamic state and member-state of NATO.

Turkey's relationship with its final neighbor, Greece, is another story altogether. The land border with Greece is only 206 kilometers long, but this is deceptive since the heavily patrolled border between the Turkish Republic of Northern Cyprus and Greek Cyprus is a de facto Turkish border, and Turkey is ringed with Greek islands along almost the full extent of her Aegean and western Mediterranean coasts. The two countries exchange slights and diplomatic insults at the slightest provocation, and have on several occasions – including the Kardak Rocks crisis in 1996 – come surprisingly close to war.

The interior of Turkey is protected on the north, east, and south by several great mountain ranges. Since ancient times these ranges have insulated the breadbasket of Asia Minor, the fertile **Anatolian plateau**. The Mediterranean, Aegean, and Black Sea coasts are likewise fertile areas for olives, fruit, and forestry. Turkey remains one of only eight nations worldwide with a net food surplus.

People

Turkey's population stands at about 70 million, and is increasing rapidly. The fertility rate in the mid-1990s was more than three children per woman, a huge figure by modern standards. A considerable minority of this population, probably some 12 million people, live in the İstanbul

Much Ado About Nothing

The ugly hand of Islamic terrorism appeared to show itself in the winter of 1994 when two Americans went missing during a ski trip to Bursa. Newpapers in the U.S. trumpeted news of the newest outbreak of terrorism until the two men turned up safe and sound in a snow cave, caught by a storm, not by Hamas. There is simply no reason for you to be concerned about becoming a victim of Islamic terrorism while visiting. For one thing, terrorist groups are usually associated with Arabs, and Turks are, as they will take pains to clarify, not Arab. Turks are simply Muslim, and tend to be a bit conservative in their views. As in North America, that simply means that they tend to be good, God-fearing folk, and the closest they will come to kidnaping you is inviting you to their home in the interest of feeding you pastries, cake and tea.

area, with others concentrated in Bursa, İzmir, Antalya, and Ankara. The population is heavily Muslim, but the republic is strictly secular. Estimates of the Muslim population run between 95 percent and 99 percent, and this number includes a **Kurdish** population (some Shiite, some Sunni) in Turkey of some 10 million people. The bulk of the population is of ethnic Turk origin.

Islam

The first questions you begin to form on arrival in Turkey will probably have to do with its minarets and mosques, the covered women and pious-looking men. Turkey is a secular nation, but its population is overwhelmingly Muslim. Most North Americans will find this religion and its trappings alien and maybe even a little disconcerting.

Islam is a vital religion, a cousin of Christianity and Judaism. The core beliefs are remarkably similar, the central cast of characters is virtually identical – Noah, Moses, Abraham, and even Jesus.

The Koran

Mohammed was born in Mecca around 570 A.D. He was a trader's son, and grew to be a trader himself. He was more than 40 years old when he received his first visitation from the Angel Gabriel, and Gabriel returned over the course of several years to deliver the word of God directly to him. Mohammed committed much of what Gabriel told him to writing, forming the core of the **Koran**. Some final chapters were passed down by word of mouth and finally incorporated into the Koran under the third Caliph, Uthman (644-656).

The Muslim God, **Allah**, remains very similar to the God of the Jews and Christians. In fact, Sura 5:83 of the Koran says "You will surely find that the nearest in affection to believers are those who say 'We are Christians,'" and this is amplified and expanded in 2:63: "Believers – Jews, Christians, and Sabians [a splinter Christian sect] – whosoever believes in God and the Last Day and does what is right, they shall have their reward with the Lord." This inclusive note has been echoed by such luminaries as the Sufi-inspired Celaddin Rumi, or Mevlana, he of the whirling dervishes. Unfortunately, this apparently clear line is muddied by 3:79, which warns that anyone who fails to select Islam will be " lost."

Within Islam there are two major sects, **Shi'ite** and **Sunni**. Turkey's Muslims are Sunni, and they worship the Koran together with a second text, the **Sunna**. The Sunna is a compilation of laws and guidelines derived from the lives of the Prophet Mohammed and his wife. The combined codes of the Koran and Sunna form the **Shariat**, or law. The Sunni caliph is a supreme judge, and this caliphate was knit to the Ottoman Imperium in the 16th Century A.D.

The Shi'ites, too, adhere to the Sunna, but they have their own caliph. Among the Shi'ites the caliph is more than the supreme judge, he is a leader, the voice of Allah, and a ruler in his own right. As a result, Shi'ites always remained aloof of the Ottoman sultan, who could never be their ultimate leader without also being the Shi'ite caliph. This schism has had bloody repercussions since ancient times, and under the Ottomans the rift was widened by Sultan Selim I's (1512-1520) bloody anti-Shi'ite campaigns in Persia.

Like the rest of the Islamic world, Turkey celebrates **Ramazan** (you may know it as Ramadan). During this period, Muslims forgo eating, drinking and even smoking from sun up until sundown. There are special dispensations for military personnel and foreigners, but if you find yourself in Turkey during Ramazan you shouldn't make a big point of eating when you find an open restaurant, and it is in poor taste to eat

The Call to Prayer

"Allah is most great. I testify that there in no god but Allah. I testify that Mohammed is the apostle of Allah. Come to prayer, come to security. God is most great."

Morning prayers have an additional verse reminding the listener that it is "better to pray than sleep." All verses repeat.

on the street during daylight. The day-long fast is elaborately broken at sunset, when huge meals appear and families gather together.

Ramazan is based on a lunar cycle, and, as a result, the dates change from year to year. Ramazan is currently going through its winter period, meaning that the days are short and the fasting is fairly painless. Summer poses a sterner test. The end of the Ramazan holiday is marked by **Şeker Bayram**, an exchange of gifts and a great celebration. Another Islamic holiday, **Kurban Bayram**, commemorates Abraham's willingness to sacrifice his son Ishmael. Families throughout the country slaughter sheep and other livestock, and it is an occasion for most offices to shut down for a full week.

Turkish Mannerisms

You're likely to meet few people more friendly than the glowering Turkish man watching you from in front of his shop. Turkish men have a habit of appearing to be somewhere between impassive and un-friendly, but they're almost always amiable and helpful.

Moreover, for all of the histrionics you're going to see in traffic jams and marketplaces, Turks are slow to anger and remarkably self-disci-plined. In what may be a testament to the importance of extended family and neighborhood community, they are unusually sane, reasonable people.

A few local habits are likely to arouse some curiosity, even resent-ment in most North Americans. The big one is "*Yok.*" When the bus is gone, the small change is exhausted, the rooms are full and the shop is closed, you will be met with "Yok," and its accompanying upthrust chin. In our culture this gesture is dismissive and rude; not so here. It simply means no; a firm, final no.

Winter in Anatolia

"As in the yards of houses in Ürgüp, so across the high country of Anatolia I had watched people preparing for winter. Gathering and storing fuel as well as food is an obsession with the inhabitants of those high, wild, unforested plains. I sympathized with the man I saw standing before his hoard of wood, heedless to the heat of the sun on his back as he reckoned up the long bitter weeks of January against the stock of logs in his yard. Was it enough? I knew how he felt – it is never enough, there isn't enough firewood in the world to quench the craving for plenty which gnaws at the wintry heart of the lover of fires."

Philip Glazebrook, **Journey to Kars: A Modern Traveler in the Ottoman Lands,** London: Penguin, 1984.

The *tsk tsk* noises (often with the aforementioned upthrust chin) are one of the Turks' great socialization tools. You'll hear it when someone is showing too much flesh, doing something unsafe, or otherwise getting out of line. North Americans accustomed to a live-and-let-live ethic are usually ill-prepared for this very judgmental chastening, usually performed by women. If someone is going way over the line you'll hear the tsk tsk in conjunction with an *Allah allah*. (Sounds like *Allah hallah*.) This phrase, meaning, more or less, "how come?" or " what's up with that?," can also simply be an expression of wonderment.

There are scores of other peculiarities, but none so important as the fact that if you go to the trouble to mime a conversation with someone, or send them a copy of a photograph, or help get their car out of a ditch, you'll have a friend for always.

The Kurds

The Kurds' story is not unique; they are a distinct people without a distinct homeland. They have their own language, culture, and traditions, and the majority of them live in southeast Turkey or just across the border in Iraq or Iran. The most famous incidents involving the Kurds were Saddam Hussein's attacks on their villages with poison gas in the late 1980s, but nowhere have the Kurds met with a great welcome. Iraq, Iran, and Turkey have spent years trying to hustle the mujjahdin-like Kurdish fighters back and forth into one another's countries, but never with much apparent success.

The NATO no-fly zone over northern Iraq has given the Kurds a de facto homeland, but no one seems ready to recognize a sovereign Kurdistan, least of all Turkey. The Turks perceive a threat to their territory in the southeast just as the GAP Project nears completion, yielding power and increasing the agricultural potential of the region, and they have been heavy-handed in their treatment of Kurds in both the political and military arenas.

There have been marked improvements in southeastern Turkey since 1999. The capture of the leader of the Kurdistan Worker's Party (PKK), Abdullah Ocalan, in 1999, seems to have cooled armed Kurdish resistance, and tensions have been easing. This is nothing short of miraculous (and may well be ephemeral); the resolve of the Turkish military deserves some credit, as do the new opportunities provided by the GAP project, and the easing of some draconian anti-Kurdish language laws—including the 2002 repeal of a ban on Kurdish-language TV and radio broadcasts. There have been no terrorist bomb attacks since the mid-1990s.

News coverage of southeastern Turkey is heavily discouraged, but everyone knows that in the late 1980s the Kurdish separatists forced

Turkey to occupy the area in force. Ever since, reports have trickled in about skirmishes and occasional battles between the Turkish military and Kurdish rebels. As happened in the American war in Vietnam, differentiating between civilians and fighters has grown more and more difficult, and not even the de facto media blackout conceals that it has been a nasty little war.

The U.S. State Department continues to caution against travel to the southeast of Turkey. No foreigners have been kidnapped or killed in years—and it was, to be clear, extremely uncommon even at the height of the conflict. Travelers by the thousands still journey through the southeast to visit sites such as Doğubeyazit, Van, Harran, and Nemrut Dağı, and most are delighted by their friendly reception. The fact remains, however, that there are threats to your safety here that you will find nowhere else in the country, and we do not recommend independent travel to the southeast.

Tobacco

Tobacco, what any visitor will soon conclude is the nation's pet vice, has been a part of Turkish culture for hundreds of years. A 1612 treaty with England opened the door to the imports of English tobacco traders, and the door that the tobacco traders opened the Marlboro man has since barged right through, offering cigarettes instead of narghile tobacco. Turks are big smokers, big even by European standards. Non-smoking North Americans, spoiled by successful anti-smoking campaigns at home, may be unprepared for smoke in taxis, restaurants, and most other public areas. Rare indeed is the public area without cigarette smoke, although anti-smoking campaigns have made some headway, and municipal buses, some private dolmuş, upscale restaurants, and good theaters now offer respite from smoking (look for *Sigarasiz* or *Sigara İçmisiz* signs).

The greatest victory in the anti-smoking campaign has been the elimination of smoking aboard buses within the country. Note also that the Muslim holy men, some of the earliest anti-smoking campaigners, prohibited smoking in mosques and other holy areas hundreds of years ago.

Narghiles were once a common sight in Turkey as in many Arab countries, and narghile tobacco is still produced on the Black Sea. These pipes have fallen out of favor among Turks these days, but some enterprising shopowners have found that visitors remain interested in indulging.

For years, if you were interested in smoking a narghile you had to go looking for it. Not so anymore. Most neighborhoods that see traffic in foreigners will have some narghile pipes available. In İstanbul, try the classic Nargileci on Çorlulu Pasaj in the Grand Bazaar near Divan Yolu – ask someone selling narghiles where it is (*narghileci nerede?*). Otherwise, there are cafes with narghiles conveniently beside the Hagia Sophia (to the left of the great church and up the street on which you find the Yuçelt Youth Hostel) and just off of Divan Yolu Caddesi in the alley with the Rumeli Café. Do remember to take a seat when you draw off one of these pipes, lest you whirl dizzily and crash to the floor.

Opium

Of the classic vices of Asia Minor, opium enjoys the least popularity today. Turkey continues to export one-third of the world's legal opium, but its success as a vice has tailed off. The government has taken serious steps to regulate the production of narcotic opium, which is a product of mature plants, by harvesting the plants while young. Legal opium has many uses in pharmaceuticals, and is a lucrative export in its own right. Although Turkey is not a source of heroin, the western world alleges that it is a major smuggling route for heroin from Afghanistan and elsewhere in Central Asia.

Turkish Language

Turkish gives the new arrival virtually no familiar benchmarks. Sentence structure is the reverse of English, and Turkish has incorporated precious few English words. As someone is bound to point out, Turkish is very systematic and logical, but then so is the computer language C++. A fat lot of good that does you on a two week visit.

Thanks to the reforms of Kemal Atatürk, Turkey now uses Latin, not Arabic, characters. These correspond roughly with English, with several notable exceptions:

Letter	Sound	Pronunciation		English Meaning
c	j	Cami	(jah-mee)	Mosque
ç	ch	Çatal	(cha-tall)	Fork
i	ee	Bin	(been)	Thousand
ı	uh	Topkapı	(top kap uh)	Topkapı Palace
ş	sh	Teşekkürler	(tey shey koor ler)	Thanks
ö	oeu	Göz	(goeuz)	Eye
ü	ehw	Yüz	(yehwz)	Hundred
ğ	(none)	Sağol	(sa-ohl)	Thanks

The Basics

English	Turkish	Pronunciation
Yes	*Evet*	*eh-veht*
No	*Hayır*	*high-uhr*
Thank you	*Teşekkürler*	*tey-shey-kur-lehr*
Thanks	*Sağol*	*sa-ohl*
Please	*Lütfen*	*lewt-fen*
Good day	*İyi Günler*	*ee-yee goon-lehr*
Good night	*İyi Akşamlar*	*ee-yee ak-shum-lar*
No, none,nothing	*Yok*	*yoke*
Many, much	*Çok*	*choke*
Good	*İyi*	*ee-yee*
Bad	*Kötü*	*koeuh-tu*

Traveling

Today	*Bugün*	*boo-goon*
Yesterday	*Dün*	*dewhn*
Tomorrow	*Yarın*	*yahr-uhn*
I will go	*Giteceğim*	*git-eh-jeh-im*
I will stay	*Kaleceğim*	*kal-eh-jeh-im*
We will go	*Giteceğız*	*git-eh-jeh-uhz*
We will not go	*Gitmeceğız*	*git-meh-jeh-uhz*
Hour	*Saat*	*sa-aht*
Minute	*Dakika*	*da-kee-ka*
Depart	*Kalkar*	*kahl-kar*
Airport	*Havaalanı*	*hav-aa-lahn-uh*
Bus station	*Otogar*	*oto-gahr*
Train station	*Tren istasiyon*	*tren is-tas-ee-yohn*
Port	*Liman*	*lee-mahn*
When	*Ne zaman*	*ney-zah-mahn*

Days

Monday	*Pazartesi*	*pah-zahr-tey-see*
Tuesday	*Salı*	*sahl-uh*
Wednesday	*Çarşamba*	*char-shum-ba*
Thursday	*Perşembe*	*pear-shem-bay*
Friday	*Cuma*	*joo-mah*
Saturday	*Cumartesi*	*joo-mahr-tay-see*
Sunday	*Pazar*	*pah-zahr*

Phrases

I want a room

Bir oda istiyorum   *beer oda ist-ee-yorum*

How much is this?
> *Bu ne kadar*   *boo nay kadar*

Is breakfast included?
> *Kahvaltı dahil mı?*   *kah-val-tuh da-heel muh?*

Where is the bus station?
> *Otogar nerede?*   *oto-gahr neh-reh-day?*

I like it.
> *O seviyorum*   *oh sev-ee-or-um*

I don't like it.
> *O sevmiyorum*   *oh sev-mee-or-um*

I want it.
> *O istiyorum*   *oh ist-ee-or-um*

We don't want it.
> *O istemiyoruz*   *oh ist-em-ee-or-uz*

Please help me.
> *Yardım edim, lütfen*   *yahr-duhm eh-deem, loot-fen*

Shame! (strong term)
> *Ayıp*   *ai-yuhp*

Numbers

10,000,000	*on milyon*	*oh-n mil-yohn*
1,000,000	*milyon*	*mil-yohn*
100,000	*yüz bin*	*yehwz binn*
10,000	*on bin*	*on binn*
1,000	*bin*	*binn*
100	*yüz*	*yehwz*
90	*doksan*	*dohk-sahn*
80	*seksen*	*sehks-sen*
70	*yetmiş*	*yet-mish*
60	*altmiş*	*alt-mish*
50	*elli*	*el-lee*
40	*kırk*	*kuhrk*
30	*otuz*	*oh-tooz*
20	*yirmi*	*yeer-mee*
10	*on*	*ohn*
9	*dokuz*	*doh-kewz*
8	*sekiz*	*sek-eez*
7	*yedi*	*yeh-dee*
6	*altı*	*al-tuh*
5	*beş*	*besh*
4	*dört*	*doohrt*

3	*üç*	*ew-ch*
2	*iki*	*ick-ee*
1	*bir*	*beer*
0	*sıfır*	*suh-fuhr*

| 450,000 TL. | *Dortyüz elli bin Turkish Lira* |
| 23,945,000 TL. | *Yirmi üc dokuzyüz kirkbeş bin Turkish Lira* |

Chapter 5

Many people come to Turkey with no intention of buying a carpet or kilim and wind up hauling three or four onto the flight home. The same may be said of the local history, which can get under your skin just as quickly (if not as expensively).

Early History

The history of civilization begins in Asia Minor, in the Anatolian plain of central Turkey. The cluster of earthen dwellings at Çatal Hüyük dates back to 7500 B.C. (near Beyşehir Lake, south of modern Konya), and evokes the pueblos of the American southwest. Çatal Hüyük was settled at the same time that people began producing specialized tools for harvesting, and, indeed, the settlement was built atop fields of obsidian, one of the first stones used to fashion simple tools.

Even at this early stage humans were, ever so slowly, beginning to gain technological momentum. Settlements were made possible by agriculture, and this, in turn, led to specialization of skills in the populace and provided traders with centers for distribution. What some wanted to trade for, of course, others wanted to take; defensive walls appeared over the course of the next 2,000 years. By 5000 B.C. Asia Minor had a network of small fortified towns that reached down into Egypt and out through Iran and India in the direction of China.

The **Bronze Age**, dating from 3200 B.C., is a time marker because it represents a dawning ability to combine two naturally occurring metals, copper and tin, to produce bronze, a tougher material. Archaeologists have identified some one dozen settlements in Asia Minor near natural metal deposits, and communities bent on mining ore further enforced the need for trade – where once there was food, now there was food, metal, metalworking technology, and, of course, the weapons and art produced with metal. Specialization of skills was gaining momentum, and has continued to do so ever since.

As technology advanced, so did the size of the young city-states. Communities increased their power through alliances and conquest, taking advantage of quantum leaps in military technology and strategy to satisfy growing demand for resources. Artisans were, meanwhile, giving those in power new things for which to fight; they began developing their metalworking skills and mastering new metal alloys to create small statues, diadems, bracelets, and necklaces. The intricate pieces in the **Treasure of Priam** discovered by Heinrich Schliemann at **Troy** date from 2500 B.C. (well before the Troy of the Iliad). This Troy, Troy II, seems to have been among the pioneers of a new sort of industry; the control of trade routes. Instead of positioning themselves to mine ore or produce textiles, the Trojans built a fortified city on a hill overlooking the mouth of the Hellespont.

Merchants, unable or unwilling to battle the contrary current and frequent north wind in the Hellespont, stopped at the mouth of the strait and did business in the marketplaces of Troy. The Trojans encouraged this with a naval force that could close the strait or demand payment for safe passage. Thus Troy profited from all the trade between east and west (as well, we assume, from trade across the Hellespont from north and south) and became the marketplace of interior Asia and Europe. Centuries of such commerce made the city prosperous.

The Hittites

The history of the region really begins taking shape in about 2000 BC, when **Assyrian** traders from the south appear in Anatolia with great stores of tin, which, combined with stores of copper (probably secured through trading elsewhere), allowed large-scale production of bronze. Better yet, for historians, the Assyrians were in the habit keeping records of their business in cuneiform script on slabs of clay. Knowledge of earlier kingdoms is largely a matter of guesswork – the Sumerians, for instance, left a large, shadowy footprint. With the Assyrians' help, however, historians have been able to reconstruct details of one of the greatest Anatolian empires, that of the **Hittites**.

The Hittites, like so many cultures to appear later, entered Anatolia from the east and soon were masters of the native Anatolian population. The new arrivals, however, were no cultural imperialists; they adopted the religion and much of the language of the indigenous Hurrian peoples. In the 20th Century B.C., these people built their first major city, Kanesh (near modern Kültepe), from which they began to dominate the rest of central Anatolia. In the 18th Century B.C., the capital was shifted back to Hattuşas (Boğazkale), and soon the Hittite Kingdom was in full flower, encompassing Babylon and the entire Anatolian plain.

The Hittites suffered through difficult periods, but for the bulk of its existence, the Hittite Kingdom (later the Hittite Empire) dominated the region. Illustrating this, in the 14th Century B.C. the widow of **King Tutankhaman** sought a Hittite prince to be her new husband. Her hopes were not realized; the son of the Hittite King Suppiluliuma I was killed on the journey to Egypt. The two empires continued in the habit of cross-pollinating their nobility, but there were some bumps along the way. Under Muwatalli II (1306-1282 B.C.) the Hittites took the field against an Egyptian invasion by Ramses II, the irrepressibly successful pharoah immortalized in Percy Byshe Shelley's *Ozymandias*. On this one occasion Ramses II was stopped dead, stalemated at the **Battle of Qadesh** (1286 B.C.) and forced to withdraw through Palestine. Upon his arrival home, the pharoah put a positive spin on the battle of Qadesh – hieroglyphs at Karnak speak only of a great victory.

After the death of Muwatalli II, the Hittite Kingdom began an abrupt decline; Agamemnon had come. Greek and Mycenaean colonists and traders had at last appeared to the west.

The Trojan War

Troy's relationship with the Hittite Kingdom is unclear. Their roots were similar, their architecture much the same, but the two kingdoms were operating in different spheres. If Homer's account of the Trojan War is to be believed, almost the whole of the mainland to the south and east supported Troy, and this might have included the Hittites and certainly included the **Paphlagonians**, or Kaşka, from the eastern Black Sea.

The Trojans never had the enduring martial success of the Hittites, but they were a thorn in side of the Greeks. An allied force of Trojans and Mysians conquered the region around the Sea of Marmara in the 14th Century B.C. and extended their territory into Thrace as far as Macedonia. Having moved so far west, the Trojans were preying on Greek settlements and colonies as well as barring entry to the Hellespont, and may well have constituted the most dangerous of the kingdoms scattered along the coast. At roughly the time of the death of Hittite King Muwatalli and the subsequent civil war among the Hittites, the **Greeks** united, and, perhaps seeking to take advantage of the strife in Anatolia, descended on Troy.

Homer's *Iliad* offers the epic account of the struggle between the Greeks and the Trojans. In the end, the Greeks stripped Troy of its lands and burned it to the ground around 1250 B.C., clearing the way for colonization throughout the Aegean and up into the Sea of Marmara and the Black Sea. Within a century the Hittite capital was also sacked and burned, probably by the Paphlagonians, and the Hittite Kingdom was completely destroyed. By 1100 B.C. even the Mycenaeans, by all accounts the great victors in the Trojan War, had collapsed. An era was at an end, and a new one was not yet under way.

The Ancient Dark Age

The success of the Greeks owed much to the introduction of quick, sturdy sailing ships, a change that shifted the balance throughout the Mediterranean and caused Asia Minor to slip into chaos. It is about the time of the Trojan War that the Egyptians tell of the coming of the Sea Peoples, most likely Greek sailors joined by refugees from Troy and elsewhere who engaged in widespread piracy, and, in many cases, sought footholds along the coasts. The whole of the Mediterranean basin was settled in this period.

Amid this upheaval, several small kingdoms succeeded in establishing themselves in Asia Minor. Refugees from the fallen Hittite Empire staked out new kingdoms deeper inland and thriving city-states emerged on the Mediterranean shore at Perge and elsewhere. By 1000 B.C. the **Phrygians** had descended on Asia Minor from Thrace, establishing their capital near Gordium. The Phrygians ranged far and wide, even forming an alliance with the Paphlagonians along the Black Sea coast and going to war against the Babylonians in the east. Having settled into the capital of their budding new empire, the Phrygians were distressed to see the **Cimmerians** (of Conan fame) swarm down from the Russian steppe, cross the Caucasus Mountains, **upset the apple cart**, then eat the apples.

The Cimmerians destroyed the Phrygian capital at Gordion in 714 B.C., and spent the next two decades belligerently sacking and looting the cities of Asia Minor as far south as Ephesus. It appears that the Cimmerians were outstanding warriors but uninspired administrators, and at the end of their rampage they dispersed and settled into the kingdoms they had conquered, melting into the local population within a few generations.

In the east, the kingdoms introduced by refugees of the Hittite Empire on the shores of Lake Van eventually cemented a coalition under Sarduri I (840-830 B.C.). This became the **Urartian Kingdom**, founded to fend off the increasingly aggressive Assyrians, and it grew powerful enough to include the bulk of Anatolia. The capital city from 810 B.C. was Tuşpa, on Lake Van, and the extent of Urartu's borders at one time reached the Caucasus in the north, Syria in the south, Cappadocia in the west and its eastern frontier penetrated deep into modern Iran. The Urartians were able to beat back the Assyrians, and under Sarduri II (753-735 B.C.) they even campaigned to the doorstep of the Assyrian capital at Nineveh. The Assyrians soon recovered and resumed their attacks, however, forcing the Urartians on two occasions to take refuge in their impregnable fortresses at the Rock of Van and suffer the destruction of their homes and crops.

In the end, the Urartians outlasted the Assyrians. The Assyrians fell to the growing might of **Persia** in 612 B.C., and Ur was incorporated into the **Lydian** Empire in 590 B.C.

Persia

Croesus succeeded a line of powerful kings to become King of Lydia in 560 B.C., and he immediately began a campaign along the coast of Asia Minor. His irrepressible armies pacified all of western Turkey within seven years, and the wealth of his capital at Sardis gained great renown – the term "rich as Croesus" has survived (albeit barely) to this day. Croesus put great stock in oracles, and the **Oracle at Delphi** was the most uncannily accurate of these. Thus Croesus, on the verge of testing his might against his greatest remaining foe, asked the oracle whether he should cross the river Halys and attack the Persians. "Make war on the Persians and you will destroy a great empire," were the words of the oracle.

Croesus heard in these words what he wanted to hear, crossing the river and verily getting his clock cleaned at the Battle of Pteria in Cappadocia in 550 B.C. Croesus retreated in disarray to Sardis, where the Persian King Cyrus' surprisingly rapid pursuit left Croesus no time to assemble a new army. The Persians seized and sacked Sardis and Croesus' empire was ruined, fulfilling the oracular prediction.

Consider that in the course of some 62 years the Persians had dominated the whole of Asia Minor, replacing four empires with a single one. It should be noted that the Greek settlements, foreshadowing centuries of conflict, did not take well to Persian administration. In the northern cities entire populations were slain or enslaved. In 540 B.C., the Persian General Harpagus marched on the cities of Lycia along the southwest coast. The collection of Anatolian and Greek peoples along that remote coast fled or fought; in the epic case of **Xanthos** – and perhaps Caunos as well – the men of the city massacred their own women and children and threw themselves hopelessly into battle against the overwhelming Persian army, dying to the last man.

Persian rule was complete on land, but the islands of the Mediterranean remained largely under Greek control, and it was from here that a major revolt by all of the Ionian cities – roughly between modern Çeşme and Bodrum – erupted in 498 B.C. Led by the greatest city of the coast at the time, Miletus, and assisted by fleets from Athens and troops from the Peloponnese, the Ionian cities scattered the Persians. Darius, the Persian King, soon mounted an overwhelming counterattack, seizing back all of what he had lost and carrying the war back to Miletus, which he sacked and destroyed in 494 B.C.

Even so, the Persian victory was incomplete. Agitation against Persian rule in Asia Minor came from aross the Aegean in Athens, and it was against this threat that Darius now moved. Seeking to root out the problem at its distant source, Darius launched a great armada in 490 B.C. The fleet of 600 ships sailed directly for Greece, where cavalry and footsoldiers sacked several towns, progressing toward Athens. The Greeks made their stand just west of Athens at Marathon, scoring a dramatic and unexpected victory that left 6,400 Persians dead to 192 of their own. The Persians fled back to their ships and sailed for Asia, and an enraged Darius was forced to begin assembling another army.

Darius did not live to see the next invasion, which was launched by his son **Xerxes** in 480. Xerxes amassed a colossal army – Herodotus gives the figure seven million, which is surely several orders of magnitude too large – and personally led his army across the Dardanelles into Europe, relying on the land approaches to Athens. At the approach of this force most enemies fled or opened their gates. Only upon arrival in Greece did the Persians meet fierce resistance, but the most valiant Greek opposition could do little more than delay a Persian army whose thirst, Herodotus reports, emptied rivers. The Greeks once again sought to make their stand at Athens, but they soon realized the futility of fighting the overwhelming Persian force and retired to the sea. Xerxes sacked Athens, winning his hoped-for victory, but the victory was hollow – no sooner had the Persians torched Athens' acropolis than the Athenians led the Greek navies in a rout of the Persian fleet just offshore.

Later that year, Xerxes retreated with a large part of his army back to Asia Minor, where he received the worst news yet: in the second year of the invasion the remaining occupation army was routed by the united Greeks at the **Battle of Plataea**. This victory was commemorated by a statue of intertwined serpents cast from the shields of fallen Persians, a trophy that now stands in the **Hippodrome** in İstanbul. Few of the fleeing Persians survived the long journey home.

Athens now sailed forth into Asia Minor, freely sacking Persian-held cities and putting remnants of the Persian army and navy to rout near Aspendos. The Persians might have been defeated once and for all, had not dissension erupted within the Greek ranks. In 432, the Spartans and Athenians became embroiled in what was essentially a Greek civil war,

the **Peloponnesian War**, during which the Persians reasserted themselves in Asia Minor and expertly played the two sides off against one
another.

The Peloponnesian War ended with Spartan victory in 406, and the
focus of the west shifted quickly back to Asia Minor. Here, a battle of
succession dragged in a great army from the west, as a young Persian
prince, Cyrus, coerced the Greeks to help him win the Persian throne
from his brother. After penetrating deep into Persia, the Greek force
defeated the Persian army, but in the course of the battle lost the Persian
prince. Without him, they had no claim to the throne, and no friends in
Persia; they found themselves stranded in hostile territory, thousands of
miles from home. **Xenophon**, their general, gives an account of the
retreat of his 10,000 soldiers through ancient Turkey in *Anabasis*, The
March Up-Country.

Alexander the Great

In the ensuing years the Persians strengthened their hold on Asia
Minor. They were represented by remarkably autonomous satraps,
including Mausolus (?-353 B.C.) for whom the **Mausoleum at
Helicarnassus** was constructed, one of the Seven Wonders of the World.
The Persians continued fighting the Lycians along the Mediterranean
coast, while in the north they came into conflict with King Philip of
Macedon. The animosity kindled in the latter of these border skirmishes
was fateful. Philip's son, **Alexander** (355-323 B.C.), inherited a grudge
against the Persian authority in Asia Minor. He crossed the Hellespont
in 334 B.C. and systematically defeated every Persian army that confronted him. After scouring almost the whole of modern Turkey for the
Persians and their allies, he met Persian King Darius III at the Battle of
Issus (near Antakya-Hatay) in 333 B.C. and routed him for a final time.

Alexander's Prophesy

Alexander's youth was filled with omens that he would grow
up to be a great conqueror, but before he set out on his invasion of
Persia he wanted to make sure he hadn't misread the signs.
Alexander visited the Oracle at Delphi in the hopes of confirming
his destiny, but was met by the priestess, who told him that, for
now, the Oracle was silent. Alexander ignored this and forced his
way toward the Temple, dragging her along. She tried to resist, but,
failing, shouted to her fellows "He can't be stopped!" At this
Alexander wheeled around and left Delphi. He had his prophesy.

Alexander went on to destroy the Persian Empire and led his armies outside the boundaries of the known world into India and Central Asia.

Alexander's military genius was overwhelming, but he failed to attend to his own succession. After altering the face of the world, Alexander died in 323 B.C. and his empire began to disintegrate. His son was just an infant, hardly fit to rule, and Alexander's many brilliant generals were soon at each other's throats. Alexander's son died within two years, probably assassinated, and the rivals for power, or **Diadochoi**, began a long, costly struggle. This is one of the most confusing chapters in history, with many of the former general of Alexander staking a claim to pieces of the empire. Many pretenders to the throne were defeated or assassinated, and others settled for small provinces.

The most successful of Alexander's proteges were **Antigonus** in Asia Minor; **Seleucus** the One Eyed, who founded a southern empire out of Syria; **Ptolemy**, who established a kingdom in Egypt; and **Lysimachos**, whose Aegean claims later formed the heart of the Kingdom of Pergamon. Even these relatively successful generals suffered grim fates; Lysimachos defeated and killed Antigonus in 301, Seleucus overwhelmed Lysimachos at the Battle of Corupedium in 281, and Seleucus was poisoned the next year by his own son. Only Ptolemy fared well, establishing his own dynasty by the waters of the Nile.

The Romans

Historians invariably paint the **Romans** as bustling, driven, and vulgar, but they were clever, too. They deserved their reputation for military acumen, but the truly astonishing thing was the Romans'administrative ability and their foreign policy cunning. This was evident in their patient and ultimately successful policy in Asia Minor.

Two of Asia Minor's most powerful kingdoms forged alliances with the emergent Romans. The **Kingdom of Pergamon** successfully sided with the Romans against the Seleucids at the Battle of Magnesia in 190 B.C., and maintained friendly relations thereafter. The **Kingdom of Pontus**, on the Black Sea, contributed to the Roman force that finally defeated Rome's great maritime rival, Carthage, in 149 B.C. During this time Rome's presence seemed limited in Asia Minor despite its clear influence in many coastal cities.

Such appearances began to fade in 133 B.C., when Attalus III of Pergamon died and bequeathed his kingdom to the Romans. This peculiar inheritance reeked of Roman intrigue, but the citizens of Pergamon had only the slightest opportunity to protest; the Romans entrenched themselves quickly. Thereafter, Rome's escalating role in the affairs of Asia Minor began to worry and anger some of its autonomous neighbors. This unease exploded under **Mithradites VI** (120-63), King of Pontus, who fanned uprisings and waged a series of wars against Rome.

Rome barely stalemated Mithradites' first campaigns, and only at great cost, but Mithradites' luck against the Romans finally ran out. The final Pontic War began in 72 B.C. and led to complete victory for the Roman generals **Lucullus** and **Pompey**, who broke and scattered the Pontic armies and pursued them to Armenia, where Mithradites ended his life. In the dying convulsions of the Kingdom of Pontus, Mithradites successor Pharnaces II was crushed in Cappadocia by three Roman divisions under **Julius Caesar**, who sent a messenger back to Rome bearing the famous account of his campaign: "*Veni, Vidi, Vici*" – *I came, I saw, I conquered.*

Cities in Asia Minor had been wary of Roman rule, but it proved an almost universally prosperous period. Secure behind Rome's distant borders and enjoying the advantages of safe commerce, cities throughout the world blossomed. Monuments, fortresses, and cities sprang up during the Pax Romana, many of them decorated by statues and stonework displaying the artistry of a wealthy age. The Romans borrowed their aesthetic from the Greeks, but seem to have been naturally deft administrators. Rome placed lands under the control of regional governors, and, excepting unusual periods of vicious taxation, populations were often better off than they had been under local rulers. At its height Rome's reach extended from England to the Arabian desert, and the Mediterranean was an Imperial lake.

The Byzantine Empire

Roman rule was enduring, but by the late third century A.D. the sheer size of the empire was proving unmanageable. To cope with the great size of the empire, Roman leaders experimented with shared rule, divided between the east and west, but this created as many problems as it solved. Add to this the excesses of various emperors, religious division, and the less glamorous matter of imperial finances and the groundwork was in place for the collapse of Roman power as it had been known. A note regarding economics in the late third century; in one famous case heavily taxed farmers were deserting the fields for the cities in such great numbers that the **Emperor Diocletian** (285-305 A.D.) decreed that men must assume their fathers' careers.

Diocletian's heavy taxation and zealous attempts to make the lower classes contribute revenue to the imperial coffers had another face as well. Diocletian was responsible for one of the empire's last, greatest spasms of genocide against Christians. During the final years of his reign, Diocletian ordered the imprisonment and execution of untold thousands of Christians, probably including **St. Nicholas**, a bishop from Myra (modern Kale/Demre). Economics and religion had always been closely connected, and such was the case now. Under the Roman empire, Christianity had blossomed among the poor and the powerless and turned into a religion of resistance. Rome understood the threat from an early date, crucifying Jesus and executing Christians for sport in Roman circuses. Diocletian understood this, too; the masses were listening to the dangerous words of Christian clerics, not their Roman emperors and governors.

As it happened, Diocletian was the last emperor to carry out a campaign of outright persecution against Christians. His successor, **Constantine**, took a dramatically different course with regard to Christianity. After assuming the throne in 306 A.D. he was famously accommodating to the religion, a religion that had grown only stronger under the onslaught of Rome under Diocletian. In this Constantine was less pious than populist: the masses in the east were largely Christian, and after uniting the divided empire and shifting the capital to **Byzantium** (later **Constantinople**), Constantine sought to curry their favor. Stories have come down to us of Constantine's vision of a cross above the battlefield on which he wrested control of Rome from his co-emperor Licinius, but the only hard fact seems to be that Constantine was baptised on his deathbed. The renewed Roman Empire at Constantinople (which always considered itself the true Roman, not Byzantine, Empire) was becoming, by fits and starts, a Christian empire.

The validity of Constantinople's claim to Roman authority was certainly buttressed when Rome fell to **Alaric** and the Goths in 410 A.D. The Byzantines, secure behind the then-indomitable walls of Constantinople, became the Roman standard bearers, but the east was to exercise great change on the character of the empire. Christianity, once thought to undermine Roman authority, was established as the state religion by Theodosius I (379-395 A.D.). Under the **Emperor Justinian** (527-565 A.D.), this left one of its indelible marks in the form of the **Hagia Sophia**, an enormous cathedral that remained the largest free standing structure in the world for 1,000 years, and stands today.

The Byzantines were masters of intrigue, with a legacy as old as Rome itself of dividing and suborning their enemies. Some emperors were masters of this, some were masters of warfare, and some, like **Heraclius** (610-641 A.D.) and **Basil II** (976-1025 A.D.), were masters of both. The latter is best known for his long campaign against the Bulgars, and the cruelty of his final victory; after capturing 14,000 Bulgars at the Battle of Cimbalongus in 1014 A.D. Basil ordered all of them blinded, with the exception of one man in each 100. The one-eyed captives were ordered to lead the others home. In the midst of the dark ages, this cruelty hardly dimmed the precious light shed by the Byzantine empire. With

Europe fallen into chaos, Constantinople was the last western refuge of culture and civilization.

The Turks

Mohammed began his teaching around 612 A.D., and the Arabs were quick to heed his call. Taxation at the time was heavy and the Byzantines were pressed hard by the Persians in the region, fertile soil for the Muslim doctrine of Mohammed to take root. Soon after his death, the Arabs coursed into the west under the flag of *Jihad* (holy war), sacking Alexandria, ravaging Asia Minor, and investing Constantinople itself. This new threat was ended by a decisive Byzantine victory in 718 A.D., but foreshadowed events yet to come.

Muslims prospered in the deserts of Arabia, eventually spilling into the Holy Land to take Jerusalem in the tenth century. At the same time, a new group of tribal warriors were emerging from the northeast and taking up the Muslim mantle. These were **Turks**, distant kin to the Bulgars and other peoples that had come from the east to challenge Byzantium in earlier years. Turkic tribes, warrior opportunists fresh from central Asia, began establishing themselves along the eastern borders and creating turmoil along the frontier. The short-lived Kingdom of Armenia, centered on Ani near Kars, was an early victim of the Turkish onslaught. The Byzantines were slow to react, and when, at last, the young, promising emperor Romanus IV Diogenes marched east to pacify the newcomers, his efforts were hamstrung by administrative errors and treachery.

In 1071 A.D., Romanus' large Byzantine army was soundly defeated at the **Battle of Manzikert** (modern Malazgirt, north of Lake Van) by Alp Arslan, leader of the Selçuk Turks. Romanus IV was captured and ransomed at a great cost in treasure and prestige, and the Selçuks won land concessions from the Byzantines.

The Byzantines were badly shaken by the loss of power in Anatolia. In the best Byzantine tradition, out of this hardship emerged a strong, able leader. Alexius I Comneni (1081-1118 A.D.) checked the Selçuks, broke a siege of Constantinople, and appeared ready for a campaign to restore control of Anatolia. However, Alexius' plans were completely undone by a most unwelcome helping hand. Anger over the loss of the Holy Lands had been percolating in the west, and in 1097 A.D. the **First Crusade** erupted out of Europe. The Crusaders marched through Byzantine lands en route to the Holy Land, and the benefit of their victories over Arab armies there were almost offset by the damage they did to their Byzantine allies. Alexius I did his best to turn the Crusade to his advantage, but the schism between the Latin and Orthodox churches deepened and relations worsened.

The hard feelings came to a head in the **Fourth Crusade** in 1204 A.D., when the Crusaders turned on their Orthodox Christian brethren and sacked, burned, and looted Constantinople itself. The Byzantines regrouped in Asia, where the Selçuk Turks were now facing difficulties of their own; Mongols had emerged from the east, crushing the Selçuk armies and seizing possession of most of their cities. The Selçuks reestablished their power with great effort, inviting newly arrived Turkish tribes to establish kingdoms on the fronteir; among these tribes were the followers of one Ertuğrul, whose son Osman would found the Ottoman dynasty.

The Ottomans

The Byzantines recaptured Constantinople in 1263 A.D., but their hold on Asia Minor had slipped away, never to return. Without the Anatolian heartland, the Byzantine Empire was a shadow of its former self, economically and militarily vulnerable. So it was that the warlike **Ottomans** settled on the Byzantine frontier at Eskişehir, south of the Sea of Marmara. The Ottomans were the product of a hardscrabble nomadic background, but the first Ottoman sultans proved much more than the mere warlords the Byzantines had come to expect.

The Sultans **Osman, Orhan,** and **Murat I** ruled from 1288 A.D. to 1389 A.D., and each proved a far-sighted administrator as well as a formidable soldier. While other Turkic settlements flared up and quickly faded, the Ottomans were patient and shrewd, marshalling their strength and avoiding confrontation except on their own terms. The Ottomans insinuated themselves ever closer to the Sea of Marmara, taking Yenişehir, then Bursa. By 1360 A.D., they were in possession of a broad expanse of land between the Dardanelles and Eskişehir, and by 1370 A.D. they had shifted their capital to Edirne, north of Constantinople.

The Byzantines watched the Ottoman conquests with increasing alarm, but were no longer strong enough to risk confrontation. Without military power, the Byzantine reliance on diplomacy was futile. The Byzantines had nothing left to bargain with; Europe regarded the Orthodox Greeks as enemies worse than the infidel Turks, and Constantinople's coffers were empty. **Sultan Beyazid I Yildirim "Thunderbolt"** began relentlessly choking off the city by sea and land in 1398 A.D. The long legacy of the Byzantine Empire seemed set to end, when, in 1401 A.D., on the verge of Constantinople's capitulation, the Tatar conqueror **Tamurlane** appeared in Asia Minor. Beyazid recognized the threat in the east, abandoned the siege and assembled an army to meet Tamurlane. The armies met at Ankara in 1402 A.D., each bearing a mystique of invincibility. It was Tamurlane who proved the better general, orchestrating a masterful battle, soundly defeating the Ottomans, and capturing Beyazid.

In the aftermath, Tamurlane's armies sacked most of the principal cities of Asia Minor. Had Tamurlane sought control of the region it would have been his for the taking, but the western campaign was simply a diversion. Tamurlane left Asia Minor in 1403 A.D. and marched back into Central Asia en route to a planned conquest of China. He died en route to China, leaving few provisions for succession and total chaos in Asia Minor.

After the departure of Tamurlane, the sons of Beyazid turned on one another, seeking control of the broken Ottoman empire. **Mehmet I** emerged victorious in 1413 A.D., and his work and the work of his son Murat II gradually restored the Ottomans to their former power.

Even with the reprieve from the siege of Beyazid, and even with civil war among the Ottomans, the Byzantines did precious little to help themselves. By 1451 A.D., 50 years after the first Ottoman siege was lifted, it was too late. **Mehmet II** (1451-1481 A.D.) assumed the throne with the express intention of seizing Constantinople immediately. For this purpose he commissioned the construction of ships, fortresses, and special artillery pieces on an unheard of scale. He choked off relief to the city as his great-grandfather Beyazid I had done, and in the spring of 1453 A.D. his army assembled beneath the massive land walls and began its siege.

After two months of stubborn, bloody fighting, the Ottomans seized Constantinople, at last accomplishing the goal for which Muslim armies had been striving for 700 years. The siege of Constantinople by Sultan Mehmet II was a turning point in the affairs of Europe and Asia both, eliminating the last legitimate vestige of Roman rule and bringing Europe face to face with the eastern armies Byzantium had long insulated them against. The sack of this city was, by all accounts, bloody, but very little worse than the sack by the Latins 250 years earlier.

If the Ottoman conquest was the death knell of a proud empire, it brought a new vitality to a city that had fallen into decay. First, Sultan Mehmet II was quick to secure the safety and trust of the existing population of the city, knowing that their skills were needed for commerce. Then the Sultan began relocating his subjects to the underpopulated city and injected vigor into the marketplaces. Sultan Mehmet was ambitious, and, as always, successful; Constantinople blossomed. Within three generations the trade generated in İstanbul, and the Ottoman Empire as a whole, brought the empire to an unrivalled state of wealth, and on the strength of this economic might the Ottoman military surged ever onward.

By the middle of the 16th century, the Ottoman territory matched the Byzantines at their zenith and included the eastern and southern Mediterranean coasts, Egypt, eastern Europe and the Balkans, the Black Sea, and all of Arabia and Persia. During the high water mark of the Ottomans in the 16th century Europe echoed with the peals of "Turk Bells," church bells rung in lament over another city fallen to the Ottoman armies. Through the 15th and 16th centuries, the Ottomans represented a terrifying mystery to the west, one with which the western armies were quite unable to cope.

The mystique faded slowly. One of the factors in the decline was the wealth introduced into the west from the New World, but a great deal of the blame must fall on the ineffective successors to Süleyman the Magnificent (1520-1566 A.D.). Süleyman himself, ruler of the Empire at its apex, must shoulder some of the blame, having instituted short-sighted economic reforms and killed his popular and promising eldest son Mustafa as a result of harem intrigue. The first hard evidence of decline, however, came under Selim II (1566-1574 A.D.), when the Ottoman navy was crushed at the **Battle of Lepanto** (1571 A.D.). For the Europeans, this success was an inspiration and a turning point, long-awaited proof that the militaries of the west could match the Turks in open battle. It was just one battle among many, but Lepanto serves as a historical marker. The warfare between the Ottomans and the kingdoms of the west remained inconclusive for the greater part of a century, but the high water mark of the Ottoman Empire had been reached.

In the absence of strong leadership from the sultan, several **Grand Viziers** emerged from the Palace Schools to husband the Ottoman Empire through increasingly turbulent times. Preeminent among these were the **Köprülüs**, three generations of Albanians who guided the empire into the mid-1600s.

Even the wisest of grand viziers would have been hard-pressed to challenge the growing might and martial skill of the west, and, increasingly, of the Russians to the north. The contrast between the broad view of Peter the Great in Russia in the late 1600s and the narrow, retrograde administrations of the sultans and viziers could not have been greater, and the Ottomans' failure to adapt took a heavy cumulative toll.

The anemia of the empire was clear in its increasing relative poverty, the erosion of its possessions, and the weakness of its armies – now reliant on advisors from England and France. By the time Russian Czar Nicholas coined his famous term for the moribund empire in the 1800s, calling it **"the sick man of Europe,"** the evaluation was universally accepted. In a peculiar twist, the states of the west now endeavored to prop up the foundering empire for fear that its collapse would open the door to Russian expansion. Since the time of Peter the Great, the Russians had stalked their southern neighbor, coveting its ports and its access to the Mediterranean. A series of wars brought the Russians ever closer to their goal – and as early as 1804 Napoleon judged that the Ottoman Empire was certain to "fall in our time." Despite the best efforts of some of the late Ottoman sultans to bankrupt the empire and antagonize its powerful neighbors, the Ottomans staggered, largely intact, into the 20th century.

But only just. Ottoman social reforms had been grudging relative to the explosive activity in Europe, but agitation against the conservative rule of the sultans grew through the latter half of the 1800s. A token form of republican rule was provisionally granted in 1908, but proved a failure. In the midst of the struggle for a relaxation of the sultan's autocratic powers, the Turks found their former vassals in the Mediterranean and the Balkans rising up and shaking of the Ottoman yoke. Most humiliating were a series of military defeats at the hands of the Romanian, Greek, and Bulgarian states beginning in 1910.

Just as Turkey was recovering from these setbacks, it was dragged onto the global stage; **World War I** had begun. The Turks weighed in on the side of Germany and the Central Powers against France and England. The Ottomans scored an unexpected early victory at **Gallipoli** under Mustafa Kemal, later known as Atatürk, but this promise was followed by dramatic defeats in Arabia. With the war's end, the Turks and their German allies shared defeat, and the **Treaty of Sevres** was designed to finally dissolve the Ottoman Empire. Most of the victorious allies were ceded tracts of Ottoman territory. İstanbul became neutral, occupied territory, and the Ottoman state was reduced to a rump of land in the interior of Asia Minor between Sivas and Eskişehir.

Kemal Atatürk

At first it seemed that the exhausted and demoralized Turks were resigned to the partition, although there was token resistance in the Anatolian interior. The British now turned to **Mustafa Kemal**, (later to become **Kemal Atatürk**) the most highly respected military man in Turkey after his leadership at Gallipoli and on the Syrian frontier, asking that he take a post in Anatolia and gauge the level of discontent he found there. Kemal was only too happy to accept this charge, but not with the spirit the British had envisioned. Upon arrival in the interior Kemal immediately drew the radical elements to him, fanning discontent over the dictates of the allies and turning on what was now a pet Ottoman government. Kemal sought out nationalist leaders, helped convene a congress, established a nationalist army, and, with the backing of Muslim clerics, eventually renounced the Ottoman government in İstanbul.

To the foundering Ottoman government, Kemal was a traitor, and, to Kemal, any government that agreed to the partition outlined in the Treaty of Sevres had committed the treachery. There was no possibility of resolving such an impasse through politics, and the British veterans of Great Game politics who were seeking to enforce the partition now sought a deux ex machina. At the behest of Lloyd George in London, Greek armies landed at İzmir and began an invasion into the interior in 1920.

This attempt to root out the rebel government at its source proved a grave mistake. The hotheaded opposition of Mustafa Kemal and his fellows to the Treaty of Sevres had remained relatively isolated to the east until Greek columns began penetrating into Anatolia. Now Turkish apathy exploded into anger; the Greek invasion shocked the Turks into seeing the grimmest aspects of the treaty signed by their leadership in İstanbul, and from throughout the country people flocked to Mustafa Kemal. The army swelled, and the nationalists at last emerged from their makeshift capital at Ankara against the invading army.

After stalemating the Greeks to close out the 1921 campaign season at the Battle of Sakarya, Kemal engineered a decisive victory in August of 1922 and drove the beaten Greek army directly back to the Aegean, which he reached just weeks later. The **War of Independence** ended with the Greeks sailing away from a burning İzmir, and the allies realizing that the genuine Turkish government was now Kemal's nationalist body at Ankara.

World War I had left Western Europe with little stomach for continued fighting, and some of the allies (Italy and France, for instance) were not pleased that the original partition had left Britain in command of the Mosul oil fields. Kemal's nationalists left the divided allies no choice other than to fight or draft a new peace. The allies chose the latter, and in the **Treaty of Lausanne** the borders of Turkey were extended to their current size (the Hatay/Antakya area was a later addition). The treaty also approved an exchange of populations, shifting Greeks in Turkey to Greece and Turks in Greece back to Turkey.

Kemal's series of dangerous gambles had paid off, and he now set about establishing a strong, western-looking nation. He set the tone immediately, making Ankara the permanent capital and turning his back on the intrigues of İstanbul. He steered a careful, peaceful course with his neighbors as only a military man could do, and carried out a raft of remarkable reforms. He abolished the fez, put women on equal political and social footing with men, changed the alphabet from Arab to Latin letters, eliminated "Arab" words in the Turkish language, created a secular republican form of government, and instituted a tradition of last names, choosing Atatürk, or "Father Türk" for himself. Kemal Atatürk proved one of the most charismatic and visionary men in history, with a rare strength of will that made him both a great revolutionary and a great nation-builder.

According to a popular story, British Prime Minister Lloyd George, surveying the wreckage of his Treaty of Sevres, shook his head and said

"A man like this comes along once a century; how could we have known?"

The Turkish Republic

Atatürk was the first president of the Republic, and remained so until his death in 1938. Atatürk's successor was one of his close friends and top generals, **Ismet İnönü**. İnönü carried forward the secular vision of Atatürk, and was careful to heed his commander's advice against entering World War II. Turkey succeeded in maintaining its neutrality despite the entreaties of various allies. Only in 1945, with the allies marching toward Berlin, did Turkey cast its lot with the winners.

In the aftermath of World War II, the Soviet Union began making claims on Turkey's eastern cities on behalf of its Armenian citizens. These claims, an extension of what was now a 300-year old tradition of Russian agitation in Asia Minor, resulted in immediate American support for Turkey in accordance with the Truman Doctrine. This also proved the foundation of what was to become a longstanding alliance between Turkey and the west.

Turkey was embraced by the North Atlantic Treaty Organization (NATO) in 1952. Turkey was that organization's stable southern anchor throughout the Cold War, and remains so today with NATO's largest standing army. The stability of the military has not been mirrored in the political arena, and has even come at the expense of domestic politics.

During the last years of İsmet İnönü's presidency, the first major popular elections were held and the country seemed ready to settle into western-style democracy. It was an abortive attempt; the military staged a coup in 1960, charging the sitting Democratic Party with bungling the economy and, ironically, undermining democracy. The principals of the deposed government were ousted and some of them, including Prime Minister **Adnan Menderes**, were executed. A new constitution was drawn up and new elections were held in 1961.

This process was to repeat itself at ten year intervals. The 1971 coup came in the wake of a deteriorating economy and leftist uprisings. The military seized power and called for new elections, and a particularly troubled period began. The island of **Cyprus**, an autonomous nation which included people of both Greek and Turkish descent, was a source of antagonism between Greece and Turkey, as well as between the Greek an Turkish Cypriots. Simmering disputes boiled over in 1973, when a Greek patriot staged a coup on the island and declared his intention to unite with Greece. The clumsy coup attempt fueled fighting between the two ethnicities, and was the invitation for which the Turks had hoped. Within 48 hours Turkish troops were ashore, seizing key towns and strategic points under the (authentic) pretense that the Turkish population was in danger.

UN negotiators, NATO, and America moved quickly to avert genuine war between Greece and Turkey, but the issues that sparked the conflict were not – and are not – resolved. UN peacekeepers were posted along the border between the Greeks and Turks (known as the Green Line), and they remain there today. The northern section of the island officially declared its independence in 1983, establishing the Turkish Republic of Northern Cyprus. "Greek" Cyprus enjoys international recognition (and is considered for inclusion in the European Union), while Northern Cyprus is recognized only by Turkey.

The Greeks weren't the only former subjects creating headaches for Turkey in the 1970s. Kurdish and Armenian minorities began agitating violently against what they considered a legacy of oppression. In this they received at least tacit support from the Soviet Union. Perhaps as a reaction against the chaos, Islamic fundamentalists began calling for a return to religious government. This only served to compound the problem, and, like clockwork, the military staged another coup in 1980.

Turkey's exercise in Islamic democracy seemed to have failed again. Bülent Ecevit, Süleyman Demirel, and Neçmettin Erbakan, all major players in today's Turkey, were arrested and imprisoned, as were thousands of others throughout the country. Amnesty International charged Turkey with 250,000 political arrests between 1980 and 1988. The restrictions and human rights violations, however, seemed to bring a degree of peace. A military general, Kenan Evren, assumed the presidency in 1980 and, once again, called for elections.

The 1990s were ushered in, remarkably, *without* a coup. The grip of the military had relaxed and political leaders seemed to have put the nation on a relatively even keel at last. A long-considered multi-billion dollar infrastructure project in the south (the GAP project) at last got under way. The Iraqi invasion of Kuwait and the Gulf even offered the Turks to take a turn on the world stage as a key supporter of the allied opposition to Iraq. Turkish President **Turgut Özal** provided the allies with military assistance and initiated economic sanctions against Iraq, a major trading partner.

The one major shadow on the Turkish landscape in the early 1990s was the escalating conflict with Kurdish separatists in the southeast. Even as the Turkish government moved to redress some of its past anti-Kurdish policies (legalizing the Kurdish language it banned in 1923, for instance), more and more Turkish troops were being posted to the southeast. Kurdish agitation in southeastern Turkey has continued to simmer and there's been no formal peace. Such a peace is all the more unlikely because Turkey's southern neighbors, particularly Syria, view

Human Rights

Turkish officials have simmered over Turkey's checkered record on human rights, sometimes intimating that Amnesty International and US-financed human rights investigators have created accusations out of whole cloth. Unfortunately, they have not. Turkey has had legitimate human rights issues, but has made remarkable progress in the past 15 years.

The easing of tensions in the southeast—and the end of martial law there—is one mark of progress. Likewise, abuses of journalists, as reported by the Committee to Protect Journalists, have eased.

In the summer of 2002, the Turkish Parliament took a promising step toward redressing ills by abolishing the death penalty (incidentally, a sentence last implemented in 1984!) and legalizing Kurdish-language education and TV and radio broadcasts. The measures probably made sense domestically, but the palliative effect on Europeans weighing Turkey's candidacy in the European Union can't be overstated.

For all of that, the real key to improvement has been the courage of Turks speaking out against political imprisonment and other crimes through an increasingly responsible and outspoken media. Turkish journalists, a courageous bunch who have seen their peers killed for their opinions, deserve particular recognition for publicizing incidents of brutality at great risk to themselves.

It remains to be seen if Turkey's progress can be sustained, but there is reason to be optimistic.

the Kurds as a lever to keep the Turkish southeast unstable and the huge GAP project from reaching completion.

Through all of this, Europe remains stuffy toward the Turks. Over the din of objecting Greeks, the European Economic Community welcomed Turkey as a member in 1995, but there seems little chance that Turkey will be invited to join the European Union despite its membership in NATO. Not all Turks are sure that EU membership would be to Turkey's advantage, anyway. Some push for stronger ties with Central Asia and the Middle East. The 1995 elections gave voice to that sentiment, when the fundamentalist **Islamic Refah Party** led by **Neçmettin Erbakan** won the largest share of the vote. Two conservative parties, led by former Prime Minister **Tansu Çiller** and **Meşut Yilmaz**, proved unable to form a viable coalition government, leaving Erbakan in a position to partner with Çiller and assume the role of Prime Minister in the summer of 1996.

The rise of an Islamic party was a stunning event in the Republic's steadfastly secular history, and it did not sit well with the military. The system of checks and balances in Turkish government provides the greatest power not to the Prime Minister, but to a committee made up largely of military men and the President, then Süleyman Demirel. The military men, forced to choose between the secular or the republican legacy of Atatürk, have always selected the former (as, in fairness, Atatürk himself did). This committee forced the resignation of Erbakan in 1997, banning him from politics and disbanding his party. A political melee among the secular parties ended with the competent and stoic Mesut Yilmaz as prime minister.

However, eliminating political parties does not remove the concerns that led to their formation; the **PKK**, the Kurdish workers party, was likewise banned to the advantage of no one. The fundamentalist Virtue Party has picked up the banner of the fundamentalists, and in October 1998 this party proved crucial in undermining the Yilmaz coalition. Against all odds, the coalition government that arrived in 1998—headed by political veteran Bülent Ecevit—enjoyed more than two years of remarkable success. Difficulties with the Kurds began easing in 1999 (in part as a result of the capture of PKK leader Abdullah Ocalan). By setting a rigid economic schedule to meet International Monetary Fund goals, the coalition steered the Turkish stock market to the best returns in the world in 1999. Better still, President Ahmet Sezer, appointed in 2000, won admirers for his determination to clean up corruption that has plagued the country. Even the catastrophic earthquake centered on Izmit in northwestern Turkey in 1999—in which an estimated 30,000 died— failed to derail the sense that things were improving.

It was too good to last. In March, 2001 President Sezer and Prime Minister Ecevit had a very public falling-out—apparently over Sezer's battle against corruption. The result: the Turkish Lira collapsed, so thoroughly that Turkey removed its artificial targets. In the space of two months, the Lira was reduced to one-half of its value, international investors were frightened away, and any confidence in the government was shaken.

Enter an American of Turkish extraction, a former IMF official named Kemal Derviş. Derviş was ceded wide-ranging powers to force accountability at state-owned banks, and make other politically difficult decisions stick. Predictably, economic belt-tightening measures have not been particularly popular in a country already enduring difficult economic times; the Ecevit coalition soldiered on as support begin to fray, propped up by a military council wary of new elections and the potential for gains by the Islamic Virtue Party.

The two men most respected in the country—President Sezer and Economic Minister Derviş—may well be tilting at windmills in their attempts to eliminate corruption and reform an economy that has run at 60 percent inflation for almost 25 years. Neither man, alas, is a politician; Turks feel their political parties are plagued with corruption, that nepotism and political favoritism cost their economy hundreds of millions of dollars a year—and they are right to feel that way.

September 11 & Beyond

The terrorist attacks on New York City and Washington D.C. raise a few questions for people interested in visiting Turkey. Some of these are answered elsewhere, but we thought it would be helpful to distill some central issues.

Secular democracy: Turkey is the world's great example of a secular Islamic democracy. The vision of Kemal Atatürk, that Turkey must cast its lot with the technological and political advances of the west, has been nurtured for almost 80 years. Even the leaders of Turkey's pro-Islamic parties support democracy, participation in the European Union, and the rights of women.

Western ties: The United States counts Turkey among its closest allies, a stalwart NATO nation that has always manned the southeastern frontier of that alliance. Turkey is host to one of the world's largest American Air Force Bases—Incirlik, near Adana—and its troops have trained with both Americans and Israelis. Turkey plays a crucial supporting role for any American action in the Middle East.

Turks and Arabs: Turks are Muslim, but they are not Arab. As rulers of Arabia—and much of Europe and northern Africa—in the heyday of the Ottomans, the Turks are under no illusions about their relationship with their southern and eastern neighbors. That is, Arabs (Shi'ites in particular) have generations-old axes to grind against the Turks, and the Turks likewise. When you hear about anti-American sentiment in the "Arab world", bear in mind that Turkey is not in the Arab world.

The Personal and Political: Having traveled in Syria, Jordan, and Egypt, we can attest to the personal kindness and friendliness of both Turks and Arabs. It is true that American policy can be unpopular, but it is also true that people anywhere in the Middle East are delighted—outright delighted—to meet individual Americans. Turks, in particular, feel an affinity for America they do not feel for the somewhat cold nations of Europe.

In the summer of 2002, Turkey finds itself at yet another watershed moment; the ruling Ecevit coalition (and the elderly statesman himself) is weak, the popular former foreign minister for the Ecevit coalition—Ismail Cem—has created a splinter party, the economy continues to struggle (helped not at all by soft tourism in the wake of 9/11), and the conservative Islamic party stands to make troubling gains in the parliament in autumn elections. As a backdrop to this, the growing possibility of a US-led assault on Iraq threatens presents a hydra-headed dilemma for Turkey: support of its close U.S. ally (whether the outright support of the Turkish army or simple rights to base attacks out of Turkey and Incirlik Air Force base) may further alienate Arab neighbors, precipitate Iraqi military action against Turkey, and result in the creation of a Kurdish state. It is a certainty that trade with Iraq will be disrupted—something that cost Turkey billions of dollars following the Gulf War.

Turkey's decisions are never easy ones, and always have repercussions far beyond its own borders. Once a physical crossroads, Turkey is today an ideological crossroads. As the greatest example of a secular Islamic democracy, it is the hope of the west, and as the greatest Muslim influence in the west, it is the hope of Islam. For all of that, in the end, Turkey stands alone.

The Byzantine Emperors

Constantine I (The Great)	324-337 A.D.
Constantius	337-361
Julian	361-363
Jovian	363-364
Valens	362-378
Theodosius I (The Great)	379-395
Arcadius	395-408
Theodosius II	408-450
Marcian	450-457
Leo I	457-474
Leo II	474
Zeno	474-491
Anastasius I	491-518
Justin I	518-527
Justinian I	527-565
Justin II	565-578
Tiberius II	578-582
Maurice	582-602
Phocas	602-610
Heraclius	610-641
Constantine II	641

Constantine III	*641-668*
Constantine IV	*668-685*
Justinian II	*685-695*
Leontius	*695-698*
Tiberius III	*698-705*
Justinian II	*705-711*
Philippicus Bardanes	*711-713*
Anastasius	*713-715*
Theodosius III	*715-717*
Leo III	*717-741*
Constantine VI	*780-797*
Irene	*797-802*
Nicephorus I	*802-811*
Stauracius	*811*
Michael I	*811-813*
Leo V	*813-820*
Michael II	*820-829*
Theophilus	*829-842*
Michael III	*842-867*
Basil I	*867-886*
Leo VI	*886-912*
Alexander	*912-913*
Constantine VII	*913-959*
Romanus I Lecapenus	*919-944*
Romanus II	*959-963*
Nicephorus II Phocas	*963-969*
John Tzimisces	*969-976*
Basil II Bulgarocontus	*976-1025*
Constantine VIII	*1025-1028*
Romanus III Argyrus	*1028-1034*
Michael IV	*1034-1041*
Michael V	*1041-1042*
Theodora / Zoe	*1042*
Constantine IX	*1042-1055*
Theodora	*1055-1056*
Michael VI	*1056-1057*
Isaac Comnenus	*1057-1059*
Constantine X Ducas	*1059-1067*
Romanus IV Diogenes	*1067-1071*
Michael VII Ducas	*1071-1078*
Nicephorus III	*1078-1081*
Alexius I Comnenus	*1081-1118*
John II	*1118-1143*

Manuel I	*1143-1180*
Alexius II	*1180-1183*
Andronicus I	*1183-1185*
Isaac II Angelus	*1185-1195*
Alexius III	*1195-1203*
Isaac II Angelus	*1203-1204*
Alexius IV	*1203-1204*
Alexius V Ducas	*1204*
(Constantinople seized by Crusaders)	
Michael VIII Paleologus	*1261-1282*
Andronicus II	*1282-1328*
Andronicus III	*1328-1341*
John V	*1341-1391*
John VI (co-emperor)	*1341-1354*
Andronicus IV(co-emperor)	*1376-1379*
John VII (co-emperor)	*1390*
Manuel II	*1391-1425*
John III	*1425-1448*
Constantine XI Dragases	*1449-1453*

The Ottoman Sultans

Orhan	*1324-1359*
Murat I	*1359-1389*
Beyazid I	*1389-1403*
Mehmet I	*1413-1421*
Murat II	*1421-1451*
Mehmet II (The Conqueror)	*1451-1481*
Beyazid II	*1481-1512*
Selim I (The Grim)	*1512-1520*
Süleyman (The Magnificent)	*1520-1566*
Selim II (The Sot)	*1566-1574*
Murat III	*1574-1595*
Mehmet III	*1595-1603*
Ahmet I	*1603-1617*
Mustafa I	*1617-1618*
Osman II	*1618-1622*
Mustafa I	*1622-1623*
Murat IV	*1623-1640*
İbrahim	*1640-1648*
Mehmet IV	*1648-1687*
Süleyman II	*1687-1691*
Ahmet II	*1691-1695*
Mustafa II	*1695-1703*

Ahmet III	*1703-1730*
Mahmut I	*1730-1754*
Osman III	*1754-1757*
Mustafa III	*1757-1774*
Abdül Hamid`I	*1774-1789*
Selim III	*1789-1807*
Mustafa IV	*1807-1808*
Mahmut II	*1808-1839*
Abdül Mecit I	*1839-1861*
Abdül Aziz	*1861-1876*
Murat V	*1876*
Abdül Hamid II	*1876-1909*
Mehmet V	*1909-1918*
Mehmet VI	*1918-1922*

Presidents of the Turkish Republic

Kemal Atatürk	*1923-1938*
İsmet İnönü	*1938-1950*
Celal Bayar	*1950-1959*
Cemal Gürsel	*1959-1966*
Cevdet Sunay	*1966-1973*
Fahri Korutürk	*1973-1980*
Kenan Evren	*1980-1989*
Turgut Özal	*1989-1993*
Süleyman Demirel	*1993-2000*
Ahmet Sezer	*2000-present*

planning your trip

Chapter 6

When to Visit - Climate & Weather

Turkey bills itself as the "world's largest open air museum," so it should come as no surprise that weather is important. You will want to write postcards home to the effect that "Using some tumbled column drums as a makeshift table, we picnicked at the Temple of Apollo,"rather than "Hands numb. Slipped in mud going up to $%#& Temple of Apollo and broke camera. Knee hurts." Generally, it is important to stick to the spring, summer, and early fall to avoid rain, cold temperatures, and in many places, snow.

The tourism season proper runs from late May through early September. What's nice is, the tourism *weather* usually runs from April through mid-October. Along the southern coast you can even milk a few extra weeks of comfortable swimming weather, but in the interior–which, for weather purposes, includes İstanbul – you cannot fudge these dates much without risking arctic conditions. When winter storms hit, they can be long and patient, blowing bitter cold down past the Russian steppe and over the Black Sea toward the Aegean. The interior becomes muddy, frozen, and windswept, and places such as Cappadocia lose some of their charm.

Even İstanbul, a city at sea level and on the same latitude as Redding, California, can become dark and (speaking of Redding) joyless in the winter. It's worth noting that during the truly cold spells, the Bosphorous actually freezes over, an event that is said to happen about once a century. The coastal areas usually remain mild in the winter months – the coast near Antalya averages 50-55° F and has some nice weather, but you cannot count on getting a mid-winter tan.

As the thermometer goes, so go airfares and room rates. So, too, go crowds. It is not uncommon to have a good part of a marquee attraction like Ephesus almost to yourself in April and May, but come August tour buses disgorge thousands of tourists – if the bay hadn't silted up and forced the Ephesians to abandon the city, the tourists certainly would have driven them out. Book ahead in the high season – Turkey is absolutely wonderful in the summer, a secret that got out about 4,000 years ago. If you do brave the inclement weather and venture to Turkey in the off season, you will be rewarded with plentiful vacancies, low rates, and friendlier, less frayed people.

What to Pack

You probably have a good idea what you'll want to bring along on your trip, but we have some words of advice. As far as dress, you can pack fairly lightly in the summer. You'll find yourself on your feet quite often, so a good pair of sturdy boots will be welcome. Turkey is fairly conservative, so once you're off the beach you'll want avoid anything too revealing. Most coastal cities are used to seeing skin, but in some smaller towns the moment you leave the beach parking lot you are in a conservative village; try to respect the local sensibilities. On the same note, women should bring along a shawl – or count on buying one in Turkey – for use in mosques and holy sites.

Chances are you know quite well how to pack. Here are a few things you might not consider: a black crayon and large pieces of sturdy paper for making rubbings of inscriptions in stone; a good flashlight, particularly handy in the caves and warrens of Cappadocia and in tunnels beneath dozens of ruins; a flat plastic sink stopper for washing in the hotel bathroom; a wash cloth (most hotels do not have them); converters for 220 volts if you're bringing any electrical devices; likewise, two-prong adapters for the electrical outlets; a Turkish phrasebook; watercolors or charcoal, even if you don't think you can draw or paint; a pocket calculator for currency conversion; and earplugs to muffle the 4 a.m. call to prayer if you're not going to be getting up. Also, if you're bringing a laptop computer, check our computer section for accessories you may want.

What to Read

Some people have been working their way through books on the area since childhood and they're still missing important pieces. If this were a class, the most fun damned class you ever had, required reading would include:

Kinross, Lord Patrick, *Atatürk, The Birth of a Nation*, London, 1964. Lord Kinross is responsible for the two works that made Turkish and Ottoman history accessible in the west; this is a long, fascinating study of the mercurial leader who fashioned modern Turkey.

Kinross, Lord Patrick, *The Ottoman Centuries, The Rise and Fall of the Turkish Empire*, New York, 1977. The second of the major Kinross books. Kinross'work is an immensely readable account.

Norwich, John Julius, *Byzantium: The Early Centuries*, London, 1988. The trilogy written by Norwich, of which this is the first, is a captivating take on the cloudy history of the Byzantines.

Norwich, John Julius, *Byzantium: The Apogee*, New York, 1992.Norwich, John Julius, *Byzantium: The Decline and Fall*, London 1995.

Herodotus, *The History* (trans. David Grene), Chicago, 1987. *The History* is an account of world affairs in the fifth century B.C. by the "father of history," a period that includes the Persian campaign against Asia Minor and Greece.

Homer, *The Iliad*, (trans. Richard Lattimore), Chicago, 1951. *The Iliad* is the tale of a pivotal week in the siege of Troy.

Xenophon, *The Persian Expedition (Anabasis)* (trans. Rex Warner), Middlesex, 1949. The account of Xenophon's fighting retreat from Persia and into Asia Minor.

Special Interest Guides

Blake, Everett C. and Edmonds, Anna G., *Biblical Sites in Turkey*, İstanbul, 1977. Discusses the Seven Churches of Revelation, and addresses the religions that Christianity supplanted.

Bean, George, *Aegean Turkey, An Archeological Guide*, London, 1966; *Turkey's Southern Shore, An Archaeological Guide*, London, 1968; *Turkey Beyond the Maeander, An Archeological Guide*, London, 1971; *Lycian Turkey, An Archeological Guide*, London, 1978. Bean's books remain the finest written on Turkey's ruins. His groundbreaking, detailed studies of Hellenistic and Roman ruins are excellent companions along the Aegean and western Mediterranean.

Ceram, C.W.; *Gods, Graves, and Scholars*, London, 1961. A wonderfully written account of modern archaeology and its major players.

Abidine, Zeynep et al.; *İstanbul and Northwest Turkey*, Knopf, New York, 1993. A beautiful guide book dedicated to İstanbul.

Dubin, Marc and Lucas, Enver; *Trekking in Turkey*, Hawthorne, Australia, 1993. The only English book of its kind for Turkey.

Misc. Ed.; *İstanbul: The Halı Rug Guide*, London, 1996. What to know and where to buy in İstanbul.

Glassie, Henry; *Turkish Traditional Arts Today*. Excellent background resource for kilims and carpets.

Barillari, Diana and Godoli, Ezio; *İstanbul 1900, Art Nouveau Architecture and Interiors*, Octavo Press, Italy, 1996. A large, beautiful account of the bleeding edge architecture of İstanbul at the turn of the century.

Karmı, Ilan; *Jewish Sites of İstanbul: A Guide Book*, Isis Press, İstanbul, 1992. A good overview of Jewish history in İstanbul, and where to find both historical and contemporary Jewish communities.

Wood, Michael; *In Search of the Trojan War*, New American Library, New York, 1985. An attractive, in-depth look at the legend and reality of Troy and the story of its rediscovery.

Recommended Literature

Gün, Güneli, *On the Road to Baghdad*, Picador, London, 1991. A whirling, jarring, fun retelling of 1,001 Arabian Nights with a Turkish twist.

Pamuk, Orhan, *The White Castle*, London, 1990; *The Black Book*, Boston, 1994. Both books are written by the favored son of Turkish literature, with The Black Book being by far the more accessible of the two.

Kemal, Yasar, *Mehmed, My Hawk*, Harper Collins, New York, 1993; *Anatolian Tales*, Writers & Readers Publishing, 1983. Kemal is the standard for Turkish authors, and these are his two most-admired works.

Twain, Mark, *The Innocents Abroad*. An American icon's account of a cruise to the old world, including his remarkably dim view of Turkey.

Tekin, Latife, *Berji Kristin: Tales From the Garbage Hills*, Marion Boyars Publishers, New York, 1996. An unusual novel about the communities on the fringes of İstanbul.

Passports & Visas

Residents of the United States, Canada, and the U.K. can pick up a three month, $45 **tourist visa** upon arrival. You'll need to have that sum in **cash**. Immigration officers at airports and seaports are usually professional and quick. In the unlikely event you're arriving in Turkey by train, bus, or car, you may find the immigration officers less professional, and less quick.

The easiest way for residents of the Canada or the United States to apply for a **passport** is to call the main branch of the local post office and follow their instructions. They have the forms you need, or, if not, they can tell you who does. Canadians can call for further information at *Tel. 800/567-6868* or (Quebec) *283-2152*, and the U.S. Passport Information office has 24-hour service, *Tel. 202/647-0518*.

Keep a photocopy of your passport with you – or exchange with your traveling partner – as a hedge against thievery. A lost passport will bring your good times to an inconvenient end, so keep some other identification with you to help the nearest U.S. consulate or embassy get you set up with a new one and get you back on your way. A friend keeps his copy in his shoe, another in a pocket sewn into his underwear.

Note: Technically, yes, you are supposed to keep your passport with you at all times. If you want to shed the passport in big cities, however, the worst that will happen is an overanxious police officer will make you return to your room and show it. In years of living there, this happened not once. You will want to make sure that you have your passport along while you are in transit, and bear in mind that police often set up automobile checkpoints along roads within İstanbul and in the country-side. A minor hassle can graduate to a real problem if you do not have your passport while in transit.

Customs

As discussed in the İstanbul chapter, since you're almost sure to arrive at Atatürk International Airport in İstanbul, you're unlikely to be pulled aside at customs. If you are, the sorts of things you aren't supposed to have you're not likely to have; more than 400 cigarettes, for instance, or five liters of liquor. Notebook computers, once illegal with a hard drive greater than, uhm, 128K, are welcome no matter what the size of the hard drive. Some of the stranger restrictions are universally ignored, but here they are anyway; five rolls of film are technically the limit, as are 2.2 pounds of chocolate and 3.3 pounds of coffee. You needn't worry about any of these unless it looks as if you're likely to start up your own business.

Customs on departing from Turkey was once a hassle, with lots of cross-referencing between receipts and numbers in your passport. Now it's as effortless as entry. If you have purchased an antique carpet or kilim you were given a receipt and a certificate; you'll want to have these handy. Export of antiquities of any kind is forbidden, although old carpets can be exported with the proper paperwork.

There was once a system in place that allowed foreigners departing Turkey to recoup the 15% Value Added Tax levied on carpets and kilims, for example. This system was never well-run, and is universally ignored today. The only way to secure the documents you need is to request them from the carpet dealer, at which point the carpet dealer will tack on an additional 15% charge that you will have to go through a great deal of bureaucracy at the airport to recoup. In short, don't bother.

Returning to the United States

Fresh food is forbidden, as are Cuban cigars, cigarettes in excess of 200, and alcohol in excess of one liter, although this last prohibition is rarely observed. More worrying, if you indulged in lots of carpets and kilims, is tax. You are allowed $400 worth of purchases tax-free, but the next $1,000 is taxed at a 10 percent rate, and thereafter matters become confusing based on the sort of item and the specific tax rate. Sure, you can fudge a little – not that we would recommend it – but the customs folks are pretty shrewd. Tax is payable immediately. Most major international airports take credit cards. For more information, contact the **United States Customs Office**, *Tel. 703/318-5900.*

Accommodations

Rooms throughout Turkey are plentiful and relatively inexpensive, but there is a tremendous range in quality. We have put a premium on finding spots with peace and quiet, places where bougainvillea climb the rails and the view is good. We like bed and breakfasts and pensions ourselves, and although you'll only rarely find a "bed and breakfast" in Turkey, you'll find our listings lean toward small, warm accommodations. We also appreciate good, well-run pensions – of which there are many throughout Turkey – and the occasional large hotel, provided it delivers on its promise. The common denominators among our finds include attention to detail, friendly management, and access to the ruins, sites and beaches that have lured you to Turkey in the first place. As a result, we tend to neglect the German and British destination resorts such as Marmaris, Kemer, and Ölüdeniz in favor of the smaller, more charming places nearby.

Make no mistake, this hardly sentences you to being a placid bookworm on your vacation. We recommend bars, night clubs, and belly dancing restaurants – not to mention ballooning, rafting, canyoning, cycling, diving and scaling sheer cliffs to poke around in cave tombs. But at the end of the day it does your heart good to have a pretty terrace, a tidy room, and a helpful staff. Beware: the best of the hotels we have selected are so nice that you won't ever want to leave the premises and actually see Turkey.

Reservations

You can make reservations for hotels in this book by simply contacting the hotel directly. We have provided fax numbers for those hotels that have them; most do. Some even have websites, which is a distinct advantage. If you're dealing directly with a hotel, the hotel should send you a list of half-board rates and other options, provided they have them.

The prices given in this book are for the high season; you may be pleasantly surprised by the rate you get if you're visiting outside of the July-early September peak season.

If you are planning your own trip and booking ahead, it is always wise to inquire about the best available rates from the sales office of a large hotel. If, for instance, you would like to stay at the Sheraton in Ankara, the hotel's sales office will be much more flexible than people at the toll-free reservation number; the cost of faxing Turkey should be more than offset by your savings. If you're staying longer than one night, on business, or use nice stationery you should get a discount. If it's the off-season in the region (which is August and September in Ankara, by the way), the sales personnel will be particularly keen to cut your rate.

If you learn that the large hotel in which you are interested is booked, ask the hotel for the names of travel agencies with whom they work. There's a strong likelihood the hotel will have rented a cluster of rooms to one of the British agencies, and that agency may have rooms.

In "Seeing Turkey on Your Own," later in this chapter, you'll find an excellent listing for resources that should help you plan and, should you wish, arrange your trip. American Express, Council Travel, Wagon Lit, and other companies also have travel management offices that can be of service.

Finally, we have accepted no money or inducements in exchange for favorable reviews of hotels, restaurants, shops, or travel agencies.

Getting a Room For the Night

The standard of accommodations in Turkey is hardly uniform, but hospitality generally is.

It is always a good idea to ask to see a room before paying and taking the key. Even at good hotels, the quality of the rooms vary greatly; those who don't ask to see the room typically get the worst room available so that later guests, who may ask to see the room first, are pleased by what they find.

Some hotels will insist that you fill out a form and provide details about your passport. There's no need for concern, it's paperwork demanded by the municipality.

Getting to Turkey

BY AIR

A few flights out of London serve Ankara, Antalya, Dalaman, and Bodrum (Güllük) directly, but virtually everyone first arrives in İstanbul (see İstanbul chapter, *Arrivals & Departures*, for more information). İstanbul's **Atatürk Airport** is served by a host of major airlines, including Air France, British Air, and Lufthansa. The national carrier, **Turkish Airlines,** is a well-run organization and is worth considering for its direct New York-İstanbul or Chicago-İstanbul flights (Note: smoking is permitted in the last few rows on these flights). Delta also serves İstanbul with direct flights. With a direct flight you won't arrive fresh, but you'll be in remarkably better shape than if you fly via Helsinki, London, or

The Jet Lag-Mathematics Trap

Turkey is 11 time zones away from the west coast of North America, eight time zones away from the east coast, which means you can fall prey to some awful jet-lag if you aren't careful. A surprisingly effective trick is to simply not to do the math. Do not start calculating how long you've been awake or what time it 'should' be, and you'll find adjusting much easier.

Frankfurt. Plus, you won't miss your connection in Europe or have to wander around an extra airport jet-lagged.

No matter who you fly with, fares to İstanbul aren't cheap – although there are reasonable fares lurking out there. In this, a good travel agent or a service such as Expedia can save you hundreds of dollars. The cheapest low-season return fare we've seen to İstanbul is $450, and this was from either the west coast or the east coast. These prices erupt in the summer, when a return fare from the west coast increases to $1,100, with the east coast having prices $2-300 cheaper.

A few of the best places to go hunting for fare information in North America are:

• **Expedia**, *www.expedia.com*
• **Turkish Air Travel Bureau**, 20 East 49th St., New York, NY 10017, *Tel. 212/888-1180, www.turkishair.com*
• **Travel CUTS**, 187 College St., Toronto, Canada M5T 1P7, *Tel. 416/979-2406*
• **STA Travel**, 273 Newbury St., Boston, MA 02116, *Tel. 617/266-6014*; 920 Westwood Blvd., Los Angeles, CA 90024, *Tel. 213/824-1574*; 17 East 45th St., New York, NY 10017, *212/986-9470*; 166 Geary St., Ste. 702, San Francisco, CA 94108, *Tel. 415/391-8407*

The UK has an excellent collection of shops with cheap airfares – the only trick is you have to book a round-trip flight to Britain. The enduring champion among London's bucket shops is **Trailfinders**, 46 Earls Court Rd., London, W8 6EJ, *Tel. 44 171 937 5400*. You can also consult the backpacker's rag, London-based *TNT Magazine* (free issue at *www.tntmag.co.uk*).

BY BOAT

If you're fortunate enough to be leaving for Turkey from Italy, there are weekly Turkish Maritime Lines ferries, one from Brindisi, several from Venice. As detailed below, you should contact **Turkish Maritime**

Lines: *Tel. 90 212 244 2502, Reservations Tel. 90 212 249 9222, Fax 90 212 251 9025.*

A wiser course may be to make reservations through the Maritime Lines' English broker, **Sunquest London Holiday Ltd.**, 23 Princes St., London, WIR 7RG. U.K., *Tel. 44 171 499 9992, Fax 44 171 499 9995.*

Antalya/Marmaris/İzmir/İstanbul-Venice, Italy

Ferries leave Marmaris and Antalya at noon on Wednesday, arriving in Venice on Saturday at 10 a.m. Departures from Venice are scheduled at 4 p.m. Saturday. In the off-season, the cost for cabins with windows starts at $350 per person, one way, increasing to $450 in the high season. Berths in interior cabins with four beds begin at $250 in the off-season, increasing to $310 in the high season. Pullman seats cost $210 in the low season. The cost of meals is included on the three-day trip. Ferrying a car costs $240 in the high season, plus port tax.

İzmir and İstanbul departures are at 4 p.m. Wednesday, arriving Venice at 11 a.m. Saturday. Prices are the same for the Antalya and Marmaris ferries.

Çeşme-Brindisi, Italy

Ferries depart Çeşme, west of İzmir, at 11 a.m. Tuesday and noon Friday. The trip takes 31 hours, arriving Brindisi at 6 p.m. Wednesday and 7 p.m. Saturday. Ferries return to Çeşme from Brindisi after a five-hour wait. Ferries do not run in the winter. One-way high-season fares range between $400 for a deluxe cabin and $180 for a berth in a four bed, internal cabin. Pullman armchair rates are $160 in the high season, and car ferrying costs $200, plus $30 port tax. Full board is included.

For information about sailing your own ship into a Turkish port, contact İstanbul's **Chamber of Maritime Commerce**, Meclisi Mebusan Caddesi No. 22, Salıpazar, İstanbul, *Tel. 212 252 0131, Fax 212 293 7935.*

Getting Around Turkey

BY AIR

Turkey is a big country, and plane flights can be a great advantage if you're short on time or short on patience.

Turkish Airlines, the national carrier, and a collection of small private airlines, the largest of which is **İstanbul Airlines,** are the alternatives for flights within Turkey. Virtually every major city in Turkey has air service, but most connections must be made either through İstanbul or Ankara (both of which have domestic and international terminals). Airfares to any point in the country are fairly uniform from İstanbul and Ankara alike; $75 one way, $125 return.

İstanbul Air has far fewer flights and serves only the prime airports – Trabzon, Antalya, Dalaman, Ankara, and İzmir – but their fares average about $60 one way, $100 for a round trip.

For information on flights when you're in İstanbul, do yourself a favor and contact **Imperial Turizm**, Divan Yolu Caddesi No. 31, Sultanahmet, İstanbul, *Tel. 212 513 9430, Fax 212 512 3291*. This small, honest agency is located directly behind the tram stop uphill from the Pudding Shop on Divan Yolu, and Saim has been of great help to ourselves and acquaintances. You can also check in by phone, fax, or email with agencies such as **Argeus** for ticketing information, İstiklal Caddesi No. 13, Ürgüp, 50400, *Tel. 90 384 341 4688, Fax 90 384 341 4888, inform@argeus.com.tr, www.argeus.com.tr*. The address and phone number for **Turkish Airlines** is: Atatürk Hava Limanı, Yesilköy, İstanbul, *Tel. 212 663 6300, Fax 212 663 4744*. You can check schedules and even book flights at *www.turkishairlines.com/*.

BY BUS

Planes have their appeal, but bus travel in Turkey is cheap, popular, and efficient. The top bus lines have spacious, comfortable coaches, coffee, comfortable seats and – on the main İstanbul routes – fresh copies of the English-language *Turkish Daily News*. Bus connections are easy in the west and along the Black Sea; faster, nicer, and often cheaper than train service.

In 1997, Turkey even legislated an end to smoking on inter-city buses. This is surprisingly well observed, but please note that the bus drivers are allowed to – and do – smoke. If you have concerns about this, make sure you get a seat towards the back of the bus (seating is assigned when you purchase your ticket). In lieu of smoking buses, most bus lines now make more frequent stops en route, ostensibly for bathroom breaks or to refuel or wash the bus, but in reality it mainly serves the nicotine-needy.

Varan (*http://www.varan.com.tr* – the site is in English, but schedule information is listed in Turkish, so Kalkış means 'Departing') is the finest bus line, followed by **Ulusoy**. In the next echelon, Kamil Koç and Metro do a good job, but, honestly, there are dozens of bus lines that offer good service, far better service than an American accustomed to Greyhound might expect. The prices are outstanding: Varan's relatively expensive service from İstanbul to Antalya – 12 hours, overnight – runs $30, and the 19 hour trip from İstanbul to Trabzon is just $35. Doses of lemon cologne, snacks, and cups of Pepsi are included; the finest non-stop bus lines serve meals.

You will probably become familiar with the **dolmuş**, a means of public transportation ubiquitous throughout the country. Dolmuş, mean-

Bus Travel with Style & Panache

"People on Turkish buses are either going home or leaving home. I never met anyone who admitted to traveling on business or state duty... This was a swift, strong Ulusoy bus, from the long-distance road fleet which binds the Turkish continent together. Every hour or so, the conductor came down the aisle with a glass carboy of cologne. Cupped hands were held out and filled; faces and necks were laved and massaged. The conversations fell away, and the passengers slept."

Neal Ascherson, **Black Sea: The Birthplace of Civilisation and Barbarism**, London: Vintage, 1995.

ing "stuffed," run more frequently than big buses, and are the main means that Turks use to get from place to place. You needn't be concerned about the "stuffed" part; dolmuş are typically fairly comfortable, and aren't allowed to get crammed full the way that minibuses in India or Africa can. Dolmuş are privately run, with rates based on the distance they take you.

In many cities the **otogar**, or bus station, is located outside of town. In such cases, there will almost certainly be ticket offices in the center of town, and from there you can get a shuttle out to the main otogar. Such is the case in İstanbul, where ticket offices are ranged around Taksim and Sultanahmet.

One final note: try to avoid the front seats – rows one through four – on overnight trips. The drivers not only smoke, they often maintain a long dialogue with their friends, and should you want to sleep through a stop you'll be bothered by noise, smoke, and cold from the open door.

BY CAR

Driving in Turkey is not a decision to be taken lightly. Turks have a remarkably more... improvisational driving style than that to which you are accustomed. Lane markers and posted speed signs seem to serve mostly decorative purposes. Vehicles pull out in front of one another, or try to pass, when doing so means their fellow drivers will have to stand on the brakes. Roads are in most cases well-signed and in good condition.

For all of its peculiarities, driving seems remarkably more civil than it is in America. If you pull out ahead of someone, they may not like it but it won't bother them. Everyone is used to being cut off or jumped in line, and there is a nice flexibility to Turkish driving when you get used to it.

Our most important advice—observed by many Turks—is simple: **Don't drive at night**. Given the livestock and pedestrian traffic in the road, the number of cars with broken lights (or with drivers who opt not to use them), the weariness of long-haul truck drivers, and your own unfamiliarity with the roads, be sure to get where you're going during daylight hours.

Several of the main highways in Turkey include stretches with toll roads, and we strongly encourage that you take them. This is no time to stick to the country roads for the aesthetic of it; the toll road was probably built because the old highway was dangerous, and there's little aesthetic pleasure to driving in the shadow of the freeway, behind a diesel smoke-spewing rig. Be sure to have smaller denomination currency available.

Road Signs

Our favorite road sign is the cow crossing sign featuring a cow with terrible posture—you'll see it everywhere. Here are some others that are a bit more important:

English	Turkish
Caution	Dikkat
Stop	Dur
Slow	Yavaş
Do not enter	Girılmez
One way	Tek Istıkamet
City center	Şehir Merkezi
No parking	Park Yapılmaz
Traffic region	Bölge Trafik
Don't be a traffic beast!	Trafik Canavar Olmayin
Press (for a ticket, etc)	Başınız

Turkey's big cities don't require a car, and in İstanbul in particular you don't really want a car. Why? First of all, you're probably staying in Sultanahmet, a short walk from whatever you want to see. Second, roads in İstanbul are tight, confusing, and subject to frequent gridlock. Third, cheap local taxis are an immensely better, more efficient and more relaxing option—note that parking is bad enough that car *owners* take cabs.

Should anything happen to your car (a blown tire, a broken muffler...) you'll find that most little roadside auto shops are able to help. There is a pretty limited range of cars, so spare parts should be a cinch, and, in general, Turkish mechanics are quick, clever, and cheap.

Road Regulations

Turks are sensible people, and drive on the right. You'll find that speed limit signs are few and far between, but you should try to stay at or below 50 kph in the city and 100 kph outside of the city. Freeway traffic moves at 140 kph, and it's okay to move with the flow of traffic.

You will, on average, run into a military or police checkpoint one out of every three days you drive. There's nothing unusual in this. You may be asked for your drivers license, or your passport. Once you clarify that you're an American or Canadian, you may find yourself helping a young jandarma to polish up his English, but you'll quickly be waved on with a "Devam Et" ("continue").

Car Rental

Outside of major cities, a rental car is a joy to have, but it's a joy that will cost you. Car rental in Turkey is more expensive than anywhere else in Europe—and far more expensive than car rental in North America. This stems from the incidence of accidents and the overall expense of operating and covering taxes for automobiles in Turkey.

We've found that the big agencies are, oddly, far more expensive than renting through some of our favorite travel agencies in Turkey— even if you are a Gold Club or AAA member or the like. Still—the big American companies with offices in Turkey are a good place to start:
- **Avis**: *Tel. 800/331-1084; www.avis.com*
- **Budget**: *Tel. 800/527-0700; www.budget.com*
- **Hertz**: *Tel. 800/654-3001; www.hertz.com*
- **AAA**: *Tel. 800/562-2582; www.aaa.com*

Using these rates as a frame of reference, you'll probably be quite pleased with the rates (and services—e.g. one-way rentals, pick-up and delivery) offered by agencies in Turkey. Here is one good, reliable Turkish agency:

Argeus Tourism & Travel, Istiklal Cad. No. 7, 50400 Ürgüp, *Tel. (384) 341-4688, Fax (384) 341-4888; www.argeus.net*. Sample rental rates for one week rental: Renault Clio, $308 high season; $238 low season: Toyota Corolla, $651 high season; $469. Includes: unlimited mileage, collision damage waiver, theft insurance, local taxes. If rental period is three days or more, no fee for drop-off and pick-up. One way rental also available.

For further comparison, check in with Istanbul's **Imperial Tourism**, Divan Yolu Cad No. 30, 34410, Sultanahmet, Istanbul, *Tel. (212) 513 9430, Fax (212) 512-3291; info@imperial-turkey.com*.

BY FERRY

Ferries within and around Turkey are very popular in the high season, and reservations are necessary. **Turkish Maritime Lines** takes bookings directly, and ordinarily has an English speaker on hand *(Information: Tel. 90 212 244 2502, Reservations: Tel.90 212 249 9222, Fax 90 212 251 9025)*. You can also make reservations through their English broker, **Sunquest London Holiday Ltd.**, 23 Princes St., London, WIR 7RG, *Tel. 44 171 499 9992, Fax 44 171 499 9995*.

Once in Turkey you can make international reservations through **Karavan Travel Agency**, *Tel. 90 212 247 5044, Fax 90 212 241 5178*.

There are either four or five cabin classes on Turkish ferries. Deluxe and "A" cabins have sea views and are the most expensive. "B" and "C" cabins are cheaper, but offer no views. Hususı, or private, cabins are available on some routes, offering semi-deluxe accommodations. Pullman chairs are also available, as is space on deck in the summer season.

Teachers, students, people 65 years and older, and children 7-12 years old receive a 30 percent discount.

INTERNAL FERRIES
İstanbul-İzmir
•Depart İstanbul 6:30 p.m. Friday, arrive İzmir 12:45 p.m. Saturday.
•Depart İzmir 2 p.m. Sunday, arrive İstanbul 9 a.m. Monday.

Double cabin fares range between $75 per person for a deluxe cabin and $30 per person for a "C" class cabin, with three levels in between. In addition, you can book a round trip from İstanbul ("Hafta Sonu Tur"), using the ferry as your hotel in İzmir on Saturday night: this increases the fare two and one-half times. Ferries run throughout the year. Meals are served three times daily, breakfast $3, lunch and dinner $10. Car transport costs $50.

A second option is the quicker İstanbul-Bandırma ferry, which connects with the Bandirma-İzmir train. This journey costs only $11.00 per person, departing İstanbul six times weekly with the Bandırma ferry. Departures are at 9 a.m. every day but Sunday, with arrival in Bandırma five hours later. Contact the main ticket office in İstanbul, *Tel. (90 212) 249 9222*, where English speakers are usually available to help you.

İstanbul-Trabzon

This ferry service operates between late May and September, leaving İstanbul at 2 p.m. Monday and arriving at Trabzon about 9:30 a.m. Wednesday. The ferry continues on to Rize, then returns to İstanbul, departing Trabzon at 7:30 p.m. Wednesday. Arrival in İstanbul is at 3 p.m. Friday. Intermediate stops can include Zonguldak, Sinop, Samsun, and Giresun. Prices range between $30 for a Pullman seat and $80 for a

"Lüks" cabin. It's worth the extra $30 expense to get an exterior cabin with a window.

Turkish Maritime Lines charges $55 for car transport between İstanbul and Trabzon. You may want to bring food along, as the food on board is relatively expensive ($10 for fixed menu lunch or dinner, $3 for breakfast). For a reservation from ports within Turkey, your best bet is to contact the local tourism information office and ask an English-speaking staffer to make a reservation for you – the Trabzon information office is particularly accustomed to this. In İstanbul you can call the Maritime Lines offices direct, *Tel. 90 212 244 2502.*

REGIONAL FERRIES
Mersin-Turkish Republic of Northern Cyprus
Mersin is the most popular departure point for ferries to Northern Cyprus, with three ferries per week. Monday, Wednesday and Friday ferries depart Mersin in the late evening, arriving at Gazimagusta by 8 a.m. For information and to make reservations, check with the tourism information office on the waterfront (Yeni Mah., İnönü Bulvarı, *Tel. 90 324 231 2710)*. Prices are expensive for the ten hour trip – $80 for a lüks cabin and $30 for a Pullman seat. The ferry rates are little better than the airline prices from İstanbul, which run $60 to $80 per person. Ferries for Northern Cyprus also depart from Alanya and Taşucu near Silifke – the latter with two hour service to Girne, Cyprus – for $29.

Trabzon-Batum, Georgia
Prices and times fluctuate, and it is necessary to complete a visa application at the Georgian consulate in Trabzon or in İstanbul. The tourism information office can be of help, as can local travel agencies such as Afacan Turizm in Trabzon.

Sinop-Odessa, Ukraine
Ferries operate sporadically between Turkey's nothernmost point and Odessa in the Crimea. As with Georgian ferries, visas should be secured prior to departure. Contact the main Turkish Maritime Lines reservation office for more information.

FERRIES TO GREEK ISLANDS
There are many small ferries serving the Greek islands offshore of Turkey, with routes including the following: Ayvalık-Lesbos; Çeşme-Chios; Kuşadası-Samos; Bodrum-Kos; Marmaris-Rhodes; Kaş-Meis. Day visits are ordinarily not penalized with heavy border fees, but overnight stays usually are. Rates vary according to Turkish-Greek relations.

BY TRAIN

Train service in Turkey is generally slow and uncomfortable, but most lines are quite cheap. You can travel from İstanbul to Van in the far southeast, a 45 hour trip, for about $20.

As interesting as the train/ferry route between İstanbul and İzmir described above is, it doesn't fit into many schedules. Two far more popular and practical trains are the **Ankara Ekspres** and the **Pamukkale Ekspres**, both of which depart İstanbul's Haydarpaşa Station. Both feature sleeper cars, departing in the evening and pulling into their destination in the early morning. Information is provided in the İstanbul chapter.

Turkey is not well connected to the sophisticated rail system of Europe, but you can link up with Budapest or Athens by rail once daily. The following train service originates at Sirkeci Station in Eminönü, İstanbul:

• Athens, Greece: $60, 8:20 a.m., 24 hours.
• Bucharest, Romania: $30, 8:45 p.m., 17 hours.
• Sofia, Bulgaria: $35, 11:20 p.m., 12 hours.
• Budapest, Hungary: $100, 11:20 p.m., 27 hours.

THE BLUE CRUISE

The term "Blue Cruise," coined by the author Cevat Şakır Kabaağaçlı, is a specific reference to plying the waters of the Aegean and Mediterranean coasts in a traditional wooden sailing ship. Statesmen and movie stars have been taking these trips for the last century, from a pre-WW I Winston Churchill to an ill-fated JFK Jr. on his honeymoon in 1996.

Fortunately, the "blue" in Blue Cruise refers to the deep azure hue of the sea, not the blood of those allowed aboard. Anyone is welcome to sign aboard a gulet cruise for four days, a week, or longer if you have the time. You'll travel from cove to cove in a wooden, broad-beamed, single-masted "gulet"—boats as lovely to look at as they are luxurious. Every itinerary includes stops at coastal ruins and sights of interest.

These trips can be shockingly inexpensive, and offer great flexibility—you can depart from points between Bodrum in the northwest and Antalya in the southeast. Weekly rates begin at **$250** per person in the off-season – a great price for a week of sun, swimming, meals, visits to ruins and beaches, and a bed.

Blue Cruise Options

There are two ways to go on a Blue Cruise:

The less expensive way is to take a cabin. Cabin charters start at $250 per person, per week in April, May, and October, and $375 per person, per week in August and September. Arrangements differ, but this price typically includes food and excludes drinks, which must be purchased separately. These trips are almost always enjoyable, but as anyone who has lived on a boat knows, your trip can be made or ruined by your bunkmates.

The more expensive alternative is to book a whole boat and crew. This makes the most sense if you have a few families together—in which case it can be cheaper than booking cabins. Chartering a boat gives you the freedom to set your own itinerary and control the atmosphere on board. The cost of chartering a three-cabin (maximum capacity six) boat, with crew, for one week is roughly $2,500; chartering a six cabin boat (maximum capacity 12) costs $4,000. This does not include food.

Whatever the arrangement you make, a few general rules apply. Most cruises depart from Antalya, Fethiye/Göcek, Marmaris, or Bodrum and will do a one-week circuit back to the same point. You're likely to have good weather anytime between May and October. Few boats book passage outside of those months.

Blue Cruise Booking Details

Before contacting the boats recommended below, you need to decide where you want to leave from, where you want to go, when you want to go, and how much time you have. Provide that information to a few blue cruise captains and operators and see what they can do for you—each of them will try to match your itinerary to where their boat(s) will be. The earlier you make reservations, the better your chances. Before making inquiries, here are a few things to note.

Unpopular stretches: Few enjoy the stretch of coast between Kalkan in the east and Fethiye in the west because it skirts the 17 exposed miles of Patara beach. Swells are prone to be large and it's not uncommon for passengers become seasick.

Point-to-point cruises: As tempting as it is to cover a lot of territory aboard a gulet, bear in mind that half the fun of it is laying at anchor. In addition, most gulet operators plan on being under way no more than four hours per day, and motoring beyond that can cost you.

Sleeping arrangements: When the weather is hot, guests traditionally sleep on deck—evening breezes (and the absence of mosquitos on the water) make this ideal. Cabins are used for changing, showering, and anything else that requires modesty.

Air conditioning: One of the latest trends in gulet construction is the incorporation of air conditioning within cabins. Cabins certainly grow stuffy and hot, so at first blush in-cabin air conditioning sounds admirable, but it isn't everything it's cracked up to be. First, it's far better to sleep on deck. Second, air conditioning requires power, more power than batteries can sustain without the motor being started every few hours—

a noisy and unwelcome proposition. Finally, boats with air conditioning cost more.

Boat types: Gulets, traditionally used as cargo ships, are broad beam ships with rounded aft sections and a single mast. Tirhandils are smaller boats, slightly banana-shaped. Aynakıç are indistinguishable from gulets except for their flat, high aft section.

Schedules: Most boats work on weekly schedules, with Saturday departures. There is some flexibility, but you should try to set your itinerary with this in mind.

Blue Cruise Boat Recommendations

All of the boats listed below offer sun sails, sun mats, toilets, bathing ladders, deck showers, kitchen facilities, sails, transfers from nearby airports/bus stations, and crew and captains that are English-speaking, conscientious, and happy to help direct you to the ruins and sights ashore. Drinks and Turkish Value Added Tax are not included.

Full Boat Charters: We have searched the docks for small, well-regarded boats to recommend in these pages. It's hot, thankless work—we'd much rather be going on a cruise than taking notes about it—so we hope you'll take full advantage. A few notes about full-boat charters: Preparation of your food is included in the price, but the food itself is often not included, as noted below—your boat will purchase food for you for between $20-$30 per person, per day. You can also shop for food yourself. (By the way, if you'd like to bring a guide along, the going rate is $100 per day plus food—inquire.)

SELINA, *Bozborun, Marmaris. Tel/Fax: (252) 456-2704; Email: sailing.selina@superonline.com; Web: None.*

The Selina, built by owner Huseyin Dolan in 1999, is not technically a gulet—it is somewhat more slender, designed for sailing. With teak decks, four cabins (one master cabin to aft, and smaller cabins to aft and port), fine food (cooked by Hüseyin or his wife Silke), and creative tilework and Picasso photos below decks, the Selina is an enchanting choice. Captain Can Saracli is young and personable, and his "crew"—the owner himself—is as reliable as can be.

Capacity: 8 guests (6 is ideal).

Weekly full boat rates (including food): Year-round; $4,500 for 8, $2,500 for 2-4.

Ports: Bodrum, Marmaris, Göcek.

GIZ, *P.O. Box 217, Bodrum 48400. Tel. (252) 316-2398; Cell: (542) 262-4636; Fax: (252) 316-1601; Email: giz@sailturkey.com; Web: www.sailturkey.com/giz/*

The 14-meter Giz ("Secret," in Turkish) is a three-cabin sloop captained and crewed by Ali Ferit Eryürek. Not a traditional gulet, the Giz is a sloop built by Ali and his father. Ali is a wonderful, engaging captain, and a fine classical guitar player; unlike many captains, Ali is strongly inclined to raise the sail.

Capacity: 6 guests.

Weekly full boat rates (not including food): April-July and September-November $2,250; August $2,750.

Ports: Bodrum, Marmaris.

CAPTAIN HIKO, *Neyzen Tavfik Cad. No. 196, Bodrum 48400. Tel. None; Fax: (252) 316-7285; Email: dina@efes.net.tr; Web: www.sailturkey.com/ hiko.*

Another three-cabin option, the 16 meter Hiko, owned by Hikmet Filis, is a gulet designed for sailing. If you'd like to stray a bit offshore and call at the Greek islands of Kos, Patmos, or Rhodes, this is a strong option. Note that the Captain Hiko is available for short trips—2 or 3 days—without a surcharge.

Capacity: 6 guests.

Weekly full-boat rates (not including food): April and October $1,750; May $2,100; June $2,450; July and September $2,800; August $3,500.

Ports: Bodrum.

ADAM VOYAGES, *Kumbahçe, Imren Sok. No. 8, Bodrum 48400. Tel. (252) 316-3764; Fax: (252) 316-4986; Email: adamvoyages@turk.net; Web: www.adamvoyages.com.*

Adam Voyages, owned by Mustafa Nalbantoğlu, owns a set of boats, ranging from the four-cabin Tirhandila to the seven-cabin Gozdem. All eight of the Adam boats feature mahogany staterooms, skilled, English speaking captains, and several offer in-cabin air conditioning. Note: Adam Voyages offers cabin charters for roughly $450 per person (with food and drink) in high season—inquire.

Capacity: 8 guests to 14 guests.

Weekly full-boat rates (not including food): Four-cabin boat, May and October $1,500; June, September $2,750; July, August $3,500: Seven-cabin boat, May and October $2,500; June, September $4,000; July, August $6,000.

Ports: Bodrum, Marmaris, Göcek.

GÖCEK YACHT SERVICE, *Iskele Mah., Göcek, Fethiye 48310. Tel. (252) 645-1730; Fax: (252) 645-1732; Email: gocekyat@superonline.com; Web: None.*

Göcek Yacht Service has a collection of 13 boats available for full-boat charter. The 13 boats include two two-cabin vessels and several eight-cabin vessels. Rates vary by boat size and season—we're including rates for the two two-cabin boats for reference. Bringing your own drinks aboard is fine.

Capacity: 4 to 16.

Weekly full-boat rates (not including food): See Rose (4 guests): May $1,675; June, September and October $2,100; July and August $2,450. Sunday (4 guests): May and October $2,450; June $2,800; July and September $3,150; August; $3,500.

Ports: Antalya, Kas, Göcek, Marmaris, Bodrum.

ADMIRAL TOURS YACHTING AND TRAVEL, *Neyzen Tevfik Cad. No. 78, Bodrum 48400. Phone: (252) 316-1781. Fax: (252) 316-2627; Email: admiral@superonline.com; Web: www.admiral_tours.com.*

Admiral is a reputable, established Blue Cruise specialist offering boats ranging from three cabins to eight cabins. Rates don't include meals, and drinks must be purchased aboard. Below are the rates for two of Admiral's smaller boats.

Capacity: 4 guests to 16 guests.

Weekly full-boat rates (not including food): Aksona (8 guests): May and October $3,000; June and September $3,900; July and August $4,800. Nuhun (6 guests): May and October $3,500; June $4,200; July, August, and September $5,100.

Ports: Bodrum, Marmaris, Göcek.

Cabin Charters

Cabin charters are the least expensive way to enjoy a Blue Cruise. Cabin charters are also favored by some up-market companies that cater to clients interested in guided trips.

CULINARY CRUISES, *P.O. Box 1913, Sausalito, CA 94966, US. Tel. 415/437-5700; Fax: 925/210-1337; Web: www.evocative.com/~turkey/tour.html; Email: info@turkishfoodandtravel.com*

Food is a highlight—or lowlight—of a Blue Cruise. To hedge your bets, consider a 10-day Bodrum-Göcek cruise or an 8-day Göcek-Göcek cruise as part of Kathleen O'Neill's Culinary Expeditions. Not only is the food good, the cooks are knowledgeable and eager to discuss their Turkish cuisine.

Capacity: 10.

Rates per person, per week (including food): $2,200 per person for 10 days, $1,800 per person for 8 days.

Ports: Bodrum, Göcek

BOUGAINVILLE TRAVEL, *Çukurbağlı Cad. No. 10, Kaş, Tel. 242 836 3142, Fax 242 836 1605. Email: info@bougainville-turkey.com; Web: www.bougainvilleturkey.com/bougainville.html.*

The helpful folks at Bougainville Travel have connections throughout the Blue Cruise world, and they're happy to do a little investigating on your behalf. They're always quick and responsive—and they have a habit of finding great, inexpensive rates. Their cabin charter rates are so inexpensive that you might want to consider renting a whole boat. Drinks are not included in the cabin charters.

Capacity: 4-10.

Rates per person, per week (including food): (high season) 2 cabin boats $545; 3 cabin boats $391; four cabin boats $332.

Ports: Kaş, Antalya, Fethiye, Göcek.

MUTLU KAPTAN, *Demre, Antalya. Tel. 242 871 5085, Fax 242 871 5594. E-mail: mutlukaptan@hotmail.com.*

The Mutlu Kaptan and Mutlu Kaptan II are boats operated by Mutlu Caner and his English-speaking brother, Mustafa. Several readers, and the authors of this guide, have found a few days or a week aboard to be a perfect tonic. The Mutlu Kaptan is part of a cooperative.

Capacity: 16.

Rates per person, per week (not including food):$425 (high season).

Ports: Antalya, Kaş, Göcek.

AEGEAN YACHT SERVICES, *Neyzen Tevfik No. 198, Bodrum 48400. Tel. (252) 316-1517; Fax: (252) 316-5749; Email: aegean@aegeanyacht.com; Web: www.aegeanyacht.com.*

AYS is a major yacht building company that now offers one of the area's largest fleets. The company maintains ships with between four and eighteen cabins, and service. Each boat has a minimum of three crew members.

Capacity: 6 to 36.

Rates per person, per week (including food): May and October $240; June $260; July and August $330; September $300.

Ports: Antalya, Kaş, Göcek.

WESTMINSTER CLASSIC TOURS, *Suite 120, 266 Banbury Road, Summertown, Oxford OX2 7DL, United Kingdom. Phone: (44) 0 (1865) 728-565; Fax: (44) 0 (1865) 728-575; Email: info@wct99.com; Web: www.wct99.com.*

Westminster is a niche, up-market travel company based in the U.K. Every year they offer a fixed set of guided, 10 to 14 day "Classical" cruises boasting exceptional range—Troy-to-Ephesus, the Dodecanese, and Antalya-to-Tarsus, in addition to the more standard itineraries between Bodrum and Antalya. Dates tend to cluster in May and September, with only private charters in the high season. The cost of these trips is high, but you're buying a guide, top-notch meals, extensive land transfers, and assurance that you're seeing Turkey's great antiquities in an the finest way possible. Westminster also offers seven-day "Painting" cruises.

Capacity: 12 guests.

Rates per person, per 14 days (including food, guides): $2,300.

Ports: Troy, Ephesus, Bodrum, Marmaris, Kaş, Göcek, Antalya, Adana.

SOUTHERN CROSS BACKPACKER'S CRUISE, *Tepe Mah. 42 Sok. No. 45, Marmaris. Phone: (252) 412-3687; Fax: (252) 412-7823; Email: interyouth@turk.net; Web: none.*

On the far end of the scale from Westminster (above), the Marmaris Interyouth Hostel operates a four-day, one-way gulet cruise out of Marmaris, taking in the Marmaris area, Dalyan, and the 12 islands before putting in at Fethiye. Boats depart every other day in summer, feature English-speaking crew, include entrance fees, meals, and permit guests to bring their own alcohol on board. The experience is a lot less sedate, and a lot less expensive, than most of the competition.

Capacity: 12 guests.
Rates per person, per four days (including food): $200
Ports: Marmaris, Fethiye.

Seeing Turkey on Your Own Terms

We strongly advise seeing Turkey independently, and if you bought this book that's probably what you want to do. You can use the hotel, yacht, and rental car listings in this book to customize your own itinerary, but in the following pages you'll find some resources that may help you arrange the details of your trip.

Our recommendation is to select a few spots and spend several days at each, but before continuing we have to concede that group tours are an excellent option if you intend to move through Turkey quickly and see a lot of things (See *The Tour*, below). If you have three weeks, you might consider taking full advantage of a two week tour and the heavily-discounted airfare that is often included, then take the third week off by yourself in the place you like best.

Turkey is a place to be explored at your leisure. Good guides have their place, and they can make your experience much richer in some ways, but your best memories will always be of finding a cave or tomb by yourself, of resting on a beach, or of having a quiet picnic atop an ancient acropolis.

Travel, Guiding, & Booking Agencies

Agencies specializing in Turkey are in the business of arranging accommodations, transfers, and guiding for individuals or groups. Different agencies specialize in different niches, and the lines tend to blur. Before setting your plans in stone, it's worth your while to contact any of the reputable agencies in the listings below and consider what they can do for you.

The agencies below are not, strictly speaking, tour group companies, although several of them do offer packaged excursions (for more information on tours, consult *The Tour*, below). The advantage of these agencies is that they can take a lot of the work out of planning your holiday; you can sketch out your itinerary, even specifying hotels and transportation methods, and they're happy to sew it into a complete whole. There is a charge for this, but given the discounts that the agencies can secure, you may still come out ahead of what you'd spend (and the time you'd take, planning independently). You may want to come up with an itinerary you like best, price it out directly with the hotels, then see whether one of these agencies can do better. Even if they can't, having the numbers of good agencies in Turkey can be of great help if you need to make plans quickly.

Most of the guiding agencies are based in Turkey, and those below have established excellent reputations. Most booking agencies, on the other hand, are based in the UK, since our former imperial rulers are far more used to dealing with Turkey than we in North America are. One of the advantages UK companies offer, too, are flight and hotel packages out of London. You can find American agencies on the Internet; *www.turkey.org* has a good listing of American outfitters and travel agencies.

Guiding & Travel Agencies

ARGEUS TRAVEL, *İstiklal Caddesi No. 7, Ürgüp, 50400, Tel. 90 384 341 4688, Fax 90 384 341 4888. E-mail: inform@argeus.com.tr, Web: http://www.argeus.com.tr.*

A travel agency based in Cappadocia, Argeus carved an excellent name for itself in tours of Cappadocia, and has extended its reach throughout the country. Argeus can book rooms, make travel arrangements, and even provide guides. An excellent contact if you have questions before traveling.

BOUGAINVILLE TRAVEL, *Çukurbağlı Cad. No. 10, Kaş, Tel. 242 836 3142, Fax: 242 836 1605. E-mail: info@bougainville-turkey.com; Web: www.bougainvilleturkey.com/bougainville.html.*

Bougainville specializes in adventure travel – sea kayaking, hiking, and scuba diving, for instance. This is an excellent resource while planning and booking your trip.

CREDO TURIZM, *Taksim Caddesi İonca Apt. No. 69/6, 80090 Taksim, İstanbul, Tel. (90 212) 254 8175, Fax (90 212) 237 9670. E-mail: credo@credo.com.tr, Web: www.credo.com.tr.*

Credo has earned a great reputation for the work it does creating itineraries for individuals and groups traveling to Turkey.

INCA FLOATS, *1311 63rd St., Emeryville, CA, USA 94608, Tel. (510) 420 1550. E-mail: info@incafloats.com, Web: http://www.incafloats.com.*

Inca Floats specializes in the Galapagos Islands, Antarctica, and Turkey; it's a strange mix, but many readers have attested to Inca Floats' collection of hotels and itineraries.

Booking Agencies

AUTHENTIC TURKEY, *20 Notting Hill Gate, London, W113JE UK, Tel. 44 071 221 3878.*

Authentic has a collection of affordable accommodations on the Mediterranean.

SAVILE ROW, *6 Blenhem Terrace, St. Johns Wood, London, NW8 OEB, U.K. Tel. 44 207 625 3001, Fax 44 207 625 8852.*

Savile Row maintains the most outstanding collection of hotels and perfectly-turned pensions in Turkey. Their free annual brochure is certainly worth ordering before you go – bear in mind that you can book a room at some of the hotels they list through another broker for a better price.

SIMPLY TURKEY, *598-608 Chiswick High Road, Chiswick, London, W4 5RT, U.K. Tel. 44 208 747 1011; Fax 44 208 995-5346; Email: turkey@simply-travel.com; Web: www.simply-travel.com.*

Similar to Savile Row but less expensive, Simply Turkey books blocks of rooms in high-quality smaller hotels and rents them directly.

SUNQUEST, *23 Princes Street, London W1R 7RG. Tel. 44 207 499 9992.*

Turkish Maritime Lines uses Sunquest as its English sales office, and the company has a good catalog of hotels throughout the country.

TAPESTRY HOLIDAYS, *24 Chiswick High Rd., London W4 1TE U.K. Tel. 44 208 235 7777; Fax 44 (208) 235-7501; Email: enquiries@tapestryholidays.com; Web: www.tapestryholidays.com.*

For the moderate price range, Tapestry has a strong selection of hotels on the Mediterranean.

Tour Agencies

Many North American travelers, having made the long journey to Turkey, feel compelled to see everything. The compulsion is understandable, and it can be rewarding, but consider Turkey's size and the distances involved. Seeing Troy, Pergamon, Ephesus, Bodrum, Antalya, Cappadocia, and İstanbul, each deserving of achaeologists' entire lifetimes, requires great energy and resolve. If you intend to do the grand tour, following in the footsteps of Alexander, consider a tour package. Two-week tours, airfare from New York included, can cost between $1,300 in the spring and fall and $1,700 per person in the summer. That price includes flight, meals, guides, transfers, entry fees, perfectly decent four star hotels, and no smoking coaches. The group tour companies secure rooms at a huge volume discount – hotels that cost $110 walking in the front door may go for as little as $15 in some seasons. You simply cannot see Turkey as cheaply and effortlessly any other way.

For cheap, thorough Turkey vacations in accommodations of good quality, we recommend **Tursem Tourism International** (*US Tel. 800/ 223-9169, 212 935 9210, Fax 212 935 9215*). Tursem offers tours at the rates mentioned above and has a deservedly good reputation and knowledgeable guides – our recommendation is confirmed by no less an authority than our own parents, who were quite satisfied by their two week tour with Tursem. A huge listing of other tour companies with U.S. or Canadian offices can be found on the Internet at *www.turkey.org*.

If you're traveling on a tight budget, also consider Fez Travel. Fez, located on "hostel row" in İstanbul's old city, offers a unique tour package that is certainly worth considering (Akbıyık Cad. No. 15, Sultanahmet, *Tel. 212 516 9024, Fax: 212 518 5085, feztravel@feztravel.com, www.feztravel.com*).

Fez buses run in a counterclockwise circuit throughout the tourism season. The buses stop at a different town each night and you can continue with them the next morning or stay put until you're ready to move on. The route winds through the best sites in western Turkey: İstanbul, Eceabat/Çanakkale (Troy, Gallipoli), Ayvacık, Bergama (Pergamon), Selcuk (Ephesus), Kuşadası, Didyma, Bodrum, Koyceğiz (Caunos), Saklikent, Fethiye, Kaş, Çiralı (Olympos), Antalya, Termessos, Eğirdir, Konya, Ürgup (Cappadocia), Ankara, İstanbul. A one-time fee of 99 Pounds Sterling (roughly $145) lets you board and disembark as you wish – the buses run daily in July and August, once every 2-3 days otherwise. You're on your own to find accommodation, with the advantage of savvy up-to-the-minute advice from Fez representatives and other travelers. This is a great way to see the country if you have some time and you can drink with Aussies and Kiwis.

Special Activities

Ruins, mosques, and beaches make everyone's itinerary, but Turkey has much more to offer. How about birding at Sultan Marshes Bird Paradise east of Cappadocia? Hiking along the Lycian Way in southwest Turkey or along the King's Road through south central Turkey? Visiting sites mentioned in the Bible? Horse trekking in Cappadocia? Skiing at Mt. Argeus? Whitewater rafting in Class 5 water? Hot air ballooning? Scuba diving? Paddling a sea kayak? Canyoning? Spelunking? Spending time on a yacht on the Mediterranean? If that's too much work, how about a tour of Turkish cuisine?

If any of this sounds appealing, you can do it on your trip to Turkey. All you need to do is ask the right people. They're listed below.

ARGEUS TRAVEL, *İstiklal Caddesi No. 7, Ürgüp, 50400, Tel. 90 384 341 4688, Fax 90 384 341 4888. E-mail: inform@argeus.com.tr, Web: http:// www.argeus.com.tr*.

Lycian Way Hiking

Kate Clow saw her dream of a hiking trail between Fethiye and Antalya come to fruition in 2000. The entire six-week hiking route (technically from Ölüdeniz to Termessos) is marked with signs and mapped, but hiking this trail requires a copy of Kate's guide book, The Lycian Way—available at Amazon.com and through Bougainville Travel (listed above).

The route is not really new—it's the restoration of a trail that is thousands of years old, one that winds past most of the regions great ruins and beaches. This is a spectacular and unique way to see Turkey, if you can spare a few days.

If you'd like to work a stretch of Lycian Way hiking into your plans, Kate's guide should provide the help you need. For consultation about the best stretches of path and to make plans for accommodation, check with Bougainville Travel at: *info@bougainville-turkey.com.*

Specialty: guided hikes and tours in Cappadocia, mountain biking, hot air ballooning, trips to Mt. Argeus, and horseback riding in the Cappadocia region.

BOUGAINVILLE TRAVEL, *Çukurbağlı Cad. No. 10, Kaş, Tel. 242 836 3142, Fax 242 836 1605. Email: info@bougainville-turkey.com; Web: www.bougainvilleturkey.com/bougainville.html.*

Specialty: Adventure travel—including scuba diving, rafting, canyoning, and sea kayaking througout Turkey. Headquartered in Kaş (on the Mediterranean).

INTER-CHURCH TRAVEL, *Middleburg Square, Folkestone, Kent CT20 1YB, U.K. Tel. (44 303) 371 1535; Fax: (44 303) 071-1100.*

Features religious tours to the Seven Churches of Revelation.

CULINARY EXPEDITIONS, *P.O. Box 1913, Sausalito, CA 94966, USA. Tel. 415/437-5700; Fax 925/210-1337; Email: info@turkishfoodandtravel.com Web: www.evocative.com/~turkey/tour.html.*

Kathleen O'Neill specializes in "food excursions," trips centered on the history and evolution of food throughout Turkey. Expeditions include Blue Cruises (listed above, in the Blue Cruise section).

Outdoor Activities

Trekking is popular in the mountainous northeast (the **Kaçkar/ Altıparmak** range) and in the **Toros Mountains** above the Mediterranean in the south. The meandering valleys of Cappadocia lend themselves to trekking, as well, as they do **horseback riding** and **mountain biking**. One excellent **hot air ballooning** company has established itself in Cappadocia in the last six years, as well.

Turkey's Çoruh River, flowing into the Black Sea in the northeast, has some of the finest **whitewater** in the world. The Dalaman and Köprüçay Rivers in the south of the country – near Dalaman and Antalya, respectively – also offer some fun, challenging whitewater and have developed into very popular rafting and kayaking spots. **Sea kayaking** opportunities have emerged since 1997, and it's now possible to rent sea kayaks in Kaş and Üçağız on the southern coast. It's high time: Turkey's long, magnificent coast is perfectly suited for kayak trekking.

Some of the best **scuba diving** in the Mediterranean can be found at several spots around the perimeter of Turkey, notably Bodrum and Kaş. You can elect to get your PADI certification over the course of a few days or simply spend an afternoon on a "discovery dive."

During the summer, **off-road** excursions into the alpine meadows (yaylalar) above the Mediterranean or the Black Sea offer an interesting glimpse into village life still relatively unaffected by tourism. During the winter, the mountains have a different appeal: you can **ski** the groomed trails at Argeus, Palandöken, or Ülüdağ, or find an outfitter to get you into the backcountry.

Taking the Kids

Turks love children. If you bring a young child with you on your trip to Turkey, she or he will be the center of attention, subject to very sincere doting that consists of cheek squeezing, gifts of candy and other treats, smiling, and much commentary. (If your child is not comfortable with being touched by strangers, Turkey may prove challenging for him or her.)

Many visitors bring their children, especially **adolescents and teenagers**. The seaside resorts are quite accustomed to Turkish and foreign families arriving en masse with children when school is out for the summer, and consequently offer daycare and childrens' activities. In general, however, there are not many child-specific activities aside from going to a playground, swimming pool, or beach. Older children are likely to be interested in the historical sites and the stories that go along with them, the sheer "oldness" of it all, but younger children might lose interest.

If you have a **very young child** along with you, you should be aware that İstanbul's sidewalks and crowds are also difficult to navigate with a baby stroller, and that breastfeeding in public is not done.

There is jarred baby food, disposable diapers, and formula available in pharmacies ("eczane") and some supermarkets, and pasteurized milk is widely available; many Turkish restaurants are also accustomed to preparing special, simplified dishes for their customers' babies and small children. Cheese, white bread, and fruit are always available, so if your child likes those, s/he will never starve in Turkey.

Some suggestions:
- plain pasta (makarna)
- pasta with grated cheese (kaşarlı makarna)
- french fries (çips)
- cheese pide (peynirli pide)
- fried cheese pastry in either triangle or 'cigarette' shape (sigara börek)
- cheese and bread (ekmek ve kaşar, ekmek ve peynir)
- cucumber-yogurt salad, without the garlic (sarmısaksız cacık)
- grated carrot salad (havuç salatası)
- cucumber slices (salatalık)
- grilled chicken (tavuk izgara)
- lamb shish kebab (şiş kebab), but be careful because this is not always tender enough
- fresh fruit (meyve)
- meatballs without spices (baharatsız köfte)
- fruit juice (meyve suyu), often has a high sugar content

b
a
s
i
c

i
n
f
o
r
m
a
t
i
o
n

Chapter 7

Business Hours

The opening hours of tourism sites and museums varies greatly, but in general museums remain open 9-5 or 9-6 in summer, occasionally with a one hour break at lunch. Most museums are closed one or two days a week, with Monday a standard off-day. Ruins are usually open in daylight hours.

Standard government office hours are 9-6, Monday-Friday, with an hour break at lunch. The government offices you'll really need, like the Visa office at the airport and the police, are always open, and some post offices (PTTs) remain open 24 hours, providing telephones and telephone cards. Standard businesses maintain 9-6 hours, open Monday-Saturday.

You may be surprised to find that restaurants and shops in urban areas stay open well past nightfall, often until midnight or later. Urban Turks do not tend to make an early night of it; you'll find families with small children out on the streets until very late.

Business hours can be quite erratic during Ramazan (see *Holidays* below).

Computers & Internet Service
Computers & the Internet

Internet cafes are fairly well established in most towns that receive any tourist traffic, and provide the obvious solution to the matter of staying in touch with e-mail from home. Rates outside of İstanbul tend to be quite reasonable; $3.50 per hour or so. You'll find that proprietors of Internet cafes tend to produce surprisingly good food, which you can eat while you compute.

If your Internet needs are more demanding, or if you need to fax from your computer, you'll find business centers at large hotels in urban centers. A few hotels in Turkey have snap-in jacks (officially, RJ-11 telephone connectors) for their phones, but not all do. You can't count on simply plugging in your computer from your room and firing off faxes or e-mail. The best large hotels offer the proper jacks, but many excellent smaller hotels do not. You have the following options:

First, determine if the hotel line is digital or analog. Most phone lines are analog, but the newer digital lines can zap your modem-card because of excessive voltage. Warning signs for a digital line include LCD displays on the face of the phone and sophisticated features. Otherwise, to determine if the line is digital you can check with reception, although they're probably not going to have the faintest idea. You can also try IBM's Modem Saver, a product designed to identify the type of line beyond all doubt.

Acoustic couplers are available at some computer stores, allowing you to use lines that are sheathed in plastic and buried in the wall in one end and buried in the phone at the other. You simply attach the coupler to the telephone headset and do what you normally do, but this method will be very, very slow.

A screwdriver, wire cutters, electrical tape and a length of cord ending in a standard RJ-11 connector of the sort that fits into your PCMCIA slot can do the same job, especially if you have a James Bond bent. Unscrew the phone bottom and fish out the line ends (or chop it in the middle, if need be). Splice the end of your own connector cord to the live line coming from the wall, plug it in and go to work. Please put the phone line back together again.

Turkey's phone noises are comprehensible to computers accustomed to North American rings and tones.

For further information consult *http://kropla.com/phones.htm* or the TeleAdapt Ltd. site at *www.teleadapt.com*.

If you need your own dial-up connection during your stay, contact Netone *(www.netone.com.tr)* for a solution. If you are a CompuServe or America Online member, you may connect and log into your account by dialling İstanbul, Ankara, İzmir, and Antalya numbers. Be aware that there may be a surcharge for this service; check with AOL or CompuServe beforehand on the cost and the dial-up numbers.

For Internet resources on planning your trip to Turkey, you need do no more than a simple search on your favorite search engine. There are plenty of English-speaking Turks on the web, and they enthusiastically broadcast information about their country and culture on their home pages.

One of the best sites comes from the Turkish Embassy in Washington, D.C. Its Web pages include a listing of American tour operators who specialize in Turkey: *http://www.turkey.org*. The *Turkish Daily News*, at *www.turkishdailynews.com*, is Turkey's only English-language daily newspaper, and reading it on the Web before your trip is a good way to get some insight into Turkish politics and culture. If you'd like to hear what Turkish sounds like and you have a RealPlayer, try the news station NTV at *www.ntv.com.tr*.

Electricity

The current in Turkey runs at 220 volts (compared to 110 at home) and the plugs are shaped differently, two round prongs like those used in Europe. Just because you have a plug adapter doesn't mean the current will slow down on its way to your favorite traveling appliance: 220 volts burns out electrical motors intended for use with 110 electricity. Post-1994 notebook computers usually have an internal adapter, but most other devices (including printers, hair dryers, and battery chargers) do not, and require a current converter.

You can find these converters at Radio Shack, and they typically have the proper outlet prongs. Even with a current converter you may subject your electrical device to undue wear and tear, although notebook computers' internal mechanisms are built for the task. Hair dryers are not; bring a cheap one.

English Language Reading Material

The *Turkish Daily News*, based out of Ankara, is the only English-language newspaper in Turkey. The News has suspect editing and peculiar news judgment, but certainly offers insight into the country's affairs.

Cornucopia Magazine is a beautiful, glossy full-size magazine focusing on Turkey. Cornucopia concentrates on literature, art, and the refined aspects of travel. The magazine is not especially practical, but it will inspire you to want to return again and again. To subscribe from North America, contact Cornucopia US Subscriptions, PO Box 3405, Sunriver, OR, 9770 (one year, three issues, $30). Email: *cornucopia@atlas.net.tr*, *www.cornucopia.net/*.

The Guide, based in İstanbul with occasional Ankara editions, offers the best calendar of İstanbul's current events available in English, together with articles on things to see and do within the city.

You will find copies of *The International Herald Tribune*, and the international editions of *Newsweek*, and *Time* in most large or frequently visited cities. Financial junkies can get the *European Wall Street Journal*, sports junkies can pick up *USA Today*, and you also have the option of

London's *Financial Times* or *The Economist*. These periodicals arrive first at the airport, second at Taksim Square and Sultanahmet in İstanbul, and on down the line until two days later, when some few *Newsweeks* are delivered in Kaş and Trabzon.

Health Services & Concerns

Before setting out for Turkey, be sure your insurance plan will cover you. Some plans neglect overseas countries or even include Europe but exclude Asia, a tricky proposition for a visit to Turkey. Turkey has socialized medicine, but that service doesn't ordinarily extend to you. Private hospitals expect immediate payment. Costs are reasonable – $55 for a check-up in İstanbul and $50 for a set of X-rays, for instance.

Top-notch urban medical care in Turkey is right at the Western standard, if lacking the equipment you would find in American hospitals. Many doctors are western-trained, and many, too, are English-speaking. Outside of İstanbul and Ankara medical care is predictably less sophisticated, but doctors are usually quite competent.

For an up-to-date list of recommended hospitals and specialists in your area, contact the Canadian, U.K. or U.S. consulates and embassies in İstanbul, İzmir, Adana and Ankara. **The emergency medical service phone number is 112**.

The Turkish pharmacy (*eczane*) occupies a more important role in health care than it typically does in North America, and the pharmacist is accustomed to making prescriptions. If you can explain your ailment the pharmacist will often have just the thing. If you're looking for a particular medicine you may have to sift through lots of boxes, since the brand name with which you are familiar will be different. The active ingredients and the manufacturer will usually be the same.

Vaccinations & Shots

There are no special vaccinations or shots recommended for visitors to Turkey. Malaria, historically a great problem along the Mediterranean coast, is no longer an issue. The eastern end of the Mediterranean, near Adana, still generates occasional cases, but the rest of the country is free from anopheles.

This is not to say there aren't mosquitoes. Along the coast, particularly in marshy towns just inland of the sea such as Dalyan, mosquitoes exist in irritating numbers. Incense coils ("spiral tütsü") are an effective defense, as are small devices that plug into electrical outlets and agitate a small tablet of pyrethrin. These burn an odorless chemical and do a good job of keeping mosquitoes at bay. Most hotels will offer one of the above, or, better yet, a fan or mosquito netting over the bed.

Holidays

Turkey has several fixed holidays every year as well as major religious celebrations that are are based on the moon cycles and whose dates change from year to year. The secular holidays can put a little crimp in your travel plans, but **Ramazan** and the main religious holidays (**bayrams**) can wreak havoc (see Chapter 4, *Land & People*). The celebrations are an excellent time to visit in some respects, but there's no denying that schedules become scrambled and transportation becomes crowded. Fortunately, this is not a great concern for most travelers at the moment, since the holiday cycle is in the middle of winter right now.

During Ramazan, Muslims are expected to forego food during daylight hours. In the hours before dawn, people rise to take large breakfasts, and in the hours after sunset families gather for large meals and celebration. Ramazan is immediately followed by "**Şeker (Candy) Bayramı**" a three-day holiday on which shops close, people enjoy the end of the daytime fasting, and children are given sweets.

The other annual major religious holiday is **Kurban Bayramı**. This is a four-day holiday following Ramazan by about two and one-half months, and it celebrates the willingness of Abraham to sacrifice his son Isaac at the behest of God. This day is to sheep in Turkey what Thanksgiving is to turkeys in America; just about every family in Turkey will slaughter a sheep, prepare a feast, and donate meat to those less fortunate. It is a joyous holiday, but the foreign traveler will find it a joyous, inconvenient holiday. Most offices close for a full week, bus schedules shift, museums and ruins close at unpredictable hours, and rooms are full.

Secular holidays, fixed on the calendar each year, are the following:
* **January 1**, New Years Day
* **April 23**, Independence Day and Children's Day
* **May 19**, Atatürk Day and Youth and Sports Day
* **August 30**, War of Independence Victory Day
* **October 29**, Republic Day

The principal dates for Ramazan, which shift from year to year, are as follows through 2004:
* Nov. 6, 2002-December 5, 2002 *Ramazan*
* December 6, 2002-December 8, 2002, *Şeker Bayram*
* March 4, 2003-March 6, 2003, *Kurban Bayram*
* October 27, 2003-November 25, 2003, *Ramazan*
* Nov. 26, 2003-Nov. 28, 2003, *Şeker Bayram*
* February 22, 2004-February 24, 2004, *Kurban Bayram*
* October 15, 2004-November 14, 2004, *Ramazan*

•Nov. 15, 2004-December 16, 2004, *Şeker Bayram*
•February 11, 2005-February 13, 2005, *Kurban Bayram*

Money & Banking

ATMs and banks are common in Turkey. Provided the credit or debit card you use is approved for use overseas (be sure to check!), obtaining money should be no problem. The question, then, is not 'Can I exchange money?'—you can—but 'What's the smartest way to exchange money?'

The answer? Pay for most purchases via a credit card you can pay off immediately on return home. For pocket money, exchange cash at foreign exchange offices as needed. Use a credit card for cash withdrawals on a limited basis, and hold a few hundred dollars of travelers checks in reserve.

U.S. Dollars: Dollars are always handy, and Turkey has such low incidence of thievery that we don't hesitate to suggest you tuck $1,000 or so in a belly pouch, along with your passport and plane tickets. For details, see "Changing Money," below.

Travelers Checks: Finding banks and foreign exchange offices willing to accept travelers checks can be surprisingly difficult. Compounding this, you pay a 1.5% premium to buy the checks at your bank, then, when you want to exchange in Turkey, you fetch rates less favorable than those earned with dollars. That said, they are a good hedge against trouble and nice to have in reserve.

Credit Cards: As mentioned, before leaving home you need to call customer service at your credit card company and confirm that your card will work internationally. Once in Turkey, you'll find that most hotels, restaurants, service stations, and large shops accept credit cards. Because your credit card will draw the best exchange rate, and because exchange rates in Turkey shift more in your favor almost every day, we suggest paying for everything you can with credit cards. (That assumes, of course, you aren't carrying debt on that card, since the incremental advantages of favorable exchange rates pale in the face of your credit card company's interest.)

Look for signs indicating "Kredi Kart Komisiyon Sıfır" – that means there's zero surcharge.

ATMs: You'll find ATM machines throughout the country. As long as you've got your PIN numbers memorized, getting Turkish Lira is no problem (be sure you know your credit card PIN number, not just your savings account withdrawal number). **Yapı Kredi** and **AkBank** are two popular Turkish banks that support most ATM exchanges and have easy-to-use English language interfaces.

ATM cash withdrawals draw favorable exchange rates, but you're probably going to pay your bank cash advance rates (typically a ridicu-

Dollar-Lira Exchange Rate

Get out the calculator. Economics is a rollicking sort of fun in a country with inflation that averages 60%. This inflation is not the result of an off-year, or debt restructuring, or a devaluation linked to the European Economic Community – it's a permanent condition. In bad spells (February 2001, for instance), the Lira has lost half of its value in the space of a few days. At the time of this writing, there were rumors that Turkey would knock six zeroes off of the Lira—but those rumors have circulated for years.

January 2003 exchange rate, est.: US$1 = 1.8 million TL.
January 2004 exchange rate, est.: US$1 = 2.5 million TL.
January 2005 exchange rate, est.: US$1 = 3.5 million TL

lous 15%-20%, beginning immediately). As a result, it's nice to rely on cash advances as seldom as possible.

Note: Every year more than $70 million in foreign currency is taken home as a memento and stuck in a desk drawer. Granted, foreign cash has some souvenir value, but you have an alternative to letting all of your Turkish Lira devalue into colored paper: **UNICEF's Change for the Good** program collects foreign currency and turns the proceeds over to charity. You should find their collection boxes at any international air terminal. For information on donations, call their New York office, *Tel. 212/503-6437.*

Changing Money

The Turkish Lira is fully convertible, and there is no black market. Money changing offices (*döviz*) can be found throughout the country. We haven't listed them in these pages because they are everywhere, and they're open long hours. Most banks also exchange money, but they are slower and less efficient than using a streetside Dovız. Exchange offices are particularly popular near heavily-touristed sites, but not exclusively so: Turks buy U.S. dollars or German Marks as a hedge against inflation. Cash exchange rates are typically posted outside each office, and can be double-checked against the daily exchange rate published on the cover of Turkey's English language paper, the *Turkish Daily News*. After making your exchange, you'll be given a receipt, and it's worth your while to count the money and check the math.

Passports are not required for exchanges of currency unless you go to the bank, and the process is ordinarily quick and painless. As mentioned above, travelers checks fetch about 90 percent of the cash exchange rate and some exchange offices refuse to accept them.

Do not exchange money at hotels. There is no advantage to it except convenience, and you're going to be walking past a döviz within five minutes of leaving the front door anyway. Hotel exchange rates are usually 20% worse than what you'll get at a döviz.

Post Offices

Turkish post offices, marked by large blue and blue **PTT** signs, have branches near the heart of every city. You will usually find telephones (see Telephone section below) and telephone cards here, as well as the postal services you'd expect.

Stamps (*pül*) for standard letters to the United States or Canada cost about one dollar, with postcards only slightly cheaper. You can buy stamps, but it's better to bring your mail to a PTT. The postal worker will weigh it, punch some numbers into a calculator, look at the numbers, punch a couple more in and, voila, give you a reasonable figure that will get your letters to their destination. Mail service is quite reliable.

If you are shipping something like a carpet home, your dealer should explain in great detail how the system works, and will often take the responsibility upon him or herself (if in doubt, however, ship it yourself to ensure that you get what you paid for). At the post office you will be expected to display the contents of your parcel, after which you can complete your wrapping job and send it along. Send the package using registered mail; someone at the front desk of your hotel should be able to help you.

Note: to ensure your postcard or letter gets where it's going, include the proper Turkish for its destination: "ABD" for the US, "Kanada" for Canada, and "İngiltere" for England.

Relieving Yourself

In what is probably an extension of the public buildings that are associated with mosques, Turkish cities have a surprisingly generous number of public restrooms. These are often located down a flight of stairs from the street level, and are usually marked "WC." **Bay** is man, **Bayan** is woman. In extremis, ask *"Tuvalet nerede?"* (where is the toilet) and someone will point you in the right direction.

The public restrooms are overseen by a worker who collects a fee and is responsible for keeping things tidy. It is not the best job, and, as will become clear, they are rarely the most fastidious of workers. Take a moment to pluck a few squares of toilet paper from the worker's table on your way in, if necessary, and be sure to pay up on your way out:

Trickery & Deceit Warnings

In general, Turkey is a scrupulously honest place, which is part of what makes it such a joy for travelers. Even so, you can't drop your guard altogether. Here are a few reasons why:

If you're a single man out walking along İstiklal Caddesi late at night, be wary of anyone who approaches you and works vigorously to steer you to a bar. Episodes are occasionally reported of foreigners being taken off by themselves under the pretext of seedy Red Light business and winding up forcibly relieved of their wallets.

Criminals have been slipping mickeys to travelers on buses and trains for decades now, and Turkey is no exception. It goes like this: someone offers you a tainted drink or snack, knocking you out. While you're blacked out they rifle your pockets and leave with your valuables. This is especially insidious because you'll be offered many things out of genuine hospitality. All you can do is have faith in your own judgment of people and a willingness to risk impoliteness. When in doubt, make a polite refusal.

Be wary of people who find out where you're going and then happen to be going the same way themselves. An Australian acquaintance traveled from Cappadocia (Nevşehir's bus station seems to figure in many of the worst stories) to Antalya with a non-Turk, booked into a hotel with him, and went down to the marina to get a boat for some fishing. Once in the boat, the hanger-on remembered something he'd left in the hotel, and ran off to retrieve it. In the process he retrieved the Australian's room key, then his belongings. The story had a sort of happy ending; the Australian found his backpack one week later being fenced in a Selçuk leather shop, his name still emblazoned on the outside. The leather shop owners, eager to get in on this happy coincidence, sold it back to him for $150.

One ploy you're unlikely to expect is pickpocketing by a crowd of older, chador-wearing women. It is a standard pickpocketing scenario: several women bump into you on a pretext, with one swiping your wallet or valuables. What's unusual is simply their appearance, which is quite disarming and can blindside even the most paranoid veteran traveler.

typically $0.25-$0.50. Occasionally you will be given a splash of lemon cologne on your way out the door.

Service stations are another option, and, finally, since you may very well have a Gore-tex coat or Tevas or non-Turkish coloring you also have the option of using hotel restrooms. Just barge in like you own the place.

Most hotels have standard sit toilets, but at some point you're likely to find yourself confronted by a floor toilet. If you've never used one, there's nothing to it. The traction pads to each side are, duh, for your feet. This system is more sanitary than the sit toilet, since you aren't in contact with anything, but it can be a little hard on the knees. Don't even think about bringing a newspaper, unless it's in lieu of toilet paper. You flush with a small bucket or hose located to the side of the hole. It's a good idea to have a stash of toilet paper with you at all times, because you're unlikely to find any in the stall if there wasn't any on the caretaker's table. If you find yourself without toilet paper, do like the Turks do and try, ahem, irrigating yourself.

Safety & Avoiding Trouble

Travelers from abroad are a precious commodity. Turkey's tourism industry has been growing at an 18 percent clip for almost 15 years, reaching a rate of 6.6 million visitors and $4 billion in revenues annually.

Turkish police officers and other officials receive extensive warnings about the importance of tourists, and the Tourism Ministry knows that a single well-publicized case of tourist mistreatment could easily put a 10 percent dent – that's $400 million – in its revenues.

After several instances of terrorism directed against tourists in 1994, the Tourism Ministry, the police, and the military set about posting guards at the country's popular tourist sites to ensure visitors' safety. In the absence of that danger there is little left to worry about. Standard crime like mugging and assault is negligible by American standards, even in big cities like İstanbul. And better still, at least from a foreigner's perspective, violent crime is rarely directed against outsiders; it usually boils up in domestic family disputes. Don't misunderstand: pickpocketing, purse snatching, and mugging do occur, they are simply very rare. If you keep your passport and cash in a money belt under your pants and your wallet in your front pocket, you should be fine.

Most of Turkey's streets are bewilderingly safe at all hours. Also note that while Turkish police may become slightly impatient with you, they will not – and should not – ever be hostile.

Defamation

Several years back in Çanakkale, an angry Australian was cursing at a pension owner and in so doing he shouted "You [expletive deleted] Turks." As the pension owner himself explained, so long as the Australian confined himself to heaping abuse on the pension owner's person, it was simply a disagreement; the moment the Australian defamed the Turkish people he had committed a crime. The Australian had one night in jail to consider this point of Turkish law.

Defamation of the Turkish people or of national institutions such as Mustafa Kemal Atatürk, the founder of the nation, is illegal in Turkey. The North American penchant for irreverence could get you in surprisingly serious trouble, so be on good behavior.

Women Travelers in Turkey

Turkish women in urban areas can wear some quite form-revealing clothing such as leggings, miniskirts, and tight T-shirts, jeans, and sweaters. Many Turkish women also favor skimpy bikinis on beaches and at pools, although typically when in the company of companions or children. Despite this, there are some realities for women traveling in the country (and especially in less-touristed areas) that you ought to know.

In general, you should have few or no problems in the touristed and urban areas of western Turkey. However, it's best to stay on the conservative side, and wear long, loose pants or skirts and sleeves that cover the arms to the elbows, just for the sake of politeness. Then again, if you're obviously a foreigner, sometimes it doesn't seem to matter what you're wearing. I have gotten as much unwanted attention while wearing formless, bulky winter clothing as I have in skimpy summer clothes.

Perhaps incongruously, I have never felt physically threatened in Turkey. Even in cases where I have been groped on a bus, I have not felt threatened—merely angry. I fear for my physical safety significantly less on a day-to-day basis in Turkey than I do in the U.S.

Here are a few things to keep in mind:

You will get stared at if you don't look Turkish (whether because of clothing or other factors). Both men and women do the staring however, and before getting offended, it's helpful to remember that staring does not have the same negative associations attached to it as it does in North America. It's largely a sign of curiosity, of noticing someone unusual. Although it is in your best interest to avoid eye contact with men, if you keep an open look on your face, and aren't afraid to smile at people, in most cases you'll get sincere, friendly smiles or 'hellos' right back. It's not to say, however, that men will not stare at you in ways you find uncomfortable.

If a man makes unwanted comments to you, the best reaction is no reaction. A response is often considered license to speak further. A noise you may hear is "Shht! Shht!," which is generally used to get attention. It's often a crude and ineffective form of courting noise, as well, and its best to just ignore it.

If you are on crowded public transportation and you suspect that you are being felt up, chances are you're right. Generally Turks do not touch one another on public transportation, unless they know each other, even when it's very crowded. And foreign women aren't the only targets.

A couple of years ago in Istanbul there was a feminist ì lavender ribbonî campaign which distributed sharp pins attached to lavender ribbons, for women to use as anti-groping devices. If you have become certain that you are being touched, you have a couple of options:

A) Move away if possible.

B) Say loudly, *"Çok ayıp!"* (chok ai-yip, much shame) or *"Ne yapıyorsun?"* (nay yap-ee-yor-sun, what are you doing?).

This latter option does not always have the desired effect, as the man you are accusing is likely to become angry and defensive in an attempt to save face. But with any luck he will be embarrassed and get off the bus at the next possible opportunity.

Along the Black Sea and in some parts of İstanbul, you may be mistaken for a prostitute (a "Natasha") by some men if you are blonde and Eastern European-looking. There has been an influx of Russian and Romanian young women into Turkey, and the unfortunate reality is that they often turn to prostitution to support themselves. Prostitution and brothels are legal in Turkey.

Bring a scarf with you (or buy one in Turkey) for covering your head in mosques and tombs.

If you're traveling alone, make it clear to the front desk manager that you want a room near other women or families. In the hotels we have recommended, however, there should be no need to do this. Ask for the **aile salonu** (family room) in restaurants if you don't see any women in the main seating area. If the restaurant doesn't have one, the proprietor should send you to one that does. Don't go into places to be social where you see only men. Your sociability will give the "wrong message."

If traveling between cities by bus, the ticket seller will seat you next to another woman traveling alone.

For advice on Turkish baths, see Chapter 8, *Shopping & Other Pleasures.*

Telephones

The Turkish phone system is quite sophisticated, and public phones are available throughout the country. Most urban Turkish lines are sleek and digital, and reaching home on a clear line is relatively easy.

There are two types of phones. The older phones, now being phased out, take **jeton**, grooved tokens that come in small (küçük), medium (orta), and big (büyük) sizes. The larger the token the greater the credit, but they are worth only 15¢, 25¢ and 50¢ apiece. Older phones occasionally let you dial into your international operator and make an international call, but you'll have to deposit more tokens every few minutes. If your token isn't being taken, stubbornly keep feeding it back in until the phone accepts it.

The new phones, well-established in urban areas and finally appearing in the hinterland (try nice hotel lobbies and the PTT offices), take **phone cards** and credit cards, not coins. These cards are available in denominations of 30 ($1.50), 60 ($3), and 100 ($5) credits. They are often sold by vendors near the phones themselves, but note that you may pay a hefty mark-up (often twice as much) over the standard price at the PTT. The new phones offer English language prompts and are a pleasure to operate. If you get 100 credits, this should be adequate for two weeks worth of local and domestic calls, but be forewarned that the credits burn off in about 3 minutes if you're calling North America. Even the new phones can be reluctant to put you through to the international operators (listed below), meaning that you may have to buy up a few phone cards and change them in the course of your conversation.

Hotel lines are predictably expensive, so, if you don't want to use a phone card at a public phone, remember to dial up your international operator from your room for calls to home. Before placing a call to North America, you may want to consult the time differences (see below under *Time*). Calling card international operator numbers are:
- **ATT**, *Tel. 00800 12277*
- **MCI**, *Tel. 00800 11177*
- **Sprint**, *Tel. 00800 14477*

Turkey's phone code is **90**: from North America dial 011 + 90 + three digit area code + seven digit number.

Time

The time difference between Turkey and the East Coast of North America is seven hours (occasionally eight when North America shifts into daylight savings). The time difference between Turkey and the West Coast is 10 hours (occasionally 11).

To put it simply, if it's 9 a.m. on Tuesday morning in Turkey, it's 2 a.m. Tuesday morning on the East Coast and 11 p.m. Monday night on the West Coast. In Turkey, you're 7-10 hours ahead of your time zone at home.

Tipping

Tipping is not an institution in Turkey. Places with a large population of foreigners are accustomed to the tipping phenomenon, but workers at small local **restaurants** are often pleasantly taken aback by money left on the table. The better the restaurant, the more likely it is that a tip is expected, but – the corollary – the more likely it is that the gratuity is included in the bill. Check to make sure. To ask whether the tip is already included, say *"Servis dahil mi?"* (ser-vees dah-heel muh). When in doubt, 10 percent tips are fine.

Pay **taxi drivers** what you owe them, rounding up to a convenient amount. Even this isn't expected outside of tourist districts. You can reward **barbers** (*kuafor*) and **masseurs** (*masör*)in Turkish baths with a small tip, although, again, in lightly touristed places they'll probably be surprised.

Tourism Offices

Offical tourism offices – marked with a big, fat white dotted "i" on a blue background – can be of great assistance throughout Turkey. The staff will usually speak some English and will certainly have some maps and brochures. They are not supposed to recommend hotels, but they can direct you to hotels and restaurants that fit a description you provide. They're happy to help you find particular hotels. Note that in some towns, Antalya for instance, travel agencies set up shop behind a big counterfeit information sign. This is pretty clear once you're inside; if they try to sell you on a particular trip or if they pitch a specific hotel, don't give them your business.

Hours vary, but most tourism offices keep normal office hours – 9 a.m to 6 p.m. with a break at lunch. We have provided the addresses and numbers of tourism offices throughout Turkey in the appropriate sections.

You can get tourism information from the **Turkish Embassy** in the U.S., 1717 Massachusetts Ave. N.W. ,Ste. 306, Washington D.C., 20036, *Tel. 202/429-9844, Fax 202/429-5649* and from the **Turkish Consulate** in New York, 821 United Nations Plaza, New York, NY, 10017, *Tel. 212/687-2194, Fax 212/599-7568.* You can also check out the official home page at *www.turkey.org/turkey.*

Water

Bottled water is not a vanity in Turkey, it's what everyone drinks. In İstanbul, the tap water tastes bad, isn't entirely clean, and shouldn't be considered potable. Outside of İstanbul, the tap water simply isn't potable.

You'll find a "Su İstasiyon" every few blocks, the place where locals stop in every few days to fill big water bottles, The only difference is the one-liter water bottles you buy at a shop cost 80¢, and locals get 20 liter refills for about the same price. If you want to fill your water bottles up at a water station that's fine, too; this way you can get in on the better prices.

The nicer hotels do offer filtered water. If you're at all unsure whether your hotel filters its water, stick to bottled water and inquire at the front desk at your next opportunity.

Chapter 8

Turkey is traditionally renowned for a wealth of goods that include kilims and carpets, ceramics, gold and silver, copper, leather, and cotton goods. You'll have no trouble being tempted - there are things to buy at every turn. The one trouble you may have is in making decisions amidst the sensory overload and jumble of options that characterizes Turkish bazaars and street life in general. But once you get your rug or bowl away from the hubbub, its individual beauty will stand out.

Haggling Primer

During the bargaining process, naivete or lack of finesse can actually work to your advantage. An American friend of ours swears by her bargaining technique, which basically strips away all the layers of pretense: she stands with the object she wants while a shopkeeper punches out amounts on his calculator and shows them to her. When, as usual, the price is high, she reacts as if the price is too high, shaking her head. 'I just stand there looking dumb,' she says, 'and the price keeps dropping.' Although all merchants have calculators at the ready, you may want to bring your own pocket calculator along to make price conversion faster and easier. It's also handy for quick checks of restaurant and bar tabs.

Tip 1: In the Grand Bazaar, resolve only to ask prices in the first five stores you enter - not to buy.

Tip 2: Don't start bargaining unless you're willing to purchase the item. If the merchant meets your price, you're supposed to buy it. It's not overly rude to

Shopping for a Fez

'Come with me,' he said, placing a disproportionately large hand in mine and leading me along a chilly corridor. He stopped in front of a door and turned a key in the lock. We stepped inside. As my eyes adjusted to the weak light, I could see that it was a fez repository. I had never seen so many fezzes in my life. They stood in wobbly stacks against the walls, fez stalagmites rising to the ceiling among lesser formations that strove for space at my feet. They lay horizontal along shelves, tubes of fezzes wrapped in brown paper which in some cases had split open and spilled to the floor.'

Jeremy Seal, **A Fez of the Heart: Travels Around Turkey in Search of a Hat**. London: Picador, 1995.

change your mind unless you've been haggling for a while. Even then, you may send the price still lower.

Tip 3: For items that are not rugs or jewelry, you can offer a fraction of the shopkeeper's first price. The shopkeeper will invariably refuse this offer, but at least it gets the bidding closer to the item's wholesale cost. And, depending on the item, your final price could get that low anyway.

Tip 4: Shops in Istanbul's Grand Bazaar are prime real estate, in the $1 million range. They do good business. Hang around and look at their wares all you want, and do not feel a sense of obligation to buy out of concern for the shopkeeper's time.

Tip 5: Do not expect to be able to bargain down the prices of gold and silver by much more than 10 percent of the asking price (although it never hurts to try); Turkish friends say that the profit margins are not as high on jewelry as they are on other items.

Tip 6: Hitting some of the coastal resort towns in late October when most establishments start shutting down for the winter will ensure you some bargains. (Although this tactic could also backfire if you are going to those resort towns for the famed nightlife, or to soak up sun on a beach.)

Tip 7: Many sellers of big-ticket items such as rugs or antiques now take credit cards. Some merchants may charge you the fee (usually 2-3 percent of purchase price) that the credit card company charges them; make sure you ask about this before striking your final deal.

Buying Kilims & Carpets

Expect to be beguiled by the many beautiful rugs sold in Turkey. Well-crafted Turkish rugs are a treasure that will outlast you, the perfect keepsake from a trip to Asia Minor. They come in a dazzling array of colors and patterns, woven, knotted, and embroidered with silk, wool, cotton, and even goat hair. There are rugs to fit every budget, from a $30 simple wool kilim to magnificent Hereke silk carpets that run well into the thousands of dollars.

There is no shortage of places to buy kilims and carpets, no matter where in Turkey you go. One of the best places is, of course, İstanbul's **Grand Bazaar**, simply because of the sheer number of dealers and variety of stock. And the rugs come from all over the Balkans, the Caucusus, the Middle East, and Central Asia - not just Turkey. Some Turkish friends tell us to avoid buying rugs in İstanbul if you'll be going elsewhere in Turkey, because prices can drop in less touristed areas. But the likelihood that you'll find anything significantly cheaper outside İstanbul is fairly low, unless you've got the time and inclination to hunt. In some towns like Kuşadası, in fact, you're sure to run into outrageously inflated prices because of the cruise ships that dock there and unload loaded visitors.

There are terrific and fortuitous stories about visitors innocently walking down a street in the Turkish interior and spotting a local fellow biking an oversized kilim up a long hill to his distributor. He sells you the rug for a song, delighted to cut out the middleman, and everyone goes home happy.

It happens. Usually, however, the carpets or kilims get to their distributor and into the hands of the shrewd rug salesmen. You will find the cheapest prices in the interior - the **Konya Bazaar** in Konya is a particularly good spot. İstanbul has a mountain of carpets, but steady tourist traffic keeps the prices higher.

Turks have been weaving kilim, a flat-weave style of rug, for almost 1,000 years. What began as a floor-covering among nomadic Selçuks has become a work of art appreciated the world over. Traditionally the patterns in carpets and kilims will mean something; common motifs include symbols for male and female fertility. For all the tradition, rugs sometimes reflect an individual weaver's humor - in some sumak pieces you can find a small car in among all the animals. Different regions produce their own distinctive designs and, commerce being what it is, rug-makers also churn out the designs that people seem to like. If you notice a striking similarity between Turkish kilim patterns, and, say, Navajo rugs, this is more than just mere coincidence. In the 19th century, Turkish rugs were brought to the American southwest to show Native Americans examples of what Europeans and white Americans would be interested in trading for and buying.

Rug sellers may tell you that a rug's high price is justified by the fact that it was made by the weaver for use in the home, not for sale. Which does not explain why the rug is now for sale. Unfortunately, carpet and kilim salesmen have also passed along their wily advice for almost 1,000 years, and today's breed of Grand Bazaar rug hawker is the end product of nine centuries of rug selling guile.

Types of Rugs

The **kilim** (kee-leem), or flat weave rug, is made by weaving yarn horizontally on the vertical 'warp.' (The warp consists of the loose threads that are like tassles at the end of the rug.) On many kilims the front and the back are virtually identical. The most common Anatolian patterns are geometric, with many triangles.

The **cicim** (jee-jeem) is an embroidered kilim, and is not usually reversible.

The **halı** (hall-uh), or carpet, is made by knotting yarns horizontally along the lengthwise warp. The yarns are then cut to a uniform height, to form the fuzzy "top" of the carpet. Anatolian carpets frequently have a distinctive double-knot on the underside, whereas carpets from other regions may have single knots. One of the more common carpet patterns is the slightly steepled rectangle, representing the mihrab, or prayer niche. Such devices indicate a prayer rug, and these can range in size from the small rugs designed for use by individuals at prayer time to the giant rugs covering the floors of mosques.

The **sumak** (soo-mak) is another flat weave rug. The threads are wrapped around the warp, not woven.

Materials

In woolen rugs, the quality of the wool is important. Machine spun wool can be more oily than hand spun wool, with the result that dyes do no hold as fast. In turn, the rug's color deteriorates more rapidly. Furthermore, machine spun wool is looser and yields less precise patterns. To distinguish machine-spun from hand-spun wool check the tails, or the warp, at the end of the rug. Hand spun wool is very tight and irregular, while machine spun wool is very regular, but loose. Hand spun wool is also more 'dry' (i.e. not as oily to the touch), while machine spun wool smells of lanolin and may feel oily.

Many rugs, both kilims and carpets, have cotton warps. Again, check the tails at the end of the rug - if you can't tell the difference by feel, cotton is usually a bright, bleached white. You can also ask - cotton in Turkish is 'pamuk.' While a cotton warp is not inherently bad, and cotton warps actually make for a tighter weave and yield wonderfully detailed and intricate patterns, they are not as forgiving as a wool warps. Cotton looks dirtier faster and is not as 'elastic' as wool. Cotton is also more susceptible to mildew in damp climates.

The most expensive rugs, aside from antiques, are carpets made with silk, and often with a silk/wool combination. The silk has a sheen to it that wool does not achieve, and feels, well, silky underfoot. Synthetics are also used in rug-making. Nylon fibers can be found in beautiful rugs and carpets, but their presence means it should cost you significantly less than a natural fiber rug. You should be particularly wary of synthetics around Kayseri. The only way to tell whether the yarns contain synthetics is to pull a small piece of the fiber out of the rug and burn it. If it melts, rather than burns, don't pay a natural-fiber price.

Dyes

Sometime between 1865 and 1879, German aniline dyes were introduced in the Ottoman Empire, and by 1920 natural dyes were effectively dead. Chemical dyes created a single, consistent color and were easier and cheaper to produce than natural dyes. The poorer of these artificial dyes would bleed, but the better dyes yielded perfectly decent products. They fade more quickly, dulling rather than curing, but artificial dyes were used, and continue to be used, in some of the finest carpets and kilims.

In 1975, efforts were begun to recreate the natural dyes, and after years of dredging up old dye recipes and experimenting, experts have recreated most of the natural colors. Camomile, for instance, yields an excellent yellow; maddar produces red; sumac and maddar combine to make purples; indigo and camomile combine for greens. The list goes on.

Natural dye production remains a niche activity (dyes from the Konya region are especially lovely), and its advantages are usually so subtle that only customers with deep pockets or exacting standards are interested in the greater expense. Natural dyes age extremely well. The colors become deeper and richer over time. Finally, natural dyes produce kilims with subtle gradations in color - a large field of yellow, for instance, will be a slightly uneven combination of beautiful yellows.

Age

When shopping for rugs, it's useful to keep in mind the distinction between 'previously owned' and 'antique.' Antiques bring in more money, and therefore some shady characters want to pass rugs off as older than they are. Antique rugs are out there, but they're very expensive and you usually have to go looking for them. Reproduction pieces are readily available, so if you're interested in a traditional pattern, you don't necessarily have to buy an antique to get it.

There are sneaky ways of falsifying a rug's age. Sometimes they're left out in the elements, sometimes they're washed in a bleach solution. Sometimes they have dirt rubbed into them to give the appearance of having been used on the Anatolian plains. Dealers who specialize in antique rugs will have the pieces professionally cleaned and repaired - and repairs should not look like the person just learned how to darn socks. Be duly suspicious, but don't let it ruin your shopping fun.

Genuinely antique rugs will be expensive because, well, they're antiques; they're hard to come by. Antique rugs have seen a couple lifetimes' use; this means that they can be more delicate than new rugs, which is something to keep in mind if you plan on stepping on yours.

Rug Shopping Tips

Measure the prospective floor or wall space in your home before you leave and convert it into centimeters. Also shop around a little to get the prices of rugs you like, if there are specialty rug shops where you live.

Find a shop on your own instead of allowing yourself to be led to one. If you buy something, 10% (sometimes far more) goes into the pocket of your guide. This is, of course, fine, but it means that your price will be at least 10% higher than had you wandered into the shop by yourself.

Select a few that you are interested in and ask about them all. Don't let on if you have a particular favorite, even though it means lavishing attention on rugs you aren't serious about. If the world of bargaining is not at all to your liking, there are also shops with fixed prices. For a few suggestions, see our İstanbul chapter shopping section.

Smell the rugs. If you smell gasoline, the material was probably treated with gasoline to hold it together. It is prone to fraying and, not surprising, it will smell like gas. If you smell chlorine, the rug has been bleached to give it a slightly aged appearance. Not only is it not as aged as the vendor may claim, after a bleaching the carpet is sure to wear relatively quickly - an heirloom for generations becomes an heirloom for 10 years or less.

If you're looking at carpets, spread the fibers and look at their roots. The best carpets made with natural dyes will have a fairly uniform color at both the end of the fiber and at its root. Less choice carpets, if not new, will be faded on the surface.

Rub a few spots with a damp handkerchief. The handkerchief should come away clean. If it does not, one of the following is amiss: a good rug has been inexpertly retouched (i.e. shoe polish, watercolors, or even felt tip markers) or the rug in question was made with second rate chemical dyes and is going to bleed a little and fade a lot. It may be a good idea to ask the dealer before doing this. If he's selling good stuff, he shouldn't mind.

You're often advised to inquire about the density of the knots in carpets, which is usually expressed in 'knots per centimeter.' You'll get answers like 32 and 42, and sometimes 72 or 116. The theory is the more knots per centimeter, the better the carpet, but it's a fundamentally irrelevant question. The dealer probably doesn't know, you don't understand what the numbers mean anyway, so our advice is don't ask about the density of the knots. Instead, look at a few different carpets and see for yourself which are tight and dense and which are loose.

If you have been sold a carpet or kilim that the dealer says is truly old, he must send you on your way with export papers certifying that your purchase is not a national treasure. Otherwise you are violating Turkey's antiquities laws.

To ship or not to ship? Although most dealers who offer you the option of shipping your rug home for you are perfectly honest in their intentions, it is probably worth your while to pay the airline's extra baggage fee if necessary than to risk your valuable new purchase.

It's understandable to feel stupid going through all of these circumlocutions, but it's a good idea to go through them nonetheless if you want to buy a rug you will enjoy for years to come. It is also understandable to fail a rug on each of the above points and still love it so much you must have it - just don't pay too much.

How do you know if you're getting a good deal? The short answer is, you don't. Ultimately, you're getting a good deal if you like the rug and you've paid an amount of money for it that you're willing to part with. One final note: Unless you're a collector, it's probably a bad idea to take the rug to a dealer when you're back in North America to ask what it's 'worth' because you may not like the answer. The worth is in your daily enjoyment of the rug and in the memories of your visit to Turkey.

Ceramics

Everyone knows about the rugs, but Turkey's bazaars will tempt you in other ways as well. Another essential element of Turkish art emerged from the kilns of İznik, where ceramics took hold in the 1400s. The **İznik patterns**, typically in gorgeous blues and turquoises (and sometimes reds), decorate many of İstanbul's greatest landmarks. These patterns have been faithfully recreated on plates and bowls by contemporary artists and fetch $20 to $150 prices in big city bazaars. If you have the luxury of time, do not make any purchases on your first shopping excursion, in the heat of the moment. Look around first.

During your spin through the bazaars, ceramics merchants will often try to convince you of a piece's quality by dinging it on the edge with a finger and letting it ring, nodding gravely and saying '*Kalite*' (quality). Ignore this senseless exercise, find what you like, get a price, gently knock the price down - even if this particular shop has 'fixed wholesale prices because we are the distributor for blah blah...' - then go back to the hotel. While there, talk to other travelers or anyone you can trust about what they would pay, and sleep on it. If you still feel you must have those bowls and like the deal you're getting, then buy. You can have your purchases wrapped in bubble wrap and cardboard for safer traveling.

İznik Ware

The Selçuk dynasty introduced tile making to Anatolia, and nowhere did it come to fuller flower than in İznik tile workshops in the 16th and 17th centuries. İznik's ascendance corresponded almost exactly with the Ottoman Empire's own rise, reaching its peak during the reign of Süleyman the Magnificent and his chief architect, Mimar Sinan. In Sinan's hands, the beautiful tiles were put to appropriately magnificent use throughout the empire, including Süleymaniye Mosque and the private chambers at Topkapı Palace.

Tiles, dishes, bowls and other porcelain-like goods were made with white clay and originally decorated with blues and turquoises. It is a trademark of the İznik workshops - in İznik, Diyarbekir, and İstanbul - that decorations are in the form of flowers or patterns. Tulips, carnations, and the Tree of Life are traditional motifs. Owing to the strict interpretation of the Koran's admonishment against idolatry, decorators were barred from making likenesses of people or creatures. If that seems odd, consider how the Muslims felt about the Christian penchant for decorating churches and homes with pictures of a Muslim prophet, Jesus Christ, after he was mutilated and nailed to a cross.

Cut off from such vivid western avenues of artistic expression, Muslim artists poured their energies into calligraphy, geometric patterns and other decorative devices (birds are often represented, an exception to the idolatry stricture). The resulting ceramic work, particularly in the case of İznik ceramics in their heyday, is beautifully artful and timeless.

As time went on, the tile makers began introducing a greater palette of colors, including reds and purples, and the patterns grew busier. By the late 1500s, the designs were increasingly muddled, and were accompanied by poorer glazes. By 1700, the İznik workshops had closed. Magnificent artwork thrives in a healthy, affluent society, and İznik's decline corresponded to mounting decadence and decay in the Ottoman Empire.

The **Kütahya** ceramic shops were peers of the İznik shops, and outlasted İznik without ever achieving the same success. Like the İznik shops, Kütahya began producing tile in the 1400s, but when İznik fell into its decline Kütahya attracted some of its artists and carried on. Some of Kütahya's business, unlike its rival, was in ecclesiastical tiles, pendants, and icons for the Christian church. Kütahya thrived into the 1700s, thereafter beginning its own slow decline. Kütahya shops finally closed their doors early in this century, and are now enjoying a tourism-generated revival. Many of the ceramics you see today are made in Kütahya.

Gold & Silver

Gold, or **altın**, holds a special place in Turkish culture. Its significance is not only as a hedge against rampant modern inflation; there is also a long history of giving gifts of gold to commemorate weddings, circumcisions, births and engagements. At wedding receptions, brides are decorated with gifts of thick gold chains and coins pinned to their chests. In rural Turkey, savings accounts often take the form of 22 karat bangles on womens' arms. Turkish savings banks with depositors would fork over the cash equivalent of just some of the estimated 4,000 to 6,000 tons of gold they are hoarding. That's about 80 grams per person.

Turkey's position as the world's seventh largest fabricator of gold jewelry is in evidence everywhere - most main streets have their own gold shops. About 30 percent of all retail gold shops in Turkey are around the **Grand Bazaar**, along with about 4,000 manufacturers. The mass producers lurk on the outskirts of İstanbul, and threaten the small-time jewelers around the Bazaar. Businesses that work only 30 kg of gold per year cannot compete with the 8 tons of jewelry produced by the seven largest firms.

There is some risk of not getting what you paid for. Jewelry manufacturers in Turkey are not obliged to have their products certified unless intended for export. However, some jewelers use serial numbers that can be traced through the İstanbul Chamber of Goldsmiths. If you stick with numbered pieces, you should be fine. Gold should also be stamped with its karat. Ask the shopkeeper to show you the daily price of unworked gold at the karatage you are interested in. The shopkeeper should have daily prices. Watch the weighing, then calculate the value of the gold and the charge for labor.

Bazaar Jewelers

'Many of the jewelers (in the Grand Bazaar) are still working in Dickensian conditions, crammed into poorly lit, unventilated rooms...yet when the final product has been finished and is held up to the light, there is a communal pride in the creation. Artisans often enter the trade as a tea-boy - it is an industry staffed exclusively by men - and make their way slowly up the ladder, for as long as they can keep their eyesight.'

From **Gold in Turkey**, İstanbul: Turk Ekonomi Bankası and IBS Research & Consultancy, 1996.

For silver, or **gümüş**, you can browse through the bazaars in many cities and towns, including İstanbul's **Old Bedesten** in the Grand Bazaar. You will find new, used, and antique silver items; bracelets in varying widths and necklaces that are woven from fine silver wires and have decorated clasps. The latter are traditionally from the **Trabzon** area on the Black Sea. Some of the finest filigree work was traditionally done by Syriani Christians in southeast Turkey, but this, like the Syrianis themselves, is difficult to find these days. Silver jewelry is also generally sold by weight. Just make certain that the stamp is 925 or higher, or else you're getting an inferior alloy instead of sterling.

Leather

If you are interested in purchasing leather goods like jackets or accessories, Turkey is the place to do it. A long tradition of leatherworking for export generally keeps the prices lower here than in western countries.

In İstanbul, a good place to start looking is the **Covered Bazaar**, but, as with everything else there, you must be discriminating. Be sure to check stitching, buttonholes, and zippers. If you are uncertain about your ability to assess quality, or if you can't find exactly what you're looking for, you can either have something made - many shops offer 24-hour delivery of made-to-order leather clothing (but make sure you're under no obligation to buy) - or you can head to some of the retail shops on **İstiklal Caddesi** near Taksim Square. You probably won't find any great bargains at the retail shops unless you locate the old-season rack, but at

The Evil Eye

This ubiquitous round blue symbol is, of course, steeped in superstition, but it can be taken quite seriously by otherwise non-superstitious and secular folks. You'll find blue eyes dangling from car exhaust pipes, from rear-view mirrors, backpacks, necklaces and bracelets, pinned to the sweaters of small children, and hanging above doors in restaurants, hotels, stores, and apartments. These blue eyes, like the real thing, are said to protect one from the evil eye. The evil eye can be cast unwittingly; even an admiring compliment not followed by 'Maşallah' (may Allah protect) can cast the eye. This has a lot to do with covetousness and acknowledging the role Allah has in creating wonderful things. Not only do blue eyes act as proof against the evil eye, they are able to cast the evil eye more readily than brown-eyes.

least you can be sure that the stitching won't come undone anytime soon. Many leather goods shops are in a neighborhood called **Zeytinburnu** (outside the city walls, just south of the E5 freeway) - the factories used to be here as well, but have since moved further out in order to improve the scent-quality of the area.

Textiles

Cotton towels are said to have gotten their start in **Bursa** for use at the mineral baths, and cotton still figures prominently in the bazaars there. The more dramatic tale is that of silk, another longtime Bursa specialty. In Byzantine times the Emperor Justinian sent a mission to China. The mission's ostensible purpose was diplomatic and religious; the real reason was Justinian's desire to cultivate silk-manufacturing in the Byzantine Empire. Several years later, the missionaries returned with the secret: hollowed-out cavities in their walking sticks hid silkworms. The Chinese secret was out, and Justinian's sturdy little silkworms helped break the Chinese silk monopoly.

Today, not much is left of actual silk cultivation in Turkey. In the mid-19th century, western silk worms were virtually wiped out by a bacterial disease. Turkish textile factories once again use imported Chinese raw silk for the production of their wares, with a single exception. As for cotton, you will have a hard time beating the standard made-in-the-USA cotton towels hanging in your bathroom at home; most of the good stuff in Turkey is produced for export, and is difficult to find in shops. There are, however, a few places to find beautiful Made-in-Turkey textiles (see the İstanbul chapter's shopping section).

Turkish Baths - Hamams

Communal baths were used in Roman times, but, as the very name 'Turkish bath' suggests, they are significant to Ottoman culture. In an age when western Europeans went without bathing, the Ottomans were very conscientious about staying clean, perhaps stemming from the cleansing rituals of Islam. Perhaps, too, the Ottomans inherited their fondness for baths from the Byzantines, who had continued the Roman tradition while it collapsed in the chaos of medieval Europe. Communal baths have been an integral part of life in Turkey for two thousand years, but with better living standards the **hamam** is slowly fading from daily life. Don't worry, though; you'll still find plenty of hamams, but your best bets are tourist spots or small towns.

The Turkish bath of the western imagination is an erotically charged place, an impression fueled by the works of various European painters. Hamams are, however, primarily places to get clean, relax, and socialize. The classical hamam design includes both mens' and womens' quarters.

If there are no separate quarters, then men and women go on separate days, or during separate hours. The mens'area is typically larger and more luxurious than the womens', and mens'hours are invariably longer.

Hamams were historically (and in rural areas still are) one of the only public places outside the home that women could socialize. A contemporary Turkish pop singer, Sibel Tüzün, stages one of her videos in a hamam, in which the women are entertaining one another with dancing and singing. This apparently still happens, although we have not witnessed it.

In recent years, some hamams in the more touristed areas have gone co-ed. Various stories circulate about female travelers who go alone to co-ed hamams being subject to unwanted sexual touching by the masseur. The only way to avoid this possibility is to go to the hamam with a male companion, or, not to get scrubbed. We would hazard to guess that most Turkish women would not allow themselves to be scrubbed by a man, and you will find neither female Turkish bathers nor female Turkish attendants/masseuses in co-ed hamams. So, when in Byzantium ...

Many Turks actually wrinkle their noses at the idea of a going to a hamam, claiming that hamams are 'dirty.' This is only true to a point. If you're sensitive about germs, have a strong allergic reaction to mildew, or have problems with chronic sinusitis, then perhaps you should avoid them. Otherwise there's no evidence that they are unsafe. To hedge your bets you can always try a watered down version of a hamam at one of the major hotels. In places like Bursa, you'll have the hamam to yourself.

The prices in touristy, historic hamams hover in the $15-$25 range. This price should include a scrubbing and massage, but when you compare that with the $5 price paid in neighborhood hamams for the same, if not better, service, you might feel gouged. You're paying for convenience, the workers' English skills, and, often, a beautiful, historic setting.

You'll find hamams fed by natural springs at **Yalova/Termal**, **Bursa**, and **Pamukkale**. (See İstanbul, Pamukkale, and Bursa for details.)

Visiting the Hamam

You will enter a reception area, the **camekan**, which in some hamams is also used for changing. Some hamams have private changing rooms where you may lock up your clothes and valuables, and others have common changing areas and small valuables lockers at the desk. Typically you pay when you enter, and pay extra for rubbing ('*keselemek*') and/or massage ('*masaj*') in neighborhood hamams. You may get tokens to give to the masseur or masseuse. You will receive a linen **peştemal** with which to wrap yourself.

Turkish Bath Suggestions

Tip 1: you may want to make a point of drinking some water before going to the hamam. Often there is bottled drinking water available for sale during your cool-down period (in addition to tea, Coke, beer, etc.), but the heat may be more difficult to bear if you're feeling dehydrated in the first place.

Tip 2: Take your shampoo and soap with you in a plastic bag, and tip money for the masseur or masseuse. Try to see how other people deal with tipping. About 20 percent of the fees charged, distributed among the attendants, is appropriate.

If you see any wooden or plastic slippers lying around, you should wear them. Not only is this for traditions'sake (the hygeine factor is negligible, especially with the wooden ones), but it may also be to protect your feet from unbearably hot marble if the heat is coming from below.

The only hard and fast rule for men is to never show your genitalia, regardless of whether you're in a co-ed or sex-segregated hamam. This is considered highly improper. Men should wear the peştemal at all times (although in some hamams, wearing a bathing suit is acceptable). Although rules for women on this may be more relaxed in some hamams, it is better to wear your underwear under the peştemal and then disrobe further depending on what you see others doing than it is to offend the other bathers and go back to the changing room to put your underwear back on (this from personal experience). Some Turkish women even wear their bras into the hamam. Use your best judgment.

You will pass through the **soğukluk** – an antechamber or passage-way of intermediate temperature – on your way to the **havlet**, the room where you perspire. Lie down on the **göbek taşı**, the hot stone slab heated from below.

Once you've started sweating and perhaps have doused yourself with water a few times (taking care not to splash other bathers or let water that has touched you back into the basin under the spigot), you will be rubbed down by the **tellak** (attendant) with the abrasive **kese**. This will loosen your dead skin. You'll be surprised at how much comes off an otherwise 'clean' body.

Afterwards, get soaped up and rinsed, and then massaged. This process, although unlike deep tissue massage, is nonetheless vigorous and remarkably relaxing in combination with the heat and steam of the bath.

If you've had enough, you can proceed from here back to the camekan, where you may wrap yourself in a dry towel, recline on lawn-chairs, and sip a beverage (paid for separately). When you're good and ready, go back to your chamber to dress.

Shave & a Haircut!

Everyone knows about the Turkish baths, but something that most male visitors find far more rewarding is a shave and a haircut. Barbers in most parts of North America do some snipping and call it good. Not so here. The haircut is followed by a shave, a long, marvelous process with a straight razor that leaves your face perfectly clean. In the likely event you've never had a shave at the barber, be sure to do it here.

With the completion of the shave the show is not over; next you will usually be fussed over with lemon cologne, flaming things, balms, and even a shoulder rub. The cost? Usually about $5 in the neighborhood barbershops of İstanbul.

Alternative Lifestyles

The 1995 Turkish film *İstanbul Beneath My Wings* stirred great contro-versy and was even banned in some municipalities for its depiction of an Ottoman sultan's homosexual activity. That the film was based in fact was beside the point. In the Turkish mainstream, charges of homosexu-ality are considered a grave insult.

There is no specific reference in Turkish law to homosexuality, but there are references to public morals and public order - community standards by another name. This makes it legal for police to take anyone "suspicious-looking" in for interrogation. There is no organized queer-bashing per se, but gays have not been allowed by the government to openly organize, stage Pride Festivals, protests, etc. Gays and transves-tites/transgendereds (lesbians are not as targeted because they are less visible) are routinely roughed up by police.

That's the bad news, but it isn't that simple. In 1996, an entertainer named Zeki Muren died during the taping of a television program. Hundreds of mourners were shown on television, weeping at his casket and his face adorned the covers of every daily newspaper. All of this public grief was, ironically, for one of Turkey's most beloved and flamboyant female impersonators, and a homosexual.

İstanbul in particular has a lively, if necessarily underground, gay and lesbian (mostly gay) culture. Other cities with homosexual-friendly establishments include Ankara, Izmir, Bodrum, and Kaş. Most of the places listed under İstanbul's Nightlife section are homosexual-friendly; none are exclusively gay. Note: It's safest finding places on your own where you feel comfortable, rather than accepting invitations you receive on the street.

For further information and listings contact: **Lambda İstanbul**, *turkiye@qrd.org*, or go the website *www.qrd.org/www/world/europe/turkey*. This page is infrequently maintained, but has some good resources which include a news archive and a guide to bars, restaurants, cafes, shops, etc., around Turkey.

Chapter 9

food & drink

Food

Americans asked to name a Turkish dish would, sad to say, name a flightless bird that goes well with cranberries or stuffing. Well, surprise: Turkey has a rich culinary tradition and your meals here should be highlights of your visit.

True Turkish cuisine is rare; it was a product of a time when women spent their days at home preparing complicated, time-consuming dishes. Precious few places prepare Turkish food way *anne* (mother) used to make it; mother's liberated now and holding down a job. What passes for Turkish food in many places is no less authentic, but it is a streamlined version of classic Turkish cuisine. To taste Turkish cuisine at its exquisite height you need to try one of the handful of places that take the time to make dishes properly; **Washington Restaurant** in Ankara and **Haci Abdullah** and the **Tuğra** in İstanbul are a few good examples.

It can be difficult to find a restaurant that does justice to Turkish cuisine, but the staples of Turkish cooking are available everywhere, and they are cheap. Stroll through a market and you'll see why Turkish food can do no wrong. Tomatoes, onions, eggplants, cucumbers, garlic, artichokes and peppers grow in great abundance, while recipes borrow from Mediterranean, Arab, and Turkish traditions. With this legacy, and these raw materials, it's almost unfair.

Turkish food emerged slowly, a product of cross-fertilization like the Turks themselves. The Turkic peoples migrated from Mongolia, bringing Far Eastern nomadic cuisine on the long journey west. A few of the

Key Food Words

Afiyet Olsun	Eat well (to those eating)
Elinize Sağlık	Health to your hands (to the cook)
Şerefe!	To your health (a toast)
İzgara	Grilled
Fırın	Baked
Et	Meat (used for red meat)
Tavuk	Chicken
Balık	Fish
Sebze	Vegetable
Meyve	Fruit
Su	Water
Süt	Milk
Ekmek	Bread
Kuru fasulye ve pilav	White beans and rice
Pide	Thick flat bread with toppings
Lahmacun	Thin flat bread with ground meat and spices, similar to pizza
Köfte	Meatballs

original Turkish dishes appear to be **mantı** (ravioli in yogurt sauce), **börek** (pastry with meat and cheese filling), and meat cooked on a skewer – **kebabs**. To this the Arabs contributed spices and breads, while the coastal areas near the Mediterranean, Aegean, and Black Sea brought fish, fresh vegetables, and fruit to the table. During the long evolution of Turkish food, the Selçuk Turks contributed a habit of baking their meat in clay ovens that evokes Indian cooking, while the Ottomans, with their 100-year domination of the Mediterranean basin, began experimenting with the classic olive oil/tomato/garlic/onion combinations so popular in Italy. The result of these many influences is a distinctive and mouthwatering local cuisine, varying by region.

Mezes

The one thing you must know about Turkish dining is the wonderful institution of **mezes**, or appetizers. "Appetizer" is an imperfect translation, since it is common for friends to gather and consume mezes and rakı without ever progressing to the entree. Excellent examples are **kalamar**, fried calamari; **patlican salata**, eggplant puree; and **yaprak dolma**, stuffed grape leaves, all of which go very well with a blue summer sky and a sea view. The meze is more than just a precursor to the meal, it is an integral part of the dining ritual.

Kahvaltı

One exception to this culture of complex food is **kahvaltı**, breakfast. North Americans accustomed to scrambled eggs, potatoes, and thick slices of bacon are in for an often-disappointing shock. First of all, pork products are not a part of the Muslim diet and will only appear at breakfast in the best of the five star hotels. Second, Turks take their breakfast simple and light; bread, cheese, tomatoes, honey, and hard boiled eggs. Again, unless you're at a first class hotel you're going to have to become accustomed to this European menu. Turks are sensible people, so you can generally expect coffee.

Drink

Coffee

When the Sultan Selim I (The Grim) conquered Yemen in the early 1500s, he installed a local governor who, stuck in Yemen for more than 20 years, turned all of his attention to the local coffee plantations. When the governor was recalled to İstanbul he brought coffee with him, and the sultan at that time, once again Süleyman the Magnificent, was duly impressed. Süleyman, in addition to his other contributions to the empire, introduced a **Kahvecebaşı**, a coffee brew master at the palace. Once established at the palace, it was just a matter of time before coffee was popular throughout İstanbul.

Skeptical Venetian traders had a taste of this hot bean liquid, and chose to take a chance with a few cases in the markets of Western Europe. It is at this point that coffee passed a crucial test. According to the popular (and perhaps apocryphal) story, a Pope took a speculative sip of the heathen drink and, on the spot, blessed it and pronounced it a proper drink for Latinate Christians, too. Owing in part to its exotic Ottoman cachet, London, Paris, and the major cities of Europe were soon importing coffee in quantity for their own aristocracies.

The dramatic tale of coffee's appearance on the world stage concludes when a great Ottoman invading force was defeated at the gates of Vienna in 1683. In the aftermath of the battle, an Austrian general discovered crates of coffee in the abandoned imperial tents and brought them within the city walls. He used the coffee to open Vienna's first coffeehouse. (One wonders, had the Turks purposefully retired from the battlefield and left men secreted in massive boxes of coffee...) The Ottoman hold on coffee production was broken soon afterward, when other nations, notably Britain, began cultivating coffee in their own possessions. In any case, for more than 100 years İstanbul was firmly established as antiquity's Seattle.

For North Americans, Turkish coffee is thick and silty; unfamiliar, but not bad. Avid coffee drinkers may not like it, not on account of its potency but because its taste is mildly bitter. It comes already sugared, unless you ask for it without: *sade*, plain; *az*, a little; *orta*, middling; *çok*, a lot. Most people take it orta. Pouring milk into the small cup will disturb the grounds at the bottom of the cup, and is not done. What *is* done, by the way, is that the cups are upended on their saucers and the grounds left in the cup are 'read' like the palm of a hand.

If you want regular coffee, you'll find mostly Nescafe, although some cafes and restaurants offer *filterkahve* (filtered coffee) and espresso drinks. If you would like milk in your Nescafe, ask for *sütlü kahve*.

Wine

At a latitude similar to California's Napa Valley, the vineyards of Italy, and France's Loire Valley, wine connoisseurs should be able to expect some delicious wines in Turkey. The country does produce some good wines, but if wine touring is a critical part of your agenda Turkey is probably the wrong place to visit.

Turkish wineries are relative latecomers to the industry, and several are state-run or state-subsidized to boot. The output of these wineries is, therefore, mediocre. It was not always so. Anatolia has an ancient-wine making tradition, perhaps the world's oldest. The first hard evidence of winemaking appears in Hittite engravings from the second millenium B.C. The Greeks, probably producing wine already, certainly began importing it from Asia Minor after the collapse of the Hittites. It was the Greeks who may first have elevated wine to its sacred – and sacramental – status in their tribute to Dionysius during the grape harvest. Dionysius was soon joined by a great many gods, Greek and Roman, pagan and Christian, all of whom were worshipped in ceremonies featuring wine.

After the settlement of the Muslims in Asia Minor at the beginning of the millenium, the ancient industry faltered and died. Although the Muslim faith warned adherents off of alcohol, it remained a vice of the sultans and ruling classes. Thus it is that the Ottoman contribution to the world of wine is nicely summed up by **Selim II** ("the Sot"), who, as his name suggests, was not afraid to have a snort or two, whatever the religious misgivings of his subjects. In 1569, Selim rerouted an invasion force intended to challenge Spain in the western Mediterranean and instead invested his Venetian allies on Cyprus. The reason? Selim wanted better wine, and a powerful adviser with a dislike for Venice lured him with the promise of tasty Cypriot vintages.

Selim II needn't have gone to such lengths to secure good wine – there has always been plenty of suitable terrain on the Turkish mainland, and since the 1920s grapes have been cultivated for wine making. If you order wine, you will be trying some of the local labels since wine imports are allowed only to a select few well-connected restaurants.

Wine is generally inexpensive, although gone are the days when $10 was the upper limit. A bottle of **Buzbağ red** ("red wine" is *kırmızı şarap*) from the government alcohol producer Tekel still costs $2 and is generally just fine. Doluca's **Villa Doluca** is the mid-market standard at $6.

Our favorite? A relatively new wine maker, **Sevilen**, has excellent merlot and cabernet sauvignons as part of its "Sevilen" label ($18). Note: Sevilen's downmarket wine—the "Evin" label—has the distinction of being the only wine the authors of this guide have ever found undrinkable. The **Kavaklıdere** label is another fixture in Turkey, and for years the Kavaklıdere Select label ($15) has graced the tables of the finest restaurants.

Turkey's principal wine-making regions are in Cappadocia and along the Aegean sea, notably Bozcaada island, near Troy. You can take "wine tours" by visiting wine manufacturers (**şarap fabrikası**) on Bozcaada and Ürgüp or **Göreme**, in Cappadocia. Göreme even hosts an annual wine festival in early September—although the festivities do not quite merit timing your visit to be there.

Rakı

Similar to Greek ouzo and other liquors in the Middle East, rakı is a licorice-flavored alcohol distilled from raisins, then distilled a second time with aniseed. **Yeni Rakı**, the common and readily available brand distributed by the government monopoly, is 90 proof and quite cheap; a liter bottle costs about $4.

There is a tradition and a culture to rakı drinking, an almost ceremonial protocol. The perfect rakı setting is a summer evening, at a table with good friends and a wide selection of Turkish **mezes**, or appetizers, and grilled fish to follow. Clear rakı is poured into a tall, slender glass, and topped off with an equal or slightly greater amount of water. The water turns the rakı a cloudy white, and several glasses later all the world becomes fairly hazy. Rakı is known as lion's milk, owing far more to its color than to the belligerence of its drinkers.

Tips for Dining Out in Turkey

- You want something to go? "To go" is *paket*.
- **İşkembe** is intestines (tripe), and tripe soup is supposedly curative for hangovers. There are lots of small İşkembeci in big cities, some with the diced tripe on a big grill out front.

- Smaller restaurants are unlikely to offer a menu. They aren't hiding them from you, it's just that 90 percent annual inflation makes printing menus an exercise in futility. Go ahead and, proferring a pen and paper, ask how much for particular items: *"Bu ne kadar?"*
- **Döner** shops display hunks of revolving chicken or lamb roasted by catalytic heaters. This meat is shaved down and stuffed into half-loaves of bread with tomato, onion, and salt. The cost for such a sandwich, a *döner sandviç*, is about 80¢ in the cities.
- In heavily-touristed places, ask prices beforehand if they're not marked on a menu, and keep a crystal clear record of your bill as you order (and expect an additional 20 percent in tax and service charge). Nothing can sour the memory of a night out like the feeling that you've been ripped off.
- **Köfte** sandwiches are sold out of carts throughout many cities. At a word from you the man will begin grilling up a handful of small meatballs, which he then packs into a half loaf of bread with some onion and tomato sauce. Delicious, and about $1 for a sandwich on a half-loaf of bread.
- If stomach ailments are a concern, down lots of yogurt to keep your stomach in good fighting shape. The food and germs here are different, so you may be afflicted with Atatürk's Revenge, but most people have no problems. Note that Ayran, a traditional drink of water, yogurt, and salt, isn't as lousy as it sounds, but it is often made with tap water – something best avoided.
- You're bound to see baked potato carts (**Patates Fırın**). To which of the toppings should you nod your head yes? We honestly can't be of any help in this matter. There are pickles, lentils, potato salad, butter, cheese, something like cranberries, several other large colorful mounds of food, and, of course, a long squirt of mayonnaise. You can watch from a distance and try to sort out what you want and what you don't – better, probably, to walk right up, nod your head saying *"her şey"* (everything), and mutter an *"Allah Korusun"* (God protect).
- Turkish pizza, **Lahmacun**, has a thin crust and a layer of spicy ground lamb and tomato sauce. It often comes with a side of lettuce, onion, and lemon. It's thin enough to be a cross between a burrito and a pizza; we love it.
- While dining at restaurants, consider ordering little bits at a time, keeping an eye on your neighbor's table for things you like the look of.
- You should take the opportunity to sample fine Turkish cuisine, but don't miss the opportunity to try the many "hazır yemek," or "ready food," places. You'll find these on every side street and in every bus

station. This will almost always be filling food cooked by men for men, best sopped up with lots of Turkish white bread.

• When in doubt, order **kuru fasulye** and **pilav** – white beans and rice. This comes with bread. Another personal, ubiquitous favorite is **patlican salata**, or eggplant salad. Almost anything with eggplant is surprisingly good, whatever your prejudices against the vegetable.

• Sauces are notably absent from most Turkish dishes, including fish.

• The greatest testament to the importance of food in Turkish culture was the hierarchy of the Ottoman Janissary Corps. These elite soldiers were organized by kitchen titles; the Chief Cooks, the Bakers, the Soup Makers, and even the much dreaded Pancake Makers. To express their dissatisfaction or anger with a sultan, the Janissaries would overturn a giant pilaf cauldron.

Sample Menu

The following list of Turkish food is on the menu at **Haci Abdullah Restaurant** in Beyoğlu, İstanbul. Haci Abdullah enjoys an unrivalled reputation for serving good, authentic Turkish food. Believe it or not, this is just the abbreviated version of the real menu. If you can't find it on their menu, it probably ain't Turkish.

Soups (Çorbalar)

Domatesli pirinç çorbası	Tomato and rice soup
Düğün çorbası	Yogurt and veal soup
Erenler çorbası	Semolina soup
Et suyu çorbası	Veal bouillon with vegetables

Dining Phrases

Breakfast	Kahvaltı	kah-vall-tuh
Lunch	Öğle yemek	oy-leh yem-eck
Dinner	Akşam yemek	ak-sham yem-eck
Bakery/pastry shop	Pastanesi	pas-ta-nay-see
Restaurant	Lokanta	lo-kahn-ta
Grill restaurant	Ocakbaşı	ojak-bash-uh
Bill, please	Hesap, lütfen	hes-ahp, loot-fen
Service Charge Included	Servis ücreti dahil	ser-vees ooch-reh-tee da-heel
Keep the change	Ustu kalsın	oos-too kal-suhn
How much is this?	Bu ne kadar?	boo nay kadar

Ezogelin çorbası	Lentil and red pepper soup
Güvec	Stew
İşkembe çorbası	Tripe soup
İspinak Kök çorbası	Spinach-root soup
Kremalı Domates çorbası	Cream of tomato soup
Mantar çorbası	Mushroom soup
Mengen çorbası	Vegetable soup
Mercimek çorbası	Lentil soup
Sebzeli pirinç çorbası	Vegetable and rice soup
Tavuk suyu şehriye çorbası	Chicken and vermicelli soup
Yoğurtlu yayla çorbası	Yogurt and mint soup

Meat dishes (Et)

Beğendil kebap	Veal with eggplant puree
Beyin tava	Fried lamb's brains
Bıldırcın pilavlı	Quail with rice
Bonfile sote mantarlı	Sauteed beef with mushrooms
Çerkez tavuğu	Circassian chicken
Çomlek kebabı	Lamb and vegetable stew
Çulluk yahnısı	Woodcock stew
Dalyan köftesi	Lamb and veal meatloaf
Dana böbrek tava	Fried veal kidneys
Dana külbastı	Grilled veal
Dana rosto	Roast veal
Dana taskebabı	Veal and vegetable stew
Fırında kuzu budu sebzeli	Roast leg of lamb with vegetables
Güvecte pilavlı pilic	Chicken and rice stew
Hindi kestaneli	Roast turkey with chestnuts
Hindi firin	Roast turkey
İspinaklı püreli kebap	Veal with spinach puree
İzmir firin köftesi	Meatballs with potatoes
Kadınbudu köfte	Fried lamb and veal meatballs
Kagıt kebabı	Lamb papillote
Kagıtta piliç	Chicken papillote
Kuzu ciğer sarma	Roulade of lamb's liver
Kuzu dolması	Lamb pilaf
Kuzu elbasan tava	Lamb baked in bechamel sauce
Kuzu fırın	Roast lamb
Kuzu haşlama	Boiled lamb
Kuzu incik	Roast leg of lamb
Kuzu incik soğan yahnısı	Lamb and onion stew
Kuzu kapama	Lamb baked with vegetables

Kuzu kavurma	Braised lamb
Kuzu sarma	Lamb roulade
Kuzu tandır	Tandoori lamb
Manisa kebabı	Meat filled crepe
Ördek fırın	Roast duck
Patlıcanlı kebap	Lamb with eggplant
Piliç dolması	Chicken pilaf
Tavşan yahnısı	Rabbit stew
Terbiyeli köfte	Meatballs in lemon and egg sauce

Grilled Meats (Et Izgara)

Biftek ızgara	Grilled thin beefsteak
Bonfile ızgara	Grilled filet of beef
Ciğer ızgara	Grilled lamb's liver
Dana böbrek ızgara	Grilled veal kidneys
Dana pirzola	Grilled veal chops
Karışık ızgara	Mixed grill
Köfte ızgara	Grilled meatballs
Kuzu pirzola	Grilled lamb chops
Kuzu şiş kebap	Lamb shish kebab
Tavuk fileto ızgara	Grilled boneless chicken breast
Tavuk şiş	Chicken shish kebab

Cold Hors D'Oeuvres (Mezes)

Bakla ezine	Bean curd
Barbunya pilakı	Pinto beans
Beyin salatası	Boiled lamb's brains
Biber dolması	Stuffed bell pepper
Enginar	Artichoke
İmam bayıldı	Stuffed eggplant
Kereviz	Celeriac
Lahana dolması	Stuffed cabbage leaves
Piyaz	White beans
Taze fasulye	Green beans
Yaprak dolması	Stuffed vine leaves
Yoğurtlu bakla	Fresh broad beans with yogurt

Hot Vegetables (Sicak Sebzeler)

Bamya	Okra and tomatoes
Biber dolması	Stuffed bell pepper
Domates dolması	Stuffed tomato
İspinak püresi	Pureed spinach
Kabak dolması	Stuffed zucchini
Karnıyarık	Meat-filled eggplant

Patates püresi	Mashed potatoes
Patlican silkme	Stewed eggplant
Sebze sote	Sauteed mixed vegetables
Türlü firin	Mixed vegetables and lamb
Yaprak dolması	Stuffed vine leaves

Rice and Pasta (Pirinç ve Makarna)

Asya pilavı	Garbanzo pilaf
Buhara pilavı	Lamb pilaf
Bulgar pilavı	Cracked wheat pilaf
Fırında makarna	Macaroni and cheese
İç pilav	Lamb's liver pilaf

Flaky pastries (Böreği)

İspanakly tepsi böreği	Spinach baked in philodough
Kremalı börek	Chopped meat baked in philodough
Kol böreği	Chopped lamb baked in philodough
Mantı/Tatar böreği	Ravioli with yogurt
Peynirli börek	Feta baked in philodough
Su böreği	Feta pastry
Tavuklu börek	Minced chicken in philodough

Fish (Balık)

Alabalık ızgara	Grilled rainbow trout
Barbunya ızgara	Grilled red mullet
Çinekop ızgara	Grilled young bluefish
Hamsi buğulama	Anchovy stew
Kalkan fileto ızgara	Grilled turbot filet
Kefal haşlama	Boiled striped mullet
Kılıç şiş ızgara	Swordfish shish kebab
Levrek buğulama	Sea bass stew
Lüfer ızgara	Grilled bluefish
Mersin buğulama	Sturgeon stew
Palamut ızgara	Grilled bonito
Sardalya fırın	Baked sardines
Sinarit fileto izgara	Grilled sea bream filet
Somon ızgara	Grilled salmon
Tekir ızgara	Grilled surmullet

Salads (Salatalar)

Çoban salatası	Chopped tomatoes, onions, peppers
Çeşitli turşular	Assorted pickles
Domate hıyar söğüş	Sliced tomatoes and cucumbers

Hindiba salatası	Chicory leaves
Karışık salata	Tossed salad
Karnabahar salatası	Boiled cauliflower
Pancar salatası	Boiled beets
Roka salatası	Rocket leaves
Salatılık salatası	Minced cucumbers and tomatoes
Turp salatası	Radishes

best places to stay

Chapter 10

This business of selecting the "Best" hotels and pensions in Turkey has become more difficult over the years. Since the first edition, we have striven to compile a list of our favorite hotels in Turkey; we continue to. In this edition, we also offer a list of our favorite budget hotels. Some of these 'budget' hotels—the Antique Pansiyon in Antalya, for instance—could easily be counted among the best hotels in the country.

Price bears on our "best hotel" choices in only the most offhand way—if it's highway robbery, it's sure to not be one of our favorites. For budget listings, we set a ceiling of about $30.

These selections are entirely subjective. Our decisions are rooted in appreciation for places that let us feel lucky to be there—not a quality that can be calculated in hair dryers, televisions, or anything else specific. We welcome any of your own thoughts. Would you like to heap further praise on a particular hotel? Did you have a bad experience? Did you find another hotel that deserves mention? Please let the authors know: *info@theturkeyguide.com* or our publisher at *jopenroad@aol.com*.

İstanbul

FOUR SEASONS HOTEL İSTANBUL, *Tevkifhane Sok. No. 1, Sultanahmet. Tel. 212 638 8200, Fax 212 638 8210 (North American Reservations: Tel. 800/332-3442). Email: huluer@fshr.com; Web: www.fshr.com. Rooms: 65. Double: $320-$2,000 (20%-30% discounts in off-season).*

The Four Seasons Istanbul opened in 1996 and immediately took its place among the finest hotels in

Europe; indeed, it was selected the finest hotel in all of Europe in 2000. This ambitious and exacting hotel is worthy of the honor.

The Four Seasons—located just downhill from the Hagia Sophia—has a grace often missing from the stuffier top-end hotels. The genius of this hotel is in the details of each room, the great basins and attractive tilework in the bathrooms, the interior shutters, the bags of potpourri hung in the closet, the appealing furniture. There is a distinct Turkish quality to this hotel in its thoughtfully conceived kilims, tilework, and small Ottoman prints and portraits.

The extraordinarily refined atmosphere is all the more remarkable given the history of this building. What is today one of the most elegant hotels in Turkey was built in 1917 as a prison. The structure you see today is substantially the same, but the traces of the old building are few (the red and blue floor tiles in some of the stairwells beside the hotel elevators, for instance). The success of the renovation and interior decoration is total. As a writer for Architectural Digest has written in an extensive feature about the hotel, "If this reinvented building still conspires to detain, it is by charm and comfort alone."

If you are unnerved by the notion of sleeping in a former prison, take comfort that long before becoming a Turkish prison, this was on the site of the principal Byzantine Royal Palace: there are pampered, well-fed ghosts here to keep the prisoners' wretched souls company. Walls and arches belonging to former Byzantine Palace of Buculeon are visible skirting the Four Seasons.

The former prison day-yard now houses the marvelous Four Seasons' restaurant, Seasons. This restaurant is run by a Venetian chef who specializes in Californian and Mediterranean cuisine. Make reservations at the hotel far in advance.

EMPRESS ZOE, *Akbıyık Cad. Adliye Sok. No. 10, Sultanahmet. Tel. 212 518 2504, Fax 212 518 5699. Email: emzoe@attglobal.net; Web: www.emzoe.com. Rooms: 19. Credit cards accepted. Open year-round. Double: $70-$85 (25% off-season discount).*

İstanbul is stuffed with small hotels, but this is our favorite of the lot, a small gem in the Sultanahmet district.

The Empress Zoe is painted in muted yellows, with appealing woodwork on the walls and bedsteads, fine metal rails and fixtures, a heavy dose of antique stone peeking from the walls, and thick slabs of rock underfoot. The decor is traditional Turkish in an environment of artistic licentiousness, with kilim and other textiles played off against dramatic full-wall renderings of Ottoman sipahis (cavalrymen) and Byzantine emperors. Every room has a bathroom finished in marble, with shower. Satellite television is available in some rooms, as it is in the public areas.

The lobby and terrace highlight the entire hotel. Both are dramatic and appealing, the lobby slightly off-kilter with its angles and arches; the terrace offering a generous view of the Sea of Marmara, with a cozy interior for after the weather turns. On the north side the hotel is leaned up against the decrepit old Işak Paşa Hamam, and this is a backdrop for breakfast in a little sliver of garden. The staff is helpful and English-speaking (the hotel is owned by an American), and the three year old hotel is the best value for money in İstanbul. If you're looking for a place to put up a family, request the penthouse here, formerly the owner's own home. The penthouse costs $115 per night.

Cappadocia (Central Anatolian region)

ESBELLI EVİ, *Turban Girişi, Çeşme Karşısı, PK 2, Ürgüp, Cappadocia. Tel. 384 341 3395, Fax 384 341 8848, E-mail: suha@esbelli.com.tr, Web:www.esbelli.com.tr. Rooms: 10. Credit cards accepted. Open March-November. Double: $80.*

In the Zelve valley just north of Ürgüp, monks spent 800 years poring over the scriptures, living simply, and slowly chipping away at the soft tufa stone to create churches, living areas, and bedrooms. Monastic life was certainly busy, but it was also exacting, and rarely rushed. The monks could take their time deciding where to carve a window out of a cliff face, where to connect two spaces with a tunnel, where to build a shelf.

Süha Ersöz purchased property in the narrow lanes above Ürgüp in 1979, and there is something in his patient approach to the creation of the Esbelli Evi that Byzantine anchorites would have appreciated. Süha Bey considered the site for years, only setting to work in 1987. He cleaned and restored three rooms cut into the living rock, rehabilitating the stone houses above. After four years of work, he began inviting guests. In the following years he purchased adjoining land and completed more rooms, one here, two there. The results were exquisite; guests were awed, and told friends. Word of the Esbelli Evi spread.

If imitation is the sincerest form of flattery, then Süha Bey is wealthy in flattery indeed. Precisely carved cave rooms, beautiful hardwood floors, cast iron bed frames, collections of books and Turkish textiles are no longer the exclusive domain of the Esbelli Evi. Nor does it have a monopoly on stone courtyards, gorgeous sitting rooms, or sweeping terrace views. The opening of several new hotels in the neighborhood that share the aesthetic of the Esbelli has only served to reinforce the immense appeal of the original.

The appeal of the Esbelli Evi goes far beyond its beauty; this is a hotel without peer in the hospitality of its host and his staff. Not the abstract hospitality of smiles at the checkout counter, but the practical hospitality of a refrigerator and bar stocked with drinks that are yours for the taking (free of charge), of a Turkish Daily News at breakfast, of a guest washing machine (the staff will hang your clothes to dry, no charge), and of anything else you might need. It is hospitality up to and including keys to the owner's car if you're in a hurry to get somewhere. It is a hospitality that has capped the number of rooms at 10, since more don't leave enough hours in the day for people to mix.

Süha Bey has created a halfway house in the old style, a place to relax. He invites you to make this your home, and likes to see guests linger over their excellent breakfast on the patio. Even better if you stroll through town until it is seemly to mix yourself a gin and tonic, then while away the hours with fellow guests on the terrace. There is much to see in Cappadocia, but Süha Bey hopes you don't have to rush to see it. Monks spent lifetimes here just sitting and looking, and they weren't as crazy as they sound. If you're going to see where they lived, you might as well see why they lived here.

YUNAK EVLERI, *Yunak Evleri, Yunak Mah., Ürgüp. Tel. 384 341-6920; Fax 384 341-6924; Email: yunak@yunak.com; Web: www.yunak.com. Rooms: 17. Credit cards accepted. Open year-round. Double: $110-$170 (10% cash discount; breakfast included).*

Yunak Evleri is in the best sense the son of Esbelli Evi. Construction was undertaken with thoughtful input from the owner of the Esbelli, and the result is impressive.

Owner Yüsüf Görürgöz began this ambitious project in 1998, taking it upon himself to renovate and renew a small community of ruined stone-carved buildings that occupied a south-facing cliffside in upper Ürgüp. Work ended in 2000, and from the moment you turn onto the cobbled entry road, curving uphill between low stone walls, you are in a compound where everything is as it should be. The centerpiece is a renovated Greek mansion that now serves as the reception and dining area, and rooms are arrayed in the cliff walls behind.

And what rooms they are: like the Esbelli Evi, each room is cut into the stone, with dark, hardwood floors as flush as the eccentric angles of the cave walls allow, metal bed frames, down comforter covers, and bathrooms clad in marble with heavy white towels. The small touches— reading lights, built-in cabinets, and patios—are marvelous. In big ways and small, the Yunak Evleri is a success.

Good Turkish buffet meals are served nightly for $15, and meet the same high standard. To get there: follow the main road from Ürgüp city center uphill toward Göreme, turning right before Surban Hotel.

Çıralı (Western Mediterranean region)

OLYMPOS LODGE MOTEL, *P.O. Box 38, Kemer/Çıralı. Tel. 242 825 7171, Fax 242 825 7173. Email: info@olymposlodge.com; Web: www.olymposlodge.com. Rooms: 8. Credit cards accepted. Open year-round. Double: $145 (half-board).*

The Olympos Lodge is one of the most beautiful little hotels in the whole of Turkey, admirably blending in behind a screen of orange trees and a large, unassumingly landscaped garden. Where most of Çıralı's hotels are rough around the edges (and wonderful in their own right), the Olympos Lodge is done to a tee.

The reception hallway leads into an octagonal dining room populated by handcrafted tables and chairs with thick felt backs. An iron and hand-blown glass chandelier hangs from above, original sketches adorn the walls, and a simple, elegant bar stretches along one side of the room. The garden is thick with mature, shading trees and plants, fragrant jasmine and colorful bougainvillea, in between which one can glimpse the sea. A new greenhouse on the grounds features a winter garden.

Scattered among the trees are the duplex guest cabins, decorated with a minimalist flair in white and blonde wood. Each room has a fan, mosquito netting, and a telephone, and as of the 1999 season each will also have air conditioning. The lawn, dotted with sculptures by Turkish artist Handan Börte Çine, is ideal for retreating in the heat of the day and having a drink. You may be joined by the rabbits or white peacocks which also make their homes there.

The Olympos Lodge does an excellent job of balancing the bucolic charm of Çıralı against the needs of fine hotel-keeping. The manager was reticent about being written up, which is one of the sure signs that his hotel deserves to be.

Kalkan (Western Mediterranean region)

TÜRK EV, *Kalkan. Tel. 242 844 3129, Fax: 242 844 3492. Email: none; Web: none. Rooms: 9. Credit cards not accepted. Open year-round. Double: $30-$40 (breakfast included).*

The Türk Ev (formerly the Eski Evi) is a small, immaculate, and creatively bustling place; it is also one of our favorite hotels in Turkey. The building is a classic, whitewashed Kalkan structure whose shaded patio leads into a pleasant, airy main room. Within, you'll find a bowl of fresh oranges here, the owners' own hand-carved wooden cradle there, and several couches on which to relax and enjoy a glass of wine. Rooms are light and spacious, and have hard wood floors, mosquito netting, balconies, and shutters. You're a short stroll from the waterfront, but the noise of mid-summer Kalkan is barely perceptible here.

Other Small Hotels of Note

İstanbul:

YEŞIL EV HOTEL, *Kabasakal Cad. No. 5, Sultanahmet. Tel. 212 517 6786; Fax 212 517 6780; Email: yesilevhotel@superonline.com; Web: none. Rooms: 25. Credit cards accepted. Open year-round. Double: $140 (25% discount in off-season).*

Safranbolu (Black Sea region):

HAVUZLU KONAK, *Mescit Sok., Safranbolu. Tel. 370 725 2883; Fax 370 712 3824; Email: none; Web: none. Rooms: 11. Credit cards accepted. Open year-round. Double: $50 (breakfast included).*

Ankara (Central Anatolian region):

ANGORA HOTEL, *Kalekapısı Sok. No. 16, Kaleiçi, Ulus, Ankara. Tel. 312 309 8380; Fax 312 309 8381; Email: none; Web: none. Rooms: 6. Credit cards accepted. Open year-round. Double: $60-$75 (breakfast included).*

LES MAISONS DE CAPPADOCE, *Semiramis A.Ş., Belediye Meydanı No. 24, BP 28, Uçhisar, Tel. 384 219 2813, Fax 384 219 2782. Email: info@cappadoce.com; Web: www.cappadoce.com. Rooms: 11. Credit cards not accepted. Open April-November. Double: $110.*

OWL'S NEST, *Kalkan. Tel. 242 837 5214; Fax 242 844 3756; Email: owlsland@usa.net; Web: none. Rooms: 6. Credit cards not accepted. Open year-round. Double: $45 (breakfast included).*

Antalya (Western Mediterranean region):

NINOVA PENSION, *Barbaros Mah. Hamit Efendi Sok. No. 9, Kaleiçi, Antalya. Tel. 242 248 6114; Fax 242 248 9684; Email: ninova@euroseek.com; Web: none. Rooms: 19. Credit cards accepted. Open year-round. Double (15% off-season discount): $40 (breakfast included). Dinner: $8.*

Fethiye (Western Mediterranean region):

OCAKKÖY, *Ovacık, Fethiye. Tel. 252 616 6157; Fax 252 616 6158; Email: ocakkoy@superonline.com; Web: www.ocakkoy.com. Cottages: 35. Credit cards accepted. Open April-October. Double: $50.*

Selçuk (Central Aegean region)

HOTEL KALEHAN, *Atatürk Cad. No. 49, Selçuk. Tel. 232 892 6154; Fax 232 892 2169; Email: ergirh@superonline.com; Web: www.kalehan.com. Rooms: 52. Credit cards accepted. Open March-October. Double: $55 (breakfast included). Restaurant.*

Kuşadası (Central Aegean region):

KISMET HOTEL, *Akyar Mevkii, Yacht Marina, Kuşadası. Tel. (256) 614-2005; Fax (256) 614-4914; Email: kismet@efes.net.tr; Web: www.kismet.com.tr. Rooms: 102. Credit cards accepted. Open April-October. Double: $110. Half-board available. Restaurant.*

Behramkale/Assos (Northern Aegean region):

ERIŞ PANSIYON, *No. 6, Behramkale Köyü, Kadırga Çıkışı. Tel. 286 721 7080; Fax none; Email: erispansiyon@yahoo.com; Web: www.assos.de/eris. Rooms: 4. Credit cards not accepted. Open year-round. Double (15% off-season discount available): $35 (includes breakfast).*

MANICI KASRI, *Yeşilyurt Köyü, Küçükkuyu. Tel. (286) 752-1731; Fax (286) 752-1734; Email: info@manicikasri.com; Web: www.manicikasri.com. Rooms: 7. Credit cards accepted. Open year-round. Double: $100 (suites $120), breakfast included. Restaurant.*

The Türk Ev is owned and run by Önder and Selma Elitez, an engaging, friendly couple who comingle their high standards of hotel-keeping and raising their daughter. If you like, the owners can make plans for small groups to spend some time aboard the small sailboat Tirace. This is an excellent refuge year round; it is ideal for single women.

If you're headed west on the main highway, the Türk Ev is located just after the Kalkan turnoff, on the left. From the end of the main road in Kalkan (just below the bus station) the Türk Ev is straight uphill three blocks.

Bodrum (Southern Aegean region)

ANTİK THEATRE HOTEL, *Kıbrıs Sehitleri Caddesi 243, Bodrum 48400. Tel. 252 316 6053, Fax 252 316 0825, Email: theatrehot@superonline.com. Web: www.pathcom.com/~antique. Rooms: 20. Credit cards accepted. Open year-round. Double: $140 (15% discount between November and April)—add $50 for half board.*

Once acclaimed as the "best small hotel in Turkey" by The New York Times, the Antik Theatre Hotel is no great secret; it just feels that way. This is a quiet, comfortable place that happens to be a beautiful hotel.

The hotel's architect, Cengiz Bektaş, built the terraced hotel for owners Zafer and Semlin Başak—Mrs. Başak was a design school colleague of the architect's and has done all the interior design and decorating herself. Every room looks out on the picturesque Castle of St. Peter through shuttered door and windows. Every terrace has its own small patio with a deliberate jumble of gravel and stepping stones and greenery sprouting by the rail, with bougainvillea crawling up wooden frames and old terracotta pots tucked in corners. On the bottom tier is a deep swimming pool, recalling in shape the curved seats of the ancient theatre. Guests gather here on summer nights, toasting the magnificent castle and bay below.

The decoration is simple whites and marble, with spare blonde wood furnishings. You'll find a candle and an old framed nautical chart or boat diagram for decoration, and take especial note of the bedspreads; the thick linen fabric comes from a weaver on the Black Sea who uses an old hand loom, and the lace is handmade as well. The corner bathrooms are particularly cleverly designed. The aesthetics and attention to detail are helped along generously by a good staff that, far from aloof, is engaging and friendly. The owners spend a fair bit of time enjoying the hotel themselves.

After all of this, it comes as no surprise that chef Arif Çenerli turns out fine cuisine every evening, putting to good use the four weeks he spends training in France every year. The patios are ideal for late evening dining, the castle illuminated and the harbor alive with lights.

ADA HOTEL, *Cataldibi Mevkii, Tepecik Cad. No. 44, Türkbükü. Tel. (216) 378-6440; Fax (216) 378-1433; Email: info@adahotel.com; Web: www.adahotel.com. Rooms: 14. Credit cards accepted. Open year-round. Double: $250-$475 ($195-$375 between October and May).*

The Ada Hotel in Türkbükü is the most refined and exacting hotel in the whole of Turkey, and one of the most expensive. This is one of only two hotels in Turkey listed by Relais & Chateau, and with good reason: it is audacious and inspired, in every way the perfect retreat.

The Ada has a humble exterior, but within it takes the breath away. The stone-walled Ada has a sprawling collection of public spaces, reading rooms, and gardens; they unfold for you peacefully, hour by hour. Take the Mahzen Restaurant, downstairs; the stone walls are softened by white drapes and tables have with crimson tablecloths to create a feeling is part Ottoman fortress, part Scottish Highlands palace. And so it is throughout, solid, beautiful, and in a place somewhere almost out of time.

Rooms are as you would expect. The suites are stunning, and even the standard "deluxe" rooms are marvelous; expect stone walls, wood trim, rich textiles, beautiful lighting, a full set of amenities, and a fruit basket upon arrival.

The Mahzen Restaurant is a marvelous indulgence; consider a reservation. A meal and a bottle of wine for two will cost roughly $75.

Selçuk (Central Aegean region)

HOTEL NİLYA, *Atatürk Mah, 1051 Sok. No. 7, Selçuk, Tel. 232 892 9081, Fax: 232 892 9080. Email: nilya_ephesus@hotmail.com; Web: none. Rooms: 12. Credit cards accepted. Open March-October. Double: $45 (breakfast included). Open year-round.*

The Nilya, opened in 1997, was a welcome addition to Selçuk. Nilgun Kaytancı has created a fine, relaxing inn on the back side of the Selçuk hill looking west. The rooms are clean and cool (the upstairs rooms have fans, the downstairs rooms do not need them) in the summer, featuring comforter covers, iron bedsteads, lace tablecloths, and old oil lamps. The hotel is unpretentious, but there are nice touches everywhere. For reading or relaxing the sitting room is ideal, a jumble of Turkish textiles cover the couches and tables, and you'll find wrought iron lamps and metal and wooden knick-knacks in every corner. In many ways, it feels like you're staying with a friend—you'll be offered a glass of wine and invited to relax.

Breakfast, with orange slices, strawberries or other seasonal fruit, pastriy, cucumber and tomato slices, cheese, toasted bread, olives, orange juice and coffee, is wonderful.

NIŞANYAN EVLERI, *Şirince, Selçuk. Tel. 232 898 3209; Fax 232 898 3117; Email: nisanyan@nisanyan.com; Web: www.nisanyan.com. Rooms: 7. Credit cards accepted. Open year-round. Double (20% discount in low seasons): $85 (hotel rates: $60).*

We don't believe it's possible to set your expectations too high; the Nisanyan Evleri (Nisanyan Houses) are magnificent. Perhaps this helps explain: during our visit in 2001, owner Sevan Nişanyan was nearing completion with a small four-room inn to augment his three impeccable individual houses. Sevan was disappointed; time constraints had forced him to forgo a second layer of frescoes on the walls of the inn; this layer he had planned to subsequently smash to expose bits of the first layer underneath.

Such is the almost preposterous attention to detail found here in the mountains above Selçuk. The houses have a few things in common: hardwood floors, high ceilings, tasteful Turkish textiles, wood furniture, CD players, and kitchens. They also have peculiarites; the recessed marble shower in one, the second floor nooks in another, the sitting room in another. Each comfortably suits five people—they're ideal for two couples—and as Sevan says "you can spend three days and still keep discovering things." A breakfast hamper is delivered each morning with coffee, eggs, bread, jams, cheese, and other seasonal groceries.

As noted above, a new four-room hotel is due to open a stone's throw from the houses, and it promises the same level of care. A few nights in Nişanyan Evleri is a marvelous tonic if you want to get away from it all. The houses are located in the heights of Şirince, and you'll need to do some steep hiking on foot.

Behramkale/Assos (Northern Aegean region)

ÇETMİ HAN, *Yeşilyurt Köyü, Küçükkuyu. Tel. 286 752 6169; Fax 286 752 6488; Email: fahir@cetmi.com; Web: http://www.cetmi.com. Rooms: 16. Credit cards accepted. Open year-round. Double: $60, half board. Restaurant.*

Well-run Turkish inns have a lot in common with ranch-style inns in the American west—the rooms are comfortable and spare, the service is attentive, and the food is plentiful. Canadians and Americans fond of that atmosphere, and of long evenings in the public area by a fire, will love the Çetmi Han. You can't retire to your room to flip back and forth pointlessly between CNN and MTV—the only TV is in the small bar downstairs.

This pretty hillside hotel is built with blocks of pudding stone carved square with torches. The building is not a restoration, but a faithful rendering of traditional buildings true to owner Fahir İskit's imagination; simple and traditional, with wine nooks along the wall. İskit bought the land perched high above the Aegean in 1990 and, retiring from a career with companies ranging from Sheraton to Citibank, commenced building in 1993. The hotel opened in 1995, introducing a new pit stop for those who appreciate Prokofiev over breakfast and true isolation. The Han has a section of waterfront on the seaside below.

THE OLD BRIDGE HOUSE, *Behramkale-Ayvacık Yol, PK2, Assos. Tel. 286 721 7426; Fax 286 721 7427; Email: oldbridgehouse@yahoo.com; Web: www.assos.de/oldbridgehouse. Rooms: 5, including bunk house. Credit cards accepted. Open year-round. Double (discounts in off-season): $50 (includes breakfast).*

The marvelous Old Bridge House inn derives its name from a 14th century Turkish bridge over the Tuzla River, a bridge located just 75 paces north of the front door. The setting, as elsewhere in Behramkale, is lovely, with a backyard that meanders endlessly back into the stone-strewn hills and quarries of the local countryside. People come for serenity, and find it; the sounds you hear are rain pattering on windows, the bells of sheep ambling past.

Owners Cem and Diana are massage therapists, and they embarked on building this as a labor of love. The love—and the creativity—shows. The public areas are spacious, with a cunning custom-designed stove for heat and a winding bridge to the computer niche that is an exercise in both sheetmetal and architectural philosophy.

The rooms are marvelous, both cozy and clever. Old wooden doors give way to carefully appointed rooms with white tile floors and big, comfortable beds. Radiators on each side of the bed help take the edge off the cool evenings. Budget travelers can take advantage of a bunkhouse, as well. Breakfast is delicious, and it's served 'til 3 p.m.

The Best Budget Hotels in Turkey

İstanbul

YUÇELT INTERYOUTH HOSTEL, *Caferiye Sok. No. 6, Sultanahmet. Tel. 212 513 6150; Fax 212 512 7628; Email: info@yucelthostel.com; Web: www.yucelthostel.com. Double Rooms: 16. Credit cards Double: $14.*

Cappadocia (Central Anatolian region):
KELEBEK MOTEL-PENSION, *Göreme. Tel. 384 271 2531; Fax 384 271 2763; Email: ali@kelebekhotel.com; Web: www.kelebekhotel.com. Rooms: 17. Credit cards accepted. Open year-round. Double: $18.*

KILIM PANSİYON, *Uçhisar. Tel. 384 219 2774; Fax 384 219 2660; Email: none; Web: none. Rooms: 9. Credit cards not accepted. Open year-round. Double: $20 (breakfast included).*

BELISIRMA EV PANSIYON, *Cami Yani, Belisirma, Aksaray. Tel. 382 457 3037. Rooms: 7. Credit cards not accepted. Open year-round. Double: $15 (breakfast included).*

Amasya (Black Sea region)
ILK HOUSE, *Gümüşlü Mah., Hittit Sok. No. 1, Amasya. Tel. 358 218 1689; Fax 358 218 6277; Email: none; Web: none. Rooms: 6. Credit cards accepted. Open year-round. Double: $32.*

Unye (Black Sea region)
PINAR PANSİYON, *Gölevi Devrent Mevkii, Ünye. Tel. 452 323 3496. Rooms: 7. Credit cards not accepted. Open year-round. Double: $17.*

Trabzon (Black Sea region)
COŞANDERE PANSİYON, *Maçka, Sümela Manastırı Yolu Üzeri 5 km. Trabzon. Tel. 462 531 1190; Fax none; Email: none; Web: none. Rooms: 14. Credit cards not accepted. Open year-round. Double: $14.*

Antalya (Western Mediterranean region)
ANTIQUE PANSİYON, *Paşa Camii Sokak, Antalya. Tel. 242 242 4615; Fax 242 241 5890; Email: fatihsertel@ixir.com; Web: none. Rooms: 5. Credit cards not accepted. Open year-round. Double (no off-season discount): $27 (breakfast included). Dinner (guests only): $8.*

Çıralı (Western Mediterranean region)
BAYRAM'S PLACE, *PK 4, Olympos, Kumluca. Tel. 242 892 1243; Fax 242 892 1399; Email: bayrams1@turk.net; Web: none. Rooms: 39. Credit cards accepted. Open year-round. Double: $20 (full board).*

Kaleköy (Western Mediterranean region)
MEHTAP PANSİYON, *Kaleköy. Tel. 242 874 2146; Fax 242 874 2261; Email: info@mehtappansiyon.com; Web: www.mehtappansiyon.com. Rooms: 10. Credit cards not accepted. Open year-round. Double: $26.*

Kalkan (Western Mediterranean region)
PATARA STONE HOUSE, *Kalkan. Tel. 242 844 3076; Fax 242 844 3274; Email: korsanltd@turk.net; Web: www.kalkan.org.tr/kalkan/korsan/. Rooms: 9. Credit cards accepted. Closed November-March. Double: $28.*

Dalyan (Western Mediterranean region)
HAPPY CARETTA, *Maraş Mah., Dalyan. Tel. 252 284 2109; Fax 252 284 3295; Email: none; Web: none. Rooms: 18. Credit cards not accepted. Open year-round. Double: $30 (breakfast included).*

Didim (Central Aegean region)
ORACLE PANSİYON, *Didim. Tel. 256 811 0270; Fax 256 811 0105; Email: none; Web: none. Rooms: 18. Credit cards not accepted. Open year-round. Double: $20.*

Selçuk (Central Aegean region)
BARIM PENSION, *Müze Arkasi Sokak, Selçuk. Tel. 232 892 6923; Fax none; Email: none; Web: none. Rooms: 12. Credit cards not accepted. Open year-round. Double: $14.*
AUSTRALIA NEW ZEALAND PENSION, *1064 Sok. No. 12, Selçuk. Tel. 232 892 6050; Fax 232 891 8594; Email: oznzpension@superonline.com; Web: www.anzturkishguesthouse.com. Rooms: 24. Credit cards not accepted. Open year-round. Double: $18 (half board).*

Behramkale/Assos (Northern Aegean region)
THE OLD BRIDGE HOUSE, *Behramkale-Ayvacık Yol, PK2, Assos. Tel. 286 721 7426; Fax 286 721 7427; Email: oldbridgehouse@yahoo.com; Web: www.assos.de/oldbridgehouse. Rooms: 5, including bunk house. Credit cards accepted. Open year-round. Double (discounts in off-season): $10 bunkhouse lodging. $50 (includes breakfast).*

i s t a n b u l

Chapter 11

The Roman Empire continued uninterrupted for more than 1,500 years, and for 900 of those years **Constantinople** was its capital. Later it became the Imperial seat of the house of Osman, capital of the Ottoman Empire; ever and always, as T.S. Eliot wrote, "the still point of the turning world." Behind the great walls of this city the visitor found a hybrid of Rome and Baghdad, a glittering collection of soaring palaces and towers, the starting-point of arcaded roads that ran on for 1,000 miles and more, home to the greatest ship-yards in the world, the finest statues, the most opulent trophies of war, and amidst a constellation of beautiful churches, the singular majesty of the **Hagia Sophia**. Here was a repository of art, architecture and learning that, in different ages, with different rulers, had no peer. Constantinople has always meant vivid things to the world; hope, and envy, and majesty.

The prosperity of the city was no accident; it enjoyed every advantage. It was protected by the greatest set of fortifications in the world and bordered on three sides by the sea. Its natural harbor provided the perfect anchorage for controlling passage through the **Bosphorous**, and merchants seeking to pass over-land between Europe and Asia were forced to cross the straits here. When the city finally fell to the Crusaders in 1204, almost nine centuries after it had been founded by Constantine, it was as much due to weakness within as the forces arrayed against it. The Latin rule of the Crusaders was hardly welcome in Constantinople, and was brief. Byzantine rule was restored later in the 13th Century, and continued until the Ottomans seized

What to Expect in Istanbul

İstanbul can appear a huge, daunting maze. An American has some preconceptions when setting down in Paris, London, and even Hong Kong, but few people arriving directly from North America know what to expect of İstanbul. Expect lots of people – the population is roughly estimated at 12 million, and the city sprawls for 100 miles. Expect lots of smoking and moustaches. Expect honking cars. Expect to see the gigantic walls and towers that kept the city safe during more than 30 sieges. Expect to see people working very, very hard for very, very little. Expect a beautiful skyline, perhaps the most beautiful in the world. Expect some women to wear Islamic headscarves, others to wear Gucci shoes. Expect to see gaudy palaces and lofty cathedrals. Expect to see cramped breezeblock apartments, mile after mile. Expect people in Sultanahmet to have a brother who owns a carpet shop. Expect to be awakened by muezzin calls. Expect tea. Expect to spend a lot of time on your feet, and a lot of money on a carpet. Expect to enjoy yourself, because İstanbul may be alien, chaotic and jarring, but it's also exciting, benign, and endlessly fascinating.

the city in 1453. The city had its own renaissance under the Ottoman Empire; it flourished under the Ottomans until the 17th century, and remained untouched by the enemies of the Ottomans until the 20th century.

Constantinople, now **İstanbul**, is filled with reminders of its magnificent history. The Bosphorous still flows past the tip of the old city, the **Golden Horn** cuts into the European shore. The city still bristles with high, strong towers, domed mosques and cathedrals, slender minarets, sprawling bazaars, and ruined palaces, but at the end of the 20th century the relics of Imperial glory are ringed by freeways, surrounded by modern office buildings, brick apartments, shops, hotels and sagging late-Ottoman wooden houses.

The muezzin awakens you with the call to prayer at the first hint of light, and you emerge into streets filled with people hawking hats, watches, fake Levis, underwear, hammers, fresh eggplants, condoms, shoeshines, and spare parts. The city is loud and disconcerting, with salesmen bickering and wheedling, tinkers and vegetable sellers wailing, gas trucks blaring their competing jingles, and everyone, but everyone, hanging from a window or filling the streets. Cars roar past, squeezing between you and the gaping holes torn in the pavement, dirty shoeshine boys elbow each other aside to importune likely-looking gentlemen, and a dissonant honking fills the air.

İstanbul is chaos, but within the chaos, order. İstanbul, home to some 12 million people, is better thought of as a great collection of small neighborhoods. The people of İstanbul are civil and kind, the family structure is powerful and neighborhoods hold their residents accountable; there is little anonymous crime and violence. The city can be aggravating, but it is safe and people are good-hearted and patient with foreigners. The least agreeable people in town will be the ones trying to chat you up in Sultanahmet, but even they are often charming, friendly, and surprisingly helpful. Especially if you want a carpet.

Unless you go looking for trouble, say in the red light areas off of İstiklal Caddesi late at night, you're unlikely to find it. This is especially true outside of the heavily touristed districts, whether in İstanbul or elsewhere in the country. In Sultanahmet and crowded areas you're well advised to be careful with your wallet, but that's just good sense anywhere. In the inimitable words of Artemis Ward, "Trust everybody, but cut the cards."

Byzantium

No one knows how long people have settled at the tip of the peninsula that is the heart of historic **Byzantium**. The first evidence of small settlements at the tip of İstanbul's peninsula – near modern-day Topkapı Palace – dates to the 13th Century BC, but these minor fishing villages were only satellites of a major trading center at Chalcedon across the Bosphorous on the Asian shore.

Tacitus wrote that when an expedition of Greeks under Byzas set out to found a new city in the 8th Century B.C., the oracle of Pythian Apollo advised them to settle opposite the land of the blind. When the expedition arrived in the area they concluded that the people of Chalcedon must have been blind not to see the defensive and commercial advantages of the spit of land directly across the water on the European shore. The peninsula was protected on three sides by the Golden Horn, the Bosphorous, and the Sea of Marmara, and Byzas' colonists completed the defensive circuit by erecting walls to seal off the tip of the peninsula.

The advice of the oracle was good: Byzantium proved a secure and thriving town. Four hundred years after the fall of Troy to the west, Byzantium was ideally suited to profit from traffic through the straits. The small Byzantine fleet could lay at anchor in the Golden Horn, emerging to challenge ships as they sailed through the Bosphorous, particularly ships fighting their way north against the current. Byzantium quickly eclipsed Chalcedon, and by the fifth century BC it had command of the straits.

An interesting cast of characters passed through Byzantium during the 1,100 years before the arrival of Constantine the Great.

Xenophon and his 10,000 came this way in 400 BC, at which time Byzantium was under the control of a Spartan governor; the Peloponessean War between Sparta and Athens had just concluded in Sparta's favor. After their long retreat from Persia, of which *The Anabasis* is an account, they were not welcomed home to the Hellenistic world as heroes – they were instead met with suspicion and ordered into fresh battles in Thrace.

Phillip II, father of Alexander the Great, mounted a siege of the Byzantium in 340-339 BC, but never entered the city in force. The siege is notable as the occasion that the Byzantines' credited the Goddess Hecate with saving the city and thereafter adopted the star and the crescent moon, a symbol that was, in turn, adopted by the Ottomans upon their seizure of the city 1,800 years later. By the time Alexander was ready to begin his famous campaign in 334 BC, Byzantium had been won over as an ally and provided ships to the young conqueror.

With the ascendance of Rome, Byzantium became an important Roman outpost, one that withstood the campaigns of Mithradites the Great of Pontus in the second and first centuries B.C. After the Roman generals Pompey, Lucullus and Julius Caesar eliminated the threat of Pontus, Byzantium entered a period of unusual stability during the Pax Romana.

The long peace drew to an abrupt close when Byzantium sided with Pescinnius Niger against Septimius Severus (Roman Emperor, 193-211 AD) during a Roman civil war. After defeating his rival in Asia Minor, Severus turned against the Byzantines with a vengeance. In 196 he leveled Byzantium, tearing down its walls and massacring its citizens and soldiery. Two years later, secure in his power, he relented and commissioned the rebuilding of a city on the site. Severus was as successful rebuilding the city as he had been in razing it; he expanded the circuit of city walls and established the great **Hippodrome** and other fixtures of the later city.

Curiously, like Severus before him, Constantine the Great first arrived in Asia Minor as an enemy to Byzantium. In 324 AD, **Constantine**, then Emperor of the West, marched against Licinius, Emperor of the East, attempting to consolidate the power of the Roman Empire. The pivotal battle in the campaign took place on the Asian shore of the Bosphorous within sight of Byzantium, which at the time was subject to Licinius' rule. Perhaps recalling the ire of Severus several generations before, Byzantium didn't hesitate to throw its gates open to the victorious Constantine immediately after the battle. This gambit worked; Constantine forgave the Byzantines their support of his rival and accepted the city's welcome. Several years later, Constantine sought to relocate the Roman capital in the stable eastern empire and away from the tumult of Rome. After narrowing his choices, Constantine chose ... Troy. Work began at the small Roman city on the Dardanelle Straits before the emperor reconsidered, halted work, and finally selected the more defensible site of Byzantium.

Byzantium was still much too humble to be a suitable imperial seat of Rome, and in 326 Constantine began an ambitious building program to render Byzantium an appropriate capital for his empire. He completed work on the **Hippodrome**, erected palaces and roads, built new land walls in a circuit that would today enclose the ruins of the **Valens Aqueduct**, beautified and repaired the churches of the city, and imported appropriate imperial tchochkes such as the 5th Century BC Bronze **Serpent Column** commemorating the Greek victory over Persia at Plataea.

Byzantium was founded anew in 330 AD after four years of renovation, and the city soon took the name of its benefactor, henceforward calling itself Constantinople.

Constantinople
The city was such a success, in fact, that one century later **Constantinople** was undergoing growth pains as its population bumped up against the land walls. The military engineers of Theodosius II endeavored to remedy this in 413 BC, but their efforts were undone by a quake 34 years later. The walls were broken in places, but the damage was not to last long. By nasty coincidence, Attila the Hun was riding roughshod over Europe at the very time that the walls were damaged, and he had long cast a covetous eye on the Roman capital. Mindful of this, the citizens of Constantinople worked round the clock, restoring the walls and even adding outer fortifications to the long circuit. A disappointed Attila took his rampage elsewhere, and the citizens of the city breathed a great, collective sigh of relief.

In the fifth century, the division between the eastern and western empire became complete, with the west spinning into chaos, punctuated by repeated sacks of Rome. Constantinople was now the greatest outpost of Roman imperial rule. In the sixth century, the ambitious Emperor **Justinian** adorned the city with its most famous landmark, commissioning the construction of the **Hagia Sophia** in 532 AD. The fame and rumor of this huge cathedral – for one thousand years it remained the largest in the world – swept aside any doubt that this was the greatest, most glorious city in the world.

Constantinople prospered during the frequent periods of Byzantine expansion, and panicked during its equally frequent contractions. No matter how grave the empire's position, however, its enemies were always frustrated by the fortifications and natural advantages of the capital city. At various times the Arabs, Goths, Avars, Persians, and Bulgars laid siege to Constantinople, and in the darkest moments different armies would approach the city simultaneously, as in the Avar and Persian campaigns of 619 AD.

Time and again, the Byzantines recoiled behind the walls of their city before striking out to reclaim their lost territories, but soon after the millennium the situation for the empire and its capital became particularly grim. Turkic tribes appeared in the east, and, spearheaded by the Selçuk Turk **Alp Arslan**, humiliated Byzantine armies and seized large tracts of Asia Minor. The **Selçuks** rolled through the Armenian buffer area, seized Ani, captured Caesera (Kayseri), and destroyed a grand Byzantine army at Manzikert in 1071 AD. For once the Byzantine resolve to reclaim lost territory was stymied; Imperial armies stood by while the Selçuks continued their campaign, seizing Jerusalem in 1077 AD and establishing themselves all along the Mediterranean and Aegean coasts as far West as Smyrna (İzmir).

"Help" now came from an unexpected quarter. The first wave of Crusades broke on Asia Minor in 1097 AD; their intent was to remove the Muslims from the Holy Land, but in fact the Latin Crusaders took every opportunity to aggravate the tensions with their Orthodox Byzantine brethren (See Crusades section in Chapter 5, *A Short History*). One century after the first Crusade, the Latins turned on and sacked Constantinople itself, and when the Byzantines were restored to power in 1261 AD their Empire had lost influence in most of its traditional Asian lands and had been shorn of its wealth. Moreover, while the Crusaders and Byzantines had fought among themselves, the Turks had dug in along the frontier.

The Ottomans

One of the most precocious Turkish tribes arose along the northern Aegean coast, established by a march-lord named **Ertuğrul**. Most of the Turkish tribes were ferocious warriors and awful administrators; not so the budding kingdom of Ertuğrul and his son, **Osman**. These Turks, who took the name Osmanoğlu (Anglicized to "Ottoman"), exhibited military acumen, evenhanded governance, and intelligent diplomacy. They gradually established a bustling state on the fringes of the Byzantine Empire, confronting and defeating a Byzantine army near Bursa in 1336 A.D.

This early success won the Ottomans renown, but they remained careful not to overreach their grasp, preferring treaties and accords to outright conflict. At this they were a remarkably quick study, matching the crafty Byzantines move for move: the Ottomans soon became hatchetmen for the Byzantines, but the hatchetmen used every opportunity to seize new territory. By 1366 A.D., the Ottomans had broken out of Asia and seized Thrace and Bulgaria, virtually encircling Constantinople. The rulers in Constantinople were initially unwilling and soon unable – to arrest the growing threat. Arranged marriages and diplomatic manipulation, two important tools of Byzantine statecraft, had lost their effectiveness in the hands of weakening emperors. By 1396 AD the land approaches to the city were blockaded and the Ottomans were preying on the ships of the Byzantines and their allies. **Beyazid I**, a gifted general and the great grandson of Osman, slowly choked off the city, waiting for the inevitable capitulation.

The surrender never came. Beyazid's armies, triumphant throughout Europe and Asia, were drawn off to meet a sudden threat in the east: the advance of **Tamurlane**. There, in the **Battle of Ankara** (1402 AD), Tamurlane shattered the Ottoman forces and captured Beyazid himself. The armies of Tamurlane took the whole of Asia Minor in the same year, leaving great piles of human heads to mark their passing, but for Tamurlane this was a mere diversion before his long-considered campaign against China. The residents of Constantinople, fearing they had been delivered from the frying pan to the fire, breathed a great sigh of relief at his unexpected departure into the east.

Alas, the Byzantines failed to take advantage of the vacuum created by Tamurlane's passing, while the shattered Ottomans demonstrated great resilience. After struggling through a ten year interregnum, the Ottomans emerged in 1413 AD with much of their former territory returned. For Constantinople, the defeat of Beyazid was only a delay, not a reprieve.

Constantinople Becomes İstanbul

Sultan **Mehmet II** ascended the throne in 1451 AD, inheriting an empire that had been put in excellent order by his father, Murat II. Mehmet immediately set to work on plans to capture Constantinople, erecting fortresses along the Bosphorous and Dardanelles to cut off support by sea and tending to other details, such as commissioning a metal-caster to create an unprecedented arsenal of heavy cannon. In 1453 the Ottoman armies drew up before the city gates and began the final siege.

As the siege progressed, Mehmet II devised an audacious scheme to dislodge the Byzantine navy from behind the heavy chain stretched across the mouth of the Golden Horn. His men secretly created a long path of rollers and hauled his ships overland to the Golden Horn from the area near Dolmabahçe Palace. The city thus cut off, Mehmet and an army of 250,000 accomplished what none had succeeded in doing for 1,000 years: breaching and storming the land walls. Ottoman soldiers enjoyed

---

That's Nobody's Business But the Turks

The name "İstanbul" is not, as often reported, a perversion of "Islam-polis." The name derives from the Greek "Eis ten polin," or "to the city," a Latin phrase that was commonly used by the Turks in reference to Constantinople, and was formalized under Atatürk.

---

three days of plunder, and all of Islam celebrated the long-sought fall of the city.

Mehmet II proved as thorough and tireless in planning the rebirth of Constantinople as he had been in planning its downfall. He imported people from conquered territories to repopulate the city and carried out ambitious construction projects, including countless public buildings and **Topkapı Palace**. Rid of the suffocating external pressures that the Ottomans themselves had created, Constantinople was a thriving metropolis within Mehmet II's own lifetime.

Ottoman rule brought a period of great security to İstanbul. Mehmet II rebuilt the city walls and added new fortifications such as the Fortress of Seven Towers (**Yedikule**), but the frontiers of the empire remained hundreds, even thousands, of miles away. İstanbul enjoyed great prosperity as the seat of Ottoman imperial power, and the Ottomans, like the Byzantines before them, decorated the capital with plunder from their territories and engineered great new private and public buildings. İstanbul owes a great debt to **Sinan**, chief architect during the heyday of the empire. Many of the mosques and türbe (tombs) scattered around the city were of his design, and he was also responsible for shoring up the Hagia Sophia and executing civil engineering projects throughout the empire.

At the height of the Ottoman Empire, which saw its greatest successes under **Süleyman the Magnificent** (1520-1566), İstanbul was once again the world's great city. At its greatest extent, the Ottoman Empire controlled almost the entire Mediterranean and Black Sea, the Caucasus, Eastern Europe, and the Holy Land, and many of the revenues returned to coffers in İstanbul. Like Constantinople before it, İstanbul benefited from the vitality of its imperial citizens and was restored to its former splendor.

The Republic

As the Ottoman Empire faded, its capital remained secure. On those occasions in the nineteenth century when even İstanbul came under threat, whether by the Egyptian Mehmet Ali in 1832 or the Russians in 1878, the world's other powers would act in defense of "the Sick Man of

Europe." It suited the purposes of the European nations, Russia included, to stand in the way of anyone else defeating the Turks or seizing their capital.

This balancing act was jeopardized at the outset of World War I, when, according to a plan advanced by Winston Churchill, Britain and France sought to force the Dardanelle Straits with warships and threaten İstanbul. If the Ottoman Empire refused to end its alliance with Germany, the British were prepared to pound İstanbul with their guns, destroying the vulnerable seaside palaces and kindling a firestorm among the city's wooden houses.

The plan failed, bogging down in Gallipolli where the Allies were undone by the tenacious leadership of young Mustafa Kemal (Atatürk). The victory at Gallipolli kept the Ottomans in the war and the straits to Russia closed. This, in turn, contributed directly to the success of the Bolsheviks and the collapse of the Czar and his armies. In the end, however, the British rolled up the Ottoman armies in Arabia and the Ottomans were forced to capitulate along with their German allies. The war had cost the Ottomans all of their possessions south of Iskendrun (formerly Alexandretta), but the peace was truly devastating. According to the **Treaty of Sevres**, the Ottoman Empire was partitioned to Italy, France, England, Russia, Armenia, and Greece, and the Marmara sea corridor, including İstanbul, became part of an occupied "control zone" whose fate was uncertain. The Ottoman Sultan was welcome to stay in İstanbul, where occupying British forces could keep an eye on him, but the only Sevres-sanctioned Turkish state was a block of land bordering only the Black Sea.

Enter, once again, **Atatürk**. The charismatic leader galvanized his people – rallying them against an ambitious invasion by the Greeks – and mounted a successful War of Independence. After driving the Greek armies literally into the sea at İzmir, diplomats of the new Turkish state, refusing to abide by the Treaty of Sevres, forced a war-weary Europe to end its plans for partition and set the borders of Turkey where they stand today (minus the Hatay spur where Antakya is located). With this accord, İstanbul and the chunk of Thrace south of Edirne were restored to Turkey and the foreign occupation of the city ended.

Atatürk, for all his love of Turkey, was not especially fond of İstanbul. It was, to his mind, a city of intrigue. The nationalist capital, originally Ankara by necessity, became Ankara by choice. Thus İstanbul, a capital for almost 1,700 years prior, became Turkey's second city. This "second city" remains far and away the largest in Turkey.

Arrivals & Departures

By Air

Atatürk Airport (Atatürk Havaalımanı) is the major hub of both national and international air travel in Turkey. Most international carriers have offices here, as do the airlines responsible for internal air travel. The Atatürk Airport serves most major cities, indeed many domestic flights take you via İstanbul. **Turkish Airlines**, *Tel. 212 663 6363*, is subsidized by the government and boasts the most flights to the most destinations, with reliable service and reasonable prices – $160 will get you a round trip to any airport in the country and to Northern Cyprus.

Some private competitors to Turkish Airlines have started to emerge, but none of them have the frequency of flights or the selection of destinations offered by the state-owned airline. Chief among the private airlines is **İstanbul Air**, *Tel. 212 509 2122*,

Before arriving, you can book reservations yourself using the Turkish Airlines website (*www.turkishairlines.com/*), or you can rely on a travel agency within Turkey to do the booking for you (see "Guiding and Travel Agencies" in Chapter 6, *Planning Your Trip*). For reservations while in İstanbul, stop in at the tiny, reliable **Imperial Turizm** office in Sultanahmet, Divan Yolu Caddesi No. 31, Sultanahmet, İstanbul, *Tel. 212 513 9430, Fax 212 512 3291.*

Arriving By Air

İstanbul's Atatürk Airport will probably be your first contact with Turkey. **Here's what to expect:**

Your first stop after arriving is the Visa/Passport lobby, where you'll wait in line to pick up a 90 day visiting visa for $45 – **you must pay cash.** After this is pasted into your passport, you'll move to one of the passport control lines. There, the date is stamped in your passport and you pass through to the baggage claim area. After claiming your bags you'll walk right past the indifferent customs inspectors; should you happen to be stopped, you're unlikely to have anything you shouldn't (see "Customs" in Chapter 6, "Planning Your Trip"). The customs officers don't care about cameras or laptop computers, if that's a concern. Fifty feet later you go through the doors to the arrivals area, exposed to the public.

This is where you will be met by your driver, guide, hotel transfer driver, or tour company representative, if you have such a thing. Otherwise, you can pick up a telephone card upstairs at the post office, distinguished by the black-on-yellow or blue-one-blue "PTT" sign. A 100 unit phone card, costing roughly $5, should cover most domestic calls during a 2 week visit, and the first of those calls can be to your hotel.

There's no need for a phone card if you know where you're headed – and the easiest way to get into the city is to take a taxi from directly in front of the arrivals area. In light traffic it's a 20 minute ride along the Sea of Marmara to the old city, Sultanahmet, and it should cost about $18 during the day (the taxi meter reads "day," or "Gündüz," between 6 a.m. and midnight, and reads "night," or "Gece" at other times, when rates double). Fresh off the plane, jet-lagged, boggled by the exchange rate, lugging all your bags and knowing only how to say Yes (*Evet*), Thank You (*Mersi*), and Nothing (*Yok*), we recommend simply taking a cab.

If you're determined to get into town cheaply, however, you do have options. Foremost, when it's completed, will be the tram-line that links directly with the airport from Sultanahmet. Construction of this line has been delayed, and was expected to be complete in 2003. If this is not yet functioning, grab one of the Havaş buses ($2), which leave hourly or half-hourly from 5 a.m. to 11 p.m. These buses can drop you between Laleli and Aksaray on the tram route to Sultanahmet (40¢) – this is probably where you're headed. Otherwise the bus continues on up to Taksim Square. From Taksim you can catch buses for most places in the city, or grab a cab – the area is teeming with them. Don't bother searching for municipal İETT buses at the airport – they don't seem to be part of the airport's transportation agenda.

Departing By Air

The international terminal ("Dış Hatlar") clogs easily, so plan to actually be there a solid two hours prior to departure for international flights, and it's wise to budget the standard one hour for domestic flights (from the "İç Hatlar" terminal). We suggest making reservations for flights out of Istanbul using the small, honest Imperial Tourism travel agency on Divan Yolu road in Sultanahmet, directly beside the tram stop. Contact **Imperial Tourism**, Divan Yolu Cad. No. 30, Sultanahmet, Istanbul; *Tel. 212 513-9430; Fax 212 512-3291; Email: imperial@superonline.com; Web: www.imperial-turkey.com.*

Most hotels in Sultanahmet will be happy to make arrangements to have you picked up by one of the private airport buses that make the rounds; check in with them. Otherwise, Sultanahmet travel agencies can make arrangements for you. In either case, the cost should be about $3.00. If you prefer, taxis are still the simplest and most reliable means of getting back and forth to the airport until one of the rail or subway lines puts through a stop.

The other alternative is the aforementioned **Havaş Airport Bus** service, departing from Cumhuriyet Caddesi (which heads north from Taksim Square towards Nişantaşı). The buses wait by a white kiosk with a green, yellow, and blue Havaş sign, just 100 feet downhill of McDonalds and Pizza Hut and just beyond the public bus stops. They depart hourly and half-hourly from 5 a.m. to 11 p.m.

Bus Routes from Istanbul

Distances (given in kilometers) and one-way prices (in U.S. Dollars) from İstanbul are as follows:

Place	Distance	Travel Time	Cost	Company
Adana	938 km	15 hours	$30	Varan
Amasra	490 km	8 hours	$15	Özemniyet
Ankara	454 km	6 hours	$25	Varan, Ulusoy
Antakya (Hatay)	1120 km	20 hours	$35	Kamil Koç
Antalya	724 km	12 hours	$30	Varan, Ulusoy
Artvin	1360 km	24 hours	$40	Ulusoy
Ayvalik	570 km	9 hours	$15	Kamil Koç
Bodrum	815 km	14 hours	$25	Varan, Ulusoy
Bursa	234 km	4 hours	$8	Ulusoy
Çanakkale	340 km	6 hours	$15	Kamil Koç
Dalyan (Ortaca)	895 km	15 hours	$24	Kamil Koç
Edirne	240 km	3 hours	$5	Çağlar Turizm
Erzurum	1229 km	20 hours	$25	Ulusoy
Fethiye	1000 km	17 hours	$25	Kamil Koç
İzmir	565 km	9 hours	$22	Varan, Ulusoy
Kas/Kalkan	870 km	16 hours	$30	Kamil Koç
Kemer	800 km	14 hours	$30	Varan, Ulusoy
Kuşadası	666 km	10 hours	$25	Varan Ulusoy
Marmaris	850 km	14 hours	$32	Varan, Ulusoy
Mersin	932 km	16 hours	$32	Varan, Kamil Koc
Ürgüp (Nevşehir)	730 km	10 hours	$20	NevTur
Patara (Kınık)	950 km	17 hours	$30	Kamil Koç
Ünye	825 km	14 hours	$25	Ulusoy
Side	815 km	14 hours	$32	Ulusoy
Trabzon	1,135 km	20 hours	$30	Ulusoy

By Bus

Sinan, the Ottoman master architect, is rolling over in his türbe (tomb). The modern Esenler Otogar is a litter-strewn concrete abomination, much more functional than the old mud-pit bus station at Topkapı, but without the aesthetic appeal. Most of the myriad bus routes servicing İstanbul terminate here, and it is often a maelstrom of touts and honking and buses locked into automotive Gordian knots.

The station is several miles outside of the city walls, and only the elite Varan and Ulusoy bus lines have stations outside of this terminal. If you're arriving at the terminal, your bus line should provide ongoing transport to Sultanahmet and elsewhere. If you need to get to the terminal, the best option is to book your bus through one of the small regional bus offices at Taksim or Beşiktaş, or to make arrangements through a travel agency in Sultanahmet such as Imperial Turizm. The price is the same, wherever you make your booking, but the satellite offices will shuttle you to the main Esenler station and spare you the hassle of getting there on your own. As discussed in Chapter 6, *Planning Your Trip*, **Varan** and **Ulusoy** offer the best bus service in the country.We suggest making reservations for Varan buses using Imperial Tourism on Divan Yolu road in Sultanahmet, directly beside the tram stop. Contact **Imperial Tourism**, Divan Yolu Cad. No. 30, Sultanahmet, Istanbul; *Tel. 212 513-9430; Fax 212 512-3291; Email: imperial@superonline.com; Web: www.imperial-turkey.com.*

See the sidebar on the previous page for bus distances, travel times, costs, and which bus companies serve which routes.

By Boat

Cruise ships dock at **Karaköy**, just across the Galata Bridge from Eminönü, which is itself just below the palace of Topkapı in Sultanahmet. There is a Tourism Information office at the site.

For information about international ferry connections (Venice, Brindisi), contact **Turkish Maritime Lines** (also see ferry listings in "Getting Around Turkey" in Chapter 6). There is usually English-speaking staff on hand, if you'd like to call yourself. They offer both information and reservation numbers: Information, *Tel. (90 212) 244 2502*, Reservations, *Tel. (90 212) 249 9222*. One travel agency that deals directly with them and has a good reputation is **Karavan Travel Agency**, *Tel. (90 212) 247 5066, Fax (90 212) 241 5178*.

For ferries along the Black Sea Coast and to İzmir, contact Turkish Maritime Lines directly. During Spring, Summer and Fall, Ferries depart for the Black Sea from İstanbul on Saturdays at 14:00, and for İzmir on Friday evenings at18:30. The ferry-train journey to İzmir departs İstanbul at 9 a.m. every day but Sunday and costs $11.00. The trip takes 12 hours.

For more information on all these cruise options, see the Getting Around Turkey section of Chapter 6, *Planning Your Trip*. Bosphorous Cruises and trips to local destinations such as the Princes Islands are covered in Getting Around Town, below.

By Train

Trains leave İstanbul regularly for destinations throughout Turkey. **Sirkeci Station** (the Sirkeci stop on the tram line, just east of Eminönü) serves the European shore, including other European countries. **Haydarpaşa Station** serves the Asian shore.

For travel within Asian Turkey, you may book a train from Sirkeci Station near Sultanahmet, after which you depart from Haydarpaşa station, or leave matters in the hands of a travel agent such as Tur-İsta, *Tel. (90 212) 513 7119*. The hub for these trains is Haydarpaşa Station, *Tel. (90 216) 336 0475*, on the Asian shore of the Bosphorous. Note that when you're looking at schedules İstanbul is usually listed "H'paşa," for the name of the railway station, just as İzmir is listed as "Basmane." To reach Haydarpaşa from the Sultanahmet area, go to the Eminönü waterfront, where you'll find the Üsküdar İskelesi building, and board a Haydarpaşa-bound ferry, leaving every 20 minutes throughout the day. On the Asian side of the Bosphorous, the Haydarpaşa ferry terminal is located at the train station, and ticket booths and train boarding areas are clear.

Trains depart daily for Ankara and Pamukkale (Denizli). Train travel is slower and more expensive than bus travel, but we recommend the İstanbul-Ankara route, in particular. It offers shades of the Orient Express charm, a dining car, and room to roam if you're claustrophobic on buses. The **Ankara Express** has sleeper cars and departs Haydarpaşa Station at 10:30 p.m., arriving in Ankara at 7:30 a.m. the next day. The cost for a berth in a sleeper car is $28 per person, one way, while seats are less than half that.

The other train of interest is the **Pamukkale Express**, departing Haydarpaşa at 6 p.m. and arriving in Pamukkale 14 hours later. The Pamukkale Express is a bit more weathered than the Ankara Express, but it also offers sleeping berths and costs $35 for a double sleeper.

Most other trains do not offer sleeping berths, but various train lines serve most of the country. The **Eastern Express** serves Kars near the Armenian border, rumbling along slowly and cheaply ($20 one way per person, arriving almost 60 hours later). Other trains include the **Fatih Express**, with an 11:30 p.m. departure to Ankara, and the **Başkent Express**, with a 10:30 p.m. departure to Ankara. Note that a ferry-train service between İstanbul and İzmir is addressed in the Ferry section, above.

Orientation

İstanbul has three distinct sections. The first is on a peninsula jutting into the mouth of the Bosphorous from the western, European shore. This is now known as **Saray Burnu (Peninsula of the Palace)**, and was the original site of Byzantium. At the tip of this peninsula are most of the great landmarks of the city, including Topkapı Palace, the Hagia Sophia, the Grand Bazaar, and the Archaelogical Museums.

The walls that once stood in a circuit along the shore have largely been taken down and their stones incorporated into the buildings of the city. The 1,300 year old land walls that separate the peninsula from Thrace are in a better state of preservation four miles to the west, a five-mile circuit of towers and multiple walls fallen in some places and pierced by highways in others. The walled section of the peninsula, Constantinople proper, has (by a somewhat imaginative reckoning) seven hills, as Rome does. The classic monuments of Constantinople's noble past are all in this area of the city, but İstanbul's population has long since leapfrogged the old city walls and poured into Thrace, as it has overcome the straits to the east and the Golden Horn to the north.

The population pressure has been intense, and changed the face of the city in the past two generations. A series of bridges now join the Byzantine peninsula with the other European shore opposite the Golden Horn. This area, known as **Pera**, was once a walled adjunct to Constantinople populated by foreign businessmen, and is best identified by the round, conically-roofed Galata Tower. What was once a distinct community is now a collection of boroughs sprawling ever further north, and now running all the way to the Black Sea. Areas that were lush forest just 20 years ago are today paved and covered with hastily-built offices and "gecekondu" (literally "built in the night"), and there is no sign of the sprawl letting up. The greatest development has taken place in a corridor along the ridge behind Galata Tower, from İstiklal Caddesi past Nişantaşı and on toward Mecidiyekoy. The communities along the European shore of the Bosphorous – Beşiktaş, Ortaköy, Bebek, İstinye, Sariyer – have lost their distinctiveness, one from another, and the length of the Bosphorous' northwestern shore is now regrettably overdeveloped.

Finally, the third section of town is located across the Bosphorous Strait in **Asia**. Modern development of the Asian shore began in earnest after the completion of the Boğazaçi (Bosphorous) Bridge in 1973, and was accelerated with the addition of the Mehmet Fatih Bridge. The Asian shore remains slightly more sedate than the European shore, with more room and better municipal planning, but it, too, is sprawling. As a drive south will make glaringly evident, İstanbul's borders are marching relentlessly south along the Marmara shore. Urban planners claim the city measures 100 miles across, and statisticians say the 12 million-person

Getting the Most Out of İstanbul

Arriving in İstanbul is a bewildering experience. The language and culture are in many ways unrecognizable; unlike Paris and Berlin, for instance, most new arrivals have little conception of how İstanbul will sound and feel. It's easy to be mildly paralyzed by the sheer size of the city, the scale of its ancient walls and its great domed mosques. Compounding this, you probably don't know where to begin.

This guide is designed to address that, dividing the city into reasonable, enjoyable days. We recommend you treat our recommendations as a sort of menu, selecting a day you want to spend and following it from beginning to end. See Chapter 3, "Suggested Itineraries."

A guidebook can only get you so far, however. One of the best things you can do is abandon yourself to the Grand Bazaar or to İstiklal Caddesi near Taksim. It takes a little time to adjust to the novelty of İstanbul and become comfortable, and one of the best ways is by immersing yourself in the city. You'll want to know a few friendly words (plus "Gerek Yok" – I want nothing – for the persistent shoeshine boys), but a wander through the city's bustling streets is an education in more ways than language practice. You'll see scenes that tear at your heart and furrow your brow, but you will too come to understand that İstanbul is a safe, non-threatening place to travel. Women traveling alone, particularly, may find aspects of the city a nuisance, but if you maintain the caution you exercise at home you should be fine; İstanbul is not dangerous by western standards.

İstanbul is packed with jazz clubs, bazaars, vegetable sellers, teahouses, Turkish baths, and boats plying the Bosphorous. Most people arrive here determined to see the grand old palaces, museums, and monuments, and find themselves delightfully distracted by the fascinating place İstanbul has become. We hope you do, too.

population estimate is probably optimistically low. The 2000 census failed to satisfactorily settle the population question: the true number of İstanbul residents remains unknown.

Detailed Advice – in English

While in town, pick up a copy of the English-language bimonthly magazine, *The Guide*. *The Guide* offers the best calendar of current events in İstanbul available in English, together with articles on things to see and do within the city. This magazine is most useful once you arrive, but if you're anxious you can get an expensive subscription (roughly $80 for six issues) by writing The Guide, Medya Pazarlama San. ve Tic., Ali Kaya Sok. No. 7, Levent, İstanbul, *Tel. (90 212) 283 2061, Fax (90 212) 280 8275.*

If you plan to spend significant time in İstanbul, you should pick up a guide specific to the city. The finest guide to İstanbul's historical sites is, far and away, *Strolling Through İstanbul* by Hilary Sumner-Boyd and John Freely. This guide is a staple of expat libraries, and is often accompanied by Freely's *The Bosphorous*, an historical account of İstanbul's famous strait.

Getting Around Town

Maps

The Tourism Information office distributes a serviceable map of İstanbul, although it is imprecise. If you plan on spending any substantial time in the city, it will be worth your while to spend $12 for a copy of *İstanbul A-Z*, a handy 400 page atlas that shows even the tiniest roads.

By Bus

The municipal bus system, İETT, provides thorough coverage of the city, but the buses are crowded and unpredictable. Route schedules are so useless they are not printed; buses generally leave the initial station on time, but İstanbul's traffic snarls are certain to delay their progress. Prices vary with inflation, but usually run between 25¢ and 50¢.

There are two distinct kinds of buses, each with a separate payment scheme. The real municipal buses, marked İETT, take small tickets (**bilet**) available at kiosks and from private vendors near many bus stops. Buy a ticket, squeeze on board, and slip it into the ticket box at the front of the bus – don't be alarmed if the metal ticket box is belching flames, they just do that sometimes.

When İstanbul upgraded its municipal buses it wisely chose to keep the older ones in circulation. The older buses, most of them a faded cream and orange, are now privately run. They do not take bus tickets, instead you pay cash once you are on board. The fare is identical to the municipal buses.

Both buses now take "Akıllı Biletler," or "smart cards." If you'll be in İstanbul for a while and using buses, buying an Akıllı Bilet may be worth your while – you can pick them up at the white bus ticket kiosks near major bus stops.

The bus terminal most useful to travelers is typically that at **Eminönü**, next to the Egyptian Spice Market and the end of the tram line. This terminus is within walking distance of Sultanahmet (the tram originating in the divider of the highway between the ferry terminals and the

Spice Market will run you up the hill straight through Sultanahmet, if you prefer). At Eminönü, buses on the inland side of the highway travel over the Galata Bridge and out along the Bosphorous, including such places as Taksim Square, Ortaköy, Bebek, Rumeli Hisar, Dolmabahçe, and Sariyer at the upper end of the Bosphorous. Buses on the Golden Horn side of the highway travel into the interior of the peninsula, including such sites as Yedikule, Edirnekapı, and Eyüp.

By Car
We tried to warn you. Driving in İstanbul is going to send your blood pressure off the scale and probably take more time than hailing taxis would. Alas. If you've taken the plunge, remember not to take getting cut off or squeezed personally; it's a different conception of traffic law, but it generally works pretty well.

People park every which way in İstanbul and don't get towed – but there is the remote possiblity it could happen to you. If you are unfortunate enough to be towed, you can find your vehicle at the nearest parking/impound lot. In the Sultanahmet area, the Bayraktar Otopark is the designated impound area; bailing your vehicle out doesn't cost too much (usually no more than $25) but the time and trouble will not be to your liking. If you need to locate your towed car elsewhere, check the up-to-date listing of lots in *The Guide* magazine or check with your hotel.

By Ferry from Eminönü
İstanbul has always been a maritime city, and that tradition is one you should endeavor to continue. Ferries and sea buses from İstanbul serve all of the nearby coastal communities, even such outlying spots as the Princes Islands and Yalova on the Sea of Marmara.

The ferry line from Eminönü offers an inexpensive and enjoyable **Bosphorous cruise**. İstanbul's antiquated – but seaworthy – ferries depart the Boğaz Hattı ferry terminal (building 3) at Eminönü every morning, leaving at 10:35 and 13:35, arriving at the north end of the Bosphorous 1.5 hours later. Ignore the "Special Bosphorous Tours" sign and look for the sign indicating a trip to "Anadolu Kavağı;" this is what you want.

The trip is inexpensive, less than $5 for the round trip on weekdays, $2.50 on weekends. The ferry is rarely crowded, and the cruise does wonders for helping get oriented after arriving. It's a municipal ferry, so you're on your own to identify the sights, and there are a lot of them. Highlights along the cruise north (in addition to the seamanship of the ferry captains as they dock at stop after stop in the powerful current) include the Dolmabahçe and Çirağan Palaces on the European (left) shore. The pretty Mecidiye Camii in Ortaköy pokes out into the strait just before you pass beneath the Bosphorous Bridge.

Just past the bridge on the Asian waterfront is the Beylerbeyi Palace, a summer lodging of the sultans and their guests. Further along the Asian shore you pass the small, ornate Küçüksu Palace in an indent on the Asian shore, followed immediately by the small, barely visible fortress at Anadolu Hisar. Sultan Beyazid I built Anadolu Hisar here at the narrowest point along the Bosphorous to choke off shipping, but his great-grandson Sultan Mehmet II was responsible for the massive, beautiful fortress on the European shore, Rumeli Hisar.

You'll note Rumeli Hisar's unique shape, which led many observers to mistakenly believe it was built to resemble Sultan Mehmet II's tuğra, or signature. Not true; it's shape simply takes full advantage of the two stone buttresses into which it is built. After passing beneath the second Bosphorous bridge – this one named for Sultan Mehmet II – you chug past a collection of pretty communities, finally arriving at Anadolu Kavağı on the Asian shore. You have two and one-half hours at Anadolu Kavağı to sightsee and sit out by one of the waterfront cafes, after which you make a leisurely return to Eminönü, pausing at Sariyer for one half hour. The trip takes about five hours, all told. Information is available at *Tel. (90 212) 522 0045*, but be prepared to hand the phone off to a Turk willing to translate.

To arrange a Bosphorous cruise aboard a privately-run tour boat, including trips complete with cocktails and meals, contact **She Tourism**, *Tel. (90 212) 233 3670*.

Other ferry trips of interest include those departing for Üsküdar (6 a.m. to midnight), and Haydarpaşa Railway Station (7 a.m.-8 p.m.) from Eminönü's Üsküdar İskele (building 2), with constant service throughout the day. The Deniz Otobusleri, or sea buses, offer quick hydrofoil service to Bostancı And Kadiköy on the Asian shore; these leave from the terminal next to the Galata Bridge and cost $1, one way.

Municipal ferries also leave the "Adalar Hattı," or Islands Terminal, bound for the Princes Islands, but people in a hurry will prefer the slightly more expensive – and much quicker – hydrofoil Deniz Otobusleri) service from Kabataş (see below). Municipal ferry service runs roughly hourly from 7 a.m. until 11:30 p.m., weather permitting, and costs $2.

By Ferry From Kabataş

Sea buses (**Deniz Otubusleri**) depart from Kabataş near Dolmabahçe, offering rapid service to the beaches of the Princes Islands and the thermal baths near İalova. Look for the dolphin logo.

Schedule 1: Leaving Kabataş, İstanbul to Heybeliada in the Princes Islands. The cost is $2.50, and you can get ferries between the islands at Heybeliada.

Weekdays	Weekends
8:40	10:15
9:25	11:45
10:55	13:45
13:40	15:45
15:40	18:50
17:15	20:20
18:50	
19:30	
20:15	

Final departure from Princes Islands is at 7:30 p.m. on weekdays, 7:00 p.m. on weekends.

Schedule 2: Leaving Kabataş, İstanbul to Yalova (Termal, Bursa). The cost is $5.

Weekdays	Weekends
8:30	9:15
11:00 11:35	
13:45 14:45	
16:10 17:45	
18:25	

Final departure from Yalova is at 7:30 p.m. on weekdays, 7:00 p.m. on weekends.

By Foot
İstanbul is the perfect place to travel on foot. It may not be tidy, it may not be peaceful, but it is always fascinating. Below are some of the best places to go well-shod, with estimated times (where appropriate) for the entire walk, loitering and dining included:

•**Sultanahmet** clearly recommends itself for those who enjoy walking, and is difficult to see without a lot of it. Seeing the sprawl of Topkapı Palace alone requires a hike, and clustered around the open area of the former Hippodrome you should visit the voluminous Hagia Sophia, the Blue Mosque, an underground cistern, the Archaelogical Museum, and the Turkish and Islamic Arts Museum. In addition, the Grand Bazaar is a ten-minute walk, directly up (west) Divan Yolu Caddesi, with a right turn just beyond Çemberlitaş, the iron-ringed column that dates back to Constantinople's founding. The best part of all of this is it's probably quite near your hotel; you're free to return for a mid-day nap at your leisure. You can plan on spending two days on your feet in Sultanahmet.

• The roiling, endless area behind the **Grand Bazaar** may seem daunting, but it's fascinating and, in the words of Ford Prefect, mostly harmless. Touts whistle, sales carts clatter, and all manner of textiles, furniture, electronics, pharmaceuticals, appliances, bronze and plasticware are piled along the narrow lanes. Enter at any point, take a left, a right, and another right and you become marvelously lost amid the chaos, finding tea shops, curio sellers, and any number of spots you would like to file away and return to later. Chances are, even if you try, you never will.

• Amid the bustling there is almost never any ill will, and once you leave the heavily touristed enclosed areas of the Grand and Spice Bazaars you're unlikely to be approached by touts, or receive much attention. So long as you're resourceful enough to hail a cab or regain your bearings when you become disoriented, it is a wonderful experience. *Duration*: until you are sick of hearing "Hello my friend" (see shopping section of this chapter).

• A walk along the defensive walls of the city, beginning at the Fortress of Seven Tower (**Yedikule**) and heading north, can be grueling, but the former outskirts of the city are peppered with curiosities. Yedikule is enjoyable to investigate, but continuing along the walls is not for the faint of heart. You can easily spend about six hours walking along the walls and exploring some of their nooks and crannies; the nooks are good, but some of the crannies are simply awful. In addition to Yedikule and the walls themselves, you'll want to see Our Lady of the Life Giving Spring (an Orthodox Church in a cemetery outside the walls) and the gorgeous mosaics of the Church of Chora. *Duration*: six hours (please see Along the Theodosian Land Walls, later in this chapter).

• A walk from Eminönü to **Taksim Square** passes through some of the most beautiful of the city's 19th century districts, along a long, wide pedestrian lane lined with boutique shops and markets. This is the place for second hand shops, old books and prints, taking in a movie, and getting a sense of life in İstanbul outside of Sultanahmet. From Sultanahmet, follow the tram tracks downhill to Eminönü. From there, cross Galata Bridge, turn left and, almost immediately, duck into the nondescript "Tünel" station. A 25¢ token will take you on a brief and historic subway ride to the top of the hill, whence you turn right, then immediately left along the main avenue. A trolley provides transportation along İstiklal, but you want to walk, right? *Duration*: three hours to Taksim Square (see İstiklal Caddesi, later this chapter).

Turkish Soccer: Cim Bom, Cim Bom Bom

For an historic perspective about Istanbul sporting passions, you could reach all the way back to the sixth century. At that time, the chariot-racing team you supported said much about your place in society—the Blues were the team of the Emperor and the Imperial ruling class, the Greens were the team of the lower classes.

Today, soccer is the national game, and allegiances no longer break down so cleanly along social lines—but there's still something to it. Atatürk was a fan of the Fenerbahçe Blue Canaries (blue and yellow), an Istanbul team with its home field on the Asian shore, and Fenerbahçe is generally considered the team of the people. Galatasaray (red and yellow), another Istanbul team with its home field in the Mecidiyeköy neighborhood, has traditionally drawn its fans from the wealthy and educated.

Those allegiances shifted in the late 1990s and early 2000s, as Galatasaray ("Cim Bom") ran rampant in the Turkish League—seizing four of five straight league championships—and established itself as a dominating force in European soccer and the pride of Turkish soccer. This success was highlighted by its run to the UEFA Championship in 2000. By dispatching such storied European sides as Borussia Dortmund, AC Milan, Leeds United, Arsenal, and Real Madrid, Galatasaray seized the UEFA Cup Championship and Super Cup Championships—the first such victories for a Turkish side. The 2000 Galatasaray team was the best Turkish League soccer team ever assembled, but even after wealthy European clubs poached coach Fatih Terim and several key players, Galatasaray's success in the Turkish League and Europe has continued.

The European experience served the Turks in good stead during the 2002 World Cup, where Turkey—fielding as many as nine players with experience playing for Galatasaray—placed third. Turkish success at the World Cup united Turkey, offering a much needed bit of good news in the face of ongoing economic woes.

Interested in catching a Turkish League game? Games are played on Saturdays (with occasional matches on Friday evenings and Sundays), and the staff at your hotel will probably be delighted to help make arrangements for seeing a game. Galatasaray plays at Ali Sami Yen stadium—affectionately known as "Hell" for opposing teams—in Mecidiyeköy—three miles northwest of Taksim Circle. The Fenerbahçe Blue Canaries play on the Asian side of the Bosphorous. Beşiktaş, with a livery of black and white, is the least storied of Istanbul's "Big Three," but its field is the easiest to find; its home field is located across the street from Dolmabahçe Palace in Beşiktaş.

• A cruise and a hike to the fortress at Anadolu Kavağı can fill a day. At the Asian terminus of the Bosphorous ferry line originating in Eminönü, at a place called Anadolu Kavağı, you can hike up a hill to Yoros Tepesi, a decaying medieval fortress. You should have three hours at Anadolu Kavağı, which is ample time to climb to the citadel and have a leisurely look around. *Duration*: Five hours round trip to Eminönü (see Anadolu Kavağı, later this chapter).

By Train

Not including the tram line (addressed below), İstanbul's only genuine local train service runs from **Sirkeci station,** *Tel. (90 212) 527 0051,* near Eminönü, around the tip of the peninsula and out along the Sea of Marmara past the city walls to Halkalı. This service covers only the European shore of the Sea of Marmara and the eastern shore of Küçük Çekmece Lake, but is ideal for reaching Yedikule and the City Walls or for an afternoon diversion.

To board the train at Sirkeci enter the main station and stay to the right. Buy tokens at the booth, use one at the turnstile, and wait at the landing for the next departure. Trains depart every 15 minutes, and run throughout the day until 10 p.m. Fare is only 25¢.

The train is also a cheap, quick means of getting to the city center from the outlying areas – including the airport-area hotels (use the Yeşilyurt or Yeşilköy stations).

The train stops at stations in each of the following neighborhoods, in order from the city center outward: Sirkeci, Cankurtaran, Kumkapı, Yenikapı, Kara Mustafa Paşa, Yedikule, Kazlıçesme, Zeytinburnu, Yeni Mahalle, Bakirköy, Yeşilyurt, Florya, Menekşe, Küçükcesme, Soğuksu, Kanarya, and Halkalı.

İstanbul also has a **trolley car** running along İstiklal Caddesi between Galata Tower and Taksim Square. If you're in a hurry, take it (the conductor takes standard İETT bus tickets). Otherwise, İstiklal is a great place for a stroll.

By Subway

İstanbul has the third oldest subway route in the world, and perhaps the first shortest: the **Tünel.** The city's antique subway route runs from the northern shore of the Golden Horn, directly behind the Galata Bridge, to the top of the hill near the Galata Tower. In a great victory for the preservation of antiquity, the route, decor, and machinery haven't changed much since service opened in 1877. In fairness, the cars have been updated at least once since 1877, the paint in the interior received a much-needed update in late 1997, and we're very fond of this subway.

The two-minute ride costs 25¢, and spares you a long walk up the hill. After crossing the Galata Bridge, turn left at the big intersection and work your way beneath or across the major street (Tersane Sokak) to the unpresupposing "Tünel" entrance on the inland side. At the first, and only, stop on the route, leave the building and turn right, then take a left onto the main pedestrian street, İstiklal Caddesi (see İstiklal Caddesi, later in this chapter).

A modern subway line was unvieled in 2001, connecting Taksim with Gayrettepe and Mecidiyeköy. This is only a commuter line – it will be of little use to most travelers. Another commuter route has long run between Aksaray, two kilometers inland of Sultanahmet, and residential areas in Thrace. This, too, has been of little use to travelers, since it goes nowhere a traveler would wish to go other than the main bus station at Esenler, and it does not directly connect to any other transit system.

Should you wish to make your way to the easternmost Aksaray Metro station on Adnan Menderes Bulvarı, you'll find that tickets are 25¢. If you are departing from Aksaray for the bus station, you will want to be careful to take the line specifying "Esenler" or "Otogar" – one of the lines deviates toward a different suburb.

By Tram

The blue- and orange-trimmed İstanbul tram line runs from Eminönü past Sultanahmet and out through Topkapı Gate (not to be confused with Topkapı Palace) toward the suburbs. The tram lines run every 15 minutes on a simple, direct route into and out of town. The tram requires its own specific ticket (**bilet**), available at a kiosk near each of the stops for about 30¢. You use the ticket to mount the landing before being whisked away. Avoid rush hours.

By Taxi

Taxi service is subsidized in İstanbul, and is thus cheaper here than in most parts of the country. Service from the airport to the Sultanahmet area – a 20 minute ride without traffic – costs about $18. Fares within the city are likewise cheap, provided the driver uses the meter properly and doesn't take advantage of the dazzling size of Turkish currency to add a zero or two to the fare. The other trick is, of course, driving you to your destination by the most circuitous route: however we recommend witholding judgment if you suspect a driver to be using a needlessly serpentine route, since you'll find that most normal routes, or non-gridlocked routes, seem fairly indirect.

Day rates (**gündüz**) are in effect from 6 a.m. to midnight. The after hours rates (**gece**) are roughly double the daytime rate. Taxi drivers are

Taxi Language

Turkish	Pronunciation	English
(name of place)	(name of place)	I am going to
'ye gidiyorum.	'ye gid-ee-yor-um	(name of place)
Sol	soul	Left
Sağa	saah	Right
Doğru	doh-roo	Straight
Dur	duhr	Stop
Ineceğim	in-eh-jay-im	I will get out.
Şurada	shoo-ra-da	Here, in this place
Orada	or-ada	There, in that place
Lütfen	LOOT-fen	Please

accustomed to small tips, but don't really expect them outside of heavily touristed areas. İstanbullus round up to the nearest convenient figure; 1.85 million TL becomes 2 million TL, and if the fare is an even 2 million they won't expect more.

Where to Stay

In town to see the sights? It's probably worth your while to stay in the **Sultanahmet** area. Most of what you came to see is here, together with a wonderful selection of smaller hotels, inns and hostels. If you're in town on business, you may want to consider one of the large business hotels on the outskirts of the convention valley, near Taksim.

Prices in İstanbul are less seasonal than in some areas, but they are negotiable in the off-season. You will often be able to secure a 20 percent discount without trying and a 40 percent discount if you will be staying for a few days, if you're visiting on business, or if you have a bit of bargaining ability.

Restored Mansions in Sultanahmet

FOUR SEASONS HOTEL İSTANBUL, *Tevkifhane Sok. No. 1, Sultanahmet. Tel. 212 638 8200, Fax 212 638 8210 (North American Reservations: Tel. 800/332-3442). Email: huluer@fshr.com; Web: www.fshr.com. Rooms: 65. Double: $320-$2,000 (20%-30% discounts in off-season).*

This hotel opened in 1996 and immediately took its place as the finest hotel in Turkey. The Four Seasons is far and away the most ambitious and exacting hotel in a city with its share of excellent hotels. The Four Seasons expects that you're here for pleasure, and sets about making everything right. In Four Seasons tradition, the İstanbul hotel is precise and lovely, with a grace often missing from the stuffier top-end hotels. The genius of this Four Seasons is in the details of each room, the great basins and attractive tilework in the bathrooms, theinterior shutters, the bags of potpourri hung in the closet. There is a distinct Turkish quality to this international hotel in the thoughtfully conceived kilims, tilework, and small Ottoman prints and portraits.

If you are unnerved by the notion of sleeping in a former prison, you might be comforted by the fact that long before becoming a Turkish prison (in the late 1800s) there was a Byzantine Royal Palace here: there are pampered, well-fed ghosts here to keep the prisoners' wretched souls company. Walls and arches belonging to former Byzantine Palace of Buculeon are visible skirting the Four Seasons.

The former prison day-yard now houses the Four Seasons' restaurant, run by a Venetian chef who specializes in California and Mediterranean cuisine. Make reservations at the hotel far in advance.

Selected as one of our best places to stay – see Chapter 10.

EMPRESS ZOE, *Akbıyık Cad. Adliye Sok. No. 10, Sultanahmet. Tel. 212 518 2504, Fax 212 518 5699. Email: emzoe@attglobal.net; Web: www.emzoe.com. Rooms: 19. Credit cards accepted. Open year-round. Double: $70-$85 (25% off-season discount).*

İstanbul is stuffed with small hotels, but this is our favorite of the lot, a small gem in the Sultanahmet district.

The Empress Zoe is painted in muted yellows, with appealing wood-work on the walls and bedsteads, fine metal rails and fixtures, a heavy dose of antique stone peeking from the walls, and thick slabs of rock underfoot.

The Finest Lodgings in Istanbul

The Best Hostels:
İstanbul Hostel, Sultanahmet
Orient Youth Hostel, Sultanahmet
Yücelt Youth Hostel, Sultanahmet

The Best Restored Ottoman House-Pensions:
The Empress Zoe, Sultanahmet
The İbrahim Paşa, Sultanahmet
The Nomade Hotel, Sultanahmet

The Best Major Hotels:
The Four Seasons, Sultanahmet
The Hyatt Regency, Conference Valley
Çirağan Palace, Yildiz/Ortaköy

The decor is traditional Turkish in an environment of artistic licentiousness, with kilim and other textiles played off against dramatic full-wall renderings of Ottoman *sipahis* (cavalrymen) and Byzantine emperors. Every room has a bathroom finished in marble, with shower. Satellite television is available in some rooms, as it is in the public areas.

The staff is helpful and English-speaking (the hotel is owned by an American), and the three year old hotel is the best value for money in İstanbul. If you're looking for a place to put up a family, request the penthouse here, formerly the owner's own home. The penthouse costs $115 per night.

Selected as one of our best places to stay – see Chapter 10.

YEŞİL EV HOTEL, *Kabasakal Cad. No. 5, Sultanahmet. Tel. 212 517-6786; Fax 212 517-6780; Email: yesilevhotel@superonline.com; Web: none. Rooms: 25. Credit cards accepted. Open year-round. Double: $140 (25% discount in off-season).*

The Yeşil Ev is the Grand Dame of Sultanahmet's stylish hotels. The Turkish Touring and Automobile Association undertook the rehabilitation of a ruined nineteenth century mansion on the site in the early 1980s, a relatively daring venture at a time when Sultanahmet was a ragged, disreputable district. The hotel opened in 1984, and this extremely convenient and atmospheric old-world hotel was an immediate success. In the decade following, Sultanahmet has been scoured and rebuilt with the Yeşil Ev serving as a model for many enterprising hoteliers.

The Yeşil Ev is designed on the lines of a winter mansion, with a conservatory downstairs and heavy carpets and drapes in the rooms. The bedsteads are brass, and the trimmed ceilings are hung with chandeliers. Be warned that this interpretation of Ottoman style is ornate, occasionally bordering on the gaudy. Brisk, simple lines were not a telltale feature of late Ottoman interior decorating, but the style is wholly appropriate in this old building, in this historic neighborhood. Weighing in on the side of the Yeşil Ev's decorating sensibilities was the late French president François Mitterand; he stayed here in 1993.

The hotel's backyard offers a spacious garden restaurant, itself worth the price of admission in congested Sultanahmet. Meals are served here in the warm months, while guests retreat to the interior in the winter.

Selected as one of our 'small hotels of note' in Chapter 10.

ALZER HOTEL, *At Meydani No. 72, Sultanahmet. Tel. 212 516 6262, Fax 212 516 0000. Email: alzer@alzerhotel.com; Web: www.alzerhotel.com. Rooms: 21. Credit cards accepted. Open year-round. Double: $70-$90 (30% off-season discount*

The Alzer is located at the southern end of the Hippodrome, across from the Blue Mosque. The hotel is a melange of rooms in an old three story building and rooms in an attached hotel building. The location,

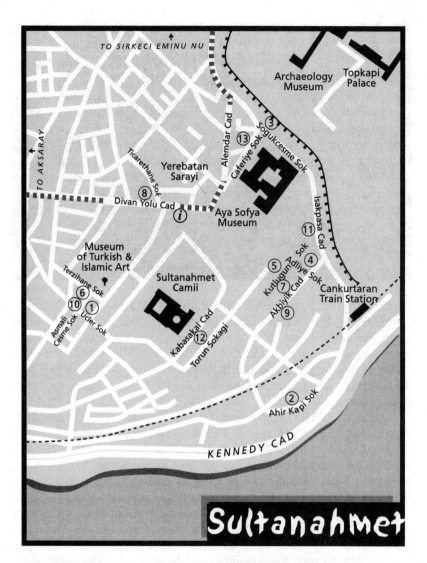

Sultanahmet

1. ALZER HOTEL
2. ARMADA HOTEL
3. AYASOFYA PANSIYONLAR
4. EMPRESS ZOE
5. FOUR SEASONS HOTEL
6. IBRAHIM PASA HOTEL
7. ISTANBUL HOSTEL
8. NOMADE HOTEL
9. ORIENT YOUTH HOSTEL
10. TURKOMAN HOTEL
11. VALID SULTAN KONAGI
12. YESIL EV
13. YUCELT YOUTH HOSTEL
(i) TOURIST INFORMATION OFFICE

■■■■■■■■■■■■
TRAMWAY TO SIRKECI TRAIN STATION/EMINONU

Negotiating for Rooms in Istanbul's Major Hotels

As discussed in "Accommodations" in Chapter 6, "Planning Your Trip," you may be able to secure a better room rate using a travel or booking agency than you'll be able to get yourself. Still, it's certainly worth trying to get a good rate on your own.

For the hotel, individual bookings are icing on the cake, always much more profitable than the rates they're able to charge to groups. Thus, the sales and reservation staff at most good hotels will be eager to knock something off of your room rate if you book ahead, particularly if you'll be staying a few days or more. You'll also want to confirm that the 15% Value Added Tax (KDV) is included in your room price.

overlooking the Hippodrome, is excellent. The Alzer's interiors are busy Turkish, with lots of knick-knacks, carpets, and kilims; bathrooms are clean, but not spotless. Several rooms have large bay windows and all have dark wood interiors and nice period details. The front rooms, with views of the Hippodrome, are the most interesting, but they get some noise from the restaurant below. Open all year, though it gets a bit drafty in mid-winter.

ARMADA HOTEL, *Ahirkapi. Tel. 212 638 1370, Fax 212 518 5060. Email: none; Web: none. Rooms: 110. Credit cards accepted. Open year-round. Double: $115.*

The Armada is built on the grounds of the former naval barracks of Heyrettin Paşa, known in the west as Barbarrossa or Red Beard. Barbarrossa made the Ottomans the scourge of the seas, but little is left of the old quarters other than some ruined foundations beneath this very nice hotel. The owners of the Armada – one of whom owns the small Kalkan Han on the southern coast – have created a relaxed and elegant hotel with large, uncluttered lobbies and decent rooms. The hotel's three floors sprawl parallel to the sea, and careful consideration has been taken to create comfortable public spaces to complement the well-equipped rooms. Rooms offer satellite TV, baths, air conditioning, mini bar, and a view of either the Sea of Marmara or the minarets of the Hagia Sophia just up the hill. The hotel uses environmentally-friendly products and olive oil soap, the pioneer of this effort among local hotels.

The staff is courteous and friendly, and the hotel is located just a five minute walk from the Hagia Sophia or the gates of the Topkapı Palace.

The Armada is an ambitious attempt to incorporate local tradition into a modern hotel. The Armada offers transfers to and from the airport. **AYASOFYA PANSİYONLAR,** *Soğuçeşme Sok., Sultanahmet. Tel. 513 3663, Fax 212 514 0213; Email: ayapans@escortnet.com; Web: none. Rooms: 63. Credit cards accepted. Open year-round. Double: $100-$120 (30% off-season discount).*

The Ayasofya Pansiyonlar are a row of remodeled Ottoman-era houses squeezed between the walls of Topkapı Palace and the Hagia Sophia. Rebuilt by the same organization responsible for the Yeşil Ev, the Ayasofya has nine houses built up against the walls of Topkapı and a tenth, with a large garden, just across the cobbled lane. The charming old houses are quite popular, although their popularity has left evidence of wear and tear in some of the rooms. The caveat offered at the Yeşil Ev applies here as well; late Ottoman decor is gold-framed, bright, and a bit gaudy. If that's not a concern, the back rooms, abutting the walls, are predictably dark and slightly discounted. The front rooms are worth the extra ten dollars.

Because the rooms have been carved out of existing houses, they vary dramatically. Some of the best rooms in the establishment are located in the third house, rooms 301-304, the former residence of Fahri Korutürk, the sixth president of the Republic. Also excellent are the 12 rooms in the Konuk Evi, the newest addition (1994) to the Ayasofya Pansiyonlar. The Konuk Evi stands on the grounds of the Ayasofya's patio garden, behind its own gate. The Konuk Evi is yet another building that has been dramatically remodeled by the Turkish Touring and Automobile Association, which also tidied up the garden area for meals in the summer. One of the secret highlights of a visit here is the old Roman Ayazma, or holy spring, located on the lower level of the garden. The ayazma, with its vaulted roof and tall columns, has been converted into a bar.

For a glimpse of Istanbul in a bygone era, inquire about the Çelik Gülersoy İstanbul Kitaplığı, a library housed in one of the buildings built against the wall. It is occasionally open on weekdays, and the prints and photographs inside depict İstanbul through the course of the Ottoman reign, in many ways a city unrecognizable today.

İBRAHİM PAŞA HOTEL, *Terzihane Sok. No. 5, Sultanahmet. Tel. 212 518 0394, Fax 212 518 4457. Email: pasha@attglobal.net; Web; www.ibrahimpasha.com. Rooms: 19. Credit cards accepted. Open year-round. Double: $90 (35% off-season discount).*

The İbrahim Paşa Hotel is housed in a restored Ottoman mansion on a side street next to the İbrahim Paşa Palace. The structure was converted for use as a hotel in 1990, with generally good results; today, this hotel has a relaxed, comfortable feel, a pleasant lobby tiled in terracotta and appointed with Turkish odds and ends, and a pretty terrace with views out over the Hippodrome and Sultan Ahmet Mosque below. Rooms have parquet floors and are well-furnished, but they clearly see considerable tour group traffic and have lost some of their fineness.

NOMADE HOTEL, *Ticarethane Sok. No. 15, Sultanahmet. Tel. 212 522 2396, Fax: 212 513 2404. Email: hotelnomade@hotmail.com; Web: www.all-hotels.com/hosted/nomade/nomade.htm. Rooms: 15. Credit cards accepted. Open year-round. Double: $65.*

This is a fine restored Ottoman house, better cared-for (and less expensive) than many of its peers. Rooms offer plain pine floors, halogen lighting, wrought iron bed frames, and small writing tables. There's an aesthetic to the best bed and breakfasts (and private homes) in Turkey – they have a nice blend of old things and new, a sense of order in clutter. This is a fine example, a comfortable spot in summer or winter. The terrace is a great escape from the crowds of the old city, offering shade umbrellas, flowers, small couches, and a good view of the "Son et Lumiere" shows at Sultanahmet. The Nomade is well-managed, and you'll find plenty of assistance when you're making plans.

SULTANAHMET SARAYI, *Torun Sok. No. 19, Sultanahmet. Tel. 212 458-0460; Fax 212 518 6224; Email: saray@sultanahmetpalace.com; Web: www.palacecuisine.com. Rooms: 36. Credit cards accepted. Open year-round. Double: $140-$160 (20% off-season discount).*

Opened in 2001, Sultanahmet Sarayi (Sultanahmet Palace) is a small oasis in the old city, offering gardens and fountains behind high stone walls. The interiors are spacious, a contemporary, oversized version of an Ottoman mansion with a clutter of columns and arches. Rooms on the south have views of the Sea of Marmara, while those on the north look out on a thickly overgrown empty lot. The muted yellow rooms are clean and offer balconies; each bathroom offers a marble-clad bathroom with a traditional marble basin. The hotel has floor heating in the winter.

Palace Cuisine, located in the garden behind the restaurant, is a fine place for a meal. The pureed aubergine and lamb (Hunkar Beğendı) is delicious, as is the tender chicken kebap; top off your meal with the delicious chocolate cake. The Sultanahmet Sarayı is located just down the street from the Mosaic Museum.

TURKOMAN HOTEL, *Asmalı Çeşme Sok. No. 2, Sultanahmet. Tel. 212 516 2956, Fax 212 516 2957. Email: info@turkomanhotel.com; Web: www.turkomanhotel.com. Rooms: 20. Credit cards accepted. Open year-round. Double: $90 (35% off-season discount).*

The Turkoman is another distinctly Turkish bed and breakfast in the neighborhood of the Hippodrome, across from the Blue Mosque. The lobby and public areas are clean and furnished with Turkish textiles, old prints of the city, and antique furniture. Rooms are quite simple and see considerable traffic from tour groups, but are kept freshly painted and maintained. The Turkoman has an excellent terrace with a gorgeous old stone fireplace and a good view of the Sea of Marmara over the Obelisk in the Hippodrome. The Turkoman is located on the Hippodrome, just around the corner from the Ibrahim Paşa Turkish Islamic Art Museum.

VALİDE SULTAN KONAĞI HOTEL, *Cankurtaran Mah., İshakpaşa Cad., Kutlugün Sok. No. 1, Sultanahmet. Tel. 212 638-0600; Fax (212) 638-1460; Email: vsultan@hotelvalidesultan.com; Web: www.hotelvalidesultan.com. Rooms: 17. Credit cards accepted. Open year-round. Double: $75.*

This is an ambitious corner lot hotel just below the gates to Topkapı Palace. The Tourism Ministry has an edict against spoiling the neighborhood's aesthetic, and the Valide Sultan is, technically, restored, although it was in reality gutted and put together anew. As a result, the hotel has more dependable plumbing and other not-so-minor features than its genuinely restored neighbors, but perhaps lacks some of their authentic aesthetic. Like many hotels in the area, the Valide Sultan has an excellent terrace, with the great dome of the Hagia Sophia above, the Topkapı walls to the side, and ships laying at anchor in the Sea of Marmara below.

Budget Hotels in Sultanahmet

YÜÇELT YOUTH HOSTEL, *Caferiye Sok. No. 6, Sultanahmet. Tel. 212 513 6150, Fax 212 512 7628. Email: info@yucelthostel.com; Web: www.yucelthostel.com. Double Rooms: 16. Credit cards Double: $14.*

Opened in 1965, when Sultanahmet saw just a fraction of the tourism traffic it does today, the Yuçelt Interyouth Hostel has a terrific, central location directly across the street from the Hagia Sophia. The hostel has grown in that time—it now offers 320 beds, most of them in dormitory rooms. This accredited International Hostel has all the features you would expect—$2 laundry, free Internet access, a book exchange, and a bar downstairs that offers belly dancing shows and live music. The terrace has a fine view out over a 15th century medresse (school) below. Request rooms 30-32 or 20-22. Be warned: the minarets of the Hagia Sophia will definitely awaken you.

Selected as one of our 'best budget hotels' in Chapter 10.

ORIENT YOUTH HOSTEL, *Akbıyık Caddesi No. 32, Sultanahmet. Tel. 212 517 9439, Fax 212 518 3994. Email: orienthostel@superonline.com; Web: www.hostels.com/orienthostel. Double Rooms: 10. Credit cards not accepted. Open year-round. Double Rooms: 10. Double: $15.*

Like the other hostels listed, the Orient is always packed with the flower of Australian, British and Americans youth, people who are eager to swap stories and share the latest traveling gossip. It gets noisy, but stays generally clean. Dorm beds go for just $4 apiece, so, mathematically, if you spend four nights here instead of at the Four Seasons just up the street, you'll have saved enough money for a free round trip to Asia on your next vacation.

İSTANBUL HOSTEL, *35 Kutlu Gün Sokak, Sultanahmet, Tel. 212 516 9380, Fax: 212 516 9384. Email: istanbulhostel@hotmail.com; Web: www.istanbul-hostel.com. Rooms: 24. Credit cards not accepted. Open year-round. Double: $16.*

The İstanbul Hostel opened in June 1998 and is pretty state of the art, hostel-wise. You have a spacious building, tidy rooms and lobbies, well-kept bathrooms, earnest workers, and lots of neat gimmicks; there's a fireplace for winter and a huge television with surround sound for movies in the evening.

In Kariye

KARİYE HOTEL, *Kariye Camii Sok. No. 18, Edirnekapy. Tel. 212 534 8414, Fax 212 521 6631. Email: none; Web: none. Rooms: 27. Credit cards accepted. Open year-round. Double: $95 (20% off-season discount).*

The Kariye is well off the beaten path but conveniently near several marvelous Byzantine and Ottoman sights. Named for Kariye Camii (The Church of St. Savior at Chora), the Kariye Hotel is a former mansion directly beside the mosaic-filled church. The mansion has been divided into 27 rooms, and the broad patio outside is used for restaurant seating in the summer. The decor is Ottoman-style, with gilt-framed pictures, carpets, and elaborate light fixtures. The rooms are nice, if slightly expensive considering the unusual location. Staying at the Kariye yields a completely different view of the city than the Sultanahmet, Bosphorous, or Taksim hotels, and affords other opportunities. Services are fewer, but the hotel has most of what you need, and you're free to linger over the frescoes at St. Savior at Chora, the Edirnekapı gate, and the ruined old Byzantine palaces at Tekfur Saray and Blachernae, near Ivaz Efendi Camii.

Asitane restaurant, located on the premises, is recommended—it is the perfect place to dine after a visit to the Kariye Camii.

In Taksim

Taksim is probably the most central location in a city filled with central locations. There's little of historical interest to see in the immediate vicinity, but it's convenient for business or an extended stay. Taksim is at the entrance to İstiklal Caddesi, a wide pedestrian avenue filled with restaurants, bars, and shops.

VARDAR PALACE, *Sıraselviler Caddesi No. 54/56, Taksim. Tel. 212 252 2888, Fax 212 252 1527. Email: info@vardarhotel.com; Web: info@vardarhotel.com. Rooms: 40. Credit cards accepted. Open year-round. Double: $60 (30% off-season discount).*

A shocking find in the mile-a-minute Taksim area. The Vardar Palace is classy, clean, well-managed, and a bargain at $90 for a double per night in the high season. There's not much of a view, but that's a small price to pay for such fine attention to detail and such a choice location. The building was erected in the 1800s and is evocative of both Selçuk architecture and the Levantine style popular at the time. The interior is attractive and open, providing a respite from the chaos outside. Rooms are well designed, with satellite television, full baths and solid crafts-manship. As always, a helpful, intelligent staff is a key to enjoying your stay; the Vardar's staff is responsive and responsible. If you stay here, have a look at the nasty and expensive "four star" establishments down the street towards Taksim Square. The hotel has a great terrace, opened in 2000.

If full, consider the **Taksim Square Hotel** a short distance back toward the main square *(Tel. 212 292 6440; Fax: 212 292 6449; Email: square@taksimsquarehotel.com; Web: www.taksimsquarehotel.com; Double: $100).*

PERA PALAS HOTEL, *Meşrutiyet Cad. No. 98/100, Tepebaşı. Tel. 212 251 4560, Fax 212 251 4089. Email: perapalas@perapalas.com; Web: www.perapalas.com. Rooms: 139. Credit cards accepted. Open year-round. Double: $220 (50% off-season discount)*

After passengers disembarked from the Orient Express, they were shuttled here. This classic hotel opened in 1892 and has been visited by a slew of famous and powerful people, ranging from Kemal Atatürk and French President Valerie Giscard d'Estaing to Greta Garbo and Jacqueline Kennedy Onassis. The Orient Express no longer operates, but the Pera Palas clings to its grand old reputation. There's old world charm to burn here, but you must pay to burn it—the posted rates of $220 are far higher than they ought to be, and you can secure deep discounts in advance.

Rooms are ostentatious but comfortable. The Pera Palas is not especially convenient to Taksim Square – its almost a full mile south – but you'll never want for a taxi here. The pedestrian avenue, İstiklal Caddesi, is just up the street, and the U.S. Consulate is two blocks away. If you're a great Agatha Christie fan, there's even an anecdote about how Christie wrote *Murder on the Orient Express* while here, somehow losing ten days and a mysterious key.

THE MARMARA, *Taksim Square, Taksim. Tel. 212 251 4696, Fax 212 244 0509. Rooms: 432. Email: info@themarmaraistanbul.com; Web: www.themarmaraistanbul.com. Rooms: 432. Credit cards accepted. Open year-round. Double: $260-$280 (30% off-season discount).*

The Marmara is an İstanbul fixture, towering above Taksim Square. It remains as convenient as ever, with marvelous views and a good, attentive staff. Rooms were redecorated in 2000, and now offer internet connections and good amenities. The room rates are higher than they should be, but you can secure deep discounts by reserving a room. The Marmara is convenient to Conference Valley just to the north.

Conference Valley
İstanbul's Conference Valley is where businesspeople are wont to stay. The valley is just one kilometer north of Taksim Square, and has a huge collection of elite hotels. The old city is 2.5 kilometers away.

HYATT REGENCY İSTANBUL, *Taşkışla Cad., Taksim. Tel. 212 225 7000, Fax 212 225 7007. Email: hyattist@hyatt.com.tr; Web: www.istanbul.hyatt.com. Rooms: 360. Credit cards accepted. Open year-round. Double: $280 plus VAT. Italian, Japanese restaurants.*

The Hyatt Regency is the finest major hotel in the Conference Valley. This is a grand, opulent hotel, far more tasteful and muted in its splendor than many of its rivals. It almost achieves that most difficult of things for a big hotel – a comfortable, friendly atmosphere. This is one of İstanbul's great hotels, with everything you'll need if you're here on business. Some room in the Hyatt have good views of the Bosphorus.

İSTANBUL HILTON, *Cumhuriyet Cad., Harbiye. Tel. 212 231 4650, Fax 212 240 4165. R; Email: hilton@hilton.com; Web: www.hilton.com. Rooms: 500. Credit cards accepted. Open year-round. Double: $280 plus VAT. Chinese Restaurant.*

The Hilton was built in the mid-1950s, and it remains a fixture in various Top 100 Hotel lists. Credit for this goes to a top-notch staff, and to considerable renovation in 2000. Between the service, the spacious grounds, the facilities, and the precise, careful decor the Hilton is an excellent choice if you're in town on business, and a not-altogether-bad option if you're here just to see the old city. The İstanbul Hilton is located in Conference Valley, and its facilities are often used during large conventions or conferences. There is no more central location if you are attending a conference in Harbiye. Half of the rooms have a view of the Bosphorus—if you stay here, insist on one.

Along the European Shore of the Bosphorous
Most of the Taksim and Conference Valley hotels overlook the Bosphorous, but there are also some excellent hotels further north. Several of these hotels are convenient to the Conference Valley, and all of them are popular for business or short stays. These hotels are inconvenient to the historical sites in Sultanahmet.

SWISSÔTEL THE BOSPHOROUS, *Bayıldım Caddesi No. 2, Maçka, Beşiktaş. Tel. 212 259 0101, Fax 212 259 0105. Email: bosphorus@swissotel.com; Web: www.swissotel.com. Rooms: 600. Credit cards accepted. Open year-round. Double: $200-$1800 plus VAT. Chinese, Japanese Restaurants.*

The Swissôtel is one of the premier luxury hotels in the city, solid, tasteful and expensive. The view commands the Bosphorous, as well as the mosques, churches and palaces of the old city. It is one of the premier vantage points in İstanbul, and the beauty of the site is combined with a generous set of amenities – including an excellent gyms, tennis courts, and a rare thing indeed, a running track. Other services are similarly good.

CONRAD INTERNATIONAL İSTANBUL, *Yıldız Cad., Beşiktaş. Tel. 212 227 3000, Fax 212 259 6667. Email: information@conradistanbul.com; Web: www.conradinternational.com. Rooms: 620. Credit cards accepted. Open year-round. Double: $185 plus VAT.*

The curving Conrad hotel is located on a promonotory above the Bosphorus. This Hilton by-product has beautiful rooms, restaurants, and facilities, and—relatively speaking—the rooms are priced to move.

ÇİRAĞAN PALACE KEMPINSKI, *Çırağan Caddesi No. 84, Beşiktaş. Tel. 212 258 3377, Fax 212 259 6687; North American Reservations: Tel. 800/ 426-3135; Email: ciragan@ciragan-palace.com; Web: www.ciragan-palace. Rooms: 322. Credit cards accepted. Open year-round. Double: $195-$5,000.*

This is where John F. Kennedy Jr. and his wife stayed on their honeymoon in 1996, as did a vacationing Hillary Clinton. President Bush stayed in 1991. The Çirağan has certainly arrived, and by a very circuitous route.

Sultan Abdül Aziz originally intended the Çirağan Palace to replace the Dolmabahçe Palace, finding Dolmabahçe too confining. Workers put the finishing touches on the Çirağan Palace – very much like the Dolmabahçe both in terms of its layout and baroque aesthetic – in 1874, but its kismet seemed bad from the beginning. Abdül Aziz was deposed in 1876 and imprisoned here. He slashed his own wrists with a pair of scissors just a few days later, which sent his successor, Sultan Murat V, spiralling into madness. Murat was then deposed in favor of Abdül Hamit II, still in 1876, but Abdül Hamit was too paranoid to live exposed on the water and commissioned a new palace at Yıldız Park. The Çirağan Palace became the prison of Murat V and the Sultan's other rivals and potential heirs, for which it became known as "The Cage."

The palace's prospects seemed to brighten in 1908, when nationalist Turks succeeded in forming a parliament and chose to house it here. The parliament, however, was a resounding failure, and the Çirağan Palace burned to the ground in 1910. The ruins still lay there 75 years later, when a group of investors began laboriously restoring the blackened ruin. Their work was completed earlier this decade, and the Çirağan has flourished.

This is one of the Leading Hotels of the World and a standard selection on the top 100 hotels list, but we have to attach some caveats.

The interiors are surprisingly gaudy, sometimes even downright ugly. The Çirağan is not far from Sultanahmet and the bulk of İstanbul's sights – except on mornings, evenings, and weekends, when the sea road gets choked with traffic. At those times, the three mile drive can take a half-hour or far longer. Finally, the best rooms at the Çirağan are the suites. These rooms are stunning with fine views out over the Bosphorous and attractive, ornate detailing. The standard rooms are just that, standard, and they not in the authentic palace, but in a new wing that was built as a hotel. Still, with one-half mile of Bosphorous shoreline, an excellent standard of service and a worldwide reputation, the Çirağan is a luxury hotel in the finest sense. Seriously, who wouldn't want to stay in a genuine Ottoman Palace?

HOTEL PRINCESS ORTAKÖY, *Dere Boyu Cad. No. 36-38, Ortaköy. Tel. 212 227 6010, Fax 212 260 2148. Rooms: 76. Credit cards accepted. Open year-round. Double: $120.*

The Princess is not frequented by visitors from abroad, owing to its location in Ortaköy, several miles up the Bosphorus from the old city. Istanbul's young and beautiful frequent Ortaköy in the evenings, one of its attractions being the Princess' own Hard Rock Café knockoff, the Rock House. If you're looking for nightlife or a different perpspective on Istanbul, this might be a good choice. Traffic along the sea road can be terrible, but the Bosphorus ferry stops here en route to Eminönü below the old city.

HOTEL BEBEK, *Cevdet Paşa Cad. No. 113-115, Bebek. Tel. 212 263 3000, Fax 212 263 2636; Email: none; Web: none. Rooms: 47. Credit cards accepted. Open year-round. Double: $100.*

The Hotel Bebek was closed for a long-overdue restoration in 2001. One can hope the restoration helps the hotel meet its potential; it has an unbeatable location directly above the Bosphorus in a pretty town that is home to the country's finest university, Boğaziçi University.

Prior to the restoration, the Hotel Bebek had been allowed to deteriorate—we're betting the restoration will make it a great option along the Bosphorus. Bebek is an interesting little borough with a cosmopolitan feel, international book and magazine shops, and cafes that include the excellent Bebek Kahve. The Bebek Hotel's Les Ambassadeurs restaurant is popular among the local B.U. students.

Princes Islands

Few visitors elect to stay on the Princes Islands. If you have limited time in Istanbul, you'll find staying on an island offshore inconvenient. If you'd like to see the city in a way few do, it's worth considering

SPLENDİD PALAS, *23 Nisan Cad. No. 71, Büyükada. Tel. 216 382 6950, Fax 216 382 6775. Rooms: 60. Credit cards accepted. Open April-November. Double: $110*

The Splendid Palas has long been the hotel chosen by İstanbullus themselves. The reason? It's tucked away from the bustle of İstanbul on Büyükada, one of the Princes Islands just three miles and three hundred years offshore of the city. There are no cars on Büyükada, just beaches, restaurants and horse-drawn carriages. There is frequent ferry service from both Kabataş on the Bosphorous and from the docks at Eminönü, so it's quite close to Sultanahmet, if you wish it to be. Büyükada is the only island served by the high-speed sea buses, nine times daily on weekdays, five times daily on weekends. This service is occasionally disrupted by high seas, but such events are extremely rare in the months this hotel is open. In the spring and fall months room prices are halved.

There's a certain English Imperial flavor to the hotel, owing to its old association with a pre-WW I English yacht club. There's a certain English Imperial tiredness to the hotel, as well, whose spacious lobbies and pleasant furnishings are all slightly worn. The hotel has an enjoyable garden and a cooperative staff – although English is not a priority.

HALKI PALAS, *Refah Şehitleri Cad. No. 88, Heybeliada. Tel. 216 351 9550, Fax 216 351 8483; Email: none; Web: none. Rooms: 45. Credit cards accepted. Open April-November. Double: $90.*

Another Princes'Islands option, this one on a slightly less convenient island than the Splendid Palas. The Halkı Palas has beautiful small rooms, spacious, open sitting area, and feels like what it is, a retreat from the city. Life on Heybeliada is slow, but hardly comatose; there are lots of small shops and restaurants where you can while away your time when you aren't in İstanbul proper. From Heybeliada you can catch normal ferries throughout the day, or the faster sea buses from Büyükada one ferry stop away. Transportation between islands is free.

Where to Eat

The Sultanahmet area has a great range of restaurants, from good, simple grills (köftecesi) to the elite Four Seasons restaurant. You can eat quite well in Sultanahmet, but to take full advantage of what the city has to offer you'll need to log a few miles in a taxi. That's a small price to pay. İstanbul's dining options are becoming ever more diverse, which is fitting for a city of 12 million.

American cuisine is one of the most successful transplants: there are dozens of McDonalds, several Wendy's and Burger Kings, two Kentucky Fried Chickens, a Subway Sandwich Shop, Arby's, and even a Dunkin' Donuts and a Little Caesars. It all sounds silly until you start craving these things after a couple of weeks away from home. You can always inquire about these restaurants at your hotel, although they're everywhere and easy to spot, and we don't make mention of them below.

Quick Istanbul Restaurant Guide

I'm in Sultanahmet and I want...

Something cheap:	Sultanahmet Köftecesi, Vitamin Restaurant, Cennet
Lunch outside:	Yeşil Ev
A good fish restaurant:	Balıkçi Sabahattin
A great, distant, expensive fish restaurant:	Körfez
A good, decent dinner:	Kathisma Restaurant
A breathtaking setting:	Sarniç Restaurant
A solid, reasonable place for dinner:	Kathisma, Rami, Rumeli Cafe
Something unique and fun:	Turkistan Evi
The finest meal money can buy:	Seasons Restaurant

I'm ready to get out of Sultanahmet and I want...

Russian food:	Rejans (Istiklal Caddesi)
A beautiful view and great food:	Susam (Beyoglu), Sunset Grill (Ulus), 29 Ulus (Ulus)
A classic Turkish meal:	Hacı Abdullah (Istiklal Caddesi)
The finest Turkish cuisine:	Tuğra (Çirağan Palace)
Italian food:	Spasso (Hyatt Regency)
Excellent Japanese food:	Takarabune (Hyatt Regency)
Ordinary fish, a lot of wheedling, and mysterious charges:	Kumkapı district
A good cup of coffee:	Myott (Ortaköy)

We used the following guidelines to determine the price of a meal in our ratings below: less than $4 per person, inexpensive; $4 to $10, moderate; $10 to $25, expensive; more than $25, very expensive. If you plan on an extended stay, pick up a copy of *Dining & Wining in İstanbul* at one of the English language bookshops.

Sultanahmet

Sultanahmet has dozens, probably hundreds of small restaurants. We've found many excellent ones, and we hope you enjoy them.

BALIKÇİ SABAHATTİN, *Cankurtaran Cad., Sultanahmet, Tel. 212 458 1824. Moderate/Expensive.*

This sprawling old Ottoman house has been converted into the best fish restaurant in the Sultanahmet area. The location is tricky; it's on Cankurtaran Caddesi, just above the rail tracks, and from above it's best accessed by descending Bayram Fırını Sokak from Akbıyık Sokak – the lane two blocks below the Four Seasons Hotel, where the hostels live – and cutting right at Cankurtaran Caddesi. Balıkçi Sabahattin (Sabahattin the Fisherman) has been in business for years, but this location is new. Ask for the seasonal fish – "Mevşimlik ne var?" means "What's in season?"

CENNET, *Divanyolu Cad. No. 90, Çemberlitaş. Tel. 212 513 1416. Inexpensive-Moderate.*

Okay, this is where half of the city's tourists go, but it's a good break from a day in the bazaar. Cennet specializes in gözleme, made in front of you and filled with your choice of potatoes, cheese, spinach, etc. The restaurant serves other dishes as well, but gözleme is the restaurant's big selling point. Meantime, while you await your gözleme you're welcome to borrow a fez from a stack and take a seat on low couches.

HAMDİ ET LOKANTASI, *Tahmis Caddesi, Kalçin Sokak, Eminönü, Tel. 212 528 0390, Fax 212 528 4991, Email: info@hamdietlokantasi.com, www.hamdietlokantasi.com. Moderate. Accepts credit cards.*

This restaurant has been serving Turks and tourists in this location, just opposite of the Egyptian Bazaar and the Eminönü bus station, since 1970. It has a wonderful terrace overlooking the Golden Horn, and serves a quality rendition of traditional Turkish meat dishes ("et lokanta" means 'meat restaurant'). Try the Patlican Kebabı, a grilled eggplant stuffed with ground lamb.

KATHİSMA RESTAURANT, *Yeni Akbıyık Cad. No. 26, Sultanahmet. Tel. 212 518 9710, Fax 212 516 2588. Moderate.*

The Kathisma is a sparkling find in the Sultanahmet area. The restaurant underwent a very successful remodel in 1996, and is remarkably attractive and reasonably-priced. More important, the food is delicious; we're fond of the roast lamb and the Kathisma Filet – steak grilled with mushrooms, cheese, tomatoes, green peppers, onion and ham, with a bechamel sauce ($9). The Kathisma used to have jazz musicians play in the evenings, and they still turn up on occasion. "Kathisma" refers to the Byzantine Emperor's personal box in the eastern stand of the Hippodrome, once located quite near here.

KONYALI, *Topkapı Palace, Sultanahmet. Tel. 212 513 9696. Moderate.* The Konyalı, the only restaurant within the grounds of Topkapı, has been serving captive audiences surprisingly good – if overpriced – lunches for many years. You can survey the offerings and make your choice accordingly. Kebaps and other grills are always good; if you're a hungry carnivore opt for the *karışık izgara*, or mixed grill. If you aren't in the mood for the prices of the crush of people, you'll have to get off of the Topkapı premises to eat.

PANDELİ, *Mısır Çarşısı (Spice Bazaar), Eminönü. Tel. 212 527 3909. Moderate.*

This is one of İstanbul's landmark restaurants, housed in the space above the entrance to the Spice Market. You enter through the main gate of the Spice Market, the public square and the Yeni Camii behind you, and immediately curl left and up a staircase. Pandeli is clad in beautiful sky blue faience, and has the slightly worn feel of most İstanbul institutions. The food is well-prepared and classic; you'll pay more here than you would at a diner in the streets below, but not *that* much; lunch for two should cost $15 or less. This is the place to forever alter your opinion of a vegetable: order anything with eggplant.

RAMI RESTAURANT, *Utangaç Sokak No. 6, Sultanahmet, Tel. 212 517 6593. Moderate-Expensive.*

Rami is located below the Blue Mosque, just down the street from the Mavi Ev Hotel. This creaky old three-storey Ottoman dwelling is a wonderful venue for a meal, filled with candles and bottled preserves and old porcelain wood stoves, and the view encompasses the Blue Mosque. The kitchen produces fine Turkish food, with appetizers running about $5.50, entrees such as shrimp stew, chicken şiş, or Hünkar Beğendi (cubes of lamb served in grilled eggplant puree,cheese, butter, and flour) costing $11. A very relaxing spot to have dinner and enjoy the "Son et Lumiere" at the Blue Mosque, although the "son" is pretty difficult to make out.

RUMELİ CAFÉ, *Ticarethane Sokak No.4, Sultanahmet, Tel. 212 517 6552. Moderate-Expensive.*

A nice spot in the heat of the day or of an evening; a cool, quiet atmosphere and a solid selection of Turkish and Italian food at reasonable prices. Shrimp casserole is $7, vegetarian dolma $5, beer $1.50.

The Rumeli Café is located just off of Divan Yolu Caddesi, up the street behind the Vitamin Restaurant. The restaurant was designed by Nikos Papadakis, the architect who restored the building that houses the Empress Zoe hotel. Just down the alley below the Rumeli Café is the **Alzer Café**, a "narghile bahçesi." The cost for a waterpipe stuffed full of tobacco and a cup of coffee is $3.50.

SARNİÇ, *Soğukçeşme Sok. Sultanahmet. Tel. 212 512 4291. Moderate-Expensive.*

The Sarniç is expensive, and the Sarniç is worth the money. Where else can you dine deep inside a stone chamber that was once a Roman cistern? The Turkish Touring and Automobile Association has lovingly restored this cistern – that was once, believe it or not, an auto repair shop. To make the structure suitable they began digging out the floor and carefully scrubbed and mended thousands of years of dirt and damage. The present floor, still some 10 feet above the old cistern floor, is deep enough. The interior of the cistern is now light and open, decorated with cast iron dividers and candlabras, wooden tables and chairs and simple, elegant place settings. The six great single-piece columns are lit by hundreds of candles and, on occasion, a roaring fire in the giant hearth. The Sarniç restoration is just one of many executed by Çelik Gülersoy and the Touring and Automobile Association.

Which brings us to the food, which is why you'd be interested in coming in the first place. The Sarniç kitchen is one of the best in İstanbul, and the meal will help complete what is probably İstanbul's most fascinating dining experience. The Sarniç offers both Turkish and international dishes, ranging from the best Turkish mezes to thick cuts of red meat and baked chicken. The Sarniç is located just down the cobbled lane from the Ayasofya Pansiyonlar, against the outer wall of Topkapı. Sarniç, sensibly enough, means "cistern."

SEASONS RESTAURANT, *Four Seasons Hotel, Sultanahmet, Tel. 212 638 8200. Very Expensive.*

Some of the restaurants in Sultanahmet are overpriced; Seasons is not. It is very expensive and it is very good. Set in the courtyard of the Four Seasons Hotel, once a prison compound, this restaurant is one of the finest in all of Turkey. Appetizers (such as deep fried prawn croquettes) run about $9, entrees (such as braised sea bass and tomato charred rack of lamb) run about $18. The setting is wonderful, with painstaking landscaping and a crispness to every detail you find so rarely in this city.

SULTANAHMET MEŞUR MEYDANI KÖFTECESİ, *Divan Yolu Caddesi, Sultanahmet, Tel. 212 638 7565.*

This is a Turkish grill, pretty much like anyplace you'll find between here and Kars. What makes Sultanahmet Köftecesi special is that it's an oasis of inexpensive, filling food in the relatively expensive Sultanahmet district. It's opposite the Hagia Sophia on Divan Yolu, just below the Pudding Shop. We eat here often when we're in Sultanahmet.

As you enter you'll want to take a moment to select your food from the steam trays – it's a grill place, so anything "izgara" (grilled) is good. Try the çorba (soup, $1.50), izgara köfte ($2.50) or tavuk şiş (chicken shish kebap, $3), salata (salad, $2), and you'll get a half-loaf of warm bread to go with it.

TÜRKİSTAN AŞEVİ, *Tavukhane Sok. No. 36, Sultanahmet. Tel. 212 518 1344. Moderate-Expensive.*

If Turkish dishes are not Turkish enough for you, the Türkistan Aşevi offers recipes from Central Asia. The restaurant is near the İbrahim Paşa Palace in a restored mansion with beautiful flat weave rugs from Üzbekistan, Turkmenistan, and elsewhere in the region. The restaurant offers friendly service with pleasant little quirks: you wear slippers while dining and their verion of *ayran*, made with soda water, is likely to suit your taste buds better than the standard kind. Try the chicken mincemeat or mixed kebap, with a big side of Turkistan rice. Readers rave about dining here.

VİTAMİN RESTAURANT, *Divanyolu Caddesi No. 16, Sultanahmet, Tel. 212 526 5086. Moderate.*

This is easy to spot, directly on the tram line on Divan Yolu Caddesi. Food is presented and you're invited to pick whichever Turkish dish you like. We prefer Sultanahmet Köftecesi, just down the street, but this place is a shade more welcoming. You're usually rushed to pick quickly; take your time. Entrees tend to cost about 2.50 apiece.

YEŞİL EV, *Kabasakal Caddesi No. 5, Sultanahmet, Tel. 212 517 6785. Moderate-Expensive.*

The garden behind Yeşil Ev Hotel is a fine setting for breakfast or lunch in the summer, if on the expensive side. It's just a few minutes from Topkapı Palace and an even shorter distance from the Hagia Sophia (the way is signed, behind the Baths of Roxelana that has been converted to a Dösim carpet shop). You can have a tomato omelette, juice, and coffee for about $9; the omelette alone is $3.50. Dinner is served here, as well, and it's serviceable but expensive French/Turkish fare. The small compound is filled with tables and shaded by an assortment of trees; fig, chestnut, apple, and maple. A fountain is located in the center of the garden, surrounded by perennial flowers.

West of Sultanahmet

ASITANE/KARİYE HOTEL RESTAURANT, *Kariye Camii Sok. No. 18, Edirnekapı. Tel. 212 534 8414, Fax 212 521 6631. Moderate-Expensive.*

This is the restaurant at the Kariye Hotel, and it's the perfect spot to have a late breakfast or lunch if you're in the neighborhood to visit the Kariye Camii/Church of Chora. The Kariye Hotel is housed in an old Ottoman building, and in the high season you can take your meal in an attractive garden alongside the Church of Chora. The kitchen serves a good selection of omelettes for breakfast, then reverts to some well-prepared Turkish dishes for lunch and dinner. The prices are reasonable.

DARÜZZİYAFE, *Şifahane Cad. No. 6, Süleymaniye Mosque. Tel. 212 511 8415. Moderate.*

When important Ottomans commissioned the construction of a mosque, they built much more than the domed structures we marvel at today. Mosques were always joined by a set of public buildings ranging from schools to soup kitchens, and the Süleymaniye, built for the most powerful Ottoman sultan, had one of the most extensive sets of public buildings. The Darüzziyafe was the soup kitchen of the Süleymaniye, and it continues to dish out food to this very day.

These days the clientele is deeper in the pockets, the menu has gone upscale, and the food is probably better. A mixed grill, always one of the better and more expensive items on a menu for meat-eaters, is $6, and it's very good. The Darüzziyafe kitchen continues to create top-quality Turkish dishes, and the setting is excellent, whether in the stone interior or the courtyard. The only jarring note, here in the mosque complex, are the occasional belly-dancing displays staged by tour groups. The restaurant is to the left as you look at the main entrance (the one you can't use) of the Süleymaniye, through a gate, and across a narrow road.

İstiklal & Taksim

İstiklal Caddesi is thick with restaurants, including several American fast-food imports. If that's not what you're looking for, there are some elegant, reasonably priced restaurants here, as well.

BİLSAK, *Şoğancı Sok. No. 7, Cihangir. Tel. 212 293 3774. Moderate. Closed Sunday.*

A bland looking building disguises one of the area's most popular bars and a great little restaurant. The menu is diverse and excellent, with curried chicken, lentil mantı, seafood pasta, and mushroom linguini. It has a slouchy, chic feel to it, with old movie posters, a great paint job, and definite appeal among trendy expatriates. The first puzzle is getting in – enter the nondescript lobby and take the elevator to five. To get here, head down from Taksim Square on Siraselviler Caddesi (passing Marmara Hotel on your right), then take a left on the street just past the Almanya Hastanesi (German Hospital) and go 1.5 blocks. Bilsak is signed, on your right.

FIVE STAR RESTAURANT, *İstiklal Caddesi, Taksim. Tel. 212 250 2440. Inexpensive-Moderate.*

If you want a quick, cheap hassle-free dinner in the Taksim area, you're probably best advised to hit a McDonalds, Wendys, or Burger King. You can also try the Five Star, an institution on İstiklal Caddesi, just a few doors in from Taksim Square. It's the one with the huge rack of chickens in the window, and it offers an inexpensive dining alternative. You select your food from a buffet line and pay for it, requesting roasted chicken (tavuk) at the register ($2.50). In a separate line the chicken server gives you the chicken in question and a helping of rice or gruel. Ask for rice "pirinç, lütfen," or the server will default to the gruel.

The big advantage to this restaurant is that, having paid in advance, there is no nastiness with an inflated bill. The food is greasy and good, but it's nothing special.

GALATA RESTAURANT, *İstiklal Cad, Orhan Adli Apaydyn Sok. No. 11, Beyoğlu. Tel. 212 293 1139. Moderate-Expensive.No credit cards.*

Many visitors find their way to Galata Tower, but only the lucky few locate this *meyhane* just uphill off of İstiklal Caddesi. Like Galata Tower, Galatea has food and entertainment, but the similarities end there. The cozy Galatea is a favorite among Turks and some expatriates, all of whom gather here many evenings to sing Turkish folk songs. The Galatea is a lot of fun, even if all you can do is hum along, drink, and eat excellent Turkish/Greek food and top notch mezes. The music lasts from 9 p.m. to midnight. Galata is closed on Sundays. As you ascend İstiklal Caddesi from the Tünel and Galata Tower, Galatea is just off to your left on the narrow Orhan Adli Apaydın lane. You might also try **Kum Saati**, which is a meyhane across the street from Galatea, and cheaper.

GALATA TOWER, *8th floor, Galata Tower, Şişhanel. Tel. 212 245 1160, Fax 212 245 2133. Daytime: Moderate. Dinner: Very Expensive.*

Galata Tower's cafe is open through the day serving coffee and some snack food. We recommend stopping in at the tower for the view and a cup of coffee, but we do not recommend the expensive floor show. There are better ways to spend $70 apiece than okay food, okay bellydancing, and weak drinks from 9 p.m. to midnight. All of that aside, the view is marvelous, and the building is genuinely fascinating. Note the plaque on the inner wall on your way up; according to the tale, long before Orville and Wilbur were a glimmer in Mrs. Wright's eye, an Ottoman scientist strapped on a pair of wings and leapt from the top of Galata tower, soaring about one mile across the Bosphorous. This appears to have worried the Sultan; the flier was exiled.

HACİ ABDULLAH, *Ağa Camii Yanı Sakızağacı Caddesi No. 17, Beyoğlu. Tel. 212 293 8561. Moderate.*

The Hacı Abdullah is an İstanbul institution, serving meals since 1876, and it has become a gathering spot for some of the city's sharpest minds. The appeal here is that often advertised but seldom found commodity, "traditional" Turkish cooking. The menu is vast, and includes dishes for the adventurous such as grilled veal kidneys and fried lamb's brains. Fortunately, there is a menu in English, and some considerably less worrisome dishes.

So exhaustive is the menu that you can find it reprinted in the "Food" section of this very book. We would encourage you to try some börek (pastries with spinach, cheese or meat), domates dolmas and biber dolmas (stuffed tomato and stuffed peppers), İmam Beyaldı (cold stuffed eggplant), and a selection of the meat and fish dishes (you can hardly go wrong). A generous dinner for two will run to $25. Alcohol is pointedly not served. Hacı Abdullah is located short walk down İstiklal from Taksim Square and right one block. Do not confuse the Hacı Abdullah with the Hacı Baba, which is close by along İstiklal. Hacı Baba – the other place – is expensive and unfriendly.

İNCİ, *İsiklal Cad. No. 124, Beyoğlu, Tel. 212 243 2412. Inexpensive.*

İnci has been serving up this neighborhood's consummate dessert – profiterol- from this location for over 50 years. Profiterol is a vanilla pudding-filled pastry slathered in chocolate sauce for all of $1.50. Eat it in this tiny shop, or take one to go (*paket*). The only downside is that they close at 9 p.m. every night. Recommended.

KAKTÜS, *Imam Adnan Sokak No. 4, Beyoğlu, Tel. 212 249 5979.*

Kaktüs is cozy cafe that also specializes in light European food. Lots of artists, intellectuals and good cheese cake. Going down İstiklal Caddesi from Taksim, take a right onto Imam Adnan Sokak, opposite the Vakko department store.

NATURE & PEACE, *İstiklal Caddesi, Büyükparmakkapı Caddesi No. 21, Beyoğlu. Tel. 212 252 8609. Moderate.*

One of İstanbul's only dedicated health food restaurants (also see Zencefil, below). Nature & Peace is quite reasonably priced and has an atmosphere you're sure to appreciate after walking all over İstanbul. The menu is varied, emphasizing health and vegetarian dishes. It is bit hard to find; walking down İstiklal Caddesi with Taksim Square at your back, take a left past the cinemas onto Büyükparmakkapı, the street with Pandora book store. The restaurant is on your left one block along.

NEVİZADE SOKAK, *near İstiklal Caddesi, Beyoğlu. Moderate.*

This small back street near the Çiçek Pasajı is filled with tiny *meyhanes*, establishments that are known for *meze*, music, and perhaps above all, *rakı*. All *meyhanes* along this strip have outdoor seating, but the irony is that none of them really feature live music anymore; instead, the musicians walk up and down the street, and solicit donations. It's a fun time, and lots of Turks go here. The best of the bunch is **Ney'le Mey'le**, but **Bade**, **Alem**, **Cumhüriyet**, **İmroz**, and others are also good. To find it, head towards Taksim on İstiklal. At Galatasaray square, turn left onto Sahne Sokak. The first right should be Nevızade Sokak.

PİA CAFE, *Bekar Sokak No. 6, Taksim, Tel. 212 252 7100.*

Go down İstiklal Caddesi from Taksim and turn right at Bekar Sokak. Cafe Pia is on the right and has two small floors. They serve light meals.

REJANS, *Emir Nevruz Sok. No. 17, Galatasaray. Tel. 244 1610. Expensive.*

Rejans offers excellent Russian food and has been a staple in this neighborhood since three White Russians fled their country during the civil war; they arrived with most of the best recipes from the old country. If you've ever been curious about borscht and real beef stroganof, this is your chance. The lemon vodka is comely and dangerous. The restaurant is located four blocks downhill of the bend in İstiklal. Atatürk himself is reported to have loved this spot. The service is not especially fine, reminding one of Ed Debeviks in Chicago.

SAFRAN, *Ezine Apartments 1/1, Balo Sok, İstiklal Cad, Beyoğlu. Moderate.*

This is one of our favorites (and not to be confused with a restaurant of the same name at the Inter-Continental Hotel). The restaurant overlooks İstiklal Caddesi from its second-story location, but you enter the building on Balo Sokak. Go up the stairs (not sure if the gorgeous, turn-of-the-century elevator works) and through the plastic beads hanging in the doorway. Safran serves both vegetarian and non-vegetarian fare in a spacious, sleek setting. The pasta dishes are good, as are all the appetizers. You will want to sit at the windows if possible. The chef and owner is a woman, which is unusual.

ŞARABİ, *İstiklal Cad. 174, Beyoğlu, Tel. 212 244 4609. Moderate.*

This snazzy wine bar opposite the Galatasaray complex serves a variety of the new breed of Turkish wines and Turkish dishes with an international twist. You may dine on the main floor or downstairs in the evocative cellar.

URBAN, *İstiklal Cad., Kartal Sok No. 6A, Beyoğlu, Tel. 212 252 1325. Moderate.*

The arched, exposed brick foundations of this café and bar are pleasingly juxtaposed with sleek modern additions of steel and glass, and make for a cozy setting to sip some coffee or eat light fare while writing postcards. In the 1920's a Jewish Patisserie was apparently at this site. To find it, walk towards Taksim on **İstiklal** and take a right onto Kartal Sokak immediately after the Galatasaray Lycee compound. Urban will be on the left.

ZENCEFİL, *Kurabiye Sokak No. 3, Taksim. Tel. 212 244 4082 Moderate.*

The vegetarian menu at Zencefil changes daily and includes specialties from different parts of the world. Only natural, locally grown ingredients are used, and they offer homemade bread, wine, and herbal teas. Open noon-10 p.m, closed on Sundays. From Taksim, go down ‹stiklal and turn right after the French Consulate. Go down the hill one block and take the first left onto Kurabiye Sokak. Zencefil is on the left.

Along the Bosphorous & Beyond

This collection of restaurants is a bit far afield from Sultanahmet, but each of them offers something special. We do recommend getting out of Sultanahmet for at least an evening for the sake of seeing İstanbullus in a more natural setting; judging ‹stanbul by Sultanahmet is like judging San Franciso by Fisherman's Wharf.

BEKRİYA, *1. Caddesi No. 90, Arnavutk öy, Tel. 212 257 0469. Moderate.*
One street inland from the sea road, Bekriya is on the upper floors of a narrow and rickety wooden Ottoman building. It has great views, a decent selection of Turkish wines, and the *meze* – apparently Bosnian style – are a real treat.

LA MAISON, *Müvezzi Caddesi 63, Beşiktaş. Tel 212 227 4263. Turkish with a French twist. Expensive.*
On the roof of the La Maison hotel (directly opposite the main gate of the Çirağan Palace) this restaurant affords you a fantastic Bosporus view, especially from the outside terrace. This tiny Beşiktaş restaurant is just a short distance from Dolmabahçe Palace and is open from noon until midnight, every day. The food here is a fusion of Turkish and French. Reservations are necessary.

KIZ KULESİ, *Kız Kulesi tower, Sea of Marmara, Tel. 216 342 4747. Expensive.*
If you saw the 2000 James Bond movie "The World is Not Enough," which was in part set in İstanbul, then you've seen Kız Kulesi, or Maiden's Tower (The maiden is Leander, of Hero and Leander fame). Kız Kulesi is a landmark at the mouth of the Bosphorus, and until recently it was little more. In 2001, a restaurant opened at Kız Kulesi, and a fine setting it is. You probably shouldn't expect Hero, or Pierce Brosnan, for that matter, to dodge the oil tankers and come swimming to the shore, but it's still a phenomenal setting for dinner and live music. You can make reservations and arrange the boat trip by calling the number above, or by calling the Klassis Hotel, Tel. 212 727 4095.

KÖRFEZ, *Körfez Cad. No. 78, Kanlıca (Asia). Tel. 216 413 4314/4098. Fish. Expensive-Very Expensive.*
A romantic fish restaurant on the Asian shore. Phone ahead to be picked up by a boat at Rumeli Hisar – the Ottoman fortress on the European shore of the Bosphorous – and the Körfez will oblige. İstanbullus agree that the fish here is the finest in the city, reserving special praise for the sea bass (levrek) leached with rock salt and baked. Dinner and drinks for two can climb quickly toward $100, but there's no denying the Körfez is a marvelous experience. Closed Mondays.

ORTAKÖY, *Ortaköy. Several moderate dining options.*
The Ortaköy waterfront is filled with inexpensive and moderately priced restaurants and cafes. Two solid choices for Turkish food are **Mor Fil** and **A la Turca**. You might also consider picking up a **baked potato** from the long row of baked potato carts in front of McDonalds. They put

all sorts of stuff on them (just point at the various condiments and hope), and they're really good. They cost about $2 apiece.

MYOTT, *Iskele Sok. No.14, Ortaköy. Tel. 212 258 9317. Cafe. Moderate.*

A forerunner of İstanbul's many slickest coffee shops, serving Italian coffee. Crowds gather here, very hip crowds, but if you can slip in this is a nice, mildly overpriced spot for pastries and coffee. Myott also serves Muesli for breakfast on weekends.

SPASSO, *Hyatt Regency İstanbul, Taksim. Tel. 212 225 7000. Expensive-Very Expensive.*

Spasso offers Italian food in an open, unusual setting. Spasso is a cross between a bistro and an art project, and it works. Food is prepared in the open and service is top notch.

SUNSET GRILL & BAR, *Adnan Saygun Cad. Kireçhane Sok., Ulus Parky No. 2, Ulus. Tel. 212 287 0357. Expensive-Very Expensive.*

Sunset Grill & Bar has one of the finest Bosphorous views in the city. Sunset serves slightly overpriced California-style cuisine, but in this setting the price isn't going to spoil your mood. In good weather you should make reservations for a table outside under one of the pavilion tents. Try the grilled prawns or the salads. The drinks are excellent. The restaurant is located just below Ulus Park on the road between Ortaköy and Akmerkez in Etiler.

TAKARABUNE JAPANESE RESTAURANT, *Hyatt Regency, Taşkışla Caddesi, Taksim, Tel. 212 232 1283. Very Expensive. Closed Sundays.*

Takarabune serves exquisite Japanese cuisine in a quiet, peaceful setting. Honda, Suzuki, and other major Japanese companies have a strong presence in Turkey, using it as their manufacturing springboard into the countries of the European Union, and this is where uprooted Japanese go for business meetings and special occasions. The food is prepared and presented with great ceremony and care, and it's delicious.

TUĞRA, *Çırağan Palace Hotel, Beşiktaş. Tel. 212 258 3377. International. Very Expensive.*

Only the finest Ottoman recipes have made their way onto the Tuğra menu. This restaurant, located in the wing of the Çirağan Palace Hotel that once was part of the palace itself, is a precious treat. The setting on the Bosphorous is marvelous, the dining area spacious and ornate, and the menu exotically unfamiliar to new arrivals. Don't let this deter you; nothing on the menu will disappoint, and the waiters are not too snooty to help. Bear in mind that few Turks are familiar with the intricacies of these dishes, and American travelers will be treated with indulgence. If you want to splurge on the finest Ottoman cuisine, the Tuğra is your place.

YİRMİDOKUZ ULUS (29 Ulus), *Adnan Saygun Caddesi, Kireçhane Sok. No. 1, Ulus. Tel. 212 265 6181. French. Very Expensive.*

Some believe this is the best restaurant in the city, and pound for pound it might be, but featherweight portions can be a problem if you have a cruiserweight appetite. International cuisine in a beautiful setting overlooking the Bosphorous – excellent in the summer. Reservations are necessary.

Seeing the Sights

Whatever your interests you will want to spend at least one or two days in the **Sultanahmet** area. After that you can take a cruise on the Bosphorous, shop in the Grand Bazaar, walk along the city walls, or visit one of the myriad museums scattered around town. We have tried to keep the sights arranged in a way that makes them convenient to one another. Follow the itineraries suggested in Chapter 3 or follow our descriptions from beginning to end and you'll see the best the city has to offer.

The reasons the Sultanahmet area is so compelling are about this many: The Topkapı Palace, the Hagia Sophia, the Blue Mosque, the Basilica Cistern, and the Archaeological Museum, plus a handful of other museums. This was the site of the ancient settlement and has always been the center of İstanbul. Once you've had spent some time here you will want to begin straying farther afield, first up the **Bosphorous** to the fortresses at Anadolu Kavağı and Rumeli Hisar, then up along İstiklal Caddesi to the Miltary Museum beyond Taksim Square, and then out to the city walls or across the Bosphorous to Aynalıkavak Kasri.

SULTANAHMET REGION: THE IMPERIAL CENTER

Sultanahmet, named for **Sultan Ahmet I**, the builder of the Blue Mosque, has a critical mass of historic sights. If you have a day, this is where you spend it. If you have a few days, you could easily spend them all here. The area is open, tidy, and busy year-round. Prepare some polite regrets for the "avcilar," literally "hunters," who will approach you about purchasing a carpet.

THE OTTOMAN PALACE AT TOPKAPI

Topkapı Palace is the greatest Ottoman museum in the world and a fascinating relic of the Empire's lost glory. Visitors can spend the day in the gardens where Sultans spent their time, look through their most private rooms and the rooms of their entourage, and reanimate the might and mystery of the palace. An immense collection of weapons, jewelry, and treasure adds color, and, finally, some of the holiest artifacts in the Muslim world are here to remind you that the Sultan ruled in spirit as well as flesh. In addition to the museums within the palace itself, there are

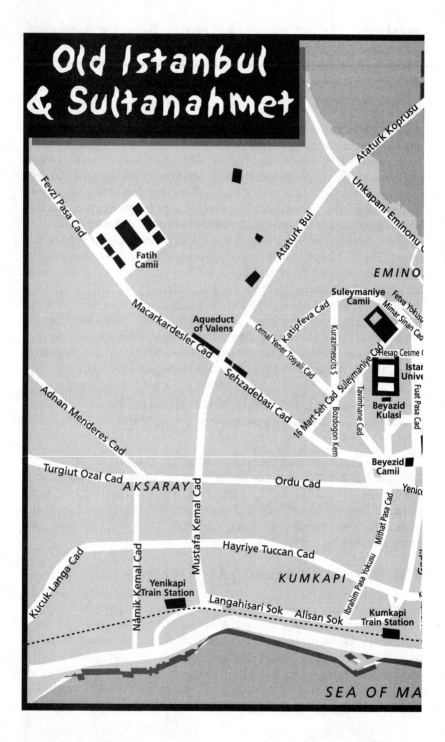

Old Istanbul & Sultanahmet

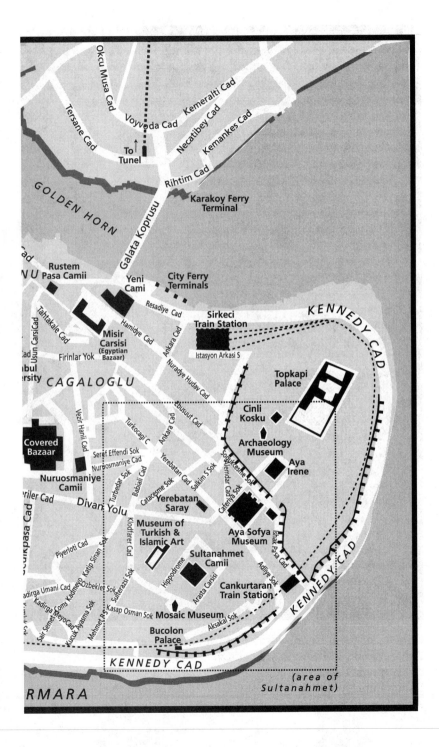

Okcu Musa Cad
Tersane Cad
Kemeralti Cad
Voyvoda Cad
Necatibey Cad
Kemankes Cad
To Tunel
Rihtim Cad
GOLDEN HORN
Galata Koprusu
Karakoy Ferry Terminal
Rustem Pasa Camii
NU
Yeni Cami
City Ferry Terminals
Resadiye Cad
KENNEDY CAD
Tahtakale Cad
Uzun Carsi Cad
Hamidye Cad
Sirkeci Train Station
Misir Carsisi (Egyptian Bazaar)
Ankara Cad
Firinlar Yok
Istasyon Arkasi S
bul rsity
CAGALOGLU
Nuradye Hudav Cad
Topkapi Palace
Ebusuut Cad
Cinli Kosku
Vezir Hanii Cad
Turkocagi C
Ankara Cad
Archaeology Museum
Covered Bazaar
Seref Effendi Sok
Yerebatan Cad
Soguk Kesme Sok
Aya Irene
Nuruosmaniye Cad
Catacesme Sok
Salkim S Sok
Alemdar Cad
Cafer Sok
Nuruosmaniye Camii
Turbedar Sok
Babiali Cad
Yerebatan Saray
eriler Cad
Divan Yolu
Museum of Turkish & Islamic Art
Aya Sofya Museum
Ishak Pasa Cad
Piyerloti Cad
Klodfarer Cad
Sultanahmet Camii
KENNEDY CAD
Katip Sinan Sok
Ozbekler Sok
Sultanazzi Sok
Hippodrome
Adliye Sok
Cankurtaran Train Station
pasa Cad
Kadirga Umani Cad
Kadmer
Kucuk Ayasma Sok
Kasap Osman Sok
Arasta Carsisi
Kadirga Coms Kadme Yo Cad
Sair Semet Meyo Cad
Mehmet Pa
Mosaic Museum
Aksakal Sok
Bucolon Palace
KENNEDY CAD
RMARA
(area of Sultanahmet)

Creating Your Itinerary in Istanbul

Monday is a particularly bad day to see the sights in İstanbul, as many of them are closed. Even on Mondays, however, you'll find something open. Closures are spread throughout the week so that there's something open every day and available for a visit. The following list, organized by the closure days, includes admission costs and hours.

Location	Price	Hours	Days Closed
Galata Tower	$1.50	cafe 8:00-21:00	(Always open)
Yerebatan			
Cistern	$2	9:00-17:00	(Always open)
Archaeology			
Museum	$2	9:30-16:30	Monday
(Cinli Kösk and Museum of the Ancient Orient)			
Hagia Sophia	$3	9:30-17:00	Monday
Museum of Turkish			
and Islamic Art	$2	10:00-17:00	Monday
Rumeli Hisar	$1.50	9:30-16:30	Wednesday
Yedikule			
(Seven Towers)	$1	9:30-5:00	Wednesday
Naval Museum	$1	9:30-17:00	Monday, Tuesday
Military Museum	$1.50	9:00-17:00	Monday, Tuesday
Beylerbeyi Saray			
(Palace)	$1.50	9:00-17:00	Monday, Thursday
Dolmabahçe			
Palace	$4, $7	9:00-16:00	Monday, Thursday
Yıldız Palace			
Chalet	$1	9:00-18:00	Monday, Thursday
Mosaic Museum	$1	9:30-17:00	Tuesday
Topkapı Palace	$4, $7	9:00-17:00	Tuesday
Kariye Camii			
(St. Savior at Chora)	$4	9:30-16:30	Wednesday
Divan Edebiyati	$1.50	9:30-17:00	Tuesday
Müzesi			

three excellent museums located in Topkapı's outer court, including the Archaeological Museum (see below).

Topkapı Palace, *Tel. 212 512 0480,* is at the head of the peninsula in Sultanahmet, within a circuit of walls directly behind the Hagia Sophia. An entrance fee of $5 is exacted at a small ticket office to your right as you approach the inner Topkapı Gate, and there is an additional fee if you wish to visit the harem.

History

Sultan Mehmet II captured Constantinople in 1453, but by that time the city was a mere shadow of its former self. Many of the city's treasures had been plundered just 200 years earlier by the Latins in the Fourth Crusade, and the subsequent governments suffered under severe economic strain largely at the hands of the Ottomans themselves. By the time the Ottomans claimed the city, parts of the metropolis were deserted and and the Imperial Palace was itself a shambles. Sultan Mehmet II "The Conqueror" was nonetheless proud of his prize and, ever industrious, he set about restoring the city and it's great buildings. He imported people from conquered territories to swell the population, commissioned a covered bazaar, and invested in other neglected infrastructure to jumpstart the city's commerce.

Finally, in 1460 he ordered an ambitious new palace complex be erected on the hill at the tip of the peninsula, replacing the temporary Ottoman administrative complex near today's Grand Bazaar. Topkapı Palace was thus created, a sprawling, walled complex that is roughly the size of the ancient city of Byzantium, and is a capital that satisfied Mehmet II and his successors for 400 years. Topkapı benefits not only from its location at the crest of İstanbul's First Hill, but from its proximity to Byzantine-era landmarks such as the Hagia Sophia.

Topkapı Palace is the soul of the Ottoman Empire at its zenith, a place of administration, education, military strategy, and spiritual leadership. As the Ottoman Empire expanded, its armies pierced deeper and deeper into Europe, and their advances were accompanied by church bells rung in grief at the news that another city, another army had fallen to the Muslims. To a cowed western world, Topkapı Palace was the mysterious and frightening source of this relentless power. Behind the impossibly distant walls of Topkapı, Ottoman sultans lived in magnificent rumor and luxury, issuing forth only to march at the head of their victorious Ottoman armies. European embassies were ignored or treated with contempt, and the Mediterranean became an Ottoman lake.

This eminence passed, but even in decline Topkapı remained a strange place. Within its walls the Imperial guard and high officials conspired with women of the harem or the chief eunuchs, maneuvering for some of the great autocratic power wielded by the Ottoman Sultan. Princes were assassinated or their prospects advanced by the military or by Grand Viziers, or by the mothers of their rival claimants to the throne. If the strengths of the Empire were manifest at Topkapı Palace, so, too, were its insular weaknesses. The haughty superiority of the early sultans deteriorated into a stubborn closed-mindedness that helped grease the long Ottoman slide from power.

The First Court of Topkapı

The Palace was built on a sprawling plan in four distinct courts. The first, outer court is immense, incorporating the entire head of the peninsula. With the contemporary addition of a road for tour buses you may not realize you are in a court at all. The main entrance is at the great gate behind the Hagia Sophia, and a paved lane leads directly to the gate of the Second Court and the main palace grounds. There is a ticket booth on the right side of the road where you'll pay $5 for entrance (see The Second Court, below).

As you entered the First Court, you may have noticed the niches in the walls. These spaces were once kept stocked with the heads of enemies of the Empire.

Much of the hewing of human heads was done by the resident Imperial guard, the **Janissaries**, for whom the huge first court was once named. The Janissaries were the elite fighting corps at the heart of the Ottoman military, and one of the cornerstones of Ottoman martial success for 300 years. As the Ottoman Empire began bringing more and more lands under its control, Sultan Orhan (1326-1361)initiated a shrewd policy with his Christian subjects. Rather than persecuting minority religions, Orhan chose to offer religious freedom to Christians and other non-Muslims, which secured their reluctant allegiance.

At the same time, he conscripted many of their young sons, converting them to Islam and inviting them to serve in the Janissary Corps. Strange as the practice sounds it was quite successful on several counts.

The conscription elevated the young Christian males to an educated, martially respected status, and it gave the Sultan a crop of young men that became full time soldiers, administrators, and military engineers in an age when warfare was a seasonal occupation. Furthermore, the Padishah's much-feared personal army served as a counterweight against rival claimants to the throne; the Janissaries were beholden only to the Sultan. In this way, the Ottomans headed off internal challenges to their power until the "devşirme," or selection process, began weakening in the 1600s and those with wealth and influence were gain selection for their own children and proteges.

As a third arm of the military, together with peasant infantry (başıbazouks) and the sipahi (cavalry) supplied by the great houses, the ably-led Janissaries were critical to the Ottoman army in the field. The Janissaries were typically held in reserve until late in the battle, then sent forward to shatter the enemy lines. Opposing armies of part-time soldiers could rarely match the Janissaries, for whom warfare was a way of life. Their commanders, Janissaries themselves, were posted to captured fortresses on the frontier to ensure loyalty to the sultan.

As the empire eroded, so did the Janissary Corps – as mentioned above, the devşirme grew lax, and the corps became highly political. By 1700, they no longer intimidated enemies of the empire, just the Sultans themselves. Several ill-fated attempts were made to eliminate the corps, but it was not until 1826 that Sultan Mahmud II succeeded in defeating the Janissaries and disbanding them permanently.

The first court is often overlooked by people who make the intuitive beeline for the central palace grounds behind the Gate of Salutations, but the buildings down the slope to the left are worth your time. The first building, near the outer wall, is the **Hagia Irene**, a much senior church to the upstart Hagia Sophia. The Hagia Irene dates back to Byzantium, and in 330 A.D. was rebuilt as the great church of Constantinople. Like the Hagia Sophia, it was repeatedly damaged and restored, although Justinian's magnificent restoration of the Hagia Sophia eventually relegated the Hagia Irene to an afterthought.

After the Ottoman capture of Constantinople the Hagia Irene became an armory and a storehouse, but under the Republic it was cleaned up and is used today for İstanbul Music Festival concerts in the late spring and early summer. Chamber music, particularly, benefits from the excellent acoustics of the Hagia Irene. For concert schedules in June and July contact the Tourism Information office.

Elsewhere in the First Court of Topkapı

Below and behind the Hagia Irene are the extensive grounds of the **Archaeological Museum** and its outbuildings. A small road lined with sarcophagi and statuary runs downhill alongside the Hagia Irene to the museums. If you continue past the Archaeological Museum you will emerge in **Gulhane Park**, at the lower end of Divan Yolu Caddesi and just down the street from the Yerebatan (Basilica) Cistern. This lower entrance to the Topkapı compound is also almost directly opposite the **Sublime Porte**, an elaborately roofed gate outside the Topkapı walls. This was the residence of Grand Viziers from the time of Süleyman the Magnificent. Most official business was done here, not in the palace itself, and "Sublime Porte" was synonymous with Ottoman power. Today the Sublime Porte enters into a police station.

If you enter the palace grounds at Gulhane, the upper path takes you to the museums and beyond, while the lower path, to the left, passes into a municipal fairground frequented by the howling, cotton-candy decorated children and young İstanbul couples. Choose wisely.

Deep into Gulhane Park, at the tip of the peninsula beneath the outer walls of Topkapı Palace, is the lonely, 50-foot tall **Goths Column**. This column standing in a small clearing, dates to a third century siege of Byzantium by the Goths: the inscription, most of which remains legible, reads *"To Fortune, who helped us gain our victory over the Goths."*

The Second Court of Topkapı

To enter the true interior of the palace you must pay at the ticket kiosk along the right side of the road as you approach. The second gate at Topkapı is the **Gate of Salutations** (Babüsselam), decorated with the Tuğra of Mehmet II, builder of the palace. For those who missed the point at the Imperial Gate, two large stones stand to either side of the gate for displaying more human heads. Salutations, indeed.

Upon entering and submitting yourself and your belongings to an x-ray scan, you that you are not in a palace at all, but in yet another park. To orient yourself, take a look at the diagram on the wall inside the gate, or at the excellent scale model.

Away to the left is the **Gate of the Privy Stables**, but the stables themselves are closed. The **Quarters of the Halberdiers with Tresses** are located in the compound with the Privy Stables behind the long western wall of the third court. The Halberdiers were simply porters and guards charged with caring for the harem, and their exposure to the beautiful residents therein compelled them to grow their hair long and wear high-collared uniforms that obscured their view (and, presumably, vice versa).

We suggest heading directly to the first real feature along the western wall of Topkapı Palace, the Harem.

The Harem

Against the long wall is a booth where you can $2 tickets for the half-hourly harem tours between 9:30 a.m. and 3:30 p.m., with an hour break at noon. This is also the place to purchase a ticket for the **Tower of Justice** above the Imperial Council chambers If you want to see the harem, you'll have to go with a tour – unfortunately the tight corridors and the large size of tour groups can render the guides unintelligible even when you manage to cram into the same room. If you are with a small group of your own, ask for a private tour ($15). In either case, it's smart to make a beeline here and make reservations for a tour; otherwise, the tours may fill up while you're elsewhere in the palace. The 300-room harem is a fascinating place whether you are interested in architecture, history, or things more prurient.

The Harem was supervised by the **Black Eunuchs**, a tradition that began when hundreds of gelded Sudanese men were brought back to İstanbul as an oddity. The Chief Black Eunuch could rise to great power within the palace, and became a pivotal player in the conspiracies of the crown princes and their mothers.

The women of the harem were invariably slaves and prisoners of war, selected for their beauty at a young age and educated within the harem. The Koran forbids such treatment of people of the Book – Muslims, Christians and Jews – but a lawyerly interpretation allowed particularly toothsome Christian and Jewish girls to be conscripted to the harem.

Yes, the Sultan could have his way with the women of the harem, but everything was subject to strict protocol that involved selection and grooming and considerable preparation. It was like a big, very promising date. The rigid, awkward-sounding structure of the harem is summed up by the fact that the **Valide Sultan** – the sultan's mother – was usually responsible for selecting and instructing women for her son, and was always quite aware of what he was getting up to.

Harem Hearsay

- Eunuchs were, it is said, selected for their ugliness.
- Women in the private harems of young heirs and rivals to the throne were forbidden to bear any children. The concubine of a prince or aspirant to the throne who showed signs of pregnancy was sentenced to death.
- Harem women were executed – sometimes by the hundreds with the ascendance of a new sultan – by being tied in bags and thrown in the Bosphorous.
- Circassian women, from the Caucasus in the northeast, were usually considered the most beautiful and formed the core of the harem population.

Some historians trace the decline of the Ottoman Empire to 1558, when Süleyman the Magnificent was manipulated by his wife, Roxelana – a member of the harem – to have his son Mustafa assassinated. Mustafa was at the time governor of northern Anatolia, a favorite of the Janissaries, and a robust, intelligent leader. His death, combined with that of another son, Beyazid, left the path clear for Roxelana's own son to become Sultan Selim II. He proved a very poor one, and the Ottoman decline began. Roxelana is famous for her influence on Süleyman, and she was the first wife of a sultan to live within Topkapı Palace. After Roxelana, wives and harem members continued living at the palace, where they became heavily embroiled in palace intrigues. Roxelana's conspiracy against the stepbrothers of her son was the first time the mother of a prince helped arrange the murders of her son's rivals, but it was not to be the last.

You emerge from the Harem tour in the third court (see the Third Court, below).

Elsewhere in the Second Court of Topkapı

Back in the second court, in the likely event you have some time before your Harem Tour, you should stop in at the **Imperial Council** chambers around the corner from the Harem. Renovation of the Imperial Council rooms were completed in 1996, and you can see parts of the original reliefs that decorated the interiors and exteriors, together with painted recreations. It was in this council chamber that the Sultan's top advisors deliberated literally under the watchful eye of the sultan, who eavesdropped on meetings of the **Divan** (Council) from an grilled area high in the wall. On Mondays and Thursdays the main Topkapı tower looming above the council chambers is open from 11 a.m. to 2 p.m., but there is a $1.50 charge next to the harem tour booth.

The **Imperial Council** chambers are further toward the west wall. Renovation of the Imperial Council rooms were completed in 1996, and you can see parts of the original reliefs that decorated the interiors and exteriors, together with painted recreations. It was in this council chamber that the Sultan's top advisors deliberated literally under the watchful eye of the sultan, who eavesdropped on meetings of the **Divan** (Council) from an grilled area high in the wall. On Mondays and Thursdays the main tower of Topkapı, the Divan Tower, is open for guided tours. There are only occasional tours on those days, between 11 a.m. to 2 p.m., costing $2. You'll want to inquire about these guided tours when you get tickets for the harem.

The **Imperial Treasury**, just beyond the council chambers, are now used as a museum of weapons. If you have a teen-age boy along, make a beeline for this place. The Janissaries once assembled in the second court to receive their quarterly wages from this hall, and it was often arranged that payday would coincide with important state visits. In the heyday of the Empire, outsiders would witness thousands of the intricately dressed imperial guards waiting in eerie, disciplined silence to receive their gold and pay allegiance to their Sultan. It is said to have made quite an impression. Today the treasury is filled with standards, maces, swords, armor, spears, rifles, and other wicked-looking paraphernalia dating from the 7th century onward. Most of the weapons are Ottoman era, including the extremely accurate Turkish war bows (tirkeş). The weapons range from the practical to the artful, with earlier Ottoman weaponry, like earlier Ottomans, being practical and particularly impressive.

On the far side of the courtyard beneath long rows of cylindrical chimneys, you'll find the palace kitchens, an original feature of the palace that was enlarged and modified – partially by the master architect Sinan in the late 16th century. The kitchens are often overlooked in the face of so much wealth and beauty, but they add a wonderful human element. More than 4,000 people are estimated to have lived on the palace grounds, many of whom expected to eat very well. Truth is, it's easier – if less fun – to identify with the harried palace cooks laboring over their massive pots and preparing exotic meats and pastries than it is to identify with the sultans.

In addition to standard cooking items, the Topkapı kitchens are now filled with display cases bearing porcelains from around the world – including Süleyman's pet collection of Chinese celadon. Other rooms have glassware and appropriately oversized kitchen utensils.

The **Imperial Council** chambers are further toward the west wall. Renovation of the Imperial Council rooms were completed in 1996, and you can see parts of the original reliefs that decorated the interiors and exteriors, together with painted recreations. It was in this council chamber that the Sultan's top advisors deliberated literally under the watchful eye of the sultan, who eavesdropped on meetings of the **Divan** (Council) from an grilled area high in the wall. On Mondays and Thursdays the main tower of Topkapı, the Divan Tower, is open for guided tours. There are only occasional tours on those days, between 11 a.m. to 2 p.m.

The **Imperial Treasury**, just beyond the council chambers, are now used as a museum of weapons. If you have a teen-age boy along, make a beeline for this place. The Janissaries once assembled in the second court to receive their quarterly wages from this hall, and it was often arranged that payday would coincide with important state visits. In the Empire's heyday, outsiders would witness thousands of the intricately dressed imperial guard waiting in eerie, disciplined silence to receive their gold and pay allegiance to their sultan. It is said to have made quite an impression. Today the treasury is full of standards, maces, swords, armor, spears, rifles, and other wicked-looking paraphenalia from the 7th century onward. Most of the weapons are Ottoman era, including the extremely accurate Turkish war bows (tirkeş). Take a look at the impressive swords carried by Mehmet the Conqueror and Süleyman the Magnificent.

The Third Court of Topkapı

The harem tour empties out at a corner of the third court, not far from the main gate, the **Gate of Felicity**. The interior of this court was given over to, of all things, lots of teenage boys. These were the non-Muslim youths harvested from throughout Ottoman lands in the devişirme to become Janissaries, administering and protecting the empire. Many of the younger boys attended school in the long buildings to either side of the gate, thereafter graduating to the military, administrative, and finance schools, or, in the case of the most promising, the Sultan's personal staff. The **White Eunuchs** were charged with teaching and administering the boys, and they ruled in this court as the Black Eunuchs ruled within the harem.

Directly inside the gate is the **Audience Hall**. This building was an audience chamber and nothing more, and the rebuilding and modifications as late as 1860 have only slightly altered the simple structure. The hall was an original feature of the palace, and the throne within dates to the 16th century. Foreign embassies were occasionally received here, although appearances by the Grand Vizier and Ottoman nobles were far more common.

Just beyond the Audience Hall is the small **Library (Kutuphane) of Sultan Ahmet III**. This is now empty of books, but it retains good tilework and is a fine, quiet building. Oddly, the books have reappeared at the mosque of the White Eunuchs, the Enderun Mosque, just to the left of the Third Court. This buildling is now used as a library for special research projects, and is closed to the public.

What you really want to see is further along the west wall past the old mosque building, the **Privy Chambers**. Until the Republic, few but the Sultan and the Grand Mufti had entered the Privy Chambers, and even the Sultan and his Imam came hither only once every year, on the Night of Power during Ramazan. At that time, the two men would enter this sanctuary and pay respects to Mohammed.

Sultan Selim I (the Grim) contributed greatly to this collection during successful campaigns that brought Mecca, Medina, Jerusalem, and Cairo under the Ottoman Empire. In the large entrance room is the Door of the Great Mosque in Mecca, the staff of Moses, a scale model of Jerusalem's Dome of the Rock, several Kaaba keys, meticulous copies of the Koran, and other Islamic artifacts such as the swords of the Caliphs. Another small room to the left rear of the entrance room contains more relics, but the holiest relics are in the room at the right front of the entrance room.

There, even on the busiest summer day you will notice a hush within. In this room are some of the most prized possessions in the Islamic world; the swords and bow of Mohammed, his footprint, his seal, and soil from his tomb. Also here, a mixture of the holy and the macabre, are hairs from the beard of Mohammed and one of his teeth. This makes one wonder about the theological consequences of cloning. Holier still are the items in the closed area to the side of this room, the Holy Mantle and the Holy Standard. The standard was raised when the Ottoman army went to war with the Christian infidels in the west or the Shi'ite heretics to the south and east.

Leaving the Privy Chambers, you pass an open stair that leads to the Fourth Court. If you bypass this for the moment, the next room in your clockwise path contains a variety of calligraphic inscriptions and Ottoman miniatures. Further along are three adjoining rooms that are now used as the treasury of Topkapı. These rooms are, appropriately, stocked with a splendid array of Imperial wealth – thrones, weapons, and jewelry. There is also a huge collection of precious stones, including the **Spoonmaker's Diamond**, an 86 carat stone found in the ruins of the old Byzantine Palace by a spoon maker, who sold it for a pittance. If that fails to impress, have a look at the emerald that weighs in at almost seven pounds.

Another curiosity is the forearm of St. John the Baptist, a desiccated old piece of bone partially gilt in gold. Creepy. Together with the armory and the holy relics, the treasury highlights the visit to Topkapı. The final room in this court, in the southeast corner, has a collection of imperial robes and clothing.

The Fourth Court of Topkapı

The deepest interior of Topkapı is not dark and mysterious, rather it is a terraced set of gardens overlooking the sea. Sultans would retire here during the day with chosen friends, relaxing in the pavilions that dot the court. Make your way up the flight of stairs to the large landing looking westward at the Golden Horn.

Here you'll find the Revan Kösk, commemorating the 1635 victory of the cruel and mercurial Sultan Murat IV over the Persians at Yerevan in modern Armenia. Another jewel of this terrace is the Sunnet Kösk, or **Circumcision Hall**, built by Sultan İbrahim in the 1640s. The İznik tilework here is what all the fuss is about; this faience is older than the structure itself, dating to the 16th century heyday of the masters at the İznik tile kilns.

The view from the terrace takes in many of the great monuments of the city; marching from left to right along the horizon of the peninsula you'll see the Beyazid Mosque above the Grand Bazaar, the Beyazid Fire Tower, the Suleimaniye Mosque, the Fatih Mosque (above the New Mosque by the Golden Horn), and, off in the distance, Mihrimah Mosque by the city walls.

Back down the stairs you pass the kiosk once occupied by the Sultan's personal physician, the **Hekimbaşı Odası**, or Physician's Room. The lower gardens had their moment of glory during the "Reign of the Tulip" under Ahmet III in the 1720s. This was one of the first times the empire looked beyond its borders and acknowledged the value of budding western institutions such as the printing press and heavy industry. Tulips, having made their way from Persia to Holland years before, became a concrete, if random, expression of the new interest. Sultan Ahmet III took a great interest in cultivating tulips, and the Ottoman elite gamely followed their Sultan's lead and pitched themselves headfirst into arts in general and the cultivation of tulips in particular. These gardens were filled with rare and valuable tulips, and of an evening the Sultan and his retinue would take dinner in the Fourth Court, the tulips lit by turtles bearing candles.

On the east side of the court, below the upper garden, the **Mecidiye Köskü** is raised on a marble terrace overlooking the Bosphorous and the Sea of Marmara. This was the last addition to the palace, and its architecture presages the Dolmabahçe Palace, built several years later by Sultan Abdül Mecit I. **Konyalı restaurant** is licensed to operate on the patio at the Mecidiye Köskü, and does a bustling business to tour groups. You'll find the setting wonderful, but there's likely to be a crowd and the food is expensive and of middling quality. The alternative is a walk all the way back out to the restaurant garden of the **Yeşil Ev** if you're in the mood for something nice, or to **Sultanahmet Köftecesi** if you're in the mood for something good, basic and, above all, cheap.

ARCHAEOLOGICAL MUSEUM, ANCIENT ORIENT MUSEUM, & ÇINLI KÖSK

The entrance to the Archaelogical Museum compound is just within and uphill of Gülhane tram stop inside the outer Topkapı Palace walls. The entrance is also accessible from Topkapı's First Court, below and behind the Hagia Irene Church. A single fee ($2) covers entrance to all of the buildings within the museum complex, *Tel. 212 520 7740* – although the Cinli Kösk and the Ancient Orient Museums have erratic schedules and are often closed. You'll find coffee served in a perfect little outdoor garden opposite the doors of the Archeaological Museum, thick with statues; it's a peaceful place to which you can retire in the heat of the day.

The entrance to the **Museum of the Ancient Orient** is immediately to the left as you enter, flanked by massive Hittite Lions. The collection here is arranged in such a way as to help clarify the history in Asia Minor. Among its most significant relics is the Treaty of Qadesh, a peace accord between the Hittite King Muwatallis and the Egyptian Pharoah Ramses II dating to the 13th century B.C. It is the oldest known peace agreement. A recreation of the avenue leading to the gates at Babylon is also on hand, an impressive entry to a city that Herodotus reported as having walls the height of a football field (he phrased it differently.)

The **Archaeological Museum** (the columned building stretched along the right side of the court) is the finest museum of antiquities in Turkey, and contains one of the most complete collection of pieces from Asia Minor in the world. Suffice it to say that upon entering the museum you are met by a giant statue of **Beş**, "Half God of Inexhaustible Power and Strength and Protection against Evil." Beş was certainly tough looking, anyway; he was the legendary equivalent of Hercules for natives of the eastern Mediterranean. For most visitors the highlight of a visit to the Archaeological Museum is the **Alexander Sarcophagus**, so called not because it was Alexander's sarcophagus – an artifact that remains unfound – but because of the elaborate decoration of Alexander's exploits on the exterior. The sarcophagus belonged to Abdalonymous, a King of Sidon in modern Lebanon, who was clearly quite impressed by the young Macedonian conqueror and revelled in his association with him.

The other attractions in the Archaeological Museum are many and extremely varied; curators have collected 50,000 artifacts here over the last century, since ancient people were like absentminded dogs, forever burying things and losing track of them.

The displays are orderly and well-captioned, particularly the excellent new section concerning the history of İstanbul. This is an interesting and remarkably lucid tour through the history of the city, offering relics from every one of the city's many ages. The curators have also erected a full scale reproduction of the Doric temple at Assos.

Within the Archaeological Museum is a room devoted to **Hamdi Bey**, the founder of the museum. This remarkable man pioneered Turkish archaeology as it is practiced today. He was the first scientist to study Nemrut Dağı and was responsible for the dig at Sidon that turned up the Alexander Sarcophagus. Colorful stories surround the crusty old archaeologist who so fiercely protected his ancient discoveries; worried that the delicate Alexander Sarcophagus would be damaged in transit, Hamdi Bey lashed himself to the massive stone object as it was hauled onto a ship.

The **Çinli Köşkü**, housed in the elaborate building opposite the Archaeological Museum, serves today as a museum of tile and ceramics. The building dates back to Mehmet II Fatih, who, like those after him, was prone to retire here during the day. Stories tell of Mehmet II whiling away the time watching princes and pages play a game called cırıt. Participants would gallop around on horses hurling javelins at one another and catching those directed at themselves. And in North America people complain that monkey bars are dangerous.

THE HAGIA SOPHIA

The least charitable description of the **Hagia Sophia** must belong to Mark Twain: "The rustiest old barn in heathendom." Most people fall over themselves in search of the proper superlative; the Hagia Sophia has, for 1,500 years, been one of the greatest works of architecture on Earth.

The Hagia Sophia, *Tel. 212 522 1750,* dominates the head of the old city peninsula, a looming jumble of domes and buttresses capped by one massive dome. The Hagia Sophia is the centerpiece of Sultanahmet, and the entrance is by the park at the bottom of Divan Yolu Caddesi.

History

The Hagia Sophia (Divine Wisdom) is the third Christian church built on this site. The first two were relatively short-lived. The first church was built by the son of Constantine the Great just 30 years after the dedication of Constantinople, but was destroyed by rioting just 44 years later in 404 A.D. The second church was dedicated in 415 A.D., but this building was destroyed in the 532 A.D. Nika Revolt that marred the beginning of Emperor Justinian's reign.

Both of the early Hagia Sophia churches are reported to have been elegant structures and centerpieces of the new Roman capital. They were conventional beauties, however, and the young Justinian had more ambitious plans for rebuilding the church. He set the mathematician Anthemius of Tralles on the task, assisted by another mathematician, Isodorus of Miletus, and the two men conceived a structure that took architecture to new figurative and literal heights. We can only assume the ever-industrious emperor was himself surprised when his designers presented plans for the new Hagia Sophia: 182 feet high, more than 24,000 square feet in area, with a dome greater than 100 feet in diameter. The nave, or open area below the dome, extends 262 feet in length, 100 feet across.

A recitation of these statistics hardly does the Hagia Sophia justice; it was a quantum leap in architecture at the time, not rivaled for a thousand years. Even those grand churches that came later – such as St. Peter's in Rome, one of the few edifices with a greater open area than the Hagia Sophia – are felt to lack the Hagia Sophia's soaring aesthetic.

For five years Isodorus supervised construction of the church – Anthemius died early in its construction. The design was mathematically sound, but in attempting such an unprecedented engineering feat the devil was in the details: hollow bricks had to be created for the towering dome, artisans from throughout the world had to be collected and persuaded to ornament the interior, great quantities of marble had to be quarried.

The Hagia Sophia was dedicated on December 26, 537, only six years after the former church was destroyed. Guests at that dedication, including Justinian, were awed by both the scale and the beauty of the new church. Justinian is quoted as gloating, *"O Solomon, I have outdone you."* The interior was faced with marble and ornate mosaics glimmered in the light of thousands of candles. No doubt the pious must have felt their belief in God confirmed, and the less-than-pious must have had some misgivings.

The cathedral had a strong hint of magic about it, but this was temporarily dispelled after earthquakes shook down the dome and the semi-dome above the apse less than 20 years after it was unveiled. Justinian lived to see his church repaired by Isidorus, a nephew of the original designer, and reopened on Christmas Eve 563. Justinian died a year later.

For the Byzantines the church was ever and always an inspiration, and Christians of every stripe traveled from around the world to see it for themselves and worship here. When the Latins took Constantinople, they worshipped here, and when the Turks took the city in Spring of 1453 it was to the Hagia Sophia that the panicked citizens fled.

According to the account of Michael Ducas, the citizens of Constantinople had retreated here in "unmeasurable multitude. And shutting the gate they stood there fervently hoping for deliverance by the angel [see below]. Then – fighting all about, killing, taking prisoners – the Turks came to the church, when the first hour of the day was not yet flown. And when they found the doors shut, they battered them with axes, without compunction." Forcing their way in, the Ottomans subdued the Greeks, then lashed them together and marched them away. The Patriarch, according to legend, chose this moment to vanish into the walls of the Hagia Sophia; various legends indicate that he will return either on the Day of Judgment or when İstanbul is returned to the Greeks.

It was later on the day after the fall of the city that Sultan Mehmet II entered Constantinople, riding directly to the Hagia Sophia. The conquering sultan wasted no time, issuing immediate orders that the church be converted to a mosque, and in that hour an imam intoned a Muslim prayer in the great hall. Workers set about soaking up the blood and cleansing and fumigating the Christian edifice that it might be rendered a suitable mosque. In later years the mihrab, mimber, and details such as the two Proconnesean marble water urns were introduced to complete the transformation to a mosque.

The Hagia Sophia was held in high esteem, the foremost mosque in the city even when Ottoman-built marvels such as the Süleymaniye and the Sultanahmet Mosques drew admirers of their own. One man who clearly spent substantial time studying this building was the master architect **Sinan**, who drew countless lessons from the structure and helped the Ottomans make a quantum leap in mosque design. Sinan was also among those who performed renovations on the old building, correcting earthquake damage and reinforcing weak areas. The minarets alongside the Hagia Sophia were erected piecemeal beginning with the northeast minaret.

Emperor Justinian

The **Emperor Justinian** must be considered one of history's most ambitious men. His long reign, 527-565, assured that his empire came into conflict with all of its many neighbors, and Justinian's generals were largely successful in pursuing his policy of restoring the former Roman empire. The emperor carefully sought to balance negotiation with the use of military force, now securing peace with the Persians to conquer the Ostrogoths and Vandals in Africa, now pacifying the Africans to deal with the Goth Totila in the west. All the while, however, enemies in the north preyed on the frontiers, taking advantage of weakness when the Byzantine army was engaged far off. The challenge was colossal, and although Justinian doubled the extent of his lands, he is judged to have ultimately weakened the empire.

The **Hagia Sophia**, Justinian's most enduring legacy, can be viewed as a testament to his visionary excesses. When Justinian came to power, the court historian Procopius reports that his predecessor had a vast reserve – 320,000 pounds of gold. Justinian dug into this reserve early and often, funding his wars (and ransoming an expensive peace with Persia), paying for civil projects such as the Hagia Sophia, the Basilica of St. John in Ephesus – even churches in newly conquered lands such as the Church of St. Vitale in Ravenna – and subsidizing fortifications throughout the empire. Ringed by enemies, Justinian had no choice in this final matter, and outposts were erected along the ever expanding frontiers of Africa, Europe, and Asia. The problem with Justinian's ambitious growth was that the gold reserve and the revenue from new territories fell far short of matching his overwhelming expenses. Justinian's recourse was simple and traditional; he burdened Byzantine citizens with heavy taxes that sapped the wealth and strength of the empire. Procopius, in a secret biography of Justinian, saw the damage the emperor was doing and referred to Justinian as "a demon in human shape."

Justinian's reign ended in 565, with the emperor 83 years old. At his death Byzantium was in full flower, having assumed a shape very similar to the Ottoman Empire at its zenith 1,000 years later, but its decline was already assured. The hold on Byzantium's western lands was tenuous. In some instances, peace was secured through tribute money, which was, ironically, coming at the expense of the poorly paid Byzantine soldiery. The empire was ripe for collapse, and, sure enough, Italy was overrun within four years of Justinian s death and the newly constructed frontier fortresses throughout Europe were soon in enemy hands.

Worse, Justinian's preoccupation with restoring the classic Roman empire in the west had left Persia to grow ever mightier in the east – helped along, again, by an annual tribute from Byzantium. Surging out of the east, one Persian force captured Jerusalem in 614, pushing on into Egypt, while a second marched through the whole of Asia Minor, encamping opposite Constantinople at Scutari. In the chaos, Mohammed, born five years after Justinian's death, galvanized the Arabs with a new religion that would in time be Constantinople's undoing. In the words of one historian, commenting on post-Justinian Byzantium, "There is perhaps no period of history in which society was so universally in a state of demoralization."

The latest chapter in the long history of the Hagia Sophia began in 1932, when Kemal Atatürk declared that the mosque would be converted to a museum. Art historians descended on the site, searching for figurative mosaics under the plaster, and discovered many in fine condition. Now, 1,450 years after the Hagia Sophia opened, it continues to dazzle a world grown used to skyscrapers and large-scale projects. That this building should still be standing is miraculous, given that it advanced so far beyond the engineering of its time. The designers of the building, Anthemius and Isidorus, must be considered two of the most visionary architects in world history.

Seeing the Hagia Sophia

You enter the grounds of the Hagia Sophia through a gate to the left of the square, paying at the ticket booth and first passing into a small garden. A smattering of columns and stone ornaments from the church are located here, as is the foundation of the former Hagia Sophia.

The first room you enter is the long, slender exonarthex along the northwest side. This opens into the **narthex**, a broader room where the first of the museum's many mosaics are found. The most famous of these mosaics is directly above the Imperial Gate – formerly said to be carved from the wood of the Ark. Christ's right hand is raised in a common sign, thumb to ring finger, identifying him as an Orthodox Christ offering a blessing: upon the book is written *"Peace upon you, for I am the light of the world."* The prostrate figure at Christ's feet is an probably an emperor named Leo VI (886-912), called "the Wise." Leo's wisdom led him to enact volumes and volumes of laws, one of which condemned the evils of third marriages. Leo, his own wives dying with suspicious rapidity, went on to have third, then fourth marriages. In this hypocrisy Leo was opposed by the Patriarch, who Leo promptly let go.

After a brief investigation of the narthex, you enter the nave, or main chamber, through the Imperial Gate. As you pass through the entrance once reserved for the Emperor and his party the Hagia Sophia opens before you, looming higher and higher. The visitor's first reaction is to the sheer scale of the interior. Architects continue to debate the merits of the world's great holy places, but many continue to maintain that the effect of the Hagia Sophia is still unmatched. The great dome's size is a marvel, achieved only with the help of light, hollow bricks and succeeding in giving the impression that it was hung from heaven by a thread.

The interior is especially striking, architects say, by virtue of the two supporting semi-domes. These partial domes open the space lengthwise (from the Imperial Gate to the apse at the front of the church), and reveal the immense dome to the visitor. Unlike later buildings that hold the dome aloft with massive piers, the designers chose to help distribute the weight with two long rows of columns on the bottom floor, and second rows lining the galleries. The towering series of columns on the lower level curtains the side aisles of the basilica.

The exterior of the Hagia Sophia is imposing, but spare. A quick glimpse at the interior reveals that the starkness ends at the door. Intricately executed stonework is on display throughout the space, marble seamlessly joined and precisely cut. The inverted bowl-shaped column capitals are elaborately carved, many of them with a round seal containing stylized insignias attributed to Justinian and the Empress Theodora. Even without the crusting of jewels and gold stripped by the Crusaders in 1204, even without the glittering mosaics that once covered the entire upper section of the basilica, even without thousands of flickering candles, the Hagia Sophia is beautiful in its detail as well as in its soaring structure.

The massive wooden **levhas**, six gold-on-black disks bearing calligraphic writing, were not installed until an 1849 renovation. The six levhas depict the names of Allah and Mohammed, as well as the first four caliphs: Abu Bakir, Omar, Othman, and Ali. An attempt was made to remove these disks after the Hagia Sophia was converted to a museum, but workers found themselves unable to squeeze the levhas through the doors. Unwilling to destroy the disks, the supervisors returned them to their places.

On the floor of the mosque are the other major Ottoman-era additions. The small raised kiosk to the left is the **Sultan's Loge**, an area reserved for the prayers of the sultan alone. This was built by Sultan Ahmet III (1703-1730), he of the tulips and turtles bearing candles. The **mihrab**, the small recessed niche facing Mecca, is located in the apse, squared with the rectangular **mahfili** at angle on the main floor of the nave. This kiosk was built for the muezzin singers. The four minarets outside were raised during the reigns of various sultans, the first soon after Sultan Mehmet II's seizure of the city.

One of the most interesting of the Byzantine features is the circle within a square inlaid on the floor of the nave. This is the oddly asymmetric site of coronations and other signal events involving the imperial personage.

Several of the mosaics in the main chamber are now visible. On the vaulted ceiling of the apse, in the front of the church, is a depiction of Mary and Christ. This image was groundbreaking, accompanied by an inscription heralding the reintroduction of mosaics at the Hagia Sophia after the supporters of icons defeated the iconoclasts in a Byzantine civil war. The Archangel Gabriel flutters to one side, also within the apse, while the Archangel Michael, to the left, is in poor condition.

High atop the nave, on two of the four pedentives – the flat-faced seams below the main dome and in the seams between the semi-domes – are mosaics of angels. To the left of the main floor are three sainted Byzantine bishops, from the apse to the back of the church, Ignatius Theophorous, John Chrysostom, and Ignatius the Younger.

Before leaving the nave, stop at the weeping column near the back of the left aisle. The column's lower section is clad in bronze, and someone will probably have a digit stuck in it. The weeping column continues to draw people seeking fertility and simple good luck.

According to one tale, an angel appeared here during a lull in the construction and ordered a boy to run off and return with his father and fellow workers. The boy scurried away to retrieve the workers, but his father cleverly forbade the boy ever to return to the church. The angel waits there still, benevolently haunting the Hagia Sophia forever. The angel, according to the story, blesses anyone who shoves their thumb in the hole in this column. It isn't necessarily enough, however, just to stick your thumb in the hole; these days it's also fashionable to twist your hand around one way, then the other, so that your fingers make a complete circle around the pivoting thumb. There's usually moisture in this hole, and no wonder, with everyone shoving their sweaty thumbs in there.

The Galleries of Hagia Sophia

Leaving the nave through one of the doors near the weeping column, turn right in the narthex and begin ascending the ramp at the narthex's end. This ramp spirals its uneven way upward to the galleries where the basilica's finest mosaics are located. You emerge in the north gallery, which extends along the left wall to the front of the church.

The galleries were the exclusive preserve of women in some periods, in others they were reserved for the imperial family. On one of the great piers in the north gallery is a mosaic of Alexander (912-913), a man content to while away his time accomplishing nothing at all. This suited his almost lifelong role as brother to the emperor (shades of Billy Carter and Roger Clinton), but became a distinct problem when his brother Leo VI (886-912) died. Alexander's listless and truculent rule created problems that would plague the empire for decades – and he managed this in a single year, after which he toppled from a horse and died. At the end of the north gallery, directly beside the apse at the front of the church, is a screen behind which emperors and ladies would sit.

In the central area of the gallery, at the back of the church above the **Imperial Door**, is a distinctive circle of green marble. This was the seat of the empress Theodora, echoing the circle of her emperor husband on the main floor.

Continuing around to the south gallery you arrive at an ornate stone screen. The purpose of this screen is unknown, but it may have been used to bar access to Church synods. Just beyond the screen in an open area to the right is the best preserved mosaic visible to the public. Christ is shown in the company of an aggrieved St. John the Baptist and Mary. This mosaic, known as the **Deisis**, clearly benefits from perspective lacking in so many Byzantine mosaics, dating it to the 13th century or later. Christ is offering an Orthodox blessing with his hand, and his eyes appear somewhat sad and thoughtful.

No wonder, he looks across the hall to the place where the Doge of Venice, **Henricus Dandalo**, was buried. Dandalo, representing Venice in the Fourth Crusade, was the driving force behind the sack and seizure of Constantinople in 1204. He lived only a single year after taking the city, and chose the Hagia Sophia as his resting place. One story holds that his body remained entombed here until the arrival of the Ottomans in 1453, and that it was the Muslims who opened his tomb and scattered his bones to the dogs; if that is the case then the Deisis was executed with the Venetian's body in place. Perhaps a more likely story is that it was the Greeks who, upon regaining their city in 1261, opened the tomb of the man who had sacked their city, enslaved and killed their people, and looted their church, and perhaps it was the Greeks who scattered his bones to the dogs. This also would cast an interesting light on the Deisis, whose Christ might be demonstrating somber approval. The inscribed lid of Dandalo's tomb has been restored to its former place.

Take a moment to note the mosaics peeking from beneath thick plaster in some sections of the gallery vaults; the ceilings here were formerly covered with mosaic patterns, and some remain covered with plaster. Continuing to the very front of the gallery you arrive at the gallery's final mosaics. To the left, closest to the apse, is a depiction of **Constantine IX** (1042-1055) and **Empress Zoe** (1028-1050). There are conflicting stories about Zoe, but it is clear she led a long and eventful life. Zoe was the heir to Constantine VIII (1025-1028), who had no sons. The elderly Constantine gave his 51 year old daughter to her aristocratic suitor **Romanus III Argyrus** (1028-1034). This was commemorated on the wall of the Hagia Sophia. Unfortunately, Romanus the diligent suitor became Romanus the neglectful husband, and, soon afterward, Romanus became dead in his own bathtub.

Now Zoe elevated her juvenile lover Michael (now Michael IV, 1034-1041) to the throne, fixing his face on the body of Romanus in the Hagia Sophia. Michael proved a competent ruler but, once again, an inattentive husband once he had secured the throne. Zoe was watched and kept at arms length, and she was banished entirely when Michael IV died of illness. Upset with her banishment, the Patriarch joined forces with the aristocracy to depose a new emperor and return the throne to the blood princess, the 65 year old Zoe, together with her younger sister Theodora.

Once more a marriage was arranged for Zoe, this time with Constantine IX. Now the mosaic of Romanus was given Constantine's head. Zoe died eight years later.

To the right of this mosaic is another of Mary and Christ, flanked by John II Comnenus (1118-1143) and his wife Eirene. The prince, Alexius, is squeezed into a tight space on the right. Alexius died at a young age, but his father was a capable and intelligent ruler.

Now return through the gallery and down the ramp, appreciating the grandeur of this building. When you decide to leave, exit through the

Hagia Sophia Mosaics

When the Hagia Sophia was originally opened in 537, the interior – including the domes, semidomes, narthex, and galleries – was almost entirely clad in mosaic tile, which, illuminated by thousands of candles, created a darkly golden second sky. Today only a few of the mosaics are visible in the old church, many of them having come to intentional harm.

Earthquakes aside, the most terrible damage to the mosaics happened at the hands of the Byzantines themselves. Following an edict by Leo III (717-741), icons were banned throughout the empire, and workers undertook to destroy images of people and animals. This was much deeper than a question of aesthetics: blood was spilled over the issue and it helped spark civil war. The work was undone after the Iconoclast period came to an end (843) and new images were created – all of the figurative images in the church were, therefore, executed after 843. The church returned to its former glory, although the decline of the Byzantine Empire resulted in a concomitant decline in the Byzantines' great church.

The arrival of the Ottomans in 1453, then, was something of a blessing. The Ottomans were ill at ease with the icons within the Hagia Sophia, but respected the great building. In accordance with the Muslim prohibition against icons the Ottomans covered the offending images, showing remarkable restraint in light of the damage done by the Christian Iconoclasts. At the same time, the vigor of the new empire meant that the church was given much-needed renovation, much of it by Sinan.

Following the conversion of the Hagia Sophia from a mosque to a museum by Kemal Atatürk in 1935, restoration efforts – already under way – accelerated. All of the mosaics visible today have been rediscovered and revealed in this century. Other mosaics, many of them simply of geometric shapes and patterns, remain hidden beneath plaster and paint – you will see parts of mosaic through holes cut in the plaster of the south gallery vaults.

Melville on the Hagia Sophia

Herman Melville visited in 1857, and had this to say:
"Saw the Mosque of St. Sophia. Went in. Rascally priests demanding "bakshesh." Fleeced me out of one half dollar; following me round, selling the fallen mosaics. Ascended a kind of horse way leading up, round and round. Came out into a gallery fifty feet above the floor. Superb interior. Precious marbles Porphyry and Verd antique. Immense magnitude of the building. Names of the prophets in great letters. Roman Catholic air to the whole."

door in the narthex opposite the ramp. This exit was the original entrance to the Hagia Sophia. The small chamber separating the narthex from the outside is adorned with a mosaic of two emperors making an offering to Mary and Christ, one, Justinian, offering the Hagia Sophia, the other, Constantine, offering the city itself. This mosaic was probably done during the reign of the great and ruthless Basil II the Bulgar Slayer (926-1025), and is remarkable because Basil II didn't insist on a mosaic of himself.

Exiting the Hagia Sophia, you enter a small **forecourt** filled with smaller buildings. Five sultans are buried here. Mustafa I and İbrahim, both known as " the mad," warranted respectable burials but not türbes of their own; they were laid to rest in the former Orthodox baptistry building. This is the first building to the left. Selim II (1566-1574), Murat III (1574-1595) and Mehmet IV (1623-1640) are buried in their own türbe in this section.

YEREBATAN CISTERN

The cistern is perfect on a summer afternoon, a cool, dark spot in the midst of the pandemonium of Sultanahmet. **Yerebatan Cistern** is located just across the street from the Hagia Sophia, in a low building near the ruined outline of the former **Milion**, or first milepost of Byzantium. *The offices can be reached at Tel. 212 522 1259.*

The cistern dates back to Byzantium, but the current, massive incarnation was built during the reign of Justinian (527-565 A.D.), incorporating pillars and other artifacts from elsewhere in the empire. A total of 336 pillars support the cistern's towering roof, and wide walkways have been installed that permit you to wander through the vast subterranean space.

The cistern fell into disuse during the Ottoman Empire, and was not discovered again until this century. A curious scholar went in search of a great cistern in the region, and discovered it by lowering himself through a hole in the basement of a local residence. The cistern was, predictably, a shambles, but its four meter-thick walls continued to be waterproof. No one knew just how far the subterranean waterways went, and there was a great air of mystery about the structure until its rehabilitation in the 1980s. Herman Melville, visiting in the mid-1800s, noted the eerie, dark interior and commented that it would be a "terrible place to be robbed or murdered in." Finally cleared out and opened, the cistern is an inspiring sight – note that a section of about 50 columns remains walled off. Chamber music is piped in, and there is a small cafe. Keep your eyes peeled for fish in the shallow water.

Midway through the cistern is a weeping column, very much like the weeping column in the Hagia Sophia. As at the Hagia Sophia, you can insert your thumb into the wishing hole on the column and twist your hand around one way, then the other in a complete circle to make a wish. Some people, skeptical of this, just chuck coins in the water nearby. The Medusa heads at the very rear of the cistern are a mystery. They may have come from anywhere – Justinian's engineers were great recyclers, particularly of Chalcedonian material from across the Bosphorous. Why they were used as column bases, one upside down, the other sideways, deep in the recesses of a cistern is anyone's guess. You can still see the snake-hair on one of the Medusa heads.

Finally, according to rumors, a few people once knew the devious subterranean routes into Topkapı Saray, using the Cistern as their entrance. Among the business conducted were rare, and presumably dangerous, abductions from the Seraglio.

Admission to the cistern costs $1.50. The Yerebatan Cistern is located at the intersection of Yerebatan Caddesi and Divan Yolu, next to the tram line and across the street from the Hagia Sophia.

The **Binbirdirek Cistern**, or Cistern of 1,001 Columns, is located behind the Palace of İbrahim Paşa. This cavernous old reservoir is also filled with columns, and at the time of this writing it is being converted into a collection of shops. The new entrance is to the west of the Hippodrome, just left off of Divan Yolu Caddesi (the tram road) as you ascend. We're not yet able to determine if the renovation is a blessing or a curse.

THE HIPPODROME

Don't come to İstanbul hoping to see the **Hippodrome**; all that remains is the ground the Hippodrome once stood on. The Hippodrome today is a grassy park immediately in front of the Blue Mosque, but at one time it was a stadium holding almost 100,000 people for large sporting events and celebrations.

The building was erected by the Roman Emperor Septimius Severus (193-211) in the process of rebuilding the city that he had earlier razed to the ground during a military campaign. The most popular past-time here was chariot racing, and the old chariot course is still identifiable by the monuments that stood in its center. The city was desperately fanatical about the teams that raced at the Hippodrome, and over time team allegiance came to have strong political and social overtones.

The most vivid example was the Nika Revolt of 532, when the Greens – named for the livery of their charioteers – rioted against the policies of Emperor Justinian, himself a Blue. The rioters destroyed the Hagia Sophia and forced Justinian to consider fleeing, but in the end he stood firm at the behest of his wife Theodora. Justinian loosed his general Belisarius, who managed to hem the rioters into, appropriately, the Hippodrome. There the Byzantine army massacred as many as 30,000 people, ending the revolt.

All that remains of the grand stadium are the centerpieces. The stadium suffered through repeated fires, earthquakes, and even, it is reported, a hurricane, to which the indignity of the Crusader's looting was added in 1204 – the **Quadriga**, a statue of four horses that stood atop St. Mark's Cathedral in Venice until they were taken down for preservation in 1995, was stolen from here by the Crusaders. Although the Hippodrome survived into the Ottoman period, it had fallen into ruin. The collapsing edifice was finally closed and mined for stone, much of which was used in the construction of the Blue Mosque next door.

As you enter the open Hippodrome area from the direction of the tourism information booth and the Hagia Sophia, you arrive first at the peculiar **Fountain of Kaiser Wilhelm II**. Suffice it to say this wasn't a fixture of ancient Byzantium; it was introduced by the German Kaiser in the late 1800s as part of his campaign to promote German/Turkish unity and, more specifically, a German-built rail line through the Ottoman Empire to the Red Sea. This Hejaz Railway was completed in 1909 and destroyed piecemeal to great effect by the British agent T.E. Lawrence during World War I. Wilhelm was lodged in his two state visits, 1892 and 1901, at an early palace at Yıldız.

The fountain's location corresponds to the former northern end of the Hippodrome, which ran lengthwise around the current grassy arcade. The **Obelisk** is the next monument along this line – the oldest object in this ancient city, dating to the reign of Thutmose III in the 16th century B.C. The Obelisk remains in good condition, its hieroglyphs remarkably well preserved after 3,500 years of weathering. Thutmose III originally erected this obelisk at the temple of Karnak in present-day Luxor. The hieroglyphic reliefs depict the pharoah making offerings to the god Amon-Ra in thanks for a great victory in Syria and Mesopotamia.

What you see now is only the tip of the original obelisk, one which measured nearly 200 feet high. Even the erection of this modest section, a mere third of the original's size, posed a unique engineering problem almost 2,000 years later when it was shipped down the Nile and across to Constantinople. Finally, under Theodosius the Great (379-395) it was raised and set on the marble blocks you see today. These blocks depict Theodosius accepting tribute from the provinces, enjoying the races, congratulating the victor, and, ahem, helping erect the obelisk. The most interesting reliefs are those lower down, demonstrating how the Byzantines set about raising the great stone. Later obelisk thievery from the Luxor area has contributed to the decoration of Washington, D.C., Paris, and London.

Next along the former racecourse is the **Serpent Column**, a trophy from the great Greek victory at Plataea in 479 B.C. The battle was fought between the united Greeks and the army of Xerxes, whose gigantic army had set out from Persia, crossed bridges at the Dardanelles, and continued by land to Greece in 480 B.C. The vast Persian army – which numbered somewhat less than Herodotus' ridiculous estimate of 5 million – had plowed through Greek resistance to sack and occupy Athens.

Their only setbacks had been at sea, and there was an air of invincibility to their land army until the Greeks met them at Plataea in the second year of the occupation. The battle turned into a rout, and the Persians were forced into a panicked 1,000 mile withdrawal towards friendly territory.

The Greek trophy names the 31 cities that contributed soldiers to the battle, and was crafted from the shields of fallen Persian soldiers. The trophy originally stood at the Oracle of Delphi – which correctly prophesied Greek victory and, Herodotus reports, defended itself from sack by the Persians with lightning bolts and a hail of boulders. Constantine the Great (324-337) ran afoul of none of this, evidently, when he removed the trophy from the Oracle site and transported it to his new capital city. Perhaps some Oracular revenge was visited on the unknown vandal – historians suspect a drunken Polish diplomat – who sawed off the three snake heads in the 1700s, one of which was found a century later and placed in the İstanbul Archaeological Museum.

The final monument is the bedraggled-looking 100-foot **Colossus**. This monument was old and rickety when it was sheathed in bronze by the Byzantine Emperor Constantine VII Porphyrogenitus (913-959), but it seems to lack the pedigree of its fellows. It dates to, at the earliest, Constantine the Great's reign. Nowadays the bronze is gone again, and the Colossus' old bones are looking their age.

THE TURKISH AND ISLAMIC ARTS MUSEUM

Across the Hippodrome from the Blue Mosque is the **Palace of İbrahim Paşa**, *Meydanı No. 46, Tel. 212 518 1385*. The palace was built for one of Süleyman the Magnificent's Grand Viziers at the height of the Ottoman Empire's power. İbrahim came to power in 1523, one year before completion of his ambitious residence, and proved an able and intelligent adviser to Süleyman, his most trusted confidante and a brilliant general in the field. The friendship between the two men was deep, and remained so through most of İbrahim's thirteen year term.

In the end, Süleyman was turned against İbrahim – as he was later turned against two of his own sons – by intrigue within the palace, particularly from his jealous favorite within the harem, Haseki Hurrem, or Roxelana. After a private dinner İbrahim was strangled and buried in an unmarked grave, his estates and belongings confiscated by the throne. The palace, considered the grandest private residence in İstanbul, was converted to a Janissary dormitory.

The palace is now converted into the **Turkish and Islamic Arts Museum**, open from 10:00 a.m. to 5 p.m. and, like most places in the area, closed Mondays. The museum has a large collection of religious art, including engravings, tiles, and calligraphy, all of which is introduced by a video that runs through basic Turkish history. The lower floor is recommended for carpet/kilim shoppers; there, in the presence of old looms, you can learn the basics about dyes, fabrics, and styles – a much more relaxed place to learn than in a Sultanahmet carpet shop. The traditional Turkish coffee house on the premises offers caffeinated help if you're unravelling under the strain of jet-lag.

To the north of the museum, three blocks in from Divan Yolu Caddesi on Klodfarer Caddesi, is the **Binbirdirek Cistern**, akin to the Yerebatan Cistern near the Hagia Sophia – ask for directions on your way toward Divan Yolu Caddesi. Binbirdirek ("Thousand and One Columns") is an immense, dry cistern, with a few less columns than advertised.

THE BLUE MOSQUE

The **Blue Mosque**, as **Sultan Ahmet Cami** is known, is probably the most striking monument in İstanbul. Unlike the Hagia Sophia, with its austere and functional exterior, and the city's other mosques, most of which have been enveloped by the city, the Blue Mosque still commands the eye with its beauty and its open location.

The Blue Mosque is best approached from the Hippodrome and entered through the front gate opposite the Turkish and Islamic Arts Museum. This approach allows you to appreciate the heap of smaller domes ascending toward the great dome high above, and will almost yank the camera from around your neck and shoot the pictures for you. You enter through the spacious courtyard, which stands beneath what was once the eastern end of the Hippodrome, and approach the main doors (in the heavy tourist season you may be directed to the left side of the mosque, facing the Hagia Sophia, and enter there).

The Blue Mosque was one of the only true interests of its namesake, Sultan Ahmet I (1603-1617). Ahmet declined to go to war in Asia, sat by while palace intrigue blossomed, and allowed the Ottoman military to decay, but the young lad found plenty of time to lend his frail help at the building site. Beyond his enthusiasm for this beautiful mosque, Ahmet resolutely failed to distinguish himself in any way as a sultan. He died curiously young, at 27.

The Blue Mosque, designed by Davut Aga, was the first in the world outside of Mecca to have six minarets. This design drew condemnation from around the Muslim world until Davut Bey offered to construct a seventh minaret at Mecca. The Blue Mosque, so named for the colors in the interior tiles, not allegiance to a faction of Byzantine charioteers in the Hippodrome, stood on par with the Hagia Sophia in Ottoman esteem, and sultans would often bypass the Hagia Sophia to worship at the Sultan Ahmet Cami. It was from here that the dissolution of the Janissary corps was announced in the summer of 1826 by a fatwa, an edict of the caliph.

The interior of the mosque is intricate, light, and pretty. The four massive columns supporting the dome replace the forest of smaller columns in the Hagia Sophia, opening up the interior in the manner popularized by Sinan in the Süleymaniye in İstanbul and the Selimiye in Edirne. The lower sections of the mosque are faced with İznik tiles from the 16th century, at the peak – and end – of the İznik workshops'brief heyday. The mimber (the slender, staired pulpit) and mihrab (the niche facing Mecca) are carved from Proconnesean Marble, quarried from an island in the Sea of Marmara.

The stonework is exacting and beautiful, although of a less precise sort than that found in the Hagia Sophia. The interior, too, is lighter, freer and less... Catholic than the Hagia Sophia. Visitors often prefer the Sultan Ahmet Cami to its moody, ancient cousin, but the Hagia Sophia is a work of greater inspiration and genius. On the other hand, the Blue Mosque is free.

MOSAIC MUSEUM

The Byzantine Royal Palace once stood on the hill now crested by the Blue Mosque, the palace grounds sprawling toward the Hagia Sophia and down toward the sea. Many of the exposed walls and foundations in this vicinity were once part of the palace, but the only significant evidence of the ancient structures are the mosaics in this museum.

Signs direct you to the **Mosaic Museum,** *Tel. 212 518 1205,* downhill of and behind the Blue Mosque on the Hagia Sophia side. You enter through a small court of shops attached to the rear of the Blue Mosque. The museum was for years a storehouse for Byzantine oddments that had been unearthed nearby, but through a concerted effort the facility has been cleaned up and organized; it's an excellent little museum. The mosaics here are in a remarkable state of preservation, insulated from abuse for centuries by marble flagstones, then by heaps of rubble and new construction. The subjects of the in-situ mosaics are well-executed hunters and their prey, some characters in popular fables thought to date to the fifth century. The path covered in these mosaics would have led, fittingly, to the Imperial box, or **kathisma,** in the Hippodrome where actual hunters and prey often provided entertainment.

The walls of the museum are covered with mosaics from elsewhere in the vicinity; all told, the mosaics in this area were thought to have included something like 75 million glass and terracotta stones. There are excellent panels that lead the visitor through the history of the Byzantine palaces here and explicate the mosaic images.

The Byzantine palaces on this site were spacious, gardened pavilions similar to Topkapı Palace, but larger. The palaces suited Constantinople, for 900 years the world's great city. In 1203 it was described thus: *"All those who had never seen Constantinople before gazed very intently at the city, having never imagined there to be so fine a place in all the world. They noted the high walls and lofty towers encircling it, and its rich palaces and tall churches, of which there were so many that no one would have believed it to be true if he had not seen it with his own eyes."* Thus wrote Geoffrey Villehardouin, one of the leaders of the Fourth Crusade who was shortly to burn, sack, and loot the city. In the aftermath of the Crusader's victory the palace was badly damaged, and after returning to the city in 1261 its Greek rulers settled in the Palace of Blachernae by the land walls, leaving the decaying Great Palace to fall into ruin. Its stones were salvaged for construction of the Blue Mosque.

NEAR SULTANAHMET

The Grand Bazaar is just up Divan Yolu Caddesi (the road with the tramway) from Sultanahmet, then down to the right. Divan Yolu was the main avenue of Constantinople, and some of its former decorations still stand. Conspicuous among them are the **Column of Constantine,** now called **Çemberlitaş,** or the banded column, because of the iron bands that help hold it erect. The column is near the upper entrances to the bazaar.

The **Beyazid Fire Tower** is another distinctive landmark atop the hill, a tall, thick tower ringed with windows. This is part of the Beyazid II complex, and was just what it claims to be, a fire lookout.

THE SÜLEYMANİYE

The **Süleymaniye** is one of the greatest works of artistry and engineering in the Ottoman Empire. You will not see a better mosque anywhere in Turkey except Edirne: you should find the time for a visit.

The Süleymaniye dominates the skyline on the hill above Galata Bridge. You can approach from this side or from the Grand Bazaar. Either way it is a short walk uphill, but a twisting one – you'll probably need to ask directions (*"Süleymaniye Camii nerede?"*).

Visiting the Süleymaniye

The Süleymaniye is a fitting monument for the man who guided the Ottoman Empire to its greatest conquests and its largest extent. **Süleyman the Magnificent** was loved by his soldiers and his people. "The Magnificent," oddly, is an appelation bestowed on him by the western countries that bore the brunt of his military power. At home he was known as "The Lawgiver," and considered a just and intelligent ruler.

Under Süleyman, the Ottomans cleared the Knights of St. John from Rhodes and cleared the eastern Mediteranean, while on land he led conquests in the east and the west. Süleyman was a contemporary of Charlemagne, but the natural rivalry between the two was never settled in battle; Charlemagne carefully avoided challenging the Ottomans in the field, where no major battle with the west had ever gone against them. The Ottomans were the scourge of the world.

And while Süleyman prosecuted wars abroad and established laws at home, his master architect, Sinan, began a fitting tribute. Sinan, with dozens of mosques already to his credit and a skilled corps of stone carvers, began work on the Süleymaniye atop the Saray Burnu's highest hill, and he was determined that it should be suitable for the ruler of the age.

One famous (possibly anecdotal) story of Sinan's exacting attention is telling: once during construction of the Süleymaniye one of Sultan Süleyman's retainers rushed back to the palace with some disturbing news: the Sultan's master architect was smoking in the partially completed mosque. Süleyman, furious, went to the building site to see for himself. Sure enough, there was the architect Sinan, calmly smoking a water pipe in the very center of the mosque. Süleyman stormed over and demanded an explanation. The old architect pointed to the dome high above, and showed the Sultan how, based on the echo of the water pipe, he was directing workmen to adjust stones in the ceiling. He was making the minute adjustments necessary for perfect acoustics, an effort that, however unorthadox, worked marvelously well. The acoustics in the Süleymaniye remain among the best in the world.

The Süleymaniye is hailed as Sinan's greatest work in İstanbul, second only to the Selimiye in Edirne. The interior is vast and fascinating, more so the closer you look. If you have visited the Hagia Sophia and the Blue Mosque, you have witnessed two very different approaches to holding aloft the great dome. This is a third. The Muslim religious ceremony dictated alterations to a great building from the Christian Hagia Sophia. In place of a long main chamber flanked by aisles, the Süleymaniye has an open central area. To achieve this Sinan rested the dome on great buttresses, then joined these to the exterior walls with galleries. This de-emphasizes the central piers so dominant in the Sultan Ahmet (Blue) Mosque and opens up the side " aisle" areas.

When you tire of admiring the structure, focus on the tiles in the interior. These are İznik tiles of the best era. If you're interested in how tiles should look and how they ordinarily do look compare a tile – a trivet, say – from the Grand Bazaar to what you see here. The İznik blues are deep, the whites have a milky quality, and the reds are sharp and precise.

After leaving the interior return to the opposite side, site of the **türbe of Süleyman** and his favorite wife, Haseki Hürrem or Roxelana. Süleyman's love for Roxelana is legend, and she is held responsible for the decline of the empire. Süleyman's eldest son, the promising, intelligent Mehmet, died naturally in 1543, deeply aggrieving Süleyman. Next in the succession was Mustafa, and he, too developed into a strong leader and a favorite among the Janissaries.

Enter Roxelana, who had already convinced Süleyman to kill İbrahim Paşa; now, wanting her own son Selim to assume the throne she slowly preyed on her husband's pride and fear, convincing him that Mustafa was planning his downfall. Süleyman ordered his son killed, clearing the way for Selim to become the next sultan. Selim was a poor sultan, and the father of poorer ones. Selim's reign marks the beginning of the empire's long decline.

If you're interested in a meal, you're in luck. The **Darüzziyafe restaurant**, one of the classic dining spots in İstanbul, is part of the mosque complex. From the türbe go back past the visitors entrance to the mosque and out the far gate, crossing a narrow street to the former soup kitchen.

ALONG THE THEODOSIAN LAND WALLS

The current circuit of land walls, originally erected in 413 A.D., still stand – they were maintained as part of the city defenses until the late 1800s. Although they are decidedly run down in places, and punctured by railways and highways in others, the five-mile long walls are an impressive reminder of the city's power. You see the section of wall along the **Sea of Marmara** upon arrival. This part of the ancient fortifications, now pierced by John F. Kennedy Caddesi, is where a tour of the walls should begin.

Yedikule (The Seven Towers), near the Sea of Marmara, is closed on Mondays, and the Kariye Camii (Church of Chora) further along the walls is closed on Tuesdays.

What Goes Up ...

The original walls of Byzantium have long since disappeared. Any remnants of those walls that were not scattered in the ferocious sack of the city by Septimius Severus in 196 AD were carted off and reused by the selfsame Severus' labor force in the construction of new, greater walls. These walls were dismantled and rebuilt further to the west as part of Constantine the Great's great vision for the city in 325-330. The new walls probably enclosed an area from the Atatürk Bridge, through Fatih, and down to the Marmara, but they didn't last long, either.

In 413, shaken by the news that Rome had fallen to Alaric's Goths (Alaric was, ironically, a former Roman general), Theodosius II's engineers and laborers set about reinforcing the city's land defenses, pushing the cordon of walls out to its current location. This wall was badly damaged in 447 by an earthquake – more than half of the defensive towers fell – but workers immediately set to work rebuilding those walls under Theodosius II, who was still ruling. The rebuilding project took on a decidedly animated aspect as Atilla the Hun approached. Two months after work began, Constantinople was again protected by its 40-foot tall main wall, now surrounded by a second 27 foot wall with 96 towers of its own. Finally, in a burst of Atilla-inspired energy, workers added a deep moat outside and below the outer walls, topped by yet another defensive wall. The flurry of activity was a success; Atilla didn't waste his time, taking his rampage elsewhere.

... Must Come Down

The walls held for another century, then another, then another. The Persians, Arabs, Saracens, Huns and Avars could seize the Byzantine Empire's land and defeat its armies, but they were always stopped short at the walls of Constantinople itself. Treasure, icons, statues and holy relics accumulated in the Imperial capital during this aberrantly-long period of stability, and by the second millennium Constantinople had the greatest concentration of artifacts in the world.

Finally, however, the walls failed on July 17, 1203, and not to the ravages of pagan hordes or Muslim armies but to the caprice of the fellow

Christians of the **Fourth Crusade**. Like all Crusades, it had been headed for the Holy Land, but became distracted by Constantinople's wealth and marched on the city with help from a sizeable Venetian fleet. The first successful siege forced the flight of Emperor Alexius III with part of the imperial treasure and left the city in the hands of a Byzantine puppet government. The people of the city revolted, assassinated the puppet leaders, and again shut the gates of the city against the Crusaders. On April 13, 1204, the Crusaders broke through the walls once again, this time ravaging and looting the city.

The wealth was scattered throughout Europe, with Venice benefiting most conspicuously, and the Latin government installed in Constantinople proceeded to sell off or give away much of the remaining art and treasure.

Constantinople fell back to the Byzantines in 1261, when Alexius Strategopoulus, commander of the revived Byzantine military, happened by and found the walls to the city unmanned and the Venetian fleet off fighting in the Black Sea. Strategopoulus was quite unprepared for this but quickly amassed his forces, fought his way through Silivri Gate, and seized the city. This delighted Constantinople's mostly Orthodox residents, who were not fond of the Crusaders' Latin rulers.

The restored Byzantine empire was doomed to undergo repeated sieges, culminating at last in the great siege of 1453. Ottoman Sultan Mehmet II put a stranglehold on the city, cutting it off by sea, then besieged it by land. Massive siege cannons pounded the walls until, on May 29, the defenders were overwhelmed and the city fell for the final time. The Byzantine Empire fell with it, but after the obligatory three days of rampage Sultan Mehmet set his immense energies to revitalizing the city. Constantinople was made the capital of the Ottoman Empire, under whom the walls were rebuilt and the treasury refilled. The city's glory was dramatically renewed as the Ottoman Empire grew to match or exceed the Byzantine Empire at its height.

Visiting the Walls - From the Marmara

Where the wall once met the sea there are the landlocked remains of a 100 foot-tall tower. Its marble-faced lower walls are hardly characteristic of the sturdy stonework elsewhere, and historians speculate that this may have been part of a small waterfront palace. Today the great tower is surrounded by the miles-long waterfront park built on filled land along the Sea of Marmara, and the tower itself is the backdrop to an apparently bankrupt outdoor theater.

The sea walls that ran in a circuit around the tip of the peninsula are missing from this section, have been destroyed by sea erosion and

Caution Along the Walls

Yedikule and The Church of Chora, two sites along the circuit of the city walls, are both on the beaten track. Otherwise, venturing along the length of these walls takes you off the touristed track and away from history and art. You'll get a solid, unfiltered dose of the social challenges of modern Turkey in general and hyper-populated İstanbul in particular. We would discourage women from walking this area alone.

There are paths or small roads along the entire length of the walls, although İstanbul's expansion has long since spilled outside the walls to the west.

The simple, sensible way to hike along the walls is to stick to the outside, where one of İstanbul's main arterial roads skirts the former moat and the walls along their entire length.

More difficult – and unnerving – are the paths along the inside and top of the walls and between the inner and outer sections. In many places, houses and warehouses abut the land walls, and, indeed, the arched recesses of the land walls offer temporary dwelling for some of İstanbul's poorer inhabitants.

The walls are not a tourist attraction, as such, and litter is strewn around their base along their length. Much of the area between the inner and outer walls has been cultivated, and is teeming with begging children and snarling dogs. Finally, climbing atop many of the walls' most inviting sections requires dexterity and a good head for heights. Despite this litany of criticism – and because of it – we find a long walk along the walls an interesting diversion and an excellent way to get acquainted with another version of life in İstanbul. You can always hop in a dolmuş or cab traveling north (to Edirnekapı, Defterdar) or south (back to Yedikule) if you're tired, or end your trek at Topkapı, midway along, and take the tram directly back to Sultanahmet.

building material scavengers. The Marble Tower's southern wall is decorated with, of all things, Metallica and Slayer graffiti.

Yedikule

The six lanes of John F. Kennedy Caddesi have flattened the wall directly beside the marble tower. On the far side of the highway the walls gradually ascend toward **Yedikule** (Seven Towers), a fortress built at this key corner of the city defenses. To reach Yedikule from the sea, pass inside the walls and cross the bridge over the railroad tracks. That road takes you to the Yedikule entrance, where admission is $1. If arriving by train from Sirkeci, follow the signs toward Yedikule, 700 feet beyond the railway station.

The Seven Towers fortress is built around the **Golden Gate**. The Golden Gate is the oldest point in the five mile circuit, a triumphal arch built by Theodosius I to commemorate a victory over the Visigoths who had defeated and slain the previous emperor, Valens. The arch was gilded and decorated with sculpture, and Theodosius II's architects were so fond of it that they chose to incorporate the arch into their defensive wall. It was a Byzantine tradition for victorious armies to return through

The Crusades

The First Crusade was conceived to wrest back Jerusalem from the Muslims, but from the earliest moments it was a headache for the Byzantines. Most of the Crusaders were crude and vicious even by the low standard of the day, leading undisciplined marches through Byzantine lands. Still, when the main Crusader armies set out in 1097 it offered the Byzantine Empire a great opportunity. The Crusaders swept through Asia Minor, rolling up the Selçuk outposts and ceding them to the Byzantine Empire, continuing on to capture Jerusalem in 1099. On balance the First Crusade helped the Byzantines, leaving them with western Asia Minor. The Second Crusade (1146) was a total failure, highlighted by the Crusader's swath of pillage through Byzantine territories en route to being slaughtered by the Turks on the frontier of the Sultanate of Rum. The Third Crusade (1189) came on the heels of two great Byzantine setbacks, one at the hands of the Selçuks at Myriokephalon (1176), and another in which the invading Normans viciously sacked the Byzantine Empire's "second city," Thessalonika. The Third Crusade itself threatened Constantinople before continuing south, where Richard the Lionhearted failed to retake Jerusalem.

Byzantine blood was in the water. The Fourth Crusade (1203) maintained the pretense of Holy War against the infidel, but from its inception the Venetian leadership viewed it as an opportunity to crush their merchant rival in Byzantium, which after some time they did. Through the darkest of the dark ages, Constantinople had burned brightly as a repository of culture and history. For almost 900 years Constantinople held out against its enemies, enduring more than 20 sieges and serving as the eastern buttress of the Christian faith. Now the city was looted and burned by fellow Christians. "So much booty had never been gained in any city since the creation of the world," boasts Geoffrey de Villehardouin, a chronicler and leader of the Crusade, not realizing how ironically tragic his words would one day sound.

the Golden Gate, but by the time the Ottomans took the city the gilding had long since vanished, and the arch was bricked up.

Soon after seizing the city, Mehmet the Conqueror ordered that a fortress be built on the spot, the headaches and concerns of a siege still fresh in his mind. A walled garrison within the main city walls – particularly one that could command access to the Sea of Marmara – would pose a problem for invaders even after breaking through the outer defenses. Fatih's industrious foresight was never tested, however. Yedikule housed an Ottoman garrison, but from the moment that Constantinople was taken, the Ottoman Empire's frontiers were hundreds of miles away. Defense of the walls became irrelevant.

In lieu of real martial action, the fortress became a treasury and a prison. The three interior towers – the largest of the seven towers that give Yedikule its name – housed an arsenal, a prison, and a treasury. The wooden innards of these towers are gone, rotted and burned away. All that remains are dark stone staircases that wind their way up to the top of the walls, and thence to the top of the towers themselves. Bring a flashlight, both as a means of finding your way up the dark stairways and of locating prisoners' sad scrawls in the stones of the prison tower.

The **prison tower**, also called the Inscriptions tower, has several stones bearing Greek inscriptions at its base. Rumors tell of a pit in the floor that was open to the sea, into which refuse, and severed human heads, were once dumped. That is the good news: Ottoman executioners here are said to have employed execution by compression of the testicles, as in the case of the deposed Sultan Osman II – although others report he died, mercifully, by common strangulation.

Inside the keep there are the ruins of several old buildings, including the telltale minaret of the former mosque, as well as some of the massive cannonballs used by Fatih Sultan Mehmet II in his assault on the city. The centerpiece of Yedikule is the Golden Gate. Even denuded of the statuary and gilding that once covered it, the Golden Gate is a beautiful triple arcade. The marble-clad pylons to either side of the Golden Gate once housed the hurly-burly of torture chambers and execution places, but these are rarely – if ever – on display anymore.

To reach the outer sections of the Golden Gate, follow the road around to the left after exiting Yedikule. After passing through the walls double back toward the sea along the outside. After entering a small portal you find yourself in the forecourt of the Golden Gate, a far more impressive site from the outside than the inside. This secluded, lush spot is excellent for a rest before moving on along the walls.

From Yedikule

The walls north of the Seven Towers are in good condition for a long stretch. Note the inscriptions atop two of the towers between the Seven Towers and the Belgrade Gate. They denote repairs made in the eighth and fifteenth centuries. The latter repairs were undertaken by John VIII Palaeologus just twenty years before the attack by Mehmet II, The Conqueror.

There is little to see at **Belgrade Gate** aside from a cannonball from Fatih's great siege cannon. Beyond the large Belgrade Gate, so named because of the natives of that town forcibly resettled here by Süleyman the Magnificent, the walls continue in good condition as far as the **Silver Gate** (Silivri Kapı). Several towers along this stretch bear inscriptions of the Byzantine Emperors who performed repairs to the land walls. The Latin Crusaders' brief rule of Constantinople ended in the summer of 1261 when the Byzantine commander Alexius Strategopoulos happened by and found the gate undefended and the Latin fleet away. He led a small force through the gate and began a popular uprising that drove the Latins out. Just inside the gate is the **Hadım İbrahim Paşa Mosque** (1551), one of the prolific Sinan's works. It is named for one of Süleyman the Magnificent's outstanding Grand Viziers.

Take a side trip one quarter mile outside the double-gated Silivri Kapı to **Our Lady of the Life Giving Spring**. This church dates back only to 1833, the latest in a string of churches that has been located by a small nearby shrine. The church and the shrine are both within a compound surrounded by – and paved with – tombstones. Inhabitants of the city have always buried their dead outside the city walls, and that custom has created a long ribbon of cemeteries from the Golden Horn to the Marmara.

To reach the church, take the left road after exiting the Silivri Kapı gate, then take the right fork (Balıklı Silivrikapı Yolu) up a small rise to the church entrance on the left. (open daily, closed during erratic lunch hours).

The shrine was founded after travelers had a vision of the Virgin Mary at the site in Byzantine times. The church, straight ahead as you enter the outer compound, is frequented by Greek travelers and residents and is lovingly decorated with engravings, woodwork, and dark, moody icons framed in silver. The **spring** (ayazma) is down a short flight of steps to the right of the inner church entrance, behind a sign written in Greek.

The waters of the spring are said to have curative, restorative properties, and even the goldfish that swim in the small, covered pool have been incorporated into the legend of the sacred spring, and are supposed to have supernatural fish powers of their own; they don't seem too extradordinary. Penitents wash themselves carefully in the marble basin, and you're welcome to treat yourself to holy water as well. There are even small containers of water available "to go," for which you can leave a donation.

The next most interesting part of the church is a nondescript square panel high on the wall to your right as you arrive at the bottom of the first flight of stairs leading to the spring/shrine. This hatch, opening into the shrine, is reported to be much more than it appears. During the heyday of the Byzantine Empire there was, some say, a tunnel from Sultanahmet, near the Hagia Sophia, directly to the sacred spring, arriving at this very spot. This astounding tunnel would have been almost five miles from end to end, a secret route used only by the Emperors and other VIPs in times of trouble. It's an absurd theory, and for all we know it might even be true.

Whether you buy into any of the tales surrounding Our Lady of the Life Giving Spring, it makes an excellent goal or rest stop as you walk along the walls. After returning to the walls, we recommend continuing along the outside as far as the huge gate at Topkapı. The most notable feature along the next stretch is the walled up **Third Military Gate**, once ornamented with a statue of the Emperor responsible for the walls, Theodosius II. The statue was spirited away in the years before the Ottoman conquest, probably peddled for cash like so much of Constantinople's artwork in those final, desperate years. The section ends at the **Mevlana Gate**.

The current name refers to the founder of the Dervish order, and is so named for a dervish tekke (a monastery or holy place) that was once located in the area. In Byzantine times the gate was known as the Gate of the Reds, taking its name from the Hippodrome faction that supervised work on this section. The gate is heavily inscribed, with great proclamations about the strength of Constantinople.

From Mevlana Kapi continue along the outside of the walls – the inner route drives you away from the walls. Just before reaching the massive reconditioned walls pierced with Millet Caddesi there is a partially buried smaller gate set into the main wall. If you scramble up between the two walls you'll find an inscription on the lintel seeking divine protection from invaders. A small pile of cannon balls just outside the old gate is testimony to the failure of the Greek prayers. If you climb over the lintel you can duck down through a gap in the wall to the left and emerge on the inside of the walls.

Edirnekapı

Just beyond this is the completely modern gate knocked through the walls for Millet Caddesi, the road down which the city's tram travels. İstanbul has pursued an aggressive beautification program in this region, rebuilding the walls and clearing out parks. A little further along, the wall is pierced at Topkapı Gate by Millet Caddesi. **Topkapı**, or

Cannon Gate, is named for Sultan Mehmet II's siege cannon Orban, which was placed just outside the walls at this point.

When Mehmet the Conqueror's army laid siege to the city in 1453, the sultan encamped near this central gate, joined by his pride and joy Orban the siege cannon. Orban joined the rest of the sultan's unprecedented artillery – the custom made cannon balls weighed 270 pounds apiece – in raining destruction on this section of walls, particularly the section in the valley to the north. To get an idea of just how impressive Orban was, have a look at the specially wrought cannon balls inside the Topkapı Gate. Still, the defenders under cunning Genoese general Giustiniani were able to repeatedly repair the breaches and fight off waves of Ottoman troops.

Continuing north down into the valley you see the disadvantages of this low section of wall, called the **Mesoteichion** (low wall). The last Byzantine Emperor made his final stand in this valley, fighting near the small military gate north of **Vatan Caddesi** (see sidebar below). At Edirnekapı, cut inside the gate and visit the **Mihrimah Camii**, directly within the entrance. This mosque stands at the highest point along the walls, and was designed by Sinan for Mihrimah, a daughter of Süleyman. Edirnekapı, the Edirne Gate (see sidebar on the next page, *The Last Emperor*), was long the major entrance to the city, and Mihrimah rises above the walls here like a talisman. This mosque is admired as one of Sinan's masterpieces. The türbe on the mosque grounds, by the way, isn't that of Mihrimah herself; she is buried near her father at the Süleymaniye.

Also in this area is one of the greatest Byzantine historical sites, the **Church of St. Savior at Chora/Kariye Camii**, *Tel. 212 631 9241*. This church is located two blocks within the city walls, and if you wind along the inside of the walls you will either find it or Kariye Camii Sokak, which leads you away from the walls and directly to the church.

CHURCH OF ST. SAVIOR AT CHORA
History
The **Church of St. Savior at Chora** was originally built well outside Constantine's city walls, thus the name "at Chora," meaning "in the country." The Theodosian walls brought the Church within their protective shell in 413.

Although the church remains on the original site, the building was completely overhauled in the 11th century and enjoyed a great revitalization when Byzantium's rulers moved to the Blachernae and Tekfur Palaces, both of which were relatively near.

The restoration work was partly structural, but immense effort was also poured into the Church of Chora's mosaics and frescoes. Because of their late date, the paintings and mosaics at the church were executed with an understanding of perspective and depth lacking in the flat, lifeless Byzantine art of earlier periods. After Constantinople fell, this may well have been the central Greek Orthodox Church, but the period of grace ended under Beyazid II (1481-1512), who ordered the church converted to a mosque. Subsequent to that the plasterers arrived on the scene and covered most of the art, and even so it is apparent that the mosque was not held in particularly high esteem.

Over the years earthquakes and neglect caused marked deterioration to the interior of the building, a process that was finally halted after World War II. The Byzantine Institute of America and California's Dumbarton Oaks Center for Byzantine Studies began carefully restoring the mosaics and frescoes, an extremely successful undertaking.

Visiting St. Savior at Chora

Today St. Savior at Chora is a museum, closed Wednesdays, and, uniquely, open on Mondays. There is a $3 entrance fee. The art within the

The Last Emperor

Edirnekapı was the place the Ottomans finally wrested from the defenders of Constantinople. The way was cleared by a simple mistake – some of the defenders neglected to close a small postern gate to the north (near the end of the main walls). Janissaries poured through, and were soon atop the walls, fighting their way toward Edirnekapy. After seizing the gate and controlling this section of the walls, Sultan Mehmet II and what remained of his 250,000 troops entered the city. The defenders were driven to their ships or killed where they fought.

There are as many contradictory stories about the fate of **Constantine XI**, the last Byzantine Emperor, as there are about Elvis. The standard story is that he fought valiantly even as the walls were overrun, and, realizing that the city had fallen, tore away his insignia and sought his own anonymous death in battle. Afterwards, his body was discovered by those loyal to him and they buried him secretly at one of the nearby churches. Character witnesses seem to accept this account of the brave king. The cynical story is that Constantine XI had unloaded his kingly raiment and was making an anonymous beeline for the boats when he was caught and killed. The most imaginative story, however, is that he disappeared, only to return at the end of time. Like Elvis.

Meanwhile, the Sultan handed the city over to his troops for three days of pillage, as was the custom. The ransacking and looting rights did not extend to the buildings, including the Hagia Sophia, which Mehmet II "Fatih" made quite clear were his.

pretty church is beautiful, and if ever there was a site where the $3 picture guidebook is worth the money, this is it. There are English language explanations within the building, but they do not elaborate on the particulars of the myriad images within.

You enter the church to the side of the exonarthex. A highlight of the interior includes a depiction of **Theodore Metochites**, the man responsible for rebuilding the church, offering a church to Christ, as Justinian does in the Hagia Sophia. Metochites was eventually forced to live his last years in the monastery on the site, and is among those buried in the south chapel.

Within the inner narthex are two domes decorated with Christ's ancestors: the upper ring of men in the southern dome lists Adam through Jacob, while the upper ring in the northern dome counts down through the kings in the house of David. One might ask questions about how God, Jesus'father, enters into such a genealogy? The most powerful image in the church is surely contained in the funerary area in the **south chapel**; the painting at the front of the chapel shows Christ breaking the gates of hell and forcing the submission of Satan. This is the Anastasis, also known as the Harrowing of Hell, and the souls of kings, saints, and even Eve (who Christ is helping from her tomb) are all being rescued. Elsewhere in this chamber are vivid images of heaven and hell, some quite grim for a funerary chapel.

The Kariye Hotel, next door, has a fine restaurant if all this apocalyptic imagery is making you hungry. If you're a glutton for Byzantine-era imagery, the **Fethiye Camii Müze** is only a ten minute walk back toward the tip of the peninsula on Draman Caddesi, which becomes Fethiye Caddesi. The old church is one block left where the road jogs sharply right. There is a $1 entrance fee to see the mosaics.

CONTINUING NORTH ALONG THE WALLS

Returning to the base of the walls, wind your way along downhill to the **Byzantine Palace**, or Tekfur Saray. The neighborhood is a little dodgy. This old palace is not on many itineraries, and the man in charge keeps some erratic hours, but if he's around or if the gates are just sitting open you might want to look around (it should cost 50¢ or less). "Palace" is hardly a suitable term anymore; this is an empty shell of a palace erected to command the view over the walls and into Thrace. Rather pretty from the outside, the interior of Tekfur Saray is fairly disappointing. The building was erected by the latter Byzantine Emperors after they seized Constantinople back from the Latin Crusaders. The palace here accompanied the Palace of Blachernae (located a small distance north), but the most interesting stories about Tekfur Saray came after Ottoman conquest when it was first a zoo, then a brothel, a pottery craft center, and, finally, a poorhouse.

The walls undergo a dramatic transformation just north of Tekfur Saray, where the Byzantine Emperor Manuel Comnenus (1143-1180) built giant new walls down to the Golden Horn. The new walls were erected in response to the weakness of the older stretch, located at an area that many invaders had chosen for their sieges. There are no traces of these sieges today, with the exception of two tombs from the Arab siege of 674 (one of which is the tomb of Eyüp below).

The final site of interest along the circuit of the walls is the former **Palace of Blachernae**, a Byzantine-era building that has been reduced to its foundations. If you thought Tekfur Saray was disappointing, we advise skipping this altogether and continuing down to the Golden Horn. The foundations of the palace are located by the Kazasker Ivaz Efendi Cami, inside the city walls and three blocks up the hill from the road along the Golden Horn. There was a palace on this site from the time of Emperor Anastasius I (491-518), but only under the late Byzantine Empire did this palace replace the former Great Palace of Bucoleon on the tip of the peninsula, east of the Blue Mosque.

In the years prior to the Ottoman conquest, the Palace of Blachernae was improved and refitted, becoming the exclusive residence of the Byzantine Emperors of the Paleologue dynasty. Two towers of the palace still stand, as do several vaulted underground chambers.

EYÜP MOSQUE

The **Eyüp Mosque** is the most important religious site in the city. Other mosques soar higher, others commemorate great Sultans, but Eyüp was built to honor the resting place of Mohammed's standard bearer and friend, Eyüp. Eyüp fell here during the first Arab siege of Constantinople in 674 and he is held in such esteem today that people from throughout the city make pilgrimages to his mosque and türbe. In the years after the Arabs broke off the siege in 678, the tomb of Eyüp was probably left undisturbed by the Byzantines as a condition of their peace agreement. In time, superstition built up around the site and residents of the city used the tomb as a talisman for summoning rain.

A second, more extravagant story holds that at the time of the Ottoman conquest the tomb had been destroyed. After taking the city Sultan Mehmet II (1451-1481) returned to the area with his greatest imam in tow and began a mystical search, wherein the tomb of Eyüp was revealed in a dream. Mehmet II uncovered the burial site of Eyüp and rebuilt the tomb, later adding an entire mosque complex.

This complex was once the site of the Ottoman coronation – the strapping on of Sultan Osman's sword – but today it is visited by ashen-faced young fellows on their way to a less rarefied coming-of-age ceremony, circumcision. The current version of the mosque and accompanying buildings was completed in 1800.

Visiting Eyüp

The Eyüp Mosque is located just outside the city walls on the Golden Horn. Several buses serve the area from Eminönü, departing from the sea-side station, not the main station on the inland side of the seafront road. Walking directly from Eminönü takes about one half hour, but the road is busy. On the way along the Golden Horn between Eminönü and Eyüp keep your eyes peeled for St. Stephan of the Bulgars, a huge, prefabricated cast iron church located on the water's edge. Parts of this church were built in Vienna and shipped here after Bulgaria won its independence from the Ottomans.

Be on your best behavior here; after the great mosques in Mecca, Medina, and Jerusalem, this is the most holy Muslim site in the world. The Eyüp Mosque is like no other site in the city, and there is almost always a large, reverent crowd.

From the parking area, the Eyüp compound is off to the left. Upon entering the courtyard the mosque is to your right, the exit of Eyüp's türbe is directly ahead. To view the türbe, go through the courtyard and turn right into the mosque's sidecourt. You will see people removing their shoes along the magnificently tiled wall and entering Eyüp's chamber. In addition to his dramatically decorated chamber, similar to the shrine of Mevlana at Konya, there is a cast of Mohammed's footprint.

Exiting and reshodding yourself, you can have a look at the mosque, originally built after the Ottoman conquest of Constantinople in 1453. The current structure dates only to the beginning of the 19th century.

After viewing the Eyüp compound, all that's left to do is to climb the cemetery hill to the **Pierre Loti Cafe**. A 15 minute walk up a long, gentle slope, tombstones to every side, brings you to the patio of the Pierre Loti, perpetually busy. Although this cafe has very little to do with the Pierre Loti who wrote so glowingly of life in İstanbul, romanticizing the city for the French, it does have an excellent view down along the Golden Horn and benefits from the fresh air of the parklike cemetery cordon.

Business here suffered during the heyday of slaughterhouses and leather production facilities that created a reek, but these are no longer in operation. Unfortunately, neither are the narghile water pipes that were once a fixture at the cafe.

İSTIKLAL CADDESI

İstiklal Caddesi is a broad pedestrian avenue in the area above Galata Tower. This fashionable district is lined with turn-of-the-century buildings and elaborate facades; all of İstanbul seems to come here on evenings and weekends. İstiklal was the European borough of old İstanbul, where the foreign traders and diplomats lived and worked, and it will feel much more familiar to you than the chaotic warrens of the bazaars.

Visiting İstiklal Caddesi

İstiklal is an interesting walk from Sultanahmet (see *Getting Around Town, By Foot* above). İstiklal is the main boulevard off of Taksim Square, so you can catch a taxi or bus from virtually anywhere in the city to Taksim and stroll down İstiklal back towards Sultanahmet. The Conference Valley hotels are located less than one mile north of Taksim in Harbiye. This account begins at the top of the tünel line and works north.

İstiklal Caddesi proper begins where the trolley route begins, and you can take a ride along the avenue for the cost of a single 30¢ İETT bus ticket. The lower end of İstiklal is thick with book shops, antique stores and shops with old prints and artwork. The most significant monument is the **Galata Tower**, a short distance downhill. This is an excellent place to stop in for a cup of coffee and one of the city's finest views (see *Where to Eat* above).

Once on İstiklal, you'll find an abundance of shops, theaters and embassies. The city's main **synagogue** is just down the street near Galata tower, and the main Catholic and Protestant churches (**St. Anthony of Padua** and the **Dutch Assembly**) are along the İstiklal to the right. Various Greek Orthodox churches are also tucked away in the side streets off of İstiklal. There are many small, good restaurants and cafes along İstiklal and along the back streets behind it. We list our favorites in *Where to Eat* above.

One of the historic sights in the Galata neighborhood is the **Galata Mevlevihanesi** and **Divan Edebiyati Müzesi**, *Tel. 212 245 4141*, a museum of the Sufi dervish order (9:30 a.m.-5 p.m., $1.50). The compound is located to the right as you begin your walk uphill toward İstiklal Caddesi. The compound was established by a descendant of Celaddin Rumi (Mevlana), the founder of the Dervish order. After Atatürk's proscription against the dervishes, the complex fell into disrepair, but has been recently restored. You can find whirling dervish shows on Sundays in the summer; times vary.

The appeal of the rest of the route is in the gorgeous, ornate facades and the endless small, interesting shops. The American Consulate is several blocks off of İstiklal – turn left on Asmalı Mescit Sokak and descend down the narrow lane to the entrance on Meşrutiyet Caddesi.

Following Meşrutiyet Caddesi uphill, you will pass a modern convention center, then arrive at the British Consulate. This beautiful building dates to 1845 and underscores the weight that the British Empire had with the Ottoman Empire in its later years.

Back on İstiklal, one of the landmarks is the **Çiçek Pasaj**, or "flower passage," a covered arcade with small restaurants and bars. You can get a tasty meal here, but the prices tend to be more than you'd expect, and the low key appeal of Çiçek Pasaj is mostly long gone. A better option is to pass through the Çicek Pasaj into the **Balıkpazarı** (fish market), a lane that is bounded by stalls for fish, vegetables, spices and lots else. A bit up the lane turn right and you'll come to a street (Nevizade Sokak) that runs parallel to İstiklal Caddesi that's choked with small restaurants with outside seating. You can also get here by continuing up İstiklal Caddesi and turning left at Mudurnu Piliç (the red and white chicken restaurant), then taking your next left. See *Nightlife & Entertainment* later in this chapter, and note that Safran Restaurant, one of our favorites, is just above Mudurnu Piliç.

As you emerge from İstiklal into the wide expanse of Taksim Square you will see a hulking Orthodox church to your right. This is the **Church of the Holy Trinity**, a 19th century institution that has predictably suffered since the population exchange of 1924. Other landmarks around the square include the **War of Independence Memorial**, the Marmara Hotel (above the city's best and most risque magazine shops), and the **Atatürk Cultural Center**, home of the İstanbul Opera. Taksim was once the main water distribution center for İstanbul, with pipes fanning out from this hilltop. Today, buses and taxis fan out from here, and so too will the new subway.

ERCÜMENT KALMIK MÜZESI

Sarayarkası Sok. No. 33-35, Gümüşsuyu, Taksim, *Tel. 212 245 1270.* Open 9 a.m. to 7 p.m., closed Sunday and Monday.

Tucked away in a restored turn-of-the century Ottoman carriage house behind the German Consulate near Taksim is the **Ercüment Kalmık Museum**. Kalmık, a prolific 20th century Turkish artist and art professor, left a legacy of diverse paintings, engravings, and art education which his wife Ayşe sought to expand upon. The Ayşe and Ercüment Kalmık Foundation began offering scholarships for art students in 1993, and finally opened this museum in February 1997 after four years of restoration and building.

On permanent display in the museum's original building are a small number of Kalmık's works. Behind the small restored building is a new annex of glass and concrete, which houses both a gallery for rotating exhibits of contemporary artists and a studio for classes in drawing and painting. Just beyond the gallery is a narrow, terraced garden, offering a peaceful reprieve from the hustle and bustle of the modern Taksim and

Gümüşsuyu neighborhoods. It is a worthwhile excursion for those interested in 20th century art.

ASKER MÜZE (MILITARY MUSEUM)

Few of İstanbul's visitors make it to the **Military Museum**, but we highly recommend a visit. With rifles and machine guns, battle standards and armor, it's great fun for the males. The museum is located north of Taksim Square in Harbiye, bordering on Nişantaşı. It is closed one hour for lunch.

Visiting the Military Museum

From Taksim Square, catch a taxi for the short ride to the museum. If you trust your sense of direction, cross the square from İstiklal and continue down the main road on the far side (there's a McDonalds on your right). Continue straight for several long blocks until you see the large police building on your right: the museum is just beyond, also to the right.

The Ottoman military had several distinct characteristics, all of them represented here. The museum's back section features old **Ottoman pavilions** of the type used by Sultans on campaign. The Ottoman sultans continued a legacy that dates back to ancient Persia of traveling with a massive retinue and recreating Imperial splendor in the field. This ostentation contributed to the mystique of the Ottoman military during its rise, and, during the decline, to its shame. No Sultan was on hand at the second siege of Vienna (1683), but in the center of a great crescent of Ottoman tents was the pavilion of Grand Vizier Kara Mustafa and his entourage. When the siege was broken and the Ottomans put to rout by a relief army, the Viennese found in the Grand Vizier's abandoned pavilion a wealth of carpets and furs, caged birds, jeweled weapons, and cases of peculiar black beans, which a clever general hauled into Vienna and used to open the city's first coffee house.

A second signature of the Ottoman military was its **Mehter**, or military band. Unlike the imperial pavilion, military music was a uniquely Ottoman invention. The rhythmic booming of martial songs preceded troops into battle, and the Ottoman's opponents are said to have been dispirited by the mere sound of the army's approach. The military band, marching in uniform as garish as the Janissaries, inspired its own troops and served as a warning in newly occupied territories. Other militaries, and college football teams, learned from the success of the Mehter, and you can still see the original go through its paces – although with artificially enhanced mustaches – at 3 p.m. in front of the museum. The dramatically percussive band is anything but dull.

The museum is divided in two sections. The back section, alongside the courtyard used by the Mehter, houses the aforementioned pavilions, captured battle standards (the Janissaries own were burned after their abolition), uniforms, and a section for Atatürk's several victorious campaigns. The front section houses the chain that was once stretched across the mouth of the Golden Horn, and also features a collection of weapons and armor.

BOSPHOROUS CRUISE

A cruise on the Bosphorous, discussed in *Getting Around Town, By Ferry* above, is highly recommended. The scenery is enchanting, dotted with mosques and fortresses, and the Bosphorous is blessedly cool during İstanbul's long, hot summers. The main sites you will want to visit are described below, starting with the fortress at the top of the Bosphorous at Anadolu Kavağı and working your way back by land from Sariyer to Rumeli Hisar, from which point you can head off to dinner at Körfez or back to your hotel. The alternative to all of this is obvious; enjoy the ferry ride back to Eminönü.

İstanbul's ferries serve the Bosphorous three times daily in the summer, departing from Boğaz Hatti east of the Galata Bridge at 10:35 and 12:45 and 14:10. For a $4 round trip price, the ferry chugs up the Bosphorous to Anadolu Kavağı. The trip takes one hour and 35 minutes, stopping at several ports along the way. There are two boats on Sunday (Pazar), at a $2.50 discount rate. Details of the route are included above in *Getting Around Town, By Ferry* .

ANADOLU KAVAĞI

If you take a public ferry, you will typically have two or three hours in the village of **Anadolu Kavağı**. There are plenty of ice cream and snack food vendors available to ease your appetite, and a number of little waterfront cafes with mildly overpriced coffee and mezes. It's not hard to linger there for your entire stay in the village, but a take the opportunity to ascend to the fortress on the hill above town.

Ferries leave daily from Eminönü's "Boğaz Hattı," one of the main terminals east of the Galata Bridge. You can also pick them up at upstream locations such as Kabataş, Beşiktaş, Ortaköy, and Sariyer.

Once you arrive at Anadolu Kavağı, the fortress is a short taxi ride or a steep hike. To reach the fortress by foot, head to the left after getting off the ferry and follow the cobbled road in front of the Midilli'li Ali Reis Mosque inland and uphill. The road follows the slope of the hill upward, bearing right. You can enter the lower compound by cutting up a path next to the small military compound, or continue to the parking area at the top. There is no fee, and there is a refreshing wind on top, much welcome when you're overheated from the walk.

The fortress, **Yoros Tepesi**, occupies the crest of two hills and commands the Black Sea entrance to the Bosphorous. Like the many other strategic points along the Bosphorous and the Dardanelles, this area has long been occupied by kingdoms vying to exact tribute from passing ships. The hilltop fortress was built to defend a small customs port at Anadolu Kavağı, formerly known as Hieron. The small anchorage was much sought after as traffic through the Bosphorous increased, and it changed hands between Byzantium, Bithnia, Pontus, and Rome. The Romans recaptured the port under Septimius Severus in 196 AD, consolidating Roman control of the entire strait. The fortress reached its zenith in the 1200s, when the walls were extended to their current size, probably under Byzantines who had been expelled from Constantinople by the Crusaders.

The fortress has been reinforced periodically, notably by the Genoese in the years preceding the Ottoman conquest of Constantinople. Soon thereafter they handed it over to the ascendant Ottomans under Beyazit I, who fumbled it away after getting stomped by Tamurlane. Along came the hyperkinetic Mehmet II, who restored the fortress as a prelude to taking Constantinople. By the time the Ottoman Empire was again threatened from the east, this time by the Russians, warfare had changed and the fortress was decaying.

Today the fortress is a vast picnic ground with an outstanding view of the upper end of the Bosphorous. There are a few nooks and crannies to poke around in, but many of them are filled with litter.

When you return to the ferry stop, you have your choice of places to dine. They all seem a bit overpriced (which, on reflection, means they're all priced appropriately), but Yedigül Restaurant, *Tel. 216 320 2180*, a fish restaurant on the water, has earned the finest reputation.

SADBERK HANIM MUSEUM

A restored Ottoman mansion along the Bosphorous shore road houses the educational and interesting **Sadberk Harım Museum**, at Büyükdere Caddesi 27-29, Sariyer, *Tel. 212 242 3813*. The mansion's modern annex is the equivalent of a four-story Cliff Notes book. The bulk of the region's numbingly long history, from the late Neolithic period (5400 B.C.) through the fall of the Byzantine Empire (1453 A.D.), is related in English and Turkish as you ascend from the first floor. Pottery, statuary, cuneiform tablets, and other relics illustrate each period, and the museum is filled with tidbits that not even the best history students remember.

For instance, Assyrian merchants introduced tin to Anatolia, which, mixed with the native copper, yielded bronze, and the Bronze Age; the

The Great Flood

İstanbul benefits from its position on the great Bosphorus Strait, commanding the sea traffic between the Black Sea and the Sea of Marmara. It was not always so.

At the beginning of the 5th Millenium B.C., scientists have concluded that the Bosphorus did not exist. At that time, the great strait was no more than an eddy at the northeast end of the Sea of Marmara, and any neolithic settlement along the Golden Horn would have been of little consequence.

All of this changed during one of the most spectacular geographic upheavals in the last 100,000 years, one precipitated by the evaporation of a great lake to the northeast. This massive freshwater lake had gradually receded, year by year, until its surface was 450 vertical feet lower than sea level. And so it would be today, were it not for a seismic event that resulted in a thin stream of saltwater finding its way northeast and cascading down toward the freshwater lake. This stream grew over time, fed by the endless volume of the world's seas, and as it grew it ran more quickly. As the seawater began rushing along the course of the Bosphorus, it scoured out the bed of the creek, in time becoming a tremendous falls, one of the largest the world had ever seen.

The rumble and mist of that great cascade served as a harbinger for the people settled in the settlements at the lakeside far away. At first their lake would have crept higher , at first at a rate of an inch every week, then inches a day, and, near the end, several feet a day. As it rose, it turned brackish; the infusion of saltwater killed the native fish and made it unsuitable for drinking. This cataclysm was probably over in little more than two years.

Little is known of the settlements wiped out in the deluge, or the fate of those that survived. The ubiquity of ancient flood narratives, as captured in the Epic of Gilgamesh and the Bible, suggests that the diaspora from the lakeside shared the terror of this event.

The best book on the topic benefits from the insights of several of the principal researchers: **Noah's Flood: The New Scientific Discoveries About the Event That Changed History**, Walter Pitman and William Ryan, Touchstone Books, 2000.

Cimmerians, vaguely immortalized in Conan comic books and movies, helped found the Lydian empire. The historical section of the museum is an excellent way for newcomers to get their bearings. Compared to the sprawling museums in Sultanahmet, it is very peaceful; on weekdays you're likely to be followed around by a museum employee who turns off lights as you leave each room.

The upper floors of the mansion itself are devoted to art and relics of the last thousand years, and are highlighted by a display of İznik and Kütahya ceramics. You can see what all the fuss over tile is about firsthand. Nearby is a display of Celadon porcelain from China's Yuan and Ming Dynasties, and while the collection may seem incongruous, it is impressive enough to have merited John Carswell's *Chinese Ceramics in the Sadberk Hanim Museum*, a table top book available at Sotheby's. You didn't come to Turkey to see the Chinese porcelain, but it is quite nice just the same. A final highlight is a section devoted to calligraphy that outdoes the Topkapı Palace.

The rest of this house has its share of oddities, but suffers from poor English documentation: a table with reliefs of Napoleon and his marshalls, displays of Ottoman medals, and even a model of a Ford Probe go unexplained; as for the latter, Sadberk Hanim was the wife of Vehbi Koç, himself a much-loved industrialist and Turkish Horatio Alger character, who made his fortune building cars..

Sariyer has several small fish restaurants lining the Bosphorous. You may also elect to taxi or bus down to İstiniye and head across the water to the upscale waterfront restaurants at Çubuklu, which has a small, fine collection of waterfront patio restaurants such as Sunset Marine, *Tel. 216 425 0721*, all of which are expensive, spacious, and have breathtaking views.

RUMELI HISAR

The "Fortress of Europe," **Rumeli Hisar**, is on the sea road on the European shore, just below the second Bosphorous Bridge. Buses serve Rumeli Hisar along the sea road, and you'll find parking. There is a $1 admission fee.

If you've taken a Bosphorous Cruise or arrived in İstanbul by bus from the Asian side, you've seen Rumeli Hisar. The fortress is built at the narrowest point along the Bosphorous, and complements the smaller **Anadolu Hisar**, the Fortress of Asia, on the opposite shore. This is the same spot that the Persian King Darius crossed into Asia on a bridge of ships in his campaign against the Scythians (512 B.C.). Herodotus remarks favorably on the Scythians' cunning, and also mentions one of their entertaining habits: they would pack into a warming hut with hot stones in the center and burn hemp, emerging with much whooping and hollering. The campaign of Darius eventually failed when the Scythians refused to give battle and made a long, meandering, hemp-inspired retreat just ahead of Darius'army. An exasperated Darius eventually gave up and marched home.

Control of the strait was always crucial, but this particular point did not return in a major historical role until late in the 1300s. At that time, Ottoman Sultan Beyazid I ordered the construction of Anadolu Hisar, on the Asian shore. This was part of his strategy of choking off Constantinople. Beyazid's scheme was foiled by the invasion of Tamurlane in 1402. By 1451, the Ottomans had recovered, and in that year Mehmet II came to power and immediately set about finishing the job his great grandfather had started: he shored up Anadolu Hisar and, with what would become typical industriousness, erected Rumeli Hisar on the European side in the space of four months.

Within Rumeli Hisar's seaside tower he positioned a set of newly forged cannons and 500 men and demanded that any ships passing through the strait submit to boarding and pay a fee. Mehmet II was delighted to hear that the first ship that attempted to run the gauntlet between the two fortresses was immediately holed and sunk. His soldiers merrily fished the survivors out of the sea and impaled them; later boat traffic stopped as ordered.

When Constantinople fell, Rumeli Hisar's purpose was served. Afterward, it housed an occasional garrison, and was at times used as a prison, but it had little military importance. Earlier this century the fortress was filled with small wooden houses, but these were cleared out in the 1970s to make way for a park. Today various international musicians perform concerts here in the spring and young couples from Bosphorous University come to neck.

Like so many old fortresses, Rumeli Hisar is a shell, but it is well worth the $1 entrance fee. Be sure to climb to the upper left tower, whose winding stair takes you up through an interior draped in vines, lit eerily from above. The column at the center was used to fix the tower's wooden flooring. Note the care taken to place a recycled Maltese cross in the floor at the tower's entrance so that the garrison could trample it on every trip in and out of the tower.

If you'd like to have lunch, you can certainly try one of the small restaurants outside the entrance to Rumeli Hisar. For a treat, head a short distance up the Bosphorous by cab to İstiniye and await a ferry from Çubuklu (they run frequently).

DOLMABAHÇE PALACE

Dolmabahçe is just two kilometers north of Galata Bridge, directly on the main sea road. **Dolmabahçe** Palace, *Tel. 212 258 5544*, is on the Bosphorous side of the main shore road, and the entrance is marked with an elaborate baroque clock tower. Buses bound from Eminönü for Beşiktaş and points north pass the palace. Dolmabahçe is closed on Mondays and Thursdays.

Arrive at 8 a.m. Gates don't open until 9 a.m., but the tour buses begin unloading hundreds of people by 8:30 a.m., even on the cusp of high season. The waiting lines are long and impossibly sluggish, the ticket takers are nasty, and if you arrive later in the day you may have to cool your heels for hours in line, jostling with sweaty people from around the world. It's fun to look at the motionless soldiers on ceremonial guard, but it ain't that fun.

History

Long before the Dolmabahçe was a glimmer in the Ottoman Imperial eye, this was the site from which Fatih Sultan Mehmet II sent his ships overland during his siege of İstanbul. Stymied by the great chain strung across the mouth of the Golden Horn (now in the Military Museum), Mehmet II completely bypassed the mouth of the Golden Horn and hauled his ships directly into the Golden Horn, advancing a step closer to his ultimate victory. Years later, Sultan Ahmet I, he of the innumerable hobbies, began ordering the deep cove at this site to be filled for the sake of his gardens. Later Sultans continued Ahmet's practice of filling this area, which yielded the name "filled-garden", or Dolma-bahçe.

It was on this auspicious spot that, in 1853, Sultan Abdül Mecit I (1839-1861) completed his new palace. His motivation may have been, in part, to distance himself from the intrigues of Topkapı Palace, but his main influence was a desire to build a palace in the style of the Europeans the sultans had come to admire.

Dolmabahçe is the culmination of the Ottomans' turn to the west. The Empire had been in obvious decline for almost a century, and the only fear the Ottomans now evoked in Europe was that their collapse would be to the advantage of another Western power – especially Russia. In order to shore up the Ottomans, western nations made loans, sent advisors, even threatened its enemies. The Ottoman sultans had grown so comfortable in this role that Abdül Mecit's palace was largely built with loans from Europe.

More vividly, in the same year Dolmabahçe was completed the Crimean War erupted, wherein Turkey's French and English allies fought off the Russians in what had once been the Ottoman's private preserve, the Black Sea. Europe battled the Ottomans' enemies and built its palaces; such a good deal, and such a sad one.

Dolmabahçe underscores the abandonment of tradition: it is a Western palace of the most extravagant kind, with rococo ornamentation and baroque flourishes. There are 285 rooms, 43 halls, and six Turkish baths; it has the world's largest mirror and chandelier, and giant elephant tusks are on hand as was anything else big and resplendent. Designed by the architect Nikolos Balyan (who was also responsible for the pretty Ortaköy mosque), the Dolmabahçe retains nothing of the Topkapı Palace's simple, functional charm.

Even after the later construction of the Çırağan Palace, Dolmabahçe was the official residence of the sultans until 1922. Afterward, Dolmabahçe was often Atatürk's accommodation while in İstanbul, although he made it plain that İstanbul was not a city he was comfortable in. He stayed here a total of three months between 1927 and 1938, and perhaps his unease with Dolmabahçe was foreboding; he died here at 9:05 a.m. on November 10, 1938. All of the clocks remain set to that time.

Visiting Dolmabahçe

Unlike Topkapı, where you can linger over those things you find interesting, you are guided through all of the buildings here. Go to the front hall after entering the grounds and join the cluster around an English speaking guide. You are herded first through the **selamlık** (residence) on a tour, in which you see several of the world's largest chandeliers, masses of crystal, cut stone, elaborate arches, gigantic carpets, and every other gaudy ornament the designers were able to pack inside. After the selamlık you are handed off to a second guide if you have purchased tickets for the harem tour as well.

The guides do a fine job of explaining the interior, which is highlighted by the **Imperial Ceremonial Hall**. This vast chamber rises almost as high as the Hagia Sophia and covers 6,200 square feet. George H.W. Bush, Helmut Kohl and François Mitterand have dined here, but that was during the summer – the palace is musty and cold in the fall and winter. For a break, the conveniently located cafe by the Selamlık entrance is surprisingly reasonable.

You can wander the gardens on your own, and, afterward, get a taxi up to Taksim Square or further up the Bosphorous to Rumeli Hisar and beyond.

MISCELLANEOUS SIGHTS OF INTEREST

A catalogue of İstanbul's sites could fill tomes. A few of the more interesting – and less interesting – historical sites are listed below.

Aşiyan Müzesi (Ethnography Museum)

Give this a pass. You'll see a sign directing you to it as you near Rumeli Hisar on the Bosphorous. The house was owned by Fikret Bey, one of Atatürk's comrades in arms, and has a fine view, but there's nothing to see that's in English or makes any sense unless you're a member of his family or you received a doctorate in Early Turkish Republican History.

Deniz Müzesi (Naval Museum)

The Naval Museum is on the waterfront in Beşiktaş. The displays are less interesting than those in the military museum, but well worth a look if you are at Dolmabahçe or Çırağan Palaces. Highlights of the collection include old naval artillery pieces and photos and paintings of naval battles in both Ottoman and Republican times.

Kiliç Ali Pasa Camii

This is one of Sinan's final works, built for a successful Ottoman naval officer who died in the company of his harem at age 90.

Kız Kalesi (Castle of the Maiden)

It isn't likely you'll be visiting this monument in the center of the Bosphorous, but you're bound to wonder what it is. This was once a customs point for ships entering the Bosphorous, and has long had a tower or fortification of some kind. It is sometimes referred to as **Leander's Tower**, a reference to the myth of Helle, Leander, and the golden ram related in the Çanakkale section.

Küçük Aya Sofya (The Church of St. Sergius and Bacchus)

This building was originally commissioned by Justinian, and is much admired by architects for its clever dome. The patron saints of the church were dear to the heart of Roman and early Byzantine soldiery. The church was converted to a mosque after the Ottoman conquest. Located below the Hippodrome in the direction of the Sea of Marmara.

Museum of Illumination and Heating Appliances

Give this a pass. It's located in the heart of Sultanahmet and includes some beautiful old braziers, stoves, and lamps, but there's nothing here that's not also included in Dolmabahçe or an antique shop near İstiklal Caddesi.

Şehzade Cami (The Prince's Mosque)

Sinan built **Şehzade** early in his long career for Süleyman the Magnificent's favorite son. The son, Mehmet, died of smallpox while still young. This is one of the most beautiful mosques in the city.

Tophane (The Cannon Foundry)

The **Tophane** is a cannon foundry dating back to Fatih Sultan Mehmet II. Under Süleyman the Magnificent, the foundry was rebuilt in its current form and became one of the most world's foremost manufacturing facilities for artillery pieces.

Aqueduct of Valens

Constantinople's system of aquaducts was elaborate, extending far outside of the city to the Belgrade Forest. This is the last great evidence of the system still intact within the city, and you're likely to pass beneath its arches as you bus or taxi through the city. Valens was a Byzantine Emperor between 364-378.

Yer Altı Camı (The Underground Mosque)

This is an underground chamber where the chain crossing the Golden Horn was once fixed, now converted to a mosque. Two martyrs of the first Arab siege are located here, in Karaköy opposite Eminönü.

Yıldız Saray (Palace) and Yıldız Park

In the hills above the Çırağan Palace you'll find İstanbul's largest park, a strip of mildly cultivated wilderness. If you need a break from urban İstanbul, this is the place. Sultan Abdul Hamid II certainly felt this way and built the last Ottoman Palace in the heights just above, maintaining his own private hunting grounds here.

The park has several small, pretty kiosks and pools, some of them restored by the Turkish Touring and Automobile Association.

The kiosks, and the buildings of Yıldız Palace itself (accessible from Barbaros Boulevard, uphill from Beşiktaş), are solidly Art Nouveau, and are interesting – if not a delight – to architects (although a stroll along İstiklal Caddesi is probably as gratifying).

Nightlife & Entertainment

Hamams

There are more than 100 Ottoman-era hamams (Turkish baths) in İstanbul alone. One of the finest examples of a classical bath in the city is the **Haseki Hurrem Hamamı**, designed by Sinan for Süleyman the Magnificent's favorite wife, Roxelana. The structure, between the Hagia Sophia and the Blue Mosque, now houses the Ministry of Culture's kilim and carpet shop, **Döşim** (see section on kilims and carpets below for further information). If you're not planning on visiting a bath for bathing purposes, then stop by Dösim and kill two birds with one stone.

Some of the more interesting hamams are:

Cağaloğlu Hamami, Yerebatan Caddesi in Sultanahmet, near the intersection with Nuruosmaniye Caddesi just uphill of the Basilica Cistern. Hours are 7 a.m to 10 p.m. for men, 8 a.m. to 9 p.m. for women. Apparently the proceeds from this bath in Ottoman times were used to maintain Sultan Mahmut I's library in the Hagia Sophia. It is now one of İstanbul's premier tourist hamams, and the prices reflect this. Cost notwithstanding, it is a beautiful place.

Çemberlitaş Hamamı, Vezirhan Caddesi No. 8, off of Divan Yolu. Hours are from 6 a.m. to midnight. *Tel. 212 522-7974; Fax (212) 511-2535; Email: contact@cemberlitashamami.com.tr; Web: www.cemberlitashamami.com.tr.* Built by Nur Banu Valide Sultan in 1580 (wife of Selim II the Sot and mother of Murat III), this hamam is supposedly based on a plan by Sinan. The original womens' section was destroyed in street widening some years ago, but still has sex-segregated quarters, of apparently equal size.

Galatasaray Hamamı, Suterazi Sokak 24, off of Istiklal Caddesi in Galata. The mens' quarters are lavishly bedecked with marble, the womens' less so. Expect to pay a lot for your luxury.

Park Hamamı, Dr. Emin Paşa Sokak No. 10 in Sultanahmet. Turn off of Divan Yolu opposite the Hippodrome. The hamam is across from Hotel Petrol and is a simple, small, neighborhood establishment.

Theater, Opera, & Ballet
Atatürk Cultural Center (Atatürk Kültür Merkezi), Taksim. If you're standing in front of the Marmara Hotel facing the Square, AKM is on your right. Built as an opera house, the AKM also houses the State Ballet, the Symphony Orchestra, and the State Theater Company. Friends generally advise against ballet, unless it's a visiting international company, and with theater you'll face the language problem. But the tickets are so inexpensive that it hardly matters.

Art Galleries
Almost all of the major banks sponsor art galleries, and publish books of Turkish artists' works. You can easily find small galleries in Nişantaşı and Teşvikiye, as well as in the small streets around İstiklal Caddesi such as: Aksanat Cultural Center, Istiklal Caddesi 16-18, *Tel. 212 252 3500*; and Yapı Kredi Gallery, Istiklal Caddesi 285-287, *Tel. 212 252 4700.*

İstanbul International Festivals
İstanbul's international festivals attract some of the world's finest performers, including Turkish ones. You can enjoy theater, film, music & dance, and jazz; tickets are inexpensive to moderate by U.S. standards. You can find out more about the festivals by asking at your hotel or the tourism information offices.

Movie Houses
Going to the movies is a popular pastime in İstanbul. Many of the theaters along Istiklal have a long history, having been built in the first half of this century.

If you missed the first run of something in the U.S., you may be able to catch it on the big screen after all. All major Hollywood films come to Turkey, not long after release in the U.S. Many other foreign films come through as well, especially during the **İstanbul International Film Festival**. The Istiklal theaters are the main venue for the festival.

Matinee prices can be as low as $1.50, but regular rates for new releases are pushing the $5-6 mark. Usually movies are subtitled in Turkish, rather than dubbed. The notable exceptions are childrens' movies, which are always dubbed. There is always an intermission, which disrupts the flow of the film but is convenient for buying snacks, using the restroom, or, of course, smoking a cigarette – which is mercifully not permitted in most theaters. Theaters usually have cafes attached, where you can buy a drink and a snack before or after the film.

Some of these theaters should fit your cinematic needs:

Atlas, Istiklal Caddesi 209, *Tel. 212 243 7576* – The main theater has very bad sound, but the smaller one is fine.

Fitaş, Istikal Caddesi, Fitaş Pasajı 24-26, *Tel. 212 249 0166* – five screens.

Beyoğlu, Istiklal Caddesi, Halep Pasajı 140, *Tel. 212 251 3240* – To find the theater, go into the passage and down the stairs ahead of you on the left.

Alkazar Cinema Center, Istiklal Caddesi 179, *Tel. 212 245 7538* – A restored theater with two screens. Look for sculptures of women on either side of the narrow arched entrance.

Emek, Istiklal Caddesi, Yeşilçam Sokak 5, *Tel. 212 293 8439* – The lobby's not much to look at, but inside is a grand old one-screen movie house.

Feriye, Çırağan Caddesi, *Tel. 212 236 2864* – This theater is along the sea road, next to the Ortaköy municipal bus stop. The modern theater has a lofty ceiling with exposed beams. Have a Bosphorus view with your pre- or post-film coffee at the indoor cafe.

Nightclubs, Bars, & Other Entertainment

İstanbul's unique summertime nightlife owes much to its peculiar geography. As in other Mediterranean cultures, Turks eat dinner late in the summer, and stay out - on the streets or at cafes and bars - even later. Outdoor restaurants, bars, and discos, especially along the Bosphorus and the Sea of Marmara, figure prominently in İstanbul's summer life (along the sea road just past Ortaköy and the first Bosporus bridge is a good place to look). In the wintertime people tend to stay at home more, but there is still a lively indoor nightlife, featuring a variety of live music, until all hours.

As in most large North American cities, nightclubs and cafes come and go in İstanbul with some regularity (wine bars have been very popular in the last year, for example). Bear in mind, too, that the half-life of many has been accelerated by the 2001 economic crisis in Turkey; in the following list we therefore recommend some of İstanbul's more established nightspots. You will also be able to find plenty on your own, especially in the Istiklal-Taksim area and the Ortaköy waterfront.

In the following list we recommend some of İstanbul's best nightspots, summer and winter. You'll notice we don't recommend bars with Turkish floor shows (usually of the belly dancing variety) aside from the very expensive Galata. Many of the places with floor shows are disreputable and you'll wind up getting gouged. There are plenty of places where you can go that will be just as lively, and, if anything, more 'Turkish' because there are Turks enjoying the atmosphere right alongside of you. Credit cards are accepted in many night spots, but you should have along enough cash for your evening out just in case (there are several cash machines from major Turkish banks along İstiklal).

Note: Although many of our favorite places are in the İstiklal area, it's probably best to avoid the deserted side streets off of İstiklal at night if you're out alone. Mugging is uncommon, but it does happen. Single men should also be wary of new friends, as explained in the Safety & Avoiding Trouble in Chapter 6, *Basic Information.*

İstiklal & Vicinity

ANDON PERA, *Siraselviler Caddesi No. 89, Taksim, Tel. 212 251 0222.* A café with a tavern on the upper floor.

BİLSAK, *Soğancı Sokak No. 7, Taksim, Tel. 212 293 3774. No cover charge. Moderate-Expensive.*

To get here, go down Siraselviler from Taksim, pass the German Hospital on your left ('Alman Hastanesi') and turn left at Dilek Market onto Soğancı Sokak. Bilsak (otherwise an arts center) is about 150 meters up on your right. Take the elevator up to the 5th floor to Beş Inci Kat (Fifth Floor), which has a great Bosphorus view. Crowded on weekends. For food details, see *Where to Eat* above. Mixed drinks are expensive. Open 6 p.m. to 2 a.m.

BÜYÜKPARMAKKAPİ SOKAK, *just off of İstiklal Caddesi, Beyoğlu. Moderate.*

This street, towards the Taksim end of İstiklal, is chock full of cafes and bars with live and canned music. Notable are the reliable **Hayal Kahvesi** and Mojo.

DULCİNEA, *İstiklal Cad., Meşelik Sok. No. 20, Beyoğlu, Tel. 212 245 1071. Moderate-Expensive.*

Dulcinea is befitting of its namesake from *Don Quixote,* a beautiful café and bar that mixes modern and antique décor. There is a cover charge when they have live music, which is often jazz. If you're heading towards Taksim on İstiklal, turn right onto Meşelik Sokak just before the walled Aya Triada church. Dulcinea will be on your right.

GRAMAFON BAR, *Tünel Meydanı No. 3, Tünel, Tel. 212 293 0786. Cover charge. Moderate-Expensive.*

The Gramafon features jazz every night except Sunday and Monday, and is a regular participant in the İstanbul Jazz Festival activities.

İSTANBLUES, *Topkapı Sarayıiçi, Darphane, Sultanahmet, Tel. 212 520 5178. Expensive. Credit cards accepted.*

If you don't want to leave Sultanahmet for your nightlife fix, İstanblues is a good option in the summertime. Inside the Topkapı Palace compounds, Darphane was the imperial mint (near the Haghia Eirene). You can eat dinner there (French and Turkish cuisine) and listen to blues, jazz, and Latin three nights a week. Open 7:30 p.m. to 1:30 a.m.

MILK, *Akarsu Sokak No. 5, Galatasaray (near İstiklal), Tel. 212 292 1119.*

We figured we should list at least one trendy disco, so this it. Local and international DJs. Open Thursday-Saturday, 10 p.m.-4 a.m.

NEVİZADE SOKAK, *near İstiklal Caddesi, Beyoğlu. Moderate.*

This small back street near the Çiçek Pasajı is filled with tiny *meyhanes*, establishments that are known for *meze*, music, and perhaps above all, *rakı* (aniseed-based alcohol). All *meyhanes* along this strip have outdoor seating, and the irony is that none of them feature live music anymore; instead, the musicians walk up and down the street, and solicit donations. It's a fun time, and lots of Turks go here. The best of the bunch is **Ney'le Mey'le**, but **Bade, Alem, Cumhüriyet, İmroz**, and others are also good. To find Nevizade Sokak, head towards Taksim on İstiklal. At Galatasaray square, turn left onto Sahne Sokak. The first right should be Nevizade Sokak.

Q CLUB, *Çırağan Palace Hotel Kempinski, Beşiktaş, Tel. 212 236 2489. No cover charge. Expensive.*

Very steep drink prices, but a breathtaking summertime setting on the palace's terrace next to the Bosphorus. In the winter they move into the ground floor of the palace itself. Q Club features Turkish and international jazz musicians, and flaunts a wine and cheese bar.

ROXY, *Arslanyatağı Sokak No. 9, Taksim, Tel. 212 249 4839. Cover charge on weekends. Moderate-Expensive.*

Go down Siraselviler from Taksim and take a left at the supermarket onto Arslanyatağı Sokak. Roxy is on the left. This rock and jazz bar/club is popular with international musicians, who are likely to show up here for jam sessions after their concerts elsewhere. No credit cards. Open 6 p.m. - 3:30 a.m.

Shopping

Whether you want the amenities of one of Europe's finest shopping malls (**Akmerkez**), the quirkiness of an arts and crafts market day (Sunday in Ortaköy), or the historic din of the Grand Bazaar, İstanbul has what you're looking for. The weekly neighborhood **pazars** - Thursdays in Etiler/Ulus, for example (in the otherwise empty lot across from Akmerkez - see Akmerkez section below for directions) - offer a 'real-life' shopping scene where you can buy everything from your weekly groceries to fingernail polish and kilims.

Remember that the Grand Bazaar and the Egyptian Bazaar are closed on Sundays, as are many shops.

THE GRAND BAZAAR

Open 9 am-7pm, Monday-Saturday, closed Sundays.

The first shopping destination in İstanbul is usually the **Grand Bazaar**, arguably the mother of all shopping malls. The Grand Bazaar is known to İstanbullus as the **Kapalı Çarşı**, or 'Covered Market,' for obvious reasons.

To get here, turn right off of Divan Yolu onto Vezirhanı Caddesi. At the Nuruosmaniye Mosque, take a left through the mosque gate. Pass through the courtyard and out the other side. One of the Grand Bazaar's entrances, on Çarşıkapı Sokak (Market Gate Street) will be right in front of you. This doorway brings you onto the Bazaar's main drag, Kalpakçılarbaşı Caddesi. Most of the Bazaar will be off to the right of this street. This may sound like a guidebook cop-out, but rather than sticking to a map, it's really much more enjoyable to let yourself get 'lost' in the Grand Bazaar. You'll find maps at most intersections.

History

The first thing you'll probably notice about the Grand Bazaar is that shops selling similar wares are all clustered together. The roots of this practice are in the guild system, which resulted from the specialization of labor, early economies of scale, and the state's desire to police prices, supplies, and tax revenues. Thus names of the streets in the Grand Bazaar - such as **Jeweler's Street** and **Quilt-Maker's Street** - reflect the guilds that are or were once making and selling their goods there.

Although this may be an urban myth, we've been told that there is still an ethic among merchants whereby a shopkeeper may refuse a sale if he's already had one that day and knows that his neighbor hasn't. This forces the customer to go next door, which spreads wealth as well as good cheer (except to the confused tourist), and perhaps wards off the evil eye to boot.

The Grand Bazaar got its start as a simple warehouse, or **bedesten,** for Mehmet the Conquerer. The area around this particular bedesten became popular with merchants, who eventually built structures from under which to ply their wares year round. As time went on, **hans** were built around this bazaar; hans were cousins of the larger **kervanserais** on the outskirts of town, places where goods could be stored and locked up. Many of the hans, which typically consist of a courtyard surrounded on all sides by a two-storied structure, are still functioning in their original capacities, as well as for the manufacture of goods. Feel free to wander into a couple as brief respite from the sensory overload of the Bazaar.

Playing the Tourist

'A fool and his money are soon parted.' P.T. Barnum would have liked it here. Bear that in mind as you ease into this capitalist spectacle, but don't let it paralyze you. If you're in Turkey for a month you can acquire some of the connections to get good stuff a little cheaper; only then do you have the luxury of not being taken for a sucker. Otherwise, you're a stranger in a strange land, baffled by jet lag and exchange rates; the odds are against you getting much of a deal. On the other hand, the Grand Bazaar has a vast amount of stuff that you can't get any cheaper elsewhere. So go ahead, wander the streets asking prices: *'Bu ne kadar?'* (Boo nay ka-dar?) - 'How much is this?' - and seeing what's to be had.

You enter the bazaar at a disadvantage: your clothes are sure to brand you as a traveler. In other words, the shopkeepers know about you. They know there's money in your pocket, know you're interested in spending it, and probably know how to string together some fair English sentences. Furthermore, they have your inherent politeness on their side - no matter how cold-blooded you think you are, you will be coerced into one or two booths and set upon with tea and hospitality.

There are the inevitable reports of people being drugged at the Bazaar. It allegedly works like this: you are offered tea, but the tea is spiked to knock you out. After you leave the booth, unscrupulous Bazaar crooks track you like Marlon Perkins tracking a tranquilized Grizzly and roll you in an alley. This is quite a tale, and it is totally unfounded. If you want to have tea in someone's shop, have tea. Shop owners and salesmen in the Bazaar may be irritating at times, but they're not criminals and in a million years they aren't going to destroy their shop's reputation by messing with a foreigner.

Pickpocketing may be a more valid concern. Although this, too, is not common, pickpocketing is on the rise, and by people you wouldn't expect, like groups of older women in headscarves. It works like this: they will feign interest in items that you are also looking at, crowd around you, talk loudly to each other and the shopkeeper, and then move on. If your wallet or another important item was in an exterior pocket, it may not be anymore. So: keep money and other valuables in a neck pouch under your clothing or in a money belt. There are also stories circulating of tourists' bags or backpacks being slashed as they wander around the bazaars.

For all of this, the Grand Bazaar is neither scary nor intimidating. It's just a big, chaotic market. Nothing bad will happen to you so long as you stay frosty. Go, shop, buy. The bazaar is fun.

THE EGYPTIAN OR SPICE BAZAAR

Open 9 am-7pm, Monday-Saturday, closed Sundays.

The **Spice Market**, or **Egyptian Bazaar** (Mısır Çarşısı), is basically a t-shaped structure adjacent to the Yeni Cami in Eminönü, constructed in the 1660s as a part of the mosque complex. It was once known for the folk remedies sold by its merchants. What's left of those remedies today are primarily spices, bins of green henna powder, loofas and sea-sponges, with other items scattered nearby. The tall brass grinders you'll see everywhere are good for either coffee or pepper; a Turkish friend says that one of his fondest childhood memories is of his grandmother roasting some coffee beans in a pan and allowing him to grind them. The tall grinders work remarkably well, and are more classic and fun than your Braun bean grinder at home. Some travelers talk about the pungent aroma of the spices being unpleasant, but we find it mild and, if anything, wonderful.

Tip: Unless you like the convenience of the packaged spices, buy in bulk. The spices will be cheaper and fresher. So, too, with the Turkish Delight and coffee.

The large doors at the foot of the 't' are the Bazaar's main entrance, right on Eminönü Square, across from the Yeni Camii's pigeon-covered steps. Inside to the left is the stairway entrance to the turquoise-tiled **Pandeli Restaurant**. The Pandeli's moderate prices, excellent Turkish dishes, and unusual setting make it one of the best deals in İstanbul. It is open for lunch only (see *Where to Eat* section above).

The real action and pungency is outside the bazaar. In the righthand arm of the 't' (if your back is facing the main entrance), your nose will lead you to Kurukahveci Mehmet Efendi coffee roasters, just beyond the Bazaar's side door. Mehmet Efendi uses Arabica beans, and sells ground coffee in brown paper packets or in sealed tins and plastic bags, whichever you like. Don't forget to ask for the English instruction sheet, because translated directions for cooking Turkish coffee are not on the packaging. Directly across from Mehmet Efendi on Hasırcılar Caddesi are some confectioner's shops, where you can pick and choose fresh

lokum (Turkish Delight) in various flavors by the kilo. Shopkeepers will give you samples to entice you to buy.

Along the outside of the bazaar that faces the bus station are stalls and stands selling fresh produce, dried fruits, cheeses, meats, olives, and nuts. Indulge in some dried apricots (kayısı), figs (incir), or dates (hurma). Outside on the other side of the 't' opposite the Yeni Camii is a **Sunday bird market** and stalls with gardening supplies. Here you can find tulip bulbs, but look at the label - the bulbs are more likely to be from Holland or Washington State then they are from Turkey, the tulip's original homeland.

Take some time to wander in the narrow streets that lead away from the ferries. In the maze of streets behind the Egyptian Bazaar you'll discover wooden utensils, fake Levis, German department store brand coats, and other everyday items. One street is filled with woodworkers, another with hardware shops, another with with plastic goods. Many of the things that you find in the shops around Eminönü are also made in workshops here, tucked away in hidden arcades, up stairways, behind walls. These are streets largely inhabited by men, craftsmen, salesmen, shopkeepers and businessmen, suggesting an İstanbul at odds with the more gender-integrated city you see elsewhere.

OTHER SHOPPING AREAS
İstiklal Caddesi

This is the most classically 'European' section of İstanbul. This hill opposite the old city has been populated for a long time, but under the Ottomans it became a borough for non-Ottoman traders and, later, diplomats. The major embassies of France, Germany, England, Russia and America are located here, although they have all been demoted to consulate status since the capitol shifted to Ankara.

Classic Greek Orthodox and Roman Catholic churches dot the avenue, as do beautiful art nouveau facades. This wide pedestrian lane is one of most popular spots for a weekend stroll, to take in a movie, or to do some shopping. Most of the shops offer clothing and household goods that probably aren't what you came to Turkey to find, but it is a wonderful excursion nonetheless. The lower end of İstiklal has many antique and collectibles shops, as described below, and just uphill from the bend at Galatasaray Square, is the **Balıkpazarı** (fish market) beside the Çiçek Pasaj, filled with spices, dried fruits, and, of course, fish. The tiny **Bünsa** shop is a reliable place to buy natural spices, sea sponges, teas, sun-dried tomatoes, etc. **Paşabahçe**, Turkey's premier glass manufacturer, also has a shop along this stretch. Look there for the beautiful and distinctive çeşme bülbül, a white and blue striped glass that goes back to Ottoman times and whose name literally means 'fountain nightingale.'

Shoeshine Boys

İstanbul's shoeshine boys, particularly in the Taksim area, are bound to get your attention. These tiny young things wander the streets late at night with their banged up shoeshine boxes, while their child colleagues offer candies or packets of tissue. Many of the urchins are persistent to the point of being relentless, especially with tourists. They'll follow you around doggedly, and you can sputter 'Git' (go) and 'Gerek yok' (not necessary) all day long without it making a bit of difference. The community often keeps an eye on the youngsters, and you'll see shopkeepers and men outside restaurants offer them some spare change. Sadly, and predictably, many of these kids are addicted to sniffing glue and live together under the 'guidance' of shoeshine pimps.

If you're strolling along İstiklal near Galatasaray Square and happen to be looking for a good deal on ceramics, you might stop by the **Aznavur Pasaj** just across from the Yapı Kredi Bank building. The kiosks on the ground floor of the *pasaj* sell ceramics with the same kinds of historical patterns and color schemes of those in the Grand Bazaar, and come at a lower price because of the lower rents. Open on Sundays.

Nisantası & Teşvikiye

These tony neighborhoods have a concentration of galleries, antique stores, contemporary design stores, and upscale clothing shops. You can easily take a taxi from Taksim to Nişantaşı - ask to be dropped off on Vali Konağı Caddesi.

Or, if you don't mind a 15-20 minute walk from Taksim, follow Cumhuriyet Caddesi past the Divan Hotel; Cumhuriyet turns left at the Harbiye Military Museum (Askeri Müze) - you want to keep going straight, onto Vali Konağı Caddesi. This puts you in great position to take advantage of some of İstanbul's prime up-market shopping.

Ortaköy/Sunday Crafts Market

Sundays in **Ortaköy** are an entertaining confusion of street vendors selling a variety of things and people stepping out for one of the city's finest views. The baroque mosque, built in the nineteenth century by the creator of the Dolmabahçe, commands the waterfront, with the 1973 Bosphorus Bridge behind. If you didn't bring your camera, this is where you grit your teeth watching the perfect light and the serene İstanbullus soaking up the sun. From about 10 a.m. until well into the evening, the pedestrian zone on Ortaköy's waterfront is filled with tables of inexpensive silver jewelry, handicrafts, and other collectibles. In good weather it's swarmed with young İstanbullus munching on huge baked potatoes and **gözleme**, filo dough cooked with your choice of filling. Have tea or coffee in one of the many indoor or outdoor cafes, stroll among the wares, and people watch.

Ortaköy, literally 'middle village,' was traditionally a mixed place, with Greeks, Armenians, Turks, and Jews all living together. The Greek Orthodox church (behind the wall opposite McDonald's) and the synagogue (on the sea road) both still attract small congregations. When the Ortaköy waterfront went through a gentrification/urban renewal phase about 10 years ago, many bars moved in and there were clashes between alcohol-swilling young people and the elders from each of the three religious establishments. They ultimately came to an agreement, and now none of the cafes near the mosque serve alcohol. Out of sight of the mosque and all along the sea road, however, there are bars and **bakkals** (small foodstuff shops) selling booze.

Even if you don't make it to Ortaköy on a Sunday, there are many little shops and restaurants where you can pass the time and spend some money. See *Where to Eat* section for restaurant recommendations in Ortaköy.

Akmerkez (Etiler)

For what it's worth, **Akmerkez** has won both the Best European Shopping Mall award for 1995 and the Best Shopping Mall in the World award for 1996. You'll find major upscale Turkish and international brands represented here. Very crowded when the weather is bad. For the Thursday pazar across from Akmerkez, simply ask anyone *'Ulus Pazarı nerede?'* (oo-loos pah-zar-uh nair-day?) and they'll point you to it. Akmerkez is open from 10 a.m. to 10 p.m. daily.

Weekly Neighborhood Bazaars

If you have the time and inclination, you might wish to visit one of the weekly neighborhood bazaars for a taste of what the non-tourist version is like. Streets get shut down for the day and vendors sell everything from fresh foodstuffs to underwear. The vast majority of Turks still do their shopping like this, and you'll see men with huge baskets on their backs, carrying groceries home for whomever will pay them. If you're heading to some smaller towns during your visit, it will be easier for you to go to a bazaar in one of those locales; for İstanbul, we recommend either the Ulus Pazari (discussed in the Akmerkez section above) or taking a taxi to the Saturday market in Beşiktaş, a neighborhood a short distance up the Bosphorus, just beyond the walls of Dolmabahçe Palace. You may simply request of the driver to be taken to the **Beşiktaş Cumartesi Pazarı** (Besh-iktash joo-mar-tay-see pa-zar-ay giddy-or-um). Note: The earlier you go, the better; the sea road becomes heavily trafficked as the day wears on.

KILIMS & CARPETS

If you want a more thorough listing, pick up a copy of *İstanbul: The Halı Rug Guide* published by Halı: the International Magazine of Antique Carpets and Textile Art ($14.50, available at stores with English-language books); it recommends rug dealers by neighborhood. As background before you leave home, you may also want to find a copy of Henry Glassie's *Turkish Traditional Arts Today*.

Everyone has his or her own favorite shop, depending on tastes, dynamics with the shopkeeper, location, and price. We make only a few recommendations, based on some personal experience and trusted recommendations. Look around, then buy where you feel comfortable with the shopkeeper, the goods, and the price.

HAZAL KİLİM & HALI, *Mecidiye Köprüsü Sok. No. 27-29, Ortaköy, İstanbul. Tel. 212 261 7233, Fax 212 261 3672.*

Hazal displays a tremendous collection of flat weave rugs and carpets in their element—a high-ceilinged wooden house just one block from the Ortaköy Mosque. We lived in Ortaköy when we first moved to Turkey, and returned to this shop on the Ortaköy waterfront again and again. The allure of the rugs at Hazal was apparent, but it took more than a year for the quality of the hand-picked stacks of rugs (and the odd carpet) to truly sink in.

The beautiful pieces and atmospheric old building are half of the equation; the knowledgeable, friendly, honest approach of Engin and Ahmet Demirkol and Orhan is the other half. The owners of Hazal reason, rightly, that their kilims will work their magic without unsolicited sales patter. A visit to Hazal (named after the Demirkol's daughter) is something we look forward to. Recommended.

DÖSIM, *Haseki Hurrem Hamamı, Ayasofya Karşısı, Sultanahmet, İstanbul. Tel. 212 638 0035.*

This shop offers carpets and kilims in a wide a range of prices and quality, but the ministry insists they are all hand made and many of them use natural dyes. Dösim is associated with the Turkish Republic Ministry of Culture and has two goals; to promote the production of traditional Turkish carpets and kilims, and to make a little money while doing so. You may recognize some of the patterns from the rugs housed in the Turkish and Islamic Arts Museum across the Hippodrome. Prices are set in Turkish Lira and posted; these prices are a good benchmark for bargaining in privately owned shops. One tip: the fixed prices are adjusted for inflation on the first Monday of each month, meaning that

Great Carpet Shops Outside Istanbul

İPEK YOLU (Silk Road), *Mevlana Cad., Naci Fikret Sokak No. 1, Konya. Tel. 332 353 2024, Fax 332 352 7658; Web: www.silkroadrugs.com.*

Mehmet Uçar, owner of İpek Yolu, has been spearheading the research into natural dyes. The lost art is now making a recovery, thanks in good measure to his efforts. What this means for you is that his shop, not far from Konya's tourism information office, has a beautiful collection of rugs. Konya has always been a marketplace for good kilims anyway, but with the revival of natural dyes they are irresistible shades of yellow, green and red. Even the least perceptive of us can appreciate these creations. Uçar has a good reputation, and is vastly knowledgeable about the business. Recommended.

AKSA HALICILIK, *Kayseri Cad. No. 38, Ürgüp, Cappadocia, Tel. 384 341 4348.*

There are carpet and kilim shops all over Cappadocia, owing in part to the tourism and in part to the fact that rugs are made in the area. We had a good experience with Muammar Sak at Aksa Halıcılık, a specialist in kilims (despite the name – halıcı means carpet maker), including a nice selection of old ones. His store is located across the street from the tourism informtion office, beneath the municipality buildling (Belediye).

in the couple of days prior you're getting the best deal relative to the US dollar. Recommended.

ADNAN & HASSAN, *Grand Bazaar.*

Adnan and Hassan are perhaps the most well-known rug dealers in İstanbul. In addition to their tourist clients, they sell to locals and expatriates, and their prices are more or less fixed. They don't put undue pressure on you, and they welcome people who would like to stop in just to learn more about kilims and carpets. The majority of their rugs are new.

SÜMERBANK, *İstiklal Caddesi, Taksim, İstanbul. Tel. 212 252 0805.*

This state-owned retail chain sells genuine Hereke silk carpets and other handmade rugs at reasonable, fixed prices.

TEXTILES

VAKKO, *İstiklal Caddesi 123-125 near Taksim Square (closed Sundays), İstanbul.*

One of İstanbul's first luxury department stores. On the second floor you can find luscious textiles at equally luscious prices. For the determined discount fabric hound, head to **Saraçhane**, on the old city side (behind the aqueduct) near the Atatürk Bridge. There you can find bolt after bolt of export-quality fabric at unbeatable prices.

İNO, *Yalıboyu Mah. No. 26, Kalkan (outside İstanbul), Tel. 242 844 2897.*
A wonderful little artisan's shop tucked into a Kalkan side street just up from the harbor. Özlen Bayram collects textiles from all over Anatolia and Central Asia, including linen veils and hamam wraps, Kurdish silk headscarves, and patterned cottons from the Black Sea. She carries items difficult to find anywhere else, such as cotton curtain panels printed with wood blocks from a workshop that has been in continuous operation since the Selçuk period (1071-1370). Ms. Bayram sells individual textiles as well as stunning handmade womens'clothing she has constructed from pieces in her collection and dyed in rich colors. Recommended.

GOLD
İstanbul is filled with gold shops. See the Gold section in Chapter 9, *Shopping*, for further information.

TEPOT, *Nuruosmaniye Cad. No. 86-88, Cağaloğlu, Tel. 212 520 7601.*
This is the jewelry shop where Hillary Rodham Clinton made some purchases on her 1996 spring break trip through the Middle East with Chelsea. The proprietor has a wide selection of traditional and modern pieces and doesn't mind people who browse. Recommended.

ANTIQUES
There are probably hundreds of antique shops in İstanbul. Some of the best are located in the **Teşvikiye/Nişantaşı** area, while recently a number have opened up in the backstreets in the **Tünel** area at the south end of İstiklal Caddesi. Remember that it is illegal to sell, buy, or export antiques that might be considered national treasures; you must get a certificate from the dealer for customs.

HORHOR BIT PAZARI, *Kırık Tulumba Sokak 13/22, Aksaray.*
A five-story flea market recently mentioned in *The New York Times* Sunday Magazine.

OLD BOOKS & MAPS
If you're interested in finding old books, maps, and collectibles, you're in for a treat. İstanbul has a number of shops, some ratty and run down, others catering to a discriminating clientele. Sahaflar Çarşısı near the Grand Bazaar is an old standby, and the Tünel district near the bottom of İstiklal Caddesi (straight ahead as you exit the Tünel subway station, look for a small lane with iron gates) is awash with stores.

SAHAFLAR ÇARSISI, *Sahaflar Çarşısı Sok., west of the Covered Bazaar.*
A tiny lane packed with used and old book sellers, also offering prints, photographs, old Ottoman contracts and official papers. Excellent collectibles. The street is crammed in alongside the Beyazid Mosque, just off of Divan Yolu to the north (uphill) and through a gate on the left.
ARTRIUM, *Tünel Pasaj No. 5/7, Beyoğlu, Tel. 212 251 4302.*
LIBRAIRIE DE PERA, *Galip Dede Sok. No. 22, Tünel, Tel. 212 245 4998.*
OTTOMANIA, *İstiklal Cad., Sofyalı Sok. No. 30/32, Beyoğlu, Tel. 212 252 8010*
Ottomania is located on a short street running parallel to Istiklal. Prices seem high, but they have prints and documents available nowhere else. Recommended.

BOOKS IN ENGLISH

İstanbul has some excellent English-language book stores that carry everything from contemporary critical theory to beautiful coffee table books on Turkey. Ara Güler's photographic tomes about Turkey are especially striking.
ROBINSON CRUSOE, *İstiklal Caddesi 389, Tünel, Beyoğlu, Tel: 212 293 6968.*
Excellent English-language section, with guides, coffee table books and an exhaustive collection of history and classics books. Located at the lower end of İstiklal Caddesi on the right side as you walk towards Taksim Square. Recommended.
DÜNYA, *İstiklal Cad. No. 469, Beyoğlu, Tel. 212 249 1006.*
Books and magazines in the major European languages, including English.
PANDORA, *Büyük Parmakkapı Sokak 3, Beyoğlu, Tel. 212 245 1667.*
A fine selection of philosophy in English, as well as books about İstanbul and Turkey. Coming from Taksim, take a left at the Benetton. Pandora is on the left. Recommended.
GALERİ KAYSERI, *Divanyolu Caddesi No. 58, Sultanahmet, Tel. 212 512 0456, Fax 212 511 7380, Email: galerikayseri@ihlas.net.tr.*
Although we had a very disturbing encounter with this shop's owner, he does have an impressive array of English-language books on Turkey, including topics on art, architecture, literature, Sufism, and Islam. Its location in Sultanahmet makes it very convenient for visitors who want to purchase books without making the trek to Istiklal Caddesi

Excursions & Day Trips

Other area excursions are treated in subsequent chapter because they deserve more than a day or two. In this section, in addition to travel agents, we've listed one main excursion north of İstanbul – **Edirne**.

Travel Agencies
The Turkish language puts up a fairly impenetrable barrier during a lot of travel planning. A reliable English-speaking travel agent makes your life much easier if you're making travel plans within the country. There are hundreds of travel agencies in İstanbul to choose from, but we reserve our highest recommendation for the infinitely patient staff at Imperial Turizm. The other agencies are helpful within their niches.

IMPERIAL TURIZM, *Divan Yolu Caddesi No. 31, Sultanahmet, İstanbul, 212 513 9430, Fax 212 512 3291; Email: imperial@superonline.com; Web: www.imperial-turkey.com.*

Saim Ata and the staff at Imperial is efficient, helpful, English-language fluent and, above all, honest. They can book planes, buses, and ferries within and without Turkey. Imperial offers a service bus from their office to the bus station. You may have some problems when trying to make arrangements with them from home, however. They give priority to people who are standing in their office. Located by the tram stop in Sultanahmet.

TUR-ISTA TURIZM, *Divan Yolu Cad. No. 16 A, Sultanahmet, Tel. 212 527 2531; Fax 212 519 3792.*

Authorized to book train travel throughout Turkey.

TURKISH MARITIME LINES, *Rıhtım Cad., Karaköy. Tel. 212 245 5366; Fax 212 251 9025.*

They can arrange international ferry travel to Venice and Brindisi, Italy.

SHE TOURISM, *Cumhuriyet Cad. 309/3, Harbiye, Tel. 212 233 3670, Fax 212 233 3673.*

She runs tours around İstanbul of fair quality, but is most useful for organizing things you cannot realistically do on your own, such as private yacht cruises on the Bosphorous and Princes Islands. Schedule well in advance.

For More Information
There are **Tourism Information offices** in the railway station at Sirkeci, along Divan Yolu Caddesi in Sultanahmet, and at Atatürk International Airport. Most offices in İstanbul have an English speaking staff member, and they are certain to have free English language maps and scads of photo-packed free literature about whichever regions are of interest. The main office is at the airport, *Tel. 212 663 6363-82.*

EDIRNE
There is precious little to see in Thrace other than **Edirne**, the former Adrianople, not far from İstanbul. Edirne is a must-see for those interested in Ottoman history and architecture. Interesting for the architec-

ture of its buildings – including Sinan's greatest work – and its Ottoman ruins, Edirne can be seen in a day from İstanbul. The city is not convenient to most travel routes, unless you are continuing into Bulgaria or Greece. This is an excellent place to bone up on mosque architecture.

Edirne, north of the junction of the Tunja and Meric Rivers, can trace its history back into the distant past. Xenophon's 10,000 probably fought battles near here on behalf of the Thracian king Seuthes, but the city never truly arrived until the much-traveled Roman Emperor **Hadrian** founded

Escapes from Istanbul

If İstanbul threatens to short circuit your brain, try getting away to one of the following spots.

Kilios: Kilios beach is located on the Black Sea by the mouth of the Bosphorous. This long sand beach is choked with İstanbullus on summer weekends, but is otherwise a good place to escape. Public buses make their way to Kilios from Sariyer.

Princes Islands: Ferries depart from Eminönü (Adalar terminal) and Kabataş for the Princes Islands (See Getting Around). These islands have pretty beaches and a relaxed pace. The islands are very busy on weekends.

Yalova (Termal): A springs wells up near Yalova on the Asian shore. The Romans took advantage of it, as did the Byzantines, and even Süleyman the Magnificent and Atatürk lowered themselves into the soothing waters. The healing powers of Yalova/Termal's hot springs are explained thusly in one of the hotel brochures: "with its radioactivity, semi-dead cells are reactivated." If you can bear up to that, Termal is a fairly quick ferry ride from İstanbul, 15 kilometers from the Yalova ferry stop. If you'd like to spend a night here, the **Turban Yalova Hotel** (Yalova, *Tel. 226 675 7400, Fax 226 675 7413.* Double: $64) is recommended, an old standby at the area, just uphill from the extensive thermal bath.

Polonezköy: This town, far outside the bounds of İstanbul, was once the Ottoman Empire's "Little Poland." It is a nice retreat from the activity of İstanbul, about one hour from the city in the mountains. It's a fine spot for an afternoon, although there are many pensions in town. The finest accommodation is a restored 1905 farmhouse. The oddly-named **Polka Country Hotel** has a relaxing feel and top-notch dining (Cumhuriet Yolu No. 36, Polonezköy, *Tel. 216 432 3220, Fax 216 432 3042; Email: polkahotel@superonline.com; Web: www.polkahotel.com.* Rooms: 15. Double: $100.)

Edirne (Hadrianopolis) to command the land approaches to Constantinople.

Through the centuries it indeed proved the key to Constantinople, and thus the key to much of the Mediterranean basin: one of Rome's signal defeats took place here when Emperor Valens and his entire army were massacred by an army of Goths in the fourth century; the Third Crusade wrested the city from Byzantine hands in 1187, paving the way for İstanbul's fall to the Fourth Crusade in 1204; and the Ottomans captured the city in 1360 and made it their capital as a precursor to cutting off and defeating İstanbul in 1453. Thereafter Edirne was a staging ground for Ottoman assaults against Christian Europe.

Fortunately artisans have lavished almost as much attention on the city as generals and pashas, leaving Edirne with a proud legacy of mosques, the ruins of the 14th century Ottoman palace, and even inexpensive baths of Sinan's design. The city retains the aura of an outpost, and the frequency of Cyrillic and Greek alphabet signs attest to the number of Bulgarians and Greeks that cross the nearby border to do business in Edirne's bustling markets. The population is estimated to be more than 130,000.

ARRIVALS & DEPARTURES
By Car
Edirne is a 2.5 hour drive up the E-80 freeway from İstanbul. The E-80 is the road that runs across the northern – Black Sea side – Bosphorous bridge, past the Esenler Otogar and continuing north into Thrace and Europe. The route has changed very little since ancient times, when a major Roman road connected Rome, the western capital, with Constantinople, the eastern capital. Keep an eye out for buses, which, as in the city, often run this route at high rates of speed, and are laissez-faire about lane markings.

By Public Transportation
Several bus companies offer service to Edirne, with buses running hourly. Edirne is a three-hour trip from the İstanbul Otogar at Esenler, unless you happen to get caught in rush hour traffic.

Cağlar Turism, *Tel. 212 658 0851*, offers nonstop service in big Mercedes buses. The cost is $4.50.

ORIENTATION
Coming from İstanbul, you arrive from the southeast on Talatpasa Asfaltı, the main road in Edirne. The road bends to the left at the city center heading in the direction of Bulgaria. Most sites of religious and historical interest are only a Koran's throw from here, exceptions being

the Kırkpınar wrestling area and the Beyazid II complex, about one kilometer to the north and northwest, respectively.

The **tourist information offices** are both on Talatpasa, the first just around the corner from Üç Serefeli (Hurriyet Meydanı, Talatpaşa Caddesi No. 17, *Tel. 284 225 1518)* and the second, main office is west of downtown (Talatpasa Caddesi No. 76A, *Tel. 284 225 5260 and 284 213 9208).* The public hospital, Edirne Devlet Hastanesi *(Tel. 284 225 4603)*, is near the Bulgarian Embassy on Talatpaşa Caddesi, out of the city center toward İstanbul.

WHERE TO STAY

Be under no illusions: Edirne caters to people on the way elsewhere and to hardcore mosque devotees. Neither group demands five star service, and neither group receives it. Hotels in this area have no more than two stars, but those listed below are clean, well-managed, have parking, phones, and at least a little English.

RUSTEMPAŞA KERVANSARAY OTEL, *Kapili Han Cad., No. 57, Edirne, Tel. 284 215 2195, Fax 284 212 0462; Email: k.saray@netone.com; Web: none. Rooms: 22 winter, 100 summer. Credit cards accepted. Open year-round. Double: $45 (breakfast included).*

In a town demonstrating the legacy of the architect Sinan, it is fitting to spend the night in a building of his design. The kervansaray, built in 1561, was one of hundreds of secure stopover points for caravans making their around Asia Minor. The contemporary history of this particular kervansaray dates to its occupation by the Russian army in the winter of 1877, when the building suffered serious damage. That damage was corrected in the early 1980s, and the building is nicely restored. It's not the fault of the restorer that the old stone hearths in each room now contain televisions that pick up Bulgarian programming.

Despite such indignities to the master architect, the kervansaray has atmosphere in its bones. You'll appreciate the domed ceilings, the old wooden doors, and the broad stone hallways. This is ordinarily the best place in town, although on weekends even the thick walls of the kervansaray may not completely insulate you from the bar downstairs.

OTEL SABAN ACIKGOZ, *Tahmis Meydany Cilingirler Cad. No. 9, Edirne, Tel. 284 213 1404, Fax 284 213 4516; Email: none; Web: none. Rooms: 34. Credit cards not accepted. Open year-round. Double: $41.*

Just four years old, the Acikgoz, just south of the Kervansaray, is one of the nattiest hotels in Edirne, with a spacious, nicely decorated lobby and friendly staff. The rooms offer fairly lousy views, but are decent and well cared for. Like all hotels in Edirne, it's centrally located.

SULTAN HOTEL, *Talatpasa Asfalti, Edirne, Tel. 284 225 1372, Fax 284 225 5763; Email: none; Web: none. Rooms: 90. Credit cards not accepted. Open year-round. Double: $38 (breakfast included).*
Officials with the tourism bureau are particularly fond of this tidy hotel, but it is not particularly appealing. Manager Mehmet Gökay is friendly and helpful, and the decor is decent. Rooms, like all of the rooms in Edirne, are fairly plain. The restaurant is open May-September.

WHERE TO EAT
Chances are your visit to Edirne is a short one, and from a dining standpoint that's just as well. With the exception of Lalezar, restaurants in the city are undistinguished. Edirne is as good a place as any to try cheap local fare.

LALEZAR, *Karaç Yolu, Edirne, Tel. 284 212 2489. Moderate.*
It is a shame to visit Edirne and not take advantage of the riverfront garden at Lalezar. This is definitely the finest restaurant in an otherwise undistinguished dining landscape, offering excellent grills and mezes. The restaurant overlooks the Meriç River and its slender Ottoman-era bridge. The restaurant is located south of town; if you don't have your own transport, get a dolmuş from in front of the PTT bound for "Karaağaç."

ÇATI RESTAURANT, *Talat Paşa Caddesi, Edirne, Tel. 284 225 1307. Moderate.*
This restaurant is located across the street from the Sultan Hotel, and it's typical of the restaurants in central Edirne; simple kebaps, köfte and soups are available at decent prices. A full meal should cost $7-$8.

SEEING THE SIGHTS
Three of the principal mosques in Edirne, the Eski Camii, the Uç Serefeli Camii, and the Selimiye Camii, offer a convenient clinic in the evolution of Ottoman architecture. The Ottomans were in all things excellent learners, and as their territory expanded they had an increasingly vast selection of architectural lessons to consider. First there were the designs of the Selçuks, like themselves Turks, which were incorporated in the early Ottoman mosques and public buildings.

Eski Cami (1414), the oldest mosque in Edirne, was built while Edirne was the Ottoman capital and deviates little from Selçuk style. The structural limitations of the old mosque are glaring when compared with the nearby Selimiye, but Eski Camii was a step in the evolution toward such ambitious buildings. In its favor, the pursuit of vast, airy spaces left behind some of the charm of the relatively confining Eski Cami, whose calligraphic inscriptions of Koranic verses are immediate and mesmerizing. Although Eski Cami's architecture has been upstaged by later mosques, it boasts an inch-long sliver of stone from the Kaaba in Mecca, located on the right – southwest – side of the mihrab. The columns on the face of the building were swiped from nearby Roman ruins, accounting for their contrast with the stone and brick used elsewhere.

Two blocks northwest of Eski Cami, **Uç Serefeli Cami** (1447) was built at the behest of Murat II, father of Mehmet the Conqueror. The name of the mosque, "three balconies," derives from the balconies high atop the northwest minaret, which was the tallest minaret in the Middle East until the construction of the Selimiye Mosque one century later. In Uç Serefeli the Turks incorporated some of the Seljuk style, but were already making improvements on it to suit their taste and to take advantage of technological advances, as evidenced in the relatively imposing size of the central dome. The forecourt and fountain of the Uç Serefeli were innovations that later became a fixture in Ottoman architecture. Reconstruction work is under way on part of the mosque, but it remains open to the public.

With the capture of İstanbul less than a decade after the completion of Uç Serefeli, the Turks had a wealth of Byzantine architecture – including the gargantuan Hagia Sophia – to study and assimilate. It was in this atmosphere that following generations of Turkish architects would fuse the Selçuk and Byzantine traditions and create a distinctly Ottoman style. Sinan, the most renowned of the Ottoman architects, constructed a mosque that is arguably the pinnacle of the alloyed style here to accompany the Eski and Uç Serefeli: the **Selimiye Mosque** (1579), atop a hill in northeast Edirne, dominates the city's landscape – and the Thracian plain below.

The mosque was built at the very apex of Ottoman power under the son of Süleyman the Magnificent, who was not particularly magnificent himself. Selim II immersed himself in wine and the harem, engaging in affairs of state only enough to precipitate the fateful battle of Lepanto, which broke the back of Ottoman naval might and signaled the decline of the empire. Selim II eventually slipped in a hamam after drinking a full bottle of wine and cracked his skull. He is probably undeserving of this legacy, the mosque Sinan considered his greatest achievement.

The Selimiye is, however, a fitting testament to one of the world's great architects at the height of his powers (he was 83 upon the mosque's completion) and to the wealth of an empire that commanded the entire eastern Mediterranean, the Middle East, and North Africa. The mosque is a quantum level beyond its predecessors, with a massive open area whose eight mammoth pillars allowed Sinan to incorporate 999 windows, one for every name of God, and achieve marvelous lighting. The symmetry of the windows is beautiful – begging the question where, in this symmetrical building, did Sinan put the odd window? The grand dome – 31.5 meters – makes the Selimiye seem fuller than even the vast

Süleymaniye. The Selimiye further benefits from its dominating position atop Edirne's hill, where it is almost completely unobscured, its galleried minarets soaring up out of the earth.

Mosque Design 101 concluded, you may want to have a look around the rest of the city. The **Beyazid II complex**, a kilometer from the city center to the northeast, is definitely worth a visit. The complex, restored in the 1970s, includes a mosque, kitchen, hospital, school, and store rooms. The design of the hospital (Darussifa) in particular was on the architectural cutting edge at the time. The **Archaeology and Ethnography Museum** and **Turkish and Islamic Art Museum**, behind the Selimiye Mosque, are each well worth the 75¢ admission price. The former traces the history of the area from prehistoric times through the Byzantine Empire.

The art museum offers further architectural information about the city's mosques, as well as a selection of glass work, weaponry, and, notably, a pavilion of the type taken on imperial campaigns. Other things to see include the **Muradiye Cami** (1436), a mosque commissioned by Murat II that demonstrates another gradation in the development of Ottoman architecture, between the time of the Eski and Üç Serefeli Mosques – it has a gorgeous prayer niche.

One of the most fascinating events in Turkey is Edirne's annual **Kırkpınar Festival**, held during one week in June or July. Activities surround Kırkpınar, but in the end it is all window dressing for the real event: **Oiled Wrestling**. Thousands of burly men pour into town each year to slather themselves with oil and wrestle in a massive round robin tournament, the winner making off with some cash and livestock, and, most important, the title "Başpehlivan" (Chief wrestler). If your arrival coincides with Kırkpınar, you're unlikely to find room at the inn, but it's worth a struggle to stay awhile and witness this greasy, manly spectacle. The tourist offices will be of great help with tickets, which should be available at the municipality (belediye).

The site of the Kırkpınar wrestling, north of town at a fork in the Tunca rivers, is alongside the ruins of the old **Ottoman Royal Palace**. This was once the equivalent of İstanbul's Topkapı Palace, but it fell into disrepair during the 18th and 19th centuries and was consumed after an Ottoman ammunition depot exploded here during the Russian offensive of 1877. The ruins are decidedly ruined, but the few remaining buildings on the once-vast grounds make for a quiet, interesting walk when the oiled-up madness isn't going on.

If you are visiting from İstanbul, you will definitely want to pay a visit to one of Sinan's baths. The **Tahtakale, Mezit Bey**, and **Sokollu** hamams are all of his design, and are all considerably cheaper than baths in İstanbul. The Sokollu Hamam, conveniently next to the Üç Serefeli Cami, is roomy and has separate baths for men and women. The smaller

Mezit Bey hamam is to the right of the statue of Sinan as you look at the Selimiye; men and women bathe at different times, but the wooden interior is superior to the Sokollu. Tahtakale, located near the junction of Sarajlar Caddesi and Eski İstanbul road south of downtown doesn't get much tourist business, and may be the better for it. Baths in each of these facilities cost about $2, with massages $4.

If it's a beautiful day and you have the time, take a walk or a short drive to the junction of the Meric and Tunca rivers. Between the first and second sections of Sinan's bridges you'll find a pleasant, lightly forested area for a picnic or simple peace and quiet. It is also on the way to Lalezar restaurant, across the second bridge and right.

Practical Information for Istanbul
Consulates
American Consulate, Meşrutiyet Caddesi No. 104-108, Tepebaşı, *Tel. 212 251 3602.* They have a public library here with slightly out of date periodicals.

Canadian Consulate, Büyükdere Caddesi No. 107/3, Gayrettepe, *Tel. 212 272 5174.*

Great Britain Consulate, N. Meşrutiyet Caddesi No. 34, Tepebaşı, *Tel. 212 293 7545.* The British Consulate Library is on İstiklal Caddesi, just uphill of the bend in the middle. Your first visit to the library is no charge.

Hospitals
İstanbul has several good hospitals and a collection of very able American and European-trained doctors. Ambulance sirens are rarely heard, because response times are too dismal to make ambulances particularly worthwhile. If you need to get to a hospital, get there yourself by taxi. For specialists, consult the U.S. Consulate, which keeps a list of recommended doctors. İstanbul's best hospitals are the:

AMIRAL BRISTOL HASTAHANESI/AMERIKALI HASTAHANESİ (American Hospital), *Güzelbahçe Sok. No. 20, Nişantaşı, Tel. 212 231 4050.*

The American Hospital is widely regarded as the city's best, with emergency service and some English speaking staff. The hospital is located in Nişantaşı in the hills above Dolmabahçe Palace.

INTERNATIONAL HOSPITAL, *İstanbul Cad. No. 82, Yeşilyurt, Tel. 212 663 3000.*

The only other hospital recommended by the American consulate. Several English speaking staff members and doctors.

Many people come down with nose and throat ailments after long flights from North America. If it turns serious, see the U.S. educated Doğan Senocak, Ear Nose and Throat, Çamlık Sok., Aslan Apt. D. 7, Etiler, İstanbul, *Tel. 212 263 1388.*

If you require blood testing or X-rays, you may be referred to a Pakize Tarzı Laboratory. One of the clinics is down the street from the American Hospital and right four blocks (Valikonağı Caddesi No. 86, Nişantaşı, *Tel. 212 241 3895)*, and another is in Etiler across the street from Akmerkez shopping center (Zeytinoğlu Caddesi, Arzu 1, Apt. K, Etiler, *Tel. 212 287 2560)*.

Places of Worship

Obviously if you're a practicing Muslim you're in for a treat. Whatever your religion, bear in mind that Mosques are houses of God, and many find them a good place to pray. If you're looking for a little more community, however, try the following places:

DUTCH CHAPEL, *Union Church of İstanbul, Postacular Sok. No. 4, İstiklal Caddesi, Hollanda Konsolosluğu, Beyoğlu, Tel. 212 244 5212.*

English language services at 9:30 and 11:00 on Sunday, with tea and coffee after the second ceremony. This is the oldest Protestant church in the city, at the lower end of İstiklal Caddesi two blocks south of the Saint Antoine Church.

ST. ANTOINE CHURCH, *İstiklal Caddesi, Beyoğlu, Tel. 212 244 0935.*

This beautiful cathedral, occasionally used for concerts during the early summer İstanbul Festival series, is still used by İstanbul's Catholic community. Mass in Italian nightly at 7:00, with English mass at 10:00 on Sundays. No Latin mass.

NEVE SHALOM, *Büyük Hendek Caddesi No. 61, Şişhane, Tel. 212 244 6675.*

İstanbul's main synagogue is located between the American Consulate and Galata Tower. Büyük Hendek Caddesi intersects with Galata Tower three blocks downhill.

Police

The local emergency number is *155*, but there's little chance of reaching an English-speaker on the other end – it is obviously a good idea to have a Turk with an understanding of the problem make the call. Police maintain a fairly high profile, so you'll probably always be fairly near an officer of the law. The bazaars have their own brand of police to settle disputes and maintain order.

Chapter 12

On your way to or from İstanbul, try to find a way to shoehorn in some of the interesting sites south of the Sea of Marmara. **Bursa** is the most intriguing city in the area, offering fascinating Ottoman relics, skiing, thermal springs and silk fabric. **İznik** and **Erdek** are both established on the sites of ancient cities, Nicaea and Cyzicus, respectively, and each is worthy of an afternoon.

Bursa

Bursa, the first Ottoman capital, remains home to some of the most important relics and monuments in Ottoman Empire. Anyone with an interest in the trappings of an ascendant empire will enjoy the tombs and mosques of the empire's first sultans, and the growth of their wealth and artistic assurance. There is little evidence of 2,000 years of habitation that predated the arrival of the Ottomans, but there is more to Bursa than history alone. People flock here for the thermal baths welling up at the foot of Mt. Uludağ, the skiing atop the mountain peak, and for markets loaded with silks and other textiles.

"Green Bursa" is also famed for the beauty of its location atop a great spur of Mt. Uludağ overlooking endless rolling hills of orchards and fields in the Bithnian plain below. Unfortunately the beauty is slipping away, sacrificed to the industrial activity associated with trade on the Sea of Marmara. Green Bursa is quickly giving way to the reds of tile roofs as far as the eye can see. The city has a population of 1.8 million and is sprawled out over an area 30 miles wide.

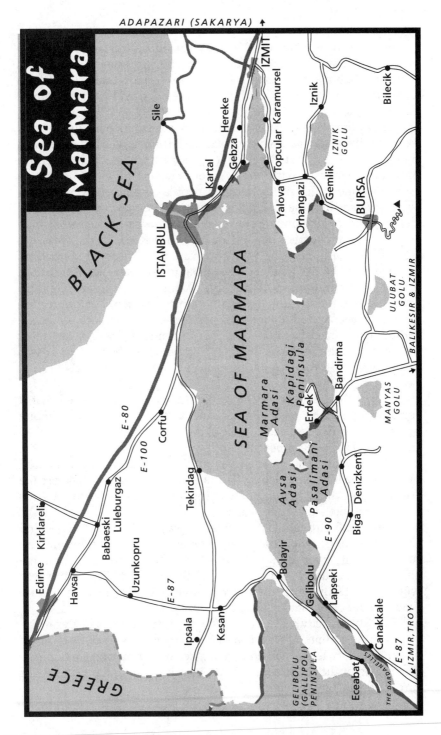

History

Bursa was founded by the Bithynian king **Prusias** in the third century B.C., and through Roman times the city was called Prusa in honor of its builder. Earlier in their history, the Bithnians had been thought of as a stubborn, warlike race, as evidenced by their obstinate attacks on Xenophon's 10,000 in 401 B.C.

The Bithnians helped improve their own reputation by inviting folk less well-liked than themselves. It was the Bithnians who imported Gaul mercenaries as proxies for their ongoing battles, but the Gauls never left, choosing instead to settle near Ankara and establish themselves as Anatolia's most universally disliked people. The Gauls were forever waging war against their neighbors, but in 230 BC they were defeated by the Kingdom of Pergamon. Soon afterward, Prusias established his city.

The city prospered, developing ties with Rome in the west and Pontus in the east. When the two realms came to blows under Mithradites VI Eupator (120-63 BC), Bithnia joined the anti-Roman armies Mithradites, a decision that proved costly. After the Roman General Lucullus' remarkable campaign against a joint Bithnian/Pontic force, the Pontic armies receded to their traditional place on the Black Sea, while Bithnia was forced to sue for peace with Rome. As part of the treaty between Bithnia and Rome, the exiled Bithnian King Nicomedes IV was restored to the throne. Upon his death he completed Rome's victory, bequeathing Bithnia to Rome.

The city's command of the fertile Bithnian plain ensured that it remained important under Roman rule, and as the Byzantine Empire grew to maturity Bursa became one of the great Imperial cities, matched in glory and strategic importance by few others. Arab raiders sacked the city in the seventh century, but it was only in 1075 that the city was seized outright. The invaders? **Selcuk Turks**, punctuating a march across the Anatolian heartland that began with the Battle of Manzikert four years earlier and 1,500 miles to the east.

This Selcuk stronghold was wrested away by the armies of the First Crusade in 1097, who, true to an arrangement with the Byzantines, turned the city over to its rightful—that is Byzantine—owners in exchange for passage & aid on the road to Jerusalem. The return was welcome, but fading Byzantine fortunes meant that, henceforth, the city would never be without fear for its security.

By 1319, the city was one of the last great redoubts of Byzantine power in Asia Minor. It was then that the city was invested by an army of Turks under a leader named Osman, the same Osman that became the first Sultan of the Empire that would bear his name—the **Osmanoğlu Imperatorluk**, or Ottoman Empire.

The Ottoman siege lasted seven years, despite relief efforts from Constantinople, and Osman died just days before the final capitulation of the besieged city. His body was carried into the city, and it remains there still: the tombs of Sultan Osman and his five immediate successors are located within the city.

Many of the most famous monuments in Bursa, such as the Muradiye, the Great Mosque, and the Green Mosque date from the early years of the Ottoman Empire, but even these structures suffered through occasional invasions and natural disasters – notably Tamurlane's occupation in 1402-3 and the quake of 1855, which toppled all but one of the minarets in the city. Bursa and its damaged historical sites were rebuilt, usually quite faithfully, allowing us to see the birth of Ottoman architecture with its attendant artwork and craftsmanship.

Arrivals & Departures

Bursa is located due south of İstanbul, but is separated from İstanbul by the sea of İzmit; thus land routes are rather serpentine. Sea-land routes are the most popular, with ferries leaving from several sites in İstanbul.

By Bus

Bursa is one of the most accessible cities in Turkey—it is directly on the way between İstanbul and many popular destinations. Among the connecting buses from Bursa: Istanbul: $6, 4 hours, hourly buses; Ankara: $7, 5 hours, hourly buses; Antalya: $10, 9 hours, hourly buses; Fethiye: $12, 10 hours, twice daily; Canakkale: $6, 4 hours, hourly buses; Selcuk: $7, 5 hours, hourly buses; Bodrum: $10, 8 hours, four times daily; Cappadocia: no direct buses—transfer at Ankara.

Note: If you are going to or from İstanbul, it's wise to ask how long the bus will take. Direct buses take advantage of ferry terminals at Yalova and Topçular to avoid the long loop around the bay of İzmit—be sure yours does.

The sprawling Bursa Bus Terminal ("Terminal") opened in 1998. It is efficient, spacious, and quite far from Bursa itself—15 kilometers north of city center. Most bus companies will provide a shuttle from the station on to the neighborhood where you wish to go (in your case, probably either Çekirge or Heykel—see *Where to Stay*). If you find yourself without transport, you can either take a taxi ($15) or a bus to the center or town (number 90/A) and a bus (number 24) or dolmuş onward to Çekirge.

To return to the Bursa Bus Terminal by public transportation, await a bus with the word "Terminal" in the window by the PTT & Emlakbank on main street (Atatürk Caddesi).

By Car

The best part of the drive between Bursa and İstanbul is that you don't need to drive too much. The car ferry terminal at Yalova, due north of Bursa, connects with Yenikapi ferry terminal in the middle of İstanbul. There are nine ferries daily, $30 per car.

Another option is to continue past Yalova to Topçular, where ferries ($12, on the half-hour) scoot back and forth between Topçular and Darica, itself a 45 minute drive from Asian shores of İstanbul. This is, generally speaking, not nearly as good as the Yalova-İstanbul direct ferry.

From Bursa to the west, well-maintained highways carry you through the gently rolling hills skirting the Marmara Sea and on towards Çanakkale The road to İzmir (via Balıkesir) follows the Çanakkale course until Karacabey, at which point it veers south, taking the four lanes with it. The road east to Ankara is solid for the first 100 kilometers, and gets even better when it joins the İstanbul-Ankara freeway.

Within Bursa, expect parking to cost $.50 per hour in the downtown area.

By Ferry

Passenger and car ferries ply the waters of the Marmara between Yalova (60 kilometers north of Bursa) and İstanbul with great regularity, and you should plan on using them.

Eight car ferries leave Yalova for Yenikapi terminal (in İstanbul, just one mile northwest of Sultanahmet on the Sea of Marmara) daily, every two hours between 7:30 a.m. (9:30 on Sundays) and 21:30. Return ferries between **Yenikapi** and İstanbul follow an identical schedule. Fare: $23 for car and driver, $4 per person. Amenities: assigned seating and a café. Time: two hours. (Ferries follow a similar schedule to Kartal, south of İstanbul on the Asian shore.)

Hydrofoil passenger ferries (Denizbus) speed between Yalova and Kabataş Terminal (in İstanbul, just two miles northeast of Sultanahmet on the Bosphorous). At the time of this writing, scheduled departures occurred several times daily between 8:30 and 6:25 on weekdays; 9:15 and 5:45 on weekends. *Tel. 216 814 1020.* Fare: $5 per person. Assigned seating. Time: one hour.

People without cars take note: Meeting a connecting bus on the Yalova side or a connecting dolmuş/taxi on the İstanbul side is easy. But, be warned, there is a reason that people seem in a hurry to disembark from these ferries. Buses and dolmuş waiting at the ferry depart as they fill up—if you straggle, you may have to sit on a half-empty bus and await the next load of passengers.

Orientation

Bursa has a long east-west axis along the base of Mt. Uludağ. Because it hugs the south face of the mountain, however, it can play tricks on you—north is down, south is up. The sights of interest sprawl from east to west along this axis—the Beyazid Complex, Ulu Mosque, the Muradiye Complex, Eski Kaplica, and Hudavendigar Mosque. Accommodations of interest are clustered in the western heights in Çekirge (where each hotel has its own marble hamam fed by geothermal springs) and around the center of town. The main east-west road, alas, has no less than four names as it moves through town—Namazgah Caddesi, Atatürk Caddesi, Altıparmak Caddesi, and, finally, Çekirge Caddesi.

Tourist Information
- **Hospital**—Devlet Haşanesi,Tel. 224 220 0020; Tip Fakultesi Hastenesi, *Tel. 224 442 8400*
- **PTT**—Main office is by Emlakbank on south (uphill) side of Atatürk Caddesi in the center of town—across the street from Ulu Mosque.

An Itinerary for Bursa

Begin at the **Yildirim Beyazid Complex** in the northeast. Spend some time there, then follow the winding streets south on foot to the Yeşil Camii and Yeşil Türbe. From there, cross the Gökdere river to the city center, still on foot. If it's nearing lunchtime, drop in at **Hacibey Iskender**, just around the corner from the Halkbank building a block from the city's central Atatürk statue. If you want to whet your appetite further, continue to city center and make your way to the **Ulu Camii** via the arcaded market area, checking the selection of textiles and other goods as you go, and perhaps picking up a newspaper or magazine. If you have questions about where to get certain items, drop in at the Tourism office—you'll be walking right past it.

After spending some time at Ulu Camii, continue to the **Muradiye Complex** ($3 taxi, frequent "Muradiye"- signed mini-bus, or a 2 kilometer walk). Get a meal at **Daruzziyafe** in the medresse of the Muradiye Complex before taking a leisurely walk through the complex itself. Worn out? How about treating yourself to a hamam at your own hotel, if you're staying in **Çekirge**, or at **Eski Kaplica** if you're staying elsewhere. Wrung out, head home for a nap and dine later, or indulge in the open buffet at the **Kervansaray Termal Hotel**.

•**Police**—*Tel. 155*
•**Tourism Police**—*Tel. 224 221 6611*
•**Laundry**—Cumcum Laundry & Internet. Location: Selimiye Mah. Bülbülce Sok. No 9—west of the city center, two blocks downhill of Altıparmak Caddesi on Selimiye Mahellesi between Ziraat Bankasi and Burgys. Hours: 9 a.m. to 7 p.m. Cost: $4 per load. *Tel. 224 223 5477.*

Where to Stay

We prefer accommodations in Çekirge. The rarity of staying in a hotel with its own geothermal spring welling up in the basement trumps the mild inconvenience of being situated 2.5 kilometers west of the city center. Bursa has one excellent luxury hotel boasting not just a spring, but Süleyman the Magnificent's own spring—Eski Kaplica. In addition, it has a few solid, non-thermal options in the center, and the aforementioned clutch of generally humble, unassuming Çekirge hotels with marble-clad hamams in their basements.

City Center

SAFRAN HOTEL, *Ortapazar Caddesi, Kale Sok. No. 40, Tophane, Bursa, Tel. 224 224 7216, Fax 224 224 7219; E-mail: kirayoglu@escortnet.com; Website: none. Rooms: 10. Credit cards accepted. Open year-round. Restaurant on premises. Double (no off-season discounts): $65 with view, $55 without (includes breakfast).*

This is the city's lone "special class" hotel. The Safran is a restored Ottoman-era mansion located on a ridge just above and to the west of the town center, one block uphill of the tombs of Orhan and Osman. Painted a bright, beautiful yellow with brown wood trim, the Safran cuts a striking profile. The interiors are a bit worn, with older carpet and a well-used lobby, and staff does not have strong English. Rooms are decently furnished with stained pine furniture and amenities such as TV and minibar. Five of the ten rooms in this three-story house have views—request one. To get there: From the center of town, head west on Atatürk Caddesi and veer up the long straight road toward the Osman and Orhan tombs.

HOTEL ÇEŞMELİ, *Gümüşçeken Cad. No. 6, Bursa, Tel. 224 224 1511, Fax 224 224 1512; E-mail: None; Website: None. Rooms: 20. Credit cards not accepted. Open year-round. Double (off-season discounts available): $35 (includes breakfast).*

The Çeşmeli is unassuming, but is meticulously clean and a fine choice in the central area. Other major hotels in the center—Kent Hotel and Bilgiç Hotel, for instance—compare very unfavorably in price, housekeeping, and, in the case of the Bilgiç, friendliness. Here at the

Çeşmeli, guests find Turkish delight on their pillow, blinding white sheets, television, showers in the room, and—İnşallah—air conditioning by Spring 2002. The Çeşmeli is owned by a woman and should be considered by women traveling alone. To get there: From the center of town, the Çeşmeli is one block down Gümüşçeken Caddesi, immediately off of Atatürk Caddesi by Vakıfbank.

HOTEL EFEHAN, *Gümüşçeken Caddesi No. 34, Heykel, Bursa. Tel. 224 225 2260; Fax 224 225 2259; E-mail: efehan@efehan.com.tr; Website: www.efehan.com. Rooms: 35. Credit cards accepted. Open year-round. Restaurant on premises. Double (off-season discounts available): $30 (includes breakfast).*

The Efehan opened in early 2001, and its price is probably too good to last—until it changes, it's a fantastic deal. The Efehan is not especially charming, but it is new, central, clean, and has some surprising touches—a glass elevator, television, wooden bedsteads, wrought iron rails, and, in the upper floors, some nice views. The staff is friendly and helpful. The lower façade even mimics the appearance of an old Ottoman house. To get there: The Efehan is one block below the Çeşmeli Hotel (see above).

Çekirge

HOTEL KERVANSARAY TERMAL, *Çekirge Meydanı, Bursa, Tel. 224 233 9300, Fax 224 233 9324. E-mail: termal@kervansarayhotels.com; Website: www.kervansaray.com.tr. Rooms: 211. Credit cards accepted. Open year-round. Restaurants on premises. Double (off-season discounts available): $170 (includes breakfast).*

Unlike most hotels in this book, the Kervansaray is not small. What makes it an exception is that, unlike most major hotels, it has a major attraction—it has been built to embrace the 600-year-old Eski Kaplıca hamam. Built in 1988, the Kervansaray Termal Hotel successfully incorporates elements of the baths in the design of the hotel, with halls and open spaces mimicking the domes and arches of the baths. The interiors are light and finished with marble and brass. Greenery cascades down from the interior courtyards, and fountains fill the halls with soothing sounds. The rooms themselves are a bit unlovely, with lots of salmon colors and gold-colored bedsteads, and some items—phones, for instance—that are a bit dated. That said, carpets were new in 2001, the halls and rooms were freshly painted, and the amenities—from pool to exercise room to in-room satellite television—are outstanding. The best rooms are those on the north, with views overlooking the greenery of Havuzlu Park. Note: guests can coordinate medical treatments with the ostensibly medicinal waters of the baths—inquire.

To get there: From the city center, head north on the main road (İnönü Caddesi) and follow the signed route to Çekirge via Haşim İşcan

Caddesi (which becomes Hamdi Tanpinar Caddesi, then Çekirge Caddesi). The Kervansaray is about two kilometers along, and stands at the intersection of Çekirge Caddesi and Zübedye Hanım Caddesi.

YEŞİL YAYLA HOTEL, *Çekirge Selvi Sok. No. 6, Çekirge, Bursa. Tel. 224 239 6496; Fax None; E-mail; None: Website: None. Rooms: 14. Credit cards not accepted. Open year-round. Double: $21 high season, $15 low season (includes breakfast).*

The Yeşil Yayla, located up the hill behind the Yıldız Hotel, is a 100-year-old house that is definitely showing some wear and tear but remains a great, cheap place to stay in Çekirge. The rooms are small, plain, and share bathrooms, but eight rooms have pleasant views, and the family that runs the hotel is friendly and a few of them speak English. The piece de resistance, as is the case throughout Çekirge, is the bath in the basement. A nondescript entrance with thin green rugs leads into a beautiful marble hamam, there at your convenience. To get there: Follow Çekirge Caddesi west, continuing uphill past the Kervansaray Termal and winding up and around another 400 meters to an intersection with Yıldız Hotel on your left—turn left and find the Yeşil Yayla on your right.

KONAK PALAS HOTEL, *Çekirge 1 Murat Camii Arkası No. 11, Bursa, Tel. 224 236 5113, Fax None; E-mail: None; Website: None. Rooms: 26+. Credit cards not accepted. Open year-round. Double (off-season discounts available): $18+.*

At the time of this writing, the Konak Palas was closed for extensive remodeling, and it is conceivable that it could reopen under a different name. Scrunched in an alley behind the Murat I Mosque in Çekirge, the Konak Palas has long been one of our favorite cheap places in Bursa—bare, simple, and possessed of a wonderful hamam. The remodeling should bring about some substantial positive changes—less draftiness and new paint and rugs—but higher prices can't be far behind. To get there: Follow directions to the Murat I Hudavendigar Camii in Çekirge, just uphill from the Kervansaray Termal Hotel, and turn into the alley between the Murat I Mosque and the Medine Tuğra Termal Hotel. The Konak Palas is kitty-corner from the mosque, in the open area at the center of the block. (Note: The Medine Tuğra Termal Hotel on the corner offers a decent rate, and is good in a pinch.)

Where to Eat

To our way of thinking, there are two places you really ought to eat while here: Kebapci İskender (often called İskender İskender), and Daruzziyafe, the former medresse (cafeteria for the poor) of the Muradiye Complex. There are other options to consider, as well. If you prefer, you can always resort to the McDonalds or Pizza Hut on the south side of Atatürk Caddesi, in the center of town.

Taste of the Town

Many towns have their culinary specialties, but Bursa's probably tops the list. None of Bursa's top-end restaurants are likely to serve you anything better than the inexpensive local fare, İskender Kebap. In the İskender, dense pieces of pide bread are covered with slices of doner kebap, which are in turn covered with a tangy tomato sauce and butter. It is served with yogurt. There are lots of small family restaurants that specialize in this dish – do yourself a favor and try one of these away from the main strip. Portions are bigger and quality is better. Iskender places are all over town, but the best ones are the little places in the streets above the Heykel at city center.

KEBAPÇI İSKENDER, *Ünlü Caddesi No. 7, Heykel, Bursa. Tel.(224 221 4615. Inexpensive-moderate.*

Just who invented the İskender Kebap is a tricky issue, but we can state with authority that Kebapci İskender has been serving this delicious dish since 1867, and has acquired the requisite skill with tomato sauce, meat, melted butter, and yogurt. And we can further state that discussing it makes our mouths water. The sign hung above this restaurant makes no bones—all it says, in massive orange letters, is "İskender." Likewise, the only prices displayed are İskender prices—$3.50 for a regular serving, $5 for a "special" serving, which is to say double the meat, and $5 for "bir büçük porsiyon," or a 1-1/2-sized portion.

To get there: Kebapçi İskender is just to the east of the Heykel, which stands at the major intersection in town—İnönü Caddesi and Atatürk Caddesi. If you're on Atatürk Caddesi in the center of town, you'll see a giant "Halkbank" sign to the east—follow that sign, duck down the street to the left of the Halkbank building, and you'll have found it.

DARUZZIYAFE, *Murat II Caddesi No. 36, Muradiye Cami Karşısı, Bursa. Tel. 224 224 6439; Fax 224 224 8007. Moderate.*

The historic setting and beautiful building aside, Daruzziyafe offers a delicious lunch and dinner menu. All of the classics of a Turkish kitchen are here, but we'd draw your attention to the Muradiye çorbası, a well-seasoned mix of seasonal vegetables and chicken, and the Hunkar Beğendı, stewed lamb in a sauce of thick pureed eggplant blended with cheese, cream, and spices. Such a meal, with a basket of bread, costs $5.50, and is enjoyed in a gorgeous old medresse, with great beams and stone pillars supporting a soaring wooden roof. The outside patio offers a wonderful view out over the city (marred somewhat by the regrettable and already-bankrupt Tower Plaza building—yes, the one with the ferris wheel). The menu is in Turkish, but a picture menu is available, as well. No alcohol is served—there are some concessions to the importance of such institutions to Islam.

To get there: The Daruzziyafe is located alongside the Muradiye Compex.

ÇİÇEK IZGARA, *Belediye Caddesi No. 15, Merkez, Bursa. Tel. 224 221 6526. Inexpensive-moderate.*

Located just 100 yards below the tourist information office in the center of town, Çiçek Izgara is a local favorite. The restaurant is housed in an appealing two-story yellow building with wood trim, on the upper floor. Arabesque music, the comfortable hubbub of Turkish families out on the town, and good grilled food make a great mix (there's no alcohol in this particular mix—Çiçek Izgara is alcohol-free). Prices are a bit higher than you'll find elsewhere in town, but not so you'd notice—köfte or şiş kebap are $2.50, grilled tomatoes $.80, rice $1.

To get there: Walk downhill from the tourism information center and around the big municipal building.

YİLMAZ RESTAURANT, *Arap Şükrü Sokak, Bursa. Tel. 224 221 6545. Moderate.*

Arap Şükrü street is the local favorite for seafood, and while opinions differ about which restaurant is the finest, we're inclined toward the Yilmaz—you might want to check this against the opinion of someone at reception before heading out. During the summer, tables are set up on the cobbled street and there is a general, enjoyable hullaballoo—rakı being imbibed, fish being grilled, and music in the air. Your meal and drinks will cost about $11 per person—more if you aren't careful about the fish you order. Be sure to order something in season, and get the price— "Mevsimlik balık istiyorum. Ne var?" means "I'd like something in season—what do you have?" With any luck, some pantomime and jotting will clarify matters to everyone's satisfaction (see the Fish Glossary in the Çanakkale section for more information).

To get there: The fish market begins on the uphill side of Altı parmak Caddesi, and the lane winds past a whole collection of Arap Şükrü restaurants and cafes.

Seeing the Sights

The rise and fall (and rise, and fall, and rise) of Bursa has erased many of its ancient landmarks, but the most recent generation remains intact. Bursa is thick with historic Ottoman mosques, markets, and mausoleums. These structures are complemented by some fascinating history; if you are in Bursa for a short stay, there are a few things it would be a shame not to see.

The Muradiye Complex

A good place to start a day of sightseeing is at the **Muradiye complex** (from Çekirge follow Çekirge Caddesi towards town, then take a soft right up Murat Caddesi for three blocks) on the west side of town. The complex was built with a mosque and school (**medresse**), but the cemetery is what truly distinguishes this site. Begin at the **Muradiye Mosque** to the left of the tombs and the school. The building was built on the orders of Murat II, a shrewd ruler who consolidated the empire and built up its resources so that upon his death in 1451 his son, Mehmet Fatih, was able to immediately set about the conquest of Constantinople. In a period of rapid architectural advancement, sure enough, the Muradiye Cami had something new to offer with the "courtyard dome" over the center of the building matched in size and height by the "prayer dome" above the mihrab at the prayer-side of the mosque. The enlarged front area was imitated later, and presaged opening up space in the mosque on a grand scale. The mosque has some beautiful tile work.

There are four major tombs in the garden behind the mosque and the school, with another eight smaller tombs of wives, dignitaries, and even concubines. The garden is well cared-for, with shaped shrubs and winding paths. Clockwise from the tomb of Sehzade (prince) Ahmet, which is the tomb to the left of the path between the medresse and the mosque, you'll find the following tombs:

Tomb of Sehzade Ahmet: There is some argument over whose bodies are here, exactly. Ahmet was a son of Beyazid II, but it might also be one of Mehmet's sons, whom Murat II had blinded upon ascending the throne. The latter Ahmet died of the plague together with his brothers.

Tomb of Murat II: The largest tomb belongs to the sultan, who asked to be buried in the earth of Bursa, and specified that a " sumptuous mausoleum" not be erected. He got his wish, more or less, with a grave within a simple building, but the artisans could not help sprucing it up a little bit with some grand old columns and later added beautifully carved wooden eaves. Murat II (1421-1451) was the final sultan to be buried in Bursa. The thick-trunked tree across the path from the entrance to the tomb was planted when the tomb was built. Murat II was the father of Mehmet II Fatih, conqueror of İstanbul.

Tomb of Prince Mustafa: Mustafa has a sad place in Ottoman history. He was the strongest, boldest, and most just of Süleyman the Magnificent's sons, but palace intrigue turned Süleyman against him. Süleyman ordered his son killed, helping clear the way for the incompetent Selim II to ascend the throne. This is a classic turning point in Ottoman history, for under a worthy successor who knows what heights the empire might have reached? Mustafa's tomb is beautifully appointed with flowered İznik tiles. Note the difference in craftmanship between the original tiles and their modern replacements – a cluster of three on the left side, another cluster of four on the right.

Tomb of the sons of Mehmet II Fatih: Mehmet's first son, Mustafa, died during a campaign in central Anatolia and was buried here. His brothers Cem and Beyazid II were left as rivals for the throne, which Beyazid assumed. Cem tried to establish his own capital in Bursa, but was driven out and forced into exile. He died a political pawn in Italy, and his brother repatriated his remains for burial here. The interior of the tomb is dazzling, with colorful gold-leaf tile, restored painting, and stained glass above a sea of blue and green tiles – a far cry from the simple resting place of grandfather Murat II.

The school is used today as a dispensary and a health center. There is some evidence of its old beauty – the tiles and stained glass at the back of the courtyard, for instance – but it is largely run down, and you'll be watched curiously if you have a look at the place.

Other Sights in Bursa

From the Muradiye, you can follow the signs one half block down the street facing the complex and visit an 18th century Ottoman house. The three-story house, its salons and parlors still decorated as they were at the time, suggests the glamour of the Ottoman high classes ($1). Continuing down takes you to the Kultur Park and the Archaelogical Museum (below); continuing up Kaplica Caddesi from the Muradiye in a winding course, you pass through remnants of the city gates atop the bluff and wind past **Şehadet Mosque**. Just prior to descending down out of the old fortress, you will see a clock tower to your left, with some structures in the park at its base. These are the **Tombs of Osman and Orhan**, the empire's first two sultans. Their tombs have changed appreciably from their original form, although they remain in the same location. The originals were demolished in the 1855 quake, and were rebuilt by Sultan Abdülaziz in 1863 in the Ottoman baroque style – in other words, the design of these tombs is even newer than the Dolmabahçe Palace in İstanbul.

Descending down out of the **Hisar** (fortress) area puts you on Atatürk Caddesi near the **Ulu Cami**. This mosque, below the intersection of Maksim Caddesi and Atatürk Caddesi, is the center of Bursa's religious life, and it is one of the finest mosques in Anatolia. Like Edirne's Eski Cami, the Ulu Cami was built just as the Ottomans began to find their own sense of style. Consider the evolution in the course of just over a century: in 1388 the empire was ruled by Murat I, a conqueror who gave little thought to art or architecture and was unable to write. By 1515, the Ottomans had become enlightened to the point that when Selim the Grim seized Tabriz and massacred all of his prisoners he spared the artists, shipping them home to help decorate his empire. Ah, the humanizing force of art! Murat's son, Beyazid I, commissioned Ulu Cami, which was completed in 1399. The construction of the mosque has an interesting story: Beyazid swore he would build 20 mosques in thanks for one of his major victories in Europe, but some of his financial people explained that he couldn't afford 20 mosques. Apparently after some haggling with Allah, Beyazid commissioned the building of a single mosque with 20 domes as a compromise. Allah may have been taking notes, considering Beyazid's grim fate (see below).

The Ulu Cami, six centuries old, is constructed out of massive stones that were cut precisely, then placed flush together without mortar. Although earthquakes have shaken the area, notably the 1855 earthquake that toppled every minaret in Bursa except one of Ulu Cami's own minarets, the mosque has held firm. The same, unfortunately, cannot be said for the 20 domes – most of them were also collapsed in the 1855 quake. Looking at them now, the perceptive person will notice how some of the domes have fine detail work, unlike the replacement domes. The imaginative person, meanwhile, can picture how the interior would have looked with gilding on all of the pillars and 700 small lanterns filling the mosque with light. Much has changed since the mosque was completed – the great entranceway was added after the invader Tamurlane wintered in Bursa, when artists carved the front doors, and one of the minarets had to be rebuilt – but in its structure, its decoration, and its delicately cut walnut mimber, the mosque retains its original spirit.

The covered markets, with a rich selection of silks and other textiles, are below the Ulu Cami in Bursa's urban labyrinth. See the shopping section below.

Getting back on Atatürk Caddesi, continue heading away from Çekirge. As you pass the PTT on the right, the tourist office is just ahead to the left. This is the town square, **Heykel**, and there are a number of good cheap restaurants in the neighborhood. Continuing on Atatürk Caddesi you cross over a small gorge. The second road to your left after the gorge is Yeşil Caddesi, and you will see the dome of the **Yeşil Türbe** ahead of you. Yeşil Türbe (Green Mausoleum) and **Yeşil Cami** (Green Mosque) stand together in this end of town, Bursa's most popular attractions.

The Yeşil Türbe (1421) was built for Mehmet I, and, no, the outside of the Green Mausoleum is not green but a radiant blue. Green, the original color, did honor to Muhammed, but the original exterior tiles were mostly lost and had to be replaced. The restorer inexplicably chose blue. The building's interior imitates the accompanying mosque on a smaller scale, and is adorned with the same fine stone and (original) tile work, and even some brooding stained glass. The same artisans that worked on the mosque turned their attentions to this tomb upon the death of Sultan Mehmet I (1413-1421). Mehmet I was the son of Beyazid I Yildirim, and had to overcome both Beyazid's crushing defeat and capture by Tamurlane and the claims of his own rival brothers. Mehmet I is characterized as more peaceful in temperament than his father, but he clearly had an iron will to emerge from the bloody interregnum and set the drifting empire in order. He was officially sultan for only eight years, but the eight years prior were absorbed with seizing control of the empire.

The **Yeşil Cami** was being built for Mehmet I, but he died just before its completion. Work on the mosque was arrested soon after his death, and among the details left unfinished was the portico before the main door. Otherwise, the mosque is wonderfully complete, lacking Hagia Sophia-inspired volume but making up for it in attention to detail and in the flourishes peculiar to the Ottoman's budding aesthetic. The mosque is decorated with the aforementioned green tiles, as well as tiles of blue that suggest the heavens above.

The highlight of the mosque is its **mihrab**. Yeşil Cami's mihrab is a massive work of ceramic that required unparalleled craftsmanship. The mihrab had to be conceived and molded in large pieces, then painted, cut into smaller pieces to fit in kilns, fired, and reassembled. Craftsmen from Tabriz, in Persia, executed this work. Little wonder, after looking at this cunningly wrought masterpiece that in later campaigns Ottoman sultans, prone to slaying pitilessly, would spare artisans from Tabriz, carting them back to the decorate the empire.

The decoration within the mosque is beautiful, with tile representing alternately flowers of the gardens of heaven, or the heavens themselves with thunderbolts and stars. Opposite the towering mihrab, the sultan's box is visible above the entranceway looking out over the interior of the building. The blues and greens of faience, textured stonework, and stained glass give this room an appropriately regal – and tantalizing – appearance. Unfortunately, visitors cannot ascend to the chambers. The vestibules off of the entranceway (themselves decorated with old Byzantine columns) have a set of stairs that lead to the chambers, but a door within the stairwell is shut and locked.

The **Turkish and Islamic Art Museum** (50¢, closed Mondays) located just down the street has a collection of decorative tile, dervish costumes, and knick-knacks from the Ottoman Empire. There are also some very old hand puppets, for which Bursa has a particular mania. Central to Bursa's puppet lore is Karagöz, a character who has a monument near Çekirge, and his friend Havicat. The characters are based on two men who worked on a mosque in Bursa in the 14th century. The older Karagöz would strike up conversations with Havicat, a Persian, and the two would inevitably fall into misunderstandings that were funny enough to bring work around them to a halt. The sultan at the time, either Orhan or Beyazid, blamed the mosque's slow progress on this mirth, and had Karagöz hanged. Havicat, saddened, left Bursa. Later, feeling sentimental, the sultan had a puppeteer recreate the antics of the two, and the shows became a hit. Television has predictably quashed the puppet shows (Mario is more fun than Karagöz), but the puppets and the name Karagöz still pepper signs around the city.

Isolated in the northeast corner of town is the **Beyazid I Complex**, with its mosque, tombs, and fascinating history. Beyazid was called Yildirim, or lightning, for his rapid marches and the speed of his decisions. He shattered the last of the great crusades in Bulgaria, laid siege to Constantinople, and his martial success further expanded the Ottoman borders in all directions. He appeared set to continue the work of the three sultans that preceded him when Tamurlane appeared in the east.

The ever-victorious Tamurlane would perhaps have been satisfied with leaving the Ottomans in peace, seizing the holy lands to the south, and marching back to pursue his dream of conquering China. However, the hot-blooded Beyazid tempted fate and goaded the eastern armies into battle, where the Ottomans were crushed at the battle of Ankara in 1402.

Beyazid himself, captured (it is said) atop a heap of Tatar soldiers, was caged and kept for Tamurlane's amusement. He lived one year in captivity while Tamurlane plowed through western Anatolia, stabled his camels in Bursa's mosques, and paralyzed Europe with fear. Tamurlane and his armies disappeared into the east the following year, never to return.

Beyazid's türbe was probably already under way when he was defeated at Ankara – it was customary for sultans to oversee the building of their own burial sites. After Tamurlane's passing, Beyazid's body was recovered and one of his sons took time out from the ferocious civil war to complete the tomb here and inter his father.

Then, in the final chaos of the interregnum, Karaman invaders from Konya, nursing an old grudge, destroyed the tomb and burned and scattered the luckless Beyazid's bones. Sultan Mehmet restored order to the empire and rebuilt his father's tomb, but later sultans refused to visit the site, scorning Yildirim's defeat and capture. The tomb itself is relatively bare, its paint long since disappeared. The mosque, too, has suffered over the years, but the structure is excellent, with marble stalactites and small "lightning" insignias in both tile and marble.

The **Archaeological Museum** (closed Monday) is located in the Kultur Park, north of town toward Çekirge. The Bursa Museum has some interesting statuary and artifacts, but is hardly the most impressive museum. There are some impressively-sculpted marble pieces, but the majority of the collection is ornamental jewelry and sculpture of little immediate interest.

The Baths

In addition to those that occupy the basement of most hotels in Çekirge, there are several historic hamams still in operation in Bursa.

Eski Kaplica: There have been baths here at the "Old Springs" since at least Roman times. They have been restored several times—including once by the Byzantine Emperor Justinian and assumed their current shape under Ottoman Sultan Murat I. Additional restoration in the last decade makes Eski Kaplica the finest hamam in Bursa. The hamam is now on the grounds of the Kervansaray Termal Hotel in Çekirge (see above). Hours: 7 a.m. to 11 p.m. Cost: $6 for men, $5 for women (a smaller hamam). Massage costs $4. *Tel. 224 233 9300.*

Yeni Kaplica: The "New Springs" is less upscale—and less expensive—than Eski Kaplica, but is hardly less old. The current structure dates to the time of Sultan Süleiman the Magnificent meaning it was built in 1522, some 100 years after Eski Kaplica, but there have been baths here since Roman times. The current structures are gorgeous, but not as well maintained as Eski Kaplica. There are three sections to the bathing complex—one for men, one for women, and one for families. The location is just across the street and downhill from Celik Palas Hotel in the Kültür Park. Hours: 6 a.m. to 10 p.m. Cost: $6. Massage costs: $4. *Tel. (224) 236-6955.*

Sports & Recreation

Skiing

Skiing is, of course, a fairly modern addition to Bursa/Uludağ's appeal, but the industry received considerable press in 1994-1995 when an American army officer and his son disappeared while skiing at Uludağ. Newspapers in North America and Europe speculated wildly about kidnapping and foul play, but the outcome was much less interesting: the two became lost while skiing in the backcountry and had to dig in and wait for a storm to pass. When rescuers located them after a three day search both were fine, a testament to the overreaction of the American press and the father's army training. It was also, alas, a testament to what lengths good skiers will go to find challenges away from Uludağ's lackluster main slopes. The mountain does have some of the best skiing near İstanbul, however, with good, plentiful intermediate slopes.

Transport from Bursa is easy – your hotel will probably help make arrangements for the 45 minute trip by road to Uludağ, or, alternately, you can stay at one of the seasonal hotels atop the mountain (see above, *Where to Stay*).

There is a cable car from Bursa to Uludağ that leaves hourly from the far east side of town ($4 round trip), but you must take a taxi the final few miles to the skiing and hotel area. The mountain's set-up is antiquated, and likely to seem odd if you're accustomed to big-time skiing in Canada and the United States; different companies – hotels, usually – own different lifts. If you are content on one or two runs, buy a day pass for a single lift. Otherwise, think about buying lift tickets for a set number of runs and venturing around the hill.

Note: **Palandöken**, near Erzurum, has Turkey's best skiing. Lodging is available at the Dedeman Palandöken, *Tel. 442 316 2414, Fax 442 316 3607*, and Turkish Airlines flies to Erzurum several times per week.

Shopping

Bursa was at the western end of the old silk road, and the city has been heavily involved with silk commerce for more than 2,000 years. In the sixth century, agents of Emperor Justinian traveled to China and returned with the secrets – and cocoons – to begin producing silk here as well. Today the bustling Bursa silk market still has local and Chinese silks, and some of them are quite cheap.

One of the reputable local outlets is **Caretta Silk Center**, Kozahan No. 233, *Tel. 224 223 5688*, on the second floor of the silk bazaar below Heykel. Caretta has almost a corner on the market in Turkish patterns – tulips and blossoms that evoke images of İznik tiles – and helpful staff.

Iznik

İznik has a peculiar and wonderful feel to it. This was an important city in ancient times, first the Bithnian capital, then the Roman provincial capital of **Nicaea**. Now, however, many of the landmarks have a Central Asian look, owing to İznik's early settlement by the Selçuks and Turks.

İznik was founded by **Antigonus the One-Eyed**. Antigonus was so named because he lost an eye in battle, continuing to fight and allowing no one to pull the dart from his eye until the battle was over. Antigonus was one of Alexander's most brilliant generals, and one of those who made claims to parts of the empire after Alexander's death. He founded İznik in 316 B.C., and it was seized from him in 301 B.C. by his rival Lysimachos. Under Lysimachos it became capital of Bithnia and remained so even after Lysimachos'own death soon afterward. The name Nicaea derived from the name of Lysimachos'wife.

Nicaea lost its primacy to Nicomedia (Izmit) in the middle of the third century, but it remained an important city. Nicaea passed to Rome peacefully, under whom it was restored to its status as capital of Bithnia. It was under Roman rule that Christianity took hold and Nicaea became an important religious center. The First Council of Nicaea in 325 settled one of the burning, divisive issues of the early Christian Church – roughly, whether Jesus was a divine entity or a mortal man possessed of the divine spirit. The latter notion, championed by Arian, was solidly defeated and denounced as the Arian Heresy. The outright divinity of Jesus Christ was established as doctrine the **Nicene Creed**.

Nicaea continued to play an important role in resolving theological disputes as late as 787, when the Iconoclastic controversy was finally ironed out here. By this time the Arabs had already flooded the area during their campaigns, and İznik had held firm, but eventually the constant attacks from the east wore down the Byzantines; İznik fell to the Selçuks in 1075, an event that badly shook Constantinople. The Byzantine Empire was able to reclaim the city shortly thereafter in the wake of the Crusaders'1097 campaign.

After the soldiers of the Fourth Crusade took Constantinople in 1204, the Byzantine royal families who fled Constantinople retreated to this city and strengthened the city walls. The displacement seems to have a bracing effect on the Orthodox refugees, and they began the gradual process of reviving their moribund empire. In 1261 they recaptured Constantinople and began reasserting their former power. The revival was to be short-lived, and İznik was to play a key role.

İznik – briefly the capital of the Byzantine Empire, a city surrounded by great, high walls, a city with a huge military garrison, and a city well within range of the armies at Constantinople – was fixed in all minds as the Imperial second city. Just 68 years after the Byzantines shifted their seat of power back to Constantinople, the Ottomans laid sustained siege to the city. Nicaea held out for two years, during which time an attempt to break the siege by Byzantine Emperor Andronicus III was beaten back at the Battle of Pelecanon (1329). Cut off from aid and unable to break the siege, the starving garrison surrendered to Sultan Orhan, son of Osman, in 1331. In Constantinople churchbells rang in mourning, a sound that would become common throughout the whole of Europe as the Ottoman successes continued unchecked for more than two more centuries.

Rather, almost unchecked. In 1402 Sultan Beyazid I, an irrepressibly successful general who was prosecuting the siege of Constantinople, was intrigued by the appearance of Tamurlane out of the east. Beyazid I gathered his armies and marched to meet him; as told elsewhere,

Beyazid's army was defeated and scattered, and the Sultan himself was captured. In the aftermath, İznik was sacked and partially destroyed, its population massacred.

Tamurlane disappeared into the east as quickly as he had arrived, and the Ottomans showed stunning resilience, reasserting their dominance in Asia Minor and Thrace. The renewal of İznik speaks volumes about the vigor of the early Ottoman Empire in its heyday. Decimated in 1403, İznik was rebuilt and rapidly developed one of the greatest ceramic workshops in the world. The heyday of the İznik workshops began at the end of the 15th century and lasted for almost 100 years, after which the Ottoman decline drastically reduced the market for faience and Persian artists captured during eastern campaigns died off. İznik's rise was meteoric, its fall as sudden. In the space of fifty years in the early 17th century most of the workshops were abandoned.

An attempt is currently underway to revive the ceramic industry, and archaeologists are at work on unearthing the old kilns and excavating the workplaces. Whatever the state of the ceramicists, İznik itself goes on about its business.

Arrivals & Departures

By Bus

İznik is a short trip from Bursa, and not far from İstanbul via the Yalova ferry. Direct İstanbul buses are rare, but dolmuş wait at Yalova for arriving ferries and are delighted to shuttle you on to İznik. İznik's otogar is inside the city walls, and the tourism office (*Tel. 224 757 1933*) and main sights are several blocks north along the east-west Kiliçaslan Caddesi.

By Car

Follow the directions to Bursa, veering off of 575 at Orhangazi and taking the 150 east, skirting İznik Gölu (Lake).

Orientation

The three mile ring of walls around İznik attests to its former importance. A walk around the circuit can be enjoyable, but it takes a little time and leads through some dodgy neighborhoods. Certainly try to stop in at the main gates in the north (**İstanbul Kapı**) and east (**Lefke Kapı**), both of which are in good states of preservation – Lefke has three separate gateways. It's fascinating for most North Americans to watch people going about their lives in a walled city, driving tractors through arched stone gates as if it were the most normal thing in the world.

For more information, contact İznik's **Tourism Information office**, Belediye Işhane No. 130-131, *Tel. 224 757 1933*.

Where to Stay & Eat

We'd suggest having a look around İznik and getting on your way. Should you take a liking to this town, we've listed some of your options (all budget accommodations) below.

BURCUM MOTEL, *Sahil Yolu (Shore Road) No. 20, İznik, Tel. 224 757 1011, Fax: 224 757 1202. Email: none; Web: none. Rooms: 9. Credit cards not accepted. Open year-round. Double: $22.*

The nicest place in town, a three-story breezeblock structure that offers views of the lake. There's nothing especially charming about the Burcum, but it's clean and has a decent setting between the city walls and the lake. Request a room with a view. The **Çamlık Motel** *(Tel. 224 757 1631)*, a short distance south, is a good second choice., a little bit south on the, is every bit as good. Both motels offer meals.

BABACAN HOTEL, *Kiliçaslan Cad. No. 104, İznik, Tel. 224 757 1623. Rooms: 42. Double: $18.*

If you'd prefer to stay in the city center, this is the sort of hotel that will do for one night. It certainly has a central location, and we found it cleaner than its counterparts at the city center. The Babacan is located two long blocks north of the otogar and two short blocks left on Kiliçaslan Caddesi. Try to get a room in back. If you don't think it will do, consider the nearby **Kaynarca Pansiyon**, three blocks to the east (Gündem Sok. No. 1, Tel. 224 757 1753; Fax 224 757 1723; Double: $21).

BALIKÇI RESTAURANT, *Göl Kıyısı, İznik, Tel. 224 757 1152. Moderate.*

This is our favorite of İznik's several fish restaurants. The location, by the lakeside at the northern end of the waterfront, is pretty. The price is hardly prohibitive, $2 for trout.

Seeing the Sights

Historically the main attraction in town was the **Hagia Sophia**, a building that dates from the beginning of Constantine's reign. The cathedral was converted to a mosque under the Ottomans, but the structure collapsed during intense fighting between the Greeks and Turks in the 1922 War of Turkish Independence. Today the ruin, near the center of town, has been partially cleared and restored and you can find mosaics from the original building.

The most interesting site in İznik today is the **Yeşil Cami**, or Green Mosque, near the Lefke Kapı. This building screams of Central Asia, and that may be because when Tamurlane sacked the town he carted off the artisans that had built this edifice and put them to work on the Registan in Samarkand. The Green Mosque is now faced partly in replacement tiles from Kütahya; it remains beautiful.

The **İznik Museum**, nearby in the Nilüfer Hatun soup kitchen, is also worth a visit. The carving around the doorway deserves to be stared at from now until the end of time, but you should, instead, enter the museum and have a look at the nice display about the history of tilemaking, old kilns, and artifacts from the city's ancient past. The other reason to visit the Museum is to inquire about the **catacomb** outside of town, to which museum personnel can direct you and for which they have keys. The catacomb is Byzantine era and – an intriguing and little-known side trip just outside of İznik.

The other appeal of İznik is obviously its beautiful shoreline on **İznik Lake**. Several restaurants have set up on the lakeside to take advantage of the beautiful view, but you can also opt for a picnic on your own in the area north of Göl (lake) Gate.

Bursa to Canakkale

The road west of Bursa is in a good state of repair, heading in the direction of Karacabey. After passing Karacabey on a bluff above the highway, the largely two-lane highway veers north to the Sea of Marmara through tilled fields of garlic, onion, potatoes, and wheat are studded with silos and farms. Nearing Bandırma, you'll see a left turning to **Kuş Cenneti Milli Park** (Bird Paradise National Park); in the spring, birders will enjoy a few hours here on Küs Gölü.

Bandırma, just north of the highway, is the site of a car ferry terminal offering direct service to Istanbul 5-8 times per day between 8 a.m. and 6 p.m. in summer. This is not a pretty town, and there is little by way of accommodation—in a pinch, consider the remarkably overpriced **Hotel Eken Prestige** *(Tel. 266 714 7600)*, Double: $90, in the city center, or the simpler, non-prestige **Hotel Eken** *(Tel. 266 714 7800)*, Double: $32. If you must stay in this region, consider staying in the prettier town of Erdek on the other side of the isthmus from Bandırma. Erdek's best options are a few stout places along the waterfront, **Umit Hotel** *(Tel. 266 835 1092)*, Double: $20; **Pınar Hotel** *(Tel. 266 835 7024)*, Double: $18); and, north of town is the upscale **Otel Gül Plaj** *(Tel. 266 835 1053)*, Double: $64.

Several Marmara islands are accessible from Erdek, including Marmara Island (Şato Motel, *Tel. 266 885 5003*) and Avşa Island (**Berlin Pansiyon**, *Tel. 266 896 4032*). Inquire at Erdek Tourism for ferry terminals. These islands are largely bare, adorned with some olive trees and small waterfront villages and, in most cases, some sprawl from vacationing İstanbullus. Marmara Island, the former Proconnesus—home to the marble quarries that yielded the finest marble in ancient Rome and Byzantium—has the best beaches.

The ruins of ancient **Cyzicus** are located six kilometers east of Erdek on the isthmus of the Kapidaş Peninsula. Most access to these ruins is blocked by unlovely development and a military base, and what little there is to see is not worth your time.

Continuing West from the Kapidağ Peninsula, the highway winds along the shore within sight of the Sea of Marmara. The highway passes several small creeks and rivers wending their way toward the sea, the most storied of these Biga Cayi—formerly the **River Granicus**, site of Alexander's first great victory over the Persians (334 B.C.). Soon afterward, the sea tapers down to the Dardanelle Straits at Lapseki. You'll find ferries between Lapsekı and Gelibolu, if your destination is to the north. Otherwise, follow the pretty highway through to the Çanakkale area.

Mithradites' Defeat

In the Third Mithraditic War (69-66 B.C.), the Roman general **Lucullus** confronted the marauding armies of **Mithradites VI Eupator at Cyzicus**. Mithradites' Pontic army was far larger than the Roman force, and it was already besieging the important Roman city of Cyzicus when Lucullus arrived in the winter of 67 B.C. Lucullus was unwilling to engage the Pontic army, and chose instead to harry its supply lines. While his small force busied itself with isolating the Pontic Army, Lucullus encamped on a hill within sight of Cyzicus. According to Plutarch's account, the inhabitants of the city believed the force to be their enemies' reinforcements, Mithradites' Armenian allies, and the Cyzicenes were thrown into despair. Some advised surrender to Mithradites. By lucky chance, a boy managed to steal his way through the cordon from outside and make his way into Cyzicus. The despondent citizens asked him if there was any word of their Roman allies. At this the youth " laughed at them, supposing them to be jesting," Plutarch writes. " But when he saw they were in earnest, he pointed out the Roman camp to them and their courage was revived."

At this point, Lucullus' strategy was already taking a toll. Mithradites army was on severe rations, and that strain was compounded by an unseasonable storm that blew in and wrecked many of the Pontic siege engines. Mithradites, realizing his plight, was forced to try to retire. While Lucullus was away with the bulk of his troops raiding a Pontic supply caravan Mithradites sent his cavalry, injured soldiers, and horses away toward Bithnia. Lucullus began a pursuit through the snow, overtaking the Pontic force at the river Rhyndacus (Kocasu Çayı) and massacring them, capturing 6,000 horses and 15,000 men. These they marched back the way they had come past Mithradites' siege army, now itself under siege. The Pontic army lost heart, and was routed in a long, harried retreat to the east that culminated in the sacking of the Pontic capital on the Black Sea.

Chapter 13

The Anatolian plain is the breadbasket of Turkey, as it was for the Ottomans and the Byzantines before them. The plateau often looks desolate, particularly in the heat of summer or during the long, bitter winters, but control of the area and its web of trade routes has been crucial since long before recorded history began in 2000 B.C. So much has changed, and so little; Turkey's capital, **Ankara**, is not far from the capital city of the Hatti pre-2000 B.C., and the city that the Hittites adopted afterward, **Hattuşas**. Another capital, **Gordion**, is just to the west of Ankara.

Ankara, Turkey's capital, carries on regardless of the weather, but some of the nearby travel destinations can be rendered inhospitable. Hattuşas, Gordion, and nearby **Cappadocia** are best avoided in the winter, although Cappadocia's hotels can take care of you despite the cold – and the region's Bizarro world landscape will still dazzle with a dusting of snow.

Ankara

For thousands of years, **Ankara** has been a crossroads and administrative center, and in a land of constant change that, at least, remains the same. If you are in Ankara, you're probably passing through, picking up a visa at one of the local embassies, or here on business. And you are in luck, because while Ankara may not get marquee billing on a trip itinerary, it has more than its share of charm. With embassies from around the world and two fine universities (Bilkent and Middle East Technical), the city has international flavor to go with its Anatolian hospitality.

Ankara is best as a staging area for trips west to Gordion, east to Hattuşas, south to Cappadocia, and north to Amasya and the Black Sea beyond. One night in Ankara is usually plenty for tourism purposes, but there's plenty to see if you remain longer. Ankara's tourism highlights include the **Anatolian Civilizations Museum**, concentrating on pre-Hellenistic history (Hittite, Assyrian, and Urartian), scattered ruins from Roman **Angora**, and **Atatürk's grand mausoleum**.

The pace here is different, and this is even reflected in holiday habits; Ankara has a July and August lull (think discount reservations) while vacationers head to the coast. Even in the dog days, though, Ankara is a pleasant place to visit.

History

Ankara is an ancient settlement, and was already old when the **Hittites** occupied it in the second millenium B.C. The easily defensible fortress here was occupied later by the Lydians and Persians, and it was still officially under Persian dominion when **Alexander** arrived in 333 B.C. After cutting the knot at Gordion, Alexander made for Ankara (then Ancyra, later Angora). The people of Ankara, however, thought better of challenging the young king and surrendered, diverting him from what would have, at best, been a damaging march through their countryside. Alexander accepted the submission of Ankara and headed south toward Cappadocia.

Ankara passed on to Seleucus after Alexander's death, but the city was seized by the Gauls who came to Anatolia as Bithnian mercenaries in 279 B.C. The Gauls dominated the local area, terrorizing their less aggressive neighbors until their great defeat at the hands of Eumenes of Pergamon in 230 B.C. Soon afterward the city was occupied by Pergamon, and was thereafter inherited by Rome after the death of Attalus III. The city's Gallic identity remained in the name of the Roman province, Galatia. Ankara was the capital of that province, and it was here that St. Paul addressed the Galatians.

Ankara's long period of peace ended with the Persian invasion of the seventh century, and after several damaging battles the Arabian Caliph Mutasim captured and decimated the town in 838 A.D. The Byzantines recovered quickly, but their hold remained weak. The city fell and was recaptured several more times, finally slipping away to the Selçuks, then the Ottomans. The Ottoman occupation dramatically interrupted when Tamurlane and Beyazid I fought the Battle of Ankara in 1402. The confrontation pitted two relentlessly successful generals against

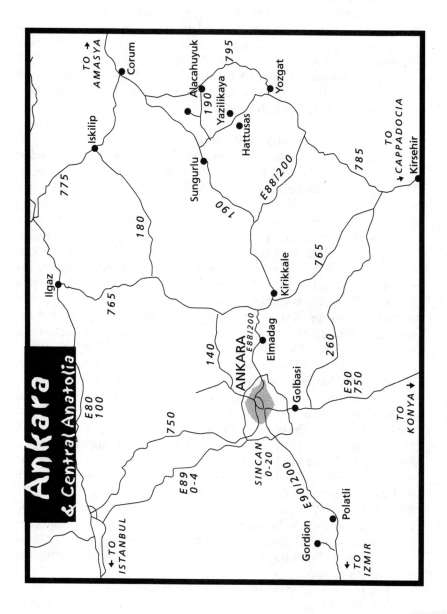

one another, young Beyazid Yildirim (Lightning) against the old, shrewd Tatar emperor. Beyazid squandered the advantage of the high ground and water at Ankara by marching out against Tamurlane who, after some shrewd maneuvering, encamped alongside Ankara himself. The ensuing battle, west of Ankara, was long and ultimately decisive, ending with the Ottoman army shattered and Beyazid captured. Ankara, like most Ottoman cities in Asia, was sacked and partially destroyed by the Tatars. The city was recovered by the Ottomans under Mehmet I in 1414. Almost 500 years later this dark period in Ottoman history was followed by a glorious moment in Turkish history.

The Founding of the Turkish Republic

Ankara was established as the seat of power in the uncertain period between the end of World War I and the Turkish War of Independence. It was chosen partly because it reflected Turkey's return to the values of the Anatolian heartland, partly because Atatürk mistrusted İstanbul, and partly because both peacemakers and rival armies were on the verge of seizing İstanbul, Turkey's last and grandest European possession.

In the years following the defeat of the Central Powers in World War I, Ankara was a hive of activity. The postwar peace had carved up the nation; Russia had a chunk of the northeast, Armenia everything east of Giresun, England everything south of Lake Van, France a block of territory extending east of the Mersin-Tokat line, Italy the rest of the Mediterranean coast as deep as Afyon. İstanbul and the rest of the northwest not ceded to the Greeks was placed in a jointly administered occupied territory. The Turks, despondent after a series of painful defeats in the Arabian theater and the subsequent collapse of the Ottoman Empire, were relegated to a chunk of the Anatolian heartland centered on Ankara. Worse, the Turks seemed resigned to this fate and showed little intention of contesting the dismantling of their homeland.

In their darkest hour, they were saved by, of all things, the Greeks. Antagonism between the Greeks and Turks had festered since the mutual atrocities of the Greek's own War of Independence in the 19th century, and, some might say, since the Greeks ransacked Troy in 1250 B.C. The post-WW I peace treaty called for the Greeks to occupy Smyrna (İzmir), and, after the judicious reluctance of the Greek King Constantine, prime minister Eleutherios Venizelos jumped at the opportunity. Greek forces landed at İzmir on May 15 , 1919, and began penetrating into the Turkish hinterland.

The Turks, written off as beaten and exhausted, were awakened by the invasion of their longtime subjects. Four days after the landing at Smyrna, the newly resolute Turks began piecing together resistance. One year later the nationalist Turks, whipped along by Mustafa Kemal (later known as Atatürk), had taken refuge at Ankara and formed an army. When the Greeks and Turks finally met, the new nationalist army was ready, stealing the initiative from the Greeks in the first battle of Inönü (January 10, 1921) and driving them back in the second (March 31, 1921). Atatürk was responsible for the military victories, as well as for fielding an army in the first place.

Atatürk distilled the anxiety and shame of the partition and the Greek invasion and, long before Adolph Hitler emerged to give racial nationalism a bad name, forged a Turkish national army. The allies, having in some ways prodded the Greeks into aggression, stood by while this army surged out of its Treaty territory. The allies, licking their wounds after the holocaust of WW I, had no stomach for further warfare. Even when the Turks drove the Greek army out of Anatolia and into the sea, neither the British, French, or Italians showed any signs of resistance. The Russians, mired in their own civil war and its horrible aftermath, were otherwise occupied.

Atatürk was careful to press his cause without provoking the allies, and the allies at no point sought to challenge him through force of arms. In the end, it was a fait acompli; the Treaty of Sevres was torn up and the The **Treaty of Lausanne** confirmed the Turkish victory, restoring their borders to the current size.

Having successfully defended Ankara, the Turkish nationalists now began to appreciate its spartan virtues. Atatürk was in favor of permanently shifting the Turkish capital from İstanbul to Ankara, and, as ever, he won the day. Ankara became the centerpiece of the new Turkish nation, and remains a sophisticated and appealing town.

Arrivals & Departures

By Air

Both internal and international flights serve Ankara's **Esenboğa Airport**, *Tel. 312 398 0000*, including occasional non-stop flights from New York City on Turkish Airlines. Ankara's airport offers direct service to several points in Turkey, but most flights continue to be funneled through İstanbul's Atatürk Airport. Among the direct flights are: Adana, 3 daily, $78; Antalya, 3 daily, $78; Bodrum, Thursday-Monday, $84; Dalaman, Friday, Sunday, $60; Erzurum, 2 daily, $78; İstanbul, 10+ flights daily, $78; Izmir, 6 daily, $70; Trabzon, 2 daily, $60.

Esenboğa Airport is located 32 kilometers outside of town. Daytime taxi rates to and from the airport are about $30; this rises to $45 at night rates. A less expensive, and quite convenient, alternative is to take a **Havaş** airport bus to and from the airport (4 a.m.-10:30 p.m). These buses run between the airport and the bus station, departing on the half-hour and taking 45 minutes in each direction.

Flying Carpets

"At the end of the twentieth century, one of the last vestiges of the Golden Age of Travel was the Turkish bus. Like the American transcontinental railroad in the late nineteenth century and Europe's Orient Express in the early twentieth, Turkey's network of long distance buses offers personalized comfort through a primitive and spectacular terrain. The buses are clean and air-conditioned, and offer snack service. The Ankara bus terminal is the most alluring of Oriental bazaars, where departure times and destinations peal in swooshy Turkish syllables. Neon signs proclaiming dozens of private bus companies brighten the passageways – proof of an entrepreneurial economy. As I approached the departure gates, drivers revved up the engines of Swedish- and German-manufactured double-decker vehicles painted in slick graphic designs, like new age versions of flying carpets."

—Tim Kelsey, **Dervish: Travels in Modern Turkey**. Penguin Books, 1997

By Bus

Ankara's otogar, **Yeni Terminal** (New Terminal), is almost deserving of a visit all by itself. The facility opened in 1995 and remains shockingly slick and organized. Buses whisk in and out with crisp precision, ticket offices are organized numerically along one long concourse, and giant information boards tell you when each bus is leaving, and where it is headed. If you're going somewhere slightly peculiar, you'll find that the best method to get where you're going is still to ask a tout which buses serve that region. The upper-end **Ulusoy** and **Varan** bus companies have separate terminals near the otogar on Eskişehir highway, but they also have ticket offices at the far western end of the terminal concourse (booths 12 and 13). Another strong bus company, **Kamil Koç**, is located nearby at booths 17 and 18. The Varan company has the following rates from Ankara: İzmir $18; Antalya $19; Alanya $21; Didim $20; Kuşadası $20; Bodrum $23; İstanbul $22.

Getting to and from the Yeni Terminal is so easy that it's jarring. Havaş buses leave half-hourly for the airport from 4 a.m. to 10:30 p.m. from the lower level, alongside the municipal buses ($2.50). Most bus companies offer ongoing service to Ankara's major neighborhoods – be sure to ask. Failing that, the recently-completed Ankaray subway line runs on an east-west axis through Ankara, passing through Kızılay in the center of town; this is where you'll want to surface. The cost of a ticket varies between $.50 and $.75, depending on the exchange rate at the moment.

For direct service to the budget hotels in Ulus, consider public bus number 198, marked "Ulus;" public buses depart from the bottom level of the Otogar.

Finally, taxis are available; expect the ride to Ulus, Kızılay, or Kavaklıdere to cost $4-$6.

By Car
All roads lead to Ankara, and most of them are in excellent shape. Konya is 255 kilometers south, Nevşehir 297 kilometers southeast, Boğazköy 200 kilometers east, Gordion 76 kilometers west, and İstanbul 385 kilometers northwest. The slick new six-lane version of the highway between Ankara and İstanbul makes the drive a pleasure.

By Train
Rail service in Turkey is not particularly good; the trains are generally old and slow and the alternatives, whether bus or plane, are cheap and quick. The Ankara-İstanbul line is an exception to this.

There are several İstanbul-Ankara trains (also addressed in the İstanbul chapter). The best of these is the **Ankara Express**, a night train with sleeper cars. If you're interested in booking tickets, bear in mind that the İstanbul train stations on the Asian shore is called "Haydarpaşa."

Two other trains may be of interest if you're headed east: Vangölü Ekspresi and the Güney Ekspresi. There's little "express" about these trains, but they're cheap and dependable. These trains alternate days, departing Ankara at 6:50 a.m. daily and rolling slowly east. They follow the same route for quite some distance, passing through Sivas en route to Malatya ($8, 17 hours); Malatya's a place of interest, you can use it as a base en route to Nemrut Dağ. From Malatya, the Vangölü Express veers off toward Van, while the Güney Express continues south toward Diyarbakır. Both trains allow you to experience a taste of the old "Trans-Siberian" railway cachet, a bustling, rolling experience of mercantile excess that goes on for days; this is an all-too "real" way to travel, for better and worse.

The Train Station (or "Garı") is one half-kilometer from a stop on the Ankaray subway line. This entrance to the Garı is located on Talat Paşa Caddesi, connected to the train station by a tunnel beneath the tracks. On Talat Paşa Caddesi, you can find taxis to Ulus, Kızılay, and Kavaklıdere.

Orientation
Ankara is a comfortable, coherent city, with lawns, broad streets, and several large parks. Diplomats from around the world mix with students

from some of Turkey's top universities, creating a cosmopolitan feel and a good nightlife. Note that tourism sites shut down on Monday.

The **Tourism Information** office is probably a bit out of your way, in Maltepe. It is a wonderful resource; the staff is smart, helpful, and mostly English-speaking, as you'd expect in the capital. The office is just across from the Maltepe subway stop (*Gazi Mustafa Kemal Bulvari No. 121, Tel. 312 229 2631*). This is the place to solicit advice, find out about trips to Hattuşas, or bring complaints from 8 a.m.-6 p.m. There is another tourism office at the airport, open 24 hours, *Tel. 312 398 0348*.

You may be coming to Ankara to pick up an ongoing visa. Here are some embassies that may be of interest:
- Azerbaijan: Cemal Nadir Sokak No. 20, Çankaya, *Tel. 312 441 2620*
- Bulgaria: Atatürk Bulvari No. 124, Kavaklıdere, *Tel. 312 426 7455, Fax: 312 427 3178*
- Canada: Nenehatun Cad. No. 75, Kavaklıdere, *Tel. 312 436 1275, Fax: 312 446 4437*
- Georgia: Ulubey Sokak No. 28, Gaziosmanpaşa, *Tel. 312 447 1720*
- Greece: Zia Ül-Rahman Sokak No. 9-11, Gaziosmanpaşa, *Tel. 312 436 8860, Fax: 312 446 3191*
- Iran: Tahran Caddesi No. 10, Kavaklıdere, *Tel. 312 427 4320, Fax: 312 468 2823*
- Iraq: Turan Emeksiz Sokak No. 11, Gaziosmanpaşa, *Tel. 312 468 7421, Fax 312 468 4832*
- Israel: Mahatma Gandi Caddesi No. 85, Gaziosmanpaşa, *Tel. 312 446 3605, Fax: 312 426 1533*
- Jordan: Dede Korkut Sokak No. 18, Aşağiayrancı, *Tel. 312 440 2054, Fax: 312 440 4327*
- Lebanon: Kızkulesi Sokak No. 4, Gaziosmanpaşa, *Tel. 312 446 7485. Fax: 446 1023*
- Romania: Bukreş Caddesi No. 4, Çankaya, *Tel. 312 427 1241*
- Russia: Kayağdı Sokak No. 5, Çankaya, *Tel. 312 439 2122, Fax: 438 3952*
- Syria: Sedat Simavi Sokak No. 40, Çankaya, *Tel. 312 440 1721, Fax: 312 438 5609*
- Turkish Republic of Northern Cyprus: Rabat Sokak No. 20, Gaziosmanpaşa, *Tel. 312 437 6031, Fax: 446 5238*
- United Kingdom: Şehit Ersan Caddesi No. 46A, Çankaya, *Tel. 312 468 6230, Fax: 312 468 3214*
- United States: Atatürk Bulvari No. 110, Kavaklıdere, *Tel. 312 468 6110, Fax: 312 467 0019*

Where to Stay
Ankara has little by way of charming, small hotels, but the city certainly doesn't want for accommodations in general. Travelers in town

to see the museum and Ankara's ancient sites are well advised to stay in the old city, the **Ulus** area. Here you'll find a good selection of budget and mid-range hotels. Foreigners in town on business or politics typically stay in the Kavaklıdere district, typically at the towering Hilton or Sheraton hotels; both are well-maintained and worthy of Turkey's capital city. The Kızılay district lies between the two in both geographic and accommodation terms.

Ulus

ANGORA HOTEL, *Kalekapısı Sok. No. 16, Kaleiçi, Ulus, Ankara. Tel. 312 309 8380; Fax 312 309 8381; Email: none; Web: none. Rooms: 6. Credit cards accepted. Open year-round. Double: $60-$75 (breakfast included).*

The Angora is the finest small hotel in Ankara, a beautifully restored Ottoman-era mansion located within the former citadel above town. The neighborhood, Kale, is home to a warren of old buildings within the bounds of ancient stone fortifications; many of these fell into disrepair as Ankara was restored under the Republic.

The renaissance of the neighborhood began with several fine restaurants; fitting that it continues with the Angora Hotel. The thick stone walls keep the interiors cool, and the setting above the city is marvelous. Rooms are well-appointed, with en suite bathrooms and beautiful Turkish decorations. To get there, follow the road from Ulus up past the above the Museum of Anatolian Civilizations on the signed road to Kale/Hisar. There, you'll find the Angora Hotel next to the Kale Washington Hotel.

Selected as one of our 'small hotels of note' in Chapter 10.

TUR İST HOTEL, *Çankırı Cad. No. 37, Ulus, Ankara, Tel. 312 310 3980, Fax Tel. 312 311 8345; Email: turisthotels@superonline.com; Web: none. Rooms: 148. Credit cards accepted. Open year-round. Double: $38.*

As the name indicates, this hotel was built to accommodate tourists in 1978. Its preeminence in the field is now something of the distant past, but the hotel still serves nicely as a midrange accommodation. Everything is a little ragged at the edges, but clean, and the hamam and sauna downstairs are most welcome during the long Ankara winter. The Turist overlooks the extensive ruins of the old Roman baths, and is located in the old heart of the city. If full, the **Otel Duman** just across the main road and down Beşik Sokak, has lower prices but is the next best option *(Tel. 312 311-0485; Double: $14).*

HİTİT HOTEL, *Hisar Park Cad., Firuzağa Sk. No. 12, Ulus, Ankara, Tel. 312 310 8617, Fax: 312 311 4102; ; Email: none; Web: none. Rooms: 44. Credit cards not accepted. Open year-round. Double: $30.*

The Hitit has an elaborate, interesting lobby and a fine location at the base of the fortress hill. The rooms are humble, but offer baths and small desks. Like most hotels in the Ulus area, the Hitit is a little ragged, but well-suited to a stay of a night or two. The Hitit Hotel is just 200 meters from the Anatolian Civilizations Museum.

HİSAR OTEL, *Hisar Park Cad. No. 6, Ulus, Ankara. Tel/Fax 312 311 9889; Email: none; Web: none. Rooms: 24. Credit cards not accepted. Open year-round. Double: $9 (plus $7 for two baths).*

The Hisar makes a virtue of its shortcomings. The modest little budget hotel doesn't claim to have 24-hour hot water, it has none at all. Instead, it is attached to a hamam where, for an additional fee, you can treat yourself to the baths. The hotel is clean and, come nightfall, quiet. Several rooms have good views. The Hisar is centrally located. The Hisar is centrally located on the road that climbs to the museum and Hisar.

LALE PALAS, *Hükümet Meydanı Telegraf Sk. No. 5, Ulus, Ankara, Tel. 312 312 5220. Rooms: 45. Double: $15.*

A tidy, exacting little Turkish hotel with downmarket charm. Run by a conservative old gentleman, and kept spic and span. Located near the Column of Julian in the center of the old town.

Kavaklıdere

SHERATON ANKARA HOTEL & TOWERS, *Noktalı Sk. Kavaklıdere, Ankara, Tel. 312 468 5454, Fax Tel. 312 467 1136; Email: info@sheraton.com; Web: www.sheraton.com. Rooms: 311. Credit cards accepted. Open year-round. Double: $165 (30-50% discount in off-season).*

ANKARA HILTON HOTEL, *Tahran Cad. No. 12, Kavaklıdere, Ankara, Tel. 312 468 2888, Fax Tel. 312 468 0909; Email: info@hilton.com; Web: www.hilton.com. Rooms: 324. Credit cards accepted. Open year-round. Double: $150 (30-50% discount in off-season).*

These two hotels have long since established themselves as the class of Ankara. It's easy to tell the two apart from the outside—the Sheraton is tall and cylindrical, the nearby Hilton is more boxlike. Within, the Hilton has a slightly more Old World feel than its peer, but otherwise it's hard to differentiate between the two. Both boast first class services, outstanding amenities, and solid, polished, comfortable rooms; these are the hotels favored by visiting NATO generals and heads of state. Each hotel has a pool, a fitness center, and a business office. As usual, these hotels are intended as line items in your expense account. You can book directly to cut 15-30 percent off the price (See Chapter 11, İstanbul, *Where to Stay*).

Kızılay

HOTEL METROPOL, *Olgunlar Sk. No. 5, Bakanlıklar, Kızılay, Ankara, Tel. 312 417 3060, Fax: 312 417 6990; Email: none; Web: none. Rooms: 32. Credit cards accepted. Open year-round. Double: $75.*

The Metropol won't wow you until you visit friends at other mid-range hotels in town. This is a great choice in Ankara's bustling Kızılay area, rating three stars from the tourism bureau on the strength of solid amenities, tidy, attractive rooms, good service, and a hospitable lobby. This is the best mid-range hotel in Ankara, with a city-center location that is convenient. The Metropol has a restaurant; nearby **Boğazaçi Lokanta** is a good, inexpensive option. **Otel Elit**, just across the street, offers similar amenities at a similar cost *(Tel. 312 417 4695; Fax 312 417 4697; Double: $70).*

ERTAN OTEL, *Selanlik Cad. No. 70, Kızılay, Tel/Fax 312 418 4084; Email: none; Web: none. Rooms: 17. Credit cards not accepted. Open year-round. Double: $27.*

The Ertan is good budget option. Its location a few blocks from the center of Kızılay lends to the air of quiet. The hotel has en suite showers in many rooms and the owners are quite helpful. To get here from the Ulus direction, head south on the main road through town, Atatürk Bulvari. You'll pass the large square and continue to Meşrutiyet Caddesi (a main east-west arterial) and turn left. Look for Selanlik Caddesi three blocks along; turn right

Where to Eat

Ankara has a fine selection of restaurants. Restaurants and cafes are constantly opening (and, sure, closing), playing to a market of foreigners, professionals, diplomats and students. The fortress atop Ankara's main hill has several of the best restaurants in the city (some say in the country), while other gems are tucked away in Kavaklıdere and elsewhere. For a change of atmosphere and food, try the **China Restaurant** in Altınparkı – we consider this good, relatively inexpensive restaurant Ankara's best-kept secret. American fast food restaurants have staked out some prime corner real estate throughout the city.

Ulus & The Kale (Citadel)

The fortified citadel above Ankara offers several fine restaurants, all of them located in old Ottoman-era mansions, with grape vines climbing through their wooden rails.

KALE WASHINGTON RESTAURANT, *Ankara Kalesi, Doyuran Sk. No. 5-7, Kaleiçi, Ankara. Tel. 312 445 0212; Fax 312 324 5959. Expensive-Very Expensive.*

An exacting Turkish acquaintance of ours maintains this is one of the only places outside of Istanbul and private kitchens where you can find true Turkish cuisine. The Washington is an Ankara institution since 1955, the work of a family which has, to answer the obvious question, ties to Washington, D.C. In 1994 the family moved the restaurant to its new location atop the fortress hill, a marvelous location in a sprawling old house that offers a patio view of the city below.

The Kale Washington is slightly more expensive than its rivals; mezes, dinner and spirits for two should cost $30 or so. The restaurant excels at making the standard dishes properly; su böreği (pastry), eggplant salad, and grills, for instance. The most dubious item on the menu is the "munched fish;" the kazandibi (milk pudding with chicken) is very good. Stay on your toes; there are serenading musicians.

ZENGER PAŞA KONAĞI, *Doyran Sokak No. 13, Kaleiçi, Tel. 312 311 7070. Expensive.*

This is another of the fine restaurants atop the old fortress, in the same mold as the Kale Washington. If you eat here, you'll have a lot of Turkish dishes the way they were meant to be eaten; homemade mantı, gözleme, lovingly stuffed dolma, and more. Zenger Paşa offers tables with a marvelous view. The Zenger Paşa is located just downhill past the Kale Washington. The **Agora et ve Balık Evı** nearby is a step down in price, offering a $15 prix-fixe menu *(Tel. 312 310 7675; Fax 312 310 1555).*

MEŞUR 49 PIDE AND KEBAP SALON, *Işiklar Caddesi, No. 9/A, Ulus, Ankara, Tel. 312 311 7260. Inexpensive.*

A good, honest hole in the wall restaurant serving food cooked by men, for men. Tavuk şiş (chicken shish) is $2, iskender kebap is $1.50, and lahmacun is 50¢. This is just a short walk downhill from the Ancient Civilizations Museum.

Kavaklıdere

SANTINI, *Sheraton Ankara, Noktalı Sok. Kavaklıdere, Ankara, Tel. 312 468 5454. Very Expensive.*

The cuisine of northern Italy in the center of Ankara. The prawns are worth squandering your expense account on, every single day.

HACİ ARIFBEY KEBAPÇİSİ, *Güniz Sk. No. 48, Kavaklıdere, Ankara, Tel. 312 467 6730. Moderate.*

A nice alternative if you're staying in the Kavaklıdere area. The kebap house is just downhill of the Hilton, offering a small garden. Good food, moderate prices, and a good reputation with the locals.

WASHINGTON RESTAURANT, *Nene Hatun Cad. No. 97, Gaziosmanpaşa, Ankara. Tel. 312 445 0212. Expensive.*

The Washington is located in a pretty old mansion, with dining in the garden outside. The menu offers Turkish dishes, with French and Russian influence.

DAILY NEWS CAFÉ, Arjantin Cad. No. 1, *Gaziosmanpaşa,* **Ankara. Tel. 312 468 4613. Moderate.**

Arjantin Caddesi, climbing uphill by the Sheraton, is lined with smart cafes. The Daily News Café is one of the best of these, with plenty of copies of the Turkish Daily News newspaper that owners operate.

TIME CAFE, *Attar Sok. No. 6, Kavaklıdere, Tel. 312 468 3393. Moderate.*
Popular among the diplomatic types. Good food and an outstanding bar. Chatty foreign service flavor until the wee hours.
PAUL, *Arjantin Cad. No. 18, Gaziosmanpaşa, Ankara, Tel. 312 427 1246. Moderate.*
A French bakery and coffee shop with two locations, the second in Bahçelievler. The croissant, by the way, is allegedly Ottoman, not French, to begin with, a puffy, flaky "crescent." A great brunch is served on Saturdays and Sundays.

Kızılay & Elsewhere
GÖKSU RESTAURANT, *Bayındır S 22/A, Kızılay, Ankara. Tel. 312 431-2219. Expensive-Very Expensive.*
This is the best restaurant in Kızılay, with traditional Ottoman décor and delicious dishes. The menu is extensive, featuring marvelous pepper steak, and kebaps that are both delicious and—for whatever its worth—beautiful to look at. The stuffed mussel mezes are excellent.
KÖŞK, *İnkilap Sokak No. 2, Kızılay, Ankara, Tel. 312 432 1300. Inexpensive.*
In the heart of the Kızılay district, Köşk has a chokehold on the local kebap business with excellent, cheap kebaps and lahmacun.
CHINA RESTAURANT (Çin Lokanta), *Irfan Baştuğ Caddesi, Altınpark, Ankara, Tel. 312 318 1207, Fax 312 318 1407. Moderate.*
Beijing and Ankara are sister cities, and these are the fruits of that relationship. The Chinese government subsidizes the prices at this restaurant as a gesture of goodwill, and apparently the Embassy personnel police the quality of the food. The setting is unbeatable, on a hill overlooking a sprawling expanse of lawn and an artificial lake at the city's Altınpark. The restaurant itself is beautiful, with wood and sliding panels in a traditional Chinese building.
Finally, best of all, the food is marvelous. A big dinner, with drinks, tea and water, won't cost more than $15. If you've been losing patience with aggressive Turkish food touts, this restaurant is a haven of serenity. The cooks, staff, and management are Chinese. Get bus 612 from Kızılay, or ask a taxi to bring you to Altınpark.
CHEZ LES BELGES, *Sahil Cad. No. 24, Gölbaşı, Ankara. Tel. 312 484 1478. Very Expensive.*
A half-hour drive south of Ankara on the Konya Highway (Konya Devlet Yolu), this small French restaurant has a pretty setting on Lake Gölbaşı. The food is excellent, the prices French ($35 per person).

Seeing the Sights
With the notable exception of Anıtkabir, most of Ankara's few historic sights are clustered on and below the city's hilltop fortress, **Hisar**, above

downtown. The fortress itself is ornamental, its southern end occupied by restaurants and the rest by an old neighborhood. There are some inscriptions built into the fortress walls, but there is no access to the towers.

Ankara's principal site, the **Anatolian Civilizations Museum**, is located down the street from the western gate of the citadel. The museum has the world's preeminent collection of Hittite and Urartian art and sculpture. If you include Hattuşas, Gordion, or eastern Turkey in your plans, this museum is a must-see. Even if you have no intention of visiting those sites, the museum is a painless, interesting education (and, besides, it's in a pretty neighborhood near some of the city's finest restaurants).

Among the things to note are the similarities between the reconstruction of the earliest known Anatolian city, **Çatal Hüyük**, and the pueblo homes of Native Americans in the United States' southwest. While pondering that, ponder this; Havasu in Turkish means "sky/water," which brings to mind the Native American root of Lake Havasu in Arizona. Note, also, the one inch by one inch tablets the Assyrians used to "publish" laws and track finances.

Among the most remarkable discoveries is a tablet bearing a message from the Egyptian Queen Nefertiti to her counterpart, Pudahepa, the Hittite Queen. The "letter" was written very soon after their husbands, Ramses II and Muwatallis II, fought one another in the great battle at Qadesh that turned back an Egyptian invasion. The correspondence underscores the close ties between the two empires, whose nobles were often of the same blood.

Downtown Ankara offers a collection of sites of little interest to anyone who's not a fan of Turkish Republican history. On a corner opposite the statue of Atatürk mounted on a horse is the **War of Independence Museum** (50¢, closed Mondays). The museum is housed in the first Turkish National Assembly building and several of the rooms are preserved much as they were when Atatürk gathered representatives from the wreckage of the Ottoman Empire and crafted a potent new renegade state. The site is designed with Turkish visitors in mind, and there are no English captions, although many of the battle maps and pictures require little explanation.

Downhill from this museum on the left side of Cumhuriet Bulvari is the Second Turkish Grand National Assembly, now the **Museum of the Republic** (50¢, closed Mondays). An English-language brochure helps guide you through the old assembly building, but there's even less here than in the War of Independence Museum.

Returning to the War of Independence Museum, take a left along Cankiri Caddesi. After several blocks you arrive at the **Roman Baths** on the left (50¢, closed Mondays). The bath ruins are extensive – with an enlarged calderium (hot pools) and tepidarium (warm pool), a by-product of the frigid Ankara winters. The site was populated since Phrygian times, but reached its zenith under the Romans when Angora was a provincial capital. There is a scatter of worked marble surrounding the site, some Roman, some Byzantine. If you've seen bath ruins along the coasts, skip it unless you're in the mood.

Cutting uphill and right, in the direction of the hilltop, you pass the **Column of Julian**. The column is tall and rifled, erected in honor of the Roman Emperor Julian (361-363). A statue of the young emperor once adorned the column, but the statue toppled hundreds of years ago. The column is now crowned with a massive bird nest, and is perhaps much improved.

Continuing uphill, you arrive at the **Hacibayram Mosque**, across the street from the big new market of the same name. The mosque is side by side with the **Temple of Augustus**. The temple is on the site of an earlier shrine of Cybele, the Anatolian fertility goddess. The Cybele shrine was converted to a temple by the Kingdom of Pergamon around 200 B.C., and when Rome appropriated Pergamon's lands it encouraged worship at the site, creating a Diana/Artemis/Cybele connection as at Ephesus. As religious sensibilities changed, so did the religious habits at the temple. Perhaps seeking to curry favor with the emperor, Angora's city fathers dedicated the temple to Augustus. After his death the history of his reign was inscribed on the outer face of the building and worship here continued, perhaps including Cybele. The final phase here, as at so many temple sites, was its conversion to a church. Note the small opening directly beneath the main altar. This area was once the holy precinct of Cybele, although its use afterwards is uncertain.

The local boys who happily show you around the site claim that a tunnel once connected this chamber to the Kale on the hill above. Given the vast tunnels at various ancient sites, it's hard to dismiss the idea out of hand; still, the claim is totally unfounded. If you take a particular interest in Latin and Greek inscriptions, the outer face of the temple will be a pleasure. As mentioned, the well-preserved inscriptions document Augustus' life, his will, and later, general history and even the expenses of the empire, like a giant stone scribble pad. Scaffolding was erected recently as part of the restoration work at the site, allowing better access to the inscriptions.

The Hacibayram Mosque takes its name from the founder of one of the dervish orders. The mosque was originally built by the Selçuks in 1290, and is a classic Selçuk design with a large wooden ceiling. It is the oldest and most important mosque in the city, although the voluminous new Kocatepe Mosque southeast of Kızılay has stolen much of the limelight. The Hacibayram Mosque is surrounded by several additions on two separate floors, with the old main building directly alongside the Temple of Augustus.

If you have a particular interest in railways, you may be interested in visiting the **Railway Museum**, very near Anıtkabır. A lot of what you need to know about Turkey's checkered railway history is detailed in T.E. Lawrence's classic *Seven Pillars of Wisdom*.

Nightlife & Entertainment

Ankara has an active nightlife. The best place to go hunting for nightspots is in the pedestrian lanes of central **Kızılay**, where you'll find ululating Arabesque singers, techno, and even swing dancing places (!) one right after the other (although, on most nights, you're better served for swing dancing by trying your luck in Kavaklıdere). This quarter is popular among students. To get here from Ulus or Kavaklıdere is easy, just go straight south or north, respectively, on Atatürk Bulvarı until you arrive at the public square at the intersection of Atatürk Bulvarı and Akay Caddesi. The pedestrian quarter is southeast of this intersection, behind the PTT.

Bilkent University has concerts on Wednesday and Friday nights during the fall, winter, and spring. Contact the ticket office, *Tel. 312 266 4382.*

Kızılay is the place to go for a **movie**, with no fewer than four theaters: **Derya**, Necatibey Caddesi No. 57, *Tel. 312 229 9618)*; **Kızılırmak**, Kızılırmak Sokak No. 21/A, *Tel. 312 425 5393*; **Megapol**, Konur Sokak No. 33, *Tel. 312 419 4492*; **Metropol Sanat Merkezi**, Selanlik Caddesi No. 76, *Tel. 312 425 7478* As is the case in İstanbul, English-language films are usually shown in English with Turkish subtitles. You should check the *Turkish Daily News* (English language newspaper) for information about what's playing where.

Shopping

If ever you are going to buy an Angora sweater, Ankara, ancient Angora, is the place. The people in the Tourism Information office have up-to-date advice on where to shop. The city's premier shopping area is **Karum Shopping Center**, located in the long, vaulted building beneath the Sheraton. The **Kızılay** area, on the north side of the first pedestrian bridge, has Ankara's English language bookshops and a collection of other stores.

Kavaklıdere winery, based out of Kavaklıdere in Ankara, releases its own Premier Beaujoulais on the third Thursday in November. For information about wine tours and wine tasting, contact the winery (or Tourism Information), **Kavaklıdere Şarapları**, Akyurt, Ankara, *Tel. 312 847 5773 (847 5075), Fax 312 847 5077.*

Excursions & Day Trips

GORDION

Gordion is located about two hours west of Ankara on the E-90 to Polatly and Sivrihisar. There are two routes, one north at Polatlı, then, 14 kilometers along, left to the site, five kilometers. The dependable route is to turn right 17 kilometers past Polatly, following the course of the Sakarya River 12 kilometers to Gordion and the modern town of Yassıhüyük.

Public transportation is possible from the Polatlı otogar, but there's no telling when minibuses will make the trip. Guided tours are arranged in Ankara; contact the Tourism Information office for information about their own tours.

Gordion has little left to show for its legacy of **Midas and the Golden Touch** and **Alexander and the Gordion Knot**. Like Troy, the evidence of a settlement here is widely scattered and difficult to make sense of, but archaeologists from the University of Pennsylvania have been busy doing just that. The **Phrygians**, a dimly understood people who reigned after the Hittites and were defeated by Persia, ruled from this city. The ruins and hillocks are difficult to appreciate, but a **museum** of recent finds has rendered a visit worthwhile. The museum contains some of the artifacts from an undisturbed royal tomb.

ANITKABIR

Atatürk's burial site is treated with something akin to religious reverence by the secularists who come here. It is a vast, impressive edifice to celebrate one of the most influential men of the 20th century.

Anıtkabır's main entrance is on Anıt Caddesi in Ankara, just off of Gazi Mustafa Kemal Caddesi, which runs from the city center at Kızılay. By public transport (transfer at Kızılay) look for buses going to Tando an, and ask for Anıtkabır. The entrance is just two blocks away from the intersection.

If you are bothered by the hasty construction technique evident throughout the country, bricks and concrete prone to immediate decrepitude, Anıtkabır will help restore your faith. Atatürk's (1881-1938) mausoleum is as visionary as the man himself. Atatürk, for all his appreciation of western dress and military discipline and alphabet, was deeply respectful of the people of his country and the Anatolian heart he believed beat in the chest of the Turkish nation.

His tomb draws on that heritage. The flourishes and baroque flair of the final sultans, as typified in Çirağan and Dolmabahçe Palaces, are discarded. In its place are Hittite and Urartian themes, and a spare, immense space approaching the tomb. Even the location is significant, atop a hill that was an ancient necropolis. Two Turkish architects, Orhan Arda and Emin Onat, captured the character of Atatürk perhaps better than they might have believed: consider that no Ottoman Sultan, possessor of Mohammed's Holy Mantle and a claim to the defender of Islam on Earth, had ever been buried in such glory. Perhaps Lenin provided a contemporary precedent; otherwise Anıtkabır hearkened back thousands of years to the Pyramids, the Mausoleum, and Nemrut Dağı. Atatürk's resting place is an ironic throwback to a time when rulers were on an equal footing with God, and this for a man who worked passionately to drive home secular lessons in his young state.

The strangest part is that Atatürk deserved it. Rarely in human history have a people owed so much to a single man. Atatürk exercised his immense will to build a nation out of broken pieces, then steered that nation, often against immense resistance, toward western thought, western dress, a western secular government, and even western alphabet and surnames. Even those who did not like the west grew to appreciate the advantages the new ideas gave Turkey over its fellow Islamic states.

In a single generation the Turks regained military status absent since the heyday of the Ottoman Empire. Atatürk secured trade relations with countries throughout the Middle East and Europe, but was careful to avoid entangling alliances that might drag Turkey into a new world war. His former second-in-command and successor, İsmet İnönü, faithful to this philosophy after Atatürk's death in 1938, kept Turkey out of WW II as part of this policy.

Anıtkabır stands atop a low hill west of town. The main entrance is at the end of a long, gently rising road. By this main entrance you walk along a long arcade lined by Hittite sphinxes, arriving at a great square below the mausoleum. This square is enclosed with museum buildings containing Atatürk's possessions and other heirlooms (note the photographs of clouds in the shape of Atatürk, one of the oddest curiosities in the exhibit.)

The towering flagpole in the courtyard was donated by Nazmi Cemal, a Turkish-American. Finally, ascending the stair past motionless soldiers (someone make a note to add Motionless Soldier to the worst jobs list), you enter the mausoleum. Anıtkabır is visited on state holidays by the president and prime minister, and there is a light and sound show on summer evenings.

Practical Information

Religious Services

The **Vatican Embassy Chapel**, 2 Sok. No. 55, Çukurca Mahalle, Çankaya, *Tel. 312 439 0041*, has an English Mass at 10 a.m. Sunday, and Masses on holy days are at 7 p.m. The **Ankara Baptist Church Interna-**

tional, Atatürk Bulvarı No. 195, Kavaklıdere, *Tel.* 312 440 6127, has services at 10 a.m. on Sundays. The **synagogue**, Birlik Sok. No. 8, Samanpazarı, *Tel.* 312 311 6200, is open only on the Jewish Sabbath.

Hattusas

The great forests of Anatolia were home to one of the world's first great Empires, the **Hittites**. The empire and the forests are long gone now but the capital city remains, and it comes as a shock to most people. Hattuşas is not the small, crude ruin that you might expect from a 4,000 year old kingdom; Hattuşas is a vast, complex city, surprisingly intact despite the 3,200 years that have elapsed since its final sack.

Tucked away amid dry rolling hills, Hattuşas, near modern **Boğazköy**, is a worthy destination, deserving of a day and benefiting from a night's stay in the area.

History

The ruins of Hattuşas represent its last, greatest incarnation under the Hittite Empire. The city – principally the section atop **Büyükkale** – had earlier been settled by the Hatti, and upon arrival the Hittites sacked it and cursed the site. Later, seeing the advantages of the easily defensible acropolis at Büyükkale, the availability of water and the excellence of nearby arable land, the Hittites disregarded their own curse and moved in. The king at the time went so far as to give himself the name Hattusili (1650-1620). The 17th and early 16th centuries marked a period of great expansion, followed by incursions into Hittite territory that culminated in the destruction of Hattuşas at the hands of the Kaşka (about 1500 B.C.), who apparently emerged out of the northeast.

The Hittites overcame the loss of their capital and launched a second campaign of expansion, and it was in this period that modern scholars deem the Kingdom ended and the Empire began. **Suppiluliuma I** (1380-1340 B.C.) is usually acknowledged as the first Hittite emperor, although the classification is almost purely academic, and the Hittite leaders are usually referred to as kings anyway. The Hittite kings occasionally moved their capital when Hattuşas was threatened, as Muwatalli II (1306-1282 B.C.) himself did around the time of an Egyptian invasion. Under Muwatalli II (1306-1282 B.C.) the Hittites took the field against an Egyptian invasion under Ramses II, the irrepressibly successful pharoah immortalized in Percy Byshe Shelley's *Ozymandias*. Ramses II was defeated, beaten at the battle of Qadesh (1286 B.C.) and forced to withdraw through Palestine. Upon his arrival home, the pharoah put a positive "spin" on the battle of Qadesh, and hieroglyphs at Karnak speak only of a great victory. Through it all, the wives of the King and the Pharoah continued trading letters and gifts, one of which, the great green stone sent by Neferteri, remains at Hattuşas today.

After the death of Muwatalli II, the Hittite Empire was shifted back to Hattuşas, but the empire was soon thrown into disarray by civil war. The timing for such chaos was bad: the Babylonians, or Persians, were threatening the southeast, the barbarous Kaşka were harassing borders in the northeast, and Greek and Mycenaean colonists and traders had at

The Hittites

Beginning around 2000 B.C., Assyrian traders from the south imported tin to Anatolia, which, combined with local stores of copper (probably secured through trading elsewhere) allowed local kingdoms to pursue large-scale production of bronze. The production of bronze weapons and art allowed the Anatolian kingdoms to thrive, and that's one story. More important, perhaps, is that the traders, being good businessmen, kept records on small tiles of clay in cuneiform script. This was a watershed; the beginning of written history (although there is some inevitable disagreement about which people intrdouced writing). Whereas earlier kingdoms – the Sumerians, for instance – left a large, shadowy footprint, the Hittites' laws, wars, and finances were immortalized.

The Hittites, like so many cultures to appear later, entered Anatolia from the east and soon were masters of the native Anatolian population. The new arrivals, however, were no cultural imperialists; they adopted the religion and much of the language of the indigenous people, largely Hurrians. In the 20th Century B.C. this alloyed race built its first major city, Kanesh (near Kültepe), from which it began to dominate the rest of central Anatolia. In the 18th Century B.C. the capital was shifted to Hattusas (Boğazkale), and soon the Hittite Empire was in full flower, encompassing Babylon in the east, all of Anatolia, the Mediterranean east of Antalya and, many believe, sections of the Aegean coast near İzmir.

The Hittite culture was not so different from the more famous culture in Egypt at the time. While it endured, so powerful was the Hittite Kingdom that in the 14th Century B.C. the widow of King Tutankhaman sought a Hittite prince to be her new husband. Her hopes were not realized; the son of the Hittite King Suppiluliuma I was killed on the journey to Egypt.

The Hittite's final legacy was one of a surprisingly restrained and fascinating set of laws. Murder and assault were punished by fines, and only rape, treason, and bestiality were punishable by death (the latter because the Hittites were wary of breeding monsters).

last appeared to the west and along the coasts. The Trojan War ended in the middle of the 13th century B.C., and in the aftermath the Greek "Sea Peoples," a confusing agglomeration of colonizing Greeks and the coastal natives displaced by their arrival, began scattering the native populations inland. This only increased the pressure on Hattuşas. Within a century of its victory at the battle of Qadesh, the Hittite Empire had collapsed. Hattuşas was sacked and burned to end the 13th century B.C. Hattuşas was only identified in the late 19th century A.D. Curiously, the burial places of the Hittite kings have proven less interesting than those of the pharoahs. Skill at war is not an indication of artistry or wealth, but considering that Muwatalli II held his own against Ramses II, and the latter's elaborate, treasure-filled burial complex, it seems reasonable to assume that Muwatalli would have been buried in glorious style. This still may have been the case, but the tombs discovered near Hattuşas have not revealed anything on the scale of the Egyptian tombs.

Arrivals & Departures
By Bus & Dolmuş
The only public transportation to Boğazköy departs from Sungurlu in the north and Yozgat in the south. Sungurlu, along the main Ankara-Samsun highway, is the most convenient. From Sungurlu, municipal buses depart for Boğazköy at 7:30 a.m. and at irregular intervals thereafter, passing in front of the Hittite Motel before veering south to Boğazköy. The Ankara Tourist office arranges tours direct from Ankara in the high season.

Dolmuş make trips back and forth, more frequently in high season. From Ankara consider joining a trip through the Tourism Information office, which offers a cheap, direct way of seeing the site with a guide.

By Car
Boğazköy is 23 kilometers off the main Ankara-Samsun road and 31 kilometers from Sungurlu. You can visit Boğazköy from Ankara on a long day trip. Seeing Hattuşas by car should take less than two hours, but adding the time spent at nearby Yazılıkaya and the museum and returning to Sungurlu, plan on making a day of it. If possible, try walking the long, steep loop road and exploring the minor stone buttresses.

Orientation
Hattuşas was the Hittite capital at the height of Hittite power, and the six kilometer circuit of the city walls is mute testimony to this dead empire. The town, located just 500 meters from the ruins, is tiny. You'll find no ATM machines, tourism information offices, or laundry. You will

find a museum, where you can pick up a $5 copy of Kurt Bittel's excellent *Guide to Boğazköy*.

Getting Around Town

Getting around Hattuşas requires lots of hiking or letting a cab drive you around. Reaching Yazılıkaya also requires a lift unless you are staying in Boğazköy and have time to walk two kilometers uphill. Seeing both sights in one day on foot under the blazing sun is probably possible, and so is heat exhaustion.

Alacahüyük, a third Hittite settlement in the area, is located 30 kilometers from Boğazköy, 14 kilometers back toward Sungurlu, then right at Salmanköy for 11 kilometers, and left to Hüyük.

Where to Stay & Eat

Boğazköy has several cheap, serviceable hotels. For a somewhat higher standard, consider staying in Sungurlu on the main Ankara-Samsun road.

HATTUSAS RESTAURANT & PANSIYON, *Boğazköy, Çorum, Tel. 364 452 2013, Fax 364 452-2957; Email: none; Web: none. Credit cards not accepted. Open year-round. Rooms: 18. Double: $15 (breakfast included).*

The Hattuşas is the most well-established pension in Hattuşas town, directly on the main road in the center of the village. The pension is owned and staffed by the Baykal family; you'll find them very helpful in preparing to see the ruins at Hattuşas. The pension also features a good restaurant, probably the best in town, and is associated with a rug shop. If full, try the **Aşikoğlu Motel** at the north end of town (*Tel. 364 452-2004; Fax 364 452-2171*).

BAŞKENT MOTEL, *Yazılıkaya Yolu Üzeri, Boğazköy, Tel. 364 452 2037, Fax Tel. 364 452 2567. Rooms: 18. Credit cards not accepted. Open year-round. Double: $17.*

The Başkent is a bare-bones hotel located one kilometer outside the Hattuşas town center on the Yazılıkaya road; it is even quieter than the hotels in Hattuşas proper. You'll find good information about the ruins, and a decent restaurant.

Sungurlu

THE HİTTİT MOTEL, *Ankara-Samsun Karayolu, Güzergahı, Sungurlu, Tel. 364 311 8409, Fax 364 311 3873. . Rooms: 25. Credit cards not accepted. Open year-round. Double: $33.*

The Hittit Motel is an unassuming place on the south side of the Çorum-Kırıkkale highway, just east of Sungurlu. The Hittit has decent, clean rooms and a garden and pool in the back. An otherwise adequate hotel gets an exotic cachet from Charles, the Prince of Wales, who spent a night in room 40 in 1992 while birding. The pool was probably full for him, but it probably won't be when you get there. The garden is a good place to return to after a day scorching at Hattuşas. The Hittit is joined with a restaurant that serves good, basic fare.

Seeing the Sights

Visiting Hattuşas

As you ascend past the entrance gate above Boğazköy, the great bastion of stone to your left was once covered with buildings and may have bridged the river. During most of the year you will probably be approached by one of the men who work with archaeologists in the digging season and asked if you would like a guide. Ideally you would have a chance to see the site and accumulate questions on one day, and take the guide along on the second. Consider seeing Hattuşas without a guide and taking one along for Yazılıkaya afterward (see below). Note: Readers report that some gentlemen at the site try to convince visitors that guides are required—they are not.

The huge foundation just uphill to your right is the **Great Temple of the Storm God**. This vast structure was dedicated to both a Storm God and a Sun Goddess, and built in the 13th century B.C. Little is known of either of these deities, although they appear to have been worshipped by the Hatti peoples well before their domination by the Hittites. As you follow the road around to the entrance, you find a large stone basin broken into different parts and decorated with the head and shoulders of lions. This was probably used as part of a ritual. A fellow nearby whittles away small lions out of green stone, or anyway, he appears to; he usually pretends to carve and buys in bulk.

Entering the precincts of the temple from this side there are several anterooms that were once guarded. The entryway opens into a hall, and another right takes you in the direction of the lower road and one of the temple chambers. The chamber is entered through three small chambers, and the chambers appear to have had deep pools of water, making access to the temple chambers difficult until someone on the interior slid a bridge across. There are small alcoves to the sides of these small rooms where guards were once posted. Statues of the two gods, each in their own temple chamber with their back to the entrance road, were the main adornment. The building would have been roofed with wood. As you exit back through the main entrance, look off to your right for a distinctive green stone. This was originally a sharp cube but it has been smoothed by weathering. This was a sacrificial stone, probably a gift to the Hittites from Queen Neferteri of Egypt.

Two of the most interesting sites at Hattuşas are rarely visited, the **stone buttresses** just up the road from the Great Temple and off to the right. These are pocked with evidence of old structures, with channels and dowels cut into leveled areas of stone. The first buttress is divided by a cleft in the rock which may have been used as a gate or, instead, had some ritual significance. There is evidence of caves cut into the bases of these outcrops. The view over the Great Temple is excellent. Just below the fork in the road is another mysterious stone outcrop. This one, called the **Kızlar Kaya**, or maiden's rock, may have had a role in blood sacrifice of the aforementioned maidens, but the deliberate shapes and channels cut in the stone are only dimly understood.

At the fork in the road continue straight (right), ascending in a loop around the interior of the former northwestern walls (now disappeared). At the top you will see signs for the **Lion Gate**, one of the three great gates still in place at Hattuşas. On the many occasions when there is no one visiting, this is one of the most silent places in Turkey, with the wide eyes of the lions staring out to the west. The lions adorn the outer gateway, giving way to a small entrance chamber that was, in turn, gated on the interior side. The sign suggests looking for an inscription here at high noon, and we can attest that it is invisible otherwise. Archaeologists are puzzled by the floor just inside of the gate, where the doors have a horizontal groove. This may have been the footing for an interior barricade.

Hattuşas' marquee site is ahead, but take some time to wander back down to the rocky outcrops in the center, most of which were carved and fashioned into small buildings and fortresses. Back on the main road, you ascend to the **Yer Kapı**, or the **Earth Gate**, so named because it dives down out of the city through a tunnel. This fascinating gate is located at the highest point in the city, and was built through a vast artificial hill that runs along the upper section of town, itself walled and punctuated with towers. The tunnel, more than 180 feet long, cuts through the center of this long, slender hill, and has puzzled archaeologists.

Another gate, the **Sphinx Gate**, is located directly above the tunnel, and appears to have been the main entrance and exit. Guesses about the purpose of the tunnel have run to the idiotic, such as speculation that Hittite soldiers may have used this route to mount sneak attacks on the enemy army, but the tunnel may well have served a ceremonial purpose for Hittite armies marching away to war. The overall appearance of this smooth stone hill – it may, too, have been clad in marble – beneath a high wall and a series of towers would have been impressive, but the rising terrain outside of the wall means it was not easy to spot from afar. Tunnels also appear to have also been used at some of the lower gates.

The third upper gate, the **King's Gate**, is so called because of a carved figure here thought to be a king. The figure has been carted off to Ankara, and was not, anyway, a king; it was probably a god, perhaps the storm god himself. A copy has been installed in its former place. This entrance was more complex than the others, with a road leading past the high southern walls and through a series of towers and compounds culminating in the gate itself. This was probably a major entry point into the city. Around the interior are a collection of temple sites, all fenced off. The stone outcrops ranged along the upper half of the interior are all accessible, but require hiking over stony ground. Among these are some outstanding examples of early architecture, with massive stone blocks combining with natural rock formations to create smooth walls and terraced surfaces for houses and temples. **Yenicekale** is the chief example of this, near the center of the interior field, and the precipitous **Sarıkale** is another example. The latter, a short distance downhill of the King's Gate and off to the left, probably had a set of upscale residences.

Just to the interior of the road is yet another outcrop, **Nişantaşı**, this one with a long inscription in Hittite hieroglyphs. The inscriptions date from the years just prior to the fall of the empire. A ramp or stair once climbed this rock just to the left of the inscription. Across the road recent excavation has yielded small chambers and what may have once been a reservoir. This area is sometimes referred to as the southern citadel.

The road continues now to **Büyükkale**, with a draw (a small valley) descending down toward the gorge below – this, too, may have been the site of a bridge across the river. Büyükkale is the location of the palace and citadel, and also the site of original settlements here. The outline of the palace is distinct, but the great collection of rooms and roads is bewildering even to those who study the site. Suffice it to say, the imperial chambers were probably located atop the buttress, looking out over the gorge.

Yazılıkaya

If you have time, consider visiting **Yazılıkaya**, where an outdoor shrine has some of the most impressive Hittite carvings in existence. A sacred road once linked Hattuşas with Yazılıkaya, probably crossing the bridge at the gorge to the south side of Büyükkale. Yazılıkaya was centered around two chambers, natural clefts in the stone, and was ornamented with various buildings as its importance grew. The last of the inscriptions here date from the final years of the empire.

The storm god, Teshup, figures prominently here as at Hattuşas, and the quality of the various reliefs are outstanding considering their age. Teshup is just one of the hundreds of dieties worshipped by the Hittites, and their rank can usually be determined by the number of horns on their hatwear. It is difficult to make sense of the great variety of reliefs, and a guide is of particular use here.

Yazılıkaya is two kilometers northeast of Boğazköy, with a road heading off toward the site from near the Hattuşas entrance gate.

Chapter 14

Cappadocia is a former Roman province, a former Hittite province, a timeless plain of softly curved stone located in the heart of the Anatolian plateau. The eerie landscape is a natural wonder: the terrain is carved into soft, rounded shapes by thousands of years of erosion, and boulders perch impossibly atop slender steeples of rock.

Cappadocia would have been a marvelous tourism destination had development never happened; fortunately, development *did* happen. The first human to dig a cave out of the soft central Anatolian stone is lost to memory, but Cappadocia is today dotted with caves and shot through with manmade tunnels and shafts. These dwellings and storehouses were surely of great use during the long, bitter winters, as they were when armies marched the great trade routes through this land, and as they certainly were to the Christian refugees who withdrew to Cappadocia to avoid persecution. Over the course of generations the warrens became more complex, their artistry, design and cunning more impressive. Cappadocia today is pocked with small holes, some giving way to a shallow room, others to painted churches, still others to great, deep labyrinths connected to one another by miles of subterranean passageways.

This is a place where the marquee sites live up to their reputation – **Göreme**, **Zelve**, and **Derinkuyu**, to name but a few. That said, the troglodytic inhabitants of Cappadocia were at work everywhere, burrowing into the stone over thousands of square miles. The region rewards those who stray from the beaten track.

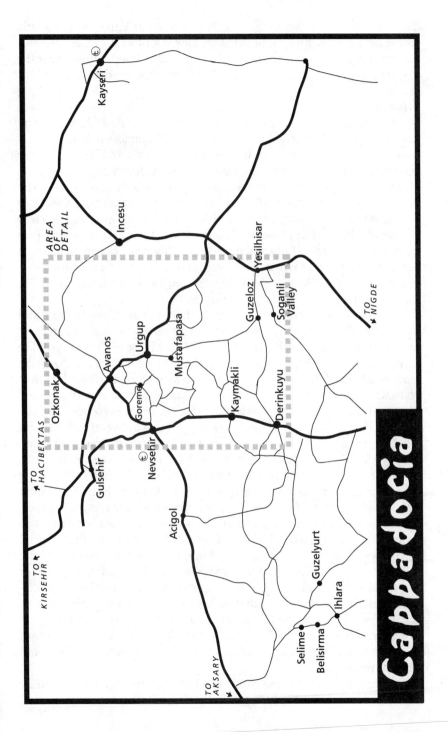

There are beautiful stone-cut churches at Soğanlı Valley to the south, impressive underground cities at Mazı, Özkonak and elsewhere, monastic complexes in **Ihlara Valley** and long, poplar-lined valleys near the Cappadocian center that are riddled with churches and caverns.

History

Cappadocia was in many respects a typical Anatolian farming community, distinguished mostly by horses (Cappadocia is a mutation of a Hittite term for "land of the beautiful horses") and by its peculiar terrain of soft stone. More important to the development of the region, Cappadocia was directly on the major crossroads of Asia Minor. The earliest trade routes wound through the area, passing under the shadow of **Mt. Argeus** and skirting the southern reaches of a natural ancient border, the River Halys (now the Kızılırmak) in their 2,000 mile run from Babylon in the East to Ephesus in the West. Other routes passed through here, principally trade roads northwest to Byzantium on the Bosphorous and north from Antioch on the Mediterranean through the Cilician Gates and on to the Black Sea, the Latin Euxine Pontus.

The land was not only a crossroads, it offered excellent farming and agriculture. That being the case, habitation predates any historical record, and it is interesting that the first true "historical records" were found in Cappadocia at Kultepe (the ancient Kanesh) near Kayseri. Assyrian traders at this Hittite city were careful to document their business transactions on clay tablets, and many of these tablets were discovered intact in the early 1900s. On the basis of this and other evidence, it is clear that the Hittite Kingdom dominated Cappadocia between 1900 BC and 1200 BC, often shifting its capital here from Hattuşas in times of danger. Scholars believe that this is the region referred to as Gomer in the Bible.

It is reasonable to assume that many of those settled here delved their homes and storehouses into the stone, retiring there in the cold of winter or in times of strife. The caves themselves offer no clues regarding their age, however scholars and archaeologists speculate that such dwellings date to 5000 BC or earlier. The oldest clear reference to dwellings carved out of stone occurs in the *Anabasis* of Xenophon, 400 B.C. During his long winter retreat through eastern Anatolia (hundreds of miles east of Cappadocia), Xenophon reported stumbling across a people who inhabited rooms in the earth beneath their homes. It would indeed be surprising if Cappadocians hadn't been doing the same for generations; after all, armies march the same roads as traders, and on occasion the Cappadocians surely found it convenient to round up their food and cattle and retire out of sight underground.

After the passing of the Hittites in 1200 BC, the region was held by numerous kingdoms, Phrygia, Lydia, Persia, and, after Alexander passed through the area in 333 BC en route to defeating Darius III at the Battle of Issus, by the Greeks. The anonymity of the agrarian region ended only in Roman times, when Cappadocia had its own small Christian Renaissance. The Roman period can be said to have begun when Julius Caesar dealt the death blow to the Kingdom of Pontus in a battle here in 57 B.C., issuing his famous report of the battle, "Veni, Vidi, Vici." Afterwards, the area was a substantial Roman province, governed out of **Caesarea** (Kayseri), and was itself occupied (as evidenced by Roman graves atop Uçhisar and elsewhere). Even so, the Romans had neither the manpower nor the desire to police the endlessly winding valleys of Cappadocia. Thus it came to be that Cappadocia became a refuge and a spiritual haven for Christians of Antioch and the eastern Mediterranean. While the Romans busied themselves torturing and murdering Christians elsewhere in the empire, the Christians who survived the early purges consolidated their views and their canon here, helping form a religion that has, in turn, shaped the world.

As early as the second century, anchorites (religious hermits) and solitary mystic Christians were settling here, and by the fourth century Cappadocia was home to a large population of Christian ascetics. The Christian gospel, with its promise of Heaven for the just and faithful, was succour to the poor of Rome, held at arms length from the largely hedonistic pagan religions. The Christian message resonated with the masses, and was amplified when the holiest of the Christians, like St. Simon Stylites in Antioch, perched atop pedestals, trusting in the promise of the afterlife. The stylites had their troglydite peers in Cappadocia, as well, monks who weathered the chill winters huddled in tiny, cramped caves in cliff walls. In a curious way, Christianity owed much of its potency among the masses to the faith demonstrated by such men.

The monks were solitary and isolated, but from beginning they created small communities. As Christianity prospered, the monks began establishing rituals and habits that were reinforced when, in the seventh century, the Byzantine Roman armies began deteriorating and Persian armies came coursing through the region. For the monks, the summers were spent tending to fields and livestock, laying in stores, and making wine, while the winters were given over to refining their underground homes, monasteries and churches. While the monks busied themselves with churches and dormitories, villagers were also eager to escape the ravages of invading , tunneling ever deeper into the soft, easily carved stone of the plains. The results of these efforts, which included **Derinkuyu**, **Özkonak**, and **Kaymaklı** to name but a few, were much more than store houses, granaries, and simple shelters; each was a defensible underground city descending hundreds of feet and many levels into the earth. And though there is no record of it, there may have been underground

How Cappadocia Happened

Everyone who visits Cappadocia wonders at the origin of its strange terrain. According to geologists, volcanic activity buried the area long ago, and the lava and ash churned up from the interior of the Earth settled and cooled into a plain of soft stone. Most of the deposits eroded quite rapidly, creating a network of ravines and channels. Other deposits, less prone to erosion, formed what are today spires, hills, and, in the extreme, the massive stone towers of **Uçhisar** and **Ortahisar**, rising far above the plain and offering a commanding view that armies and traders would later come to appreciate.

The same phenomenon explains "**fairy chimneys**." These are the slender, tapered shafts of stone topped with great boulders. In such cases, a hard stone protected the softer stone directly beneath it from erosion, until, in time, the surrounding soft stone was worn away entirely.

There are parallels here with Petra in Jordan and the mesa cliff dwellings in the southwest United States, but the sheer scale of the human-carved caves and warrens and underground cities here is entirely unique, and a function of the particularly malleable stone. That said, it seems a disservice to continually emphasize the "soft" in "soft stone." Have a feel for yourself when you visit: tunneling into this rock took a lot of work.

fortifications far earlier; fanciful modern drawings of Roman soldiers attempting to storm the subterranean hives of Cappadocians probably have a kernel of truth to them.

With the arrival of the Turks, things changed. Persian and Arab armies had broken into Asia Minor on many occasions, but armies of the Byzantine Empire were always equal to the task and drove them back into the east. Soon after the Battle of Manzikert in 1071 A.D., however, the Selçuk Turks drove the Byzantine armies into the west permanently and settled into Cappadocia to stay. The clerics and the people of the land could not hide out forever; they had never intended to live their entire lives underground. Over time, the local Christian population emerged from their dwellings, assimilated the Muslim Turkish newcomers and were in turn diluted. Through the next centuries the external threat that compelled people to delve cities into the Earth waned, and the monastic wealth that permitted the creation of cavernous, beautifully decorated churches, too, slipped away.

The Christian inhabitants remained until the exchange of populations in 1923, when the Greeks from Turkey were replaced with Turks from Greece. It should be noted that, notwithstanding cookie cutter breeze-block apartment construction found on the outskirts of most towns, houses built partially underground remain the standard. What is more, such subterranean buildings provide the finest hotels in Cappadocia.

Cappadocia provokes intense curiosity. The best information available is in Spiro Kostof's *Caves of Gods*, Oxford Press; *The Dictionary of Christian Lore and Legend*, Thames & Hudson Publishing; and Guillaume de Jerphanion's *Une Nouvelle Province de l'Art Byzantin*.

Arrivals & Departures

By Air

Turkish Airlines serves Kayseri's tiny **Erkilet Airport** from İstanbul twice daily between June and mid-September, once daily in the off season; departures from İstanbul are at 9:20 a.m. Monday to Thursday, 7 p.m. Friday to Sunday, with additional times in summer. There are ordinarily two weekend flights in the winter. Flights depart Kayseri at 11:45 a.m. Monday to Thursday, 9:15 p.m. Friday to Sunday. One-way flights between İstanbul and Kayseri on Turkish Airlines cost $73.

Erkilet Airport is a military airport and has almost nothing in the way of civilian amenities. The only civilian traffic in and out are the Turkish Airlines flights, and they're capped at two per day and fly only between Kayseri and İstanbul. You're sure to notice a strong military presence at the airfield.

Getting from Erkilet Airport to central Cappadocia: If you're flying into Kayseri, you'll want to see if your hotel in Ürgüp, Goreme, Üçhisar or elsewhere in central Cappadocia has arranged transportation; Kayseri is 55 kilometers from Ürgüp. If your hotel doesn't provide transportation of its own, you'll find that cooperative shuttles from both Ürgüp and Göreme meet many Kayseri flights at the airport. Do make arrangements beforehand with Argeus Travel *(Tel. (384) 341-4688*, see below); it is the Turkish Airlines liaison, offering shuttle service for $5 per person to Ürgüp, $6 to Göreme. Be forewarned; less expensive dolmuş drivers are prone to run out of petrol by a carpet shop.

Your alternatives are to taxi into Kayseri and get an ongoing bus to Nevşehir, or to take a taxi directly to Cappadocia (Ürgüp is 55 kilometers away and will cost roughly $55). Public buses do not serve Erkilet Airport.

At the time of this writing the new airport at Nevşehir was not being served by commercial carriers. In theory, this airport should be available for flights from Ankara and Istanbul; it is more convenient than the airport at Kayseri. Fares and schedule information can be found at the Turkish Airlines website: *www.turkishairlines.com.*

By Bus
Nevşehir is the main transit hub for Cappadocia, and the final stop for many of the major inter-city buses such as the Nevtur or Göreme buses on which you probably arrived. If you take our advice, you'll have booked through to Ürgüp or elsewhere in Cappadocia. You should be shuttled on to your final destination in central Cappadocia by a separate bus.

Pay no attention to touts who claim that Ürgüp, Göreme and other towns are closed for winter, or have no water, or are under medical quarantine. All of the towns in the region, Ürgüp, Uçhisar and Göreme, particularly, are busy year-round and are eminently preferable to the stolid city of Nevşehir.

You should be aware that this bus station is mildly notorious for the irritating persistence of its touts and as a point at which people happen upon travel partners who steal from them. It's really not that bad, but you would be wise to treat it as a Turkish Mos Eisley: "You will never see a more wretched hive of scum and villainy."

When you leave the town where you're staying, whether Ürgüp, Göreme or elsewhere, you will be shuttled to the Nevşehir bus station, and here you'll transfer to your ongoing bus.

Most bus traffic departs early or late, with İstanbul buses typically arriving in the morning and departing in the evening. Large carriers such as Ulusoy and Varan do not serve the Cappadocia region. Instead, the local lines NevTur *(Nevşehir, Tel. 384 213 1171)* and Göreme Turizm *(Nevşehir, Tel. 384 213 0191)* serve cities throughout the country and provide direct service within Cappadocia to Ürgüp, Göreme, and Uçhisar, in addition to main offices at Nevşehir.

The two bus lines serve an identical set of cities. Göreme Turizm buses depart from Nevşehir for Ankara at 9:00, 11:30, 14:30 and 17:30 ($8, 4 hours); Kayseri seven times daily between 6 a.m. and 5 p.m. ($3, 1.5 hours); Fethiye once daily at 21:00 ($20, 12 hours); İstanbul three times daily at 9:00, 20:00 and 21:00 ($17, 10 hours); Konya twice daily at 19:00 and 21:00 ($7, 2.5 hours); Antalya, three times daily at 19:30, 21:30 and 22:30 ($15, 9 hours).

It's worth noting that only these two bus lines can be depended on to bring you directly to towns in Cappadocia; many other bus companies, particularly those on the Aegean coast and Mediterranean coast, will bring you part of the way (usually to Aksaray in the west, Kayseri in the east), from which point you'll need to catch an ongoing bus to Nevşehir. The good news is, buses between these cities and Nevşehir are frequent.

If you're on your way to Nemrut Dağ, make your way to Kayseri and transfer to Malatya (three-four times per day). Several agencies in Cappadocia can help with arrangements.

By Car

The roads to Cappadocia from all points west are heavily traveled and in good condition. The journey from İstanbul takes some 8 hours (the most direct route is on the E-89 to Gölbaşı, just west of Ankara, then the E-90 through Şereflikoçhisar, turning east at Aksaray).

From the Antalya area you'll want to go via Konya, but there's some question which was is fastest; with the recent improvements, it's probably fastest to take the 400 Highway due east to Manavgat, taking the left turn on 695 (marked for Akseki), then north to Konya via Beyşehir, then east to Cappadocia via Aksaray. The classic route from Antalya to Cappadocia, now perhaps a bit slower, was the 650 highway due north to Isparta, then to Eğirdir and around Eğirdir lake, and east to Konya. This still has the advantage of passing through the pretty town of Eğirdir.

Orientation

Cappadocia has several pretty small towns with excellent pensions and hotels. We are most fond of Ürgüp, and we have organized this chapter around a stay in Ürgüp, with trips radiating out from there.

If you prefer to stay in Uçhisar, Göreme, or even in a smaller village such as Mustafapaşa, you'll find that complete hotel and restaurant information is available in these pages as well.

Cappadocia is a daunting place, with much to see. We highly recommend spending at least three days here – that's just sufficient to see the major sites with a little grace, and perhaps squeeze in some hiking, biking or horseriding through the various valleys (see *Cappadocia By Foot & Hoof*, below).

Nevşehir, mentioned above as the transit hub, is convenient to the roads west, and has several large hotels. At the far end of the spectrum, Göreme, a town at the bottom of a valley east of Nevşehir, has a slew of cheap pensions and a predictably boisterous nightlife. Falling somewhere in between are the towns of Ürgüp and Uçhisar. Both are graced with some of the finest accommodations in the country, but Ürgüp, the larger of the two, has more fine hotels and easier access to other sites in the valley (it is home, too, to the most reputable guiding company in Cappadocia).

Urgup

Morning in **Ürgüp**: the air is clean with a trace of wood smoke, the sky a vast chalky blue, and swifts whirl madly clockwise, around and around. The mesas on the near horizon are undercut by entrances and windows in the stone, and off in the east snowcapped **Argeus** rises out of the mist.

Ürgüp is a clean, pretty town near the heart of Cappadocia. It is convenient to rarely-visited monastic valleys and the popular sites of Göreme and Uçhisar alike. In addition, it has its own rock-hewn dwellings in a great ridge of stone running into town from the west.

Some of the modern development leaves much to be desired, but the upper, western part of town, traditionally known as Esbelli, remains filled with beautiful stone houses, many of which are now being restored. We think of Ürgüp as the perfect place to spend time after a flight in from North America or after a few frenetic days in İstanbul. It's a wonderful place to relax, and an excellent hub for visits throughout the area.

The tourism information office is located east of the town center by the museum on Kayseri Caddesi, *Tel. (384) 341-4059, Fax (384) 341-4059.*

Arrivals & Departures

Ürgüp is 20 kilometers east of Nevşehir and 55 kilometers west of Kayseri, and dolmus offer service in all directions. The dolmuş drivers became embroiled in a turf war with their fellows in Goreme for two years, but that has ended, at last, and you can now take dolmuş on a counterclockwise "ring tour" from Ürgup to Zelve, then on to Avanos, and, finally, Goreme. This is an inexpensive ($4) and liberating way to see the marquee sites of Cappadocia. You can also get a dolmuş directly to towns in every direction, whether Uçhisar, Mustafapaşa, Avanos or Nevşehir. Bus offices are located in the otogar.

Where to Stay

The tight, winding lanes of western Ürgüp are filled with hundreds of stone houses that fell into disrepair after the exchange of Turkish and Greek populations in 1923. Many of the houses in the upper, western end of town have been rebuilt as hotels in the image of the justly lauded Esbelli Evi. The marvelous result of this construction is that a half-dozen of the finest hotels in the whole of Turkey are located here, sharing the same few hundred meters of narrow, cobbled lanes.

ESBELLİ EVİ, *Turban Girişi, Çeşme Karşısı, PK 2, Ürgüp, Cappadocia. Tel. 384 341 3395, Fax 384 341 8848, E-mail: suha@esbelli.com.tr, Web: www.esbelli.com.tr. Rooms: 10. Credit cards accepted. Open March-November. Double: $80.*

In the Zelve valley just north of Ürgüp, monks spent 800 years poring over the scriptures, living simply, and slowly chipping away at the soft tufa stone to create churches, living areas, and bedrooms. Monastic life was certainly busy, but it was also exacting, and rarely rushed. The monks could take their time deciding where to carve a window out of a cliff face, where to connect two spaces with a tunnel, where to build a shelf.

Süha Ersöz purchased property in the narrow lanes above Ürgüp in 1979, and there is something in his patient approach to the creation of the Esbelli Evi that Byzantine anchorites would have appreciated. Süha Bey considered the site for years, only setting to work in 1987. He cleaned and restored three rooms cut into the living rock, rehabilitating the stone houses above. After four years of work, he began inviting guests. In the following years he purchased adjoining land and completed more rooms, one here, two there. The results were exquisite; guests were awed, and told friends. Word of the Esbelli Evi spread.

If imitation is the sincerest form of flattery, then Süha Bey is wealthy in flattery indeed. Precisely carved cave rooms, beautiful hardwood floors, cast iron bed frames, collections of books and Turkish textiles are no longer the exclusive domain of the Esbelli Evi. Nor does it have a monopoly on stone courtyards, gorgeous sitting rooms, or sweeping terrace views. The opening of several new hotels in the neighborhood that share the aesthetic of the Esbelli has only served to reinforce the immense appeal of the original.

The appeal of the Esbelli Evi goes far beyond its beauty; this is a hotel without peer in the hospitality of its host and his staff. Not the abstract hospitality of smiles at the checkout counter, but the practical hospitality of a refrigerator and bar stocked with drinks that are yours for the taking (free of charge), of a *Turkish Daily News* at breakfast, of a guest washing machine (the staff will hang your clothes to dry, no charge), and of anything else you might need. It is hospitality up to and including keys to the owner's car if you're in a hurry to get somewhere. It is a hospitality that has capped the number of rooms at 10, since more don't leave enough hours in the day for people to mix.

Süha Bey has created a halfway house in the old style, a place to relax. He invites you to make this your home, and likes to see guests linger over their excellent breakfast on the patio. Even better if you stroll through town until it is seemly to mix yourself a gin and tonic, then while away the hours with fellow guests on the terrace. There is much to see in Cappadocia, but Süha Bey hopes you don't have to rush to see it. Monks spent lifetimes here just sitting and looking, and they weren't as crazy as they sound. If you're going to see where they lived, you might as well see why they lived here.

Selected as one of our Best Places to Stay – see Chapter 10.

YUNAK EVLERİ, *Yunak Evleri, Yunak Mahallesi, Ürgüp, Tel. 384 341 6920, Fax: 384 341 6924, Email: yunak@yunak.com, Web: www.yunak.com. Rooms: 17. Double: $80. Credit cards accepted. Open year-round. Double: $110-$170 (10% cash discount; breakfast included).* Yunak Evleri is in the best sense the son of Esbelli Evi. Construction was undertaken with thoughtful input from the owner of the Esbelli, and the result is impressive.

Owner Yüsuüf Görürgöz began this ambitious project in 1998, taking it upon himself to renovate and renew a small community of ruined stone-carved buildings that occupied a south-facing cliffside in upper Ürgüp. Work ended in 2000, and from the moment you turn onto the cobbled entry road, curving uphill between low stone walls, you are in a compound where everything is as it should be. The centerpiece is a renovated Greek mansion that now serves as the reception and dining area, and rooms are arrayed in the cliff walls behind.

And what rooms they are: like the Esbelli Evi, each room is cut into the stone, with dark, hardwood floors as flush as the eccentric angles of the cave walls allow, metal bed frames, down comforter covers, and bathrooms clad in marble with heavy white towels. The small touches—reading lights, built-in cabinets, and patios—are marvelous. In big ways and small, the Yunak Evleri is a success.

Good Turkish buffet meals are served nightly for $15, and meet the same high standard. To get there: follow the main road from Ürgüp city center uphill toward Göreme, turning right before Surban Hotel.

Selected as one of our Best Places to Stay – see Chapter 10.

KAYADAM, *Esbelli Sok. No. 6, Ürgüp. Tel. (384) 341-6623; Fax (384) 341-5982; Email: kayadam@kayadam.com; Web: www.kayadam.com. Rooms: 5. Credit cards accepted. Open April-November. Double: $70 (breakfast included).*

The Kayadam ('Troglodyte') is another stone-carved hotel, a restoration of cave houses carved into a pier of rock untold centuries ago. Everything in this neighborhood is measured against the Esbelli Evi, and the Kayadam fares well: rooms are lovingly decorated, offering extensive nooks and peculiarities. Each room is decorated with old pots, books, baskets of dried flowers, and old wooden jugs. The owner, Attila Ciner, is a geology professor—what more appropriate profession!—who is better able than most to explain the circustances of this geological oddity. To get there: follow Esbelli Sokak straight uphill past the Esbelli Ev (the way is signed). If full, consider the nearby Elkep Evi *(Tel. 384 341-6000; Fax (384) 341-8089; Email: elkepevi@superonline.com; Web: www.elkepevi.com; Double: $60).*

ASIA MINOR HOTEL, *Istiklal Cad. No. 42 Ürgüp,. Tel. (384) 341-4645; Fax (384) 341-2721; Email: cappadocia50@hotmail.com; Web:*

www.asiaminorhotel.homestead.com. Rooms: 10. Credit cards accepted. Open year-round. Double: $30-40 (breakfast included).

The Asia Minor, renovated in 2000, is located in a distinguished 200 year-old Greek house on the road into Ürgüp from the west. The renovation has left the Asia Minor one of the best relatively inexpensive hotels in Ürgüp, with clean, spare bathrooms and rooms hewn back into the cliff wall behind. Rooms offer high wood ceilings and attractive textiles. You'll find a lawn forecourt whose centerpiece is a small fountain.

HİTTİT OTEL, *İstiklal Cad. No. 46, Ürgüp. Tel. (384) 341-4481; Fax (384) 341-3620; Email: none; Fax none. Rooms: 15. Credit cards not accepted. Open year-round. Double: $40 (breakfast included).*

The Hittit Otel offers standard, non-cave rooms with thoughtful, friendly service. Rooms are solid and clean, with a few in an older building and more in a modern structure. The most remarkable feature of this hotel is beyond the garden behind the hotel; a short flight of stairs leads up into an opening in a sheer stone bluff where a bar has been created. That room is just part of a very old network of shafts and tunnels, including shafts leading directly up and a natural spring that the owner has blocked to create his own underground reservoir.

PANSIYON SUN, *Hamam Sok. No. 6, Ürgüp. Tel. (384) 341-4493; Fax (384) 341-4774. Rooms: 7. Credit cards not accepted. Open year-round. Double: $15.*

This is a fine, friendly little backpacker pension in the center of Ürgüp. The structure leans back into a fairy chimney and is partially burrowed into it. The lobby and rooms – several of which are in caves – are filled with characteristically Turkish flotsam and jetsam, old doors, textiles, and crafts. The Ürgüp Hamam is located next door.

Where to Eat

It is a surprise that a town with accommodations as impressive as those in Ürgüp is so bereft of fine dining. We recommend a few decent restaurants below. As this book went to press, a promising new restaurant, Kervan, was opening in the city center. Inquire.

ŞOMİNE, *Cumhuriyet Meydanı, Ürgüp, Tel. 384 341 8443. Moderate.*

The Somine is located in the main square at the center of town. The hotel offers seating on a pleasant terrace, and most dishes are decent if small. Grilled chicken will cost $3.50, and spicy Adana kepap $2.50

OCAKBAŞI, *Terminal Üstu, Ürgüp, Tel. 384 341 3277. Moderate.*

This is the premier kebap house in Ürgüp, widely acclaimed by the locals. There is ordinarily someone on hand who can speak English, but you may need to order by pantomime. It is a classic Turkish grill, with food cooked by men, for men. The restaurant is located on the up a set of stairs at the rear of the bus terminal.

KARDEŞLER PIZZA RESTAURANT, *Suat Hayri-Dumlupınar Cad., Ürgüp, Tel. 384 341 4357. Inexpensive.*

When we're in Ürgüp, we invariably find our way here in the center of town across the road from the main square. Big, friendly proprietor, Mehmet Sofularlı offers excellent borek and the local specialty, stew (güveç) in a clay pot sealed shut by baking bread. He saws through the bread "lid" at your table, revealing the eggplant, tomato, onion, garlic and (optional) meat still boiling. Neat trick, and good food; you hardly even need to know Turkish to enjoy his loving description of tandir güveç.

TURASAN WINERY, *Çimenli Mevkii, Ürgüp, Tel. 384 341 4872, turasan@turasan.com.tr.Inexpensive.*

The Turasan Winery offers a great opportunity to test the wines of an ancient wine-making land. Bottles cost $2-$9, and you can accompany your wine-tasting with dried apricots, figs, and other fruit. The wine tasting room is open until 8 p.m. in the summer, 5 p.m. in the winter, and is located just down the road from the massive Turban Hotel in western Ürgüp below the Turban Hotel..

KARAKUŞ, *Mustafapaşa Yolu (Pancarlık), Ürgüp, Tel. 384 341 5353, Fax: 384 341 5356. Moderate-Expensive ($29 per person, with drinks).*

If you're in the mood to be entertained by one of the local floor shows, we suggest checking with someone at your hotel for advice; the quality of food and dancers varies dramatically from year to year. These belly-dancing and whirling dervish shows can be a great time.

The Karakuş has stood the test of time, offering a meal and drinks followed by whirling Mevlevi Dervishes. With drinks, an evening here will cost about $30 per person. Karakuş is located south of Ürgüp on the Mustafapaşa road.

Seeing the Sights

The overwhelming fabulousness of Cappadocia is all around you, and Ürgüp is but an hors d'ouevre. What there is to see in Ürgüp is above the center of town, on the one-way road looping northwest toward Goreme. This is the direction of the Esbelli district, and cliffs to either side are carved into rooms and passageways, some of which were exposed when erosion sheared the outer walls away.

If you wind around and up toward **Yeşil Point** (Green Point) you'll find a good view out over town (and be $.50 poorer for having done so – you must pay to enter the "Temeni Wish Hill View Point" on top).

If you pay to enter (it's just barely worth the $.50) you'll find a small türbe to Kiliçarslan, a local hero who is the namesake of a great Selçuk warrior. There is also a small building housing a collection of old photographs, including many that include the old Greek Orthodox Church of St. Yuannis. This was once the greatest Orthodox church in a region that was heavily populated by the Greek Orthodox and had a constellation of largely Orthodox towns such as Ürgüp itself, Mustafapaşa (formerly Sinassos) and İbrahimpaşa (Babayan).

You can find carpet/kilim shops all over Cappadocia; Kayseri, just to the east, was once famed for its textiles, and that legacy is carried on in towns such as Göreme and Ürgüp. In Ürgüp, we had an excellent experience with Muammar Sak at Aksa Halıcılık,, a specialist in flat weave rugs (kilims). His store is located across the street from the tourism information office, beneath the municipality buildling (Belediye).

Saturday is market day in Ürgup.

Wine Tours

The oldest depictions of wine drinking are Hittite engravings, so it should come as little surprise here in the former heartland of the Hittite Kingdom wine production continues. Your hotel or the tourism information office can help pinpoint the various wineries in the area, most of which have simple facilities for welcoming visitors and offering wine tasting.

Most of the grapes cultivated in Cappadocian vineyards – many of which are located between Ürgüp and Kayseri – find their way into Turasan wines. This winery has been in operation since 1943, and what began as a 3,000 liter capacity business under Hasan Turasan has blossomed into a 2 million liter per year operation run by his grandson, also Hasan.

In upper Ürgüp, the **Turasan Şarapçılık**, Çimenli Mevkii, *Tel. (384) 341 4872, turasan@turasan.com.tr*, has a wine-tasting room just down the street from the Turban Hotel and near the Esbelli Ev. The tasting room is a long, slender cave filled with low wooden tables and traditional Turkish handicrafts. The tasting room is open throughout the year, from 8 a.m. to 8 p.m. during summer and 8 a.m. to 5 p.m. in the winter. The price range of the bottles is $1.75 to $7.50, and the quality of the wines is as good as anything on the market in Turkey (by the way, the "Kavaklıdere Select" label by Kavaklıdere is generally considered the finest in the country, and the main "Turasan" red stacks up quite well against it).

VISITING CAPPADOCIA

Cappadocia is home to rock-cut churches, monastic caves, and underground cities beyond count, sprawling over thousands of square miles. No matter how much time you spend here, you will miss marvel-

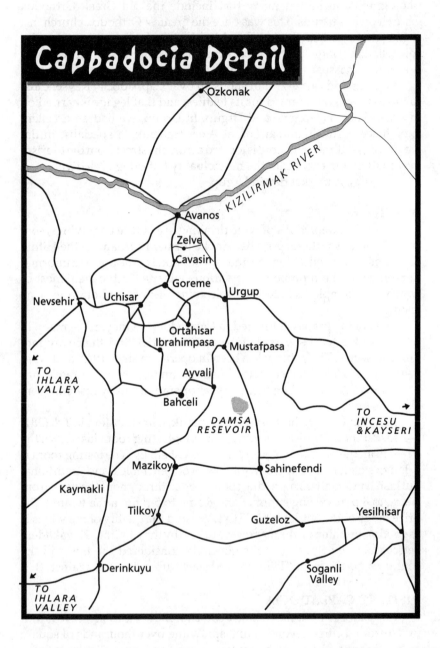

Cappadocia Detail

Ozkonak

KIZILIRMAK RIVER

Avanos

Zelve

Cavasin

Goreme

Nevsehir Uchisar Urgup

Ortahisar
Ibrahimpasa Mustafpasa

TO
IHLARA
VALLEY

Ayvali

Bahceli

DAMSA
RESEVOIR

TO
INCESU
&KAYSERI

Mazikoy Sahinefendi

Kaymakli

Tilkoy Guzeloz Yesilhisar

Derinkuyu Soganli
Valley

TO
IHLARA
VALLEY

ous sites. The only way to see Cappadocia thoroughly is to buy a house and live here.

If you accept the fact that you can't see everything there is to see, you'll find that Cappadocia is a good place to simply relax. Choose a few things that sound most interesting and visit them on your own or in the company of a guide.

You can see all of the major sites by public transportation and judicious taxi rides – some places, such as Göreme Open Air Museum, Zelve, Derinkuyu, and Kaymaklı, are easy to see by dolmuş. Many smaller sites require a rented scooter, motorcycle or car. Be sure to bring a **flashlight**, a light jacket for the cool interiors, and (who knows) a long piece of string or breadcrumbs. Most of the valleys and underground cities in the area have an admission fee of between $1 and $3.

Getting Around

The Cappadocia chapter is arranged in spokes radiating from Ürgüp for ease of use, but you'll find that you'll often head out on one route and loop back by a different route.

Here are some good day trips from Ürgüp:
• Devrent Valley, Zelve, Paşabağ, lunch at Avanos, Özkonak Underground City.
• Göreme Open Air Museum, lunch in Göreme, hike to Cavuşin through Kızılçukur Valley, return to Göreme, Uçhisar fortress.
• Derinkuyu Underground city, Ihlara Valley.
• Mustafapaşa, Mazi Underground City, Soğanlı Valley.
• Ortahisar, hike, bike or horseride to Pancarlık or İbrahimpaşa.
• An early morning at Sultan Marshes National Park, a bird sanctuary to the southeast.

How to See Cappadocia

Taxis charge roughly $55 for eight hours of shuttling three or four people–prices fluctuate according to the season and your bargaining ability. Rental cars are ideal, and scooters ($25 per day), motorcycles ($30 per day) and bikes ($8 per day) provide other options.

Unless you have such transportation and a doctorate in Byzantine art, a guided trip can prove useful. Cappadocia is filled with oddities, with new peculiarities down every hole and around each corner. A good guide, with years of experience in the area, can explain what you're looking at and even give you tips on how to spend your unguided time.

Bear in mind, however, there are distinct problems with guided tours that are compounded by some of the poorly run local guiding companies. Although guided tours do take you to the most interesting sites, they won't leave you with time to get off the well-worn paths and poke around in out of the way areas. Nowhere is straying from the beaten path more tempting than here, where you can duck into a cave and emerge 50 feet up on a cliff face. With a guide you are on someone else's clock, which isn't always enjoyable on your own vacation.

Second, guides take you on a circuit that can get congested, and run-of-the-mill guides are inclined only to show you what they want to show you. You may stand in line while 200 feet away a collection of churches sits empty.

Third, the amount of time spent visiting the ruins can be equivalent to, or even less than, the amount of time spent at carpet, pottery, and rug-weaving shops. Perhaps you don't mind, but if you do mind then the detours and delays of a guided tour can be frustrating. Bear in mind that your tour guide, or his company, will receive a commission on items you purchase; that's how the business works.

Finally, several guiding companies tend to burden their guides with far too many clients; thus, even if you don't want to visit pottery shops you may be sharing your day with someone who does.

There are many guide companies in Cappadocia, few of which have established a strong reputation. Argeus Travel Agency in Ürgüp (Istiklal Cad. No. 13, Ürgüp. Tel. (384) 341-4688, Fax (384) 341-4888; E-mail: inform@argeus.com.tr; Web: www.argeus.com.tr) is head and shoulders above the rest. Argeus has higher rates than its competitors by some 30%, charging $65 per person per day—this includes guiding, entrance fees, a la carte lunch and drinks at good local restaurants, and transportation. They also offer use of a minivan and driver (gas included) for $70. If you can afford their rates, they're worth the premium price: Argeus deals honestly with its clients, skips side trips to pottery or carpet shops (unless you insist), feeds you at top-notch restaurants, and has a brace of knowledgeable guides. Their main office is in Ürgüp, but you can make arrangements with Argeus from anywhere in Cappadocia.

The company occasionally works with American outfitter REI, and is Ürgüp's licensed agent for Turkish Airlines offering shuttle service to Kayseri (70 kilometers). You can rent bikes here, join a guided trip, arrange horseback riding, rent a car, book a plane, or make reservations at a hotel elsewhere in the country. The Argeus office, just up the street from the city center on the road into town from Göreme, is an eddy of tranquility where you're welcome to sit down and craft your plans with their informed help.

At a lower price point, and a reduced—but decent—level of service, we suggest Alan Turizm, Yunak Mah. PK 55, Ürgüp *(Tel. (384) 341-4667; Fax (384) 341-2025)* and Stone Park Tourism, Istiklal Cad. No. 19E, Ürgüp *(Tel. (384) 341-8897; Fax (384) 341-5348; Email: tours@stonepark.com.tr; Web: www.stonepark.com.tr).*

Cappadocia By Hoof & Foot

For the fortunate few who are able to take some time in the region, there are several excellent alternatives to seeing Cappadocia by bus, car, or dolmuş. A thriving industry has blossomed in horse trekking, bicycling and hiking.

There are horseriding outfits in several towns in Cappadocia, but the most reputable is **Beyaz Yele** (White Mane) run by a Frenchwoman, Berengere Şentürk. Her stables in Ürgüp, opening onto a landscape of tufa cones and valleys, are filled with 20 strong horses. The "Land of Beautiful Horses," from which Cappadocia drew its name, is no longer; horses no longer run wild here, and these horses are from Urfa, near the Syrian border.

You can take a half-day or day horseriding trip out of Ürgüp, and longer trips of up to 8-10 days are available if you are an experienced rider. On some trips you'll cover 45 kilometers in a day. Excursions are available between April and October and cost roughly $50 per person, per day in the high season. On longer trips, accommodation is provided in private houses or camps, with equipment transported by van. For more information, contact Beyaz Yele at Karandere, Sucuoğlu Sok. No. 12, Ürgüp, *Tel. 384 341 5175, Fax 384 341 8089.* You can also make reservations directly through Argeus Tourism, *Tel: (384) 341-4688; Fax (384) 341-4888; Email: inform@argeus.com.tr; Web: www.argeus.com.tr.*

Bicycle Trekking, long the province of another local woman, has been thrown into some uncertainty now that the woman has moved to India. Argeus, the outfit she worked with, can still arrange bicyling tours if you wish. Argeus is also one of the several agencies that rents mountain bikes daily (a full day should cost about $9).

We recommend several hikes within these pages, notably (Kızılçukur (Red) Valley, Güvercin (Pigeon) Valley, Kılıçlar (Swords) Valley, and Pancarlık Valley, but this is only a little of the hiking and exploring that is available. If you'd like to set out on a longer trek by foot, you can certainly find ways to do so, whether you go from town to town or pack a tent along. Check with Argeus Tourism or another reputable tourism company for the best routes.

Cappadocia By Air

Lars Möre and Kaili Kidner have been running hot air balloon trips in Cappadocia since 1992. That was when Lars, then operating hot air balloon trips in France, had an opportunity to lead a trip through the valleys of Cappadocia and realized the value of what he'd discovered.

is the Cappadocian terrain beautiful and marked with the
ousands of generations, it lends lends itself perfectly to
through its steep valleys. As they pilot their balloons
through the valleys, dipping into them and popping back out, you're
allowed a serene glimpse of this soft stone world.

Balloon trips are ordinarily scheduled for the early morning and take
roughly three hours from beginning to end, with 1.5 hours in the balloon.
It's traditional to end the trip with a glass of sparkling wine, fond
memories, and a dented pocketbook; the rates vary a little through the
season, but are generally about $230 per person. Note that Kapadokya
Balloons Göreme, otherwise known as Cloud Nine, is the only properly
licensed hot air ballooning company in Cappadocia; rogue operators
move into the area occasionally and we'd warn against flying with them.
Contact **Kapadokya Balloons Göreme**, Göreme, TR-50180, Nevşehir,
*Tel. (384) 271-2442; Fax (384) 271-2586; Email: fly@kapadokyaballoons.com;
Web: www.kapadokyaballoons.com.*

NORTH OF ÜRGÜP
Devrent, Zelve, Paşabağ, Cavusin, Avanos & Özkonak

Devrent Valley

Just north of Ürgup on the Avanos road, the **Devrent Valley** dives
down off of the roadway in the direction of Zelve. The road passing
through the valley is a popular place to stop and take in the view, and
many tour buses stop in the thick of the "fairy chimneys" to let you
marvel at the strange cones and pick out the age-worn shapes in the
stone.

Zelve

Zelve is one of the featured attractions of Cappadocia, an area long
inhabited by monks who carved monasteries, churches, and storehouses
out of the steep slopes of three neighboring valleys. All three narrow
valleys radiate south from the ticket booth and parking lot just south of
the Ürgup-Avanos road. Admission is $4 per person, and the valleys are
open during daylight hours, 8 a.m. to 7 p.m. in the summer, closing at 5
p.m. in winter. Parking costs $3.

Cappadocia is filled with places that challenge your phobias, your
fears of height and tight places, and Zelve is no exception. The windows

and doorways in the stone valley walls open into passages and stairways that emerge high above or cut straight through to the next valley. You'll need sturdy clothes, no fear of getting dirty, and a flashlight. The valleys are particularly beautiful first thing in the morning, when tour groups have not yet arrived and the site is achingly quiet. Christians settled here very early, perhaps as early as the first century AD, and they began work on cooperative monastic living quarters in the fourth and fifth centuries.

The community thrived under the Byzantine empire, and at one point early in the second millenium Zelve is thought to have been populated by some 5,000 people. Under the Byzantines, Cappadocia was overrun by Persians, Arabs, and other non-Christians, but the Byzantines always regained control. Such was not the case after the 11th century, when it came under the steady control of the Selçuks, the dominion of the Sultanate of Rum. Although this area remained inhabited until 1952 (when Turkey forced the inhabitants out for reasons of both safety and, perhaps, tourism dollars), it was never again a vital monastic complex after 1200 AD.

There are tunnels and rooms and multi-storied buildings beyond cataloguing in the Zelve valleys, and you could easily spend the better part of a day here. Most tours will spend a couple of hours here.

Among the things you'll not want to miss is the huge, partially collapsed structure against the right wall of the right valley; stairs and bridges have been constructed to let you investigate what was once a central monastic building. Across this valley is a warren of rooms radiating into the bluff, and a long, tight tunnel that emerges in the center valley.

The facades of many of these rooms and churches have collapsed, evidence of the erosion that forced the modern inhabitants to relocate.

If you return to the road and head west, you'll next pass Paşabağ to the left, a pretty valley filled with rock-cut dwellings and fairy chimneys. There are several small cafes and restaurants here, as well as a Jandarma located within a fairy chimney.

Cavusin

Çavuşin is not a site to visit if you're only in Cappadocia for a short visit, but if you're looking for a good destination for a hike – or a good place from which to set out on hikes – it's perfect. The town is located to the east of the main road between Göreme and Avanos, five kilometers north of Göreme (a roadsign names the two beautiful valleys into which paths lead, Güllüdere and Kızılçukur, or Red Valley). A track for hiking

Great Cappadocian Hikes

Cappadocia is perfect for getting out and walking. Hikes lead through dozens of local valleys, skirting impressive cliffs, crossing streams, and, of course, leading you to obscure churches and caves all the while. The most popular of these hikes is is the path from the road near Ortahisar that leads through the Red Valley (Kızılçukur) to Çavuşin (see "Red Valley" section, below). Pigeon Valley (Guvercin), which begins east of Uçhisar and empties out at Göreme, is another popular hike. Our advice: ask at your hotel for the nearest, most interesting hike—everyone has their own.

or bicycing leads to Çavuşin from Göreme, beginning by "Kaya Camping" between Göreme and the Göreme Open Air Museum; this route takes you into the Red Valley.

There is a small village at Çavuşin where you'll find some simple tea gardens, restaurants and pensions. The best pension in Çavuşin is the **In Pension** *(Tel. (384) 532-7070l; Fax (384) 532-7195; Email: in_pension@hotmail.com; Web: www.mephistovoyages.com.)*, Double: $20, whose owner Ahmet Kilinç is an excellent guide for the nearby valleys— he even has a wheeled contraption for hauling customers unable to walk.

The first of the churches near Çavuşin, **Ayvalı Kilise (The Church of St. John)**, is the oldest surface church still standing in the region, dating to the 6th or 7th century. It is located on a ridge just above town, and remains worth a visit even after a collapse in 1962. If you're coming by the track directly from Göreme through Kızılçukur Valley, you'll enter into Çavuşin town and want to take a right to get there, or to begin the trail on towards Paşabağ and Zelve. The trail passes up behind the Ceviz (Walnut) tea garden.

Also at Çavuşin is a place known simply as the **Guvercinlik**, or "Dovecote." An image within commemorates the visit of Nicephorus II (Phocas), a native of Cappadocia who rose to become military governor of Anatolia, then Byzantine Emperor (963-969). In a series of rapid campaigns against the Byzantine's bitter enemies he earned the nickname "White Death of the Saracens" and seized key Saracen towns including Aleppo, all of which helped propel him to the Imperial throne. In addition to his martial acumen, he was devout. These were two of the three ideal characteristics for a Byzantine Emperor, but he lacked the political shrewdness that was the third great characteristic and he was assasinated in 969. The northern wall of the Guvercinlik has images of two horsemen, one of whom some believe to be John Tzimisces, a fellow general and comrade of Nicephoras Phocas who was responsible for the assassination in 969.

From Çavuşin, you can hike the **Red Valley** south in the direction of Ürgup or you can continue over the ridge and east to Zelve. On the latter route there is an intersection at the valley rim that takes you down to Paşabağ on the Zelve road.

Avanos

Once the principal city in the region (it had a major Temple of Zeus in Hellenistic times), and again the principal tourism destination in Cappadocia for some years, **Avanos** has been eclipsed by the towns of Ürgüp, Göreme and Uçhisar. Even with the smaller central Cappadocian towns bleeding off its tourism income, Avanos continues to bustle and remains a center of commerce. In particular, it is home to a thriving rug weaving and pottery industry. You're likely to find yourself stopping, willingly or not, at a pottery shop where you'll find demonstrations of pottery-making as well as a lot of finished product on sale.

A UPS office is located in the center of town, should you wish to ship goods home, and that's also where you'll find the Tuvanna Restaurant (moderate). If you're passing through town and in need of a bite, you'll see this fine little Turkish eatery; treat yourself to the tavuk saç tava (a stir-fried chicken and mushroom dish) or any of the Turkish staples such as şiş kebab.

Where to Stay

There is little reason to visit Avanos now, given the excellent accommodations that have become available in the center of Cappadocia, but you can find very good accommodations here if you so choose.

THE SOFA HOTEL, *Orta Mahalle, Avanos. Phone/Fax (384) 511-4489; Email: sofa-hotel@katpatuka.org; Web: www.katpatuka.org/sofa. Rooms: 30. Credit cards accepted. Open year-round. Double: $50 (breakfast included).*

The Sofa has long been the standard in Avanos, a sprawl of buildings, caves, and passages opposite Haci Nuri Bey Konağı Museum. The hotel has clearly been here for years, consequently it has a mix of beautiful old doors, worn carpets, old samovars, and pretty old ceilings. Rooms are well-maintained, and the staff is helpful and friendly. Meals are served here, including great breakfasts, and there is an outdoor grill for preparing your own meal in the summer. To get there: The Sofa is located on the Avanos side of the Kizilirmak River, just inland and left of the bridge.

KIRKIT PANSIYON, *Hakkiefendi Sokak No. 12, Atatürk Cad. Avanos. Tel. (384) 511-3148; Fax (384) 511-2135; Email: kirkit@gediknet.com;*

www.kirkit.com. Rooms: 13. Credit cards accepted. Open year-round. Double: $24 (breakfast included).

The Kirkit, located in an old Ottoman house in downtown Avanos, is a decent hotel option. It suffers, in our estimation, from a vaguely predatory feel: the owners run a carpet shop around the corner and a travel agency, as well. It's a bit hard to tell whether they're friendly or you're being made. The owners also run the Karballa Hotel in Güzelyurt, a more pleasant option by far. The quality of rooms is uneven; in all cases they are appointed simply and kept clean.

Ozkonak Underground City

Özkonak is a small village in the hills above Avanos. The town has little by way of tourist infrastructure, little more than a souvenir stand.

Less refined than Derinkuyu and Kaymaklı, this underground city is in some ways far more fascinating. Özkonak may have once been as large as Derinkuyu and Kaymaklı, but large sections have not yet been explored. Features of those cities such as the great rolling defensive stones are present here, too.

One distinctive aspect of Özkonak is the drainage system, not present in other underground complexes. The city appears to have been designed by people who had the advantage of critiquing other underground complexes. The oft-quoted population figure for this city is inexplicably 60,000 people (40,000 more than the figures given for Derinkuyu), which seems completely preposterous. Fewer than 5,000 live in Özkonak today.

Perhaps more interesting than what you see inside the officially exhibited part of the underground city is what you'll see if you wander off the road toward the stream. There, more underground rooms that are presumably connected to Özkonak have been exposed by recent erosion. Within, you'll find giant millstones and clay storage containers in situ. Winemaking basins lined in plaster give credence to the idea that these underground cities once had rooms lined in plaster.

To reach the underground city ("Yeraltı şehir") pass through Avanos and follow the "Özkonak/Göynük" road north. The road is signed for the Özkonak underground city 11 kilometers past Avanos. The Kayseri road is slightly more roundabout, but also posted. Dolmuş depart Avanos for Özkonak about once every two hours from in front of the PTT, and are especially frequent on market days in Avanos (Friday) and the weekend.

WEST OF ÜRGÜP
Ortahisar, Uçhisar, Göreme, Nevşehir, Kaymaklı,
Derinkuyü, Ihlara Valley & Selime Monastery

Ortahisar

Ortahisar (literally, middle fortress) is so named for its position between the formations at Uçhisar and Ürgüp, and was once part of a series of watchtowers. A quiet village hugs the base of this towering bastion of stone, and the town can be reached by taking the turn off of the main Nevşehir-Ürgüp road for 2 kilometers. The fortress is laced with tunnels and rooms, more so, even, than the Uçhisar fortress; many of these now stand exposed after the outer walls collapsed. This is a more difficult place to visit that the tower at Uçhisar; the access route is steeper and more demanding. There is a $1.50 admission fee, and Ortahisar is open from 7:30 a.m. to 8:30 p.m. in the summer, daylight hours in the winter.

The town itself has a few small hotels, restaurants, and curio shops befitting a place that receives only a minor share of the tourism in the region. There is a good map of the town and its surroundings in the center of town above a telephone booth.

As the map indicates, there are two alternatives from Ortahisar. Some impressive painted churches are located in the Balkandere valley, which is most quickly accessed by following Hüseyin Bey Camii Sokak and continuing into the ravine below Ortahisar. One of the rewards along this trail is the Balkandere Kilise (with frescoes in a fairly poor state), and if you continue you'll find yourself in the tinier town of Ibrahimpaşa four kilometers later.

The second alternative is to follow the winding dirt track toward Pancarlık Kilise. Pancarlık Kilise and its compound is some 6 kilometers along this road, and the route from the center of Ortahisar is well-signed.

Uçhisar

On the rim of the valley, above both Göreme and Ürgüp, **Uçhisar** clings to the side of Güvercin (Pigeon) Valley in the shadow of a giant buttress of natural stone. This buttress, with its dominating view of the valley below, has been a watchtower and a fortified waypoint on the roads through Cappadocia since Persian times, if not before.

Uçhisar is a peaceful town, less heavily touristed than either Göreme or Ürgüp, although there is a great influx of French in the summer and in the off season it becomes positively somnolent, and most hotels shut down.

Arrivals & Departures

Uçhisar is just off of the main Nevşehir-Ürgüp road. Dolmuş whiz back and forth south of town throughout the day, with some veering off just west of Uçhisar to dive down into the valley below and Göreme. Dolmuş serve Uçhisar directly, as well, trolling for fares on the main road in the upper section of town by the PTT.

Where to Stay

LES MAISONS DE CAPPADOCE, *Semiramis A.Ş., Belediye Meydanı, No. 24, BP 28, Uçhisar, Tel. 384 219 2813, Fax 384 219 2782. Email: info@cappadoce.com; Web: www.cappadoce.com. Rooms: 11. Credit cards not accepted. Open April-November. Double: $110.*

French architect Jacques Avizou came to Cappadocia as a tourist in 1987, returning home with photographs, tourist chotchkes, and inspiration. Since then he has returned annually, often flying back to Orly Airport with more substantial souvenirs, such as title deeds. Through his Turkish company, Semiramis, Avizou has renovated a clutch of houses and studios in the center of old Uçhisar, doting over them and mending them in exacting fashion. There are five houses and two studios currently available, and Avizou is restoring other houses as well.

Examples of the condition in which Avizou found each of his houses abound in Uçhisar; many others in the neighborhood are in a state of neglect and disrepair, their stones poached for other projects, their inner walls caked with the soot of thousands of open fires and their floors thick with dirt from their use as pens for goats and sheep. Avizou has taken it upon himself to restore these houses, and he has had great success.

There is a peculiar architectural legacy in Cappadocia, with arches, stairs, and rooms carved into valley wall, finished with blocks of stone that are themselves fluted or scored in simple, symettric patterns. Avizou has embraced this legacy, but he has extended it as well. Each of the houses he rents has its own unique character, each sprawls into unexpected nooks and crannies, and each has a patio and its own private view out over Pigeon Valley with a small garden and grill.

"Les Maisons" are not hotel rooms; there are no meals, no phones (other than at the main Semiramis office by the post office in the center of town). Each house and suite is equipped with a kitchen, and you should solicit advice on some Turkish recipes from the Turkish caretakers while here.

Six houses are intended to accommodate six, two houses accommodate four, and three studios sleep two people. In every case, there is plenty of room to spare

Selected one of our favorite small hotels.

KAYA OTEL, *Uçhisar. Tel. (384) 219-2007; Fax (384) 219-2363 Rooms: 60. Credit cards accepted. Open April-October. Double: $64.*

The Kaya is the Club Med offering in Cappadocia, and is highly regarded. The building is decorous and attractive, offering stone block rooms looking out over the valley. The pool and grounds have a welcome bit of cool greenery during the hot Cappadocian summer. The restaurant, too, is the best in Uçhisar. The standard of service is adequate; Kaya is not the friendliest hotel in the area, but it is clean, enjoyable and efficient.

KILIM PANSIYON, *Uçhisar. Tel. (384) 219-2774; Fax (384) 219-2660. Rooms: 9. Credit cards not accepted. Open year-round. Double: $20 (breakfast included).*

In a region filled with great, inexpensive hotels, the Kilim Pension is among the best. Owner Mehmet Türke is engaging and helpful, and has done a fine job of renovating this 150 year-old building. The views out over Pigeon Valley are gorgeous, and Mehmet offers daily walks into Pigeon Valley—occasionally accompanied by a picnic.

Rooms are pleasant and clean, if a bit hacked together, and most are carved into the wall of the ridge or covered in stone arches. To get there: The Kilim is located down the cobbled lane from the main intersection in Uçhisar, just past the Efes Restaurant and up a small hill.

Selected one of our favorite budget hotels.

LES TERRACES D'UÇHISAR, *Eski Göreme Caddesi, Uçhisar. Tel. (384) 219-2792; Fax (384) 219-2762. Rooms: 16. Credit cards accepted. Open year-round. Double: $23.*

This is another of the better hotels on the ridge above Eski Göreme Caddesi, run by Suzie Vernon, a French woman who opened this hotel in 1996. The building makes good use of its public spaces and has clean, simple rooms with showers; request a room with a window. Meals are served in the small dining area, and the quality of the food makes dining in an excellent option. There is typically an English-speaker on hand, the daughter of the proprietor. If full, consider La Maisons du Reve (Tel. 384 219-2199) a bit further downhill.

Where to Eat

Uçhisar remains a small town at heart, and, charming though that may be, there aren't many good restaurants from which to choose. You'll find that many hotels – including, we bet, your own – serve meals that are your best bet.

EFES LOKANTA, *Eski Göreme Caddesi, Uçhisar, Tel. 384 219 2620. (Inexpensive-moderate).*

This is the best relatively inexpensive restaurant in Uçhisar, located down the cobbled lane that begins at the center of town and angles beneath the tower toward Göreme. You'll find that if you have neither French nor Turkish, menu selection may be a roller coaster. Be sure to try an appetizer of İmam Bayaldi ($1.25), and the Saç Tava ($3.25), a plate of grilled chicken, is a good entree. Soups are $1.25, beer is $2, and wine is $7.

CENTRE RESTAURANT, *Belediye Meydanı No. 27, Uçhisar. Tel. (384) 219-2111. Moderate.*

The Centre is located in the center of town, near the main intersection. The chef used to work at the Club Med nearby, and prepares French dishes with a great variety of fresh, delicious produce. Outdoor dining is available in the summer months.

BINDALLI RESTAURANT, *Ürgüp Caddesi, Uçhisar, Nevşehir, Tel. 384 219 2690, Fax 384 219 2363. (Moderate-Expensive).*

The restaurant at the Kaya Hotel serves up excellent buffet lunches for $8 per person, and if you find yourself in Uçhisar around lunchtime it's a good place to take a break. The restaurant serves a well-conceived combination of traditional Turkish fare and food from around the world. Breakfast and lunch only.

Seeing the Sights

The **Uçhisar fortress**, which dominates the skyline in all directions, is well worth a visit. This natural shaft of rock was tunneled long ago and appears to have been fortified during by the Romans, who are have left some tombs at the top of the fortress. From the top of the fortress you have a commanding view of the plain below, as well as of other natural fortresses in this circuit, such as those at Ortahisar and Ürgüp. The fortress – like so many things in Cappadocia – is as interesting as you are daring, with tunnels and shafts shooting every which way, and caves winding around the exterior of the rock. There is a $1.50 charge to enter the fortress, and the carved stone "lobby" has a gift shop.

From Uçhisar, you can take several paths down into Pigeon Valley and follow trails north to Goreme, three kilometers away.

Alparslan Horseriding, *Tel. 384 219 2944*, is located on Eski Goreme Caddesi, the long cobbled lane that cuts across the ridge below the fortress.

Goreme

Göreme is just 3 kilometers north of Uçhisar, one kilometer west of the **Göreme Open Air Museum**. Located deep in a valley at the head of several valleys, Göreme has become the center of budget travel in the area. The town has a raucous feel to it, and teems with backpackers in the high season. There is no official tourism bureau in town, but there is a tourism information cooperative at the bus station.

Some consider Göreme the prime location within Cappadocia, and it is certainly convenient to Pigeon Valley and the Göreme Open Air museum. Still, small hoteliers, carpet sellers, and restaurateurs have run a bit amok

Arrivals & Departures

Dolmuş leave for Göreme from Nevşehir hourly throughout the day, passing just west of Uçhisar on the way. There is also dolmuş service directly to Ürgüp and Avanos. In the high season, Göreme is on the dolmuş "ring tour" that passes counterclockwise to the tourism hubs in Cappadocia (Ürgüp, the Zelve valley, Avanos, Göreme, and back to Ürgüp). This ring tour operates from May to October, with dolmus leaving hourly, and charging fares from point to point. The dolmuş stop is at the otogar in the middle of town.

Where to Stay

Göreme's identity is firmly entrenched: this is the backpacker's town. Budget cave hotels are everywhere, and many of them are quite good. In recent years a few slightly upscale hotels have opened, giving the well-established Ataman Hotel some direct competition.

ATAMAN HOTEL, *Göreme, Nevşehir. Tel. (384) 271-2310; Fax (384) 271-2313; Email: info@atamanhotel.com; Web: www.atamanhotel.com. Rooms: 48. Double: $130 (half-board).*

The appeal of the Ataman Hotel has eroded somewhat over the years as charmless modern rooms have been added for the sake of catering to tour groups. At the same time, room rates have risen beyond reason; there are more beautiful, less expensive alternatives in Uçhisar and Ürgüp. For all of that, there remains much to appreciate: the beauty of this hotel has always been in its cave rooms and network of subterranean passageways mined into the hill behind it, and in the terrace overlooking the poplar-lined creek emptying out of Pigeon Valley. Should you elect to stay here, be sure to request a cave-room; many of the other rooms, while carefully decorated, are disappointing.

KELEBEK MOTEL-PENSION, *Göreme. Tel. (384) 271-2531; Fax (384) 271-2763; Email: ali@kelebekhotel.com; Web: www.kelebekhotel.com. Rooms: 17. Credit cards accepted. Open year-round. Double: $18.*

Getting to the Kelebek from the bus stop in the center of town requires a hike to the ridge above Pigeon Valley, but the hike is worth it for the best budget accommodation in Göreme. As advertised, the Kelebek (butterfly) offers the best view in town from a series of terraces and sitting rooms. The standard of rooms is mixed—several are carved into stone, two in the peak of a fairy chimney, in fact. Other rooms are purpose built with tufa stone, and less charming. There are three—yes, three—honeymoon suites. If you like, you can call from the bus stop and they'll pick you up to spare you the walk.

Selected one of our favorite budget hotels.

KÖSE PANSIYON, *Göreme, Nevşehir. Tel. (384) 271-2294; Fax (384) 279-2577. Rooms: 16. Credit cards not accepted. Open year-round. Double: $16.*

It seems a shame to stay in Göreme and not stay in a cave room, but thousands of backpackers can't be wrong. This hotel is a perennial favorite of budget travelers, offering all of the things that you've come to expect from backpacker hotels; great information, movies, book exchange, cheap meals ($4 dinner), and inexpensive options for viewing the sites of Cappadocia. The Köse has a pool. The Köse is located north of the otogar, left past the PTT.

Should it be full, try a similarly-priced stalwart backpacking pitstop, **Paradise Pension** *(Tel/Fax (384) 271-2248)*. **Tabiat Pension** is a third good pension option, in the center of town past the main mosque on the left, is well-managed and tidy *(Tel. 384 271-2660; Email: tabiatpension@hotmail.com)*, Double: $14.

Where to Eat

Many hotels offer dinner, and your fellow guests can attest to whether it's worthwhile. For an evening out, there are several good dining options.

KONAK TÜRK EVI, *Göreme. Tel. (384) 271-2463. Moderate-expensive.*

Konak Türk Evi, the Old Turkish Inn, is a beautiful, 165 year-old building in the little-visited side of Göreme on the opposite side of the canal from the center. The restaurant within is somewhat expensive, but the food is worthy of its attractive setting. Try to arrange reservations for seating in one of the beautiful old rooms upstairs (check with reception at your hotel). There are some dissonant chords amid the wood and old textiles; they have the pool-playing dog poster prominently displayed. Mezes run $3-$4, entrees such as the karışık izgara (mixed grill) run $5-$7.

ORIENT RESTAURANT, *Orta Mahalle Okul Sok., Göreme. Tel. (384) 271-2346. Inexpensive-moderate.*

A lot, meaning a lot, of restaurants have opened in Göreme intent on making fast money, but the Orient has for years been reliable and honest. It probably helps that it's a bit away from the center, on the Uç hisar road across from Cafedocia and Kapadokya Balloons. The food is good, the prices are reasonable, and the atmosphere is relaxed. Try the biber dolma (stuffed peppers, without meat) and the cacik as starters, then move on to tavuk şiş or whatever moves you.

CAFEDOCIA, *Orta Mahalle Okul Sokak No. 6, Göreme. Tel. (384) 271-2900; Fax (384) 271-2901; Email: cafedoci@indigoturizm.com.tr; Web: www.indigoturizm.com.tr/cafedocia. Inexpensive-moderate.*

Cafedocia is a good restaurant and bar on its own merits, never mind the fact that it's also an Internet cafe. Entering Cafedocia, you find yourself in an oasis of American-ness, with burgers for $2.50, chicken curry for $3, beer $2, and, even, omelettes for breakfast ($1.50). The ambience is sedate, dark, and interesting, and the food is good. There's a selection of English language papers and magazines and, of course, Internet access. The cost for access is about $2.25 per half hour (a little steep), and there were only two terminals when we visited, so you may have to wait for Nigel to read all about Tottenham's match against Leeds before you can log on. Note: many carpet shops use free Internet access to lure you, but a pay-as-you-go Internet café is probably far cheaper in the long run.

ATAMAN HOTEL, *Göreme, Nevşehir. Tel. (384) 271-2310; Fax (384) 271-2313. Expensive.*

Abbas Ataman opened his restaurant in 1986, and it became popular enough that he opened a hotel to go with it in 1993. The cuisine at the Ataman is overwhelmingly rich, baked shrimp, quail, sauteed artichokes and chicken, followed by heavy, decadent desserts. That said, the restaurant has endured some turnover with chefs, and some readers of this guide have complained about the quality. We still favor this restaurant, but the fluctuating quality makes it worth checking with your host or guide before treating yourself. The cost is roughly $24 for a prix fixe meal.

Seeing the Sights

Göreme village is itself a sight, and it's worth your while to wander along the stone lanes past the many cave houses. Two blocks above the town center near the Magic Rock House Pension (we cringe when we write that name) you'll find a cobbled lane with big metal vats filled with dye lining the walls.

Nearby is the entryway to the **Halk Eğitim Merkezi**, a national cultural center that in this case is devoted to the making of carpets. Inside find women at a series of looms and a room devoted to creating natural dyes in large bronze vats. If you're at all curious about the production of carpets, this is a very worthwhile stop, especially so if you're in the company of a guide: there is no English language documentation to explain the process.

Pigeon Valley

Pigeon Valley extends from Uçhisar down to Göreme, offering an excellent hike in both directions. The trail along the valley floor offers a hushed, pretty walk past tombs, caves and churches – as you would expect, dovecotes for collecting pigeon guano pock the valley walls. A small stream follows the course of Pigeon Valley down to Göreme, emerging near the Ataman Hotel; you can walk either up into this valley or down toward Goreme from Uçhisar.

Kizilcukur (The Red Valley)

The Red Valley is an excellent destination for those interested in a relatively easy hike through the undulating Cappadocian landscape. To get there, follow the highway 6 kilometers out of Ürgüp in the direction of Göreme, following a signed turning for "Kızılçukur" north (right) beyond Ortahisar. Three kilometers along you'll find a small car park and someone collecting a fee (dawn-dusk, $1).

Many come to the top of the valley simply to watch the sun set; better to hike into the valley and back out, or to hike clear through to Çavuşin on the Göreme-Avanos road. The trail winds along ridges and twists down into valleys of steepled stone, passing small tunnels and chambers. Hidden in these valleys are several marvelous stone-cut churches; without someone along to guide you, they can be difficult to find—trust to the well-worn trails, and bring a flashlight. Just one kilometer from the road is one of the most stunning churches, Direkli Kilise (The Church of Columns). As you descend along the main trail, look for a flat buttress of stone on your right. In the side of this particular stone outcrop there is a series of six manmade 'windows', pocked with pigeonholes and decorated with black and white geometric figures. The approach dips sharply into a gully and ascends immediately, cutting left to the final opening; it leads to a stair within. Suffice it to say, the church is marvelous—a fine reward for its own discovery. Further along in the valley are other churches, principally the Beyaz Kilise (White Church).

Goreme Open Air Museum

This is the most impressive site in Cappadocia. Monks living here carved out a cluster of churches and habitations above a small, fertile valley, decorating their holy places with painting and frescoes. Many of the frescoes remain in good shape, although most are marred in some way, usually with their eyes gouged. Again and again while in Cappadocia you will see frescoes and paintings defaced in this way. This practice was supposed to "kill" the images, according to iconoclastic Muslims. In addition to the damage done on religious grounds, standard vandalism has taken a toll. Sadly, many frescoes were also damaged by the people who created them; in later years, Greek Orthodox residents chipped bits of the art away for use in healing balms.

Tickets to the Open Air Museum are $4.50, quite expensive by the standard of Turkish museums. That price does not include access to the Karanlık Kilise (Dark Church); the cost of admission for this one church is $5 per person, and if you are moved by masterful Byzantine painting, is well worth the price..

The Churches

The first church you'll see is located just outside of the gates, and you'll need to have a ticket to visit. **Tokalı Church** is one of the crowning glories of Cappadocia, a beautiful cave church ornamented with remarkably well-preserved frescoes. The church is located outside of the main gate of the Göreme Open Air Museum, down the road toward the car park. The beautiful detailing of the columns and arches within Tokalı perfectly recreate the interior of a barrel-vaulted church, although it serves no structural purpose here.

The current foyer was once the extent of the church, but over time the larger interior space was hollowed out, and with the end of the Iconoclastic period in 843 A.D., the monks were free to decorate the interiors with representations of Christ and other figurative images. Note the difference in the artwork; the outer section is painted directly on stone, while the interior chamber is covered with frescoes. The life of Christ is represented on one section of the arched ceiling in six long rows, separated in the center by depictions of the apostles. The lower level was a crypt, the long troughs filled with bones of people and clerics from the community. UNESCO restored parts of this church after a collapse in the 1960s.

Within the park all of the churches are signed, each given a name that has something to do with the art within the church or a significant feature of it. The **Elmalı Kilise**, or **Apple Church**, was so named for the simple reason that an apple tree once stood before the entrance; it does no longer.

Cappadocian Symbols

Cappadocian churches and monasteries are carefully decorated with innumerable inscriptions and other forms of art. When the iconoclasts banned figurative art, monks began forming **rebuses** to depict important stories.

Here's what the symbols represent:

The Cross – Christianity.

The Fish – Both Jesus Christ and Christians were symbolized by the fish. The Greek letters in "fish" were also strung out to form a holy acronym meaning Jesus, son of God, saviour, while Christians considered themselves fish caught in his holy net.

The Pigeon – It stands to reason that this bird, so important to the people of these valleys, would stand for peace and fertility, as well as the Holy Spirit.

The Peacock – The adoption of Christianity.

The Deer – Resurrection.

The Lion – Victory.

Grapes – Baptism, or Jesus.

The Chicken – The annunciation.

The Triangle – Someone espousing the Holy Trinity, an evangelist.

The Rabbit – Sin, Sexuality.

The Insect – Satan.

The images within are in an excellent state of preservation. The central dome of this church is decorated with an image of Christ holding a book in his left hand and making a classic Byzantine blessing with his right, representing the Trinity. The archangel Michael is depicted on the dome immediately behind him and above the main apse (some say the spherical object in his left hand is the "apple" to which the name of the church refers).

It is interesting to juxtapose the Apple Church with the **Church of St. Barbara**, nearby. The artwork within represents a "before" (Church of St. Barbara) and "after" (Apple Church). During the Iconoclastic period in the 8th and 9th centuries the Orthodox were not permitted to create figurative images, an edict that weighed heavily on the Cappadocians. The decorators of the chapels and churches relied instead on symbols to convey their message; in the Church of St. Barbara we have an unspoilt example of this. It is likely that this is how the Apple Church appeared before a benefactor paid for figurative artwork to be created instead.

In the Church of St. Barbara, and elsewhere in Cappadocia, you'll find some comingling of figurative artwork and images in some churches. As is the case here, this is the result of later frescoes only partially covering the original symbolic art; small wonder, given the time, skill and (perhaps) expense that would have been necessary to decorate an entire church.

St. Barbara is herself represented within the church, on the north wall. As the story goes, she was slain by her father for converting to Christianity, and he was, in turn, struck down by a bolt of lightning. For no immediately obvious reason, she is a patron saint of architects and soldiers. You'll also notice the mounted figures of St. Theodore and St. George, two soldier saints, and, above them, an interesting series of symbols. There are at least two theories about this series; the first suggests that the insect represents Satan, and that he can only be thus depicted because his evil is nullified by the symbolic crosses to either side. The second theory suggests that the odd creature is a token once borne by the Byzantine army, yet another indication that this church may have been a place of worship intended for soldiers.

The barrel-vaulted **Yılanli Kilise (Snake Church)**, is so named for the great fresco depicting, again, the Saints Theodore and George slaying a great serpent. They are joined by Constantine the Great and his mother, St. Helena; she is said to have divined the location of the True Cross, and is shown carrying it with her son. Constantine and Helena appear again on the other side of the vault, this time accompanied by St. Onophrius, a bearded man making a warding gesture. St. Onophrius was an Egyptian hermit in the 4th Century who distinguished himself through self-denial. A more interesting tale tells us that St. Onophrius is in fact an old bearded woman. It seems that as a young girl Onophrius sought God's intervention to help steer her away from the temptations of the flesh, and God granted her wish by transforming her into an old man. St. Onophrius is the patron saint of weavers.

The **Çarıklı Kilise (Church of the Sandal)** was closed for restoration as this book went to press, but the images contained therein were in poor condition when work began. The church derives its name from the indentations in the floor, and a host of saints are depicted.

The **Karanlık Kilise**, or **Dark Church**, was reopened in early 1997 after a long restoration project. As mentioned above, there is a surcharge for anyone wishing to visit this church of $5. This surprisingly high price is warranted due to the vivid, complex images depicted within, but most visitors will have plenty to see without paying a premium to visit this church.

That said, the images of the Dark Church are marvelous and rich. The artwork inside was once exposed only to the light of a single window, and the darkness, combined with surprising good fortune vis a vis vandalism, have made these the most arresting frescoes in Cappadocia. The interior was exposed after a section of the facade broke off and collapsed, but restoration completed in 1997 has resealed the church and created an entirely new entrance.

The images within the Dark Church concern many things, but some of the most striking depict the final episodes in Jesus' life. There is the Last Supper, in which Judas betrays himself by being the first to "dippeth with me in the dish," as St. Mark reports Jesus foreseeing. In another image, the same Judas figure, who you'll note is included among the haloed, prepares to betray Jesus with a kiss with the spears of the gathered Roman soldiers as a backdrop. He appears to lament that decision in the crucifiction scene, wherein Jesus is pierced in the side and the suffering of Jesus and Judas alike is compounded when Jesus is offered only a sponge soaked in vinegar to slake his thirst. The blue backdrop of the images in the Dark Church is unusual, and for good reason; that pigment was created with lapis lazuli, and was remarkably expensive. It appears that as many as nine wealthy benefactors contributed to the creation of the artwork within the Dark Church.

The Open Air Museum has a great collection of other churches, monasteries and refectories, as well, and is usually overrun with tourists. If you can spare the time, it's good to pack some food along and budget a long while to visit the churches, climb through the tunnels overlooking the valley below, and avoid standing in long lines.

Nevsehir

The regional hub in Cappadocia is **Nevşehir**, but that does not mean you want to stay here. Aside from the **Selçuk fort** on the crest of the hill above town and the relaxed byways of **Nar** (old Nevşehir) across the gorge, there's very little to see. You are sure to pass back and forth through town, but you needn't feel inclined to stay.

The **tourism information office**, Atatürk Bulvarı, *Tel. 384 213 3659*, is staffed by people who are often disinclined to actually give you any, and they're strongly inclined to keep you staying in town.

Arrivals & Depatures

Nevşehir is a transit hub on the western end of the Cappadocian plain, with roads fanning out toward Mersin, Konya, and Ankara. If you arrive in the area by bus, you will probably be dropped off at Nevşehir's main bus station, out of town to the north. As discussed in Cappadocia,

Arrivals and Departures, if you arrive by bus in Nevşehir you should be transferred on to Ürgüp, Göreme, or wherever you're ultimately headed. Nevşehir's major dolmuş stop is on Atatürk Caddesi near the tourism office and a little east of the major intersection at the center of town (Lale Caddesi and Atatürk Caddesi). Dolmuş bound for the towns of Ürgüp, Üçhisar, Göreme and the other towns of central Cappadocia stop here, and if you are using public transportation you'll become familiar with this place. Dolmuş also serve the underground cities of Derinkuyu and Kaymaklı and sites farther south, such as Niğde – you'll see the signed turnoff. You can also get a dolmuş from the main Nevşehir otogar for Açıksaray (in the direction of Gülşehir), although it's difficult to visit all eight of the subterranean monastic complexes using public transportation.

Where to Stay

Given the strange and delightful accommodations available to the east of Nevşehir, we advise bypassing accommodation here and selecting someplace in Ürgüp, Uçhisar or Göreme.

HOTEL KAPADOKYA DEDEMAN, *Ürgüp Yolu, Nevşehir, Tel. 384 213 9900-9915, Fax 384 213 2158. Rooms: 349. Double: $120.*

This is Cappadocia's lone five star hotel, with satellite television, pools, basketball. The Dedeman chain is very well run, and this hotel is no exception. If you need convenience and the standard amenities of a major hotel, this is the place.

Kaymakli Underground City

From Nevşehir, the Niğde road leads directly south through Kaymaklı and Derinkuyu, both of which are located by the main road.

Contrary to popular belief, "Kaymaklı" is not Turkish for bad posture. This cramped underground city is south of Nevşehir on the way to Derinkuyü, easily accessible by car or dolmuş from Nevşehir. This complex has fewer floors than its neighbor Derinkuyu, but snakes into the earth in a tighter, more disconcerting way. This is not a place for the faint of heart or the bad of back.

Kaymaklı is, if anything, more complex than the open sections of Derinkuyu. It is interesting to see the differences in tunneling and internal design; note, for instance, the holes for passing along messages from floor to floor. The offset, staggered floors within underground cities such as Kaymaklı have helped them survive earthquakes in the region; in the case of Kaymaklı, the city is spread out over one square kilometer and many older houses in the area have direct access to it. As in

Derinkuyu, the people of this village had access to well water from within their cities. It is also thought that when the population retired underground it was in the habit of dumping its waste into the section of river furthest downstream; unfortunately what was downstream to Kaymaklı was upstream to Derinkuyu. Despite this, as mentioned in the Derinkuyu section, some excavators suspect there was a great tunnel linking the two cities. As at Derinkuyu, there is an arrow system to help you determine whether you are ascending or descending.

Derinkuyu Underground City

Along with Kaymakly, this is the most-visited underground city in Cappadocia, and deservedly so. It is south of Kaymaklı, directly on the main Nevşehir-Niğde road, so it is simple to reach by car or by dolmuş from Nevşehir ($1.50).

Derinkuyu is a nondescript town, within which, at the southern end, there is a parking lot on the east side of the road. The entrance to the underground city is here, and it's well signed. Try to avoid Derinkuyu between 10 a.m. and 3 p.m. during high season, when you have to squeeze in between huffing, sweating busloads of people.

The entrance to Derinkuyu Underground City is a humble staircase that opens into a large chamber, which is in turn attached to further chambers descending eight floors and 180 feet deep. Upon entering, the bulk of the city is around to your right, while livestock areas, the school, and the winery are off to your left.

According to one account this city was besieged three separate times by the Arabs, to no avail. The Arabs could not dislodge the Christians, who were supplied with food and water from an underground river, and they could not seal them in since the natives could burrow out at will. You will see huge stone disks in situ that were intended to block off passages in times of siege.

There has long been talk of a wide tunnel that extends from Derinkuyu to Kaymaklı – almost six miles – but although it is possible, it's not been proven. The problem is, great sections of both underground cities remain unexcavated – at Derinkuyu, the section visitors see today is probably 15 percent of the entire city. Arrows direct you through the maze, and if you can take the tight spaces and the huddle of people you'll definitely want to descend all the way to the old chapel at the root of Derinkuyu. One final spur of tunnel dives down to the lowest accessible section of the city, where you look out at a vertical shaft extending to the water below and to a pinpoint of natural light far above.

Ihlara Valley

In a region full of wonderful oddities, this is frequently the favorite. If you are staying in central Cappadocia, a large part of **Ihlara Valley** can be seen in a single day combined with, say, a trip to the underground city at Derinkuyu. Bear in mind that Ihlara Valley is some 200 kilometers from the towns of central Cappadocia, round trip. Start early, bring a small pack full of food, clothes you can get grubby, a good book and some hiking boots or comfortable sneakers.

The Ihlara Valley is defined by sheer cliffs to either side of the **Melendiz River**. The river valley is a thick ribbon of green, sharply contrasting the sere grasses of the plain above. What makes Ihlara peculiar instead of merely dramatic is the collection of painted churches, dormitories, and individual dwellings that honeycomb the walls. The monks who inhabited this valley (formerly Peristrema), lived austere lives, but they were no fools; this gorge is a beautiful, peaceful, thriving place filled with whirling birds and wide-eyed frogs. Trails follow the valley from its head at the town of **Ihlara**, past tiny **Belisirma** village 7 kilometers north, and continues 5 kilometers to the point where the gorge opens again at the town of **Selime**. In the spring, sections of trail may be flooded. Churches and monastic dwellings are located on either side of the Melendiz (more a stream than a river); the Melendiz is spanned by several bridges.

Arrivals & Departures

By Bus

Buses serve Ihlara and Selime from Aksaray, the regional transportation hub. There is no public transportation from Nevşehir or central Cappadocia—tour groups make their way from central Cappadocia to Ihlara almost daily. Municipal buses depart Aksaray for Selime, Ihlara, and Guzelyurt to the east at 7 a.m., 11 a.m., 1 p.m., 3:30 p.m., 5 p.m., and 6 p.m. ($3.50); the last departure from Ihlara is at 5 p.m.

Given the heavy tourist traffic from central Cappadocia, you should be able to secure a ride back to Cappadocia aboard a tour bus for a few dollars.

By Car

Ihlara town, at the head of the valley is a one and one-half hour drive from Nevşehir in central Cappadocia. Follow signs directing you to the underground city at Derinkuyu, then follow the signed west turning to Ihlara Valley. Another route follows the main highway from Nevşehir toward Aksaray, taking the left turn at the town of Gökce just beyond the kervansaray at Ağzıkarahan.

Where to Stay & Eat

Most people make Ihlara part of a day trip from central Cappadocia. If you choose to spend a night near Ihlara, you'll find yourself well-served by accommodations in the area. The best choices are located in Ihlara town, at the upstream end of Ihlara Valley, and in Güzelyurt 8 kilometers away. There is a single pension in Belisirma, midway down the valley, and several acceptable hotels in Selime at the far end of the valley.

In Ihlara

AKAR PANSIYON, *Ihlara. Tel. (382) 453-7018; Fax (382) 453-7511; Email: none; Web: none. Rooms: 20. Credit cards not accepted. Open year-round. Double: $15 (including breakfast).*

Akar Pension is one of two well-established hotels in Ihlara, located in upper Ihlara directly on the main Ihlara-Selime road. Rooms have balconies, clean white walls, and are decently-appointed. You'll find a small market to suit your picnicking needs. A new building was underway at the time of this writing. The hotel is 1.5 kilometers from the entrance to Ihlara valley. If you're a guest, owner Cengiz Akar is happy to provide a ride to or from Belisirma or Selime as part of your hike in the valley. The other top-flight pension is the **Pansiyon Anatolia** *(Tel. 382 453-7440; Fax 382 453-7439; Rooms: 12; Double: $16)*, located 100 meters off the main road, also northwest of central Ihlara town.

STAR HOTEL & RESTAURANT, *Ihlara Vadisi, Irmak Kenarı, Ihlara, Aksaray. Tel. (382) 453-7676. Rooms: 12. Credit cards not accepted. Open year-round. Double: $9 (including breakfast).*

The restaurant at the Star is a good place for a bite before or after a trip through Ihlara Valley, owing to its absolutely fascinating location. $5 buys a fixed menu lunch of trout, rice, pide, and salad. We know of few better ways to whet your appetite before the meal than poking around the natural bridge at the headwaters of the Melendiz. Just a few paces from the restaurant is an ancient baptistry carved into the stone wall. Further along is the arched natural tunnel from which the river emerges. On the face of the wall on the far side is a separate channel that ducks into a tunnel; the room at the entrance was a winemaking room. The hotel is extremely spartan, with thin rugs, serviceable beds, and squat toilets. The Star is located just a stone's throw from the small otogar in the center of Ihlara.

In Güzelyurt

KARBALLA HOTEL, *Çarşi içi, Güzelyurt. Tel. (382) 451-2103; Fax (382) 451-2107; Email: kirkit@kgediknet.com; Web: www.kirkit.com. Rooms: 20. Credit cards accepted. Open March-October. Double: $34 (breakfast included).*

This is the most compelling accommodation in the Ihlara Valley region, located in the former Kızlar Manastir (Girls' Monastery). The structure, built in 1857, has been reworked with monk cells as guest rooms. The stone-walled, arched rooms are basic and comfortable, with kilims, small desks, and the names of Orthodox saints, befitting their former residents. The grounds include a swimming pool and a small private outdoor theatre. The former refectory now offers good, filling meals popular among tour groups. Open buffet lunches and dinners cost $7, and are recommended. Get thee to the nunnery.

Güzelyurt is home to a small underground city, the entrance to which is in the middle of town.

In Belisirma
BELISIRMA EV PANSIYON, *Cami Yani, Belisirma, Aksaray. Tel. (382) 457-3037. Rooms: 7. Credit cards not accepted. Open year-round. Double: $15 (breakfast included).*

Belisirma, midway down the valley, is a quiet spot that sees foot traffic from Ihlara's many visitors. The Ev Pansiyon, at the top of the path in Belisirma just north of the mosque, is the sole pension here. This is a fine pit stop if you're hiking the entire valley. The Ev Pansiyon, run by the friendly Necati Karsandı and his family, offers a nice terrace and good food—a meal of kuru fasulye, piliç, soup, salad, and cacık costs $4. In the town below, directly on the river by the bridge, you'll find two popular lunch restaurants—Belisirma Restaurant on the east bank and Aslan Restaurant on the west bank. Meals at either place cost $4. A road winds down the western wall of the gorge, and tour buses frequently pick people up in Belisirma.

Selected one of our favorite budget hotels.

In Selime
ÇATLAK RESTAURANT & HOTEL, *Ihlara Vadi Ici, Selime, Aksaray. Tel. (382) 454-5065. Rooms: 18. Credit cards not accepted. Open year-round. Double: $20 (breakfast included).*

Once in Selime, most people have a bite to eat, then visit the spectacular monastic ruins nearby. Çatlak Restaurant, just downstream of the trailhead on the Melendiz River, is a great place for a break. $3 will buy you a good meal of salad, rice, trout, tomato, and bread; there are plenty of other grilled dishes, as well. Seating is arranged along the bank under a grape arbor. If you will be staying the night here, the owners of the Çatlak Restaurant recently opened a solid hotel one kilometer north of the trailhead—they'll be happy to give you a ride. **Piri Motel and Camping**, *Tel. (382) 454-5114*, also north of the trailhead, is also a decent

Orthodox Death Rites

In many of the churches of Cappadocia you will find shallow trenches in the stone by the entrance, and often elsewhere throughout the interior. These were sacred places where the keeper of the church deposited the bones of people in the community after the flesh had rotted. When the bones were clean, they were bathed in water or wine and kept within the confines of the church. The clean white of the bones was a symbol of the purity of the soul, and the loss of flesh meant that sin, too, was being left behind.

The bones in most of these churches are long since scattered.

option. The owners of both hotels can provide some useful guiding services.

Seeing the Sights

There are two entrances to the valley at its south end, one in Ihlara village and another atop a high stair that begins between Ihlara and Belisirma. We'll begin at the south gate, where you pay a $2 entrance fee (8:30 a.m. to 5:30 p.m.).

There were more than 90 churches along this 13 kilometer stretch of the Melendiz River, and many are still intact. The churches at the upstream end of the valley show more eastern influence in their frescoes, while those downstream are more Byzantine, perhaps suggesting later occupation. As at Göreme and Zelve, peasants damaged many of the frescoes around the eyes in order to "kill" the spirit within the painting, and simple vandalism has compounded matters (particularly in recent years).

You can spend many delightful hours investigating Ihlara on your own, but the company of a guide is quite useful to ensure you find and understand all of the great sites in Ihlara Valley.

The southern end of the trail winds through tilled fields bordered by slender cottonwoods. Small caves pock the walls, but **Kokar Kilise** (The Church of Good Odors), is the first significant church as you leave Ihlara, on the left (western) bank. Kokar Kilise is carved in the form of a simple basilica, and it has striking symmetry and charm. The barrel-vaulted ceiling has a great Maltese Cross surrounded by patterns in reds, yellows and greens, and there is a great host of saints arrayed on all sides. To the left as you enter are some badly defaced images of the early life of Christ, and on the right are the final scenes of the betrayal and crucifixion. The inscriptions are clearly influenced by the east, referring to the Persian names of some characters rather than their Greek equivalents. Continuing down the river on the same bank is **Pürenli Seki church** (The Church of the Terraces). This church is difficult to reach, located 75 feet above the level of the river; the frescoes within are damanged. Further along is **Ağaçaltı Kilise** (The Church Beneath the Tree). On the wall opposite the entrance is a fresco of Daniel in the lion's den. The vaulted right chamber has a depiction of the flight into Egypt.

Past the entrance stair on the same side of the river is **Sümbüllü Kilise** (The Hyacinth Church). This two-story monastery has an elaborate façade and some frescoes within. Backing up and crossing the river to the east bank you arrive at the most well-known church in the valley, **Yylanlı Kilise** (Snake Church). This church is firmly in the Eastern Orthodox fold. The churches of upper (southern) Ihlara were built and adorned by Orthodox Christians whose faith was rooted in fear of Satan and hatred of what they considered his greatest tool: woman.

The art within Yılanlı Kilise is badly damaged and requires use of a flashlight to see properly. The snakes who give this church its name are reptilian demons busily repaying women for their sins; four woman are depicted being bitten in various ways as punishment for neglecting children, committing adultery, disobeying a husband, and calumny. Another grim image is that of the forty *Christian Martyrs of Sebaste* forced into freezing water and forbidden to leave until they renounce their religion. This 39 of the men refused to do; one did. A Roman guard then reveals himself as a Christian, strips, and enters the pool. An exasperated devil looks on, grimacing.

Upsteam on this side of the river is a badly damaged monastic complex—**Karanlık Kale** (The Dark Fort). Turning back downstream, the walls are filled with churches and monastic dwellings in various states of repair. **Karagedik Kilise** (The Church of the Black Collar) is found several hundred meters further along, and is unusual in that it is not a rock-cut church—it's built above ground. Back on the west bank, is **Kırk Damalti Kilise** (The Church of St. George), notable for a cameo mention of the Selçuk Sultan Mesut II (1283-1298). This church is on the west side of the valley as you approach Belisirma from the south. This is quite a late date for Orthodox artwork in Cappadocia, and the mention of a Selçuk Sultan is also quite unusual; it is thought that the benefactor of this church was the wife of a local governor under the Selçuk Sultan. The couple is depicted, she in Byzantine dress, he in Selçuk style.

The final major churches before reaching the village of Belisirma are also located on the west bank; **Bahattin Samanlığı Kilise** (Bahattin's Granary Church) and **Direkli Kilise** (Church of Columns). The former, named for the man who used to store his hay here, has extensive frescoes depicting scenes of Christ recorded in the Bible. The latter, within sight of Belisirma, has a central dome "supported" by six columns. Frescoes depict several saints.

Most visitors go no further than **Belisirma**, opting to dine at the Aşlan Restaurant on the west bank or Belisirma Restaurant on the east bank, then head home on one of the buses that awaits here. This is all the more reason to consider hiking the final 5 kilometers to Selime. This section is lightly traveled and small paths wind up to churches such as **Ala Kilise** (The Mottled Church) and chambers in the valley wall. The trail terminates just down the road from the magnificent Monastery/Fortress at Selime.

The Monastery/Fortress at Selime

The Monastery and Fortress at Selime (8 a.m.-6 p.m., $4; the same ticket serves for Ihlara Valley) has a stupefying collection of sights; a rock-cut monastic complex, a fortified warren of chambers, and four marvelous rock-cut churches. Somehow, this site remained off the beaten track until the late 1990s, at which point work was done to open it up to tourism. Today, this is an immensely gratifying site to visit, and one that definitely rewards fearless climbing and the services of a local kid to guide you.

The entrance—and ticket taker—is located just above the Selçuk Ali Pasa türbe by the roadside. From the entrance, rock-cut steps lead to a series of rooms and tunnels. The lower tunnels are high enough that passersby could bring their camels and horses within, using the caves as a caravansaray. Note the loops and troughs cut into the walls.

There is a winemaking room near the base of the compound, and you'll find a kitchen higher up. To the right across the face of the stone wall is the entrance to the monastery, which has several levels and a great central chamber with meter-thick columns where one can easily imagine monks intoning.

From within the monastic complex, a guide can direct you to the stairs and ladders that ascend, level by perilous level, through the stone, out onto the exposed face of the rock, and on up to a series of rooms high in the cliff wall. The ascent and descent is rewarding, but very dangerous. According to local guides, this easily-defensible warren was the fortress of Ali Paşa (interred in the turbe marked "Selime Sultan" by the roadside), a local 13th century hero who did battle with evildoers from the safety of this refuge.

Back on solid ground, there are four different churches in an excellent state of preservation. All of them are arrayed around the monastic complex, with several of them off to the right (south), in the direction of the Ihlara Valley trailhead. Derviş Church has fine frescoes on the left wall, depicting Jesus and the Apostles.

One other topic of note; villagers will lead you to a section of town where, they say, scenes from the first Star Wars movie—"A New Hope"— were filmmed.

SOUTH OF ÜRGÜP
Mustafapaşa, Mazı Underground City,
Soğanli and Eski Gumuş

Pancarlik Valley

Pancarlık (Beet) Valley is one of the lesser sites of Cappadocia, but it is impressive by any other standard. Two kilometers south of Ürgüp, in the direction of Mustafapaşa, there is a signed turnoff west for Pancarlık. Another two kilometers on a well-maintained back road brings you to Sarica Kilise and Kepez Kilise, two churches in the valley south of and below the road. Both are located within a single stone buttress, featuring the inverted architecture common to rock-hewn churches; the barrel vaults, domes, and columns serve no structural purpose, they simply mimic the architecture of above-ground churches. There is evidence of old frescoes, but only simple red on white patterns remain.

Another half kilometer along the road brings you to the central part of Pancarlık Valley. Here, a ticket taker dwelling in a small cave by the parking lot may collect $1 from you. The main church, unlocked when the ticket-taker is present, is decorated with elaborate frescoes in greens and reds, and the figures here are of unusually good quality, with expressive eyes. In the valley below there is a cluster of dwellings and, as elsewhere, hundreds of dovecotes carved out for pigeons. Throughout Cappadocia their guano was collected and tilled back into the soil.

Pancarlık is also a good point from which to set out on a hike winding seven kilometers up toward Ortahisar. To do so requires a walk from the main Ürgüp-Mustafapaşa road or a taxi ride directly to Pancarlık. Once in Ortahisar you will be able to get a dolmuş.

Mustafapasa

Mustafapaşa, formerly Sinassos, is a pretty village just 6 kilometers south of Ürgüp. This town retains much of its Orthodox heritage in the Church of St. Basil and in the buildings of the town, and the "Greek" feeling of this town is stronger than elsewhere in Cappadocia. Charming though the town is, it is not heavily touristed, save tour buses that stop in during the day. In addition to the church, which is worthy of a visit, there is a winery near the Old Greek House should you spend more time in town.

Dolmuş pass through town both north and south every hour.

Where to Stay & Eat

THE OLD GREEK HOUSE, *Sahir Cad. No. 12, Mustafapaşa, Ürgüp. Tel. (384) 353-5306; Fax (384) 353-5141; Email: none; Web: none. Rooms: 13. Credit cards not accepted. Open year-round. Double: $35 (breakfast included).*

The Old Greek House is just that, a sprawling old 19th century stone and wooden building built around a spacious courtyard. Each of the rooms is a classic, barrel-vaulted affair, and the public spaces include a grand courtyard, cavernous sitting rooms, and old Turkish baths. This is a wonderfully spacious and airy structure, with grapes vines twined through overhanging lattice and the chirping of birds in the distance. A few tour groups find there way here, but few others.

The Old Greek House is noteworthy for its excellent restaurant. Meals are taken in the courtyard or in large, high-ceilinged rooms inside. Meals are prepared by hand; this is some of the best Turkish food you will have, often cooked in a great stone tandir oven. A big, filling lunch or dinner for two will cost you no more than $8-$9.

LAMIA, *Mustafapaşa, Ürgüp.. Tel. (384) 353-5413; Fax (384) 353-5044; Email: lamiahouse@turkport.net; Web: none. Rooms: 5. Credit cards not accepted. Open March-November. Double: $50.*

Lamia is located on a hillside behind Mustafapaşa, up the road signed "Sinassos." The hotel, tucked in behind a nondescript stone wall, has been built on the model of the stone houses in the area, and has rooms that are filled with personal touches—like your own room at home, but with better furniture. You'll find old Ottoman porcelain stoves and Ottoman knick-knacks. Owner Lamia Arslan oversees her domain with great attention and care.

OTEL SINASSOS, *Mustafapaşa, Ürgüp.. Tel. (384) 353-5434; Fax (384) 353-5435; Email: none; Web: none. Rooms: 60. Credit cards no accepted. Open year-round. Double: $34 (breakfast included).*

The Sinassos is, at its core, also a vintage Greek house. The hotel is clean and well-run, and is a fine choice in the mold of the Old Greek House. The hotel has a well-restored dining area in the main house.

MONASTERY PENSION, *Mustafapaşa, Ürgüp.. Tel. (384) 353-5005; Fax (384) 353-5344; Email: monasterypension@yahoo.com; Web: none. Rooms: 11. Credit cards not accepted. Open year-round. Double: $17 (breakfast included).*

The Monastery Pension has been in business since 1968, and is a solid budget/backpacking option in Mustafapaşa. Some rooms are located in old arched stone rooms, others are in a new building and are unlovely, but serviceable. The pension has its own underground stone chamber, which serves as a disco. The nearby Atasoy Pension (Tel. 384 353-5378) is another good budget option.

In Ayvalı
GAMIRASU CAVE HOTEL, *Ayvalı Köyü , Ürgüp..* Tel. (384) 354-5820; Fax *(384) 354-5815; Email: gamirasu@hotmail.com; Web: www.gamirasu.com. Rooms: 14. Credit cards accepted. Open year-round. Double: $60-$80 (half-board).*

Gamirasu is a recent addition to the constellation of Cappadocia-area hotels. The Gamirasu has clearly taken its cue from many of the best hotels in the Cappadocia area, with success. One advantage this hotel has that others do not is its location in Ayvalı village, a postcard-perfect stone village in which this hotel is the lone concession to the tourism market. The village is five kilometers west of Mustafapaşa.

If you really want to get away, this is a good place to do it. If you really want to stay in a place where holistic energy is aligned the way you like, we suppose this is the place for you, too. The owners are doctors of alternative medicine, and the hotel offers organic food, holistic work-shops, and beds without metal ("if there's metal in the bed, it cuts the energy," we were told).

The Gamirasu is located in a large compound with large public spaces, dining areas, and patios. Most rooms are not cave rooms, but a few are. The situation of the hotel, built into the wall of a cliff above small Içeri stream, is pretty. The principal disadvantage to the Gamirasu is its somewhat remote location, but the owners are happy to make arrangements for you.

Mazi Underground City

There is a seldom-visited underground city at the town of Mazı southwest of Mustafapaşa; coming from Ürgüp you'll want to veer right at the intersection marked "Ayvalı." Another 8 kilometers on you reach Ayvalı, and you'll continue another 16 kilometers to Mazı, which has a posted turnoff. Another road heads directly west to Mazı from the Ürgüp-Güzelöz road south of Cemil.

You can also reach Mazı by taking the 10 kilometer road from Kaymaklı. Note that if you want to reach Mazı by public transportation, Kaymaklı and Mustafapaşa are your best bets – but even at the height of summer dolmuş are very infrequent. We don't recommend it; hitch.

Mazı Yeraltişehir (Mazı Underground City) is delved back into a ridge and is quite extensive. The main entrance opens into several large chambers and this collection of rooms (which includes winemaking rooms and a church) is connected to rooms higher in the ridge by a series of long vertical shafts. If you're nimble and intrepid, you'll want to ascend through the lighted shafts (they rise to rooms on four levels), and this course eventually ducks back out into open air on the ridge above Mazı.

There's a lot to this underground city, including tombs in the upper section, and you'll want to find a guide (although, in all likelihood, a guide will find you; İrmaz Yenicay, a typhoon of a local woman, is likely to be the one who takes you under her her wing).

The underground city is lit electrically, but given that unaccountable power outages are not unusual, you're well-advised to bring along a flashlight or headlamp. The entry fee is $1.50, and if you're shown around by a local they're going to expect a token of appreciation, even if their help was unbidden. You'll see how useful such help is, and a few dollars is fair compensation.

Tour buses do find their way to Mazı, but, generally, it is ideal for getting away from the lines and crowds during the summer.

South of Mustafapasa

If you don't take the first turn for Mazı, back on the Ürgüp-Güzelöz road the Keslik Monastery and Churches is just south of Mustafapaşa, 100 yards off of the main road. The complex is currently being restored by a private firm contracted by the government. Some feel the restoration is regrettably ambitious. There are three different churches in the complex, the interiors of which are damaged but retain some beautiful and unusual frescoes (the restoration may encompass a cleaning of the interior art at some point). The restored sections of the monastery do produce a good sense of what such monastic communities must have been like, with dining areas and living areas in addition to the churches. Admission costs $1.25 (9am-5pm daily) and is collected by the same local guide who may show you through the complex for a small fee.

Cemil Kilise is located just a few kilometers south of Mustafapaşa. This is an Orthodox church standing above ground in the town of Cemil. The paintings within the church weren't completed until 1913-1914, but the "new" paintings covered over frescoes far older. This church is off the beaten track and often closed, but it is a finer structure than that at Mustafapaşa.

The Churches of Soganli Valley

Soğanlı is the site of a collection of outstanding rock-cut churches, including some with a somewhat different character than the churches you find in the Göreme-Ürgüp area. This area appears to have been settled by Armenian Christians at some point, judging by the simulated architecture carved into some of the stone formations found here.

These churches are located little more than 50 kilometers south of Ürgüp, and they have only recently started to receive a volume of visitors. Public transportation is possible, but it is difficult, involving dolmuş to Güzelöz from Ürgüp, then on to Soğanlı— these dolmuş are infrequent, and most locals hitch back and forth. Before you arrive at the ticket gate there is a long stone stair up the ridge to the right of the road, and it takes you to Tokalı Kilise (Buckle Church), a striking building amid a collection of cave rooms. This is just the most obvious of several such compounds secreted in the valley walls, and an hors d'oeuvre to the structures further down the road.

At the entrance to town there is a "Dur" ("Stop") sign and a ticket booth (a sign reads "Gise, Bilet") where you'll be charged $1.50. Soğanlı is located at the point where two valleys meet, and the road you arrived on forks near the center of town. Follow the fork to the right, crossing a bridge. It has to be noted that Soğanlı means, literally, "with onions," but onions are not grown here, and the meaning of the name is lost.

The best place to get a meal in town is the Soğanlı Restaurant, Tel. 352 653 1016 (inexpensive), very near the intersection in the center of town. The owner, Ziya Baba, serves a good selection of Turkish standards on the patio in front of the restaurant, and you would do well to try the local kiremit tava, a mix of onion, tomatoes, eggs and green pepper, similar to another Turkish specialty, menemen. Rakı and beer are served as well. There are a few pensions in town, as well, including the new Emek Pansiyon.

The first church compound down this road, that of Karabaş Kilise (Dark-Head Church), has a series of interconnected room dug back into the ridge. The church itself stands behind a wooden door and is oddly designed, with three smaller naves parallel to the main nave. Much of the art within is badly damaged by graffiti, but you'll find images of the birth of Jesus and the communion of the apostles in good condition. The church derives its name from the haloes of the saints depicted; they have grown dark as a result of oxidation.

The road continues a short distance, then terminates in a small parking area. Next to the parking area on the right is the Yılanlı Kilise (Snake Church), so named because of the depiction, above and to the left in the central nave, of a woman suckling snakes. This is damaged and difficult to make out, but there are other, better images of the last judgment. Elsewhere in the compound, the rooms of which open on the central courtyard, several rooms dive deeply back beneath the ridge and contain passageways that continue some distance.

Cross the parking area and follow the trail across a stream bed and through a stand of poplars. The trail then ascends back toward **Soğanlı** and arrives first at **Kubbeli Kilise** (the **Domed Church**) and then at **Saklı Kilise** (the **Hidden Church**).

The Domed Church is inappropriately named. The conical roof is precisely *not* a dome, and suggests that this buttress was crafted by Armenians for whom conical spires were standard on their churches. The interior is complex, but has suffered badly the ravages of time. You enter from uphill through a collapsed wall and find, within, a spiral staircase that has broken in several places. There are many windows (and holes) in the walls of the structure that provide outstanding views out over the valley. Frescoes within are worn and defaced, and the lower stories contain a warren of rooms with broken columns, dovecotes, and graves.

Just a little further down the valley you'll find the Hidden Church, and although it is not obvious, neither is it especially well-hidden. The church has several deep rooms, squared columns, and is on multiple levels. You can hike up and around the spur to the churches in the next valley, a beautiful walk against the backdrop of the high valley walls, but it's faster to return to your vehicle and head back down the road, recrossing the bridge and bearing right up into the next valley.

You pass back through the center of Soğanlı, and about 500 meters along you'll come to Geyikli Kilise (Deer Church) to the left of the road, unsigned as of late 1998. The name of the church derives from the scene with St. Eustis in chase of a deer, not knowing that the holy spirit has manifested itself in the deer. The Deer Church is in very poor condition, and if you're becoming glutted with churches you may want to skip ahead to **Tahtalı Kilise** (Wood Church, or Church of St. Barbara).

The Church of St. Barbara, named for a patron saint of soldiers, is to the right of the road, across a small streambed. The church has vivid images of Christ harrowing hell for souls, releasing those shackled there. The art within this church is the oldest in the immediate area, dating to the 10th century, and is perceptibly less well made than the 11th century images in The Dark-Head Church.

From Soğanlı you will head back to Güzelöz and you can go directly north through Mustafapaşa to Ürgüp, or you can head west to the underground city of Derinkuyu.

Eski Gumus

This is far to the southwest of Soganlı, but it's too fine a site not to include. The rock cut church of Eski Gumuş is located 85 kilometers south of Nevşehir, roughly 47 kilometers south of Derinkuyu in the foothills of the Taurus Mountains. As you're driving south on the Nevşehir road, take the left turn (signed "Eski Gumuşler) one kilometer before Niğde and go about seven kilometers. A visit to Eski Gumuş is probably a relatively long trip out of your way, but if you can squeeze it in it's worthwhile. This former monastery is seldom visited.

The monastery remains in excellent condition; it is adorned with startling, intact frescoes on a background of blue, probably a color created with crushed lapis lazuli. The condition of these frescoes is in many places finer than any in Cappadocia excepting only the Dark Church at the Göreme Open Air Museum.

The monastery, which dates to about 1000 A.D., is on a unique plan and is accessed through a short stone tunnel that opens into a large central courtyard. The entrance tunnel itself is interesting – the slit in the roof appears to have been intended to spy on, or dump hot oil on, visitors.

The central courtyard is surrounded on all sides by rooms and the great church. The frescoes in the church, partially restored by the British Archaelogical Institute, depict early chapters in the life of Christ, the Annunciation, Nativity, and the Magi. There is an interesting chamber in the upper section of the monastery with further painted images directly on stone of purely secular interest: they appear to be scenes from Aesop's fables. Aesop, as it happens, is thought to have been a member of the court of Croesus in Sardis some 1,600 years before this monastery was created.

Adding to the aura of mystery about the cunningly-designed monastery is the fact that other chambers are being found beneath the surface, and many speculate that Eski Gumuş may open into an underground city.

Konya

The interior of Anatolia is insulated from the Mediterranean by several long, daunting mountain ranges. Konya stands near the southern walls—the Taurus mountains—and has long helped control the southern passes to the Mediterranean.

Konya, Roman Iconium, has been a significant city for several millennia, but the reminders of Hellenistic and Roman times are few. Visitors today come to see traces of the Selcuk empire based here between the eleventh and thirteenth centuries, and the place where Sufi mysticism was born. The cool blue and green tiles of the holy places, the precise stonework of old facades, and the strong religious belief of Konya's people contribute to an atmosphere that is unique in western Turkey.

History

Konya was inhabited before 3000 B.C. by people living on Alaeddin Tepesi, the site of today's Alaeddin Camii and the former palace of the Sultanate of Rum. Konya's early history is fragmentary, but the town changed hands repeatedly, falling under Hittite dominion, then passing to the Phrygians, who were defeated by the Lydians, who were themselves defeated by the Persians in 546 B.C. The subsequent centuries were full of such monotonous activity; even Alexander thought the story was tired in 333 B.C., skipping past the city and leaving it unmolested. Rome brought respite from the repeated invasions, but the peace was similarly dull; whatever empire controlled Konya, the city's lot was the same, a trading post on the road to somewhere better.

Konya's long slumber ended with the appearance of the Turks, when the Selcuks established their capital here after defeating the Byzantines at the **Battle of Manzikert** in 1071. The Selçuks held the city in great esteem, founding here the Sultanate of Rum, as the Selcuk kingdom was known. The kingdom suffered growing pains as the Byzantines and the Crusaders, not to mention rival Muslim forces, sought to bring it down. Still, the Selcuks put their stamp on the region, and the city itself, with mosques and public buildings of intricate beauty.

The high water mark of the Sultanate was under **Sultan Alaeddin Keykobad** (1219-1237), who ringed the city with new defensive walls and buildings. During this period it could fairly be said that the Sultanate of Rum, with its great respect for learning and science, was one of the few bright spots in a world gone dark. It was not to last. In the years before Alaeddin's death, bands of Mongols began to emerge in the east, drops of rain presaging the storm to come.

The Selcuks scrambled to prepare themselves against the emergent threat; in 1243 the Sultanate entered into a truce with the Byzantine Empire, hoping to unite in the face of the Mongol threat. Byzantine assistance did the Selcuks precious little good. Later the same year the Mongols plowed through the Selcuks and their allies at the Battle of Köse Dağ, dividing up the lands in eastern Anatolia. The loss did not cost the Sultanate of Rum its capital city, which remained under Selcuk control, but the Selcuks were forced to seek an expensive peace.

The Sultanate remained on the brink of collapse for long years afterward, eventually losing the capital, then gaining it back in 1276. The last Selcuk Sultan was killed by the Mongols in 1307, and the Mongols were themselves supplanted by another ascendant Turkic power, the Karamans.

Another Turkic power was rising in the north. An obscure Turkish march lord, Ertuğrul, was posted to northeastern Anatolia by Selcuk Sultan Keykobad to help insulate the Sultanate from interference by the Byzantines. As it happened, the decay and collapse of the Selcuk Empire in the south and the rickety Byzantine Empire in the north proved the perfect climate for the birth of the Ottoman Empire. Ottoman power grew quickly, and within one century the Ottoman Turks were transcendant in Asia Minor. Sultan Beyazid I established that beyond question by seizing Konya itself after defeating the Ottoman's great Turkish rival, the Karamans, at the **Battle of Ak Tchai** in 1393. The classic storyline was ruined, however, after Tamurlane crushed Beyazid at the Battle of Ankara in 1402. Beyazid died, the prisoner of Tamurlane, in 1403.

In the chaotic aftermath of Tamurlane's two-year rampage through Asia Minor the Ottomans retreated and the Karaman Turks recovered Konya, later revenging themselves on Beyazid I by seizing Bursa and scattering his bones to the dogs. The Ottomans did not retake Konya until 1466, 13 years after the fall of Constantinople.

Arrivals & Departures

By Bus

Most major bus companies have offices in Konya. Some rates and departure times include Izmir, 0:30, 7:30, 10 a.m., 2:30, 6:30, 11 p.m.; $11. Ankara, hourly; $6. Antalya, 6:30, 9, 11 a.m., 12:30 p.m., midnight; $8. İstanbul, 7, 8:30, 10 a.m., 10:30, 11 p.m.; $14.

Your bus company should offer service to downtown Konya (say "şehir merkezi'ye gitiyorum"). Barring that, minibuses marked "Sehir Merkez" depart frequently, as do rail cars on Konya's rail line one block away. Both options cost 30¢. A taxi to the main hotel area near the Mevlana Museum costs $5.

By Car

Konya is typically seen en route between Cappadocia and either Antalya, Alanya, or Silifke on the Mediterranean.

There are two three major routes headed south from Konya. The westernmost route is the slickest and most popular (From Konya, the Isparta road past Eğirdir, then south from Isparta to Antalya). If you're headed to Alanya, take the Beyşehir Lake route, then follow the 695 south via Akseki. If you're headed to Kızkalesi, the Silifke road via Karaman is stunning and in great condition, descending past the magnificent ruin at Alahan through a stunning gorge.

Orientation

Most hotels, restaurants, and museums are clustered along the axis of Mevlana Caddesi between **Alaeddin Tepesi** in the center of town and the **Mevlana Museum** to the east. The otogar is located several miles north of the town center, and each bus company provides service to the city center, as do minibuses marked "Sehir Merkezi" and a tram line. To get into town by car, strongly consider navigating around the ring road and entering via the Konya-Ankara road from the north—other routes tend to get you lost.

The extremely helpful Tourist Information office is located on Mevlana Caddesi No. 65, near the Mevlana Museum *(Tel. (332) 351-1074; Fax (332) 350-6461)*.

An Itinerary for Konya

The one must-see spot in Konya is the **Mevlana Museum**. Begin your visit early in the day; budget an hour for your visit, unless Sufi mysticism is of particular interest. From the Mevlana, walk due west on the main road (Mevlana Caddesi) and cross the harrowing roundabout to Alaeddin Tepesi, where you'll see the few remaining traces of the former Selcuk palace beneath an open concrete dome as well as (far better) the **Alaeddin Mosque**, which dates to 1221. Recrossing the road from Alaeddin Tepesi to the north (by the ruined palace walls), you'll find the marvelous entrance to the **Karatay Medresse/Museum** (9 a.m-noon, 1:30 p.m.-5:30 p.m.; $1) kitty-corner from the Huma Hotel.

After seeing the masonry and tilework on display within, continue the counterclockwise spiral around the outside of the traffic circle to the **Ince Minare** (9 a.m.-noon, 1:30 p.m.-5:00 p.m., closed Mondays) and view the wood and stone work on display within. If you arrive during lunch, no problem—there's a McDonalds a few paces away, and Saydam Hünkar Restaurant just beyond that. After eating, continue the spiral around the roundabout past news stands (don't be fooled by Herald Tribunes published a year earlier). When you arrive at the stone Catholic church, head off to the right down Numune Sokak—three blocks along is the **Archaelogical Museum** (9 a.m.-noon, 1:30-5:30, closed Mondays; $1). After enjoying the artifacts within, you have every right to hail a cab and head back to the hotel. If you prefer, veer right after leaving the Archaeological Museum to see the distinctive **Aziziye Mosque**—with the most grand entrace gate in the city, and stunning minarets faced with sky blue tile—and the bazaar beyond.

Where to Stay

Accommodation in Konya leaves much to be desired. Because even the most expensive hotels are quite stolid, we'd advise opting for a less expensive place for the night. Note: Our hopes are pinned on the Ipek Yolu Pansiyon, which we visited in 2001, but was still under construction. There are rumors that Hilton may introduce a hotel in the area in 2002.

HOTEL BALIKÇILAR, *Mevlana Karsısı No. 1, Konya 42020. Tel. (332) 350 9470; Fax (332) 351 3259; Email: balikcilar@ihlasnet.com.tr; Web: www.balikcilar.com.tr. Rooms: 51. Credit cards accepted. Open year-round. Restaurant on premises. Double (25% off-season discount): $85 (breakfast included).*

Long the class of Konya's hotels, the Balıkçılar is clean, decent, and centrally-located, but is neither charming nor priced well for what you get. The Balıkçılar offers a lobby with cobblestone floors and eerie green lighting, rooms with small balconies and conveniences, and somewhat indifferent cleaning and service. That said, the location is excellent—just across the street from the Selimiye Mosque, 100 meters from the Mevlana Museum. Konya's a dry town, and this is one of the few hotels that offers a bar. The terrace is directly across from the Selimiye Mosque.

OTEL DUNDAR, *Feritpaşa Mah. Kerkük Cad. No. 34, Konya. Tel. (332) 236-1052; Fax (332) 235-9130. Rooms: 106. Double: $100. Credit cards accepted. Open year-round. Double (25% off-season discount): $100 (breakfast included).*

The city's lone four-star hotel, the Dundar is ambitious and hums with tour bus traffic. Everyone in town agrees it's the best place, what with bidets and CNN and all, but it has aged a lot just since its establishment in 1995. It is not a particularly rewarding way to spend $100.

YENI KÖŞK & ESRA HOTEL, *Yeni Aziziye Cad. Kadılar Sok. No. 28, Konya. Tel. 332 352 0671; Fax (332) 352-0901. Rooms: 47. Credit cards accepted. Open year-round. Double (no off-season discount): $20 (breakfast included).*

The Yeni Köşk (whose ownership purchased the adjoining Esra Hotel in 2000) is a relief after hunting through Konya's backstreets for a decent, reasonably-priced place to stay. There's nothing flashy about the Yeni Köşk, but it provides nice, clean, well-maintained rooms with phones and television. To get there from Mevlana Caddesi, turn onto Aziziye Cad. next to Sumerbank, then take a right at Kadılar Sokak. The nearby Bey Otel is a decent second option.

ŞIFA HOTEL, *Mevlana Cad. No. 11, Konya. Tel. (332) 350-4290; Fax (332) 351-9251. Rooms: 37. Credit cards accepted. Open year-round. Double (no off-season discount): $17 (breakfast included).*

The Şifa offers spartan, decent accommodation, second only to the Yeni Kösk in the lower price range. The şifa is located on the north side of Mevlana Caddesi, and is subject to some street noise. **Şifa Restaurant,** across the street, is well-considered and inexpensive.

IPEK YOLU PANSIYON, *Sedirler Sok., Konya. Tel. (332) 352-7658; Fax (332) 352-7658; Email: ipekyolu@sim.net.tr Web: www.silkroadrugs.com. Rooms: 8. Credit cards accepted. Open year-round. Double (25% off-season discount): $35 (breakfast included).*

At the time of this writing, the Ipek Yolu Pansiyon is not open; it is due to open in 2002. The Ipek Yolu (Silk Road) is located in an old Konya house near the Mevlana Museum, a building that is being restored by Mehmet Uçar, pioneer of natural dye kilims (see Shopping, below). The old wooden house has high ceilings, double-paned windows, built in cupboards, and a lovely terrace overlooking the Selimiye Mosque. If the Ipek Yolu lives up to its promise, it becomes far and away the finest accommodation in Konya.

Alternative accommodations

The aforementioned Mehmet Uçar hails from Esenler village 120 kilometers south of Konya in the foothills of the Taurus Mountains; he is happy to make arrangements for people to stay with families in the village. The villagers ask $15 per person per night, a fee that includes breakfast, lunch, and dinner. Guests are welcome to spend their days hiking nearby, reading, or pitching in with work; the village has phone service, minibus service once per day, and electricity. For further information, e-mail Mehmet at *ipekyolu@sim.net.tr.*

Where to Eat

The food landscape in Konya is dominated by the Köşk restaurant, but there are several decent places for a meal, including the Sifa Restaurant (mentioned with Şifa Hotel, above) and a McDonalds in city center.

KÖŞK LOKANTA, *Akçesme Mahallesi, Topraklık Cad. No. 66, Konya. Tel. (332) 352-7848. Moderate.*

The Köşk is an old local home, long since converted into Konya's finest restaurant. Traditional Turkish cuisine is served in the high-ceilinged rooms of the old mansion, a fine atmosphere for delicious food. Borek pastries, soups, and entrees such as Tirit and Fırın Kebap are all wonderful. Do yourself a favor and order a dish with yogurt, or simply order yogurt as a side—it's homemade and delicious. No alcohol is served, in good Koranic tradition. To get there: The Köşk is located 200 meters south of the Balıkçıiar Hotel.

SAYDAM HÜNKAR RESTAURANT, *Zafer Meydanı No. 19, Konya. Tel. (332) 353-4865. Moderate.*

A few steps from McDonalds on the west side of the roundabout in the middle of town, this is a great, inexpensive place to get a bite in the middle of the day. You're invited to select the food you would like. Kebaps—including Beyti, Urfa, and Patlican kebaps—cost less than $2.

OPERA RESTAURANT & BAR, *Meram Bağları, Konya. Tel. (332) 325-0009. Moderate-Expensive.*

If you're in Konya for a few nights, take the opportunity to visit the Meram neighborhood one evening and dine at the Opera. This quirky French/Turkish restaurant is well off the beaten track, but offers good food and a nice ambiance—as well as drinks with dinner. Open year round.

Seeing the Sights

Most people spend a day in Konya, if that. Use the itinerary provided (above) to make the best use of your time.

Konya's great site is the **Mevlana Museum** (open daily except Mondays, 9 a.m.-5:30 p.m.; $1.50). The pacific green-blue conical tower of the edifice is visible from a distance, directly above the tomb of one of Islam's great religious philosophers and mystics, **Celaleddin Rumi**, later known as Mevlana. Mevlana's works fill 22 volumes of poetry, and his lectures and letters form a daunting collection.

Tourists pay $1.50 on entering the mosque complex; Turks pay 25¢, in a clear violation of Mevlana's ecumenical teachings. You leave your shoes outside of the interior building. The tombs are located in a cluster below the ornate interior of the tiled tower. Mevlana is buried here, together with his father, wife, children, and some family friends. The interior of the museum is filled with cunningly wrought Korans, rugs, wood stools and Koran stands, and musical instruments. Some of the latter are **neys**, the reedy flutes whose whine is so appropriate and haunting within the complex or during a dervish ceremony. There is usually ney music in the background during your visit. Away from the confines of the Mevlana Museum you're unlikely to seek out ney music; it seems to be an acquired taste.

Dervishes still whirl at tourist dinner places throughout the country, but they truly whirl in December in Konya. During the week leading up to the anniversary of Mevlana's December 17th death, dervishes whirl for real at a gymnasium in Konya; the former grounds are no longer large enough to accommodate their many visitors. The dance is riveting, with dervishes whirling in their snow white dresses, while a dervish master walks among them, ensuring that they are performing properly.

Before the dance, the dervishes drop their black coverings and emerge in white to whirl their way closer to God, symbolizing the abandonment of their earthly cares. Mevlana's teaching inspires deep curiosity among most people unfamiliar with it, but the good-hearted

The Father of the Dervishes

Celaleddin Rumi was born on September 30th, 1207, the son of a renowned religious philosopher. The family migrated west from Afghanistan in the face of Mongol expansion, settling in Konya at the behest of Alaeddin II in 1228. Upon his father's death, Rumi assumed the role of religious teacher (Mevlana), and was soon held in the same esteem enjoyed by his father. He lived to the age of 66, his teaching corresponding to some of the most trying times in the Sultanate's short reign; the Sultanate's armies were beaten by the Mongols in 1243, the city occupied several years later.

Mevlana's Sufi message of dedication to Islam was tempered with a powerful message of toleration and loving one another. His teachings combined bits and pieces of familiar philosophy, but had one manifestation that was dramatically new: to this day Mevlana's most famous teaching is that an epiphany of love is possible by whirling, the left hand face down, the right hand face up. The position of the hands indicates the receiving of blessings from Heaven and the passing of those blessings along to mankind. Other teachings were more strictly ascetic, befitting a Sufi, such as 40 day periods of bread and water. In general, however, Mevlana's teaching was neither stark nor unyielding:

Come, come again, whoever, whatever you may be, come
Heathen, fire worshiper, sinner in idolatry, come
Come, even if you have broken penitence 100 times,
Ours is not the portal of despair and misery, come.

kernel of his philosophy is probably there in front of us the entire time, in the giddy whirling of the dervishes.

The **Selimiye Mosque** is near the museum, in the direction of Alaeddin Tepesi and near the tourism information office. The Selimiye is one of several mosques in Turkey celebrating Sultan Selim II, who was a governor here before ascending the throne. The mosque was not completed until 1587, a 29-year project from beginning to end. The mosque is imposing and pretty within, suiting this religious city, but suffers a little in comparison to Selim II's other mosque, Edirne's Selimiye. The latter building is usually cited as the greatest Ottoman architectural achievement and Sinan's piece de resistance. Selim II was an uninspired sultan, but inherited an empire at the height of its wealth and glory from his father, Süleyman the Magnificent. Mosques were built for him because there was money for such projects, not because he was particularly deserving.

Alaeddin Tepesi, or "the hill of Alaeddin," is 400 meters further east along Mevlana Caddesi, peculiarly situated in the middle of a large traffic roundabout. The most distinctive feature here is the concrete canopy, intended as protection for the precious bits of wall remaining from the former Selcuk palace.

Above and behind the old palace walls are a collection of çay bahçesilar, or **tea gardens,** ascending toward a structure atop the hill. This building is the **Alaeddin Mosque,** which houses a complex of tombs and former meeting areas and libraries. The interior is decorated in blue and white tile, and recent renovations have mixed new wooden roof panelling with a collection of Iconium's old Hellenistic and Roman columns.

Most of the redecoration has the feel of a YMCA, but there's no disguising the beautiful bones of this structure. The Selcuk's contribution included the gloriously precise **mimber,** or slender prayer platform. The tombs of the earliest sultans are in the courtyard and at the bottom of a stair; scattered around the courtyard are Meşud I, Kılıçarslan, Rukneddin Süleyman II, Giyaseddin Keyhusrev I and Alaeddin Keykobad I, Keyhusrev II, Izzeddin, Kılıcarslan IV and Keyhusrev III, the sixth to sixteenth rulers of the Sultanate of Rum (1116-1283).

Crossing the road near the palace ruins, you'll find the **Karatay Çini Eserler Müzesi** (Karatay Tile Museum), kitty-corner from Huma Hotel. Here, much of the best work is in the medresse (school) structure itself, from grand stone entrance to the stunning tiled dome depicting the heavens. This is an impressive exhibit, with hundreds of oddly shaped tiles and Escher-like patterns.

Another example of fine Selcuk craftsmanship is just a few paces southwest (still hugging the perimeter of the traffic circle)—the **Ince Minare and Medresse** (Thin Minaret and School). Restoration work on the portal was under way in 2001, but the distinctively Selcuk tilework of the minaret remains in fine condition. The interior houses a collection of Selcuk carving and art—well worth, to our minds, the $1 admission.

Konya's **Archaeological Museum,** south of the roundabout at the small stone Catholic church, is deserving of a visit. Empires and kingdoms have littered this region with artifacts and statues for thousands of years, and Konya enjoys the spoils—including artifacts from Çatal Hüyük. The finest pieces in this interesting museum are the sarcophagi, one of which depicts Hercules performing his 12 tasks.

Shopping

Among those harmed by Konya's relegation to "lunch break" status on the standard trip itinerary are the local **kilim shops.** Shed no tears for them, they still sell plenty of kilims, but trade is down. This is good news for kilim buyers, as Konya has rich a kilim-making tradition.

We are wary of recommending kilim and carpet dealers, but if you are in the market for high quality pieces, consider **Ipek Yolu** (Silk Road), Mevlana Caddesi, Bostan Sok. No. 14A, Konya, *Tel. (332) 352-7658*. The owner, Mehmet Uçar, exports to the United States and has a solid reputation in the business. He has helped pioneer the rediscovery of traditional natural dyes (see "The Dye is Recast" sidebar, below), in order to create vivid, rich, permanent colors. We're probably the only people who say we aren't getting a commission who really aren't.

The Dye is Recast

Most natural dye recipes were lost during the twentieth century as artificial dyes came into vogue. Small wonder—artificial dyes were less expensive, easier to use, and readily available.

Alas, artificial dyes have also proved to be far, far less permanent than natural dyes, and natural dye rugs are now at a premium.

Enter Mehmet Uçar, one of several men acknowledged for having pieced together many of the lost dye recipes. This is a trickier proposition than it sounds. Consider that to create a specific color, the dye maker must know the plants to use, where and when to harvest each plant (including the nature of the soil), the heat and time for cooking and steeping the plant, and the recipe for mixing, if necessary.

Mehmet has sat down with old-timers in villages throughout the Taurus Mountains, picking their brains for clues about this rich red, or that deep green. In the end, he has had great success, but only after much trial and error—including an error that could have killed him. While boiling and stirring a mix with mullein, in search of a warm, mustard yellow, the fumes knocked Mehmet out—had he not had a helper on hand to drag him clear, the fumes might have killed him.

Excursions & Day Trips

Çatal Hüyük, which archaeologists reckon to be among the oldest civilized human settlement yet discovered (it dates to 7500 B.C.), is located about 55 kilometers from Konya. To get here, turn off of the Konya-Karaman road near İcericumra for Cumra. At Cumra, located at a rail intersection 14 kilometers from the main road, you take the signed road another 20 kilometers to Çatal Hüyük. Public transportation will not get you here; you'll have to drive, find someone in Konya headed that way, or bus and hitchhike. We don't recommend hitchhiking, and, at any rate, there's not much traffic out here.

The site is not much more than a series of partially excavated mounds (work by a team from Oxford University is ongoing).

Gökyurt is a rarely-visited, little known extension of the Cappadocian cave complexes, with several elaborate churches carved from the stone. Gökyurt is near Alahan in the mountains beyond Karaman on the Silifke road.

Eğirdir

Eğirdir is a mountain town built on the shore of Eğirdir Gölu. This great lake is squeezed between the Karakuş and Kuyucak mountain ranges, and Eğirdir is itself built up on a long, slender spur of Davras Dağı that descends gradually into vivid blue water. The character of the town is mixed, part lakeside resort, part working mountain town, and part army town (there's a training base for Turkish commandos on the İsparta road winding up out of town). Eğirdir is surrounded by national park land; the hillsides are thick with apple orchards, the lake is good for rowing or swimming, and the mountains are ideal for trekking, with stretches of the ancient Royal Road still visible.

Eğirdir is not why people come to Turkey in the first place, we realize that. There is, though, something clean and good about this town that makes it a perfect interlude en route between the coast and the interior.

History

This spot has been inhabited since at least Hittite times, and it was a waypoint on the great Persian Royal Road from Sardis to Babylon. As such, it was the site of ancient kervansarays, and still has vestiges of its ancient structures recycled into the local mosque (Ulu Camii) and the mosque complex (which today includes a school converted into an upscale market).

The Selcuks left some evidence of their passing in slender minarets, but Eğirdir has probably been too well-populated for too long not to have broken down and recycled most of its historic landmarks. Other than the minarets, it is the aging fortress at the neck of the isthmus that suggests the age of this place. The fortress, a Byzantine structure rebuilt by the Selcuks, has been reduced over time to an incomplete set of walls.

The mountain ruin of Sagalassos, some 30 kilometers away, was a significant city in Hellenistic times – significant enough for Alexander the Great to besiege and capture it. If you're without your own tranportation, trips to Sagalassos can be arranged through your hotel.

Arrivals & Departures

Bus: This is a frequent stop for public buses (and tour buses) making their way the looping route from Antalya to Cappadocia or vice versa. You'll see the buses stop in at the base of the isthmus and people taking lunch, enjoying the look of the water and mountains after the flats of Konya. You can get several buses daily from here for Ankara ($9, 7 hours), Antalya ($5, 3 hours), İstanbul ($14, 11 hours), İzmir ($9, 6 hours), Konya ($7, 4 hours), and Nevşehir ($12, 6 hours).

Car: If you're en route from Konya or beyond to Antalya (or vice-versa) then Eğirdir is right on your way. The roads east and west are both in good condition – in fact that's why this route is generally favored over the more direct route Konya-Manavgat-Antalya.

Train: Yes, the train pulls into the station a few kilometers outside of Eğirdir. This is the southeast end of a rail spur that heads off to the Aegean coast at İzmir.

Orientation

Eğirdir is at the south end of Eğirdir Lake, and its best feature (other than the sheer outstandingness of its setting) is a long causeway that joins the town to a collection of pensions and houses well out in the lake. You'll find two small clusters of hotels and pensions, one at the tip of the causeway in the lake, the other on the "mainland" not far from the otogar.

Where to Stay & Eat

You have your choice; you may stay at a hotel on the mainland, near the good beaches but in a setting of middling romance, or you can head out to the tip of the peninsula. Dolmuş bound for the tip of the peninsula leave from a spot across the street from the bus station. There are restaurants on Yeşilada (the "Green Island" at the other end of the causeway), but most pensions serve good, big meals. Yes, fish is often on the menu.

ADAC PANSIYON, *Yeşilada Mahalle No. 4, Yeşilada, Eğirdir, Tel. 246 312 3074. Rooms: 9. Double: $24.*

Adac is just about the first thing on your right when you cross the causeway and arrive at the island at its head. This is a clean, simple place with great views. As with all hotels, seek a room with a view.

HALLEY PANSIYON, *Yeşilada Mahalle No. 6, Yeşilada, Eğirdir, Tel. 246 312 3625. Rooms: 9. Double: $17.*

The Halley pension, like many pensions in Eğirdir, is long on backpacker charm, meaning it's clean, friendly, bustling with travelers, full of information, and wont to be a little noisy. If all of that sounds all right to you, then head out to the end of the peninsula and stay. The

Halley serves meals, offers a rowboat for guests, and is a fount of information about hikes in the area; if you're interested in a trek, it's worth stopping in for some advice. Guests should ask for a room upstairs room with a lake view. The Halley Pansiyon is located on the main road of the island on the right just after you come "ashore."

If the Halley is full, check in at whichever pension looks best; there are many fine choices, including the neaby **Göl Pansiyon** and the **Paris Pansiyon** on the opposite side of the island.

KÖSK PANSİYON, *Yazla Mahalle No. 37, Yeşilada, Eğirdir, Tel. 246 31 6350. Rooms: 8. Double: $17.*

The Kösk Pansiyon is located around the shore of the lake from the center of town, has quick access to the swimming holes. The Kösk is always tidy and the owner has all sorts of information about the area you may find of use. Call upon arrival and he'll shuttle you over to the hotel.

EĞIRDIR HOTEL, *Kuzey Sahil Yolu No. 2, Tel. 246 311 4992, Fax 246 311 4219. Rooms: 51. Double: $34.*

This is the solid hotel choice in Eğirdir, with rooms, showers en suite, and TVs. That said, if you're going to stay in Eğirdir we'd almost hope you stayed at one of the small pensions out on the peninsula. The Eğirdir Hotel is located across the isthmus from the otogar, on the northern (İsparta) side near the PTT.

MELODI RESTAURANT, *Yeşilada Mahalle. Tel. 246 311 2443. Moderate.*

You're sure to be pleased with the food at your own pension, but if you're in the mood for dinner out, try the Melodi on the southeast tip of Yeşilada. This is an unassuming little spot, but it serves up a great collection of bass, crawfish, and even shrimp. Prices are very low by normal seafood standards, about $3 for an entrée. Note that you can rent a rowboat at the tiny bay near the Melodi.

Sports & Recreation

One of the best things to do in Eğirdir is to rent a rowboat (or borrow one from your hotel) and paddle around the southern shore of the lake. You can go swimming at Yeşilada, but there's no suitable beach there. Most people prefer the sand beach at Altınkum Plaj, a little more than 2 kilometers away from the center of Egirdir on the İsparta road. There's a small fee for use of the beach, roughly $.50 per person, and dolmuş serve this spot from town.

Hiking is the other great attraction here, so if you have time to spend consider a trip south toward Kovada Gölü; you'll find stretches of the ancient King's Road (see Sardis) between Sardis and Babylon. Herodotus marveled at this highway, and it remains to this day.

Finally, if Cappadocia hasn't whet your appetite for being below the earth, consider a side trip to Zindan Cave near the town of Aksu, some 30 kilometers southeast of Eğirdir. The cave is located next to the headwaters of the Eurymedon River, the river that reaches the sea at Aspendos. A temple to the river god Eurymedon stood here, and its ruins remain. The statue of Eurymedon has been transported to the museum at İsparta. The cave, part of the temple precinct, requires use of a flashlight.

Chapter 15

the black sea coast

The **Black Sea coast**, from Akçakoca to Trabzon, is Turkey's most peaceful frontier. The ancient allure of Troy and Ephesus, the mystique of İstanbul and the temptation of the Mediterranean beaches attract most of Turkey's visitors. This is understandable, but at least consider a spin out along the Black Sea. Languishing, or thriving, along this moody sea are sites that are older, more significant, and less understood than their counterparts in well-traveled Turkey. Even the climate seems to conspire to keep tourism interest low; the rain arrives in late August and continues at a tropical rhythm until October, when the temperatures begin to drop. May and June are warm again but wet, leaving July and the bulk of August as the ideal time unless you can deal with afternoon rains.

The moist climate has also encouraged dense greenery, which has in turn done its level best to hide or obscure the ruins scattered across the landscape. Still, for a few months of the year, this is one of the most rewarding places to travel in Turkey today. You don't need to forgo beaches nestled beneath Hellenistic city walls; they're here, too. You don't need to hole up in fleabag pensions; we've found plenty of good hotels, and some that are wonderful. You don't need a car; bus transport along the Black Sea coast is easy and cheap, on good, well-maintained roads. You don't even need to be wary and weathered; Turkish honesty and decency is at an extreme in these little traveled areas. Every time we think we're ripped off on the Black Sea, we're adding incorrectly.

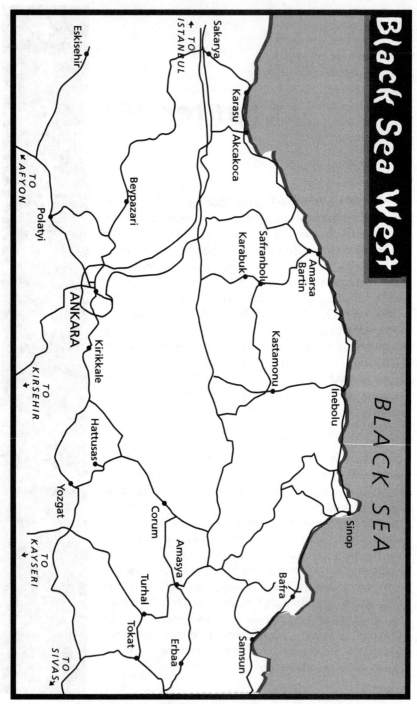

Black Sea Seasonal Fish

Season	Fish
Dec./Jan.	Hamsi
Feb./Mar.	Istavrit, Hamsi, Kalkan (small)
April/May	Barbuniye, Mezgit, Kalkan (small)
June/July	Midye (mussels), Kefal, Mezgit, Istavrit, Iskarpit, Barbuniye
Aug./Sept.	Zargan, Palamut, Lufer, Istavrit, Hamsi, Iskarpit, Barbuniye, Mezgit
Oct./Nov.	Palamut, Lufer, Hamsi, Mezgit

Note: Shrimp (karides) are not native to the Black Sea. **Alabalik**, freshwater trout, is always available.

What you do need along the Black Sea route is a willingness to climb and hike and, at the end of the day, not quite understand what you've seen. Somewhere beneath the vegetation and thousands of years of history are traces of the Amazons, Jason and the Argonauts, the Kingdoms of Pontus and Phyrgia and Rome, the Armenians, Hittites, and Urartians, the monasteries of Sümela and Georgia, the outposts of the Trapezuntine Empire, and, finally, the Ottomans. Archaeologists have been hard at work along this coast for a century, but it's slow going; the known sites are a tangle of mystery and rumor, and no one knows what else lay unknown in the thick undergrowth.

The first stretch, from **Akçakoca** to **Amasra**, is off the main highways and particularly peaceful. The coast between **Amasra** and **Sinop** is dotted with perfect little beaches and quiet fishing villages, but lodging is rare - often in the form of a guest room. Just east of Sinop the main highway emerges at **Samsun** and carries most İstanbul and Ankara traffic on toward **Trabzon**, then on to the Georgian Republic.

Akçakoca

Most visitors bypass **Akçakoca** en route to Amasra and sites further east. It is a popular holiday spot for Turks, with several decent hotels and good beaches.

History

Akçakoca has always played a minor role in Black Sea affairs. As the port town for Prusias ad Hypium, 15 miles inland at modern **Konuralp**, it often did bustling trade, and its rich plantations of hazelnuts were a major source of income, then as now. The town, called Diapolis, carried on under Bithnia, Pontus, Rome, and Byzantium, but its only remaining fortification is a small Genoese keep to the west of town. This fortification was built in the 1200s and handed over to the Ottomans one century later. Two of Sultan Orhan's generals, Akçakoca and Konuralp, seized this territory around 1355, leaving their names to the conquered towns. They are celebrated in a statue at the town center, by the new mosque (although Orhan is mislabeled Osman).

Akçakoca continues churning out hazelnuts, and there is a festival to celebrate the pending harvest on the third weekend in July.

Arrivals & Departures
By Bus
Several bus companies offer service to Akçakoca, leaving you at the intersection west of town. From there it is a simple matter (during daylight hours) to get a dolmuş into town. The route into town passes the Hotel Akçakoca and follows close to the beach, leaving you in the city center. The tourist information office is one block away on Cumhuriet Meydanı. You can continue on to the Diapolis by foot, or take another bus on the Kale route that passes Tezel Kamping, the city's best pension/campground.

Ulusoy has daily service to the area from Ankara and İstanbul, but Üstün Erçelik offers the most frequent buses.

By Car
From the south and west the quickest way to Akçakoca is following the main E-80 highway to Düzçe, then following the 655 through Konuralp to the coast and following the signs left into Akçakoca. A brand new highway along the Black Sea coast from Karasu in the west was still under construction at the end of 1996. To the east, the highway hugs the coast as far as Ereğli, then ascends into the mountains, emerging just west of Zonguldak.

Orientation
Akçakoca is only a pilgrimage for Nutella lovers. This quiet town has had only glancing attention from the tourist masses making a beeline to the southern beaches, and is the better for it. The beaches in the area are excellent - along a 20 mile stretch, half of the coastline is beach, most of it deserted. To the west the coastline is both prettier and less accessible, and there is an excellent sand beach about five kilometers west of town.

The **tourism information** office is near the dolmuş stop at the center of town, on Cumhuriet Meydanı, *Tel. 374 611 4554, Fax 374 611 4448.*

Where to Stay & Eat

As at most mid-sized towns on the Black Sea, the Tourism Information office is a clearing house for people willing to rent out their homes or rooms in their homes.

HOTEL AKÇAKOCA, *Ereğli Cad. No. 23, Akçakoca, Tel. (374) 611-4525; Fax (374) 611-4440. Rooms: 76. Credit cards not accepted. Open April-October. Double: $60.*

The Hotel Akçakoca was the first four star facility on the Black Sea coast. This is a nice, unpretentious holiday spot on a long expanse of gritty sand beach. Tennis court, pool, cafes, a restaurant, and several bars.

DİAPOLİS HOTEL, *İnönü Cad., Akçakoca, el. (374) 611-3741; Fax (374) 611-3790; Email: none; Web: none. Rooms: 120. Credit cards not accepted. Open April-October. Double: $50.*

Diapolis is one of the most appealing hotels in Akçakoca, overlooking Akçakoca's small port. Its restaurant is an excellent place to watch the sun set while boats chug home after a day fishing.

TEZEL CAMPING, *Hürriyettepe Mevki, Akçakoca, Tel. (374) 611-4115; Fax (374) 611-4115. Rooms: 12. Credit cards not accepted. Open year-round. Double: $9.*

Charming little campground/pension on terraces above a cliff, with a stairway leading down to the surf. The rooms are no-frills, but the staff is friendly and there is, lest we forget, a perfectly situated clifftop bar. On the western side of town.

Outside of Akçakoca

MESEN HOTEL, *Edilli Köyü, Çanak Çanak Mevkii, Akçakoca, Tel. (374) 611-4436; Fax (374) 611-2574. Rooms: 20. Credit cards not accepted. Open April-November. Double: $45.*

Isolated outside of Akçakoca, this small hotel is away from whatever hustle and bustle Akçakoca has, ideally located for relaxation. The hotel has a small pool, sauna and in-house restaurant. To truly get away, try one of the bungalows.

Seeing the Sights

The fortress to the west of Akçakoca is badly ruined, hardly even yielding good photographs. Ruins enthusiasts will be likewise disappointed by the ruins of Prusias ad Herculeum at Ereğli, which were picked over for building material by Sultan Mehmet II's work crews while Rumeli Hisar was under construction. The area's finest ruins are at **Prusias ad Hypium** in Konuralp, 20 miles inland from Akçakoca. A small museum at the site has sarcophagi and other things of interest. Prusias ad Hypium was one of three cities founded by Prusias, the King of Bithnia.

The other cities were Prusias ad Herculeum (now Ereğli) and Prusias ad Olympium (now Bursa).

Cave enthusiasts will be pleased with the meandering **Caverns at Fakıllı**, just 8 miles from Akçakoca (follow the signs from the bridge intersection on the east side of town near the Hotel Akçakoca. Continue following signs, finally taking a left at the Fakıllı mosque. Park in front of the Kayalar Aile Çay Bahçesi). Bring a light and some grubby clothes; the caves wind through some tight, muddy spots. Local boys will be happy to guide you – there's even a small underground lake if you descend far enough. This is, experts say, not the cave the ancients called The Cave of Hades, the route by which Hercules entered and escaped the underworld. That cave is in Ereğli, not far to the east.

The Fakıllı cave is, nonetheless, a remarkable spot, with a little of its own history: Turks are supposed to have holed up within the cave when the region was Greek-occupied after WW I. It is a one and one-half hour walk from the entrance of the cave to its (blocked) end, with many more hours required to explore its nooks and crannies. Electric lights are strung deep into the interior, but a flashlight is necessary insurance. If no one is around to show you, the electricity box is just inside the entrance.

The next stop on the Great Caves of the Western Black Sea excursion are the aforementioned **Caves of Hades** (Cehennum Mağarası), one half hour east by dolmuş or car. The caves are located in the northwest of Ereğli, about 400 feet inland of the Black Sea on the ancient river Acheron - the river of the dead. The river of the dead is more realistically suspect today, its waters carrying effluent from the industrial plants lining the river out to the sea. The ruins of **Herecleias ad Pontus** are scattered around the northeast section of Ereğli.

The ancient town was at one time quite extensive, but in its current condition it doesn't merit a visit. Fatih Sultan Mehmet II, the conqueror of Constantinople, raided the site for material while building Rumeli Hisar on the Bosphorous. Ereğli is renowned for iron production, a smoke-spewing industrial town not well suited to most conceptions of a beach holiday. Iron lovers will want to stop by the Erdemir factory.

Waterfall Hikes

Back in the Akçakoca area, consider a hike to one of the two waterfalls just inland, **Aktaş Selalesi** and **Sariyayla Selalesi**. If you lack your own transport, contact the Tourism Information office in the center of town. They arrange occasional tours, and the tourism information director is exceptionally helpful.

Safranbolu

Safranbolu is a favorite getaway within Turkey, and for good reason. This small mountain town is located 83 kilometers inland of Bartin on the Black Sea highway, and features several beautiful hotels and pensions. In 1994 Safranbolu was placed on UNESCO's World Cultural Heritage list in hohor of its wealth of well-preserved 18th and 19th century Ottoman houses. These Ottoman-era buildings, in one of which you'll probably stay, are part of Safranbolu's appeal; the rest is its relaxed pace.

Arrivals & Departures
By Bus

Most buses serve Karabük, an industrial town 10 kilometers west of Safranbolu. From Karabük, dolmuş serve Safranbolu every 15 minutes until 7 p.m. ($.50). The Ulusoy bus company, one of Turkey's two best, serves the town.

By Car

The road from Ankara is in great shape, being frequented by many Turkish parliamentarians. Follow the freeway to Gerede, turning right on the E80 highway, then left at the Karabük/Safranbolu intersection. From the north, a small, scenic two-lane road climbs from Bartın along the Gökirmak river, reaching a 4,500 foot summit at Ahmet Usta Gecidi.

By Train

The daily Ankara-Zonguldak train stops in Karabük; the trip to Ankara is 3.5 hours, $7. From the Karabük train station, grab a taxi to Safranbolu ($9) or make your way to the bus station and get a dolmuş there.

Orientation

The Tourism Information office, *Tel. 370 712-3863*, is located two blocks from the otogar; the road is signed.

Where to Stay

Safranbolu is packed with tourists on weekends in the summer months; prices are 20% or so higher on Saturday and Sunday evenings. The hotels we recommend, below, offer dining; to eat out, consider the Kadioğlu Şehzade Sofrası. There are several restaurants in the old section of Safranbolu, where these hotels are located

HAVUZLU KONAK, *Mescit Sok., Safranbolu. Tel. (370) 725-2883; Fax (370) 712-3824; Email: none; Web: none. Rooms: 11. Credit cards accepted. Open year-round. Double: $50 (breakfast included).*

This is the hotel that started the trend in Safranbolu. This mansion was lovingly restored by the Turkish Touring and Automobile Association—the same organization that ignited the creation of good hotels in Istanbul's old city with Yeşil Ev. As at Yeşil Ev, the Havuzlu Konak is decorated in period furniture; brass bed frames, ornate mirrors, pleasant sitting rooms, and Turkish textiles. "Havuzlu" means "with pool", a reference to the pool on the grounds. The restaurant on the premises is the best in town.

Selected one of our favorite small hotels.

TAHSIN BEY & PAŞA KONAĞI, *Hükümet Sok. No. 50, Safranbolu. Tel. (370) 712-6062; Fax (370) 712-5596; Email: none; Web: none. Rooms: 26. Credit cards accepted. Open year-round. Double: $42 (breakfast included).*

This is not a single restored mansion, but a set of three. All three buildings date to the 19th century and have been refitted to serve as hotels. When you enter off the cobbled lane outside you'll find rich, welcoming public spaces thick with textiles and lace. Continuing up broad wooden staircases rooted in stone, you climb to a room with high ceilings, thick walls, and windows that take in the village below. As is the case in most restored mansions, bathrooms have been squeezed into closets and other imaginative spaces; expect this. If you prefer, book a stay at a private home via the Ev Pansiyonculuğu Geliştirme Merkezi—that is, House Pension Development Center: *Tel. (370) 712-7236;* Double: $29-$38).

Seeing the Sights

Most people come to Safranbolu for the relaxed pace, the mountain air, and the beautiful restored Ottoman buildings that serve as hotels. In addition, most people leave with some local crafts, including lace, preserves, and olive oil—and there are, of course, shops offering kilims and carpets. The central shopping area is located at the foot of the 17th century Köprülü Mehmet Paşa Camii, named to honor one of the powerful Grand Viziers who hailed from the Köprülü family.

Wandering the cobbled lanes of Safranbolu, you see a wealth of stone walls and, behind them, the shuttered windows of beautiful old buildings, each with second floor rooms that jut out over the road.

Among the other principal buildings is the Izzet Mehmet Paşa Camii, an 18th century mosque named for another resident of Safranbolu who had been a Grand Vizier. This mosque, larger, more prominent, and more heavily decorated than its fellow by the bazaar. The Kaymakamlar Evi (Governor's House) is located above the Paşa Hotel west of the town center, and is open from 9 a.m. to dusk. This house, and it's voluminous courtyard, offers fascinating insight into the life of an Ottoman regional governor.

Amasra

Amasra is one of the highlights of the Black Sea. You arrive after winding through lush hills, finally descending to a long spit of land - really a tiny archipelago linked to the mainland by a narrow isthmus and a small bridge. Amasra's natural advantages have made it an important trading center for thousands of years, and although its primacy has been brought to an end by the more easily accessible ports at Zonguldak, Ereğli, and elsewhere, Amasra still supports a thriving fishery.

Amasra's industrial loss is the traveler's gain. Amasra today is an infrequently-visited combination of historic ruins, natural beauty, a sand beach, a small, interesting museum and vigorously healthy, friendly people. Even the bread is wonderful.

History

The early history of the area is unknown, but the city was settled by Greek colonists, calling it Sesamos, which in time became Amastris and, eventually, Amasra. Homer refers to Sesamos, but the best thing he can think to say about it is that it is where "wild mules are engendered." The leader of the Paphlagonians is described as "the equal of Ares," but, three lines later, is stabbed through the chest and killed by Menelaus. Amastris supplanted Sesamos in the fourth century B.C. and soon fell under the sway of the Kingdom of Pontus, based in Amasya and Sinop. Amastris paid for its allegiance when the Roman General Lucullus, pursuing the routed Pontic King Mithradites VI, stopped here and sacked the town.

Amastris recovered, but its later history was undistinguished. The city was always a haven for ships and a commercial center, and the Romans held it in a little esteem. Rivals for the throne of the Byzantine Empire struggled over the town, but its strategic location atop an isthmus, with a secondary position higher up on Boztepe, made it difficult to take by force. Sultan Mehmet II used a remarkably indirect strategy. As a prelude to taking Amasra he secured the Bosphorous, the Dardanelles, besieged and took Constantinople, seized the towns near Amasra, and seized Trabzon. Only then, with a reported 50 healthy soldiers defending the city walls and a ragtag collection of pirates at sea, did the sultan sail and march his army to Amasra (1461). After a long bleak look at the alternatives, Amasra opened its gates without a fight.

Arrivals & Departures

By Bus

Most people come to Amasra via Bartin (dolmuş between Amasra and Bartin are half-hourly and hourly, 75¢). The roads are good and frequently traveled, with several bus companies serving Bartin from İstanbul, Ankara, and other major towns. The alternative route to Amasra is from the east, via the remote and dramatically undulating road from Cide. Getting to Cide is itself a chore, but from there dolmuş frequently come and go to Bartin via Amasra.

Özemniyet bus line serves Amasra direct from İstanbul, a six hour trip. İstanbul departures are at 9:00, 12:00, 15:00, 19:00, 21:00, and 23:30.

Orientation

Amasra is ideal for relaxed exploration. Even on August weekends the town is relatively uncrowded. Our favorite accommodations in Amasra are small house pensions; we recommend some below. For more, check in at the tourism information office on the east side of the isthmus, just south of the mosque.

Where to Stay

Amasra's hotel selection is cheap and generally uninspired. Space is sold by the bed, so if you'd like solitude make this clear *("Bir oda istiyorum")*. You'll pay for all of the beds in the room. Expect some bugs and squat toilets, and pick up a mosquito coil or device.

The helpful folks at the tourism information office *("Turism Danişma Şubesi")* are located near the end of the neck of the isthmus, just south of the mosque. The office is on the corner. They can direct you to these hotels and other family-run establishments.

OTEL BELVÜ PALAS, *Küçük Liman Cad. No. 20, Amasra, Bartin, Tel. (378) 315-1237. Rooms: 11. Double: $14.*

The Belvü Palas has offered spacious budget accommodation for almost 30 years. Rooms are stolid, but the terrace and balconies overlooking Amasra's western (quiet) bay are quite nice, and the location is central.

AMASRA OTELI, *Büyük Liman iskele Cad. No. 59, Amasra, Bartin, Tel. (378) 315-1722; Fax (378) 315-3025. Rooms: 8. Credit cards not accepted. Open April-October. Double: $16.*

The Amasra Hotel is modest, but it's one of Amasra's best. The location is convenient, clean and offers appealing views in two of the eight rooms. The rooftop bar next door troubles some, however. The hotel is located by the base of the walls at the eastern end of the isthmus. Otel Timur, nearby, has a similar standard (Gen. Mithat Ceylan Cad. No. 57, Amasra, Bartin; *Tel. 378 315-2589; Fax 378 315-3290; Double: $18)*

BÜLBÜL PANSİYON, *Boztepe Mah., Uçpalamar Sk. No. 38, 74300 Amasra, Bartin. Tel. (378) 315-1288. Rooms: 3. Credit cards not accepted. Open year-round. Double: $12.*

This is a family pension, owned by the Bülbül family at the end of Uçpalamar Sokak. The guest rooms are in an extension of the house, and you're treated like an extension of the owner's family. Charming and quiet, with views of the western bay, a kitchen, and the family's own boat. Follow Küçük Liman Caddesi through the isthmus around to the left, passing through a gate, cross the old stone bridge to Boztepe, enter another gate, and turn left on Uçpalamar Sokak.

MUKADDER CEBECİOĞLU *(owner, not hotel name), Tel. (378) 315-3244. Rooms: 7. Credit cards not accepted. Open year-round. Double: $15.*

Small, spartan apartments overlooking the eastern beach, atop the walls of the citadel. A small stove and kitchen area, but otherwise no frills whatsoever. A great place to hole up for a while and sit out on the balcony. Bring mosquito coils. Mrs. Cebecioğlu doesn't speak much English, so if you call to make reservations, consider doing so with the assistance of someone at a hotel in Istanbul or elsewhere.

Where to Eat

Amasra has many good, small restaurants, and it is hard to find seafood cheaper in any town you'd enjoy being in. Don't miss the greasy, ketchupy fried mussel *(midye)* sandwiches sold out of carts in the summer.

CANLIBALIK RESTAURANT, *Kücük Liman Cad. No. 8, Amasra, Bartin, Tel. 378 315 2606. Moderate.*

An Amasra institution since 1945. One of the town's two status restaurants, but it still offers good, cheap food. Mezes are $1.30, fish range from $1 for barbuniye (mullet) to $6 for istavrit (mackarel). Beer is 70¢, rakı 80¢.

LİMAN LOKANTASI, *Büyük Liman Cad., Amasra, Bartin, Tel. 378 315 2148. Moderate-Expensive.*

The Liman may be a bit less charming than the Canlı Balık, but no one can argue with the freshness of its fish. The purse seiners pull up right in front of the restaurant and the Liman is among the first to see what they've brought back. The Liman is at the end of Büyük Liman Caddesi beneath the city walls. Prices are akin to Canlı Balık.

Seeing the Sights

At the lower, southwestern end of the island (the left, as you look away from the mainland) an ancient road winds through several gates from the isthmus toward the island of Boztepe. As you look below you'll notice the peculiar Byzantine tower jutting into the sea. This tower, called

Direkli, is thought to be an old watch tower or lighthouse. On the same spur of land is the foundation of a much older Hellenistic building, perhaps a temple to Poseidon, the sea god popular among the Amastrians.

The island attached to the northwestern shore of Kaleiçi is called **Boztepe**. It is reached via a small bridge. The small strait below the bridge was cleared in 1995, recreating the natural moat that existed in Hellenistic times. The double-gated archway is just about large enough to squeeze a car through, and the local residents do (as evidenced by the gouges scraped through the stone). Once through the gate, follow the small roads up the right side of the island, ascending sharply along the old walls until they terminate at the point of redundancy - the cliffs below served well enough.

From there, cut left and across the island, taking in ruined walls. Tucked away on the southern face of Boztepe, just above the present town, are large square cuts in the stone, rooms dating to at least Hellenistic times. Local boys will show you some graves and bones they shouldn't. The view from the top is predictably brilliant. At the far western point you can shinny down the long, flat sloping rock to the seaside like the local kids do, and trace the course of the fallen walls.

The main citadel is on the main hill at the end of the isthmus, now the center of Amasra town. The old Genoese-era walls and gates are still in place, and the gates remain in use. There is a Byzantine church within the compound, now unroofed and in ruins.

When you tire of the beaches and wandering the Amasra's winding streets, Amasra's **museum** is pleasantly small and concise ($1). There's nothing here worth traveling from Ottawa or Los Angeles for, but it's well worth a short walk down Amasra's cobbled lanes. The museum has a fine collection of Hellenistic and Roman statues and inscriptions gathered at Amasra, and the workmanship on the statuary is very good. Take a moment to look at the snake carved from a single block of stone, which you'll appreciate even if you don't appreciate snakes. There are

Tea Gardens & Backgammon

On your way back from Amasra's museum, stop in at one of Amasra's many relaxed, friendly beachfront **tea gardens** (çay bahçesi). You can retire in the trees for a cheap beer or a sandwich and a game of **tavak** (backgammon). This is an obsolete phenomenon in most parts of Turkey – real estate this outstanding is usually trampled with pricey waterfront disco spots. Enjoy it while you can.

also some Byzantine and Ottoman items here to round out the collection, and an interesting set of inscriptions in the garden surrounding the museum.

Sports & Recreation

Beaches

Most people, reasonably, make a beeline for the long sand beach on the **eastern side** of the isthmus and stake out a space. It's busy on summer weekends, but nothing like the lines of roasting people in Marmaris or Kemer. The east side of the isthmus may be the conventional place to swim, but anywhere around the islands is good. On the western side of the isthmus, in the **Küçük Liman**, kids play like otters beneath the Direkli tower, for instance, and on the eastern side of Boztepe.

Boating

Renting a boat is inexpensive and easy. A small fleet of rowboats ($1.50 per hour) and motorboats ($5 per hour) awaits on the north (fortress) side of the main beach. A guide will be happy to escort you around and deliver pleasant patter, but a better idea is to bring some food and paddle out around the sea wall - weather permitting - and back to the outer side of town, perhaps stopping off for a look at the monastery ruins on uninhabited **Tavşan Island**. A motorboat can get you to the beach at **Çakroz**, in the east, in 45 minutes.

Caving

The **Gürcuoluk Mağarası**, near Çakroz town, is fairly deep and worth visiting. Check with the Tourism Information people about getting to and from this labyrinth.

Along the Coast from Amasra to Sinop

Most people opt to skip the coastal route between Amasra and Sinop, instead taking the relatively quick inland route to Sinop or Samsun via Kastamonu.

If you choose to hug the coast you'll be rewarded with fine views along a winding road that serves village after tiny village. Some of the towns have small hotels, some have little beaches. The next significant town is **Cide**, followed by **İnebolu**, but most people find even these provincial centers too, ah, provincial. The smaller towns, too, while pretty, are not necessarily places you will, or should, feel comfortable

Mithradites, He Died Old

Mithradites' name lives on. The long lived scholar-king is reported to have mastered 22 languages, and secured his long reign by building up his immunity to various poisons by sampling them little bits at a time. Prisoners and criminals paid dearly for Mithradites' curiosity, and were often forced to test his various antidotes and exotic concoctions. The King's methods certainly saved him from various intrigues, but in the end he was ironically stymied in an attempt to end his own life with poison after the Romans had pursued him to his last refuge in Armenia. In desperation to avoid falling into Roman hands, Mithradites had one of his servants run him through with a sword.

spending the day on the beach. Your best bets, if spartan accommodation and isolation from other travelers is what you want, include:

Tekkeönü: A ruined isthmus fortress is off to the west of Tekkeönü's town center.

Gideros Koyu: This pretty natural harbor 12 kilometers west of Cide offers some accommodation.

Cide: at the eastern end of a long stretch of sand and gravel beach. This, with İnebolu, is a transportation hub, more or less, and you can get minibuses several times daily to the east, west, and south (Kastamonu). The **Cafe Yalı Restaurant and Pansiyon**, east of the town dock and near the beach, is the destination of choice (or very little choice) for the occasional visitors.

Denizkonak: 27 kilometers east of Cide, has a camping site upstream of a pretty beach.

Akbayir: 42 kilometers east of Cide, has some small pensions and the standard access to a small cove.

İnebolu: There was once a great Hellenistic city on this site, but the city (probably the former Ionopolis) has only the barest trace of its antiquity. Mostly, the old fortifications have become retaining walls for a pretty assortment of Ottoman houses on the city's main hill. The houses have not been converted into pensions, the ruins are disappointing, and the waterfront is gravelly and, to the east, industrial. If you choose to stay, the bread is marvelous and there are some cheap pensions. The best in town is the **HOTEL DENİZ**, *Zafer Yolu Cad. No. 18, Inebolu, Tel. 366 811 3448, Fax 366 811 3449*, on the east side of town across the road from the sea. Across the street from the beach on the west side of town, the **SAHIL PENSION** is recommended over the generally poor hotels in town.

The favored dining spot is the obvious choice, the **CANLIBALIK LOKANTA** at the city center by the PTT. Prices are reasonable ($1 beer). For excellent, even cheaper food, try the Palmiye, just inland on Cumhuriet Caddesi. Many dolmuş and minibuses will drop you in İnebolu on the sea road at the center of town, but the genuine otogar is four blocks inland on the east bank of the İnebolu River. If you've made it all the way to İnebolu, treat yourself to the local köfte, which some Turks consider the country's finest. The regional bread is also heavy and excellent. A road crawls steeply inland to Kastamonu from here.

Sinop

The history of **Sinop** is longer and more glorious than any other city on the Black Sea, but the city has little left to show for its rich heritage. Today the town is a fairly busy port city located off the beaten track, but is less pretty than Amasra or Amasya. There are good beaches nearby, and some beautiful natural scenery.

History

There have been settlements at Sinop since well before the Bronze Age (3,000 B.C.), but details are difficult to find. Visitors to this region were clearly impressed by the great natural harbor at Sinop. Like those who came after, the first settlers probably established themselves on the isthmus south of Sinop Burnu. Herodotus reports that the Cimmerians founded a city here in roughly 700 B.C., fleeing persecution by the Scythians along the northern Black Sea. The Cimmerians themselves were ferocious by the standard of Asia Minor and went on to sack and destroy towns throughout the area.

At roughly the same time the Cimmerians arrived, perhaps slightly before, settlers from Miletus on the Aegean are also thought to have built a town here. Whether the settlements were simultaneous is not known, but the Milesian legacy was lasting, and this colony, in turn, established other towns to the east including Cerasus (Giresun) and Trapezus (Trabzon).

The name **Sinope** was an invention of these settlers. The name supposedly derives from Sinope, the beautiful Amazon daughter of a minor god. Sinope caught the eye of Zeus, who desperately sought to consummate his godly love with her. Sinope, with Amazon resoluteness, refused his advances, prompting Zeus to offer her any wish if she would change her mind. Sinope agreed, wishing that she be allowed eternal virginity. Zeus, outwitted, took this well and allowed Sinope to live out her life here.

The next great character in Sinop's history was its wry son, the philosopher **Diogenes**. Diogenes (the Cynic) was well known for his disdain for common beliefs; he lived outside in a tub and exercised his bodily functions in full view, obeying his own appetites for sleep, food, and sunlight in the way he chose. No wonder he was sent packing by the people of Sinop, but while in Corinth he was well enough respected that Alexander sought him out. Finding the old philosopher sunning himself, Alexander asked if there was anything he could do for him. Diogenes replied that, yes, there was: Alexander should stand back out of his light. This startled Alexander and delighted his friends. Later, while his entourage was joyously recalling the story, Alexander said *"Nevertheless, if I were not Alexander I would be Diogenes."* On another occasion, when someone was comparing Diogenes' life unfavorably with that of Aristotle, Alexander's tutor in the court of Philip, Diogenes said simply *"Aristotle dines when Philip chooses, Diogenes when Diogenes chooses."*

Sinop was conquered by Pharnaces I (185-169 B.C.), King of Pontus. His successor Mithradites III consolidated the young kingdom and shifted the capital here from Amasya. Sinop remained the capital of Pontus for a full century, and was decorated as befitted one of the most powerful cities in the world at the time. The Pontic kings were careful to stay on good terms with the Roman Empire, which was emerging on the Mediterranean, and Pontus contributed to the force that subdued Rome's hated enemy, Carthage.

With Carthage out of the way, however, Rome became increasingly belligerent. Pontic resentment came to a head under Mithradites VI Eupator (the Great), who lived from 120-63 B.C. A series of Mithraditic Wars ensued, in which the Romans were forced to directly intervene against the Pontic King, who styled himself as a liberator of the heavily taxed Roman subjects in Asia Minor.

Mithradites' kingdom proved no match for the Roman Empire, however, and his armies no match for the Romans, either. Between 90 and 69 B.C. some of Rome's finest generals first stalemated and finally defeated the Pontic armies, seizing Mithradites' homeland and driving the King across Anatolia into Armenia. General Pompey's pursuit continued even there, and with the Roman victory over Armenia at Tigranocerta Mithradites ended his own life.

Sinop was destroyed following an earlier defeat by Lucullus, and slowly built its way back up. Both the Romans and the Byzantines made great use of this port city, far and away the best natural harbor on the southern Black Sea coast.

Russian ships shelled Sinop in 1853, an attack that decimated the Turkish fleet and killed more than 2,000 Turks. The "Massacre of Sinop" stirred up anti-Russian sentiment in both France and England and helped precipitate the Crimean War. The most recent footnote is the relatively recent passing of a U.S. Air Force facility atop the Sinop peninsula. With the end of the Cold War this facility was closed; many residents of Sinop worked there and seem to have fond memories of the facility. English is predictably common.

Arrivals & Departures
By Bus
Sinop is not directly on the main bus route, which emerges from the interior at Samsun and heads east, but there are hourly buses from Samsun. Dolmuş serve Sinop from both Boyabat and Cide in the west. The otogar is located alongside the outer city walls. Dolmuş serve the center of town, continuing on to isolated Karakum beach. They also head in the other direction, toward Kumsal beach.

By Car
From the west, either follow the coast road from Cide – slow going – or do what most people do and cut north just before Boyabat. The road descends through the misty, green highlands and emerges on the coast road just east of Sinop.

By Ferry
The Black Sea ferry arrives from İstanbul on Tuesdays at 10 a.m., departing for points east at 2:30 p.m. The ferry returns on Thursdays, departing at 5 p.m.

Getting Around
By Tour
For tours around the area, the best choice is **Sinop Tours**, *Kıbrıs Caddesi No. 7, Sinop, Tel. 368 261 7900, Fax 368 261 0810,* run by the Mephistophelian Adem Tahtacı. Sinop Tours does an excellent job organizing boat tours, cruises, cave trips, and guided day trips that take in the area's natural beauty - an American working in the area described the tip of Ince Burnu northwest of Sinop as looking like Tierra del Fuego. Most tours cost between $15 and $20.

Where to Stay & Eat
Sinop's accommodations are scattered along the east side of the isthmus, with the concentration of cheaper spots just below the main city walls, another half kilometer into town from the outer walls by the otogar.

The restaurants along the waterfront serve good, fresh fish—of them, Saray Restaurant has the best reputation. Fresh seafood or mussels should cost $3-$6. On the street behind the waterfront, Akvaryum Canli Balık Restaurant near Meral Hotel is a bit cheaper and offers food every bit as good.

VILLA ROSE, *Kartal Cad. No. 9, Sinop. Tel. (368) 261-1923; Fax (368) 260-1016; Email: none; Web: none. Rooms: 6. Credit cards not accepted. Open year-round. Double: $58 (breakfast included).*

The Villa Rose is located a few minutes above Sinop as you cross the isthmus and ascend onto the peninsula. This is the sole bed and breakfast in Sinop, stuffed with Turkish knick-knacks. Dinner is served in the high season.

OTEL 57, *M. Kapı Mah., Kurtuluş Cad. No. 29, Sinop, Tel. (368) 261-5462; Fax (368) 261-6068; Email: none; Web: none. Rooms: 20. Credit cards not accepted. Open year-round. Double: $28 (breakfast included).*

Probably the nicest spot in town. An odd location on the top of the isthmus, but that just means you're a four minute walk from the waterfront. Clean and interesting, with a pleasant second floor lobby and, of course, breakfast. If full, consider the decent Hotel Meral a block down Kurtuluş Caddesi (*Kurtuluş Cad. No. 1, Sinop; Tel. (368) 261-3100;* Double: $15).

OTEL MELIA KASIM, *Gazi Caddesi No. 49, Sinop, Tel. (368) 261-4210; Fax (368) 261-1625. Rooms: 57. Double: $32.*

This centrally-located hotel was once Sinop's status address, but the deterioration of its rooms—and the noise of the nightclub on the ground floor—has undermined its position. It remains among Sinop's best, situated on the eastern bay just beyond the old city walls. The hotel boasts in-room television, complete with the Turkish movie channel Cine5, full baths and other amenities. Request a room on the top floor to insulate yourself from the nightclub.

Other reputable pensions include the **KARAKUM PANSİYON**, in a quiet location beyond town on the peninsula, and the **IKIZLER PANSİYON** overlooking the harbor.

Seeing the Sights

The **fortress** that straddles the isthmus was the last in a long line of fortifications on the site, the handiwork of the Selçuks. Today the outer walls bisect the isthmus at the otogar, to your left on entering town. Just inside the outer fortifications on the southern (right) side is a large keep, a 19th century addition to the fortifications. You'll notice it appears to be in good condition; it should be, as it is the regional prison. The main road follows the crest of the isthmus. The inner walls of the town, farthest from the mainland, divide the city. Two large gates are still in use, and atop the walls is the **Burç Çay Bahçesi**, with cheap tea and excellent views.

The beaches on the southern side of the isthmus are the most immediately tempting, and that's good. The undercurrent on the north side - and out along the northern side of the İnce Burnu peninsula - are notorious, and should be avoided unless you spot bright, reliable people (read: not teenage boys) swimming there. The beaches along the developed southern and western shore have safe swimming, such as **Kumsal** and **Karakum**. **Sarıkum** (Yellow sand) beach 20 kilometers west is also supposed to be safe.

The **Sinop Museum** in the center of town has an average collection, unless you are a particular fan of Byzantine art. There are several Byzantine paintings recovered from a Byzantine palace at the site, as well as an assortment of ornaments, vases, and a few gruesome weapons. The Sinop area is of keen interest to anthropologists and archaeologists. An interdisciplinary team that includes students at the University of Chicago has been pursuing research in the area, interested in the tiny settlements that sprang up in many of the small, isolated coves around the region. The museum is set on a plot of land that has the foundations of the former Temple of Serapis, an Egyptian god you might not expect to find way up here; according to Tacitus, Hellenistic worship of Serapis may have even begun here.

For an out of the way jaunt, try a drive around the **Erfelek** area, just south of the inland westbound road. The area offers atmospheric old houses in the heavily wooded mountains. If it's a Friday, you're in particular luck; it's slaughtering day, and the kebaps here are reputed to be the best in Turkey.

While wandering around Sinop, keep your eye peeled for Tarzan Kemal, a 50 or so year-old guy who walks around town in a loin cloth. You'll know him if you see him.

Amasya

The eastern end of the Black Sea is covered in forests and topped with alpine meadows. The Ankara-Trabzon route passes near Amasya en route to Georgia and the former Soviet Republics. You want to make Amasya your first stop, and perhaps your last as well.

Amasya is a small, fascinating town on the road from Ankara to the Black Sea. Amasya is near the route most people take to the Black Sea, and a far more interesting destination than Samsun on the seaside. The town sits in a narrow river valley, its old houses hanging over the edge of the usually placid Yeşilirmak River. A great fortress looms directly above town, originally of Pontic design and later restored and improved by the Byzantines and Ottomans. This city, once the capital of the Kingdom of

Pontus, is further decorated with the tombs of its former kings and an interesting collection of Ottoman buildings. The days of glory seem to be in the past now, but Amasya maintains a tidy, bustling spirit and makes an interesting diversion for one or two nights.

History

As is the case in so many places where nature offered an ideal site for fortification, Amasya's citadel area was probably settled quite early, but no traces have been discovered under the fortifications built and rebuilt in the thousands of years since. Amasya began to emerge from obscurity at the time of Alexander's campaign. Alexander's conquests only grazed this area, but the turmoil of the young king's victories and the chaos that followed allowed a dynasty started in 337 B.C. to grow near the shores of the Black Sea. The borders of the Pontus were initially modest, well within the area delineated by the modern cities of Sinop, Samsun, and Amasya.

The Pontic kings took advantage of the 301 B.C. defeat and death of one of the most initially successful Diadochi, Antigonus the One Eyed, and established Amasya as their capital in 300 B.C. under **Mithradites I**. The Pontic kings clung to the Persian system of rule while the Persian Empire itself was crushed under Alexander's heel. The budding kingdom played a cautious diplomatic game with the rivals for Alexander's empire, alternately forging alliances and fighting against the Seleucids, and went on to foster a similar relationship with the Romans. Mithradites V went so far as to contribute men and arms to the final Roman campaign against Carthage (147-146 B.C.), at the same time pushing the borders of his own kingdom south into Cappadocia and the heart of Anatolia and west until it came into conflict with the Kingdom of Bithnia based at Nicaea, modern Iznik.

Amasya lost some of its importance after Pharnaces I established a new Pontic capital at Sinop. The Roman General Pompey underscored Amasya's continued importance, however, by razing it to the ground during the final stages of Mithradites VI's (120-63) failed anti-Roman wars. Near the end of Mithradites' reign, the writer **Strabo** was born in Amasya. Strabo would later travel much of the world and amass more than 17 volumes of historical and geographical facts, only a few of which survive today.

Amasya was chosen as a Roman provincial capital, then faded into obscurity during the Byzantine years. The area was overrun by Arabs, retaken by the Byzantines, and passed back and forth between various local lords before falling to the Ottoman Sultan Beyazid I in 1392. According to one account, Amasya's citadel was one of the few places in Asia Minor to remain in Ottoman hands during Tamurlane's rampage of

1402-1403, and it was from here that Beyazid I's son Mehmet I embarked on the campaign that won for him his father's empire.

Amasya maintained an important role under the Ottomans thereafter as a frequent staging area for campaigns into the east and as a proving ground for Ottoman princes. The most momentous events in Amasya's later Ottoman history were the earthquakes that often rocked the city, including three times in the past three centuries. Finally, Atatürk came here via Samsun in 1919, ostensibly as a British agent seeking to pacify the Turks. His intention was far from what the British thought, however; Atatürk's first order of business was to meet with several Turkish separatist leaders and begin organizing the nationalist movement that, four years later, ended with the restoration of Turkey.

Atatürk's arrival at Amasya is commemorated on its anniversary, June 12, with a week long festival.

Arrivals & Departures

By Bus

Amasya is not directly on the highway between Samsun and Ankara, but many buses swing through town anyway. The otogar is about two kilometers northwest of town, and it is frequently served by dolmuş as well as taxis. A rail line passes through Amasya en route to Samsun from Sivas, but buses are preferable.

Buses serve many cities on the Marmaris and Aegean directly; some nearby destinations and distances to note: Ankara (Sungurlu/Hattuşas) buses depart several times an hour, five hour trip, $12 ($6); Samsun buses depart once an hour, two hour trip, $7; Kayseri buses depart in the morning and evening, eight hour trip, $13.

By Car

Amasya is 130 kilometers south of Samsun on the Black Sea, 261 kilometers north of Nevşehir, and 528 kilometers northeast of Ankara. The distance from Hattuşas is 157 kilometers. Roads to the north, west, and east are in good shape.

Orientation

Apart from the train and bus stations, Amasya is fairly compact and easy to see on foot. The citadel is the most daunting walk, a half hour hike up a steep incline, but is well worth the effort.

The **Tourism Information** office is at *Mehmet Paşa Mah., Mustafa Kemal Paşa Cad. No. 27, Tel. 358 218 5002, Fax 358 218 3385.*

Where to Stay

ILK HOUSE, *Gümüşlü Mah., Hittit Sok. No. 1, Amasya. Tel. 358 218 1689; Fax 358 218 6277. Rooms: 6. Credit cards accepted. Open year-round. Double: $32.*

Guests roundly enjoy both the architecture of the İlk House and the architect responsible for it, Kamil Yalçin. Yalçin has been working incessantly around Amasya since renting and restoring the İlk Pansiyon in the late 1980s, and among his current projects are a boardwalk on the river and restoration of some riverfront houses. These good intentions, combined with painstaking detail and tempting prices have made this hotel a standard first stop on the Black Sea circuit. Request the light, spacious room 3; if you don't get it, the others are good as well. Breakfast is $3, dinner is $8. Open year round.

Selected as one of our favorite budget hotels.

YUVAM PANSİYONS, *Atatürk Cad. 24, Amasya, Tel. (358) 218-1342; Fax (358) 218-3409; Email: ariecz@superonline.com. Rooms: 20. Credit cards not accepted. Open year-round. Double: $26.*

There are two Yuvam Pansiyons under the same ownership; the second of the two (whose address is listed above) is housed in the more appealing building. The decor in both buildings is rural Ottoman, with appealing wooden furniture and kilims. The courtyard serves as a dining area in the summer, and a wooden house in the garden is used for additional accommodation in the summer. Another of the Amasya's genuinely friendly places to spend the night. Open year round.

MELİŞ PANSİYON, *Yeniyol Cad. Torumtay Sok. No. 135, Amasya,Tel. (358) 212-3650; Fax (358) 218-2082. Rooms: 12. Credit cards accepted. Open year-round. Double: $37.*

This special class hotel is located in the west of town in the neighborhood of the Gök Medresse Mosque. This is one of Turkey's "special class" hotels, with television and good amenities. Decor is busy Ottoman.

Where to Eat

Hotels have their own restaurants with good set price meals, but if you want to venture out for dinner try the ŞEHİR KULUBU, *Tel. 358 218 1016*, on the north shore of the river beneath the fortress. This club opens its doors to visiting foreigners. Among the cheap, filling restaurants, ELMAS KEBAP SALONU, *Tel. 358 218 1606*, is highly esteemed among kebapçis in the area; it's a good, cheap place for kebap and rice. The kebap salonu is located directly off the main square.

Seeing the Sights

Amasya's **fortress** dominates the heights above a bend in the Yeşilirmak River, as it has for at least 2,200 years. The summit of the hill was once crowned with the Pontic acropolis, which had a temple to the Persian god Ahura, akin to Zeus. Today the fortress is a shell, but the views are tremendous and there are stone cut chambers and even long, descending tunnels on the grounds.

These tunnels, occasionally found on hilltop fortresses in the Black Sea region, were probably used to guarantee the citadel's water supply, but may have had a religious role, probably associated with Mithra or Ahura. The towers date from the Pontic Kingdom but the walls have been extended over time by various rulers; note their former course down to the river, where they encircled the northern town.

The **rock tombs** lining the cliff below the citadel are also interesting. This somewhat perilous collection of tombs was for the burial of royalty, but there is little evidence for which tomb belonged to which king. Mithradites is always a good bet, since, over the course of 260 years, there were six kings named Mithradites plus an earlier Mithradites who was an ancestor to them all. Still, the one identified tomb is that of Pharnaces I, (185-169 B.C.), and it appears unfinished. Pharnaces helped expand Pontic control over the Black Sea, paving the way for the capital to shift under his successor, Mithradites IV (169-150 B.C.).

One of the nearby tomb entrances connects to a tunnel leading down from the acropolis, but, deeper down, the tunnels are choked with the debris of several thousand years. A group spearheaded by the local governor and assisted by Kamil Yalçin of the Ilk House (see *Where to Stay* above) has discussed an effort to clear the tunnels. The **Pontic Royal Palace** (called Kızlar Saray, or Maiden's Palace) was located on the terrace just below the tombs.

Most of the sights within town are from the last 800 years. Particularly interesting is the **Bimarhane Medresse**, an insane asylum completed in 1308 under the Mongols, who occupied the area until the arrival of the Ottomans. This interesting old building, long since roofless, has an ornate facade, and is not far inland from the tourism information office. The insane asylum was dedicated by a Mongol lord to his wife. The museum, located in an old house, has both archaeological and ethnographic areas, the former with a mishmash of items found in the region, some pieces dating back to Hittite times.

Ünye

Ünye rarely makes it onto itineraries for the simple reason that no one knows about it. The city is itself boilerplate, offering the barest glimpse of its former importance. Ünye, however, is located just to the east of long stretch of sand beaches that are well served by pensions and hotels. Inland, the lush green interior hides some truly fascinating sites, sites that, at the least, you'll want to stop by on your way through the area.

History

Precious little is known about the history of Ünye, but it seems clear that if there is any truth to the stories of **Amazons**, they once lived in this area. The legendary range of the Amazons is bounded by Thermodon (modern Terme) on the west and Giresun on the east. No hard evidence of their existence has ever been discovered, but even the most ancient writers, skeptical of many things, had no doubts that Amazons existed.

Ünye Kalesi was pre-Byzantine, and probably pre-Roman. Tunnels at the site like those at Amasya, together with a rock tomb at the entrance, suggest that the fortress was erected by the Kingdom of Pontus, but even this might have been built on an earlier foundation. The settlement on the coast was known as Oiniaon in ancient times, eventually yielding the modern name, Ünye. Pompey either sacked or accepted the surrender of the fortress from Pontus during his campaign, and the city was subject to Roman control after 63 B.C. Ünye's fortress maintained a garrison, but it largely faded from view for several centuries. There are mentions of the popularity of Ünye wine, although wine is no longer made in the area.

Several Turkic tribes seized and held the city after the Empire of Trabzon began deteriorating. The Ottomans took the town as a prelude to the capture of Trabzon in 1459.

Arrivals & Departures

By Bus

If you are arriving from the west, keep your eyes peeled several miles before Ünye, where the beach and hotels are located. The main otogar is located three blocks inland of the PTT; this is where dolmuş depart for Ünye Kalesi. Another bus and dolmuş station is located just to the northwest of this intersection on the sea road; dolmuş headed west and east are green and white, while those heading inland are red and white. Dolmuş serve Kumsal beach (the good hotel strip) half-hourly.

Ulusoy is the best bus company running the Ankara-Trabzon route, with Metro another good option.

By Car

The main coast highway passes right through Ünye. The strip of good hotels is to the west of town on the main highway.

Orientation

Ünye has beaches to all sides, including Çamlık, Gölevi, and Uzunkum, although you're likely to be satisfied with the beach directly below wherever you're staying. Ünye retains fragments of its old walls, but the compelling things are outside of town. Check in at the tourism information office for more nearby sights, including the tombs at Delikkaya and other fortresses.

Ünye's **tourism information** office, *Tel. 452 323 4952, Fax 452 323 4952,* is usually staffed by some very helpful and English-savvy people.

Where to Stay

In Ünye proper there are a few desultory options, but there are several nice pensions, hotels, and campgrounds at Kumsal Beach to the west of town. The pensions at city center remain open in winter. The hotels below are in order from west to east along the highway.

OTEL KUMSAL, *Ataturk Mah., PK 9 Kumsal, Ünye, Tel/Fax (452) 323-4490. Rooms: 32. Double: $45.*

A longtime favorite in the area. The Kumsal (just across the road and west from the Pınar Pansiyon) has the relaxed, lazy atmosphere you'd hope to find, with a sauna and television in the room (and VCRs and videotapes floating around). The in-house restaurant serves good Turkish food.

PINAR PANSİYON, *Gölevi Devrent Mevkii, Ünye, Tel. (452) 323-3496. Rooms: 7. Credit cards not accepted. Open year-round. Double: $17.*

The Pınar is simply one of the nicest pensions in Turkey. It comes as a surprise here along the Black Sea coast, a carefully maintained large house with old wardrobes and other nice furniture in spacious, tidy rooms. Guests have access to the kitchen, as well as the patio outside amid the lush, colorful garden. Ünye beach is just across the road. The owner, Münir Altınay, is a kind, helpful man who built the house and maintains it as a hobby. The hotel is on the inland side of the highway.

Selected as one of our favorite budget hotels.

ÇAMLIK MOTEL, *Sahil Yolu, Ünye. Tel. (452) 312-1333. Rooms: 14. Credit cards not accepted. Open March-November. Double: $21.*

The Çamlık Motel is run by the municipality, situated in a little pine forest two kilometers west of Ünye. Rooms are simple and clean, and you have access to a restaurant with well-regarded kebaps and a sand beach.

OTEL BURAK, *Atatürk Mah., Ünye. Tel. (452) 312-0186. Rooms: 14. Credit cards not accepted. Open year-round. Double: $14.*

The Otel Burak is a simple, friendly spot in the center of town, near the otogar. We prefer the hotels to the west of town, but if you want to stay in town, this is a serviceable option.

Where to Eat

Most hotels have their own restaurants, and pensions let you cook for yourself. Dining in Ünye is a matter of selecting good, hearty fare that any one of a number of restaurants can offer.

ADANA MUTFAĞI KEBAP HOUSE, *Atatürk Mah., Ünye. Tel. (452) 312-4334. Inexpensive.*

This is a good place to get a quick bite in Ünye town. The kebap house is located opposite the Belediye building.

ÇAMLIK RESTAURANT, *Atatürk Mah., Ünye. Tel. (452) 323-4447. Inexpensive.*

This restaurant is reputed to have the best köfte in town, and it is delicious. The Çamlık is located 1.5 kilometers west of town.

KALEDİBİ LOKANTA, *Ünye Kalesi Altı, Ünye, Tel. (452) 323-4978.*

A small, excellent trout restaurant just a short distance below the path to Ünye Kalesi. Two trout, bread and a salad cost about $4.

Seeing the Sights
Ünye Kalesi

Ünye Kalesi is located just five kilometers inland of the main highway just off of the Akkuş road. Check with the Tourism Information office for an area map if you're heading up on your own.. The fortress appears ahead and left as you ascend into the valley on Akkuş road, and you take the road that dips to the left as you approach, which then ascends to the trailhead about 700 feet past Kaledibi Lokanta (it is a leisurely 25 minute walk to the top).

The fortress is very much in the tradition of Black Sea citadels; it crowns a sheer crag, offers several defensive rings, has steps and buildings carved in the living stone, and is, today, overgrown and open free to the public. Upon arrival, you enter between two great pylons just below an old rock cut tomb. One of the pylons is fixed to the crag at the left, the second stands free on the right. These walls are probably Hellenistic, thus Pontic. The most adventurous, and those with no concern for tearing holes in their clothes, can take the difficult, steeper path to the left and scramble along old staircases, through thick bushes, and past old walls to the lower cave. Otherwise, wind around to the right and approach the cave from below. The lower tunnel is an impressive piece of work, 15 feet wide and eight feet high, a perfectly arched and sealed staircase descending at a ridiculous 35 degree angle - an impossible descent now that the stairs have worn and weathered. The peculiarity of this tunnel is leavened by its abrupt end less than 50 yards deep, the result of either collapse or intentional filling.

On the same terrace, before ascending, you can examine some old walls and cuttings in the stone, as well as an overgrown upper gate. Be careful of uncovered cisterns. The ascent to the next level squeezes between two great stones, emerging in a flat, open area looking out in the direction of the sea. On the northern rim, facing the sea, is a broken sarcophagus. Stairs have been carved into the final great stone outcrop at the center, but before ascending the solid - if rickety looking - wooden ladder, round the corner to the left.

Here you find the entrance to the upper tunnel. Like the lower tunnel, it is cut steeply and neatly into the stone, descending rapidly in the direction of the sea, five kilometers away. Unlike the lower tunnel, this tunnel has no apparent end. Toss a smooth stone or marble into the tunnel and listen. And listen. This is an eerie place, and rumors swirl in town; some say it is an old well, others an ancient shrine, others an escape tunnel. Tearing yourself away from here, ascend the ladder to the acropolis, where more steps and foundations are carved in stone, and from where you have an excellent view in all directions.

Toskoparan Cave

Perhaps the most truly weird site in Turkey is four kilometers to the east of Ünye. **Toskoparan Mağarası**, or the Toskoparan cave, is less than two kilometers off the main coast road. To get there, stay to the left at the first main intersection by the cement plant and look for the battered sign on the right. Follow the path just to the right of the landowners' stairs through a thick hazelnut grove. As you ascend you'll see the rock cut tomb carved into the surface. The tomb is not unusual, and reports of art in the interior are greatly exaggerated. The tomb is only vaguely interesting if you've been through the Lycian coast or Cappadocia, where they'd carve something like this before breakfast.

Returning to the path, continue following the trail around the stone buttress. Arriving at the uphill face, look carefully at the regular courses of one and one-half foot wide layers of stone, and the seams in the rock, and the sealant that is corroding in those seams. Toskoparan Mağarası, on close examination, appears at least partly manmade, like a low, squat pyramid. A winding path leads to the top of the hill, which offers traces of old cut stone. Continuing around the buttress you arrive at a great trench along the face of the rock; when we visited in 1996 a work crew was digging out this trench under the watchful eye of some armed soldiers.

During the 1922 exchange of populations, we were told, a Greek took with him a map indicating that five meters directly beneath a sign carved into the stone there were gates to this hollow formation, and a treasure of gold. Having bought rights to the map, a small team of investors secured digging rights from the Turkish authorities and spent four days digging for treasure at the proper spot. Our initial impression of strangeness was vouchsafed by the diggers; this was once a site of worship, may well be hollow, and some speculation about its origin involves, yes, space aliens. No treasure was recovered, but the trench remains and curiosity mounts.

Ancient Home of the Amazons?

Farther afield is a battered, ancient fortress commanding the heights above Terme, ancient Thermodon, the former home of the Amazons. **Karpu Kale** requires a substantial drive out of the way, and is only accessible by car. Turn inland of the main coast highway at Terme, 26 kilometers west of Ünye. From here to **Salıpazar** is 20 kilometers - there are some signs, but ask for the correct road to Salıpazar (*"Salıpazar'a gidiyorum. Salıpazar nerede?"*). The turn-off is just before Salıpazar. If you miss it, from Salıpazar follow signs toward Yenidoğan, and once out of Salıpazar keep your eye peeled for battered signs. While on the mountain road, stay to the left at each turn (most of which are signed), continuing for 10.5 kilometers from the town center. The roads in the mountains above are rough and winding, but in pretty good condition.

Upon emerging in full view of the mountaintop fortress, pull up by the Suluca Koyu sign and hike 25 minutes from there. The upper sections, within the old mountaintop compound, are steep and usually wet - be extremely careful. Some may want to content themselves with the lower sections. The site has not been adequately explored, and most of what is believed is speculation. This was clearly an ancient site, perhaps Paphlagonian, or, based on sheer speculation, Amazonian. The hilltop is crowned with a ring of walls, where walls are necessary, and at the summit are cisterns and stone-cut rooms, long since collapsed. The view down over the Thermodon valley is glorious.

Giresun

Like Terme, **Giresun** has a direct tie to tales of the Amazons. The small island just offshore of Giresun to the east, now known as **Giresun Adası**, was probably the one mentioned in the tale of Jason and the Argonauts. The city has only a few things to see, and unless you want to spend time nosing around the island of the Amazons, you'll probably want to use it as a break on the way to Trabzon or, nearer, Tirebolu.

History

Giresun may have been an Amazon stronghold, as evidenced by their association with little Giresun Adası just offshore. The island was thought to have been an **Amazon shrine**, but by the year 400 B.C. there was no trace of the fierce women warriors. At that time Xenophon's

10,000 stopped here on their long march home, finding a normal Greek settlement, one of the colonies of Sinop.

Their stay was uneventful, although they were much intrigued by the native Mossynoici people they found just to the west. *"When they were in a crowd they acted as men act would act when in private, and when they were by themselves, they used to behave as they might do if they were in company; they used to talk to themselves, and laugh to themselves, and stop and dance wherever they happened to be,"* reported Xenophon. Most startling were the wealthy boys fed on boiled chestnuts until *"they were practically as broad as they were tall,"* and decorated head to toe in flower tattoos.

Pharnaces I, King of Pontus, seized the city in the second century B.C., after which it was known as Pharnacos until the Romans destroyed

The Amazons

According to the legends, the ancient land of the Amazons was bound by Themistikos (near Terme) on the west and an island - probably Giresun Adası - on the east. Themistikos was the capital city. The Amazons allowed no man to live among them, and to sustain the tribe they mated anonymously with men of the inland tribes in the middle of the night. Boy children they returned to the inland tribes, girls they kept and raised as Amazons. One custom was to sear the right chest to stop the right breast from growing and interfering with spear casting. Their only known shrine, on their Black Sea island, was devoted to a war god.

When Homer chronicled the Iliad in the eighth century B.C., there were no Amazons left. He refers to them as Bronze Age contemporaries of Troy in the centuries before the Trojan War. If this is the case they were contemporaries, too, of the Hittites, perhaps bounded by the Kaşka on the east and the Trojans far to the west.

The problem is that evidence is all apocryphal - Hercules fighting for the girdle of the Amazon queen, King Priam of Troy and Theseus battling invasions of the women warriors, Bellerophon sent against them on an impossible mission. The stories are legion, but the hard evidence is slim. Some have suggested that Amazons were simply matriarchal tribes living along the Black Sea before the arrival of the Greeks, but most of us can't help believing that there is an element of truth to the tales. As Arrian, Alexander's biographer, wrote in the second century A.D., "I cannot bring myself to believe that this race of women, whose praises have been sung so often by the most reputable writers, never existed at all."

the kingdom. Giresun was one of the many Pontic strongholds quashed by the Roman General Lucullus, who not only sacked the city but, adding insult to injury, took its cherries. Cherries grew naturally in this area, and Lucullus, fond of the fruit, shipped some seeds home to Rome where they became justly popular. Lucullus is sometimes credited with changing the name of the city from Pharnacus to Cerasus, Latin for cherry, but he was only restoring the city's former name.

The Kingdom of Pontus, however, was not dead yet. Pharnaces II (63-47 B.C.) used Giresun as a base to begin cautiously restoring the broken kingdom after the death of his father, Mithradites VI, the Great. Pharnaces II worked doggedly at rebuilding key fortresses and piecing together an army, and was rewarded by a victory over Rome that opened the way to Cappadocia and Bithnia. From the ruin of his father's last days, Pharnaces seemed on the verge of restoring the Kingdom of Pontus, when he ran headlong into Julius Caesar at the battle of Zela in central Anatolia. In just four hours, Caesar routed Pharnaces' army and destroyed Pontus forever, and it was in recalling this brilliant, rapid battle he said laconically, "*Veni, Vidi, Vici.*"

Giresun's fortress was restored and used into Byzantine times, then taken over by the Trapezuntine Empire in its desperate rearguard action against the Ottomans. The Ottomans took the city in 1461. Giresun marked the eastern border of Turkey in the post-World War I partition.

Arrivals & Departures
By Bus
Giresun has constant bus service to both the east and west, with Ulusoy and Metro bus companies offering the best service.

By Ferry
Westbound ferries arrive at 1 a.m. Thursday, eastbound ferries at 5 a.m. Wednesday.

Where to Stay & Eat
The eastern Black Sea coast is notorious for its "Natashas," prostitutes who often hail from the former Soviet Union. Many cheaper hotels cater to the trade, and often it is obvious. Occasionally it's not. Stick to hotels with the word "Aile" (family) in them. Strongly consider staying on Girsesun Island if at all possible, or in Tirebolu further east.

KIT-TUR OTEL, *Arifbey Cad. No. 2, Giresun, Tel. (454) 212-0245; Fax (454) 212-3034. Rooms: 50. Credit cards accepted. Open year-round. Double: $40.*

Giresun's status address, with a nice lobby and helpful staff. The rooms are perfectly decent; don't expect too much, but you'll find them clean and simple. The lobby is the most pleasant in town.

ER-TUR OTEL, *Çapulacilar Sok. No. 8, Giresun. Tel. (454) 216-1757;* *Fax (454) 216-7762; Email: none; Web: none. Rooms: 18. Credit cards not accepted. Open year-round. Double: $24.*

The Er-Tur offers good value for money. The hotel is tidy and well-managed. You'll find the Er-Tur just off of Osmanağa Caddesi near the Belediye.

BULUT OTEL, *Fatih Cad. No. 10, Giresun, Tel. (454) 216-4115. Rooms: 14. Double: $10.*

A budget option located away from most of the other budget hotels, west and behind the tourism information office on the far side of the park.

DENİZ LOKANTA, *Alparslan Cad., Giresun, Tel. (454) 216-1158. Moderate-Expensive.*

The "sea restaurant," has, predictably, an excellent selection of fish. Somewhat expensive by the local standard, a full meal will cost about $11. For less expensive dining, consider the cheap 'steam-tray' restaurants clustered by the Belediye (municipal building); of these, we prefer Halil Usta Pide and Kebap.

On Giresun Adası

GİRESUN ADASI, *Giresun Island, Tel. (454) 216-4707. Camping; $5 per night.*

If you have a tent along—or arrange for one in town--the best place to stay, bar none, is the former temple island of the Amazons. The caretaker is resupplied with necessities every three days, but you'll want your own stove and food along. There is no charge, great swimming, and perfect little campsites. This is the best kept secret on the Black Sea coast. See the site description below for information on getting to the island.

Selected one of our favorite budget hotels (err... campsites).

Tirebolu

Tirebolu is located east of Giresun, en route to Trabzon.

EREN PANSİYON BOARDING HOUSE, *Plaj Mevkii, Tirebolu, Tel. (454) 411-4600. Rooms: 12. Credit cards not accepted. Open year-round. Double: $12.*

Eren Pansiyon, one-half hour east of Giresun at the western end of tiny Tirebolu town, is a quiet, enticing budget option. The Eren is stark and clean, and it is located across the highway from a perfect sand beach. Each floor has its own kitchen and the town's nicest restaurant is a stone's throw away. Tirebolu boasts an old Ottoman castle. Dolmuş depart for Giresun hourly.

TRİPOLİS PLAJ-RESTAURANT, *Plaj Mevkii, Tirebolu, Tel. (454) 411-4339. Moderate.*

Tucked away between a stand of trees and a hill at the base of

Tirebolu town, this is the obvious (and right) choice if you're staying at the Eren Pansiyon.

Seeing the Sights

Giresun has two interesting places to visit. The first is the citadel looming above the city. On your way uphill toward the hilltop fortress, take a moment to appreciate the valor of a distinguished Ottoman soldier. While storming the fortifications, one of Sultan Mehmet II's lieutenant's had his head lopped off by one of the Trapezuntine defenders; no matter, Seyit Vakkas fought on valiantly, leading the attackers up the hill. His comrades, much impressed, erected a türbe that still stands next to the road up to the fortress.

Even with your head still on, it is a steep walk up to the **citadel**, which now encloses a city park and fills with children and picnickers on weekends. The walls make a long circuit, and the entrance is at the site of the original main gate. The walls and buildings within are badly damaged, and the addition of layers of soft earth have made the layout of the old structure difficult to understand. Even so, the large compound with its commanding view is compelling. What remains of the walls is mostly Selçuk and Trapezuntine, but the raw steps and footings carved in the rocks at the summit date back to an earlier time, perhaps Pontus, perhaps before.

On the western side of the hill, within the citadel compound, is a series of large **caves**. Rumors swirl about another northern cave, since collapsed. Locals say it led to a labyrinth beneath the citadel. Another entrance was supposed to have been to the left of the main gates, now hidden behind houses. Yet another tunnel wound down to the area near the **museum** on the east. Some even say a tunnel extended to the Giresun Adası offshore, a distinct impossibility.

If you have the time, the island of **Giresun Adası** is the other thing you should try to see. Since the tunnel option doesn't work, you need a boat. There is no ferry service, but one of the fishermen along the shore will agree to shuttle you out and back for $10 or less. The Çerkez Lokanta east of town usually has a few men with boats available, as does the Uç Kaya harbor nearer town. You can also contact (or have the information office contact) the island's Turkish-speaking Grizzly Adams-looking caretaker, Yusuf Dinç, *Tel. 454 216 4707*. He occasionally has time to shuttle people across, for a fee.

Giresun Adası is thought to be the Amazon's sacred island, Aretias. This was the site of their altar to the war god, the place where Jason and the Argonauts landed and were attacked by birds dropping darts.

The Amazons worshipped a black stone on their island, according to the second century B.C. account, and that stone remains on the island today. The "mystic power source" remains an object of veneration; once a year, during the **Aksu Festival** in the third week of May, people of the area gather at the mouth of the Aksu Çayı, on the mainland, and boat out to the island to visit the stone. Circling the stone three times - once for every point of the rock touching the earth, the mystic number three - is supposed to bring good luck and fertility, but the rock juts out into the sea and is virtually impossible to negotiate without getting wet. Other parts of the ritual include jumping into and out of a metal pot hanger and tossing pebbles, representing troubles, over your back and into the Aksu.

Whether this is residue of the Amazons is anyone's guess. The walls that once surrounded the island are mostly fallen, although a fairly intact large tower still stands on the west side, looking out toward Giresun.

The most substantial ruins are those of a Byzantine monastery in the middle of the island. Large amphorae once filled with wine are now inhabited by croaking frogs. The island has several campsites, with beautiful, peaceful views to all sides, but few people are aware of them and the campsites are rarely used.

Trabzon

Trabzon's days of charm and glory are mostly behind it. The town is a hub of the bustling suitcase trade over the border with Georgia and it is an important port, but it is a gritty, industrial town in the throes of tremendous growth even by Turkish standards. The population has doubled to almost one million in just seven years. There are several interesting things to see in Trabzon, but the best sights are in the interior or along the coast in either direction.

Many people check into Trabzon in order to see the Sümela Monastery, but that's not necessary. If you'd just as soon avoid Trabzon's bustling urban scene you can; on the other hand, Trabzon is a vital, interesting city whose past is not yet completely buried and whose present can be intriguing.

Our favorite observation is that the burgundy and blue Trabzonspor soccer club banners waving throughout the city mimic the colors in Trabzon's glorious sunsets. Speak well of Trabzonspor, one of the Big Four teams in Turkey, and you will make friends here quickly.

History

Trabzon's history is long and impressive. **Xenophon** is among the first to mention the city, which was well-established when his fugitive army descended out of the mountains in 400 B.C. The city was located on a small plateau above the Tabakhane Dere, a site so advantageous that the relatively unprotected harbor barely dented the city's growth. Trapezus, as it was first known, was settled by people from Sinop. These colonists originally came from Miletus soon after the Trojan War broke the stranglehold on Hellenistic commerce.

Trabzon's high water mark was in the 12th and 13th centuries. With the Latin capture of Constantinople, the rulers of the Byzantine Empire scattered into Anatolia. The Comnenis took advantage of their family ties and settled in Trabzon, founding a Greek Orthodox splinter empire out of the broken bits of Byzantium. The new empire of Trebizond proved a short-lived success. The rulers of this peculiar little empire were adept at playing their predatory neighbors off against one another and securing their alliances with one currency they are said to have had in abundance - beautiful princesses. Even after the Byzantine empire was reestablished at Constantinople the Comnenis were content with their corner of the Black Sea, nestled among the Orthodox monasteries and good trade routes.

The pressure mounting on the Trebizond Empire, however, was immense. Even with fortresses at the mountain passes and lining the sea approaches, the empire was prey to ceaseless incursions from the east and harassment along its southern border. The empire's troubles were compounded with the conquests of Tamurlane, who rode roughshod over the whole of Anatolia in 1401. When, in 1402, Tamurlane vanished into the east, Trebizond struggled to right itself, but its brief golden age had passed.

In 1453, the Trapezuntine Empire, shot through with fabled decadence and vice, stood by as the Ottomans seized Constantinople. In the aftermath, **Sultan Mehmet II** demanded and received substantial tribute from Trabzon. So might affairs have continued, had not the cautious Emperor John IV died and been replaced by his hot-headed brother David. Emperor David secured an alliance with the ever-more fragile Venetians and Genoese, and arranged a further alliance with Uzun Hassan, a Turkish prince who held sway in the east. Having made these arrangements, the Emperor David demanded a reduction in tribute. The Sultan's response was a sudden attack by land and sea, rolling up the enemy outposts on the Black Sea by siege and negotiation.

The Emperor David's erstwhile allies proved useless, with even the formidable Uzun Hassan's armies melting away at the Sultan's approach.

When the Ottoman armies arrived at Trebizond, completing the encirclement begun by the navy, Emperor David met the Ottoman's rapid march with an equally rapid capitulation. The terms of the peace were akin to total surrender: the population was enslaved and deported, the palace stripped of valuables, and Emperor David became a pet on a short leash. The Emperor, and the other males of Comneni blood, were executed at Yedikule in İstanbul in 1564.

The execution of the Comneni males was to end, once and for all, the hereditary claims to the throne of Constantinople, but Sultan Mehmet II's efforts were partially undermined by the irrepressibly beautiful princesses of Trebizond. Sultan Beyazid II fathered Selim I (The Grim) by one of the captured princesses, thus ensuring Comneni blood in the veins of the sultans themselves.

Arrivals & Departures

Trabzon's airport is three kilometers to the east of town along the shore of the Black Sea. Turkish Airlines has two flights daily (except Thursdays) to İstanbul during the low season; check the times, but at the time of this writing departures are at 6:10 a.m. and 4 p.m.; departures from İstanbul are at 8:25 a.m. and 8:15 p.m. The cost is $70 one way. Turkish Airlines operates a shuttle bus between the airport and their office across from the park on Atatürk Alanı (at Kemerkaya Mah. on Meydanı Park (Tel. 462 321-1680).

By Bus

Trabzon is Turkey's northeastern hub, with service throughout the country. The otogar is two kilometers east of the city center, inland of the main highway. Ulusoy is the premier carrier along this route, with Metro and As Turizm also offering buses with good service and decent ventilation. All three companies have offices on the main square and offer service to the otogar.

Among the destinations and rates: Ankara, 11 hours, $30; Artvin, 4 hours, $6; Erzurum, 6 hours, $10; İstanbul, 20 hours, $35; Kars, 12 hours, $20,

By Car

The Black Sea highway from Samsun is in good condition, but it is extremely busy with truck and bus traffic. Many bus and truck drivers make the İstanbul-Trabzon stretch in a single shot (often continuing East as far as Baku, Azerbaijan), and they get a shade ragged as they barrel along this highway. Drive by day.

By Ferry

If you're fortunate enough to have the time, you can take a two day cruise to/from Istanbul aboard a car ferry. This service is available between late May and September, leaving İstanbul at 2 p.m. Monday, arriving at Trabzon about 9:30 a.m. Wednesday. The ferry continues on to Rize, then returns to İstanbul, departing Trabzon at 7:30 p.m. Wednesday. Arrival in İstanbul is at 3 p.m. Friday. There are several classes, with prices running between $30 for a seat to $105 for a first class cabin.

İstanbul Maritime Lines charges $55 for car transport between Istanbul and Trabzon. Bring food along, as the food on board is relatively expensive and of uncertain deliciousness ($10 for fixed menu dinner, $3 for breakfast). For a reservation from contact the Istanbul Turkish Maritime Lines offices at İstanbul, Tel. 212 249-9222; Fax (212) 251-9025. English speakers are always available. There is a Turkish Maritime Lines sales office in England, as well: **London Sunquest Holiday Ltd.**, 23 Princes St., WIR 7RG, London. *Tel. (44) 171 499-9992; Fax (44) 171 499-9995.*

In Trabzon, your best bet is to contact the tourism information office and ask them to make a reservation for you - they are accustomed to this.

Orientation

Before racing off to see Sümela, take the opportunity to have a look around Trabzon. Tucked away throughout the city are sights from the city's Byzantine heyday, some of them well-preserved. The Hagia Sophia is more than two kilometers west of the city center.

The tourism information office *(Tel. 462 321-4659)*, once conveniently on the main square, has migrated two blocks west, by the Nur Hotel in the shadow of the Iskender Paşa Mosque. The staff here is extremely helpful, and can assist with arrangements for ferries or securing a hotel.

Getting Around Town

Within town, Trabzon has a good public transportation system. Most people stay near the main square ("Park"), and dolmuş from the north side of this square (Atatürk Alani) are marked for "Ayasofya" (Hagia Sophia) or "TIP" (otogar). The airport bus originates two blocks north.

The most common mode of transportation is the peculiar, and excellent, dolmuş car arrangement. Compact station wagons are operated like dolmuş, traveling along set routes through town. Tell the driver your destination and he'll let you know whether you should get in. Fare is roughly the same as the bus (30¢).

Where to Stay

Trabzon has a mediocre selection of hotels, with a few pleasant exceptions. Budget hotels are plagued by garrulous Georgian and central Asian businessmen and "Natashas," as prostitutes from across the border have come to be known. Note: at the time of this writing, the **Hisarsaray Pansiyon**, a pretty, restored mansion across from the Fatih Büyük Mosque in the Kale, was closed; if open, it is worth considering (Zağanos Cad. No. 22; *Tel. 462 326-3132; Fax 462 326-2669;* Double: $32).

ZORLU GRAND HOTEL, *Kahramanmaraş Cad. No. 9, Trabzon. Tel. (462) 326-8400; Web: (462) 326-8458; Email: zorlu@zorlugrand.com; Web: www.zorlugrand.com/zorlueng.htm. Rooms: 66. Credit cards accepted. Open year-round. Double: $180 (70% discounts available).*

The Zorlu Grand, opened in 1999, is the sole 5-star hotel on the Turkish Black Sea coast. It is also the most ridiculously overpriced hotel for 400 miles in every direction, and the reservation office knows it—enquire about discounts in advance. The hotel is comfortable and central, with satellite television and the other amenities you would expect. If they stick on price, you'll find almost the same standard at the **Hotel Usta** for a fraction of the cost (Telgrafhane Sok. No. 1; *Tel. (462) 326-5700; Fax (462) 322-3703;* Double: $55).

OTEL ANIL, *Güzel Hisar Cad. No. 10, Trabzon. Tel. (462) 321-9566; Fax (462) 322-2617. Rooms: 45. Credit cards not accepted. Open year-round. Double: $24.*

The Anıl is well-established as the lodging of choice for most travelers en route to Sumela Monastery and beyond. It is a plain, blocky building, but the staff is helpful and the rooms are pleasant, clean, and generally quiet. The hotel is conveniently near the tour offices, city center, and non-stop hustle of commerce-sodden Trabzon. Call ahead (the Tourism information office can help) to secure a discount.

OTEL NUR, *15 Meydani Cami Sok. No. 4, Trabzon. Tel. (462) 326-7282; Fax (462) 321-9576. Rooms: 13. Credit cards not accepted. Open year-round. Double: $22.*

The Nur is a decent, serviceable hotel located next to the Tourism Information office, behind the Iskender Paşa Mosque. Rooms have en suite showers and phones.

CHURCH OF SANTA MARIA (Santa Maria Katolik Kilisesi), *Istiklal Mah., Sümer Sok. No. 26, Trabzon. Tel. (462) 321-2192; Fax (462) 326-7950. Rooms: 15. Credit cards not accepted. Open year-round. Double: Donation.*

This is an intriguing accommodation option, a boarding house in a Catholic Church. In a city with the rampant vice of Trabzon it's a wonder the priests and nuns have time to keep the modest rooms tidy, but as you would expect, they do. The church has been a halfway-house for 130 years, and in the winter of 1999 five new rooms were added. If you phone from the otogar you can even get a lift. You are welcome to use the kitchen and do your own laundry, and you pay what you feel is right ($20 per night is reasonable). This can get downright expensive for good, conscience-ridden Catholics. Some English is spoken, as well as Italian, French, and Turkish.

The Church of Santa Maria is located only 200 meters downhill (north) from the square at the center of town; follow the path toward the seaside and when the stairs begin you'll see the church on the right. Ring the bell that looks like a light.

Towards Sumela
COŞANDERE PANSİYON, *Maçka, Sümela Manastırı Yolu Üzeri 5 km. Trabzon. Tel. (462) 531-1190. Rooms: 14. Credit cards not accepted. Open year-round. Double: $14.*

The Coşandere solves the Trabzon accommodation problem by getting you out of Trabzon. An industrious family on the Sümela Road, 40 kilometers inland, opened a restaurant ten years ago, and in 1995 added a small guest house. The guest house is set above the same stream that spills past the Sümela Monastery, high on a slope in a grove of hazelnut trees.

The ten room farmhouse-inn is at the top of a steep gravel path, with small spare rooms built of wood and stone. The restaurant offers the only food for miles, but it is cheap and excellent. For breakfast (and lunch and dinner) treat yourself to an omelet and trout, breaded with corn meal and pan fried.

To get here follow the directions toward Sümela by car; the Coşandere is just across a small bridge five kilometers past Maçka. Getting there without your own car is tricky, but not too bad. The first solution is to make your way there aboard one of the many minibuses bound for Sumela Monastery. The second solution, if you arrive at Trabzon in the afternoon, is to call ahead (or have someone call on your behalf—the tourism information office will help) to be sure there is a room available and request to be picked up. Take a Maçka minibus and get out at the end of the line, by Maçka's town square. From here, phone the Coşandere ("Bu akşam pension'da kalacağiz. Şimdi Maçka merkez'da bekliyoruz. Geliyor musunuz?"). This should get your point across: "Tonight we're staying at your pension. Now we're waiting in Maçka. Can you come?"). Someone will be along shortly to give you a ride - if your party is greater than two, someone may make the trip in the bed of the family's pickup.

Selected one of our favorite budget hotels.

In Rize
DEDEMAN RIZE HOTEL, *Ali Paşa Köyü, Rize. Tel. (464) 223-5344; Fax (464) 223-5348. Rooms: 82. Credit cards accepted. Open year-round. Double: $75.*

The Dedeman, one of a chain of four- and five-star hotels throughout Turkey, is all by itself to the west of Rize—one hour east of Trabzon. It makes up for the lack of westerners by doing bustling business in folks from Georgia and elsewhere in the former Soviet Union. The hotel has its own slender strip of beach, satellite television, sauna, pool, restaurant and attentive service. The Dedeman is located just off of the main Black Sea highway, so dolmuş and minibuses between Trabzon and Rize pass this way frequently.

Where to Eat

You didn't come to Trabzon for fine dining, and that's a good thing. Trabzon's restaurants tend to offer substantial, traditional food. Trabzon has been welcomed into McDonalds' wide embrace (on the main square).

KIBRIS RESTAURANT, *Trabzon. Tel. (462) 321-7679. Moderate.*

A good, filling meal of mezes and köfte izgara washed down with a couple of glasses of beer will cost about $7. Traditional Turkish fare, served on patio tables on the east side of the main square. Nearby, on the southern side of the square, Çınar Lokantası is another good, convenient option.

ZINDAN RESTAURANT, *Zağnos Tower, Kale, Trabzon. Tel. (462) 322-3232. Moderate-Expensive.*

This is by far the most interesting restaurant in Trabzon, located in a tower of the city walls near Gülbaharhatun Mosque. It's not unusual to find tour groups here, dining on an extensive menu of fish, grills, and Turkish mezes. The walls are pierced with windows on the sea below.

In Akçaabat

KÖSK RESTAURANT, *İnönü Cad., Akçaabat. Tel. (462) 228-3223. Moderate-Expensive.*

Acclaimed for a hundred kilometers in both directions, the Kösk is worth the trip from Trabzon. The restaurant is across the street from the Hotel Sümela. Try the seasonal (mevşimlik) fish, which will be cheaper and almost certainly delicious. Lüfer (bluefish) and palamut (bonito) are always good choices.

Seeing the Sights

One of Trabzon's great sites, the **Hagia Sophia**, is more than two kilometers west of the city center, requiring either a dolmuş-car or an "Ayasofya"-bound bus, both of which depart from the lower end of the main city square. The Hagia Sophia has been marvelously restored, largely through the efforts of a team from the University of Edinburgh, Scotland. Restoration work began in the 1950s, ending centuries of neglect by the Ottomans, who covered over the frescoes and used the Hagia Sophia as a mosque. Today the Hagia Sophia is a museum, closed Mondays, and there is a $2 entrance fee.

The Hagia Sophia (Divine Wisdom, the same name as İstanbul's great cathedral) was erected by Emperor Manuel I in the 13th century on the site of an older, smaller church. The structure is on a much more modest scale than the vast İstanbul cathedral of the same name, but Trabzon's Hagia Sophia benefits from the immense talents of Selçuk stone workers who pitched in during construction. The truly distinguishing characteristic of the church, however, is the quality of its frescoes. The paintings are titled with English plaques, although you need to know that the pendentives are the joints between the top of two arches and the dome on top, and north is toward the sea.

Some of the most striking of the many vivid frescoes within are in the narthex, where Christ's miraculous acts are depicted. The vibrant paintings are a quantum leap from the flat Byzantine artwork of earlier centuries, and this has been traced to a late 11th century journey by monks from Europe. These monks brought with them a book whose vivid illustrations used tricks of depth and scale, forever altering the art of the places they visited. The clock tower alongside the church was here before the Comnenis began construction of the Hagia Sophia.

Just off the main road through the citadel, Uzun Yol, is the **Ortahisar Cami**, also called **Fatih Büyük Cami**, formerly an Orthodox church. The basic structure of the Panaghia Chrisokephalos, as it was once called, dates to the 10th century, with extensive remodeling in the 13th century heyday of the Trebizond Empire. During the reign of the Comnenis, this church was the site of their coronation ceremonies, and was appropriately resplendent with a golden dome. Comneni family members were buried on the church grounds.

Like most churches of the period, the Panaghia Chrisokephalos was decorated with frescoes that are now either plastered over or fallen. The church is a fine engineering exercise, with ascending vaults and arches that create a dramatic effect. The building has changed very little in the past thousand years, although a stairway had to be removed to fit a wooden mihrab, and the stone floor, like the frescoes, is covered over.

Due south of Ortahisar Cami, the road climbs to the centerpiece of old Trebizond, the hilltop **Golden Palace of the Comneni**. Be warned, the palace is neither golden nor even palatial. Follow one of the likely looking paths through backyard gardens to the ruins. Children are very likely to come along and offer to show you around (disputes develop: what the boys call "dungeons" the girls call "kitchens"). The highest tower is topped by a flag and visible from a distance.

While the Trebizond Empire controlled affairs in its corner of the world, this palace was its glorious centerpiece. The author Rose Macaulay in *The Towers of Trebizond* has helped fix the beauty of this labyrinthine palace in our minds, but it can be difficult to square that image with the tumbling and overgrown ruin found today. Vines, grasses, and trees have sprung up amid the palace walls, taking advantage of Trabzon's fecund climate. Once the home of royalty, of galleries, wind towers and great audience halls, the eastern palace is now a warren of small residences and garden plots. After winding your way to the outer ramparts, you can scale to the top and look out over the western city. This was once just a remote corner of a palace that straddled the hill from east to west. The western battlements rise directly out of the shallow valley on the west side of the hill, and that, at least, remains quite dramatic. Most of the interior sections have collapsed or burned, but you can still get a sense of the palace's size. This was part of the upper keep, one of three terraced levels that descended toward the sea.

Gülbaharhatun Cami, located across the bridge to the west of the citadel and one long block south, bears the name given to the beautiful and generous Comneni princess, Maria. Gülbaharhatun, or "spring rose" was among the spoils of Fatih Sultan Mehmet's conquest of Trebizond, and she was introduced into the harem of his son Beyazid II. She was a great favorite of Beyazid II, and bore him the son that became the next sultan, Selim I.

The apple, it seems, fell far from the tree. No spring rose, Selim was called Yavuz, or "the Grim." He was a great conqueror with little regard for human life, slaying his grand viziers and attendants with the same alacrity his armies showed in massacring Shi'ite armies and doubling the size of the empire. Historians say nothing about the relationship between young Selim and his mother, but it can be said that the mother won a measure of vengeance for the Ottoman massacre of her male relations, the destruction of Trebizond, and her own "imprisonment" within Beyazid II's harem: Selim forced his father Beyazid II from the throne in 1512 and probably poisoned him.

For his mother, the lad showed much more respect. In the same year, 1512, Selim began construction of a mosque in his mother's ancestral home. Gülbaharhatun is interred in a türbe alongside the mosque.

Nightlife & Eentertainment
Hamams

Both the Sekiz Direkli Hamam and Fatih Hamam are interesting, attractive Turkish baths. The **Sekiz Direkli**, *Moloz Mevkii, Tel. 462 322 1012*, or Eight Column bath is open to women on Thursdays from 8 a.m. to 5 p.m. The **Fatih Hamam** is open to women on Wednesdays at the same hours. A bath and full scrub costs $6.

Sumela Monastery

Sümela Monastery is one of Turkey's great sights, however construction work is expected to continue until 2000. With much of the structure teetering there was no choice but to begin restoration in 1990. As often happens, however, the restoration is robbing the site of some of its mystery. The process is necessary, but somewhat regrettable and inconvenient.

History
It all began when St. Luke painted a black figure of Mary on a piece of the True Cross. Two Athenian monks set out along the Black Sea in the fourth century, at the time of Theodosius the Great, bearing with them the holy icon. Led by dreams and visions, they came upon a cave high above a remote area and established a small church and monastery there, with the icon as its centerpiece. In ensuing years the monastery grew into both an Orthodox religious center and a Byzantine outpost guarding one of the most important passes into Trabzon. Justinian and his general Belisarius are said to have visited and caused a series of lookouts to be built as an early warning system for the city below.

The Persians and Arabs who besieged Byzantium in the seventh century thus had good cause to sack the monastery, and did, although monks were able to spirit away most of the valuables and religious icons and reestablish the monastery when the threat ebbed. Trabzon helped secure funds for the rebuilding project. The monastery continued in its role as a guardian of the critical Zigana Pass down to the Black Sea, and was occasionally attacked by bandits, which led the monks to begin constructing the high walls now in place.

Under the Trapezuntine Empire, Sümela rose greatly in esteem, and **Emperor Alexius Comneni III** (1349-1390) chose the monastery for his coronation and helped fund construction and decoration of the site. The Trapezuntine Empire was, however, nearing its end. When Fatih Sultan Mehmet II seized Trabzon in 1461, he showed characteristic - but remarkable - indulgence of his Christian subjects and left the monastery in peace and the monks with most of their lands intact. While Sultan Mehmet II's grandson **Selim I** (1512-1520) was governor of Trabzon he once fell ill on a campaign and was restored to health at the monastery. In thanks for the monks' help, Selim - a frequent visitor during his eastern campaigns - bestowed lavish gifts on the monastery, including five ornate oil lamps.

The monastery continued to thrive for centuries, and at one point the Ottomans made it a virtual dumping ground for troublesome priests. The population declined from an estimated 1,000 monks and nuns to just 100 by the end of the 19th century, but contributions and alms continued to pour in. Armenians retreated to the monastery during the purges prior to WW I. During the severe economic crisis and warfare of the time the monks were forced to abandon the monastery.

Following the war, the Treaty of Sevres partitioned Turkey, and Sümela was now located outside of Turkey in a Russian/Armenian administered zone, under the oversight of a French governor. The French governor helped restore the monastery, but the partition was never really enforced before Kemal Atatürk's nationalists routed the Greek occupation army in the west and Turkey reclaimed its current lands. The monastery's long life came to an abrupt end in the summer of 1923, when the monks were deported to Greece in the exchange of populations.

Arrivals & Departures

By Bus Tour from Trabzon

Several companies run tours from Trabzon to Sümela, and the tours are both cheap and fairly informative. The best of the tours is offered by **Afacan Tour**, Iskele Cad. No. 40C, Trabzon, *Tel. (462) 321-5804, Fax (462) 321-7001*, with buses departing at 10 a.m. from in front of their offices, just just downhill of Usta Hotel on Karaoğlanoğu Caddesi from the main square. The cost is $6 per person. Ulusoy also offers a tour one half hour later, departing from the south side of the square near the Çınar Lokantası.

By Car

The main southern E-97 highway out of Trabzon, serving Maçka, Bayburt, and Erzurum, also takes you in the direction of Sümela. At Maçka follow the signs to the left marked Sümela and Maryemana, which ascends the left side of a steep gorge, crossing back and forth as you ascend. The ticket booth is 17 kilometers along, and there is a restaurant and gift shop at the trailhead.

Where to Stay

The **Çosandere Pansiyon**, listed in Trabzon's *Where to Stay* section, is located halfway up the Maçka-Sümela road. There are also eight bungalows available at the Sümela trailhead, open year round. Reservations at the bungalows are necessary, however; have the tourism information office call ahead, *Tel. 462 331 1061*.

Seeing the Sights

In addition to a charge at the entrance to the park, there is another fee at the top of the trail. The **monastery** is built into a great natural cave high above the valley floor. The ascent from the parking lot is steep and the trail is usually a little muddy. After a determined 15 minute climb you begin catching glimpses of the monastery's dramatic face, eventually and you ascend a long staircase beneath the old aqueduct and enter the compound from above.

Sümela's facade is one of the best-preserved parts of the monastery, so don't be surprised to descend into what is mostly a set of ruins. If it appears a bomb must have gone off, one did. In the aftermath of the monk's abandonment, an explosion destroyed part of the interior; the Greeks accuse the Turks, the Turks accuse the Greeks. Adding to the damage, the venerable collection of wooden houses burned in the 1930s.

The current restoration work may undermine the mystery of the site, but it has certain clear advantages; you now begin to understand the layout of the interior. The highlights are the chapel and the holy spring. A spring on the underside of the cave's roof drops a trickle of water down through open space into the "fountain," and this water was considered to have healing and purifying properties. The same fountain was also used as a cistern, and connected to the aqueduct.

The chapel, like most of the buildings and frescoes hugging the back wall of the cave, is fairly well preserved. Vandals have gone to great pains to chip away at and scar the many images here, but a beautiful collection of art remains. In many cases the frescoes are at least two layers thick, done and redone over a period of centuries. Despite the damage, the Greek writing and artwork is still largely intact, and you can make out several Biblical tales in the succession of panels by the main church, including the Creation. In the interior of the church - the first thing constructed - are Jesus and Mary paintings that shimmer on the rare occasions when sunshine breaks through the clouds.

During the exchange of populations, the monks were wary of bringing the monastery's great collection of valuables and icons along and secreted them in a hole near the smaller church outside the compound, along the upper path. Later, in secret, they recovered their treasures. There is an alternate path down to the restaurant and parking lot from here.

Chapter 16

Eastern Turkey, generally defined as everything east of Cappadocia and south of the Black Sea, offers fascinating traveling. Historically, you will find fortresses of ancient Ur, mountaintop Bagratid churches, the great tomb at Nemrut Dağ, the Armenian ruin of Ani, and, yes, swimming cats. Better, perhaps, is the hospitality of the people who inhabit this vast land.

The fighting between Turkey and Kurdish separatists in the southeast has eased in recent years. During that long conflict, the U.S. State Department advised against travel to that part of Turkey; and still does as this is written. Still, the atmosphere is much improved, owing to the capture of PKK leader Abdullah Ocalan on the one hand, and the easing of some anti-Kurdish laws on the other.

This book focuses on the northeast, a short distance from the Black Sea, but also provides a blueprint for traveling from Antakya in the southwest to Artvin in the northeast.

Northeastern Turkey

Artvin is the northern gateway to the east. The landscape undergoes a dramatic transformation as you ascend out of the Black Sea basin, leaving its lush greenery behind. The northeast interior of Turkey was once the territory of the **Bagratids**, Christians with a great love of churches and monasteries; many of these monasteries remain today, and are the goal of travelers who head inland. However the landscape and the stark culture alone should lure you through the passes and into the interior.

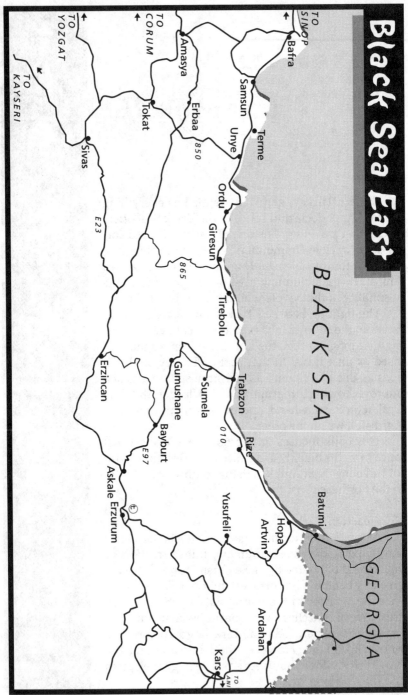

Hikes in the **Kaçkars** are popular, rafting on the **Çoruh River** can be arranged, and for those of you who want to see what the State Department insists you shouldn't, we give you details for a trip through the east. Note that a car is the best way in the northeast corner of Turkey for getting to and away from the monasteries, and that viewing the **Georgian churches** is extremely slow, difficult, and tedious by bus and dolmuş. Conversely, you should stick to major forms of public transportation for any travel southeast of Erzurum, where you are safer from (extremely rare) terrorism than you would be in a car.

Artvin

Artvin is historic, but has little historic to see. The fortress guarding the mountain pass below is on the grounds of a military installation, thus off-limits. Otherwise Artvin is a simple, quietly bustling town with staggering views and quick access to some of the Georgian monasteries. You get the sense that something has changed with your arrival here; the heat lightning, the watchful people, and the steep, barren, silent landscape can be unsettling. You are in the east.

History

The creases in this mountainside have always been used as trade routes, and Artvin sits atop one of the most important routes, following the Çoruh River down to the Black Sea. The distant history of the area is lost, although it was certainly occupied under the Arabs in the seventh century. The Georgians of the **Bagratid Kingdom** established themselves in this mountainous region in the early ninth century, and their rule lasted until the 13th century.

Most of the monasteries and churches date from the 9th and 10th centuries. The Bagratids control of the mountain passes made its neighbors wary of invasion, and the Bagratids proved very able at repelling invaders; only the Selçuks broke through and successfully seized the Bagratid cities (in 1071), and they were forced out just 30 years later. With the Bagratid collapse, the Ottomans seized these lands under Selim I, and they remained crucial to the Ottomans' eastern defenses until the Russians forced the passes during the Russian war of 1886-87.

At that time the Russians seized Kars, Erzurum, and Ardahan, penetrating as far as Artvin. The lands were restored in the Treaty of Lausanne in 1922.

Catching a Buzz in Artvin

The honey in the mountains west of Artvin is infamous. Twice, once during Xenophon's passage in 400 B.C. and again during the Roman General Pompey's campaign against Mithradites in 65 B.C., armies were ravaged by the hallucinogenic effects of the local honey. Pompey's army suffered the most: during their journey through the area the natives left great quantities of honey out for the soldiers to eat, waiting for the men to descend into delirium and illness before attacking and butchering hundreds of helpless soldiers.

Arrivals & Departures

By Bus

If you have arrived by public transportation, you should probably keep going to Yusufeli. The monasteries near Artvin almost all require a car, although taxis will gladly help guide you around the area. Artvin's otogar is located at the riverside, but Artvin itself clings to the mountain slope high above, even above the fortress. From the otogar to the city center you can walk (three hours straight uphill) or catch the minibus at the otogar for 30¢, a ten minute ride.

Public transportation can be excruciatingly slow if you are on a schedule. Buses from Artvin serve Ardahan, Kars (once per day), Yusufeli, Erzurum and other northeast towns, as well as Trabzon, and there is one bus daily continuing all the way to İstanbul.

By Car

Getting here is half the fun. From the direction of the Black Sea you wind your way up the Çoruh River through great gaps in the local mountain range. On the journey, along a surprisingly good road, you're treated to glimpses of old fortifications, many of them tumbled, but some of them, like the old Ottoman post at Borçka, in good condition. From Erzurum in the opposite direction you descend through similarly stark terrain. Upon arrival at the Artvin's otogar, you see a slender tower high above on the far side of the river, a defensive position dating to Selim I's eastern campaigns.

Orientation

The road to Artvin climbs up more than a dozen switchbacks, finally turning onto a relatively flat road called **İnönü Caddesi**. The city's restaurants, hotels, and government buildings are all located here. The city's former lament that it had nowhere flat enough for a soccer field has been solved with a large concrete platform across from the PTT.

Where to Stay & Eat

HOTEL KARAHAN, İnönü Cad. No. 16, Artvin, Tel. (466) 212-1800; Fax (466) 212-2420. Rooms: 48. Credit cards not accepted. Open year-round. Double: $35.

The Karahan's rooms have a Frankensteinian aspect, as if made with odds and ends from the building supply, but it's charming just the same, and by far the best lodging option in Artvin. Guests who come here typically have just a few things on their mind—hiking in the Kaçkars, visiting the Bagratid monasteries, and visiting the city of Ani. The owners at the Karahan expect this, and have helpful advice and suggestions. The hotel's front rooms have gorgeous, endless views. The restaurant serves good, hearty food. One of the Karahan brothers also has a pension in Altıparmak that can be a useful base (listed below).

OTEL KAÇKAR, Hamam Sok. No. 5 (below İnönü), Artvin, Tel. (466) 212-3397. Rooms: 24. Credit cards not accepted. Open year-round. Double: $14.

The Kaçkar offers clean rooms and a kitchen. The hotel is located below Artvin's centerpiece Valiliğli building just off the main street. Ahmet-Bey runs a remarkably tight ship, far superior to most of the budget competitors in town.

KAFKASÖR TATIL KÖYÜ DAĞ EVLERI, Tel. (466) 212-5013.

This is a collection of bungalows in an alpine meadow, some 30 minutes from Artvin. Vacancies can be hard to find in the summer. Phone ahead and enquire.

EFKAR LOKANTA, İnönü Cad., Artvin, Tel. (466) 212-2963.

At the bend in the road as you begin your descent out of Artvin, Efkar has a good, inexpensive menu. The most noteworthy thing about the Efkar is surely the almost-perilous view; it is perched at the edge of a sheer drop-off above the fortress and valley below.

Seeing the Sights

Visiting the Churches & Fortresses Near Artvin

You won't be able to miss the fortress perched above the Çoruh River as you enter town. This is reportedly a fascinating spot, but you'll be unable to visit until the Turkish Army moves to a new location. The picturesque ruins date from the campaigns of Selim I, the Grim. It was Selim who plowed through the enemies that had plagued the Ottomans' eastern borders, wiping out several Persian armies and sacking cities well into modern Iraq. At the end of his campaign he fortified the passes in eastern Anatolia, of which this was one.

The reason for visiting Artvin is to visit the Georgian monasteries nearby. The bulk of these are on the highway linking Artvin to Şavşat, an area sometimes compared to Greece's Mt. Athos. Nearest Artvin is the **Hamamlı Church**, south on the main 950 highway and left at the intersection for Şavşat. Nine kilometers from the intersection a road turns off abruptly for Hamamlı, a harrowing five kilometer drive. The village has a 10th century church with several large paintings. Descending back to the road at the bottom of the gorge, several battered old yellow signs lead you to monasteries above the gorge. Some of the churches and monasteries require a hike, such as that at **Pırnallı**. Following the gorge you emerge at a formidable Bagratid fortress just west of Şavşat. Six kilometers northeast of Şavşat is another church in modern Cevizli, this one offering reliefs of Georgian luminaries.

Returning back toward Artvin, the Ardanuç road cuts off across a bridge to the left and passes south through the spectacular **Cehennum Deresi Kanyonu**, or Hell's Creek Canyon. Unfortunately the Ardanuç road doesn't get you anywhere but Ardanuç, but there you are rewarded by beautiful views and a ruined Bagratid fortress. **Ardanuç** was the Bagratid capital from the 9th century onward, and the clifftop citadel is a 12th century Bagratid structure. In the interior of the battered old fortress is an old Georgian church.

On the road between Artvin and Erzurum, beyond Yusufeli, are several more excellent monasteries and churches, highlighted by the church at **Ösk Vank** and, further south, **Haho** (Bağbaşı).

Trekking in the Kaçkars

There are innumerable trekking options in the region. Below we detail one such trek, but you may want to get input from a local guiding company with experience such as Usta Tours in Trabzon, the Kaçkar Outdoor Sports Center located at the Çiçek Palas Hotel in Yusufeli, one of the guide-run pensions in Ayder such as Cağlayan Hotel, or even, well before arriving, from **Alternatif Turizm**, İstanbul, *Tel. 216 345 6650*.

You should, however, be able to collect information from backpackers emerging from the opposite direction or convince someone to draw something up. If this seems chancy, it is and it isn't; trails are in good shape and receive steady use, and the main trail across to Ayder is pretty clear. If you take a wrong turn, someone will be able to set you right soon enough. If you choose to follow the valley to the Altıparmak massif there's no getting lost, you follow the valley. The Turkish Tourism Ministry publishes a mountaineering guide with a vague map of the Altıparmak-Ayder route.

We describe a route takes you directly through the mountains from south to north, and assumes you won't want to return for a car. From Trabzon, get a bus into Yusufeli, 75 kilometers south of Artvin. The town has an old west mining town flavor to it, although the image is skewed by people putting in at the class 4 and 5 Çoruh River and itinerant trekkers (for information on rafting, contact). Zeytinlik, downstream, has a hot springs at which most rafting trips end and people relax. If you need accommodations in Yusufeli, try the Barhal Hotel overlooking the river.

From Yusufeli get one of the several daily dolmuş headed toward Barhal/Altıparmak, climbing up and out of barren Yusufeli to the moist greenery of the mountains. You want to set out on your trek from Yaylalar, another hour further west, but you may want to spend at least one night here. There are several small family pensions at Barhal, and someone will almost surely offer lodging if you emerge from the dolmuş. If you have any choice in the matter, check in at the **Karahan Pansiyon** (*Tel. (466) 212-1800*, Double: $25); this delightful place is built in the tradition of the area, with long wooden porches and good views. The owners are accustomed to the needs of people who intend to trek across the range to the north and can be a great resource. Nearby **Marsis Pansiyon** is another good option (*Tel. (466) 826-2002*; Double: $24) where you can make plans for your trek.

The **Barhal Kilise**, a 10th century Georgian church, is in great condition and merits a visit. After days and weeks in Turkey, this church is simply jarring; it looks nothing like the domed and barrel vaulted structures so common in Turkey. Barhal Kilise, like others of the Georgian churches, has the tall, slender lines of a western European cathedral.

You may set out from here, but the way is long – five days long. Better to continue to Yaylalar, where, again, you can stay a night or more in a pretty wooden lodging with communal kitchen and wood stoves in the rooms.

You can get directions from here for the route across to **Ayder**, a village on the northern slope; head to the end of the road, then take the trail via Döbe. In Ayder, you'll find several pretty wooden bungalows, a fine hot springs, and dolmuş to Pazar on the Black Sea coast. Among the pleasant wooden hotels at Ayder are the **Cağlayan Hotel** (*Tel. (464) 657-2073*; Double: $20), **Pirekoğlu Hotel** (*Tel. (464) 657-2021*; Double: $14), and **Fora Pansiyon** (*Tel. (464) 657-2024*: Double: $24). All of these hotels are accustomed to trekkers; they can help arrange a guide for you (many are owned by guides) if you strike out on the trails to the south.

The Eastern Circuit

This book offers a traveling circuit that has developed in the past few years, and on which you can be fairly confident of safety. Driving a rental car would offer great freedom, but it remains wisest, while in the southeast, to travel by day using public transportation.

In the following pages, we offer only the bare necessities for a clockwise course through the towns nearest the principal sites in the east; Kars, Doğubeyazit, Van, Malatya, and Şanliurfa. En route, you will want to grill other travelers and the staff at your hotels during your travels.

Kars & Ani

Buses serve the city of Kars from Ankara, Trabzon, and even İstanbul ($12, $9, and $22, respectively). A remarkably cheap train also wends its way all the way from Haydarpaşa station in İstanbul. The winding, 44-hour route passes through Ankara, Kayseri, Erzincan, and Erzurum; the entire trip costs less than $15. A far more convenient option is to fly into Erzurum or Trabzon via Turkish Airlines' daily flight from İstanbul at 6:30 a.m., via Ankara at 8:15 a.m.

Kars has long served as a linchpin to the security of Asia Minor; its loss to the Turks spelled the slow-motion decline of the Byzantine Empire, and it has been fought over as recently as the 19th century, when it was occupied by Russia. Even today, the Turkish military has a strong presence. Poverty also has a strong presence; this is an unforgiving landscape, and one in which the long battle against the PKK has taken a toll.

Arriving in Kars, your first stop is the **tourism information office**. Here the friendly and somewhat bored staffer will check your passport and issue a permit for visiting Ani (which is in a restricted zone along the Armenian border). Sometime before departing for Ani you must stop off at the Kars Museum to pick up your ticket for the ruins, and you should consider a quick run around the museum while there. The city's fanciest hotel is the **Hotel Karabağ** (Faikbey Cad. No. 84, Kars; *Tel. 474 212-3480; E-mail: 474 223-3089;* Double: $55); the **Güngören Hotel** (Halit Paşa Cad. Millet Sok. No. 4, Kars; *Tel. 474 212-5630; Fax 474 223-4821;* Double: $42) is another good option; the **Hotel Temel** (Kazımpaşa Cad. No. 4, Kars. *Tel. 474 222-1276; Fax 474 223-1323;* Double: 30) has been a decent choice for years, and was being renovated as this went to press.

The following day you need to make a 43 kilometer trip to Ani, whether under your own power, by taxi, or as part of a tour; the tourism information office makes arragements. The cost of a trip is typically $50 or so, including waiting time; the more people you have to split the tab, obviously the better.

Ani is worth the trouble. This city was one of the grandest in the world, the centerpiece of Armenia at the height of its power at the end of the first millenium. Many of the beautifully crafted churches are still recognizable, particularly **St. Gregory**. The stonework here provided inspiration for the Selçuks who, under Alp Arslan, seized the city in 1063. The city's decline was dramatic, as successive conquerors from the east, first the Turks, then the Mongols, then the Tatars, damaged and ultimately destroyed the city.

Doğubeyazit & Ishak Paşa Palace
From Kars, head south to **Doğubeyazit**. Buses make the two-leg trip via Iğdir several times daily. The city has a interesting circuit of walls, but is not especially appealing. It is, however, in the foothills of **Mt. Ararat** of Noah's Ark fame. Ararat treks are increasingly difficult to arrange, with occasional PKK (Kurdish rebel) incursions in the area, but you can enquire with a local travel agency. There is a large population of Kurds here, accompanied by a large population of soldiers.

The sight you must see is five kilometers from the city center, **Ishak Paşa Palace**. The palace is four kilometers uphill. Dolmuş make the trip infrequently, and taxis are glad to offer a ride for about $10 both ways. The Palace was built for the local governor, an almost completely autonomous lord of this far-flung Ottoman province. The grandeur of the palace, completed in 1801, reflects the pasha's ability to keep a little something from the tax money generated in his realm. The Silk Route wound past, and one important provincial business was tolling passing caravans. The palace is decorated with beautiful stonework, and almost half of the interior space was dedicated to the paşa's harem. As incredible as the palace is, it was more ornate still before the Russians took advantage of their brief possession of this land to cart off many of the most beautiful relics to the Hermitage Museum in St. Petersburg.

Accommodations in Doğubeyazit are uniformly disappointing. Among these, the cleanest and most hospitable are the **Otel Isfahan** (Isa Geçit Cad. No. 26, Doğubeyazit; *Tel.* 472 215-5289; *Fax* 472 215-2044; Double: $28), the **Işakpaşa Hotel** (Ismail Beşikçi, Doğubeyazit; *Tel.* 472 215-5243; Double: 30), and, at the cheap end, the budget **Saruhan Hotel** (*Tel.* 472 311-3097; Double: $10).

Van & Hoşap Kalesi
From Doğubeyazit, take one of the frequent buses to **Van**. This stretch of road skirts the Iranian border before veering off toward **Lake Van**. The otogar is outside of town, but shuttle buses ordinarily meet arriving buses. Van has an airport, with twice-daily flights to/from Ankara.

Van is located at the ancient capital of **Urartu**, a land populated with an industrious people who emerged from the wreck of the Hittite Empire. They figure prominently in the Bible; Urartu and Ararat, for instance, are written consonant for consonant identically in the vowelless characters of the time. **Van Kalesi**, the Rock of Van, was their original citadel, reinforced and rebuilt through the years, with the final improvements by the Byzantines and Ottomans.

Most of the basic fortifications, such as the long trenches, were built by the Urartians. This citadel still commands the surrounding area from its bluff between the town and the lake.

The lake is vast and well over 1,000 feet deep. The **museum** in town has a striking collection of near Eastern pieces. **Çavuştepe**, 20 kilometers south of Van, was the Urartian royal citadel, and on the same road, 59 kilometers from Van, is **Hosap Kalesi**, a Kurdish fortress dominating another sheer peak. This mazelike castle, located near Güzelsu, was built by Kurdish separatists in the 17th century; that much, at least, has not changed.

Van has a much better selection of hotels than Doğubeyazit. At the upper end, the **Büyük Urartu Hotel** (Hastane Cad. No. 60, Van; *Tel. (432) 212-0660; Fax (432) 212-1610*; Double: $90) by the hospital is a solid hotel with rates that are subject to negotiation; **Hotel Büyük Asur** (Turizm Sok. No. 5, Van; *Tel. (432) 216-8792; Fax (432) 216-9461*; Double: $38) is a well-trafficked and nicely managed option with a good terrace just off of Cumhüriyet Caddesi, south of the PTT; the **Akdamar Hotel** (Kazım Karabekir Cad. No. 56, Van; *Tel. 432 216-8100; Fax 432 212-0868*; Double: $55) is a good choice just west of the intersection with the Van Gölü and Van Seyahat bus companies.

You can try to catch the ferry across Lake Van to Tatvan and bus from there, but the ferry keeps irregular hours and is typically commandeered on the whim of the army. Outside of Fridays and Saturdays it is often better to bus directly on to Malatya from Van.

Malatya & Nemrut Dağı

Malatya has a few interesting sights, but is most useful for its convenience to **Nemrut Dağı**. Kahta in the southwest is closer to the peak and well accustomed to booking trips to Nemrut Dağı, but is itself a difficult place to reach.

Getting to Malatya is not difficult. Frequent buses serve Malatya from Kayseri, Şanliurfa, Van, and Karamanmaraş. From Malatya there are also daily Turkish Airlines flights to/from Ankara ($60 one-way); the departing flight leaves at 5:30 p.m. and is scheduled to allow continued service to İstanbul.

Upon arrival in Malatya stop in at the tourism information office. The staff arranges tours to the Nemrut Dağı. Minibuses typically depart in the early afternoon, arriving at the top four hours later for sunset.

After getting this initial view, often with some helpful information about the surprisingly unimpressive Antiochus I, for whom this was built, you descend to a small hotel. After dinner and some cards you sleep, with a second trip to the summit at sunrise. This, plus the ride back to Malatya and breakfast, costs $32. There are more thorough ways of seeing Nemrut Dağı, but this is a remarkably good option, and less expensive by hundreds of dollars than the deals arranged by most of the people you see at the mountaintop.

If you are spending a night in Malatya—as opposed to staying atop Nemrut Dağı as part of the tourism information trip—you'll find some decent lodging options. The **Malatya Büyük Otel** (Yeni Cami Karşi, Zafer Işhanı No. 1, Malatya; *Tel. 422 321-1400; Fax 422 321-5367;* Double: $27) is in the bazaar, two and one-half blocks north of the tourism information office just beyond the Yeni Cami; **Hotel Beydağı** (Darbakhane Sok. No. 26, Malatya; *Tel. 422 322-4611; Fax 422 323-2258;* Double: $25) is just west of the Malatya Büyük Otel, a block behind the PTT; the best budget option is the **Otel Park** (Atatürk Cad. No. 17; *Tel. 422 321-1691;* Double: $14) one block east of the Tourism Information office, beyond the Belediye.

Chapter 17

The Eastern Mediterranean has always been, and remains, a major crossroads. Central Asia, Africa, and Europe pivot on the axis near present-day Antakya: Hittite armies checked the advance of the Pharoahs, Alexander broke the back of the Persian Empire in open battle at Issus, and Romans, Byzantines, Arabs, and Ottomans have marched here. The legacy continues; a great international pipeline from Kazakhstan is being built to terminate at Ceyhan, near Tarsus on the coast.

The character of the coast varies. The Syrian border is mountainous, with the Turkish region (the Hatay) encircling the great natural Iskendrun Bay. West of Antakya (ancient Antioch) the coast opens into vast low-lying plains, these covered with rich alluvial soil; the wide-open spaces of the Çukurova plain (Bibilical Goa) and the gentle curve of the coastline earned this place the ancient name of "Smooth Cilicia." Continuing westward, an abrupt change occurs at Silifke; Smooth Cilicia gives way to "Rough Cilicia," 300 kilometers of inhospitable, mountainous terrain that drops abruptly into the sea. The roughness was not only textural; pirates and outlaws have often thrived in the area, free of meddlesome notions of law and order. Beyond Cilicia the Eastern Mediterranean proper ends at Alanya, and the coast eases into floodplains that end at Antalya.

The roads from the Eastern Mediterranean into central Anatolia have always been few, constrained by a few celebrated passes. The first of these, inland of Silifke, is where Frederick Barbarossa marched the armies of the Second Crusade, dying at a river crossing. The second, and greatest, of these, is a great natural cleft in the Taurus Mountains due north of Tarsus; there stand the Cilician Gates, key to the interior.

Antakya

Even in its heyday as the provincial capitol of Roman Syria, Antakya was never a city of great size. Its location brought lucrative commerce to its doors, of which it ever kept a share, filling the coffers of businessmen, conferring great power on its rulers, and helping evangelists reach a cosmopolitan audience. It was here, then, that St. Peter established the first known Christian church, and Antioch remained a center of Christian thought and learning for those critical hundreds of years when the religion was virtually unknown, then actively persecuted.

Antakya is close to the Syrian border, and you will find its citizenry closer to Arabs in appearance, cuisine, and praying habits than people elsewhere in Turkey.

Antakya stands in a river valley flanked by mountains, and precious little of its long-faded glory remains. The principal sights are the cave church of St. Peter, the glorious collections of mosaics in the museum and elsewhere, and the Titus and Vespasian Tunnel.

History

Antioch was founded in 300 B.C., soon after the death of Alexander the Great, by one of the conquerors former generals, Seleucus Nicator (321-280 B.C). The city bore the name of the general's father. The Seleucid Empire, virtually unknown today, was arguably the most successful of the empires founded by Alexander's successors. In the wars of succession among the four principal diadochoi, Lysimachos defeated Antigonus in the Battle of Ipsus in 301 B.C., after which Seleucus defeated Lysimachos at the Battle of Corupedium in 281 B.C. With this victory, Antiochus effectively seized control of a three-quarters share of the known world—from India in the east to Greece in the west, leaving out only the African lands of Ptolemy. Selecus died soon after the battle, at the moment his empire was at its very zenith of power; the borders of this empire were unsustainable, and in short order the legacy of Antiochus was an empire, if such is the right term, in Syria.

The Seleucid Empire endured for more than 200 years, growing wealthy and decadent off the commerce that flowed past its gates. The empire was conquered, and Antiochus seized, by the Armenian Tigranes the Great in 83 B.C. In short order, Tigranes was defeated by the Roman

Lucullus, and Antioch found new stability as the Roman capital of Syria in 64 B.C.

Antioch continued to prosper under Roman rule, becoming one of the principal cities of the far-flung empire. Merchants, soldiers, and saints made their way here; the latter included Saints Peter and Paul, who found among the cosmopolitan citizens of Antioch rich soil in which to plant the seeds that would someday flower into the Christian church. Not only did Christianity take root here, hybrid religions did so, as well. Many of the fine points of Christian theology were first argued here--the Arian Heresy, for instance, which deemed Christ a man like any other, imbued with the spirit of God but a mortal entity, not a holy one.

Even as Rome declined and was replaced in the east by the rule of Constantine in present-day Istanbul, Antioch remained powerful. The great city fell at last not to armies, but to a tremendous earthquake that toppled its towers and broke its magnificent walls. Historians tell us that hundreds of thousands were killed in the sixth century catastrophe. Soon afterward, Persian armies emerged from the east to sack the city, and Byzantine efforts to reassert control of Antioch were short-lived; the history of the seventh century and beyond is one of onslaught after onslaught: Persians, Saracens, Arabs, and Turks, to name but a few. Crusaders seized the city and established a kingdom here in the late 12th century, but this, too, was not to last: in 1268 the city was besieged and taken by Egyptian Mamelukes, who burned, looted, and destroyed it.

This final defeat ended the primacy of Antioch in the region. Other cities arose, and Antioch faded from history for centuries, only regaining something of its stature under the late Ottoman Empire.

Arrivals & Departures
By Bus

Antakya's main otogar is just 500 meters north of the center of town, on the east side of the river. Bus service is frequent in all directions, including into Syria:
• Ankara: $14, 10 hours, 6 per day
• Antalya: $14, 14 hours, 5 per day
• İstanbul (transfer to Cappadocia at Aksaray): $20, 17 hours, 8 per day
• Damascus, Syria: $12, 8 hours, 2 per day
• Aleppo, Syria: $8, 4 hours, 4 per day

Orientation

Antakya is divided by the Asi River (the ancient Orontes), with most hotels and restaurants (and the museum) clustered around both sides (particularly the east side) of the Ata bridge, which is itself at the terminus of most roads from the west. The tourism information office is one kilometer north of the central roundabout by the Rana bridge on Ataturk Caddesi *(Tel. (326) 216-0610)*.

Where to Stay

Antakya has many lodging options, but precious little deserving of recommendation. Tourism to the city remains limited, and hotels reflect that.

ANTIK BEYAZIT HOTEL, *Hükümet Cad. No. 4, Antakya 31070. Tel. (326) 216-2900; Fax (326) 214-3084; Email: bbeyazit@hotmail.com; Web: www.antakya.com/antikbeyazitoteli. Rooms: 27. Credit cards accepted. Open year-round. Double (off-season discount available): $80 (breakfast not included).*

The Antik Beyazit is housed in a mansion dating from the last years of the Ottoman Empire. The restoration to the exterior is diligent; the rooms within are solid and decent with A/C, even if they do not live up to the promise of the building itself. To get there: from the east side of the river across from the Archaelogical Museum, follow Hükümet Caddesi south, veering inland.

BÜYÜK ANTAKYA HOTEL, *Atatürk Cad. No. 8, Antakya 31070. Tel. (326) 213-5860; Fax (326) 213-5869. Rooms: 72. Credit cards accepted. Open year-round. Double (off-season discount available): $85 (breakfast not included).*

This is the largest hotel in Antakya, and its reputation as the finest in town remains despite signs of neglect—worn carpets and bathroom grout that's dark with mold. For all that, it continues to have the best set of amenities in town (including A/C), and the service is good. To get there: The Büyük Antakya is located just north of the turnabout by the Archaeological Museum.

ONUR HOTEL, *Istiklal Cad., Istiklal Sok. No. 14, Antakya. Tel. (326) 216-2210; Fax: (326) 216-2214. Rooms: 36. Credit cards accepted. Open year-round. Double (off-season discount available): $43 (breakfast included).*

Opened in 1999, this is one of the newest hotels in town, and a fine compromise between the expense of the nicer hotels and the shoddiness of the budget hotels. Rooms offer air conditioning and television. To get there: The Onur is about 250 meters south of the Otogar on Istiklal Caddesi; from the town center, follow the river north on the east bank until just past the footbridge, then veer inland and follow Istiklal Caddesi north.

Where to Eat

The food of the Hatay, as the region is known, is predictably influenced by Syria; expect to feast on dates, hummous, and spicy dishes seldom found elsewhere in Turkey.

SARAY RESTAURANT, *Hürriyet (Hükümet) Caddesi No. 19/1, Antakya.*

The Saray is a mainstay of Antakya dining, both inexpensive and excellent. Food is served in a garden courtyard, or within if you prefer. The Saray is just across the bridge from the Archeological Museum, on the south (downstream) side of the Ulu Camii and inland of Tivoli Restaurant.

Seeing the Sights

If you do nothing else while in Antakya, visit the **Archaeological Museum** (8:30 a.m.-noon, 1:30 p.m.-5 p.m., closed Mondays. $3), home to the world's finest collection of mosaics.

Entering the museum, you are greeted by two statues of Venus, a marker that the museum does not concentrate on mosaics to the exclusion of all else. From the entry hall, you move through four large mosaic salons, the first three of which feature mosaics recovered from ruins near the sea at Daphne.

The centerpiece of the first salon is the Four Seasons, a second century AD mosaic depicting a boar hunt. Other mosaics here, and throughout the museum, are well signed. In the second salon, a depiction of the rape of Ganymede by Zeus (in the form of an eagle) is the most arresting. The third salon has several interesting mosaics—including a hunchbacked Priapus and villagers attacking an evil eye—but the central feature is a glorious mosaic of Oceanus and Thetis from the fourth century. The fourth salon features mosaics from Antakya and Tarsus, including a fine hunting scene, Dionysius in true Dionysian revel, and Orpheus pacifying wild animals with his lyre.

Mosaics continue into the hall, but the fifth and sixth salons feature more workaday collections of coins, statues, and sarcophagi. The range of artifacts is impressive; some are Assyrian and Hittite. The garden also has several fine mosaics.

Leaving the museum, you might want to consider a detour to **Konak Sinema**, which shows blockbuster American films in English with Turkish subtitles. In the heat of summer, this is a fines respite from the heat. The cinema is located immediately behind the PTT, across the roundabout from the Archaeological Museum.

Crossing the river from the museum to the east bank and heading north (upstream) and inland, you'll enter the **Antakya bazaar**. This is a fine place to browse for figs and dates, textiles, and anything else you fancy. The bazaar extends north as far as the otogar.

Saint Peter Church (Senpiyer Kilisesi; 8 a.m.-noon, 1:30 p.m.-5 p.m., closed Monday; free) is located three kilometers northeast of the center of Antakya, a $3 taxi ride or a 45 minute walk. To get there from the east bank of the Asi River, head northeast until you hit Kurtuluş Caddesi, then head due north until you come to the signed turnoff for St. Peter's Church; the church is carved into the hillside another 500 meters on.

The validity of claims that St. Peter preached here have been questioned, but there is no denying that this is the oldest known place of Christian worship. For the first embattled Christians, their religion was grounds for ostracism, even execution, and the meetings were held in secret. To the left of the apse is a collapsed tunnel that is said to have been an escape tunnel for those first Christians. In time, as Christianity won a foothold in the Roman Empire, the grotto was improved; mosaic floors were introduced in the fourth century, the façade in the 12th century by Crusaders who settled at Antioch. The dripping water within the cave is credited with healing powers.

Orthodox and Roman Catholic services continue to be held at the Church (Sunday mornings and afternoons, respectively). The Church is maintained by the Catholic Church, and you can contact the caretakers directly (*Tel. (326) 215-6703*). The hillside is honeycombed with tunnels, and a path winds up to reliefs that include the mysterious relief of a veiled figure looking out over the city.

Southwest from Antakya: The **Monastery of Saint Simeon** is located 7 kilometers south of Uzunbağ, near Karaçay on the Antakya-Samandag road, and is not serviced by public transport (you can find taxis in Karaçay). The monastery is named for Simeon Stylites the Younger, who, like the Elder before him, ascended a slender column in the 4th century AD and stayed there for 25 years. The depth and faith of this commitment attracted other stylites—dozens, perhaps hundreds of Christian ascetics ascended columns of their own. In addition, an entire monastery complex was constructed at the foot of Saint Simeon's column. The base of Simeon's column remains, as do the foundations of the monastery.

Continuing west to Samandağ, turn right to Çevlik, 6 kilometers north. The **Titus and Vespasian Tunnel** (8 a.m.-dusk; $1.50) is really a system of channels and a tunnel, built for the purpose of preventing flooding in nearby Seleucia as Piera and forestalling siltation of the ancient harbor there. This marvel of Roman civil engineering requires a good bit of hiking, and you will need a flashlight: someone will be on hand to help you climb up, along the channel, and on to an old Roman bridge, from which you can access the tunnel. The seaside town of Çevlik is fairly charmless.

North from Antakya: **Bakras Castle** is located 4 kilometers west of the main highway, south of Belen. This fortress was first built in the 4th century AD, and was substantially improved upon by the Knights Templar, whose legendary military engineers erected a system of fortresses along the Mediterranean that included Crac de Chevaliers. As the power of the Templars waned in the region the fortress fell to the Arabs, from whom it was wrested by Ottoman Sultan Selim the Grim in the sixteenth century. The fortress rarely receives visitors, but is accessible by foot from Bakras village. To get to the village you'll want a car.

East from Antakya: If you intend to cross the border into Syria at Bab al Hawa/Cilvegözlü, you will do well to have made Visa arrangements beforehand. The It is usually possible for U.S. and Canadian citizens to make a border crossing without a Visa, but it will cost a premium ($100 versus $60) and add excitement; dull border crossings are always best. If your passport contains stamps from visits to Israel, you will be denied entry to Syria. You can make arrangements for a Syria visa from home or in Ankara (see Ankara section).

Adana

Adana is the fourth-largest city in Turkey, the urban manifestation of the rich plains of Çukorova. There is little to recommend this city, but its airport and location on the E-5 Highway near the intersection north through the Cilician Gates means it might fit into your plans. Adana is just 12 kilometers from the military airfields at Incirlik.

History

Adana is thought to be located on the site of the Hittite city of Danunas. The great age of the city's foundation did not translate into commercial or political importance, however; bracketed by Antioch to the east and Tarsus to the west, Adana was ever an afterthought in the region. For all that, the agricultural wealth of the Çukorova Plain meant that Adana thrived, and under the Romans it received considerable attention, including the great stone bridge that still spans the Seyhan River. The city fell to Ottoman Sultan Selim the Grim in 1515.

Arrivals & Departures

The Adana airport has daily flights to and from Ankara, Izmir, and Istanbul, as well as less frequent direct flights to international destinations including Northern Cyprus. The Adana airport is located 4 kilometers west of town, and a taxi will cost you $5.

The otogar is also located west of Adana, north of the airport. Minibuses, dolmuş, and bus company service buses offer frequent service to the center of town. In town, most bus companies have offices just north of the main E-5 highway on Ziya Paşa Caddesi, just west of the Tourism Information offices.

Orientation

Adana is bisected by the E-5 highway (which goes by the name Turan Cemal Beriker Bulvarı), and the north-south axis of the city is Atatürk Caddesi/Saydam Caddesi. The Tourism Information office (Phone: (322) 359-1994) is located at this intersection, and most hotels are tucked into the streets southwest of that office. A U.S. Consulate is located north of town on Ataturk Caddesi, at the intersection with Vali Yolu, *Tel. (322) 453-9106.*

Where to Stay

Adana traffics in business people and military officials, and there are several excellent hotels catering to them. The lack of tourism, however, has done little to incent Adana's hoteliers to create good mid-range accommodations, however.

OTEL SEYHAN, *Turhan Cemal Beriker Bulvari No. 18, Adana. Tel. (322) 457-5810; Fax (322) 454-2834; Email: info@otelseyhan.com.tr; Web: www.otelseyhan.com.tr. Rooms: 140. Credit cards accepted. Open year-round. Double (off-season discount available): $125 (breakfast not included).*

The Seyhan is the status address in the center of Adana, equipped with all the amenities you would expect of a top-flight hotel. To get there: The Seyhan is locted on the north side of the main highway through town, just west of Atatürk Caddesi.

ADANA SURMELI HOTEL, *Inönü Cad. No. 151, Adana. Tel. (322) 351-7321; Fax (322) 351-8973; Email: none; Web: none. Rooms: 116. Credit cards accepted. Open year-round. Double (off-season discounts available): $90 (breakfast not included).*

A step down from Otel Seyhan, the four-star Surmeli is a solid hotel in its own right. Amenities include air conditioning, television, and minibar. To get there: Adana Surmeli is opposite the Ethnography Museum in the neighborhood behind the Tourism Information office.

HOTEL MERCAN, *5 Ocak Meydanı, Melekgirmez Carşısı, Adana. Tel. (322) 351-2603. Rooms: 24. Credit cards not accepted. Open year-round. Double (off-season discounts available): $18 (breakfast included).*

A clean, decent option in the budget range, offering en suite showers and attentive, knowledgeable staff. To get there: head south from the Tourism Information office on Saydam Caddesi, turning left after the roundabout on 5 Ocak Meydanı and continuing one block.

Where to Eat

Adana Kebap is famous throughout the country, a spicy alternative to standard Turkish lamb kebap. What better place to sample it than in the town for which it is named? Non-Turks are likely to get more expensive rates than Turks, and a gratuity might be added into your bill.

YENI ONBAŞLAR, *Atatürk Cad., Adana. Tel. (322) 363-2084. Credit cards not accepted. Inexpensive.*

Known for good Adana kebap as well as for its great location at the intersection of the main highway and Atatürk Caddesi across from the Tourism Information office, Yeni Onbaşlar is a good spot for a cheap, filling meal.

Seeing the Sights

Within Adana, the most interesting sight is a work in progress. The **Sabanci Merkez Camii**, located where the highway crosses the Seyhan River, is a massive mosque being built by the head of the spectacularly wealthy Sabanci family. According to the literature, the mosque will be the largest in the Middle East, but at the time of this writing it remained incomplete.

South of the mosque, the **"Tas Kopru"** (Stone Bridge) is a sixteen-arch bridge constructed during the reign of Roman Emperor Hadrian; incredibly, it remains in use today.

The **Archaeological Museum** (8:30-noon, 1 p.m.-5 p.m., $1.50), on the west bank of the river on the north side of the main highway, is a good place to while away an hour. The sarcophagi and statuary have been recovered from throughout the region

Dolmuş depart from the south side of the highway across from the Sabanci Camii for the beaches at Karataş, 50 kilometers due south of Adana.

Sights Near Adana

Traveling east from Adana, you will see **Yilan Kalesi** (Snake Fortress) atop a peak to the south, 12 kilometers west of Ceyhan. The origin of the name is unknown; rest assured it has more to do with legend than with snakes at the site. With your own transportation you can follow a road three kilometers south of the highway to visit the fortress, and see a fine example of medieval military engineering, complete with towers, cisterns, inscriptions, and a fine, unobstructed view out over the Seyhan winding away toward the Mediterranean.

With your own vehicle, two isolated, fascinating historic sites can be seen in a long day trip from Adana to Anavarza and Karatepe. Without your own transport, seeing just one of these two sites will take most of your time.

Anavarza (Anabarzus) is located four kilometers east of the Ceyhan-Kozan highway, 23 kilometers north of Ceyhan. Public transportation between the highway and Anavarza is rare, despite the town at the site of the same name. The ruins of the medieval fortress on the site loom above the Cukurova plain, built atop a great bluff. A walled settlement has been present here since at least the seventh century BC; its ruins date from the Roman and Byzantine Empires, with finishing touches put on by a period of Arab and Armenian rule.

Anavarza has been badly damaged by earthquakes, but the damaged remains definitely reward the intrepid. Within town, the modest **Anavarza museum** displays a beguiling mosaic of Thetis; the road continues through a manmade defile cut into the limestone slope, with the stadium off to the right and the walled city to the left. Exploring the walled city will yield churches, rock-cut tombs, arches and several buildings; more difficult, and rewarding, is the grueling hike up the rock-cut steps behind the theatre to the medieval fortress. The fortress, constructed in the 8th century by Haroun al-Rashid, was improved under its subsequent occupants, the Armenians, to become a gem of military engineering deemed impregnable. The earthquakes that have wracked this area have badly damaged the fortress and the Armenian Church within, but it remains a fascinating example of military engineering. Bring water and a bite to eat.

Karatepe (8 a.m.-noon, 1:30 p.m.-5:30 p.m. during summer; abbreviated hours in winter) is even further afield, set on a hill that juts out into an artificial lake. Karatepe was the key to rediscovery of the language of the Hittite Empire, one of the most significant archaeological sites in Turkey. For the beauty of its sculpture and inscription, as well as its setting within the borders of **Karatepe Aslantaş National Park**, a visit to Karatepe is rewarding. This is a fine place to bring a picnic lunch.

In theory dolmuş should ply the route between Kırmıtlı and Karatepe, but they run so rarely as to be miraculous. The direct route from Adana is via the freeway, through Ceyhan and on to the Kadirli turnoff at Osmaniye; from the turnoff, follow the posted route to Kırmıtlı and on to the national park. From Anavarza, follow signs to Kadirli, continue just beyond in the direction of Andırın, then follow the winding track 20 kilometers to Karatepe. There is a park entry fee of $2 per vehicle and $.75 per person, as well as a $1 fee to enter the museum. The site has facilities, most of which are designed to serve the excavation work that has been ongoing since the early 1970s. Because this excavation continues, you will be asked to surrender your camera upon entering the site; all visitors to the palace grounds are guided.

A palace for kings was probably built on this site soon before 1200 B.C., within a generation or two of the sacking of Troy. It is likely that the zenith of this palace corresponds to the date of the many inscriptions found within, near to 730 B.C. By this time the Hittite Kingdom was a fading memory, carried forward in memory and a fading language by a few soon-to-be extinguished kingdoms in eastern Asia Minor. The end of these kingdoms seems to coincide with the abandonment of this site; it was virtually unused for millenia afterward.

Entrance to the palace grounds is gained through the southern gate, ten minutes along a path through the pines. The gate stands guarded by worn lions and sphinxes. The many pictoral inscriptions (orthostats) are quite recognizable—most depict a specific king (Asitawandas) at feast and at play in his palace. The ruins within are limited, but they have the richness of all recent finds—most of what you see has been unearthed in the last three decades, and some of it has not yet been documented in journals and reports. The most significant section of town is near the north (lower) gate, again flanked by lions and sphinxes. It is here that archaelogists discovered inscriptions in Phoenician and hieroglyphic Hittite; these were the levers used by Professor Helmuth Bossert and a team of linguists and historians to crack the Hittite language in 1947.

Cukurova

The slopes of the Taurus Mountains rise from the shores of the Eastern Mediterranean, on the southern coast of Turkey, in a steady ascent from the white, foam-fringed rocks to the peaks. They then spread inland, at a tangent to the curve of the coast. Clouds in white masses always float over the sea. The coastal plains between the mountains and the shore are of clay, quite smooth, as if polished. Here the soil is rich. For miles inland the plain holds the tang of the sea, its air still salt and sharp. Beyond this smooth ploughed land the scrub of the Çukurova begins. Thickly covered with a tangle of brushwood, reeds, blackberry brambles, wild vines and rushes, its deep green expanse seems boundless, wilder and darker than a forest.

--Yaşar Kemal, *Memed, My Hawk*. The Harville Press, London, 1997

Kizkalesi

The vast Cilician plateau is bordered in the west by the Göksu river near Silifke. It is here that the long, smooth roads from the east fork—one climbing north through a high, stunning gorge toward the Anatolian plain, the other ascending the steep western track along the coast of rough Cilicia. While hardly undiscovered, the area sees relatively limited tourism given its critical mass of stunning sights at Kizkalesi, Kanlidivane, Uzuncaburc, and Cennet ve Cehennum; what tourism there is is centered on the white sand beaches and fairy-tale castle of Kizkalesi.

History

This crossroads region is dense with interesting ruins, and the sea castle at **Kizkalesi** (Maiden's Castle) is one of the most interesting—and certainly the most photogenic—of them all. The fortress is located 190 meters offshore, built atop a barren stony island that was the refuge of pirates for long centuries before Byzantine admiral Eugenius commissioned its construction in 1104. The Maiden's Castle gains its name from a tale, worth retelling if not believing. Once upon a time, an early death from snakebite was foretold for a princess. Her father the king, much distressed, had a castle built offshore for the princess, thinking to outfox fate by keeping her far from snakes. Alas, a fruit basket delivered to the princess concealed the snake, as prophesied, and it delivered the fatal bite to the princess.

The fortress, paired with the larger **Corycus fortress** on the mainland just east of Kizkalesi town, formed part of a great defensive cordon along the eastern Mediterranean. This network, constructed and improved during the long reign of Emperor Alexius Comnenus, were part of Byzantine retrenching against the Turks and Arabs in the grim aftermath of the Byzantine defeat at Manzikert in 1071. Alas for the Byzantines, most of their fortresses were in the hands of Selcuks, Arabs, and even their Crusader "allies" within a century; Kizkalesi and its sister Corycus passed peacefully to the Armenians, then the Latins. The fortress was seized by force by the Karaman Turks in 1448, from whom it was wrested, in turn, by the Ottomans in the 1480s.

Corycus was originally settled long before the time of Herodotus, who mentions it. Its fortunes waxed under Roman rule, but the temples and structures of the city were pulled apart to strengthen the medieval fortifications, and little can be seen today outside of the two fortresses.

Arrivals & Departures

The roads to the east are straight and clear. The road from Silifke north is in excellent shape, and follows a beautiful route that winds high above the Göksu river and on to the low plains near Mut, then on past the ruins at Alahan and to the mile-high Sertavul pass beyond. The two-lane road to the west begins crawling upward just beyond Silifke, and is soon hugging sheer valley walls, winding high above the sea on its way toward Anamur. If you are driving, the road west requires patience.

Buses pass through Kizkalesi frequently in both directions (east and west), and you can secure tickets from bus agencies in town. Silifke is a major transportation hub, so if you are heading north or west you can find tickets at the bus station there. Adana: two hours, $3, hourly; Ankara: seven hours, $13, five times daily; Antalya: nine hours, $10, hourly in summer; Cappadocia (Nevşehir, via Mersin): seven hours, $12, six times daily; Konya: four hours, $8, half-hourly.

Orientation

Kizkalesi town is built up between a fine sand beach overlooking Maiden's Castle and the coast highway. This small town is given over almost entirely to the business of tourism, and is certainly less idyllic than it once was, but it remains a pleasant place to spend a few days. Thre is no tourism information office.

Where to Stay

With its fine sand beach and picture-postcard setting, Kızkalesi is the most pleasant place to stay in the region, although many of its accommodations are the worse for wear. The hotels listed below are all fine choices; each of them has staked a claim to a section of the beach.

CLUB & HOTEL BARBAROSSA, *33790, Kızkalesi. Tel/Fax (324) 523-2089; Email: clubbarbarossa@ixir.com. Rooms: 103. Credit cards accepted. Open year-round. Double (30% off-season discount): $70 (including half board).*

The Barbarossa is the best of the hotels in the increasingly cramped area built right up against the beach. The whitewashed buildings are fanned out toward the sea, built around a large pool and 150 paces of green lawn that opens onto the sand. The grounds are pleasant, with climbing vines, palm trees, and a liberal scatter of column drums and amphorae. The rooms are decent, with air conditioning, television, and views over the grounds and toward the sea. Buffet meals are served outside through summer. To get there: the Barbarossa is near the western end of the Kızkalesi beach.

HOTEL SAADET, *33790, Kızkalesi. Tel/Fax (324) 523-2173; Email: none; Web: none. Rooms: 12. Credit cards accepted. Open year-round. Double (20% off-season discount): $35 (including breakfast).*

Hotel Saadet, on a lane just east of Barbarossa Hotel, is a gem. Opened by a young German-born Turk, Timur, the Saadet is small, ambitious, and exceptionally clean. The location, down the street from the beach, is convenient, if not scenic. The details of each room are unusually fine and, well, German; wire-hung halogen lights, double-paned sliding glass balcony doors, nice furniture, and quality fixtures in the bathrooms. Phone, TV, and air conditioning in rooms. The service is friendly and helpful. To get there: turn at the Barbarossa sign, then take the next left toward the sea.

HOTEL RAIN, *33790, Kızkalesi. Tel. (324) 523-2782; Fax (324) 523-2040; Email: info@oztoprain.com; Web: www.oztoprain.com. Rooms: 18. Credit cards accepted. Open year-round. Double (20% off-season discount): $35 (including breakfast).*

Like the Saadet, Hotel Rain is antiseptically clean, with spacious rooms, tile floors and little in the way of views. This is a fine choice. The hotel has its own section of beach just 100 feet down the road, and rooms have air conditioning, but no TV. The hotel's owners also run a café, a travel agency, and a jeweler; expect some cross-promotional inquiries while there.

HOTEL YAKA, *Kızkalesi. Tel: (324) 523-2041; Fax (324) 523-2448; Email: yakahotel@superonline.com. Rooms: 16. Credit cards accepted. Open March through October. Double (20% off-season discount): $30 (including breakfast).*

The Yaka is set back from the waterfront some 100 yards, far enough to offer a little elbow room. Rooms offer balconies, air conditioning, ceiling fans, and coffee-makers, but the location back from the beach isn't ideal. Bathrooms are unattractive, but clean. The restaurant on the premises serves food at standard prices for the area.

Where to Eat

All the locals who can't afford to open a hotel have opened restaurants; you'll not be wanting for dining options. There are a few spots in town that stand out. The common wisdom is the best dining is in the waterfront fish restaurants at Narlikuyu, a few kilometers west; we did not find the restaurants there to warrant their reputation.

SULTAN ABLA, *Barbaros Oteli Sokak, Kızkalesi. Tel (324) 523-2597. Open year-round. Credit cards not accepted. Inexpensive.*

Located on a back street 150 meters from the beach (behind Kilikya Hotel, near the Titanic Restaurant), Sultan Abla is the closest thing left to a local secret. The house specialty is mantı—best described as mini-ravioli—($2); other excellent dishes are stuffed eggplant and stew ($1.50 apiece) and our favorite, the Icli Kofte ($2).

CAFÉ RAIN, *33790, Kızkalesi. Tel. (324) 523-2782; Fax (324) 523-2040. Credit cards accepted. Inexpensive/Moderate.*

The Café Rain, inland some 100 feet behind the Café Nur, boasts better food and better prices. The Saç Tava—meat stewed in tomato sauce with garlic, onions, and peppers—is delicious ($3.50). Other bar food, including sandwiches, are decent. As at the Hotel Rain, you might be encouraged to try the owners' other local businesses (and the travel agency really is quite good).

HONEY RESTAURANT & BAR, *Kızkalesi. Tel. (324) 523-2438. Open year-round. Credit cards not accepted. Inexpensive/Moderate.*

The Honey, whose signage reads "Save the Planet," is the most atmospheric spot in town, and you can't miss it as you enter town—it's on the highway across from the Kızkalesi Mosque. Tucked away under the Honey's wood eaves, amid the hanging plants, you're likely to find a couple of German expatriates sipping a drink and having an omelette ($1.50), schnitzel ($3), or kebap ($2.25). A great retreat after you've had too much sun.

In Narlikuyu
INCI BALIK RESTAURANT, *Canatan Sok. No. 19, Narlikuyu. Tel. (324) 723-3281. Open year-round. Credit cards not accepted. Moderate.*

The setting for the Inci Balık and its fellow restaurants is lovely, on a shallow, chalky-blue bay. Each restaurant is perched above the sea, and serves fresh seafood, primarily çupra (sea bass), levrek (sea bream), and lagos (snapper). Lunch will cost $8, and prices should be fixed before breaking bread.

Seeing the Sights

Given the critical mass of interesting sights in the neighborhood of Kızkalesi, the area is lightly touristed. We'll address the sights within Kızkalesi town first, then turn our attention to the rewards further afield.

Upon arrival, your eye (and your camera lens) will be drawn to the impossibly beautiful sea **castle of Kızkalesi** 190 meters offshore. The great circular towers punctuate a high inner wall and a somewhat lower sea wall, and the castle occupies the entire island on which it was built.

Small boats ferry visitors back and forth to the island throughout the day—enquire at the long pier near the eastern end of the beach ($4 for a round trip) or check with your hotel. You can also get to Kızkalesi under your own power by renting a paddleboat ($5 for two hours) or, if you're in good shape, by making the 190 meter swim.

Once on the island, you'll want to have some sandals or shoes along to make the most of your exploration. Entrance is via the gate in the east wall (above which you'll note a dedication inscribed in Armenian) and once within you can climb a set of stairs and follow trails along the battlements. There is little of note within the castle, but you will find many cisterns and fine views out over the sister castle on shore.

The **land castle at Corycus** is worthy of a visit as well; less scenic but more interesting than its waterbound counterpart (dawn-dusk, $2). The fortress, located just east of town—certainly within walking distance—is surrounded by a moat (now dry) and a double circuit of defensive walls. The walls and buildings are built largely of stone recycled from ancient Corycus (whose ruins and tombs are scattered east of the fortress). Entrance to the fortress is afforded through breaches in the sea wall and through the arched sea gate; it is from near here that a slender mole once connected the land and sea castles.

Entrance to the inner keep can be gained from the east side; it is here that the fortress was most heavily fortified, and the former gates are located here. Within the inner section you will find three Armenian churches and a single cistern.

To see the other sites in the region, it's best to have your own transportation or to join a guided trip. Öztop's Rain Travel Agency is recommended; located on the same street as Hotel Rain, they offer affordable day trips to the prinicipal sites in the region. Öztop offers different trips from one day to the next; here are a few we recommend. Trip 1: Cennet & Cehannum, Uzuncaburc, Aya Tekla, with lunch: $25. Trip 2: Alahan monastery, with lunch: $30. Trip 3: Adamkayalar: $8. Trip 4: Kanlidivane: $25.

East of Kızkalesi

To the east, **Adam Kayalar** (Man Rocks) is the site of a set of high reliefs carved in the wall of a deep, scenic gorge 7 kilometers northeast of Kızkalesi. The set of reliefs appears to date to Roman occupation of the area. Getting there is the trick; the road is now signed, but at the site you must hike westward more than a kilometer on foot, after which you descend an ancient stair carved from living rock. Rumors of treasure secreted in the cliff wall have led treasure hunters to seriously damage several of the reliefs, but they remain impressive.

Kanlidivane is located further to the east. As you drive east from Kızkalesi, you pass the husk of the ancient island fortress of Sebaste three kilometers along; the site is now on dry land, and the area is peppered with tombs and other jetsam—it does not warrant a stop. Six kilometers beyond, find the signed turnoff for Kanlidivane. From there, the road winds in and up to Kanlidivane (ancient Kanytelis).

The name Kanlidivane, derived from "place of madness and blood," derives in equal parts from the crimson color of the cliff walls and the rumors that swirl around the chasm at the site, into which, it is said, criminals were once hurled to their death. It is certain that this chasm was once central to worship of Zeus, the same strain of Zeus worship practiced at Uzuncaburç.

Access to the ruins is from the car park on the southwestern side of the chasm, and a 50 foot Hellenistic-era defensive tower looms nearby. Alongside is one of several Byzantine basilicas on the site, this site clearly having maintained its sacred legacy long after Zeus-worship was abandoned. The high reliefs visible on descent into the chasm are thought to date to the ancient temple of Zeus, and the people represented may be priests of that temple. Elsewhere at the site, the principal ruins of interest are some well-preserved tombs and a great cistern carved into the stone and partially covered with an arched roof; this within the cemetery in use today.

North from Kızkalesi

Returning to Kızkalesi, the next set of sites are arrayed to the north and west. Near at hand, just 7 kilometers from Kızkalesi is Narlikuyu, site of several popular fish restaurants (see *Where to Eat*) as well as a tiny museum that preserves an excellent mosaic. The **Narlikuyu Museum** (9 a.m. to 5 p.m., $1) is entirely devoted to a fine mosaic that was once the floor of a bath complex associated with a late-Roman era palace. The three Graces Aglaia, Thalia, and Euphrosyne, daughters of Zeus, are depicted dancing together in the company of fountains and birds; well worth a stop if you appreciate mosaics.

Two kilometers uphill from Narlikuyu are the **caves of Cennet and Cehennum** (Heaven and Hell), one of the principal attractions in the area. You'll find a tourism complex at the lip of the "Heaven" gorge, where restroom facilities and refreshments are available. The sites are open from 8 a.m. to 5 p.m. daily, later in summer, and cost $1.25 per person, with an additional $.50 for the asthma caves some 300 meters away. You can make your way here using public transportation—either by hiking 1.5 kilometers from the main road uphill to the caverns, or by taking a taxi directly from Kızkalesi.

The main Gorge of Heaven is not visible until you are standing on its edge. Expect to spend one and one-half hours descending into the gorge, lingering at the cave, and climbing back out. Descent into the gorge is by a steep stone stair that doubles back along the floor of the chasm and leads to the chapel standing at the mouth of the "Hell" cavern. The sinkhole is lush and full of birdsong, in contrast to the sere landscape above.

The mouth to the cave of Hell, directly behind the fifth century chapel of Virgin Mary at the base of the gorge, is enormous. Making a descent into it from the chapel of Virgin Mary is a fine idea, even for people uneasy with caves, since it is well lit and you never leave sight of the entrance. The stone stair that descends into the cavern is built of great marble blocks; marble has many virtues, but traction is not among them, so be careful. For those who make their way to the bottom of the cavern, you'll be rewarded by the sound of rushing water deep below; the Styx, it was once thought, when this was believed to be an entrance to Hades. Progress beyond this point is blocked today. It is interesting to note that the freshwater river you hear is probably the very river that upwells in the sea near Narlikuyu.

Ascending back out of the chasm on a warm summer day, the restrooms and drinks available at the visitors center will seem heavenly indeed. The Chasm of Hell, just northeast of the gorge of Heaven, is another sinkhole; this one is not accessible to the public. According to legend, it is here that Typhon, father of the Chimera, was temporarily imprisoned by Zeus.

The final cave of interest in the Cennet and Cehennum complex is 300 meters along. Astim Mağarası, the Cave of Asthma, is thought to be soothing to asthma sufferers owing to its high humidity.

The beautifully laid walls of a former **Temple of Zeus** stand hard by the Cennet visitors complex. The regular and irregular stone courses were laid with typical second century B.C. Hellenistic artistry, leaving barely a seam between them. The great walls are surmounted by later Byzantine stonework.

The road to Cennet and Cehennum continues north and joins the Silifke-Kırağıbucağı road near Imamlı; from there, the road climbs roughly 15 kilometers to the great ruins of **Uzuncaburç** (Diocaesarea/Olba). The ruins here are of the sacred precincts of a temple of Zeus; the residential settlement (signed "Olba") is located four kilometers along. Olba, as the sacred precincts were known at their foundation early in the first millenium B.C., was dedicated to supporting a temple of Zeus. The temple complex truly began to prosper around 300 B.C., when one of Alexander's warring generals founded the port city of Seleucia ad Calycadnus (modern Silifke) and passed along some of his largesse to the sacred sanctuary at Olba. Substantial ruins of the great temple built at that time remain today.

As Roman rule expanded into the eastern Mediterranean, the temple city adopted the name Diocaesarea and was a Roman provincial seat in good standing for two centuries, printing its own coinage and prospering on both its sacred reputation and the north-south trade that passed through the area. As Christianity drove out competing religions in the early Byzantine empire, Diocaesarea's temples were repurposed for Christian worship; it was only the long decline of Byzantine power in the region that sapped the strength of the city. By the time the Byzantine empire collapsed in the fifteenth century Diocaesarea had been abandoned by all but goatherds for many lives of men. It is in part owing to the gradual decline that many of the great monuments of the city remain in outstanding shape; they were rarely recycled for other uses. There is a modern town near the site today.

You are rewarded for your 3,000-foot climb from the seaside by cooler air, pine forests, fine views, and an interesting set of ruins and tombs. One of the first structures you will note on your approach is a tall tomb with a pyramid roof on a hill to the south of the sacred complex.

This structure was once topped with a statue of the deceased. Like the stature, any grave goods were plundered long before modern times; entrance is prohibited.

As you enter Uzuncaburç town you will find a collection of shops and markets, including a PTT. While here, stop in at a shop for "kenger kahvesi," a local coffee infused with acanthus. It is acanthus leaves you will find decorating columns and other stonework throughout the city. A short road east of the village climbs to the high rectangular tower that gives Uzuncaburç its name—literally "tall tower." This 70-foot tower, built of great courses of stone and pierced with slits for archers, is closed to the public for reasons of safety, but is a marvel worthy of the time. This tower was once an integral part of the city walls built to surround the sacred precinct.

Descending into town and following the signs south, you come to a parking lot (dawn-dusk, $1.50) alongside a ceremonial entrance gate. Only the right half of this impressive entranceway stands, with pedestals protruding from the front of the columns where statues once stood. The entrance, which was part of the circuit of defensive walls, dates to the beginning of the fifth century A.D.

The theatre, just east of the parking area, was excavated in the 1980s by the Turkish Tourism ministry. From the theatre, the principal ruins are all located past the ceremonial gate and along a long colonnade. The broad colonnaded street is strewn with fallen stonework, many pieces of which are inscribed or decorated with reliefs. To your right you will see the nymphaeum, or baths complex. This structure was made possible by an extensive system of Roman-built aqueducts and irrigation channels that routed water from the Lamus river to the northeast.

The greatest monument in Uzuncaburç is ahead and left of the colonnaded way. A forest of columns stands on the site of the **Temple of Zeus Olbios**. The temple was place of pilgrimage for hundreds of years, and was converted to a church at the time of Theodosius the Great. Today, 30 of the original 70 columns remain standing, giving the visitor a very complete sense of the plan and dimensions of the ancient structure. The adaptations that were made to the structure to convert it to a proper church have been removed as part of a recent cleanup effort; the bulk of the damage probably occurred during a great fire, traces of which are still visible. It is not known whose beautifully carved sarcophagus abuts the northern wall of the temple.

The colonnaded way ends at the Temple of Tyche. Five of the temple's beautiful, single-shaft columns remain standing, topped by their ornate Corinthian capitals and a long architrave. Tyche was the goddess of chance, popular throughout Rome, and favored in many cities for her protection of cities from harm. From the Temple, the last principal site of interest is along another arcaded road left of the colonnade d way on which you arrived; this brings you to the City Gate. The walls to either side of the gate have fallen, but the gate remains in a good state of preservation.

With additional time, consider investigating the ruins at the "other" Olba, four kilometers along at the town of Ura. Likewise, the mausoleums at Demircili, on the Silifke road just 8 kilometers from Silifke, are impressive; consider stopping by on your way back to the coast.

Leaving Kızkalesi via Konya

The spectacular ruins at **Alahan** can be seen in a day trip from Kızkalesi, but require several round-trip hours of driving—the site is 20 kilometers beyond Mut, itself 84 kilometers from Silifke). If you plan to use the (excellent) road between Silifke and Konya, you'll pass two kilometers from Alahan, and can hike, hitch, or ,ideally, drive the steep track to the site. If you are headed up on foot, you can see Alahan high above at the first turn so you're aware what you're getting yourself into.

At the time of this writing, no fees were collected at Alahan; open dawn til dusk.

Alahan is one of the most breathtaking sites in the whole of Turkey. The setting high above a pass is arresting; the structures built at the site are well-preserved and ingeniously constructed; the site is compact and infrequently-visited. You can spend one hour at the site and leave feeling satisfied you've seen what you came to see.

The monastery at Alahan is an extension of the Christian refuges that extend hundreds of miles inland in the direction of Cappadocia, culminating in great subterranean churches and cities carved into the tufa stone. At Alahan, and elsewhere in the walls of the Göksu gorge, you begin to see tombs and dwellings carved by monks and other Christian refugees.

The parking lot is set into the hillside, with a steep dropoff to the south (right). Ascending a set of stairs, you pass a complex of caves. This cluster of grottoes, undercut in the stone ridge, is thought to have been the first settlement at Alahan, dating back to the arrival of the first Christian ascetics and probably far earlier. The grottoes include the cave church, a large space 30 feet high and 30 feet deep, and small dwellings extend out along the stone spur jutting in the direction of the highway below.

The first structure on the terrace is the Evangelists Basilica, little of which remains standing other than its beautifully carved doorway. The richness of the carving is something you will see throughout Alahan. The doorposts feature acanthus leaves and vines, and support a lintel with reliefs of two faces and of angels carrying an emblem of Christ. Interesting, too, are the inner faces of the posts, since they suggest more about the struggles of Christianity as it tried to take root in this high places. On the left post Gabriel stands over an ox and a man representing Mithra; on the right post Michael towers over two women representing the fertility goddess Cybele/Artemis.

The parking lot is set into the hillside, with a steep dropoff to the south (right). Ascending a set of stairs, you pass a complex of caves. This cluster of grottoes, undercut in the stone ridge, is thought to have been the first settlement at Alahan, dating back to the arrival of the first Christian ascetics and probably far earlier. The grottoes include the cave church, a large space 30 feet high and 30 feet deep, and small dwellings extend out along the stone spur jutting in the direction of the highway below.

The first structure on the terrace is the Evangelists Basilica, little of which remains standing other than its beautifully carved doorway. The richness of the carving is something you will see throughout Alahan. The doorposts feature acanthus leaves and vines, and support a lintel with reliefs of two faces and of angels carrying an emblem of Christ. Interesting, too, are the inner faces of the posts, since they suggest more about the struggles of Christianity as it tried to take root in this high places. On the left post Gabriel stands over an ox and a man representing Mithra; on the right post Michael towers over two women representing the fertility goddess Cybele/Artemis.

Continuing east along the terrace past more caves in the ridge above, you arrive next at the baptistry. The baptistry has a small chapel with two naves, in the second of which the baptism pool is magnificently carved in stone in the form of a Maltese Cross, fed by a now-dry water channel that pierces the northern wall. Continuing, you pass four arched tombs in the north wall, including the tomb of Tarasis, the man responsible for founding a true monastery on this site in the fifth century. On your right, with its back to the valley below, you will notice a spendidly carved 10-foot high stone marker. This significance of this "aedicula," or memorial, is not known, but it is another fine example of the stonework of the Alahan monks.

The terrace path comes to its obvious conclusion at the Eastern Church. This church is in a marvelous state of preservation. Only the dome of this magnificent structure has collapsed; its walls and columns all stand, against all hope. The arcaded façade of the church is beautiful, and the structure itself is a marvel, with a north wall of living stone, and arches rooted ingeniously in the rock. Where the structure ends and the bedrock begins is often difficult to tell. On the façade, postholes above the arcade helped support a wooden narthex; it is unfortunate that we have no idea what these skilled workers of stone might have done with woodwork. You can climb the hillside above the Eastern Church and continue out along the western spur; there are caves and tombs tucked away all over the hillside, and you'll see others hewn into boulders by the highway far below.

Upon leaving Alahan, Alahan Restaurant back on the main road offers "et mangal," or grilled meat, not to mention marvelous views out over the gorge; this is a fine place to take a break.

From Kızkalesi to Alanya

The coast road west of Silifke ascends the sheer mountain walls of rugged "**Rough Cilicia**," climbing and descending time and again. The two-lane road is in fine condition, but it requires patience, time, and passengers who aren't prone to carsickness. Rough Cilicia draws its name from the ancient name for region ("Smooth" Cilicia refers to the flatter and more forgiving terrain to the east), and includes the great south-pointing spur of land with Anamur at its tip. Rough Cilicia is peppered with small ruins (principally those at Anamur 121 kilometers west of Silifke) and at Alanya, 231 kilometers west of Silifke.

Most travelers along this rump of coast choose to rest halfway along--overnighting at Anamur, visiting Mamure Kalesi three kilometers east of the town and Anamurium four kilometers west. Anamur has a very modest selection of accommodations: **Dragon Otel** is located just 100 yards from Mamure Kalesi on the main coast road, offering direct access to a huge expanse of beach, 12 rustic, flyscreened bungalows, and meals (Bozdoğan Köyü, Anamur, *Tel. (324) 827-1355, Fax (324) 827-1684*; Double: $14; meals are served). In town, **Hotel Dolphine** is the best of some bland options, set just back from the road opposite the waterfront gozleme and baked potato restaurants (İnönü Cad. No. 17, Anamur, *Tel. (324) 814-3435, Fax (324) 814-1575*; Double: $22; meals are served).

Anamur's two ruins are quite different from one another. **Mamure Kalesi** ($1, 8 a.m. to 5 p.m.) is an ancient fortification whose current incarnation dates to Selcuk domination of the area in the 13th century; today it has remarkably intact galleries within the towers, and paths that pierce the southern wall and bring you to the sea gate. There is a small, working mosque within the walls of the fortress.

Anamurium ($1, 8 a.m. to 5 p.m.), four kilometers west of Anamur, has an altogether different character; this is a far older site, a sprawl of ruined buildings that probably dates to the Phoenician settlement of this section of coast. The settlement evolved into a substantial Roman settlement; the residents are thought to have benefited from maritime commerce with Egypt—this is the closest point to Egypt in Asia Minor, and its abundant timber was a lucrative export. The city was badly damaged in a 6th century earthquake, and rocked by Arab and Saracen raiders soon thereafter; it never recovered. Today, an asphalt path winds 400 meters down through the ruins to a small beach; there is a theatre just below the path, and above the path are a collection of houses and tombs—many of which offer mosaics. In fact, mosaic hunting is the most enjoyable aspect of a visit to Anamurium; several excellent in situ mosaics are located in the baths complex above the path, just west of the necropolis. There is a network of goat trails throughout the area, and picking your way through the gorse bushes to the various broken tombs you will find many interesting mosaics and frescoes.

From Anamur, the coast road begins an immediate ascent, looping up, then back down to sleepy coastal villages such as Melleç, 17 kilometers along, and Kaledran, 29 kilometers along. In the spring roadside stands punctuate the hair-raising drive with offers of honey (buz) and small local bananas (muz); those with the time to venture inland will begin to see the distinctive yellow or brown ruin markers some 50 kilometers along: Antioch ad Cragum, Nephelis, Yalan Dunya, Cestrus, Selinus, and Lamus are all located east of Gazipaşa—the main town between Anamur and Adana.

Beyond Gazipaşa, the coast road passes a scatter of ruins and a fortifications at ancient Iotape (just 15 kilometers from Alanya, shortly before the scenic Kale Restaurant), and passes signed turnings for the ruins at Naula and Laertes. The many ruins in this area are little-visited, and only **Antioch ad Cragum** should distract any but the most die-hard ruins-hunters. Antioch ad Cragum, with ruins scattered along footpaths near the modern village of Guney, is located atop mountain walls that drop into the sea. The site affords dramatic 180 degree-plus views, and its ruins—primarily a necropolis jutting into space above the sea and a fortress punctuated with medieval towers—are picturesque, but not outstanding.

Alanya

Alanya has much to offer—a nearly-intact Selcuk-era fortified city, extensive sand beaches, and even one particularly interesting hotel. The city itself (population 140,000) is a generally unlovely sprawl, and in the summer months it is thick with package tourists, most of them fair-haired folk from northern Europe. You'll find the 'old city', the center of town on the east side of the isthmus, a fairly bustling place offering banks, bars, internet cafes, magazine shops, and other welcome spots.

History
Alanya sits like a punctuation mark at the western border of Rough

Cilicia, on a spot where a huge stone buttress that rises from the gentle surrounding landscape in dizzying fashion. The remarkable situation of the headland and anchorage at Alanya would have recommended itself to the earliest settlers, but it leaves no footprint in history until a passing mention in the fourth century BC. Only in the early second century BC does Coracesium, as the settlement was known in Roman times, appear in a substantial way.

Like so many ports in the region, Coracesium trafficked in lumber and piracy; this latter industry, in particular, helped local corsairs amass wealth sufficient to challenge the supremacy of the Seleucid kingdom in the eastern Mediterranean. The wealth, alas, was insufficient to defeat the Seleucids; the corsairs were soundly defeated and Coracesium pulled more tightly into the orbit of the Seleucid King Antiochus VII. It is not apparent that Seleucid rule did much to discourage piracy; it remained a burr in the side of local shipping until being crushed during the great Roman campaign under Pompey in 67 BC. The great battle of that campaign took place in the sea offshore of the Alanya headland.

With piracy brought to heel, the city settled in under Roman rule, prospered, and mostly slipped from the pages of history during the long Pax Romana. The only notable exception is early in Roman rule, when Marc Antony briefly presented the city—and its rich timber—to Cleopatra.

Centuries passed. As Roman, then Byzantine, grip on the eastern Mediterranean began to loosen in the third and fourth centuries, raiders from the east began to prey on Coracesium (the Byzantine Kalonoros). The city faded.

Ownership of the great headland passed back and forth, principally between the Byzantines, Arabs, Persians, and—just after the first millennium—the Armenians. Overwhelmed by the onslaught of the Turks out of the east and displaced from their native lands along the periphery of Asia Minor, the Armenians established themselves throughout Cilicia. Armenia Minor, as these lands were known, was really a patchwork of kingdoms ranging from Antioch in the east to Alanya in the west; their successes were many, but their setbacks were, as well. In whole or in part Armenia Minor was at various times made subject of the Byzantines (under John II), the Latin Crusaders, the Arabs, and the Selcuk Turks. After two centuries of this uneasy existence, Alanya was seized outright by the Selcuk Turks at the zenith of their power under Sultan Alaeddin Keykobad I in 1221. The Armenian rulers of the city fought briefly, then negotiated a price for surrender and withdrew to the east.

The full military potential of the site was not realized until the arrival of the Selcuks. Sultan Alaeddin's great wealth, combined with his perspective as a military commander who had once prepared to besiege the great rock, inspired him to rebuile the fortifications at the city on the plan you see today. The long, steep ascent was intersected by multiple gates, and commanded by 6500 meters of wall and 140 towers; state-of-the-art shipyards were built, and the great Red Tower erected by the marina as protection. It is under Alaeddin that the city took an early version of its present name, "Alaiya."

The fortress at Alanya was built to be impregnable, and it might well have been; the Selcuks never had an opportunity to find out. Just 21 years after Alaeddin's seizure of Alanya, the Selcuk Empire was broken and scattered at the Battle of Kosedağ by the Mongols. The capital at Konya was sacked, the Selcuk Sultans reduced to vassals, central authority undone, and Selcuk garrisons like the one at Alanya left largly on their own. Despite all of this, the newly-rebuilt city of Alanya enjoyed relative prosperity for several more decades. The eventual withdrawal of the Mongols after great defeats in 1260 and 1274 created a vacuum the Karaman Turks were eager to fill. By the beginning of the14th century most of the jewels in the former Selcuk crown—including Konya and Alanya—were in the possession of the Karamans.

The Karamanid Dynasty, a bitter rival for power with its Ottoman cousin, held Alanya for more than 100 years, eventually selling it to the Mameluks in 1427 for funds to fuel their struggle with the Ottomans. For their part, the Mameluks had emerged from Egypt to help sweep away the remainders of Latin, Mongol, and Armenian rule in Cilicia. Alas, the days of both dynasties were numbered; the ascent of the Ottoman Empire was not to be slowed. Antalya had already fallen to the Ottomans; Constantinople would fall in 1453, Trabzon in 1461, and an Ottoman army under Mehmet the Conqueror's Grand Vizier Gedik Ahmet Paşa seized Alanya in 1471.

Arrivals & Departures

A broad ribbon of highway follows the gentle sweep of coast west to Antalya, with almost constant connections by bus or dolmuş. To the east, the highway continues its smooth run for 15 kilometers before beginning the long, winding ascent along "Rough Cilicia" toward Anamur and Mersin far beyond.

Bus companies have offices in the heart of the old city along Iskele Caddesi (on the eastern side of the isthmus), and offer shuttle service to the otogar. Our favorite bus company, the luxury outfit Varan, offers the following alternatives west and north in the summer: Ankara, departures twice daily at 9:45 p.m. and midnight, $19, 9.5 hours; Istanbul, departures once daily at 6:45 p.m., $23, 13.5 hours; Izmir, departures once daily at 9:15 p.m., $18, 9.5 hours. From the main otogar, you'll find hourly buses west toward Antalya ($3, 2 hours) and points beyond, and a handful of companies that make the run to Anamur and Mersin along the somewhat harrowing coast road to the east ($6, 4 hours to Anamur; $10, 8 hours to Mersin). Those heading east should make reservations.

Ferry service connects Alanya with Girne, Northern Cyprus three times weekly (Monday, Wednesday, and Friday at 3 p.m. Round trip fare is $50 (not including $12 port tax), with trip time of three hours. Tickets can be purchased at Fam Tour, Damlatas Cad. No. 53, Alanya; *Tel. (242) 513-9597; Fax: (242) 512-1931; Email: famtour@antnet.net.tr.*

Orientation

Alanya is 135 kilometers east of Antalya, connected by a fine stretch of road. The highway continues along the Alanya waterfront as Atatürk Caddesi (with the Cevre Yolu—or 'ring road'—looping inland). The waterfront road passes inland of the great rock of Alanya, with the Alanya Museum and tourism information office located several blocks south of Atatürk Caddesi on Ismet Hilmi Balci Caddesi (on the western side of the isthmus behind the beach), and the heart of the old city—with restaurants, banks, and the starting point for the road to the top of the great rock (the well-signed Kale Yolu)—located several blocks south on the eastern side of the isthmus.

The otogar is located three kilometers west of town, one block inland of Atatürk Caddesi, and is served throughout the day by public buses ($.50). The tourism information office, across the street from a beachfront park, is open from 9 a.m. to 5:30 p.m., closed at lunch *(Tel. 242 513-1240)*, and is the variety that charges for maps.

Where to Stay

Accommodation in Alanya is serviceable, but boilerplate; only one hotel clearly earns our wholehearted recommendation.

BEDESTEN CLUB HOTEL, *Içkale, Alanya. Tel. (242) 512-1234; Fax (242) 513-7934. Rooms: 30. Credit cards not accepted. Open year-round. Double (half-board): $60 (30% off-season discount).*

The Bedesten is the crown jewel of Alanya's hotels; it is a jewel that could stand some polishing, but even so it is a stunning find high atop the great buttress of Alanya's outer citadel. The hotel is housed within the compound of a Selcuk Kervansaray built here by Sultan Alaeddin Keykobad in the years when he was converting the fortress at Alanya into one of the most forbidding on the Mediterranean. Some rooms are located in the arched stone rooms that once served passing traders, others in a spacious old Turkish Han. The compound offers a swimming pool, spacious patios, and outdoor restaurant seating that commands a view of the arc of coast to the west.

Among hotels, only the Bedesten sits high on the rump of Alanya's great buttress. This offers a unique opportunity to explore the upper reaches of Alanya, including nearby Suleimaniye Camii, and, uphill to the south, the upper citadel. One of the most compelling sights in the upper city happens to be on the grounds; a massive, empty cistern is cut into the stone beneath the kervansaray and accessible by stair.

The hotel is clean and well-maintained, and rooms—which differ greatly one to the other—offer the necessities, including air-conditioning but not television. You'll probably find some contemporary touches of décor, tilework and carpentry that are unfortunate.

A taxi from town far below costs $5; the hotel offers shuttle service to Kleopatra Beach and charges $35 for transportation to or from the Antalya airport. Half-board is recommended (see "Where to Eat").

HOTEL KAPTAN, *Iskele Cad. No. 70, Alanya, 07400. Tel. (242) 513-4900; Fax (242) 513-2000. Rooms: 57. Credit cards accepted. Open year-round. Double: $45 back view, $60 sea view, breakfast included.*

The Hotel Kaptan is a traditional four star, six-story lodging option overlooking the marina and the Red Tower on Iskele Caddesi. The hotel is clean, safe, and well-maintained, offering little touches in your room like credenzas and television with foreign channels. The Kaptan offers a central location, attentive service, air-conditioning, a swimming pool, and good views (albeit at the risk of some late-night noise from the bars to the north and below). To reach the hotel, follow the signs south of Atatürk Caddesi toward the Red Tower; it is 150 meters beyond the Temiz Hotel (the best nearby alternative, at just $20 for a double).

SUNNY HILL HOTEL, *Sultan Alaeddin Cad. No. 3, Alanya, 07400. Tel. (242) 511-1211; Fax (242) 512-3893e. Rooms: 73. Credit cards accepted. Open year-round. Double: $42, breakfast included.*

The Sunny Hill is located on the 'quiet' side of the isthmus, on the slope above Damlataş Mağarası and the tourism office. The Sunny Hill is the best of the 'beachfront' hotels, although it is actually a ten-minute walk from the beach. Rooms offer satellite television, air-conditioning, and many have patios with a view to the northwest. Buffet lunch and dinner is available for $5 and $9, respectively.

HOTEL MARINA, *Iskele Cad. No. 80, Alanya, 07400. Tel.: (242) 513-4321; Fax (242) 513-9611; Email: hotelmarina@usa.net. Rooms: 28. Credit cards accepted. Open April-December. Double: $16, breakfast included.*

Hotel Marina is another of the blocky hotels lining Alanya's eastern marina, offering decent, inexpensive accommodation. Rooms and public areas are not particularly appealing, but they are clean. One oddity of the Marina is that air conditioning units can be rented for $5 per night; money well spent in the blistering summer months. The Marina Hotel is located just inland of the Red Tower, and can get some of the sound from the marina.

Where to Eat

Dining options abound in Alanya, with most of the good restaurants located along the marina along the eastern shore benath the Kale.

BEDESTEN, *Içkale, Alanya. Tel. (242) 512-1234; Fax (242) 513-7934. Open May-December. Credit cards not accepted. Moderate.*

As detailed in the "Where to Stay" section, the Bedesten is perched high above Alanya within the outer fortress (a $5 taxi ride from town center). Dinner taken on the patio is breathtaking, with the lit battlements and Suleimaniye mosque in the foreground and the city and sea far below. The prix-fixe meal ($11) is a hearty complement; typical of a meal is a course of dolma and bread, followed by a plate heaped with pide, grilled chicken, grilled onions, tomatoes, and peppers, and fries.

OTTOMAN HOUSE, *Damlataş Cad. No. 31, Alanya, 07400. Tel. (242) 511-1421. Open year-round. Credit cards accepted. Moderate.*

Ottoman House is generally thought to offer the best dining in Alanya, and our experience was good. True to its name, Ottoman House is a 19th century Ottoman house with 4 meter-high ceilings and solid stone and woodwork. Some aspects of the décor have been allowed to deteriorate, but in the upstairs and outdoor dining areas everything is spotless—and the hallmark Turkish dishes are well-prepared. Cold mezes run $1.50, grills and other entrees $6 to $8. The prix-fixe menu—mezes, mixed grill, salad, wine, and coffee—comes in at a slightly expensive $12. The Ottoman House offers the following disclaimer: "Please don't be afraid to try something new. If you don't like your choice we shall immediately replace it with another dish." If you have children along, a small playground and collection of animals will help keep them entertained.

ADANA OCAKBAŞI, *Otogar karşısı, Alanya, 07400. Tel. (242) 511-2342. Open year-round. Credit cards not accepted. Inexpensive.*

Adana Ocakbaşı is a local favorite for grills, located alongside the Otogar. There's no need to make a special trip here, but if you're already at the otogar, take advantage of Adana Ocakbaşı. This is a great place to while away your time while awaiting your bus. If you're looking for a good, inexpensive place nearer to the town center, explore Hukumet Caddesi and Gazipaşa Caddesi just north of the eastern marina, near Yeni Camii.

Seeing the Sights

Alanya has a small museum and a diverting bazaar (inland of Atatürk Caddesi, due north of the marina), but the true reasons to visit the city the ruins of the citadel and Red Tower, the nearby beaches, and a trip by boat around the horn of land that supports the fortifications.

The citadel (**Iç Kale**) towers above the city, and is reached via a steep, winding road more than two kilometers long. The road ("Kale Yolu") is well-signed, originating just behind the marina at the intersection of Iskele Caddesi and Damlataş Caddesi. Taxi fare is a fairly well-spent $4, but you might prefer to make the hike yourself (there are more than a dozen little stands offering lace, gozleme, tea, drinks, and ice cream as you ascend). In its ascent, the road cuts through fortification walls that descend to the **Red Tower**; on foot, you can examine the Selcuk-era gate alongside the modern road; it is a heavily fortified right-angle gate intended to blunt the momentum of attackers.Upon reaching the summit, you'll find tickets for entering the Iç Kale are $4.50 per person (9 a.m.- 8 p.m.). Signs ask that visitors refrain from picnicking at the site, but tidy picnickers are happily indulged. Iç Kale is certainly a good place to enjoy a meal before the long descent.

The first impression a visitor has, particularly having just ascended to the inner fortress, is one of awe. The site towers so far above the sea below that the only sound you hear is the wind; you can barely make out the details of the mint (darphane) and monastery (manastir) on the jagged slopes of Cılvarda peninsula far below.

The grounds of the citadel are well-maintained. Off to your left as you enter are a covered set of cisterns, once meant to help address the limited availability of fresh water on the site. Along the northern wall, near the ruined barracks, are the remnants of a small, appealing building that served first as a Byzantine Church of St. George, later as a mosque.

At the western end of the inner fortress is a high platform known, fairly or not, as "Adam Atacağı" (the place for hurling men). This is, predictably, a place of great interest for visitors, and looking down at the sheer drop to the rocks and sea below may weaken your knees despite the modern addition of a high iron fence.

If time and fitness allows, descend from Iç Kale on foot. This way you have the opportunity to follow the course of the walls downhill, enjoy the views, stop at the occasional café, and visit the Suleimaniye Camii and the cisterns at the Bedesten Hotel.

The walls descend to the marina on the eastern shore, terminating at the Red Tower (Kızıl Kule) and Shipyard (Tershane) just south of the modern marina. If you are descending on foot, paths wind downhill from within the main outer gate. Small lanes pass between interesting old wooden houses, eventually winding past a great, empty tower that once served as the arsenal (tophane) for the fortress, and on to the Red Tower.

The Red Tower is Alanya's trademark image, and rightly so. This Selcuk-era fortification cuts an imposing figure, looming high above the marina. The Red Tower was erected just five years after Selcuk occupation of Alanya, and was likely one of the first steps in the overhaul of the site under Sultan Alaeddin Keykobad.

As you make the full circuit around the foot of the tower on your way to the entrance ($2, 9 a.m. to 8 p.m.), your high school physics lessons will come back with a start; rocks, chunks of mortar, and anything else the defenders of this fortress elected to hurl down would have had time—or close enough—to reach terminal velocity on the way to your head. The gate is not grand, it is an intentionally cramped four feet-high, another impediment for the attacker (and us). Within, you find the 100-foot tower divided into five floors and wrapped around a core that served as the garrison's cistern. As you ascend, you'll find military artifacts on many floors--cannonballs, chain mail, swords, bows and arrows, firearms— and textiles, lamps and period clothes on others. Climbing the high stone stairs you have plenty of opportunity to peer down from the vantage point of an attacker; be careful that little ones keep well clear.

From just outside the entrance to the Red Tower, a cement path descends toward the water alongside a sea wall. This inauspicious path winds down to the massive **Selcuk Shipyard**, the only building of its kind remaining in the world. Five great, arched bays—each measuring 120 feet in length and more than 20 feet wide—are contained in a single building. The scale of the facility is immense, and it remains in remarkably good condition. Ducking through a small gate in the north wall, you find yourself in great chambers that are open to the sea and fairly well lit thanks to holes pierced in the walls. The shipyard is in such fine condition that it offers an unusual glimpse of the military and engineering acumen of the Selcuks; just beyond the lap of waves at the mouth of the edifice, you can almost hear hawsers being cut and timbers being hammered into place.

The **marina**, just north of the Red Tower, is the place to set out on a cruise around the great rock of Alanya. Most trips depart by 10 a.m., so make arrangements a day ahead or make your way to the marina early in the day. A typical itinerary is five hours, including lunch, with stops at several caves, principally the Pirates Cave (Korsanlar Mağarası) and the Phosporescent Cave (Fosforlu Mağarası), opportunities to swim, and a cost of $15 per person.

The favored beach in the immediate neighborhood of Alanya is **Kleopatra Plaj** (Cleopatra Beach), a coarse sand beach to the west of town. For a fine sand beach, you can travel west to Incekum (dolmuş make this trip every 30 minutes in the high season); Kleopatra Plaj is quite satisfactory for most folks. Not far from the eastern end of Kleopatra Plaj is Damlataş Mağarası (9 a.m. to 7 p.m.; $1); this warm, humid cavern is located near the tourism office and is popular among people with arthritis and asthma.

Chapter 18

West of Alanya, the Turkish Mediterranean coast becomes more forgiving and offers dozens of fascinating way-points. The first stretch of coast, centered on Antalya, is detailed in this chapter. The central Mediterranean coast is popular, dotted with holiday villages, resorts, and golf courses; we direct you to some of our favorite accommodations in the region and the marquee ruins near at hand.

Antalya

Antalya (population 450,000) is a good base from which to see many of the most interesting ruins in the ancient world. Among the nearby sites are **Termessos**, easily defensible in its mountain fastness; **Perge** sprawling between two mesas; **Aspendos**, whose ancient theater is the best on earth; **Sillion**, perched atop a barely accessible bluff; and **Selge**, high in the interior at the end of a deep, beautiful gorge. Away to the east are **Side**, **Alanya**, and the sites of **Rough Cilicia**. Away to the west are the marvels of the Lycian coast.

Antalya has a few ruins of its own, but its greatest assets are a central location, an airport, Setur Marina just west of town, and a thicket of sprawling old wooden houses now converted to hotels and pensions in the

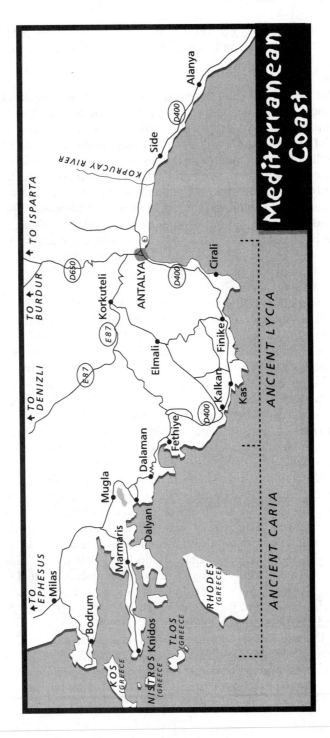

city's old quarter, Kaleiçi. There is one tiny, pleasant beach at the foot of Kaleiçi, larger Konyaaltı Beach to the west, and Lara Beach to the east.

History

One version of Antalya's foundation has it that **King Attalus II** of Pergamon (160-139 B.C.) sent forth his minions to find the perfect site for a beautiful new city, and those minions picked this spot. Beautiful though the site certainly was, perched in the greenery on the cliffs above the Mediterranean, a more realistic reason for Antalya's founding was its strategic position commanding the wide **Bay of Antalya**, the first major anchorage west of the Lycian Mountains. Attalus II's search for a port city coincided with the high water mark of ancient civilization in the region; Side and Aspendos to the east were near the height of their power, as were other coastal cities to the west. Rome was extending its influence into the eastern Mediterranean, and had completed a trading deal with Side. **Attalus II**, needing a secure port of his own, built a city here and named it Attaleia, after himself.

The Kingdom of Pergamon hardly had time to build the city before Attalus II's successor, Attalus III, broke up the kingdom, willing most of it to Rome. Antalya did not pass immediately to Rome, and pirates and other ne'er do wells moved in, taking advantage of Antalya's fine bay (the world's navies still anchor there). The **Roman Empire** had little tolerance for interference in its trade and waged several brutal campaigns to clear the area of piracy, the most notable under Pompey in 66 B.C. Afterwards, the region was cleared of pirates and port cities such as Antalya came directly under Roman control. Rome, unfortunately, used the eastern Mediterranean as a dumping ground for its shadiest noblemen, and local governors systematically looted and abused the coastal towns. Unlike Perge and Aspendos, however, Antalya's brief history had left it with little to steal or desecrate, and the city grew apace while its venerable neighbors were stripped and brought low.

Antalya's fortunes never seriously declined, although for many years it remained a footnote to the activities at Perge and Aspendos. Eventually the inland cities began to fade, but Antalya, with the last good anchorage easily accessible by road from the east, continued to thrive under fairly steady Byzantine rule. Crusaders used the city in their forays to the Holy Land, but they fumbled the city away to the Selçuks, who adorned it with some of its landmark monuments. The Ottomans finally seized the city in the expansion campaigns of Beyazid I (1389-1403), capturing it from their Turkish rivals, the Karamanlıs. The city remained an important commercial center throughout the Imperial period, eventually assuming the dominant role along the Mediterranean. Following WW I, Antalya was partitioned to the Italians in the Treaty of Sevres, and

It's a Pirate's Death for Me!

A pirate tale you don't usually hear: While still a young Roman officer, young **Gaius Julius Caesar** was seized by pirates on his way to Rhodes and held for ransom. The charming young Roman developed a friendship with the pirates in the weeks he awaited payment of the ransom, playfully telling them that someday he would crucify them all for his current indignity. One account even says that he was insulted when the pirates failed to ask a high enough ransom, and voluntarily increased it fivefold. When payment arrived from Caesar's friends in Miletus the parting was tinged by sadness. Several years later, Caesar was helping the powerful Pompey in his effort to clear the eastern Mediterranean of pirates, and it so happened that Caesar's past captors fell into his hands. According to the policy of the times, and his own past assurances, Caesar was compelled to crucify the pirates - but out of sentiment for their past acquaintance he had their throats cut first.

was occupied by the Italians between 1918 and 1921, when Kemal Atatürk seized back the Turkish heartland and all of the allies abandoned their claims.

Today Antalya is one of Turkey's main industrial centers, and the hub for tourism along the southern coast. The World Bank-funded tourism zone near Kemer is fed through Antalya's airport, and even without this help the city is a natural destination for connoisseurs of ruins and fine accommodations.

Arrivals & Departures

By Air

Antalya's economy hinges on processing sesame, cotton, and tourists. The latter industry has been carefully masterminded to funnel through Antalya's airport and disperse in the huge resort hotels between here and Tekirova in the west, Side in the east. Turkish Airlines offers nine nonstop flights between Istanbul and Antalya every day during summer, and two nonstop flights between Ankara and Antalya; $80 per person. Flights to most other points in Turkey cost roughly $90, but the flights are routed via either İstanbul or Ankara and include a layover. Turkish Airlines fares from New York, with a stay of less than one month, are $760 in the high season, $600 in low. West Coast departures cost an extra $400.

Many hotels are happy to arrange for your transfer from the airport into town; inquire when you make reservations. If not, you may choose between taxis ($13 fare to Kaleiçi—the old town), or the blue/green livery of the Havaş Airport buses (leaving the airport nine times daily, as dictated by flight arrivals). The Havaş buses cost $2 and drop you off at the main Turkish Airlines office by the tourism information office, 500 meters west of Kaleiçi. For more information, contact **Turkish Airlines**, Cumhuriet Cd. Özel Idare İşhanı Altı, *Tel. 242 243 4383.*

By Boat

Antalya's Setur Marina, west of town at the far end of Konyaalti Beach, is host to a sizeable fleet of gulets, and is a fine place to begin a Blue Cruise. The marina at the base of Kaleiçi is home to boats, as well, but most of them are of the day-trip variety.

By Bus

Antalya's main otogar is now several kilometers distant from the Kaleiçi district on Kazim Özalp Caddesi. The major companies (Kamil Koç, Ulusoy, and Varan) are represented, as are a handful of smaller competitors. There is service to almost every major city in Turkey. Kamil Koç serves the Lycian coast to the west. Varan, one of Turkey's premier lines, offers non-smoking buses to and from İstanbul for $20, Ankara for $15, and İzmir for $15. Taxis into Kaleici should cost less than $8, and there is dolmuş service.

Many dolmuş pass through the otogar, but the official dolmuş station is to the east of Kaleiçi. From Kaleiçi follow Cumhuriyet/Atatürk Caddesi east to the Doğu Garaj parking lot, on your right. Some dolmuş (Serik, for instance) must be met even further down Atatürk Caddesi at the Mevlana Caddesi intersection.

By Car

Roads radiating out from Antalya in all directions are well-maintained. The northern road, to Isparta, is the most popular route for people making their way to Cappadocia (via Konya); its ascent into the Taurus mountains is beautiful. The western road hugs the coast until Tekirova, after which it ascends through pine forests in the direction of Olympos and beyond. To the east, the road is broad and flat all the way to Alanya, after which it begins a somewhat harrowing route along the precipitous Cilician coast.

If you are staying in Antalya's Kaleiçi district and you are using a rental car, be sure to have crystal clear directions before entering Kaleiçi itself—losing yourself in the tight, winding lanes of Kaleiçi in the heat of summer is no fun.

Orientation

The city is laid out along the clifftop, sprawling east to west. To reach Kaleiçi follow signs directing you toward Kaleiçi or "Liman."

Antalya is a base from which to see nearby ruins, but its own are not particularly compelling. They are worth appreciating on your inevitable way past. The major ruins of Selge, Aspendos, Sillion, Aspendos and Termessos are listed below in *Seeing the Sights*.

The **tourism information** office is on the main waterfront road, three blocks west of Kaleiçi, Cumhuriyet Caddesi, *Tel. 242 247 0541.*

A Not-Quite Secret Beach

Mermerli (Marble) Beach, so-named because of the jumble of marble columns strewn in the crystal clear water offshore, is located a short walk from hotels in Kaleiçi. The water offshore is warm, with the exception of chilly spots where fresh water wells up from the surface. The presence of the beach is hardly secret, but before 1 p.m. on hot weekdays, you're likely to have it almost to yourself. The trick is to arrive shortly after the sun creeps above the cliff walls; between May and August, that means getting there at about 10 a.m. After 1 p.m. you'll have more company, but even then Mermerli Beach tends to remain lightly visited. One reason for this (here's the other trick) is that access to Mermerli Beach isn't free; a $2.25 fee is charged at the Mermerli Restaurant entrance, that includes use of the deck chairs.

Where to Stay

The Historic Preservation Society and the Turkish Touring and Automobile Association have conspired to bar development of new buildings in Antalya's old city, Kaleiçi, so this thicket of charming 100- and 200-year-old patios and compounds is safe. We suggest that you stay here (unless the Sheraton three kilometers west is more your style).

Rates given are for the high season and are typically one-third lower in the fall and spring, and can drop dramatically in the winter. Rates are typically set by the municipality, so haggling is not technically necessary - but it always helps. Breakfast is usually included.

If you are in Antalya with a small group, you may want to inquire about renting an apartment. Daily rates begin at $35. Inquire at the tourist information office.

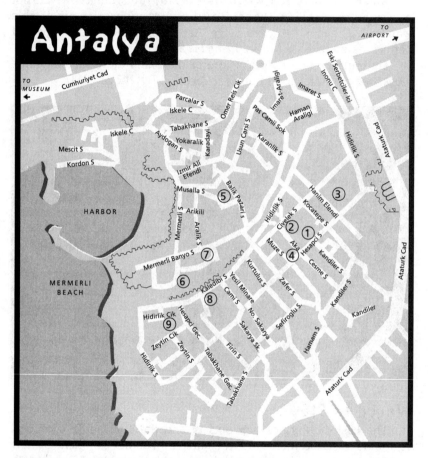

HOTELS

1. Villa Perla
2. Antalya Pansiyon
3. Ninova Pansiyon
4. Alp Pasa Hotel
5. Argos Hotel
6. Aspen Hotel
7. Dogan Hotel
8. Dedekonak Pansiyon
9. Bacchus Pension

ANTIQUE PANSIYON, *Paşa Camii Sokak, Antalya. Tel. (242) 242-4615; Fax (242) 241-5890; Email: fatihsertel@ixir.com. Rooms: 5. Credit cards not accepted. Open year-round. Double (no off-season discount): $27 (breakfast included). Dinner (guests only): $8.*

This grand old (almost 300-year old!) house has walls one-half meter thick, cool interiors, upper floor ceilings almost 12 feet high, and fine old woodwork and paned glass sitting areas throughout. Such features are marvelous, but in Kaleiçi they are not unique; unique is the food from the kitchen—some of the finest Turkish cuisine we have had—and the engaging hospitality of owner and chef Fatih Sertel, who runs the Antique Pansiyon with his Dutch wife Emmy. Unique are the sensibilities of the owner, who has pared the number of rooms from eight to five to help ensure good relations among his guests.

The back patio is unassuming, but it changes at dusk, transformed by candlelight on the hibiscus, by stars high above, and by food that has a fair claim to being the finest in Antalya. It is in such places as this that Turkey fulfils its promise; the laughter of sunburned guests, bottles of good, inexpensive wine, mezes prepared with first press olive oil, entrees that are delicious and plentiful, Lavazza filter coffee, and the reassurance of a nearby bed.

The Antique Pansiyon puts us to the test; giving the Antique Pansiyon's full measure risks full bookings when we, ourselves are next in Antalya. To get there: from Cumhuriet Caddesi enter Kaleiçi by the clock tower, then turn left by the minaret at Tekeli Ali Paşa Mosque onto Paşa Camii Sokak. The Antique Pansiyon is on your right a short distance along, opposite Dedehan Pansiyon.

Selected one of our favorite small hotels

VILLA PERLA, *Barbaros Mah., Hesapci Sok. No. 26, Kaleiçi, Antalya. Tel. (242) 248-9793; Fax (242) 241-2917; Email: info@villaperla.com; Web: www.villaperla.com. Rooms: 11. Credit cards accepted. Open year-round. Double (25% off-season discount): $70 (breakfast included). Dinner: $10.*

The Villa Perla is one of the finest examples of a restored Ottoman house in Kaleiçi. The house, entered through a spacious patio where meals are served, is two stories high with high ceilings. Both levels, connected by a great stair with a foundation of stone, look back out onto the patio and the ivy-covered wall behind through paned glass walls. The interiors are open and relaxed, with cushions and magazines for whiling away your time out of the heat. It's the feeling of these public spaces that make Villa Perla special. The rooms and their bathrooms, squeezed into spaces where other rooms had once been, are peculiar in the way of all of Kaleiçi's old houses. All rooms feature air-conditioning.

The matron (Inci, or "Perla") has run things here since 1990, and has a loyal following. The standard of the in-house restaurant is on par with others in Kaleiçi, not quite meeting the promise of its location. There is a very small pool in the courtyard, used mostly by oranges that drop from the trees above. An interesting note: this was for a short time the Italian consulate. The Italians picked this from among all the houses in Kaleiçi, and they knew Antalya well - it was their provincial seat during Italy's brief reign in the region following the World War I partition of the country. To get there: From Hadrian's Gate, go straight along Hesapçi Sokak; Villa Perla is on your right several blocks along, by the Alp Paşa Hotel.

ATELYA PANSİYON, *Barbaros Mah. Civelek Sok. No. 21, Kaleiçi, Antalya. Tel. (242) 241-6416; Fax (242) 241-2848. Rooms: 21. Credit cards not accepted. Open year-round. Double (20% off-season discount): $30 (breakfast included). Dinner: $10.*

Entering the spacious courtyard of the Atelya Pansiyon, you cannot help but relax. The courtyard is bedecked with green flowering things and traditional Turkish tchochkies — couches covered in kilims, antique wooden cabinets, metal and ceramic vessels. The Atelya's rooms are divided between a large, 160-year old Ottoman house and a newer structure across the street (room numbers in the 300 series). Rooms in the old house are the better, more intriguing option: 203 and 207, for instance, have traces of old Greek frescoes; 208 is spacoius and offers views toward the sea beneath the eaves. All rooms in the old house have high ceilings, wood or tile floors, showers, and, in the upper rooms, air-conditioning.

NINOVA PENSION, *Barbaros Mah. Hamit Efendi Sok. No. 9, Kaleiçi, Antalya. Tel. (242) 248-6114; Fax (242) 248-9684; Email: ninova@euroseek.com. Rooms: 19. Credit cards accepted. Open year-round. Double (15% off-season discount): $40 (breakfast included). Dinner: $8.*

This spacious 100-year old Ottoman structure has high ceilings, wood floors, and a peaceful, stone-walled garden with orange trees that won an award in 1996 for the most beautiful garden in Antalya. The rooms are small and spartan, but the ceilings are high and all but four naturally cooler rooms downstairs have air-conditioning. A large common room boasts a fireplace and a television. A wonderful place to return to after a day searing on the beach or at the ruins. To get there: From the clock tower, turn right, then left at Paşa Camii minaret, left at Felek rental car office, then turn up the Hamit Efendi Sokak, beside Hotel Bougainville. (During our visit in 2001, there was no street-facing sign.)

Selected one of our favorite small hotels.

MINI-ORIENT HOTEL, *Barbaros Mah. Civelek Sok. No. 30, Kaleiçi, Antalya. Tel/Fax (242) 244-0015. Rooms: 10. Credit cards not accepted. Open* *year-round. Double (15% off-season discount): $20 (breakfast included). Dinner: $8.*

The Mini-Orient Hotel is another hotel located in a grand old house; the house, in its bones and its restoration, is similar to the Antique Pansiyon Hotel (above); its restoration a decade ago was carried out by the same man, Fatih Sertel. Dark wood ceilings, walls half a meter thick glass-paned walls; no, they don't make them like they used to. Rooms are simple, with bathrooms wedged into all of them. The three upstairs rooms are larger, better, and more expensive (by $5 per night). Standing fans are available. To get there: Right at the clock tower, left at the Paşa Camii minaret, go several blocks, then turn right at Oskar Sinema.

ALP PAŞA HOTEL, *Barbaros Mah., Hesapçi Sok. No. 30-32, Kaleiçi, Antalya. Tel. (242) 247-5676; Fax (242) 248-5074; Email: info@alppasa.com; Web: www.alppasa.com. Rooms: 57. Credit cards not accepted. Open year-round. Double (15% off-season discount): $60-$90 (breakfast included). Dinner: $15.*

The Alp Paşa is housed in several old mansions that date back 200 years; their transformation into a hotel was completed in 1995. This is today one of the most popular hotels in Kaleiçi for group tours. The hotel has high, ornate wooden ceilings, foundations of marble blocks, and a pretty setting around a pleasant (and often busy) garden. The quality and style of rooms varies greatly; suffice it to say that even the cheapest rooms are pleasant and air-conditioned, and the more expensive rooms are marvelous. The prices listed are with reservation—posted room prices are much higher. Buffet dinner costs $12. To get there: Right at the clock tower, left just past the Paşa Camii minaret, left at Oscar Sinema, and left after about 20 meters (one block from Villa Perla).

ASPEN HOTEL, *Kaledibi Sok. No. 16-18, Kaleiçi, Antalya 07100. Tel. (242) 247-0590; Fax (242) 241-3364; Email: aspenhotel@superonline.com; Web: www.aspenhotel.8k.com. Rooms: 40. Credit cards accepted. Open year-round. Double (40% off-season discount): $110 (breakfast included).*

The Aspen set the standard for Antalya's finer hotels, with its central building in a restored 150-year old Ottoman house and a network of pretty, multi-level, landscaped patios, fountains, and a pool. Its balconies are decked with flowers and the gardens are filled with aged marble and manicured plants. The quality of the rooms is uneven, alas, and most are housed in a large, modern building built for the purpose. You will find plenty of amenities—including room service and air conditioning—but unless you have a view room such 206-210 or rooms 500 and above, the Aspen is a solid choice, but not remarkable. (Note that the Aspen's nearby competitor, the Marina Hotel, is another upscale hotel with modern trappings; it is more expensive and less appealing.)

TUTAV TÜRK EVI, *Mermerli Sok. No. 2, Kaleiçi, Antalya, Tel. (242) 248-6591; Fax (242) 241-9419; Email: turkevi@tutavturkevi.com. Rooms: 20. Credit cards accepted. Restaurant. Open year-round. Double (20% off-season discount): $75 (breakfast included).*

Readers of this guide swear by the charms of the Tutav Turk Evleri, both its setting and its service. The evleri (or houses) surmount the ancient walls of Antalya, overlooking the marina and the bay beyond. Rooms do not take advantage of the view, and are filled with furniture that is a bit over-the-top Ottoman gaudy, but they are certainly decent and well cared-for. To get there: Follow Uzun Çarşı Sokak several long blocks downhill from the clock tower, turning left at Mermerli Sokak.

DOĞAN OTEL & PANSIYON, *Kılıçaslan Mah. Mermerli Banyo Sok. No. 5., Kaleiçi, Antalya. Tel. (242) 241-8842; Fax (242) 247-4006; Email: info@doganhotel.com; Web: www.doganhotel.com. Rooms: 30. Credit cards accepted. Open year-round. Double (20% off-season discount): $50 (if reservation; breakfast included).*

Blurring the lines between pension and hotel, the Doğan is comprised of three old, restored houses. The restorers of these houses restored them thoroughly, for better and worse—they are a bit bland. Still, the air-conditioned rooms are pleasant (rooms 118, 125, 136, and 137 have the nicest views), and the lush patio garden is a relaxing place, provided that the music from the patio bar doesn't drown out the sound of the fountains. The pool, installed in 1996, is a practical alternative to most of the decorative kidney-shapes in the area. To get there: head right at the clock tower, left at Paşa Camii minaret, then straight for 200 meters. The 12-room La Paloma Pansiyon, run by the same ownership and opened in April 2000 is a fine alternative that maintains a similar standard.

Budget

DEDEKONAK PANSİYON, *Kılıçaslan Mah., Hıdırlık Sok. No. 13, Kaleiçi, Antalya. Tel/Fax (242) 247 5170. Rooms: 10. Credit cards not accepted. Open year-round. Double (20% off-season discount): $20 (breakfast included).*

This small pension and restaurant, in a recently-restored 150-year old house, is one of the better values in Antalya. The vaulted ceilings, marble floors, and white tile give it an appealing, clean aesthetic, and the small garden is very pleasant. Ask for a room with a view (manzaralı oda). To get there: Turn right at the clock tower, left just past the Paşa Camii minaret, continuing two blocks past Oscar Sinema.

KARYATIT HOTEL, *Kılıçaslan Mah., Kadıpaşa Sok. No. 9, Kaleici, Antalya. Tel. (242) 244-0054; Fax (242) 244-0055. Rooms: 24. Credit cards not accepted. Open year-round. Double: $20 (breakfast included).*

A decent inexpensive choice, offering air-conditioned rooms in a restored old building. The building embraces a pleasant garden, and

483 CENTRAL MEDITERRANEAN COAST

hanımeli (honeysuckle) flowers hang from the rails. To get there: from the Karaali Park side of Kaleiçi, head into Kaleiçi by Sofra restaurant for one block, turning left onto Kadıpaşa Sokak.

NOSTALJI PANSIYON, *Atatürk Cad., Kocatepe Sok. No. 4, Kaleiçi, Antalya. Tel. (242) 244-0006; Fax (242) 247-9065. Rooms: 10. Credit cards not accepted. Open year-round. Double: $20 (breakfast included).*

A restored old house, with air-conditioning, double-pane windows and a pretty garden ringed with ivy—a surprisingly good deal, although its proximity to Atatürk Caddesi means some noise in evenings. To get there: from the Karaali Park side of Kaleiçi, head just 20 meters into Kaleiçi by Sofra restaurant.

Outside of Kaleiçi

SHERATON VOYAGER ANTALYA, *100 Yıl Bulvarı, Antalya. Tel. (242) 243-2432; Fax (242) 243-2462; Email: reservations.voyager@starwoodhotels.com; Web: www.sheraton.com. Rooms: 400. Double: $210-$180. Restaurants.*

Many giant hotels deteriorate rapidly and pitifully. A select few escape that fate. The Sheraton, an Antalya institution, is taking the latter course. The grounds are a bucolic pleasure, the rooms are done to a tee, service is engaging, and you'll often find a rose or some Turkish Delight in your room at the end of the day. Five star "full service" hotels sprang up in bunches in the early 1990s, but few were done with the precision and evident care taken with the Sheraton.

Guests at large hotels usually encounter a raft of silly indignities that include indifferent service and extra charges for the health club, hamam, or fresh squeezed orange juice. The Sheraton carefully avoids the appearance of parsimony, although you'll still pay a fee for the squash or tennis courts, and outside phone calls are, as usual, staggeringly expensive. Note that room prices are always negotiable by fax or e-mail beforehand, and published rates drop to $155-$130 in the off season.

The hotel is located atop Antalya's waterfront cliffs, with dedicated park and convention center land to one side and Antalya's outdoor sports facilities behind it. The acclaimed Antalya Archaeological Museum is just a short walk away. The location leaves plenty of room to run or stroll and watch the sun set.

Where to Eat

The old town, site of the Antalya's finest lodging, is also the place to find good food. Many of the accommodations we list offer dinner for guests; it's probably worth your while to dine out once or twice, however. There are many places serving cheap, fresh-squeezed orange juice, and small stores offer a delicious array of fruit preserves. Big Mac attack? You'll find a McDonalds on the heavily-trafficked road that rings Kaleiçi, just inland of Karaali Park on Atatürk Caddesi.

SIM RESTAURANT, *Kılıçaslan Mah., Kaledibi Sok. No. 7, Antalya. Tel. (242) 248-0107. Open year-round. Credit cards not accepted. Moderate.*
Turnover among kitchen staff is the bane of guidebook writers; so much the better that the best-kept dining secret in Kaleiçi is owned by its chef, Süheyla Edipoğlu. The Sim is an unpretentious place, squeezed into a vine-covered alley with a few tables outside and more in the graffiti-scrawled interior. On our first visit, nearly despairing of finding a good, inexpensive dining option in Kaleiçi, we enjoyed eggplant tightly stuffed with rice, dill, pepper, and tomato, served with toasted bread, cheese, and tomatoes. The table was adorned with fresh-cut flowers; Süheyla was adorned with a smile. That light repast, perfect in the heat of the afternoon, cost $1.50. A price-fixe four-course dinner, with an entrée of stew, kebap, or seafood, is $8 well-spent. "We are only a restaurant," reads the menu; a polite way of saying "We don't cater to a captive audience of guests—our food has to be outstanding." Outstanding it is.

To get there: follow Paşa Camii down in the direction of Mermerli Beach; at Doğan Hotel (near Oscar Cinema), turn uphill, pass Kleopatra Pansiyon, and turn right.

CHANG QING CHINESE RESTAURANT, *Imaret Sok., Dönerciler Çarşısı Arkası No. 28, Antalya. Tel. (242) 247-6587. Open year-round. Credit cards accepted. Moderate-Expensive.*
Particularly popular among those disembarking from Blue Cruises, Chang Qing has Chinese ownership and well-regarded food. Portions are light, but the cost isn't extravagant--spring rolls, almond chicken, sweet and sour beef, chow mein, and drinks, cost $20. To get there: Chang Qing is just within Kaleiçi, behind the clock tower on Cumhuriet Caddesi.

TATLISES LAHMACUN, *Barbaros Mah., Atatürk Caddesi No. 54, Antalya. Tel. (242) 247-2560. Open year-round. Credit cards not accepted. Inexpensive.*
If you're in the mood for something quick, cheap and delicious, make your way toward McDonalds on Atatürk Caddesi (following the flow of traffic south past Hadrian's Gate), and duck into Tatlises instead. Tatlises restaurants are Turkey's answer to McDonalds, in fact—a "Turkish pizza" fast food franchise founded by Turkish arabesque singing super-star Ibrahim Tatlises. Two lahmacun, costing $.75 apiece, constitute a meal, more or less.

LA TRATTORIA, *Fevzi Çakmak Caddesi No. 3C, Antalya. Tel. (242) 243-3931. Open year-round. Credit cards accepted. Expensive.*
La Trattoria is justly known for offering the finest Italian food in Antalya. How to get there: Go to Atatürk Caddesi, outside Hadrian's Gate, and follow the flow of traffic around past the police station—La

Trattoria is on your left.

CLUB 29, *Kaleiçi Yat Limanı, Antalya. Tel. (242) 241-6260; Fax (242) 247-5937. Open year-round. Credit cards accepted. Expensive.*
Club 29 is the smartest restaurant in Antalya. You enter the spacious, vaulted interior of this former warehouse through grand wooden doors and are ushered between thick black curtains. Dining tables are lined up in rows, punctuated by dark couches and tables strewn with Turkish and English-language magazines. The wood ceilings are held high aloft by great stone arches, and the arches are pierced by windows that command a view of the marina entrance and the Mediterranean beyond. Outside those windows, a sweeping balcony dotted with plants fills up with diners at sunset. Mezes begin at $4; entrees such as lamb filet with mint sauce and greens or risotto with porcini mushrooms cost $10; desserts cost $8; the wine list ranges from $15 to $45. The adjoining night club is where the jet-set come to dance.

TUTAV TÜRK EVI, *Mermerli Sok. No. 2, Kaleiçi, Antalya. Tel. (242) 248-6591. Open year-round. Credit cards accepted. Expensive.*
Asked to recommend a hotel restaurant that is open to the public, we would point you to the restaurants at Tutav Türk Evi. The location, within the ancient city walls, is sublime, and the quality of food has been consistent for several years. Tutav Türk Evi features the Pink House and Green House restaurants, as well as the Kale Bar. Watching the onset of dusk from the battlements over mezes ($6) and a plate of grilled fish or steak ($10) is a treat.

MERMERLI RESTAURANT, *Mermerli/Kaleiçi Banyo Sokak No. 25, Antalya. Tel. (242) 248-5484. Moderate.*
Mermerli Restaurant, atop the stair that descends to Mermerli Beach (see sidebar above), offers one of the finest views in Kaleiçi to accompany food that is better—and less expensive—than you might expect. After spending time baking on the beach below, the open, airy restaurant is a fine refuge. Meze ($1 to $3), beer ($1), and köfte ($2.50) go down well here, accompanied by unrestricted views west past the warships laying at anchor in the great bay, and, beyond, Bakırlıdağ and the Bey Mountains climbing out of the haze. In the foreground, smaller vessels slice through the sea toward the marina just below. To get there: follow Paşa Camii Sokak to its end (the name changes to Mermerli Banyo Sokak) at the southeast corner of the harbor.

NATURAL INTERNET CAFÉ, *Cumhüriyet Meydanı Antalya. Tel. (242) 243-8763. Open year-round. Credit cards not accepted. Inexpensive-Moderate.*
This is a great place to check your Hotmail account and catch up on your web surfing, a friendly spot with inexpensive café fare and fast connections at $1 per hour. The Internet café is on the lower courtyard of

Republican Square, just west of Kaleiçi on the waterfront side of Cumhüriyet Caddesi. Food is reasonably priced, comes in good-sized portions, and is surprisingly tasty.

Seeing the Sights

The principal attractions of Antalya are clustered around the warren of the old town, **Kaleiçi** (literally, "within the fortress"). Kaleiçi is perched above a small, perfect bay, one that remains in use today as it was two thousands years ago. Far to the east and west, high cliff walls descend into the sea, backed by parks and pedestrian thoroughfares.

It's likely that the first true sight you see as you approach Antalya's old city will be the **fluted minaret** (Yivli Minare) located near the main entrance to Kaleiçi off of Cumhuriet Caddesi. Bundled red-brick columns form the shaft of the fluted minaret, a distinctive creation built in the early thirteenth century for Selcuk Sultan Alaeddin Keykobad. The minaret was originally attached to a converted Byzantine church, but it is all that remains of the original structure.

Standing just inland of the minaret at the entrance to Kaleiçi is a commonly-referenced landmark, the **stone clocktower** (Saat Kulesi). Inland of the clocktower is Antalya's open bazaar, while behind the clocktower Uzun Çarşı Sokak descends past broken old walls toward the marina.

If you'd like to see what Antalya looked like in days of yore, stop by the painstakingly-restored digs of the **Suna-İnan Kıraç Research Institute on Mediterranean Civilizations** within Kaleiçi (Barbaros Mah., Kocatepe Sok. No. 25, Tel. (242) 243-4274; open 9 a.m. to 6 p.m., closed Wednesdays; $.50). The buildings were restored from 1993-1996, and the Institute and its archives were established to conduct archaeological and ethnographic research on Mediterranean cultures. In the garden of one of the buildings is the meticulously restored Greek church of St. George. On exhibit are historic photographs of old Antalya, and the art collection of Suna and İnan Kıraç. Note the beautiful pebble mosaic floors. The Institute is open 9:00am–6:00pm, closed Wednesdays. A visitors' cafeteria and gift shop is also at the site.

Continuing on around the Cumhuriet/Atatürk Caddesi ring road, keeping Kaleiçi to your left, you can't miss **Hadrian's Gate** (130 A.D.). Most cities in Asia Minor commemorated the visit of Roman Emperor Hadrian, and Antalya was no different. The triple-arcade marble gate built to honor the emperor is one of the few traces of that ancient city. Further south, in the direction of traffic on the one-way street, you'll pass McDonalds en route to Karaali Park, within which is the Hıdırlık Kulesi, a cylindrical tower on the clifftop overlooking the bay. The building dates to the second century A.D., but its use is unknown; it is thought to have been a watchtower or tomb. The park is pleasant on warm evenings; young couples stroll in the company of chaperones a few paces behind and wheeling bats in the trees above.

The most impressive historical sights in Antalya are housed in the **Antalya Museum** (closed Mondays, $3.50). The museum can be reached on foot from Kaleiçi, but it's a hike: take advantage of the tram line ($.30 tickets) or a "Konyaaltı" minibus. The collection at the Antalya museum is among the most well-organized and carefully-presented in Turkey. We highly recommend setting aside half of a day for a visit here. You will appreciate the information in the exhibits here during excursions to nearby ruins, and the education goes down easily with the pleasure of seeing a marvelous collection of sculpture. Highlights include a room with statues of Greek and Egyptian gods, from Athena to Zeus; a register explains their roles and powers. An inscribed chunk of Saint Nicholas' skull is also on hand.

You will find, also, a stern rebuke to the Museum of Fine Arts in Boston in the front court. There, the bottom half of a statue is displayed, together with a photograph of the perfectly matching upper half now on display at the American museum. Turkey continues to be burned by thievery of antiquities, and is understandably outraged when a respectable foreign museum benefits from the practice. The museum is a long walk or a short cab ride from the Kaleiçi along the waterfront road, Cumhuriet Cadessi.

Sports & Recreation
Beaches

In addition to **Mermerli Beach**, located just below Kaleiçi (see sidebar), there are two large expanses of beach to either side of the old city. The long band of **Konyaaltı Beach**, beginning just beyond the Archaeological Museum west of Kaleiçi, joins Antalya to the resort areas in the west. Konyaaltı offers large stretches of free public beach, but is pebbly and not particularly clean. Better, **Lara Beach** ($.50 entry, $3 for chairs and umbrellas) is a sand beach, generally well maintained. You can catch dolmuş for either beach (helpfully signed "Konyaaltı" and "Lara," respectively) from Cumhuriet Caddesi at the entrance to Kaleiçi.

Boating

A boat tour out of Antalya is enjoyable - although perhaps redundant if you've already had the good fortune to have a gulet cruise. Particular companies are as evanescent as their reputation, so the best policy is to get a personal recommendation: Regatta and Dragon are recommended *against*. The Kaleiçi harbor is filled with tour boats and their touts.

Itineraries vary little: a five hour tour will usually include a short sail out to **Rat Island**, where pirates once holed up. Your day is divided between swimming and some mild sightseeing at the island. Lunch is served. The cost is about $14 per person, but you can do better. Another destination is the **Lower Duden waterfalls**, a shorter trip.

Blue Cruises

Antalya's **Setur Marina** is the eastern hub of blue cruises, trips on which you can spend a few days or a week aboard a single-masted wooden sailing ship. As addressed in Chapter 6, *Planning Your Trip*, these trips are quite reasonably priced (prices are highest in August) and are just about the best thing you can do while in Turkey.

Golf

The **National Golf Club**, *Tel. 242 725-4620*, is located in Belek, one-half hour east of Antalya. The course has an 18-hole championship course and a nine-hole par 3 course, as well as a driving range.

Rafting/Canyoning

Several companies lead guided rafting tours down the lower Köprüçay (Eurymedon) River as well as "canyoning" day trips through a steep, beautiful gorge east of Side, allowing you to swim, jump, and clamber your way down. We'd sugggest making your arrangements via the well-connected adventure travel agency **Bougainville Travel** in Kaş *(Tel. (242) 836-3142; Fax (242) 836-1605; Email: info@bougainville-turkey.com; Web: www.bougainville-turkey.com)*. Of the agencies based in Antalya, **Medraft** has the best reputation: Konyaaltı Cad. Derya Apt. No. 68-16, Antalya, *Tel. (242) 248-0083*.

For rafting trips from Antalya, you will take a 50 minute bus ride to Side to join rafting trips before their 9 a.m. departures. Some rafting trips include half-day visits to the distant ruins of Selge combined with a half-day descent down the Köprüçay River by raft.

Cinema

There are several theatres in Antalya. As elsewhere in Turkey, all American films are presented in English with Turkish subtitles. The two most convenient theatres are **Oscar Sinema**, in the center of Kaleiçi at the intersection of Paşa Camii Sokak and Zafer Sokak, and **Kultur Sinema** on Atatürk Caddesi near Karaali Park, with its back to Kaleiçi. If you're not pleased with the offerings at either cinema, see what's showing at **Sinema Megapol** *(Tel. 237-0131, in the Meltem district, near the Sheraton)* and **Batı Sinema** *(Tel. 247-8625, six blocks inland of the clocktower on Milli Eğemenlik Caddesi)*.

Shopping

Antalya's **Bazaar** is just outside the Kaleiçi area in the direction of the otogar. Antalya has a slew of international retailers, including Benetton and Ralph Lauren. This is in addition to the regular assortment of shops selling leather, carpets, and other Turkish goods.

Excursions & Day Trips

Using Antalya as a base you can see all three of the the ruins to the east in a day - Aspendos, Sillion, and Perge. If you have patience for more, you can even brave the tourist feeding frenzy at Side. Selge and Termessos, distant and isolated, pose the biggest challenge for visitors without their own transportation, and even with your own transportation will account for more than half a day. The following ruins are listed in order from east (Selge) to west (Termessos).

SELGE

This remote city is difficult to reach, but rewarding for those who persevere. The site is high in the mountains above the **Köprüçay River**, surrounded by cedar forests and stone that bears a resemblance to the bizarre landscape of the Cappadocian interior. The ruins are at an elevation of 3,000 feet, and get only determined visitors; their inaccessibility has helped preserve them from museum-funded depredation. Plan on spending more than three hours at the site; take a lunch along, a sweater for the altitude, and, as always, lots of fluid.

If you're driving, turn off the main E400 road five kilometers east of the Aspendos turn off, passing through Taşağıl to Beşkonak, 37 kilometers inland. Ignore the first set of Selge signs, continuing to Beşkonak and then a further 18 kilometers to Selge, following the signs to Altınkaya/ Zerk. Six kilometers beyond Beşkonak turn left at the Altınkaya sign, cross the bridge, and follow the road right and up the final gravelled 11 kilometers.

Dolmuş serve Beşkonak, but from that remote town you must cross the Köprüçay River and ascend another 18 kilometers. There are a few taxis in Beşkonak willing to shuttle you to the site for a flat fee, but it begins making more sense to arrange a full day ruins excursion unless you really want to see the ruins on your own. Anyway, you begin to understand why invaders like Pergamon's Attalus II usually gave up.

History

Oddly, the residents of Selge had a running feud with their equally inaccessible and recalcitrant western neighbors, the residents of **Termessos**. Why the two fairly distant cities came into conflict is unknown - perhaps over control of the mountainous interior in between - but their antipathy was evident whenever a third party invader would march on either one of the cities. When Alexander besieged Termessos the people of Selge dropped what they were doing and raced to his assistance. After Alexander abandoned the siege, the people of Selge were only too happy to lead him against another of their Pisidian allies, Sagalassus. The Termessans, for their part, were happy to return the favor when Selge provoked Attalus II to attempt an invasion.

Both cities succeeded in resisting these and countless other sieges, and Selge was ordinarily left alone in its lofty perch. During the prosperous early Roman years, an estimated 20,000 people lived in this town, a seemingly remarkable number for so inhospitable a site, but the citizens traded heavily in wine, olives, livestock, and a local perfume made with the resin of the styrax bush. The trade augmented the toll business, but in time the trade routes shifted (and perfume tastes changed) and Selge's importance waned. Selge, initially ranked behind only Side in the esteem of the Byzantine Empire's Mediterranean bishoprics, dropped quickly out of sight in the 400s.

Visiting the Ruins of Selge
Selge is notable for the beauty of its situation, as you begin to understand on the long, winding ascent to the old city. The deep gorges and peculiarly weathered stone are blanketed with coastal cedars in the lower climes, then heartier pines - and light-hued styrax bushes - at the higher elevations. The old Roman bridge that you cross on your ascent has given its name to the former Eurymedon River; Köprüçay, or "Bridge River."

Selge is built in the heights above Zerk, where the road terminates. The theater, facing you, initially dominates the ruins. This theater has a predictably excellent view, and may have been large enough to hold half of Selge's Roman-era population, 10,000. At the foot of the theater is the large market square, or **agora**, while to the south - the right as you look out from the theater - a long **stadium** runs in the direction of the slope and the city walls. The ancient town occupies the high ground south of Zerk, and is ringed by a wall.

The walls, mostly broken or borrowed on the Zerk side, are in good condition on the far side of the slope, on the southern face of the hill. A necropolis is located in the section of town just above the theater, with another necropolis on the eastern spur. Some of the stones bear inscriptions in Pisidian. The city's truly dominant feature is the **Temple of Zeus** standing on a spur above the rest of the town, in what amounts to the acropolis of Selge.

ASPENDOS

Aspendos is home to one of the world's great ancient theaters, with other ruins on the hill just above.

The route is well signed if you're driving, three miles north off the main road east of Antalya between Serik and Side. Aspendos can also be reached easily by public transport. Take a bus or dolmuş to the Serik otogar and transfer to an hourly Aspendos-bound dolmuş. Fare to Serik from Antalya or Side is $1, and the Aspendos leg is 40¢. There is also a coven of taxis waiting at the Aspendos turn-off on the main road, their meters ratcheted up full blast - no need to have them wait at the site, there are always other taxis (and the hourly Serik dolmuş) to bring you back.

You can also visit by tour. Every Antalya and Side tour company includes Aspendos in a one-day trip that also includes Manavgat Falls and Perge, with average rates of about $22 and a trip to a carpet shop or jewelry store cutting deeply into your time.

History

Aspendos is an Anatolian name, so there was probably a settlement here before the arrival of colonizing outsiders. According to an apocryphal but accepted theory, the colonizers in question were Trojans fleeing the ruin of their empire in the 13th century B.C. This theory was popular in the ancient world, where cities around the Mediterranean basin, Rome included, sought to cultivate a worthy, if revisionist, heritage by establishing roots among the Trojan heroes. If in fact the Greeks did colonize the area, it was probably already settled by Asian natives of some stripe, perhaps Hittites.

The citizens of Aspendos were not particularly good at warfare, and it's no wonder their trade routes were preyed on by the Pisidians at Termessos and Selge, but their spotty martial record is at least entertaining. The city followed the normal course in the region, falling under Lydian, then Persian, control. While still a Persian possession, Aspendos was the site of a critical battle between the Greeks and Persians. Persian **King Xerxes**, desperately trying to recover from the failure of his Greek invasion, gathered the remnants of his army and navy near Aspendos in 467 B.C. The Athenian navy, having won over the Lycian cities to the west, advanced eastward and descended on the Persian encampment. The naval battle went quickly and predictably to the Greek admiral Cimon, who followed up his success the same evening by outfitting his army with captured ships and uniforms and crushing the confused and demoralized Persian and Aspendian soldiers at the mouth of the river Eurymedon.

Having been thus fooled, in 333 B.C. the citizens of Aspendos sought to use some guile of their own. They made a great declaration of peace with **Alexander the Great** on his approach. Alexander accepted the terms and busied himself with the siege of Sillion to the west. Aspendos' citizenry then used the breathing space to begin fortifying and arming their city against Alexander. Messengers informed Alexander of the treachery, and the young general, already exasperated by the time-consuming siege of towering Sillion, marched his army back to Aspendos. The illicit building effort was of course unfinished, and the conqueror's unexpected arrival caused much consternation. The town fathers cowered, paid double the initial tribute, handed over hostages, and accepted a garrison.

The heavy payment aside, Aspendos' fortunes rose following Alexander's arrival in 333 B.C. Piracy blossomed along the coast, but Aspendos probably had a tidy stake in the pirating business. In fact, the Roman onslaught that finally broke local piracy (70 B.C.) had a deleterious effect on local affairs; Rome saddled Aspendos with a series of avaricious governors who famously stripped the city of its sculpture and artwork.

Aspendos remained a viable city throughout the first millennium A.D. - the theater was built in the second century A.D. - but its fortunes waned. The Byzantines had a respectable city at the site, and the ruins of a grand basilica are atop the hill behind the theater. Arab depredations finally drove the Byzantines away, and the Selçuks occupied the deteriorating city from the time of **Alaeddin Keykobad I** (1219-1236 A.D.). Under the Selçuks the long-empty theater came to life again; its stage building became headquarters for the local Selçuk governor.

Visiting the Ruins of Aspendos

The parking lot is located directly beneath the grand Aspendos **theater**, which is the finest Roman-era theater in the world today. Unless you are in town for the June **Balat Arts Festival** (contact the Antalya Ministry of Culture for schedules, Tel. 242 243 3810) the sublime acoustics are squandered on foreigners' experimental hooting. The theater is like the many others in Turkey, only more complete. The statues that once lined the top of the theater are missing, as is most of the detail from the stage, but the theater is fundamentally the same as it was when it was built in the late second century A.D. during the reign of Marcus Aurelius (161-180). According to one theory, the massive theater was built to compensate for Aspendos' decline into relative unimportance.

Perhaps the most wonderful thing about Aspendos' theater is that it attracts tour groups to the exclusion of all else. The only entrance fee at Aspendos is for the theater ($4), and the rest of the site costs nothing to visit. The theater is not particularly more interesting than those at Perge, Ephesus, or elsewhere unless you have a background in Roman architecture. The gentle hill above the theater has the balance of the city's ruins. The trail begins to the right of the theater. The right fork takes you out past a sprawling temple building and continues out past several smaller structures to the old city walls, pierced in a draw by the old Northern Gate.

As at Sillion, there are several **deep cisterns** scattered around the site; be careful. To the west of the gate is the **aquaduct**, an astounding piece of engineering. The aquaduct carried water to Aspendos from the foothills to the north, delivering it in under enough pressure to supply the entire town through terracotta, lead-reinforced pipe. The entire aquaduct structure is some 80 feet high, even with the top of Aspendos' hill. The aquaduct's course within the city is impossible to determine.

The stadium and necropolis at the eastern foot of the hill are in bad shape, overgrown and broken.

As mentioned, the stripping of Aspendos began in 60 B.C. and has been carried on today by the world's museums. The town center offers several large, nondescript structures and the foundations of others, but the statues and ornamentation that accented Aspendos are long gone. One of the last remaining pieces of interest is a white column bearing Greek inscriptions.

SILLION

There are three yellow signs along the main D400 road indicating Sillion. The westernmost sign takes you through Abdullah Rahman, where another sign directs you to the right toward the Sillion mesa. If you keep your eye on the imposing Sillion mesa, however, any of the occasionally confusing roads will bring you to the gravel parking area at the southern side of Sillion and the small store. If you feel lost, say *"Sillion istiyorum. Sillion nair-duh?"* (I want Sillion. Where is it?) and at least get a general point in the direction of the ruins. The roads are perfectly manageable.

Leave your car at the small refreshment stand on the southwest (Antalya, sea side) and have a look at the battered metal historical marker sign, as it is the only tourism-friendly object at the site.

No dolmuş serve this remote site, but it is less than 10 kilometers from the main road. On a Serik or Side-bound bus from Antalya ask to be dropped off at the Belek turn-off, where taxis can take you directly inland to the site. This is most sensible in small groups, since transport and a few hours at the sight will cost about $20 or $25.

History

Sillion arrived on the historical scene with a bang, when it defied **Alexander the Great** in 333 B.C. Alexander immediately marched on

Sillion and besieged the city. The siege of towering Sillion rapidly promised to become time consuming, however, and Alexander wanted to move along. Alexander, gritting his teeth at the citizens hurling boulders down on his troops and dancing mockingly atop the outcrop, eventually withdrew to Aspendos. As a result, this is one of the few places to have successfully held its own against the conqueror.

Sillion emerged from obscurity during Alexander's campaign only to lapse back into obscurity once again. How earlier and later conquerors dealt with the city is unknown - probably in much the same way Alexander did, cutting it off and letting it fall in good time of its own accord. It was always associated with Perge, even claiming the same legendary and fabricated founder, Mopsus. Both the Byzantines and the Selçuks maintained garrisons here, and some of the ruins are of their creation.

Visiting the Ruins of Sillion

Reaching the top of Sillion requires a 30-minute climb from the valley floor to the top, plus exploration time. Allow yourself three hours at the site. To reach the top either rent a lad to show you the way or follow the path that meanders gradually upwards to the right of the mesa, cutting back up past a spring. You can reach the top by a fairly direct route up this south side, or follow the old road as it climbs the west (left) side of the mesa and doubles back. As at most sites, try to be here before the heat of the day. You are likely to have Sillion virtually to yourself.

Sillion's ruins are curious. After passing the outer ramparts and checkpoints and scrambling to the top, you'll find yourself in heavy undergrowth with walls and buildings poking out. It's a disorienting place, so get your bearings to assure a swift and hassle-free descent.

The first reward for the sweaty hike up the ridge into Sillion is appreciation for Alexander's frustration. The city was perfectly defensible with strong walls augmenting the sheer rock faces. The remaining rewards are for determined bushwhackers, because the upper area of Sillion is thick with underbrush. First, work your way into the middle of the city, behind the great Hellenistic walls, and poke around for a stone doorway. Here, on the inside of a door jamb, is the longest example of the undeciphered Pamphlian writing. It has been partially destroyed by a deep rectangular hole cut into the jamb, and was apparently recycled as a doorjamb after a more dignified role elsewhere.

Continue past the old Hellenistic walls to the southern edge of the mesa. Be careful: the upper level of Sillion is pocked with **deep cisterns**, and their flared openings are convenient for falling through and inconvenient for escape. To the southwest is Sillion's **theater**. The theater was built into the top of the hill, but its lower sections have toppled away, crashing to the earth hundreds of feet below. Only the upper rows of the theater remain, and all the world is its stage.

Beyond this, further along the southern edge, are several small buildings and a number of deep fissures. The most intriguing of these fissures is located just in front of a temple structure, separating the temple from the main body of Sillion. There is a small Hellenistic bridge spanning the narrow chasm. The fissure itself may have once had a sheer, **secret path** winding down to the valley floor. This is partially supported by a tunnel sunk into the earth below the city in the neighborhood of the fissure's opening. The path, if it was indeed a path, is no longer suited for any traffic whatsoever; the fissure now is a treacherous jumble of fallen stone. The temple itself is constructed of both blocks of stone and living rock, but there is no indication of its denomination. At the far eastern edge of Sillion is a tower with a predictably magnificent view of the Pamphlian plain below.

The aforementioned tunnel requires effort and determination to reach. After descending from the top, circle back around to the left by whatever paths you can find. The explorer George Bean describes the tunnel, which he speculated to be a water channel, as two feet wide and 75 feet long, with several rooms at the end. Bean visited the site about 30 years ago, and we have yet to locate it ourselves, but we wish anyone intrepid enough the best of luck.

PERGE

Perge sprawls along a plain between two high hills. One of the hills once held the former acropolis; that is gone, but most of the city's public buildings remain. Perge is the closest and most convenient ruin to Antalya.

Perge is the easiest of the ruins in the Antalya area to see. If you're driving, follow the main coast road (E400) east out of Antalya to Aksu, 13 kilometers on. Just after entering Aksu from Antalya look for a sign directing you left to Perge, one mile off the main road.

Dolmuş and normal buses serve Aksu en route to cities further east. Aksu buses depart from the main otogar, and are the best option; dolmuş make a broad circuit around the center of town, meaning a long walk east on Cumhuriet Caddesi to Doğu Garaj or the Mevlana Caddesi intersection.

History

Until the upstart Antalya came along in the second century, Perge was the first major city east of the **Lycian Mountains**. Owing to its (former) coastal location and its position near the Cestrus River (Aksu

Çay), trade funneled through the area and it was already established at the time of the **Trojan War**. Hittite records mention a city called Parha on the Kashtraha River, which seems a match for Perge on the Cestrus. Then as now, Antalya probably produced an abundance of crops, including citrus.

Perge did not enjoy the defensive advantages of its truculent neighbors Termessus and Sillion, nor did it share Aspendos' bad judgment; when **Alexander** arrived in 333 B.C., Perge welcomed him, appointing guides and whatever assistance he asked. Alexander moved on quickly, ensuring his flank was secure before continuing north and east to confront the retreating Persians, but in the aftermath Perge's position among the Pamphlian cities was elevated. Following Alexander's death, Perge passed back and forth between all of the principal rivals for Alexander's Empire, but after Pergamon and Rome united to defeat the Seleucids in 188 B.C., the kingdom spawned by Lysimachos, Pergamon, won control of the city.

Even at this time, the port at Side was considered much superior to Perge's shallow bay. King Attalus II of Pergamon, clearly dissatisfied with Perge's diminishing value as a port, sought to establish his own port city, Attaleia, modern Antalya, in 160 B.C. This nearby city would eventually supplant Perge, but not for centuries. The Roman period burdened the town with some inept and corrupt governors, but was generally a time of prosperity. In the first century Perge reached its greatest historic extent, a population of 100,000.

Among Perge's advantages over the upstart Antalya was a renowned **Temple of Artemis**. This temple, mentioned in Strabo's *Geography* and on inscriptions still at the site (search through the tumbled inscriptions inside the pylons of the Hellenistic gates), has not been located. It may have been dismantled and scattered by especially thorough Christians.

Two large basilicas at Perge establish that the city was still powerful into the fifth century B.C., but the one-two punch of siltation and a new rival with a superior bay eventually sent Perge into decline. The city's great arcades and lanes have become the province of goat herds.

Visiting the Ruins of Perge

As with so many cities that once were built on the ancient shore, Perge can be hard to envision. Upon arrival clamber up the **theater** (if restoration work is complete). When it was built, the theater would have looked directly out over the sea, which continued on around the acropolis hill to the left, on the far side of the ruins. The course of walls remains in good shape, excluding the theater and stadium just below, but including everything north of the parking lot, including the acropolis hill.

The ticket booth is by the parking lot beyond the theater. Admission costs $3. The necropolis is outside of the city proper east of the parking lot. Just before entering the city, the tomb of **Plancia Magna** is to the right. Plancia Magna was a wealthy priestess of Artemis who contributed generously to buildings and statues in Perge - you will find inscriptions of her name here and at the Antalya Museum. Continuing now through the outer gate you enter a great paved area with a variety of levels; this was the site of the **baths**, which began at the frigidarium, progressed to the tepidarium, and ended in the hot water of the caldarium. The scale of these baths is impressive.

Two great rounded pylons constitute the inner, older gate. This **Hellenistic Gate** was rendered into a pretty municipal centerpiece by the aforementioned Plancia Magna after the outer gates were erected. The semicircular court, with its twelve niches and two smaller niches, honored many of the city's great men. Included among them were some members of Plancia Magna's own family (M. Plancius Varus and C. Plancius Varus), as well as the irrepressible **Mopsus and Calchas**, who were a sort of Homeric Rosencrantz and Guildenstern. Following the Trojan War these two Greek heroes are said to have sailed south, and many of the Mediterranean cities seized upon them to create a Homeric pedigree. In fact Perge was already well established when the Trojan War ended. Some of the inscriptions have been replaced in their niches, with others scattered around the floor of the court.

The main marketplace is just inside the Hellenistic Gates, and a wide paved lane continues directly to the acropolis. This lane was once covered, and runs on either side of an open-air **water channel**. The details of ancient city planning are often impressive, and this is such a feature; given the area's warm summer temperatures, a colonnade with water flowing past would have been greatly appreciated by the citizens of the town. If you continue to the base of the hill, you find the water issuing from an elaborate fountain. **Cestrus**, god of the local river, probably reclined atop the fountain.

If you wish to continue to the acropolis, continue up the dirt paths behind the fountain. The acropolis' ruins are unimpressive, and defensive walls skirting the hill are not visible. Rather than working your way through the thick undergrowth atop the hill, you should follow the trails left, west, toward another set of baths. These baths are directly at the end of one aquaduct course, and require some bushwhacking to reach.

TERMESSOS

Termessos is not an easy ruin to visit. It requires a hike of 20-30 minutes, and much more if you want to see all there is to see here. The effort is rewarded.

By car, follow the main highway north (650) from Antalya toward Isparta, turning right at the Korkuteli turnoff (E87). Along this road you may run into some slow-moving vehicles with signs on top saying "Surucu Adayi." As you might expect, these are student drivers, and this road is one place where they practice; try not to alarm them. Some 25 kilometers along you will see the entrance to **Güllükdağı Milli Parkı** to the left, at which you pay an entrance fee (at a place corresponding closely to the former Termessan toll site), and continue nine kilometers to Termessos. It'll cost $3 for your car (driver not included), and $1 per person.

Before you enter or after you leave, consider visiting the Karain Caves on the opposite side of the highway, seven kilometers north. If you've arrived with a car and you have some time, it's worth the trouble. This is the spot with the oldest evidence of human civilization in Turkey. Material found in the caves dates to the Paleolithic Age, before 10,000 B.C., and the cavern may have also been the site of religious ceremonies in Hellenistic times. The caves are seven kilometers off of the Korkuteli road (E87) opposite and just east of the Güllükdağı/Termessos turnoff.

By public transportation, it's more difficult. Take a Korkuteli dolmuş and ask to be dropped off at the Termessos intersection, at the entrance to Güllükdağı Milli Parkı. In summer you should find taxis waiting to shuttle you the nine kilometers to Termessos for $5. In the off-season be content with collecting enough people for a taxi from Antalya to the site - $50 total, or stick with the guided tours. You can hazard the dolmuş to the gate, still, but you may have to hitch to the site.

History

The **Solymi**, as the people of Termessos called themselves, had a unique reputation for skill at warfare from an early date. They crept into Homer's tale of Bellerophon as the indomitable warriors against whom the young hero is sent to battle (Bellerophon, of course, gets the better of them by hurling rocks down from soaring Pegasus). Homer's tale dates to the eighth century B.C., but the martial skill he immortalized was still in evidence many centuries later, as when, in 333 B.C., Alexander uncharacteristically called off a siege here.

Termessos was one of two cities in Turkey to repel **Alexander the Great**, and, unlike his abortive siege of Sillion, Alexander had time to make a game attempt. Alexander even had the eager assistance from the people of distant Selge, who saw his arrival as an excellent opportunity to settle an old score with Termessos, their fellow Pisidians. Arrian, chronicling the campaign of Alexander, mentions a skirmish at the site, Alexander's encampment outside the walls, and the arrival of fresh troops from Selge anxious to besiege the city; then, after all of this, Arrian breezily says that Alexander marched on to Sagalassus.

Termessos eventually came around on its own, cooperating with the world Alexander had recast. Soon after Alexander's death, **Alcetas**, one of Alexander's infantry generals, withdrew here after suffering a shattering defeat at the hands of Antigonus. Alcetas, one of the many men who made a bid for parts of Alexander's empire, was welcomed here, and the city endured a siege by Antigonus. With the siege stalled, Antigonus coerced a group of older Termessans to assassinate Alcetas, which they did while the younger Termessans who supported the general were fighting outside the city walls. In the aftermath the younger Termessans began to destroy their own city, later relenting and giving Alcetas a suitable burial in an elaborate tomb. Some suspect that his tomb is the one located on the western wall of the valley above a dirt track that winds towards the spur of the mountain.

The Termessans continued to rely on their ability to withdraw behind their natural defenses. They were at war with the entire Lycian League at the end of the third century B.C., a war that the Lycians never chose to prosecute to the extent of a siege. Termessos was often at odds with its neighbors, and even in times of relative peace the ongoing feud with the people of Selge was simmering. Roman administrators seem to have sized up the situation quickly, leaving the city an unusual degree of autonomy and partial exemption from taxes.

Termessos is clearly defensible, but the visitor must wonder how the natives supported themselves. The answer appears to be through **tolls** levied on the Korkuteli road, which was heavily trafficked owing to the difficulties of the Lycian coast. The city faded in the third century A.D., never to regain its former power.

Visiting the Ruins of Termessos

Termessos is a beautiful ruin, in many places thickly overgrown with shrubs and trees. Its distance from the sea probably spared it much of the archaeological depredation that has stripped other sites in Turkey.

The parking lot is located one half mile below the town, and you'll want to be carrying water with you as it's easy to work up a sweat on the climb. Before heading up, have a look at the **Propylon of Hadrian**, a grand entrance gate to a temple just above the parking lot to the west. The gate was dedicated during Hadrian's second century B.C. whirlwind tour of his empire. Below the parking lot, wrapping back down around the hillside, is a necropolis with beautiful reliefs of lions, symmetric patterns, and Medusa heads on the side of the sarcophagi.

Returning to the parking lot, you can enter Termessos the same way people entered - or tried to enter - the city two millennia ago, following the King's Road along the left ridge up a cleft between two high hills. The approach gives you some appreciation of the site's defensive advantages.

As you climb you'll see city walls rise to your right, perfect courses of stone. The path cuts right through the former city gate, on which you'll see inscriptions on the interior. This was a **dice oracle**. No hurly burly of secret ceremonies and rites here; Termessans would roll dice and read the corresponding fortune. These oracles, found throughout the ancient world, Turkish archeologist George Bean called, aptly, "curious monuments to human credulity." Continuing up the path you arrive at the great gymnasium to your left and a fork in the path.

If you're in a hurry, continue on up the path. Otherwise, continuing to gawk at the stonecraft that the Termessans used in the gymnasium, continue down the gradually sloping path. This trail passes more sarcophagi and terminates above a deep valley, with Mt. Solymi ranged above and to the left. If you elect to scramble around on the walls here be mindful of the cisterns.

Return to the main path and continue up into the city. Heading left toward the theater (Termessos is well signed) you follow the old stone road with its intricate drainage system. If you continue on past the Stoa

South from Ephesus

"Bestiarii, the professional slaughterers, fought lions and tigers, bears and bulls, but these as often fought each other, or alligators, or hippopotami (imagine the time that it takes for a great defenceless hippo to die, for no big cat could throttle it or break its neck, and only shock and exsanguination would bring it mercy as small parcels of flesh were torn from it under the leather hide), or slew a host of such defenceless creatures as deer, giraffes and ostriches. Suetonius noted with seeming pleasure the death of 5,000 animals in one day at the inauguration of the Roman Colosseum, and Trajan saw 3,000 slaughtered in two days; even if these great numbers died only on Imperial occasions, and the ordinary venatio accounted for comparatively few, those smaller figures must be multiplied by the number of theaters spread across the Empire, and the frequency of the occasions; scale too must have had its effect, for there would be little point in filling the great circus of El Djem in Tunisia for the death of a single ostrich, though it might have made a flurry in Termessos. Five centuries of slaughter wiped out the Caspian tiger, the Assyrian lion, and the Numidian forest elephant - the tough pygmy that carried Hannibal over the Alps."

- Brian Sewell, **South from Ephesus; Travels in Aegean Turkey**, Arrow Books Limited, 1988.

of Osbaros to the left you'll come to the theater, and it's gorgeous. This theater looks out over a distant corner of Antalya and the sea beyond, and it remains in excellent condition.

The stage area was the site of some late remodeling so that wild animals could be released and slaughtered without danger of the animals dragging audience members from their seats. This theater, with a capacity of no more than 5,000, was a relatively minor venue for the brutal entertainment of the time.

Leaving the stadium, you can veer left and visit the upper gymnasium and, beyond it, the splendid wreck of the Temple of Zeus Solymi on the point. Nothing here is intact, but one must suspect that all of the pieces – the column drums, lintels, inscriptions, reliefs – are there in that jumble awaiting reassembly. The stone here is so fine that struck with metal it rings

Heading back over or around the hill toward the city center you'll pass a collection of buildings, including a minor Temple of Artemis that is still standing. Ahead you come to the heroon of an unknown king, and, just beyond, you find part of the solution to the question you've probably been wondering: Where did this stone come from?

The cisterns provide an answer. The main set of linked cisterns atop the city is highly unusual, and clearly the result of great labor. It is thought that the stone for the city was quarried here from the bedrock. The engineering of these cisterns, indeed the engineering of the entire mountain fastness, boggles the mind.

The trail drops back down toward the western ridge past the Corinthian temple. A trail heads up to a fire lookout through a necropolis high above, while a spur heads off toward the tomb of Alcetas another 800 meters on.

There are a few tombs and structures out this way, and tomb of Alcetas is located above the path against a stone outcrop. Alcetas' cave tomb has been preyed on in the very recent past by antiquities thieves – you can see where they chipped out part of the high relief of a horseman and the entirety of his shield.

There's not all that much to see, anymore, but it's interesting nonetheless. The damaged relief of the soldier on horseback at the entrance is inconsistent with Alcetas' career as an infantry general; the tomb is thought to be his, anyway.

Chapter 19

Turkey's Western Mediterranean coast, often referred to as the Lycian Coast, extends roughly between
Phaselis in the east and Dalyan in the west, encompassing some of the most picturesque terrain in Turkey.
Mountains rise from the sea like blades, and the rugged
landscape was the last section of the Mediterranean to
be pacified by the Romans. The cities in the region
formed the Lycian League, a body led by six cities -
Xanthus, Patara, Pinara, Tlos, Myra and Olympos - that
now constitute the core of Turkey's most fascinating
and beautiful set of ruins.

Waves of development have hit the eastern edge of
the Lycian Coast, knocking the charm out of the cities
near Kemer for the sake of beachfront holiday play-
grounds. The World Bank has helped Turkey finance
the slew of resort hotel operations here, envisioning the
Turkish Riviera as a highly profitable tourism destination. The region has all of the requisite characteristics:
mountains tumble directly into the sea, pine forests and
fragrant flowering plants give way to long sand and
pebble beaches, and of course there are ruins.

The only problem, ironically, is the intense development. The streets of Kemer resemble nothing so
much as a sunny Atlantic City boardwalk. Large hotels
squat behind columns and columns of beach umbrellas,
and with the influx of tourists has come the inevitable
wave of carpet, ceramic, and knick-knack hustlers.

There are some nice hotels in the lot, but in high
season they range upwards of $100 per night. If that's a
concern we recommend skipping past the hotel zone to
Çirali/Olympos, a plummeting 7 kilometers below the

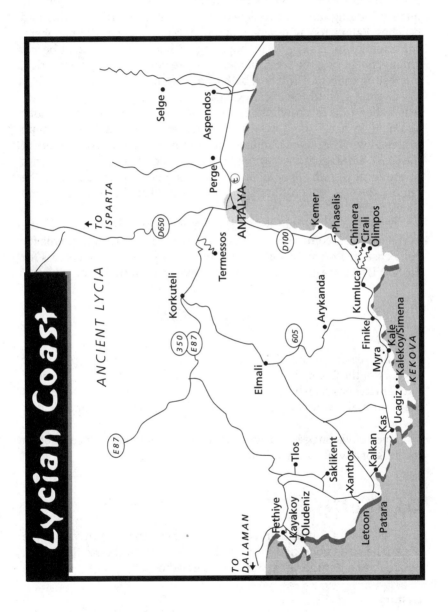

main coast road. The ruins and the wraith-fire of the Chimera merit a visit to this stubbornly undeveloped oceanside village. Continuing east, the **Kaş/Kalkan** area is marvelous, offering antiquated fishing-village charm, quality lodging, and convenience to many days worth of ruins and beaches. **Patara**, too, wins a recommendation for its sleepy atmosphere, convenience to ruins, and its boggling 16 kilometer fine sand beach. Finally, anchoring the western end of the region, **Dalyan** boasts a rich, interesting collection of ruins, baths, and beaches.

Getting around the Lycian Coast is remarkably easier than it once was, when pirates prowled the coastline and a particularly ferocious strain of Lycians, the Termessans, extorted money at the mountain passes. A winding, scenic, and well-maintained road serves the length of the coast, although it is occasionally forced miles inland by the vagaries of the local terrain. The Antalya and Dalaman airports bookend the region, through which Kamil Koç and Pamukkale buses pass several times daily.

A number of the sites in this chapter are ruins only, with very little in the way of accommodations. You can pick any number of towns for your base, with Antalya or the Olympos area your leading choices for Eastern Lycia (there's a greater range of places to stay in Western Lycia).

EASTERN LYCIA

This region is one of Turkey's garden spots, the very place that Alexander the Great chose to settle in for the winter in 334 B.C. Some of its character has been buried beneath walls of hotels, and we recommend that you make your way to Phaselis and continue to Olympos/Çıralı beyond.

If you envision peaceful mornings with bougainvillea twined through the rails of a whitewashed hotel, go west!

Phaselis

This beautiful little ruin has three beaches beneath a cover of pine trees. The air is good and you can go for a swim in the southern bay, where Alexander the Great himself once bathed.

History

Phaselis' origin is similar to Manhattan's in New York City. Colonists from Rhodes arrived in the area and rightly judged this site to be the perfect piece of land. They found a shepherd nearby and arranged to purchase the property from him - never mind that he probably didn't "own" it anyway - for a supply of dried fish. The shepherd accepted the offer and the Rhodians settled in to build a perfect little fortress town. In any case, but there was probably some sort of port at the site during the Phoenicians' explorations in the second millennium B.C.

Phaselis' three harbors, one on the southwest, two on the northeast, were ideal for warfare as well as trade, and in the latter pursuit Phaselis proved very successful, trading timber from the interior. Their first historic battle went less well. Phaselis sided with the Persians against the Athenian Cimon in 467 B.C. Cimon, in hot pursuit of Persian King Xerxes' fleet following the Greek victories at Salamis and Plataea, wanted to roll up the Persian defenses along the entire coast before squaring off against the main body of Persians.

Cimon settled in for a siege of Phaselis that led to a Phaselitan capitulation, the terms of which were money and the assistance of the Phaselitan navy against Xerxes. Cimon went on to crush the Persians at the Eurymedon River, near Aspendos.

The Sisoe

With tombs to discover and great mysteries to solve, some historians still find the time to speculate about the Phaselitans' hair. The citizens of Phaselis wore a sisoe, a hairstyle that is forbidden in the Book of Leviticus in the Bible (the writers of the King James Bible, somewhat at a loss, translate this as "thou shalt not round the corners of thine head."). What, exactly, a sisoe was is unknown, although it may have been a shaved head with a long topknot, as popularized by Baal worshipers and Yul Brynner as a Native American in Western movies.

Phaselis' peculiar situation between the territories of Lycia to the west, Pisidia to the north, and Pamphlia to the east helped give it an independent character in choosing policy. When the Persian satrap **Mausolus** (377-353) of Helicarnassus sought to reestablish Persian rule in Lycia, the Lycian League (of which Phaselis was an occasional member) waged a long, successful war for its independence, while Phaselis chose to come to terms with the Persians.

The Phaselitans' ongoing allegiance to the Persians didn't cloud their good sense. When **Alexander the Great** began marching through Lycia to the west, accepting the peace offers of Xanthos, Pinara, and Patara, Phaselitan envoys approached him with a golden crown, vowing allegiance. With the summer campaign season drawing to a close, Alexander chose to winter in Phaselis (334-333), reportedly helping dislodge a small Pisidian fortress just inland as a favor to his hosts. Phaselis shared the Lycian's fate after this, eventually being given back to their colonizing forebears, the Rhodians, as part of a Roman peace agreement.

When the pirate **Zenicetes** built a small piracy empire out of Olympos, he seized Phaselis as well. With the two best ports on the long, sheer coastline west of Antalya, Zenicetes had excellent bases from which to control local shipping. In 67 B.C. Pompey judged the pirate's continued depredation of Imperial Roman shipping to be an official burr in his saddle and launched the campaign that bloodily cleared the area, area, finally drawing the two towns into the Roman fold. Phaselis flourished through Roman times, eventually succumbing to the persistent invasions of the Arabs and finally disappearing in the medieval period.

Arrivals & Departures

Phaselis is two kilometers off the road between Kemer and Tekirova. If you arrive by public transportation expect to walk the two km - taxis rarely wait at the main road. The road is gently sloping, with a ticket gate just before entering the ruins. Dolmuş from Tekirova go directly to the Phaselis gate, if there is enough interest.

Where to Stay

We would advise a day trip to the site and continuing to Antalya in the east or Çıralı in the west, but if you intend to stay in the area consider Tekirova just 4 kilometers west. At the high end is the **Tekirova Corinthia** (*Tel. 242 821-4750; Email: info@corinthia.com; Web: www.corinthia.com;* Double: $120) on the waterfront; at the budget end is the **Phaselis Pension** (*Tel/Fax 242 821-4507;* Double: $27), well-signed off the highway.

Seeing the Sights

Phaselis' location alone is worth the $2 price of admission. Pine trees pad the earth with needles, and sand dunes have engulfed parts of the old town. There are many well-shaded areas and you can swim in the southern bay. The large north harbor, to your left upon arriving at Phaselis' parking lot, is below the necropolis. This harbor was inferior to the other two and little used. Parts of the wharf of the smaller, central harbor are visible. This harbor, protected to the north, or Antalya, side by a long breakwater was topped with a tower. This harbor could be closed with a chain. The third harbor, on the opposite side of the isthmus, was Phaselis' main moorage.

The **acropolis** was probably the site of the **Temple of Athena**, in which Achilles' spear was housed. How the Phaselitan's came by this item is unknown, but it might have made a great impression on Alexander,

Hiking the Lycian Way

The summer of 2000 saw the fulfillment of a seemingly impossible dream, the linking of a series of trails between the heights above Ölüdeniz beach and the heights above Antalya, 500 kilometers east. The trails you follow are worn by the foot traffic of goatherds, who are, themselves, following trails created thousands of years earlier. It is a rare opportunity to see the fortresses, rock-cut tombs, bridges, and ancient cities of southern Turkey at the pace of their creators. A trek along even short stretches of the trail will be punctuated by thrilling vistas, gorgeous beaches, hillsides dotted with alpine wildflowers, nights in the huts of goatherds, and fortunate meetings along the way.

The Persian General Harpagus marched west along these trails and Alexander the Great marched his east hundreds of years later. You are welcome to conduct your march in either direction, or to pick the most appealing sections. The entire trail is suited to backpackers with tents and cooking gear, but if you would prefer to hike legs of the trail by day and check into small hotels by night, that's easily done as well.

By now it's clear that the authors of this guide recommend finding a few days for hiking along choice sections of the Lycian Way—for its own wonderful sake, and, too, because it makes subsequent days on a Blue Cruise or elsewhere in Turkey so much the sweeter. A few of the many shorter hikes you might consider:

• The 16 kilometer trail between Akbel and Patara, taking in the magnificent Patara aqueduct; overnight at Patara.

• The 15 kilometer trail between Ovacık and Faralya (Butterfly Valley); over night at Butterfly Valley.

• The 18 kilometer trail between Karaöz and Adrasan along the precipitous Taşlık Burun; overnight at Adrasan.

The Lycian Way has its own $18 guidebook: The Lycian Way, published in 2000, ISBN 0953921808. This book, written by the woman who spearheaded the trail network, Kate Clow, comes with trail maps and detailed directions. For assistance arranging day hikes, overnight stays, or creating a multi-day itinerary, contact Bougainville Travel (Email: bougainville@superonline.com – see Kaş section).

who, in his stop at Troy, had danced naked around Achilles' tumulus. The exact site of the temple is unknown, and Phaselis has not yet been worked over by archaeologists (although, local guides say, the holes in the floor of the theater are the work of some amateur archaeologists-cum-treasure hunters). The acropolis is relatively barren.

The final significant structure at the site is the marble **gateway** at the south end of the main avenue by the south harbor. This gateway was dedicated to the Roman Emperor Hadrian (117-138 A.D.), and ceremonial gates seem to have been the potato salad of Hadrian's traveling potluck – "you're making him a gate? But *we're* making him a gate!"

Olympos/The Chimaera

This place is, in a nutshell, why you have come to Turkey. In the evening the meltem blows in off of the Mediterranean, lights come on in the village, and it's quiet enough to hear the wind, and the sea, and the barking of dogs. You leave the ruins, or the beach, or the living fire at Chimaera, and head back through the orange groves to town for a good, filling meal.

Adrasan beach is 4 kilometers long, protecting a narrow, fertile plain that stretches between two great spurs of Tahtalı Dağ. The ruined Hellenistic city of Olympos is located at the southern end of the beach. The Olympos ruins rise above a pretty estuary that empties into the Mediterranean beneath an old Genoese fortification. The ruins here are scattered and rough, half-buried in thick vegetation.

The Chimaera is located in the hills behind the northern end of the beach. Here, a clearing is ablaze with inextinguishable fire, as it has been for thousands of years. Ancient mariners used this flame as a benchmark, and the ruined temples to Hephaestus and other gods make clear that it was central to religious ritual.

This is a national park, meaning that development is prohibited. The only hotels are small pensions and two-story affairs tucked away in orange groves. The area is frequented by backpackers who've heard of it through the grapevine, gulet passengers, and others who don't mind the rusticated accommodations.

History

The city of Olympos sounds quite important, but, actually, it wasn't. It was a decent sized town, but never became famously embroiled in warfare or politics (which, many would say, speaks well of the local inhabitants). The city held enough sway that it had maximum votes among cities of the Lycian League, but it seems to have been a fair-weather member, and was usually overlooked when a new conqueror sought to bring the League to heel. Olympos drew its name from **Mt. Olympos**, towering directly above. This is one of a handful of Mt. Olymposes scattered around Turkey.

Olympos' history, if not dramatic, was interesting. Owing to the proximity of the blazing **Chimaera** - whose flames have for thousands of years burned so brightly that they serve as a beacon to passing ships - Olympos became a sort of pilgrimage. Olympos was linked to the flames of the Chimera by a paved road, and the residents of the city worshipped **Hephaestus** (the Roman Vulcan), the god of fire and metal smithing. Curiouser still, the area became central to worship of the god **Mithra**, a warrior religion that grew to be hugely popular among the Roman soldiery and competed with Christianity into the fourth century. Mithra worship involved secret ceremonies and initiations that now appear destined to remain secret. Locally, the ceremonies took place with the Chimaera as a backdrop.

Mithra worship was imported by a pirate named **Zenicetes**, who seized the city and made it his home at the beginning of the first century B.C. Zenicetes' piracy was so successful, and so irritating, that the Roman general Pompey sailed to the region with a huge Roman force. Pompey completed a determined and bloody purge of the area's pirates in 67 B.C., and Olympos was incorporated into the Roman empire soon thereafter.

Olympos eventually became an honest Roman town, but by the third century A.D. pirates had returned to the winding Lycian Coast and resumed preying on local shipping. Olympos continued to make do, however, and under the Byzantines a church was established atop the old pagan worshipping sites near the Chimera and a fortress was built on a hill above the beach. In the 12th century, the Genoese expanded the Byzantine structure, establishing a fortified trading post at Olympos. This venture was a ringing success for almost 200 years, but the rapid expansion of the Ottoman Empire on land and at sea forced the Genoese out, out, out. The old city has been its serene, dilapidated self ever since.

Olympos' great structures have collapsed or been shipped off to the world's museums, so the ruins are less a tourist attraction than the backdrop of a tourist attraction. The determined ruins enthusiast can nonetheless pick over these ruins for hours with gratification, finding arches bursting up out of thick vegetation and ancient walls above the meandering river.

Arrivals & Departures

There are two routes from the main highway down to the Olympos area. The northern route brings you to the village of Çıralıwhere most of the hotels we list are located. Çıralı is at the center of the 4-kilometer

The Chimaera

The Chimaera was one of the most formidable beasts of mythology, the monstrous spawn of **Typhon**, himself the son of Gaia. Typhon was powerful enough that a concerned Zeus connived against him, succeeding in shackling the giant god in the bowels of the earth, eternally consumed in flames. Typhon's offspring was a gargantuan thing, with a snake's long, reptilian tail, the belly of a goat, the chest and forelegs of a lion, and a firebreathing goat head. There are some variations on this theme, but it is in any event a terrible and fearsome combination. This misshapen creature was given to terrorize the people of ancient Lycia, descending on them unawares and burning their cities.

Against this terrible monster the Lycians had no recourse. Their savior arrived in the unlikely form of a young man named **Bellerophon**, who arrived in Lycia bearing coded instructions for his own assassination. He had run afoul of his previous host, who mistakenly believed the lad to have had an affair with his own wife. The Lycian King at the time, Iobates, obligingly sent Bellerophon off on the impossible task of battling the Chimaera. The resourceful young man, however, was a favorite of Athena. Visiting his plight, she lent him the bridle with which to tame and mount Pegasus, formerly Perseus' winged horse (by the way Perseus was claimed as an ancestor by, you guessed it, the Persians). Astride Pegasus, Bellerophon set off to battle the Chimaera.

For this purpose he had fashioned a great spear of lead, which he hurled into the creature's furnace mouth from high above. As Bellerophon hoped, the spear melted as it fell, raining into the monster's innards and killing it. The Chimaera's resting place is still marked by guttering flame. Bellerophon, for his part, returned to Iobates unexpectedly triumphant, and eventually unseated the wily old King and assumed the throne himself. Glaucus, one of the famous Lycians who fought alongside the Trojans in The Iliad, claimed to be his grandson.

beach, convenient to the ruins and the Chimaera. The southern route brings you directly to the ruins of Olympos and a collection of budget accommodations that includes Kadirs; there are no stores or services here.

Note: the two roads do not join – be sure to select the correct one.

By Bus

Public transportation to Çıralı is tricky, but it's getting easier. There is allegedly direct dolmuş service to Çirali from Antalya's main otogar once daily, Monday through Saturday, except in winter or when the whim of the driver says otherwise. Dolmuş leave from Antalya in the afternoon (making stops along the highway), returning to Antalya in the morning. There is direct dolmuş service between Çıralı and Kumluca once per week on Friday mornings.

What most people do is get one of the frequent buses to Kaş or Demre/Kale and get out at the "Çirali 7, Yanartaş, Chimaera" sign. Dolmuş make the steep journey up and down the hill a few times a day in the high season, and taxis will always be on hand unless it starts pouring down rain and you really want one. A lot of people wind up hitching a ride into town. There are daily dolmuş to and from Kumluca in the west, whence you can get wherever you're headed.

By Car

After a long ascent from the east you arrive at a sign telling you quite clearly "Çiralı 7, Yanartaş, Chimaera." This is the best of three alternatives, and if you're coming from the west we suggest this route as well, unless you're just dropping by Olympos for a day trip (or going to Kadir's; see below). In that case take the turnoff closer to the Olympos Panorama Berg Otel farther west.

Orientation

Çıralı has no banks and few amenities; bring Lira. There are a few hotels at the bottom of the road just before town, after which you reach a store just opposite a concrete bridge; this serves as the dolmuş station.

To get to the beach and Olympos, head southwest (right). You may need to ford a stream, but a bridge is built for this purpose by the Olympos Lodge each season. The beach has coarse sand and pebbles, and Olympos is 1-2 kilometers along. There is a $1 entrance fee at Olympos when the guard is on duty.

The trailhead for the Chimaera is located about 3 kilometers north of Çirali on the ridge up behind the beach. The path in to the Chimaera is about 1 kilometer.

Where to Stay & Eat

With the exception of the Olympos Lodge, accommodations in Çıralı and Olympos are pretty basic. That's a lot of the charm. Hotels typically offer their own dining, and there are lots of small open air **kebapcıs** open along the beach in season. Restaurants see a lot of turnover, literally. The municipality occasionally bulldozes beachfront restaurants, owing to the fact that this area is protected from development and the beachfront restaurants violate the local code.

The best meal in town is at the Olympos Lodge, but we've found that food everywhere is hearty and good. The kitchen at the Canan Pension on the road into town is recommended. In the off-season the trees are filled with oranges and lemons, which you can have mashed into juice. Çıralı is largely spared mosquito problems by its location on the beach, but they can be an issue in the freewheeling backpacker treehouses on the other side of the beach at Olympos.

Çıralı

OLYMPOS LODGE MOTEL, *P.O. Box 38, Kemer/Çıralı. Tel. (242) 825-7171; Fax (242) 825-7173; Email: info@olymposlodge.com; Web: www.olymposlodge.com. Rooms: 8. Credit cards accepted. Open year-round. Double: $145 (half-board).*

The Olympos Lodge is one of the most beautiful little hotels in the whole of Turkey, admirably blending in behind a screen of orange trees and a large, unassumingly landscaped garden. Where most of Çıralı's hotels are rough around the edges (and wonderful in their own right), the Olympos Lodge is done to a tee.

The reception hallway leads into an octagonal dining room populated by handcrafted tables and chairs with thick felt backs. An iron and hand-blown glass chandelier hangs from above, original sketches adorn the walls, and a simple, elegant bar stretches along one side of the room. The garden is thick with mature, shading trees and plants, fragrant jasmine and colorful bougainvillea, in between which one can glimpse the sea. A new greenhouse on the grounds features a winter garden.

Scattered among the trees are the duplex guest cabins, decorated with a minimalist flair in white and blonde wood. Each room has a fan, mosquito netting, phone, and air-conditioning. The lawn, dotted with sculptures by Turkish artist Handan Börte Çine, is ideal for retreating in the heat of the day and having a drink. You may be joined by the rabbits or white peacocks who also make their homes here.

The Olympos Lodge does an excellent job of balancing the bucolic charm of Çıralı against the needs of fine hotel-keeping. The manager was reticent about being written up, which is one of the sure signs that his hotel deserves to be.

Selected one of our favorite small hotels.

ARCADIA HOTEL, *Çıralı. Tel/Fax (242) 825-7340; Email: arcadia3@superonline.com; Web: www.kemernet.com/arcadia. Rooms: 5. Credit cards accepted. Open year-round. Double: $75 (breakfast included).*

The Arcadia, opened in April, 2001, is an excellent new addition to

Çıralı on the foreshore of the eastern section of beach. Guests stay in five separate bungalows, sharing a central building for meals and drinks. The bungalows are beautifully crafted of pine, spare with small features such as beautifully worked fly screens and built-in wine racks. Everything seems to be done with great deliberation by the builder, Ahmet. The grounds, bare when we visited in early 2001, will be planted and should begin taking shape in 2002.

A long expanse of beach separates the Arcadia from the sea, and a raised platform under the screen of trees enjoys the evening meltem breeze. The owners, former co-owners of Oba Hotel in Ölüdeniz, prepare excellent food, and accompany meals with lattes from Ann's espresso machine. The Arcadia is located 1.5 kilometers east of the center of Çıralı by the bridge.

AZUR HOTEL, *Çıralı. Tel. (242) 825-7072; Fax (242) 825-7076; Email: info@md-tours.net; Web: www.olympos.de. Rooms: 8. Credit cards accepted. Double: $60 (breakfast included).*

The Azur is one of Çıralı's nicest hotels, boasting a marvel of a garden, thick with roses, climbing vines, palms, and all manner of flowering plants. The hotel is divided into several low cottages around this wonderfully heterogeneous garden (bananas, dates, avocado, pomegranates, zucchini). Rooms are spacious and plain, making this a good choice for families—particularly given that the hotel has a sandbox, an aviary, and rabbits to chase. Meals are served and half-board accommodations are offered for $10 more per person. At the same standard, also consider the **Aida Hotel**, owned by the brother of the Azur and located just 100 yards south (*Tel. 242 825-7323; Fax 242 825-7272; Double: $50).*

CIRALI PANSIYON, *Çıralı. Tel. (242) 825-7122; Fax (242) 825-7175; Email: ciralipansiyon@superposta.com. Rooms: 20. Credit cards not accepted. Open year-round. Double: $23 (breakfast included).*

Çıralı Pansiyon is one of several clean, spartan, inexpensive hotels in Çıralı. This hotel offers screened windows, air-conditioning, balconies, and a good restaurant in a large main room. The Çıralı Pansiyon is located just up the road east of the concrete bridge at the entrance to town. **Canan Pansiyon** (*Tel. 242 825-7251*) at the mouth of the valley at the entrance to town is another good budget option—one with remarkably good food. Also consider the **Jasmin Pansiyon** (*Tel. 242 825-7247, Email: jasminpension@hotmail.com*) alongside the raised irrigation channel just south of the center of town.

Olympos
Olympos shares the long beach with the town of Çıralı 2 kilometers east, but the two are connected neither by road nor in spirit. Çıralı is

relaxed and quiet, while the kilometer-long stretch of road above the ruins of Olympos is wild, free-living, and free-loving. Olympos is reached via different 7 kilometer spur from the highway than Çiralı, with a dolmuş stop and a food booth at the intersection.

KADİR'S YÖRÜK TREE HOUSE, *Olympos, Kumluca. Tel. (242) 892-1250; Fax (242) 892-1110; Email: treehouse@superonline.com. Beds: 150. Credit cards accepted. Open year-round. Double: $20 (full board).*

Kadir's is located about 1.5 kilometers above the ruins of Olympos, on the road that climbs to the highway. It is now just one of dozens of places along this stretch of road that boast raised wooden bunkhouses, but it is the most famous—featured in Outside magazine in March, 2001. Kadir's sits in a deep valley and resembles a MASH unit, with the almost round-the-clock hum of cards, chess, drinking and South Park on the VCR. Internet access is available.

Seasoned, cynical backpackers are happily processed here, churned through Kadir's $9-per-night-all-you-can-eat-breakfast-and-dinner-included wonderland. The setting is beautiful, but mildly distant from the ruins and the beach. Mosquitoes can be a problem in the high season. Guests looking for relaxation and quiet are barking up the wrong tree.

To get there without your own transportation, disembark at the turnoff and await a taxi, an infrequent minibus, or await a passing car.

BAYRAM'S PLACE, *PK 4, Olympos, Kumluca. Tel. (242) 892-1243; Fax (242) 892-1399; Email: bayrams1@turk.net. Rooms: 39. Credit cards accepted. Open year-round. Double: $20 (full board).*

Bayram's Place is cut from the same cloth as Kadir's and benefits from a location 1 kilometer closer to the Olympos ruins. It also offers an atmosphere less raucous than Kadir's, although it's every bit as packed with backpackers. There are several rooms with en suite bathrooms, and they get the same full board treatment as everyone else; as the hostess told us, "this is where people come to get back on budget."

Selected one of our favorite budget hotels.

Seeing the Ssights

Olympos is divided by the slough; on the near side the **acropolis** is a steep scramble, but rewarding for its complex network of walls and broken towers and, of course, its excellent view. In the thick vegetation below, accessed from the river by a well-worn path, is a colossal gateway, ornately decorated and surrounded by fallen blocks and pillars.

This presumed to have been a **temple**, its back to the reedy area north of the ruins, but the divinity in question is unknown. It is a true prize to

Olympos: The Movies

In late 1996, Armand Assante, Bernadette Peters and a large cast descended on Çıralı to film "The Odyssey." Locals were hired by the hundreds as extras, and carpenters built palaces on the shore. The movie—like "Jason and the Argonauts" filmed here in 1999— was hardly memorable, but it it offered the residents of the area something out of the ordinary.

The locals, for their part, gave big time Hollywood's month-long stay mixed reviews: the money wasn't bad, but stage crews erected giant fans to blow mist over the sets, and everyone came down with head colds.

stumble upon in the tangle of undergrowth. Not far along are Roman era baths complete with the Romans' beloved mosaics.

Continuing upriver you come to the ticket booth and a small set of backpacker hotels and restaurants just beyond. Across the ancient bridge - or, for our purposes, the sand choked mouth of the stream - you find more remnants of the ancient city, including industrial waterfront structures from the time when the river opened into a serviceable lake. Immediately across the bridge is a Byzantine church surrounded by Greek and Roman structures. The highlights of this bank are the wreckage of the theater a little inland and above the stream, and, above that, Olympos' **necropolis**. The necropolis has a smattering of tombs - not, oddly, Lycian in style, despite Olympos' important place in the Lycian defensive alliance.

Inscriptions abound - again, not Lycian script - including one 24 line inscription that is a letter oracle of the kind found at Termessos. The messages were presumably thought to offer advice from beyond the grave. The Genoese fortress sprawls on the steep hillside south of the beach above tall fissures in the cliff face. Most of the fortress walls are fallen, but individual buildings, towers, and chapels still stand. There appears to have been an entrance to the fortress directly from the sea through at the cliff bottom (the interior side has collapsed. A great stone pier, mostly hauled or washed away, pokes out into the sea.

The **Chimaera** (Yanartaş) is best visited from Çıralı, a sometimes steep hike into the mountains above town (it is a 45 minute walk from Çıralı to the trailhead plus another 25 minutes up to the lower Chimaera). The parking lot is about three kilometers north of Çıralı(follow the signs), and the flames of the Chimera itself are a further two kilometers along a winding trail. You have arrived when you see the ruins of a great temple to the right of the path, and, above it, a large church still decorated with frescoes. Above the church the flames spout at various openings in a large stony area, burning on water and stone.

Amateur scientists and frustrated vandals quench the flame with dirt, but the flames burn on beneath the earth and re-erupt later. The flames are most arresting beneath the canopy of stars late at night, but you'll definitely need a flashlight for the hike. Guides and residents of the area can lead you to a second Chimaera fire higher on the hillside.

WESTERN LYCIA

This is the rugged Lycian Coast that daunted sailors and soldiers alike. The once-indomitable terrain has been made a bit accessible by a good highway—albeit one that has some winding, mildly-harrowing stretches.

Finike

Finike is a sleepy little town that hasn't been overwhelmed by the influx of tourists because there hasn't been much of one. Finike is not ugly, it's just plain. An ambitious marina has not attracted the hoped-for yachting crowd, and what remains are people passing through en route to Arycanda and Limyra (see *Excursions & Day Trips* below).

Arrivals & Departures

You pass through Finike on your way between Olympos and Kale/Demre, and you may wish to make an inland detour to Arycanda. The Arycanda ruins are located up the excellent Elmalı Road, 41 kilometers along. This road turns inland from the main coast road in the Finike city center on the west bank of the Yaşgöz Çayı, formerly the Arycandus. If you are without rental car, the Finike otogar is several hundred feet up this road, and minibuses for the interior depart from the otogar hourly. Elmalı dolmuş can drop you at the Arycanda turn-off (Arıf village), from which the ruins are a one kilometer hike.

Catch a return dolmuş, which run between 7 a.m. and 6 p.m., later in the summer.

Where to Stay & Eat

Accommodation here is uninspired. In a pinch, here are some places that will do.

ŞENDIL PANSİYON, *Finike, Tel. 242 855 1660. Rooms: 22. Double: $15*
Alaadin Şendil has been running a hotel here for years. Rooms are
tidy and simple, hot water is guaranteed, and the establishment is open
year round.

PARIS PANSIYON, *Finike. Tel. (242) 855-1488. Rooms: 8. Double: $15.*
The Paris Pansiyon is in the heights above Finike, up a long staircase
150 meters south (toward the marina) from the otogar. The Paris offers a
fine view of the sea from the terrace.

ALTIN SOFRA RESTAURANT, *Liman ici, Finike. Tel. (242) 855-
1281. Inexpensive.*
The Altın Sofra is always busy, and offers the best dining in town.
The restaurant is located at the west end of garden that backs up the
marina, and offers vaulted wooden ceilings, a bar, and remarkably
inexpensive food. Entrees such as kebaps and grilled meat cost just $2-$3,
and meze are a startlingly cheap $.80. Petek Restaurant, located on the
main road at the entrance to the marina, is a quieter choice with a good
reputation.

Seeing the Sights

Other than the fortress and the waterfront fish restaurants, Finike's
best feature may be a new **Turkish bath** by the otogar. Women's days are
Saturday and Sunday. Finike's finest beach is five kilometers west, **Gökliman
Plaj**. The new coast road passes long stretches of beach to the east of town,
but these are unpopular. There are some tiny beaches along the winding
section of road to the east and west, but parking can be difficult.

Excursions & Day Trips
ARYCANDA

As Turkish archaeologists continue their archaeological dig at
Arycanda, ruins aficionados are becoming a little breathless in their
praise of the site. The work has elevated Arycanda from a minor backwa-
ter ruin (of the kind scattered liberally throughout the region) to a major
find. The ruins are not only substantial, they're gorgeous, with thick
stone-walled buildings climbing toward the Temple of Helios above.

History

Arycanda's position atop an eagle's nest controlling the main Elmalı-
Finike pass through the Toros Mountains suggests a role similar to the
one enjoyed by Termessos, charging for access to a toll road through their
land. The city predates Greek settlement, as evidenced by its patently un-
Greek name. Little is known about these people beyond Plutarch's
denunciation of the Arycandans as a lazy bunch of spendthrifts.

Visiting the Ruins of Arycanda

Like other inland cities, Arycanda was spared the ravages of nineteenth century archaeologists/treasure hunters. The ruins are in a remarkable state of preservation, descending **Mt. Akdağ** in a series of tiers. The upper terrace is the site of a Hellenistic stadium, which was built coeval with the nearly perfect theater below. During the Roman period reconstruction was undertaken on the theater. The lower terrace is the site of an almost intact Roman bath, missing only its roof. Mosaics can be found here, and note that fresh water sometimes still flows through the town, carried in by an old water system. The necropolis is perched just above the baths in a series of buildings.

One of the most arresting structures in the city is the odeon on the middle terrace; it opens on to the grand marketplace, itself suspended above a backdrop of mountains. Similarly, the Temple of Helios, off to the left of the stadium as you approach from below, is stunning, green and silent.

Demre (Kale)

Demre is roughly on the site of the former Lycian city of **Myra**. The ruins of that city, and the legacy of its most famous citizen, St. Nicholas, are the highlights of a visit here. Accommodation is available. Note that the official name of the city is Kale, but the locals continue to call it by its traditional name, Demre. This all becomes especially confusing if you are going to Kale, or "Kaleköy," otherwise known as Simena, in nearby in Kekova Bay.

History

Myra was another of the Lycian League's chief cities, commanding the large plain that is today choked with tomato greenhouses. The city like Priene, was once astride a navigable bay, but the silting of the river narrowed the watercourse until it narrowed all the way out to the sea near the Andriake garrison. The contemporary names of the ruins at the site, the sea necropolis and the river necropolis, hearken back to a time when the sea was much nearer, and the river's course much wider and closer.

Myra appears little in the historical record, typically lumped together with its fellow intractable Lycian cities chafing under outside rule or raiding sites elsewhere in the Mediterranean. The city and its two garrison towns (the aforementioned Andriake and Sura) carried on independently, pirates to the east and uncertain Roman rule to the west. In 42 B.C., the Romans were forced to assault the city to bring it under their control (although the Myrans proved more flexible than their allies at Xanthus, submitting after the Roman navy broke through the defenses at Andriake). St. Paul put in here briefly during his travels, but his visit is overshadowed by a later Christian, St. Nicholas.

Perhaps owing to the fame of St. Nicholas, Myra became the provincial capital of Lycia in the fifth century, although this success evaporated as the Byzantine Empire was beset by waves of Persians and Arabs in the 600s. The river's continued silting and intermittent invasions from the east finally undid the city, which faded into agrarian obscurity.

Arrivals & Departures

By Bus
Dolmuş leave Demre for Kaş and Fethiye frequently between 7:45 am and 11 p.m., and they depart for Antalya until 8:45 p.m. The daily bus to Üçağız passes through town around 5 p.m. Demre's otogar is on the main road, one quarter mile shy of the city center, inland. The Church of Saint Nicholas (Noel Baba) is signed to the left at the city center intersection, and Myra is also signed, straight through town to the foothills behind.

Andriake in Demre/Kale is remote from transport and hotels, but much closer and cheaper to visit (from-$6) than Kaş.

By Car
Demre is at the western end of a large alluvial plain, and the road westward toward Kaş is forced up the mountain behind Myra. The main road takes a circuitous route through town, but it is well signed in both directions and toward Myra. To reach the docks at Andriake, follow the Müze Caddesi road past the Church of St. Nicholas due west.

Orientation
Follow the signs from the main coast highway to the city center (merkez), which is posted with yellow signs for Myra and Noel Baba Kilesi (The Basilica of St. Nicholas). Myra is built up against the foot of the mountain inland of town.

The tourism information office for Demre is in **Kaş**, *Tel. 242 836 1238, Fax 242 836 1238.*

Where to Stay & Eat
Demre does not particularly recommend itself for overnight stays, but if time prohibits continuing east to Kaleköy, Kaş, or Kalkan or west to Çıralı, you'll find some decent options. You'll find several serviceable restaurants clustered around the Church of St. Nicholas, all accustomed

to feeding busloads of tour groups; this is a good place to get some beans and rice at the bus-stop lokanta.

ANDRIAKE HOTEL, *Finike Caddesi PK 62, Demre. Tel. (242) 871-2249; Fax (242) 871-5440. Rooms: 52. Credit cards accepted. Open year-round. Double: $35 (breakfast included).*

The Andriake Hotel is the best in town; the ribbon-cutting ceremony at the end of 1996 was attended by former Prime Minister Tansu Çiller herself. The Andriake ranks three stars and offers air conditioning, television, balconies, and minibuses to local points of interest—principally the beach at Andriake, the Myra necropolis, and the Church of St. Nicholas. The hotel is frequented by tour groups, and has a restaurant.

HOTEL KIYAK, *Merkez Girişi, PK 65, Demre. Tel. (242) 871-4509; Fax (242) 871-2093; Email: kiyakhotel@hotmail.com. Rooms: 24. Credit cards accepted. Open year-round. Double: $16 (breakfast included).*

The Kıyak is good, clean lodging option just across the street from the Andriake Hotel. The interior is dark, but rooms are decent and usually busy with budget travelers. Note that catalytic heaters provide heat in the winter, and that the water heater is wood-fueled. The Kıyak brothers, who own the hotel, offer a popular boat trip to Kekova almost daily. The cost per person is $10, lunch not included. If your destination is Kekova, consider joining the daily boat trip at 10 a.m. in summer. In a pinch, the bland Şahin Hotel in the town center will do (*Tel. (242) 871-5686*).

IPEK RESTAURANT, *Gökyazı Mah., Müze Cad. No. 28, Demre. Tel. (242) 871-5088. Moderate.*

This is the best of the tour-group restaurants in the neighborhood of the Church of St. Nicholas. The food is the same decent quality found at the other restaurants, but the ambiance and service are superior.

Seeing the Sights

The **Basilica of St. Nicholas** (Noel Baba Kilesi) dates to the eighth century, and is obviously built on a far more grand scale than the chapel used by St. Nicholas himself. There is a $3 entry fee, a small price to pay if you are a sailor, virgin, pawnbroker, or Russian seeking spiritual guidance. The church is interesting but not especially exceptional.

The current incarnation of the basilica was pieced together by a Russian prince in 1862, and makes use of recycled stones bearing old pagan inscriptions to Artemis and her ilk. The conspicuous broken tomb within the church's southern aisle may be that of St. Nicholas, but that is as dubious as the claim by the Antalya Museum that they are displaying the skull and jaw of the old saint. Note the small looped passage behind the apse, identical to the passage in the chapel on the lowest level at Derinkuyu in Cappadocia.

On Dec. 6 every year, the Greek Orthodox Church still observes the feast of St. Nicholas at the site, a tradition that blossomed in England during medieval times.

The Story of Father Christmas

Who really knows how legends grow and perpetuate themselves, but the kernel of truth left in St. Nick's tale is no deeper than the name, St. Nick. Before settling in for a long winter's nap, the rosy-cheeked children may be surprised by some of the differences between the traditional and actual accounts of the saint's life.

St. Nicholas grew up in Patara, west of Demre, in the third century. The details of his upbringing are vague, but he appears to have been elected bishop in Demre during the reign of Diocletian (285-305 A.D.). His good deeds won him fame throughout the Mediterranean, but what deeds, and how good, is impossible to tell. One story foreshadows a modern Christmas tradition: told of a poor man unable to provide his three marriageable daughters with a dowry, St. Nicholas stole up to the house one night and dropped three small bags of gold down the chimney - or, more likely through a window opening. These anonymous gifts were credited with saving the young women from lives of prostitution. Other tales are less familiar: St. Nick refusing to suckle at his mother's breast on the sabbath, or St. Nick resurrecting three dismembered lads (an act that would have put Christ's resurrection of Lazarus to shame).

The truth of St. Nicholas' life is difficult to separate from the folklore. In the end St. Nicholas was probably murdered as part of Diocletian's anti-Christian pogroms.

Whatever his fate, St. Nicholas' fame and reputation appeared to blossom in the centuries after his death. In the seventh century a church was erected in his name at Constantinople, and he was adopted by pawnbrokers, children, the Russian nation, and even the suspicious pairing of sailors and virgins as a patron saint. A Byzantine named Simon Metaphrastes wrote a preposterous account of the saint's life in the early 900s, perpetuating all of the rumors that had circulated during the past 500 years. This account helped make St. Nicholas more popular than ever, and surely contributed to the next grim chapter: in 1087, a motley bunch of merchants from Bari sailed to Myra. There, ignoring the animated resistance of some clerics, the merchants disinterred the myrrh-covered bones of St. Nicholas and hauled them back to Italy. These bones fetched a fine price among those under St. Nicholas' protection, and were popular both as talismans and medicinals.

For those who complain that Christmas has become too commercial, it's also interesting to note that prior to the theft of the bones, the Greek Orthodox clergy at Myra's Church of St. Nicholas turned a nice profit selling myrrh they claimed came from a bottomless supply in St. Nicholas' tomb.

Ruins of Myra

The **ruins** of Myra are inland of the Church of St. Nicholas on Yeni Cami/Alakent Caddesi, west of the church. The Myra ruins are a fine bit of tourism sleight of hand. The ticket booth is located at the westernmost part of the site, and allows entrance to the Myra theater and the "sea" necropolis. After running a gauntlet of mystifying curio sellers (porcelain rabbits and ducks, Santa Claus statuettes) you arrive at the base of the hill. A few tombs are down at ground level, but the majority are on the steep ridge and cliff face above. Signs discourage climbing, but curious folk will be sorely tempted. The collection of largely inaccessible tombs is pretty, but most visitors find little else beyond, sigh, another theater and a $1 entrance fee (7:30 a.m.-7 p.m. summer, 8 a.m.-5:30 p.m. in winter).

For the intrepid, Myra offers much more of interest. Instead of turning left at the yellow "Myra 200 meters" sign, continue on the same road (Guvercinlik Cad.) for another 1,500 feet, rounding the southeastern spur of the mountain, and turn left at light pole #34. Continue to another road just after light pole #20 and take another left by the concrete cistern. The road heads directly into the draw past more tombs and climbs the ridge to a big new industrial building halfway up the slope. If you climb to the top of the mountain, you find the battered ruins of the old **acropolis** and a Selçuk **fortress**.

If you want a jumble of ruins to yourself, the ascent virtually guarantees it. The large exterior walls are a Byzantine construction, while the inner, more finely hewn walls are Lycian, dating to the fifth century B.C. The hilltop also has the remains of a watch tower and a Roman-era temple.

The most interesting ruins in the area are in the **river necropolis**, to the left of the aforementioned acropolis road just before it begins climbing out of the valley. You can approach the base of the hill from the popular sea necropolis by winding your way right through greenhouses or by following the directions toward the acropolis. The ruins of the river necropolis are fun to look through, but only if you have a good head for heights; many of them require heavily exposed scrambling. You will see the tombs as you approach, carved into the rocky mountainside, and there is an ancient network of steps and paths cut into the stone to help ascend to them. Many of the paths have fallen into an understandable state of disrepair.

The tombs in the area are often adorned with lengthy Lycian inscriptions and even artwork. The two most interesting tombs - some of the best in the whole of Lycia - are also three of the most obvious, on the eastern flank of the mountain between the acropolis road and the sea necropolis. The two tombs are on the left side. The first, more easily accessible tomb is decorated with reliefs of the deceased's family, four to one side of the opening, four to the other. The interior columns of the tomb itself are topped by the heads of lions in a curiously Hittite style. They were once decorated with paint, but the paint has worn even less well than the stone itself.

The second tomb is accessible after a long ascent topped with a mildly nasty carved stair. This tomb, the finest of a good lot, has a square opening divided with living stone into four panes, the bottom frame broken. A group of people, presumably the family, is carved in relief to either side of the tomb. To the right is a peculiarly Egyptian-looking relief of a woman offering a small box to the deceased (myrrh, for all we know, which some have suggested was the root of the name Myra). These tombs were almost certainly carved after the 5th century B.C., but the Hittite and Egyptian imagery could hearken back to the Lycians', sometimes referred to as the Lukka or Lukki, persistent raids and warfare against both great empires.

Excursions & Day Trips
ANDRIAKE

Andriake (Çayağzı) is three kilometers from Demre. Follow the road in front of the Church of St. Nicholas (Müze Cad.) away from the city center; signs guide you, but it's basically a beeline. Scheduled boats depart Andriake for Kaleköy (Simena)/Kekova at 10 a.m., but there are always captains on the docks willing to shuttle you there or take you fishing for a little extra money. Fishing will cost at least $20 for 5 hours, and a special charter to Kaleköy (Simena) is typically $25 for the boat. The trip from Andriake to the Kekova bay is shorter than the trip to Kekova from Kaş, but the scheduled departures here are less regular.

Little is known about Andriake. The town was founded as a garrison port for the metropolis of Myra up the Androkos River. Today Andriake is overgrown and partially buried in fine white sand. This is a shame for archeologists, but generally good news if you like beaches. The beach at Andriake is long, but it is rather polluted and populated mostly by young boys. Foreigners are somewhat uncommon, and it is not a comfortable place to lie in the sun for a woman traveling alone.

A new port here has renewed Andriake's historic role as a seafaring terminus – boats frequently ply the old routes back and forth between the dead cities to the west and the dead city here.

The new road winds along the Androkos River in what was once one of the coast's finest bays. The **ruins** of the former town are distributed to either side of the old bay, with the majority of ruins inland of the new road and another collection of walled ruins on the opposite shore in the area behind the restaurant. A pedestrian bridge allows access to the far (northern) bank, where the beach is located. The buildings on the road shore were dedicated to commerce from Myra and include a great granary built during Hadrian's reign (117-138 A.D.). On the far shore there were also commercial buildings, although fewer. The necropolis is further inland on the northern bank, outside the ring of walls.

Sura
Several kilometers west of Demre on the main highway is another of Myra's outposts, the minor ruin of **Sura**. This city stood on the western road, then as now. The scattered ruins are located in the vicinity of the second turn as you ascend from the plain. The perfectly rectangular walled city guarded the upper entrance to Myra's plain, and may have been immediately above a navigable section of river or sea, today a soupy marsh.

Sura's only distinction from the garrison towns that pepper the Lycian Coast is that it was host to a **"fish oracle."** Priests of the oracle would feed fish chunks of meat and make their determinations on the basis of what food the fish ate. This sounds ridiculous until you visit other of history's great budget oracles at Termessos and Olympos.

Andriake's Temple of the Fish Oracle was associated with **Apollo**, who was also the patron of the great oracle at Patara. The Doric Apollo temple is located below the main town, and a spring still trickles past. There are no fish here anymore to offer prophesy, nor have there been since oracles were given the kibosh by Theodosius the Great (378-395 A.D.).

Kekova Bay

If you want sheer escape, **Kekova Bay** is your place. Two small seafront towns are located at the site, **Kaleköy (Simena)** and **Üçağız**, and both of these fishing and farming villages remain what all of the developed towns along the Mediterranean claim to have once been: pretty and unassuming spots with thick cascades of bougainvillea, whitewashed buildings, and lush greenery. Here, too, there is an overwhelming collection of Lycian ruins - it is here we saw a weary old spaniel dog eating from her bowl while lying prone in her stylish doghouse, a Lycian tomb with a hole punched in the front. The **Teimussa ruins** in Üçağız are related to the ruins just outside the mouth of the bay at Kaleköy, ancient Simena. Capping this, sunken ruins sprawl into the bay, and **Kekova Island** is just offshore.

Visitors stay here for weeks at a time, taking advantage of the town's several pensions and private guest houses. Writers, burnout victims, and backpackers take up residence and are lulled by the peace of the little town. The only "disturbance", besides a rogue rooster crowing well before dawn, is the activity on the waterfront, where several daily tours from both Kaş and Andriake/Demre visit the town and anchor offshore. That remains a fairly benign sort of irritant, although it has served to nudge food and accommodation prices upwards. You can't rent a place in Üçağız for pennies, but it won't cost you much more than $10 for a double in winter, $20 in summer. Everything's negotiable, of course, and if you want to stay for a while your bargaining power rises accordingly.

Also, between the good paved road connecting Üçağız and the main Antalya-Fethiye highway and the frequent yacht and tour boat visits, Üçağız manages to be a lot closer to civilization than it might appear - if you must have your *Herald Tribune* or *Turkish Daily News*, you can have it shipped in with a little something for the trouble.

A couple of years ago we heard tell of a new, more highway-like road that would be punched through to Uçagız from Demre, but at the time of writing there was no evidence of this yet.

Arrivals & Departures

By Bus

The main highway passes between Demre/Kale and Kaş; the road to Üçağız from the main highway is 16 kilometers, and there is nothing at the intersection—neither shops nor taxi stands. You can try to hitch--most people spare themselves the trouble and simply pay to be ferried to Üçağız the port near Demre (see below). That said, there is a dolmuş to Üçağız from the east. During the summer dolmuş leave Üçağız for Antalya at about 8 a.m., at the discretion of the driver. After arriving at Antalya the dolmuş waits until about 3 p.m., then heads back west to Üçağız. The dolmuş passes through Demre on its way to Üçağız - on those days it is running - sometime after 5 p.m.

By Boat

The best way to get to Kale or Üçağız is by boat from Andriake port (just west of Demre). From the Demre otogar, get a taxi to the waterfront ($5), and you'll have no problem finding someone to ferry you to Simena/Üçağız —rates are roughly $15 for the ride. If you're making your way to Simena/Üçağız from Kaş, consider paying your way aboard one of the daily boat trips that stop in at Simena/Üçağız ($12)—they depart in the morning.

By Car

A taxi from Kaş costs about $35. If you have your own vehicle, the turnoff for Üçağız is posted just three miles east of the Kaş/Antalya/Elmali intersection, taking you 16 well-paved but curvy miles down through the mountains. En route you pass through Kılıçlı, a fairly lifeless valley town that is the unlikely site of the ruins of Appolonia. The Appolonia ruins are atop a hill just south of town; nothing is known of the town. Üçağız has a main parking lot by the waterfront, from which you can get your bearings.

Kaleköy (Simena) is just outside the mouth of the bay, around to the left as you look out at the sea from Üçağız, and is an even better retreat. Kaleköy's sole contact with the outside world is by boat - no one has yet managed to put a road through to the inaccessible village. If you have a rental car you can park it in the lot at the end of the road; you may want to make arrangements if you're staying a boatride away in Kaleköy.

The trip from Üçağız to Kaleköy/Simena by small launch takes 15 minutes and costs whatever the market will bear—generally about $3. Otherwise, you can walk along a pretty and rocky footpath between the two, along which you're likely to cross paths with some turtles. Walking takes 45 minutes. Kaleköy has its own collection of small guest houses and pensions, and the same casual litter of Lycian ruins, including a Byzantine fort atop the hill behind the village.

Orientation

Üçağız is the larger of the two towns, but they are both quite small. There are no banks or ATMs, just a few small stores and a post office (in Üçağız).

When you bestir yourself to investigate the region, you are in for a pleasant surprise; there are several necropoles of stone tombs in the area, a Templar fortress at Kaleköy, and old Lycian ruins across the bay on Kekova Island. The island protects the small bay, deep and navigable in some places, shallow and peculiar in others. The peculiarity arises from the staircases carved out of living rock that descend into the depths, and from a sprawling collection of submerged buildings and tombs.

Where to Stay & Eat

Kaleköy is the more charming of the two towns, by dint of its sloping location, its tiny size, the presence of a hilltop castle, and its preternatural quiet--there is something restful about a town without cars or access by road. The quality of restaurants is similar in both towns; the fact that Kaleköy has no touts again recommends it. One note about water in Kaleköy; it is shipped in, and you'll be advised to use as little as possible. If you don't mind the brine, bathe in good, clean sea.

Some of the most charming accommodations in Kale book blocks of rooms to the upscale Savile Row Tours and Travel agency. You might want a copy of their annual booklet if only to inspire you: 39 Savile Row, London, W1X 1AG, UK, Tel. (0171) 287-3001.

Üçağız

ONUR PANSİYON, *Üçağız, Kekova. Tel. (242) 874-2071; Fax (242) 874-2266. Rooms: 8. Credit cards not accepted. Open year-round. Double: $20 (breakfast included).*

This waterfront pension is unprepossessing, but it is the sort of place where people are pleased to stay for months on end. Rooms are spartan but clean. The restaurant on the premises is well-considered, offering seafood for $4-$5 and fresh mezes for $1. The Onur is located just west of the marina at the end of the road. The nearby Baba Veli Pansiyon, at the end of the road to your right after you descend into town, is another good option.

LEYLA PANSİYON, *Üçağız, Kekova. Tel. (242) 874-2038; Fax (242) 874-2039. Rooms: 6. Credit cards not accepted. Open year-round. Double: $14.*

Ms. Aliçavuşoğlu rents out six rooms in her sprawling house, and this is a good budget option two blocks behind the waterfront. The pretty garden has a fine Lycian tomb as its centerpiece, and is an excellent place to while away the time. Upon arrival, follow the road that runs parallel to the waterfront, past the Fisherman's Inn, and another 100 feet to the Kekova Market. Inquire at the market with Ahmet Aliçavuşoğlu.

FISHERMAN'S INN, *Üçağız, Kekova. Tel. (242) 874-2024. Inexpensive-moderate*

The Fisherman's Inn is a fine, dark, wood-trimmed hideout with $1 beers, good snacks, and an interesting mix of customers. This relaxed little spot, run for years by Uğur Yilmaz, is just up the road from the marina, across the road from Onur Pansiyon.

Kaleköy/Simena

MEHTAP PANSİYON, *Kaleköy. Tel. (242) 874 2146; Fax (242) 874-2261; Email: info@mehtappansiyon.com; Web: www.mehtappansiyon.com. Rooms: 10. Credit cards not accepted. Open year-round. Double: $26.*

The Mehtap's great feature is a stunning, simple wooden porch wrapped around several rooms and a restaurant. The Mehtap, uphill from the dock and slightly left, commands a view of Kale and the archipelago. Irfan Tezcan, the relaxed, friendly proprietor, has been in business since 1982 and has honed the art of hosting. You'll find a small lending library, excellent food (like Irfan-Bey's palamut), and pleasant, clean rooms. Get the price of the meal before you order.

Selected one of our favorite small hotels.

KALE PANSİYON, *Kaleköy İskele. Tel. (242) 874-2111; Fax (242) 874-2110. Rooms: 7. Credit cards accepted. Open April-October. Double: $25.*

Perched just above the water, this little pension offers fine views over the bay and is run by Salih Can, a helpful man who can help direct you around the area and make arrangements. This pension (like the nearby Nesrin's Bademli Ev, Tel. (242) 874-2170, Fax (242) 874-2093) is included on Savile Row's clutch of Mediterranean hotels intended to epitomize relaxed living. Salih owns a good restaurant (bearing the same name) next door; outside tables are arranged on a covered wooden patio that extends out over the sea. Another good options in Kaleköy is Murat Pansiyon; all of the pensions are within within two minutes walk of the boat landing.

CAFE ANKH, *Kaleköy. Tel. (242) 874-2171. Inexpensive.*

Ahmet and Hasan Takır built this small café on the stony slopes above the sea. Ice cream acts as a lure, attracting the guests of Blue Cruise boats that moor in the Kekova area. The other offerings are also quite good, making the short walk to the eastern side of Kaleköy worthwhile. There's a small landing below the Ankh where you can stake out a place in the sun and swim.

Seeing the Sights

Üçağız, ancient Teimussa, is almost entirely in the form of a sprawling **necropolis** - and it's easy to wonder whether the unwalled area wasn't simply the necropolis for nearby Simena. Teimussa is a city without history, known only from a few inscriptions. If it was more than a necropolis for Simena, it may have been a small associated fishing village - there are sunken piers just offshore. The name Üçağız derives from "three mouths," identical to the Greek "Tristomo," which refers to the mouth of the small Üçağız bay and the two narrow mouths of the Kekova Bay to either side of Kekova Island.

While looking through Üçağız's beautifully crafted collection of tombs, fashioned with such care and artistry, you cannot help but be impressed with the efforts the living made for the dead. The tombs here were not made for citizens of this small town, people who were by no means great Lycian kings and queens.

Sarcophagi lie scattered throughout the little town, but the main section of the ancient town is supposed to have been located to the east, behind the Koçlar Turizm pension. An especially picturesque tomb is located here, perched atop a stone with a natural cleft.

If you've arrived by boat you've already begun seeing ruins in the shallows beneath the sea, and the greatest concentration of these curiosities is on Kekova Island. The Üçağız side of the island is liberally sprinkled with structures just beneath the surface; mostly small chambers and stairways, with more sarcophagi. This section of Kekova, called **Tershane** (or boatworks), is supposed to have been the main necropolis for Simena, in modern Kaleköy. The structure that gives the area its name is a long stone building near a sand beach on the northwest side of the island. The locals suppose it to have been a boatworks, although it also suggests a small church. Unfortunately, the bulk of the remaining walls collapsed in 1996. More ruins are located in the thickly overgrown interior. Good boots and heavy pants are handy for a real investigation. Tiny islands jut from the sea throughout the bay, many of them cut and quarried for building material

Continuing now along the leeward side of the island and crossing to the mainland we arrive at the final town in this idyllic archipelago, **Simena** (also variably Kale or Kaleköy). Simena is located at the eastern entrance to Kekova Bay. Such a fine, well-protected bay needed some protecting of its own, to which end the pretty **Crusader Fort** was built atop Simena's steep hill. The present form of the fortress derives from the Knights of St. John, although there was doubtless a fortification prior to the 13th century. Based on the likely occupation of pirates and Crusaders, it seems this perfect little bay was seized for its remote character, its excellent harbor, and its ability to control shipping lanes. Merchants must have made a wide detour around this spot.

The path to the castle is direct, and the view from the ramparts is excellent. There may be a guard waiting nearby to extract an entrance fee of about $1.50. While atop the fortress you can take in the entirety of Kekova Bay, as well as the steeply descending town below. The town's present scattering of houses probably varies little from its Hellenistic forebear, indeed the modern houses incorporate the same stone quarried by the residents of Simena. A seven row theater carved into the bedrock inside the castle looks out over the turquoise sea, the ruins of a small bath lay near the pier, and a necropolis descends in the direction of Üçağız.

You can rent rowboats in Üçağız and, obviously, Kaleköy/Simena, where they constitute the main mode of transportation.

Sports & Recreation

The Kekova Island area seems to have been designed with sea kayaks in mind, and we are fortunate that one company rents them:: **Bougainville Travel**, Çukurbağlı Cad. No. 10, Kaş, *Tel. (242) 836-3142; Fax: (242) 836-1605; Email: bougainville@superonline.com; www.bougainville-turkey.com.* **Bougainville** offers day-long kayaking tours in doubles and singles (putting in at Üçağız, transportation from Kaş included, $35, or weekly tours for $324) and kayak rentals to experienced boaters ($24/day). Their instructors/tour leaders are all certified kayak guides, but if you can convince the Bougainville folks you know what you're doing you can rent the boats.

Paddles, skirt, flotation device and a map of the suitable campgrounds on and near Kekova Island are all included. Bougainville also has sleeping bags and tents if you haven't come prepared for outdoor adventure.

Turkey's Southern Atlantis?

The sunken ruins at Kekova are fascinating, and beg several questions. Chief among them, why, when so many ancient cities in Asia Minor were left high and dry by siltation, quakes, and slight drops in the sealevel, did Kekova drop into the sea? One theory is that the ruins haven't sunk at all; there may have been a local tradition of hewing sarcophagi and small buildings out of stone already in the water. In other words the ruins may have come presunk. Any examination of ruins such as the sunken gates at Aperlae disputes that theory.

It is more likely that a regional seismic dropped the Kekova area into the sea while leaving Myra to the east and Patara to the west high and dry. Unlike those cities, there was no siltation at Kekova to keep it landlocked.

Kas

Kaş has long been a pit stop on the great backpacking road, past Kuşadası, on the way to Kathmandu. When the new coast road was laid in 1980 the beaches and sparse ruins of Kaş seemed a natural pit stop.

We prefer the accommodations of **Kalkan**, just 25 kilometers west, but Kaş is a bit larger and more cosmopolitan, and certainly offers less expensive hotels and meals. Another appealing aspect of Kaş is that it offers boat tours to Kekova.

History

Before this city was Kaş it was Antiphellos, sister city to Phellos in the mountains above. The inland city slipped out of the historical record by the first century B.C., but coastal Antiphellos thrived under Roman rule.

The city benefited from maritime trade, but was shielded from invading armies by the screen of mountains lining this section of coast. Only when the maritime power of the Byzantine Empire fell into decay and the Arab corsairs began maruading the coast did the power of the city wane. Pliny the Younger, the Cliff Clavin of antiquity, notes that Antiphellos produced excellent sponges.

Arrivals & Departures

Kaş is on the main coast road, easily accessible by car or bus. Buses depart regularly for Bodrum (six hours, $15) and Fethiye (two hours, $4) to the west, and Antalya (four hours, $8) in the east. At least one İstanbul-bound bus is available per bus company, per day (15 hours, $21).

Orientation

The very-helpful **Kaş tourism information office** is located just inland of the harbor on Cumhuriet Meydanı No. 5, *Tel. (242) 836 1238, Fax (242) 836-1238*. The town has ATMs, banks, a hospital on Hastane Caddesi *(Tel. (242) 836-1185)*, grocery stores, rental car agencies and a laundromat (Habessos Laundry, Uzun Çarşı Antik Sok. No. 5).

Where to Stay

There are some decent hotels in Kaş, but they are not as appealing as their neighbors to the west in Kalkan. The more expensive of these hotels are in the waterfront Küçükçakıl district just east of the marina; the less expensive—and in some way preferable—hotels are just west of the mosque by the marina; additional hotels are scattered on the huge rocky peninsula west of town.

HERA OTEL, *Küçükçakıl Mevkii, Kaş. Tel. (242) 836-3062; Fax (242) 836-3063. Rooms: 40. Credit cards accepted. Open April-October. Double: $62.*

The waterfront façade of the Hera Hotel is built to resemble an Ionic Temple, making it a landmark when you approach from the sea. Rooms are decent and clean, and offer a wide range of amenities—satellite TV, minibar, air conditioning, a small pool, and a swimming platform on the sea. The hotel is modern and not particularly charming, but you're sure to be comfortable. The nearby **Otel Medusa** *(Tel. (242) 836-1440; Fax: (242) 836-1441;* Double: $52) is another quality alternative. Both hotels are located around Küçükçakıl Caddesi east of the Kaş marina.

OTEL SARDUNYA, *Hastane Cad. No. 56, Kaş. Tel. (242) 836-3080; Fax (242) 836-3082. Rooms: 16. Credit cards accepted. Open year-round. Double: $32 (breakfast included).*

The Sardunya is located just above the water to the west of the marina, and offers a good value for the price. Ten rooms offer a sea view, each simple, clean, and clad in stark white tile. A splendid cascade of bougainvillea almost obscures your sea view. Avoid the back rooms—they are a bit cooler through the day, but don't get the evening breezes the way the waterfront rooms do. The Sarduniye has swimming from a small landing below the hotel.

YALI PANSIYON, *Hastane Cad. No. 11, Kaş. Tel. (242) 836-1132; Fax (242) 836-3487. Rooms: 5. Credit cards not accepted. Open year-round. Double: $14.*

The Yalı, open since 1985, is a good budget hotel. With its old, clean tile floors, en suite bathrooms, and lovely balcony perched above the sea, this offers a better standard than many more expensive areas in the area. In addition, you have access to a kitchen and freezer, and you can swim from the rocks just below. Fans are available in summer. The Yalı Pansiyon is located next to the ruins of a Hellenistic temple just west of the waterfront marina. **Kaş Hotel**, just west and across the road from Yalı Pansiyon, is also a decent budget choice and offers air conditioning (*Tel. (242) 836-1271; Fax: (242) 836-2170;* Double: $24).

On the Peninsula

Dozens of hotels have sprung up on Çukurbağ Peninsula. Many of these offer good quality accommodation, but they are a bit antiseptic and hardly convenient—public transportation around the sparsely-populated peninsula is infrequent. All of that said, there are some good things to be said for these hotels, particularly if you have your own vehicle.

CLUB ARPIA, *Çukurbağ Yarımdası, Kaş. Tel. (242) 836-2642; Fax (242) 836-3163; Email: none; Web: none. Rooms: 19. Credit cards accepted. Open February-October. Double: $27 ($38 half-board).*

The Club Arpia is the best value for money on the peninsula, offering the same amenities available at its peers at just $38 for two, half-board. Rooms have fans, air-conditioning, and balconies; they are not particularly lovely, but they are clean and well-maintained. A path descends from a garden to a swimming platform on the sea far below. Since being taken over by Bougainville Travel in 2001, the Arpia is sure to be well-managed. The Arpia is four kilometers outside of Kaş. The neighboring **Savile Kaş Residence**, operated by Savile travel, is an extraordinarily upscale version of the Arpia (*Tel. (242) 836-2300; Fax (242) 836-3054; Email: info@saviletours.com; Web: www.saviletours.com.* Double: $98).

Where to Eat

CHEZ EVY, *Terzi Sokak No. 2, Kaş. Tel. (242) 836-1253. Moderate-Expensive. Dinner only.*

This cozy side-street restaurant, owned and run by a French expatriate, serves the best French food in Turkey—and some of the least expensive. We cannot recommend it highly enough.

Evy is an accomplished chef who for many years cooked aboard yachts. Leaving that behind, she had great success with Gramofon restaurant in a tony Istanbul neighborhood, then moved to Kaş, and the southern coast is much the better for it. Chez Evy is crammed with Turkish antiques and textiles, and patrons cluster around low, intimate tables covered by crisp white linens. In the summertime you sit under jasmine blossoms on the patio in back.

It is Evy herself who completes the scene. Your first sight of her will probably catch her immersed in the act of cooking; one hand stirring, the other sauteeing vegetables, one eye on a timer, another on her sous-chef. This, Evy takes seriously; the rest is good fun. Circulating through her dining room, she is friendly, garrulous, and a good judge of appetite; she might size you up and assign you a meal, and you're fortunate if she does.

Which, at last, brings us to the food. It is marvelous, and it comes in quantity. Take, for instance, the pepper steak: it is a thick, specially-butchered cut, bathed in delicious cream sauce and accompanied by a mound of crisp potatoes and other seasonal vegetables. Or the leg of lamb; served on a platter with a great butcher knife, the garlic-infused meat affixed to a silver handle and steeped in its own juices. The menu is mind-bending, the Turkish wine list—Evy prefers the Seviler label—excellent, and the cost of an entrée $8-$10. Reservations are recommended.

SUN CAFÉ RESTAURANT, *Hükümet Cad., Kaş. Tel. (242) 836-1053; Fax (242) 836-1924; Email: suncafe@hotmail.com. Moderate-Expensive.*

The Sun Café offers good, plentiful food in a great outdoor setting. The restaurant, set behind an old building on the waterfront, has a large, terraced patio blessed with a fine garden and its own Lycian tomb. The walls are draped in ivy and bougainville. The menu has sportfish from May to September—early in the year, for instance, a cut of tuna or swordfish will cost $6, for instance. Sun Café is located just inland of Mercan Restaurant, 35 meters from the water.

ERİŞ RESTAURANT, *Gülsoy Sok. Orta Sok. No. 13, Kaş. Tel. (242) 836-2134. Moderate-Expensive.*

Eriş Restaurant, located down the lane from the tourism information office in an old Ottoman house, is generally thought to have the best traditional Turkish food in Kaş. Mezes cost $2-$3, and entrees cost $5-$7.

BAHÇE LOKANTA, *Anı Mezar Karşısı No. 31, Kaş. Tel. (242) 836-2370. Moderate-Expensive.*

A lovely garden restaurant just uphill of a conspicuous city center rock tomb. Excellent mezes and a wide selection of vegetarian dishes.

Seeing the Sights

Lycian sarcophagi are scattered around town, and remnants of Antiphellos are located just west of town, beginning with the foundation of a temple uphill from the mosque and continuing along the waterfront to the ruins of the theatre. This 26-row theater often remains humming into the wee hours, as rogue campers and the guests at nearby Kaş Camping strum their guitars and commune with the Antiphellians. If you stay in town you can also visit the base of the hill behind town, where rock-carved tombs are located.

The sea in the immediate vicinity of Kaş isn't too clean, as you're likely to notice. Two beaches, **Küçük Çakil** and **Büyük Çakil**, offer good swimming not far away. Otherwise, get a dolmuş to **Kaputaş Beach** in the west. Another alternative is to go on one of the several boat tours out of Kaş (see below).

The ruins of the Lycian valley to the west are described later in the book. Ruins also pepper the mountains above, principally the remarkable Byzantine fortress at Dereağzi. This fortress is located at the confluence of two rivers that become **Demre Çayi**—the river that descends to the port at Andriake in Demre. The foundations of the fortress are hewn into the living stone and built with polygonal masonry, a testament to the great antiquity of the site. These are topped with cobbled Byzantine-era walls, marking its fortifications against the depredations of Arab and Saracen invaders in the eight and ninth centuries. To get there, follow the highway east out of Kaş, turn left at the main intersection toward Gombe and Elmalı, and turn right at Kasaba on the road signed "Çatallar"— which, by the way, is next to the magnificent ruin of Arykanda (see Finike section). The trailhead to the ruin of Dereağiz is three kilometers south of Dirgenler.

Sports & Recreation
Boat Tours

The daily Kekova boat tours depart at 10 a.m. from the town's main harbor, located between the tourist information office and the central mosque. These tours pack a big boat full of people and set out for the sunken city, Kekova Island, and pull in at Uçağız or Kaleköy for a bite. The cost is $15 per person, and should include lunch and a stop for swimming. Another tour chugs off in the opposite, western direction, visiting some of the impressive sea caves along the coast, passing through the Kalkan Bay and calling at small islands. Kahramanlar has been around for years and tends to have standard prices.

Another sailing possibility is the boat trip to **Meis**, a Greek island just offshore. This is one of the busiest small ferry routes in the country, kept bustling by foreigners leaving Turkey for an afternoon to get their travel visas renewed as well as standard tourists. The Greek community of Meis and the Turkish community in Kaş have been conspiring to give Turkish/Greek relations a good name, cooperating between themselves and doing their best to tone down the ongoing disputes between their respective nations.

For an afternoon on Meis, turn your passport in to Rekor Turizm the day before traveling. That office will run your passport through the port authority so that you can sail the following day. Travel time is just over one-half hour. Spending an afternoon in Meis does not require a special visa, but if you intend to stay longer than a single afternoon you'll be asked to fill out a form. Cost of a single day excursion is $22, plus $20 if you need to renew your Turkish visa. This is subject to change in the same way that relations between Turkey and Greece are subject to change.

A Victory for Common Sense

In 1996, a diplomatic crisis erupted between Turkey and Greece over a collection of guano-spackled rocks in the Aegean Sea. The dispute was precipitated when Greek nationalists planted the Greek flag on the Kardak Rocks. The rocks are uninhabitable and of no practical use, but their possession has consequences (minor ones) for maritime and mineral rights. Turkey reacted by sending commandos in to remove the flag and plant the Turkish flag in its place. In the speace of days latent ill-will between nationalists on both sides exploded; two NATO member-states exchanged barbs and inched toward real military confrontation.

Enter diplomats from the EU and the US...and the good people of Kaş. Several nationalist journalists arrived in Kaş at the height of the conflict, hoping to plant a Turkish flag on some rocks near Meis. Fortunately, their attempt to rent a boat for the purpose was firmly and sensibly refused. The dispute eased. Diplomacy and good sense won the day.

Diving, Walking, & Sea Kayaking Tours

Scuba diving lessons are an interesting local possibility, with 6 day P.A.D.I. deep water certification courses costing $350, including equipment. Or you can simply go on a day-trip discovery dive, receiving instruction and the chance to see ancient amphorae and anchors not far below the water's surface. Experienced divers pay $30/half-day to see some actual ship wrecks in what is considered some of the best diving in the Mediterranean.

Bougainville Travel is a reliable, experienced, and enthusiastic company, handling diving in addition to an excellent range of walking, hiking, and biking tours in the region and sea kayak rentals/trips out of Kekova Bay. Bougainville also boasts Turkey's only certified diving instructor for disabled people (who provides this service on a volunteer basis); their dive-boat is wheelchair accessible. Contact **Bougainville Travel**, *Çukurbağlı Cad. No. 10, Kaş, Tel. 242 836 3142, Fax 242 836 1605, bougainville@superonline.com.* Bougainville can also make rental car and plane reservations for you (they are an official Turkish Airlines ticketing agent), and they offer reasonably-priced Internet access. Recommended.

Shopping

Like Kalkan, Kaş has a lot of shops with art and crafts. In addition to the requisite leathers and carpets you'll find some interesting silver work. One good, honest silver shop is **Mencilis Art**, Uzunçarşı No. 17, Kaş, *Tel. 242 836 2897.*

WEST TO KALKAN

Kalkan

Kalkan is spared the fate of some of its formerly pristine and charming peers (Marmaris, Kuşadası, Kemer) by its geography and its judicious laws concerning development. The heart of the town, clinging to a mountainside above a picturesque little port, is protected from development.

There are a few jarring notes, such as the colorful Pirate's Club hotel in the west of town and an explosion of hotels on the outskirts—hotels that are to the Kalkan vernacular what Frankenstein was to the homo sapiens vernacular. For all of that, Kalkan itself strikes a fine balance between resort area and quaint Turkish coastal town.

Arrivals & Departures

The coast road from Kaş to Patara runs just a few hundred meters above town. Kamil Koç offers dolmuş and regular bus service in the area, serving Kaş hourly, Antalya and Fethiye seven times daily, with İstanbul departures at 7 p.m., Ankara at 4:30 p.m., and Marmaris at 8:30 a.m. Pamukkale's buses maintain a similar schedule, with an additional İzmir route at 10 a.m. and 10 p.m. Additional service is added in the high season.

There are dolmuş to Patara beach hourly in summer, and regular service to Kaş hourly in summer via Kaputaş Beach.

Orientation

Kalkan is a simple fishing village; no ruins, no mythology. The town is picturesque; a cascade of whitewashed stone buildings that descend steeply toward a small marina. Kalkan was founded 150 years ago by settlers from Meis, and it retained a large Greek population until the exchange of Turkish and Greek populations in 1923.

Kalkan caters to Turks and Europeans on holiday, as well as to those cruising the Mediterranean by gulet or yacht. You'll find international newspapers (near the PTT in the upper part of town), foreign exchange offices and an ATM (also near the PTT at Ziraat Bankası), excellent arts and crafts sellers, and a critical mass of strong hotels.

Where to Stay

The flower of accommodation in the region is found here. Choices include several excellent small hotels and a brace of outstanding pensions. All of the hotels below offer dinner in the high season.

TÜRK EVI, *Kalkan. Tel. (242) 844-3129; Fax (242) 844-3492. Rooms: 9. Credit cards not accepted. Open year-round. Double: $30-$40 (breakfast included).*

The Türk Ev (formerly the Eski Evi) is a friendly, immaculate, and creatively bustling place; it is also one of our favorite hotels in the whole of Turkey. The building is a classic, whitewashed Kalkan structure whose shaded patio leads into a pleasant, airy main room. Within, you'll find a bowl of fresh oranges here, the owners' own hand-carved wooden cradle there, and several couches on which to relax and enjoy a glass of wine. Rooms are light and spacious, and have hard wood floors, mosquito netting, balconies, and shutters. You're a short stroll from the waterfront, but the noise of mid-summer Kalkan is barely perceptible here.

The Türk Ev is owned and run by Önder and Selma Elitez, an engaging, friendly couple who comingle their high standards of hotelkeeping and raising their daughter. If you like, the owners can make plans for small groups to spend some time aboard the small sailboat Tirace. This is an excellent refuge year round; it is ideal for single women.

If you're headed west on the main highway, the Türk Ev is located just after the Kalkan turnoff, on the left. From the end of the main road in Kalkan (just below the bus station) the Türk Ev is straight uphill three blocks.

Selected one of our favorite small hotels.

KALKAN HAN, *Kalkan, Tel. (242) 844-3151; Fax (242) 844-2048; Email: kalkanhan@superonline.com; Web: www.kalkanhan.8k.com. Rooms: 16. Credit cards accepted. Open March-October. Double: $65 (breakfast included).*

The Kalkan Han set the tone in Kalkan, and continues to epitomize its simple, elegant ideal. Haydar Karabey, designer of the hotel, spearheaded the establishment of the town's far-sighted zoning standards. These standards prevented giant hotels from sweeping away what makes Kalkan so appealing. The whitewash and dark wood trim match the local vernacular perfectly; the stone, wood, and tile give the hotel its clean, simple lines. Rooms are of decent size and spartan, with ceiling fans, air conditioning, well-appointed bathrooms, and balconies along the upper floor.

At the time of this writing, dinner was no longer being served on the terrace above the Kalkan Han—which is unfortunate. The other misfortune visited upon the hotel has been improving—the Moonlight Bar and Disco several doors west has been forced to stifle its late-night noise since 2000; prior to that, the noise was awful. The Han is located at the upper end of town just uphill from Kalkan's single entry road.

PATARA STONE HOUSE, *Kalkan. Tel. (242) 844-3076; Fax (242) 844-3274; Email: korsanltd@turk.net; Web: www.kalkan.org.tr/kalkan/korsan/. Rooms: 9. Credit cards accepted. Closed November-March. Double: $28.*

The Patara Stone House, formerly Patara Pansiyon, is one of the oldest buildings in Kalkan. Owners Claire and Uluç have steadily improved the sprawling, whitewashed building over the years, and today it is a fine, inexpensive guest house. The age and peculiarities of the building should help explain the occasional slanting floor, crooked door, or wedged-in bathroom—it's all well done. Rooms are simple and offer fans. The Patara Stone House is located just inland of the small marina lighthouse, and benefits from a good breeze in the evening. The flower-covered terrace is beautiful.

Selected one of our favorite budget hotels.

VILLA MAHAL, *Kalkan. Tel. (242) 844-3268; Fax (242) 844-2122; Email: villamahal@turk.net; Web: www.kalkan.org.tr. Rooms: 14. Credit cards accepted. Closed November-March. Double: $90 (breakfast included).*

The Villa Mahal is a marvelous, startlingly white hotel across the bay from the Kalkan marina. Villa Mahal is the best upscale hotel in Kalkan, at once intimate and very professional. Rooms are clean and well-appointed, and the patios and balconies are dotted with potted plants. The hotel has its own swimming platform on the stony Kalkan bay. To get there: a signed road descends from the main highway one kilometer east of Kalkan.

ÖZ KALAMAKI, *Kalkan. Tel. (242) 844-3649; (242) 844-3654. Rooms: 10. Credit cards not accepted. Open year-round. Double: $22 (breakfast included).*

Restored in 1999, the Öz Kalamakı is now one of the best pensions in Kalkan. A lovely terrace commands a view of the full arc of Kalkan bay; with its deck chairs, couches, and a grill for summertime cooking, this is a great place to spend an evening. Within, you'll find pristine white tile floors and rooms with cream curtains, screened windows, and pine furniture. There are no mosquito nets, but fans are provided. The Kalamakı is located at the center of town on Yalı Boyu No. 51A.

PASHA'S INN, *Kalkan. Tel. (242) 844-3666; Fax (242) 844-3077; Email: fbalaban@superonline.com. Rooms: 7. Credit cards accepted. Open year-round. Double: $23 (25% discount in off-season).*

The Pasha's Inn shares the aesthetic of the other good Kalkan hotels; tile floors, thick walls, whitewashed exteriors, and wood trim. You'll find both mosquito nets and standing fans, and electric heat in the winter. Dinner is served on the terrace on many evenings. To get there: head straight down the main road from the bus station, turning right at the Alley Bar.

Bezirgan
Bezirgan is a postage-stamp town perched 3,000 feet directly above Kalkan (a steep fifty-minute drive), and was once the home of Kalkan's residents during the hot summer months.

OWL'S NEST, *Kalkan. Tel. (242) 837-5214; Fax (242) 844-3756; Email: owlsland@usa.net. Rooms: 6. Credit cards not accepted. Open year-round. Double: $45 (breakfast included).*

The Owl's Nest, tucked away high in the quiet yayla town of Bezirgan, is the perfect escape. Wild-haired owner Erol Şalvarlı and his wife Pauline returned to this town after years as a restaurateur in Kalkan and has converted an old family dwelling and erected a new one. The new rooms are more comfortable, but the heart of Owl's Nest is the three-room, 60-year old building 100 yards away—request a room there, unless you're visiting in the snowy off-season. In the old building, you'll find stone floors, great timber beams, thick walls, recessed windows, and fireplaces in each room. You'll also find the necessary modern touches— the shower and generator for instance—and some remarkable little touches typical of old Turkish farm houses. There's nothing to do in Bezirgan; you're here to relax, enjoy the meals at the Owl's Nest ($20 per person for lunch and dinner), read, and take walks in the countryside.

Selected one of our favorite small hotels.

Where to Eat
Kalkan boasts 125 restaurants, many of them seasonal places that cater to visitors; most of them are good, and most of them have somewhat high prices. Your hotel probably offers evening meals; inquire. Remember that Chez Evy, a magnificent French restaurant, is one-half hour east in Kaş.

SULTAN MARINA, *Kalkan. Tel. (242) 844-2680. Moderate-Expensive.*

Opened on the Kalkan waterfront in 1998, the Sultan Marina is owned and operated by Mustafa Güney, a former İstanbul restaurateur.

You can sit outside behind a low rail overlooking the harbor; the interior is nice, too, simply and tastefully decorated with a mounted swordfish head on the wall, shelved wineglasses, and skylights. Prices are not bad for a place right on the water (appetizers are $1.50-$3.50, and special main courses are in the $5-$7 range) and the menu is filled with traditional Turkish dishes such as patlıcan böreği (eggplant pastry), güveç (casserole served in an earthenware pot), shepherd's lamb, and pan-fried seafood. Two other waterfront restaurants—the nearby **Aubergine Restaurant** *(Tel. (242) 844-3332)* and the Korsan Restaurant at the east end of the marina—are also recommended, offering similar prices.

TANGO RESTAURANT, *Yalıboyu Cad. No. 36, Kalkan. Tel. (242) 844-3790. Credit cards accepted. Open April-October. Moderate-Expensive.*

The Tango is a Kalkan standard, serving some of Kalkan's best food since 1986. This is a good choice for a night out, with an excellent, imaginative set of mezes including pureed squash with garlic and mushrooms, stuffed peppers, and carrot pate (all $2.50-$3). Entrees such as grills and köfte cost $5. To get there: The Tango is located in upper Kalkan, just uphill of Kalkan leather in the block above the garden.

BELGIN'S KITCHEN, *Yalıbolu Mah. No. 1, Kalkan. Tel. (242) 844-3614; Web: www.kalkan.org.tr/kalkan/belgin/. Moderate-Expensive.*

Great effort has been taken to make Belgin's Kitchen look like a nomad tent, with grass mats, cushions against walls, low round tables, oil lamps, and Turkish textiles draping the walls. A good deal of effort is likewise taken with the food, but perhaps not enough to justify the relatively high prices. Soup and mezes cost $1.50-$2 and entrees such as Beğendi Kebap (tomato and lamb on a bed of thick aubergine sauce) cost $5-$8.

Seeing the Sights

Kalkan has no ruins of its own, but it is a marvelous base for visiting the great Lycian ruins to the west—Patara, Xanthos, Letoon, Tlos, and Pınara. Nor does it have great swimming, although you can swim east of the marina and across the bay by ferry on purpose-built landings. Better still, Kalkan offers convenient access to two marvelous beaches; picture-postcard **Kaputaş beach** five kilometers east ($1.50), and the 16-kilometer white sand beach by the ruins at Patara 17 kilometers west ($2.50). In high season, two dolmuş depart in each direction every hour between 9 a.m. and 6 p.m. from the bus stop in front of the municipal (Belediye) building.

Daily boat tours depart out of Kalkan for the nearby sea caves and small islands that dot the bay—you can make arrangements at the waterfront. You can make arrangements for a Kekova Boat Tour departing from Kaş—with the shuttle to Kaş included--for $22. Any time you're in the neighborhood of Kaş, it's worth your while to compare any plans you make with **Bougainville Travel** in Kaş *(Tel. (242) 836-3142; Fax (242) 836-1605; Email: bougainville@superonline.com* – see the Kaş section). In Kalkan, **Adda Tours**, Yalıboyu Mah., *Tel. (242) 844-3610; Fax (242) 844 3501*, arranges boat trips, trips into the interior, and a canoeing trip from Xanthos down the Esen Çayı 17 kilometers to Patara Beach.

Shopping

Shopping is a primary form or recreation among visitors to Kalkan, as you'll observe by the sheer volume of little boutiques distributed throughout the town. Oddly, ATM machines are in remarkably short supply. You'll find one in the upper area of town by the PTT at Ziraat Bankası; within the bank you'll also find a döviz (foreign exchange). Failing that, don't worry: everyone seems happy to take dollars.

If you're at all interested in textiles or reasonably-priced handmade womens' clothing, be sure to look for İNO (Yalıboyu Mah. No. 26, Kalkan, *Tel. (242) 844-2897)*, a wonderful little artisan's shop tucked into a side street just up from the harbor. Özlen Bayram collects textiles from all over Anatolia and Central Asia, including linen veils and hamam wraps, Kurdish silk headscarves, and patterned cottons from the Black Sea. She carries items that would be difficult to find anywhere else, such as hand-embroidered Uzbek kaftans and cotton curtain panels printed with wood blocks from a workshop that has been in continuous operation since the Selcuk period (1071-1370). Ms. Bayram sells individual textiles as well as stunning handmade womens' clothing she has constructed from pieces in her collection and dyed in rich colors. Also of note is the Tufanlar Silkroad Collection in the center of Kalkan.

Finally, there is a reason Kalkan is so silent and peaceful in the morning; everyone has been out all night at the local bars and dance places, which are theoretically kept muffled after midnight, and often surge right through Kalkan's periodic power outages on the strength of their generators.

WEST TO PATARA

The road from Kalkan is a winding two-lane affair, cutting up and over a spur of the Taurus mountains, then descending to the great plain of Esen Çay. The distance is short—little more than 20 kilometers—and at the crest you can opt to jog inland and climb 3,000 feet through İslamlar to Bezirgan. The route, relying heavily on second gear, windes past cliff

tombs and alabalik (trout) restaurants to the high summer retreat—
yayla—of the people of Kalkan.

Patara

Patara (Gelemiş town) has Turkey's finest beach, 16 long kilometers
of clean white sand. Development is prohibited and access is basically
limited to the entrypoint behind Gelemiş—the easternmost point of the
beach. Walk far enough along the hot white sand beach and you are
guaranteed a section of pristine sand to yourself.

Now a long, pure stretch of white sand, Patara Beach was once
punctured by a perfect little port, that of the Lycian city Patara. The bay
was choked with sand morethan 1,000 years ago, and the city is now
disappearing beneath sand dunes.

Gelemiş, the town that has sprouted just inland of the ruins, has a
relaxed charm and remains largely unblemished by development—but
has just enough to make you feel welcome. Tip: Take real shoes with you
when you go to Patara – the sand will cook your feet if you're wearing
sandals or Tevas.

History

Patara's history is peculiar among the four major Lycian cities
located in the Esen Çayı Valley, owing first to its ancient roots and second
to its role as a transportation hub. Patara stems from Pttara, a word in the
ancient Lycian dialect that predates the arrival of the Greeks. How much
evidence of the town's advanced years is still located at Patara no one
knows, since much of the site has been lost to the advance of sand dunes.

One of the greatest mysteries is the whereabouts of the Temple of
Apollo, a famous oracular shrine based in Patara. This temple was built
to accommodate a god who was thought to retire to Patara during
winter—the only season in which the Oracle issued its oracular state-
ments. Traces of the temple, thought to have been built on a grand scale
rivaling that of Didyma, have not yet been found.

Patara first appears in the historical record in an inscription at
Xanthos in 400 B.C. The two cities were always closely linked by trade,
with Xanthos–12 kilometers northeast—making great use of the Patarene
harbor. The Xanthos inscription postdates the first recorded cataclysm to
befall the region, when the Persian Harpagus led his armies into the
valley seeking to subjugate Lycia and was forced to witness the self-
immolation and battlefield suicide of Xanthos' entire population. The
catastrophe at Xanthos would surely have sent shock waves through its

neighbor Patara, who, historians surmise, quickly capitulated following the destruction of Xanthos.

The cosmopolitan attitudes of the sea-trading Patarenes irked the conservative, agrarian Xanthians, and the people of Patara surely scoffed at their inland cousins. As a result, the bond between the citizens the two cities was evidently a little elastic - on at least one occasion they went to war - but they were generally close allies.

Their alliance formed a kernel of the Lycian League, which was assembled under Pericles in the early fourth century B.C. to maintain independence from the Persian Satrap Mausolus. As a result of naval victories won largely on the strength of Patarene naval power, the Lycian League was able to set down roots. Alexander, passing through the area in the fouth century B.C., was welcomed as a fellow foe of the Persians, was ushered through the area without incident.

The League faded in the third century B.C., and accounts of Patara are few until the first century B.C., when Mithradites VI, King of Pontus, brought his long campaign against Rome to the walls of Patara. The Pontic King ordered the construction of great siege engines from the sacred trees at Letoon. His siege engines failed, and Patara withstood the siege long enough for the Pontic armies to withdraw in the face of a threat from Rome. What is more, 19 years after felling the holy trees Mithradites VI had lost his entire kingdom and taken his own life.

Just 46 years after the Pontic siege, Julius Caesar's assassins Cassius and Brutus assaulted Lycia during a Roman civil war. As before, the citizens of Patara looked on as their Xanthian allies committed mass suicide rather than surrender. And, as before, the citizens of Patara saw the night sky filled with the burning of their sister city, and, diplomatic where their allies were unyielding, surrendered to the Roman generals.

St. Paul passed this way briefly, not even stopping long enough to give a speech. Another famous Christian, Nicholas, spent his childhood in Patara before joining the clergy and moving to Myra, where he was eventually sainted. The rise of Christianity eventually spelled doom for one of Patara's greatest attractions, the oracular Temple of Apollo. Pagan oracles, such as the temple, were ultimately condemned by Theodosius the Great. Patara's fortunes faded further still when siltation finally closed the harbor, after which the city began its long, slow submersion beneath the sand.

A final event with bearing on the ancient history of the site occurred in 1842, when the battleship HMS Beacon anchored offshore for six months and waited while a huge team of British sailors cut apart the ruins of Xanthos and Patara and packed them into 78 huge crates. These they loaded aboard the Beacon and sailed back to London, where they remain on display at the British Museum.

Arrivals & Departures
By Bus

Dolmuş to Patara from Kalkan depart hourly in summer, once every two hours (or so) in winter. Dolmuş to Patara from Fethiye leave 2-3 times daily in summer; most pass by the intersection 5 kilometers from the beach en route to Kalkan and beyond; you can await a dolmuş bound for Patara at the intersection, or get a taxi ($4-$6).

By Car

Gelemiş is just three kilometers off the main coast road, 15 kilometers from Kalkan in the east and 12 from Kinik in the west. Patara is 2 kilometers beyond Gelemiş. Whether you're headed to the ruins or the beach, you're going to use the same road—and pay the same $1 entrance fee.

Where to Stay & Eat

Gelemiş, often simply referred to as Patara town, has some decent accommodation, but sees remarkably little tourist traffic. Most visitors opt to stay in Kalkan and take day trips to Patara; if you prefer to stay in a place that is quieter, closer to the beach, and offers a far slower pace, you might consider Gelemiş.

MERHABA HOTEL, *P.O. Box 23, Patara. Tel. (242) 843-5199; Fax (242) 843-5133; Email: mithat_unnu@hotmail.com; Web: www.geocities.com/krpole/patarahp.html. Rooms: 10. Credit cards not accepted. Open year-round. Double: $35-$42 (breakfast included).*

This is a lovely little hotel in a splendid setting on a west-facing ridge above the road to the Patara ruins and beach. Dr. Mithat Ünnü and his wife run the Merhaba Hotel with an antiseptic iron fist; Mithat Bey is an avowed enemy of mosquitos, and a fine hotelier. You'll find laundry service, mosquito netting, a generator, a good bar, and simple, spartan, meticulously cared-for rooms. Is there hot water? "Not just hot water," cries Mithat Bey, "boiling water!" He will regale you with the marvels of his elaborate water filtration system, given half a chance.

The doctor was forced out of İstanbul following the military coup in 1980. He has made the most of his exile, practicing medicine and opening this hotel in 1989. Rooms have balconies and desks, but you'll want to spend your time at the small lobby bar or down the road at the beach. A fixed-menu dinner is served every evening for $5-$7. To get there, follow the signed road straight through the outskirts of Patara town in the direction of the ruins—just before reaching the gates, take a signed left turning to the Merhaba Hotel.

XANTHUS HOTEL, *Patara. Tel. (242) 843-5015; Fax (242) 843-5069. Rooms: 16. Credit cards not accepted. Open year-round. Double: $32 (half-board).*

The Xanthus is a sprawling hotel on a hill just above the entrance to town. The Xanthus is ambitious, with a pool and tennis court, but neither of the two is guaranteed to be in working order. The hotel has a nice setting that has been allowed to go a little to seed in an inexplicably British way. The Xanthus is located on a ridge east of Patara town.

HOTEL SISYPHOS, *PK 57, Patara. Tel. (242) 843-5043. Rooms: 16. Credit cards not accepted. Open year-round. Double: $35.*

Just to the left as you enter the main part of Patara, the Sisyphos is a simple, decent hotel with a small pool and a pretty vine-covered terrace. The restaurant is a good choice if you're not dining at your hotel, offering chicken curry, crepes, and even banana splits.

HOTEL BEYHAN PATARA, *Patara. Tel. (242) 843-5096; Fax (242) 843-5097; Email: info@patarabeyhanhotel.com; Web: www.patarabeyhanhotel.com. Rooms: 122. Credit cards accepted. Closed November to February. Double: $60 (half-board; 20% discount in winter).*

The Beyhan Patara is the lone big hotel in Patara, with a commanding view of Patara beach from atop a hill west of town. There is consensus in town that the Beyhan ruins the skyline, but that doesn't seem as big a deal when you're on the balcony of your room looking out at a spectacular view of the sea. Rooms are air-conditioned and decorated with vividly purple décor. The hotel offers service to the beach several times per day. The view from the terrace is beautiful; a $1.50 beer in the late afternoon breeze goes down quite well. To get there, turn off the main road through the center of town and follow the road up the hill; you can't miss the hotel on the ridge above.

MEDUSA BAR & CAMPING, *Patara. Tel. (242) 843-5193. Inexpensive-Moderate.*

The Medusa has been serving up inexpensive sandwiches, wine, and beer in high style for years. Owners Pamir and Natalie Yılmaz open their doors at 10 a.m., serving omelettes and coffee, and continue until 11 p.m. The décor, with posters of jazz genealogy and Kurt Cobain, is comfortable, and you'll always find good music on tap. The Medusa attracts a strange set of expats and young collegiate types, and conversations that begin normal are likely to veer strange. The owner is a fount of knowledge about the ruins and is willing to explain what he knows. The Medusa is near the center of town, on the side road from the Patara beach road. The minibus station is across the street.

Seeing the Sights
The Patara Ruins

The first indication of the ancient city is Kısık Boğazı, the cleft in the high rock walls as you enter Patara. This pass once walled and fortified, giving way to a small valley. In Patara's heyday the bay reached deep into the valley, probably as far as the T-junction that passes for the city center. The majority of the Patara ruins skirted the eastern side of the former bay, roughly following the course of the main Patara road. The road was widened in 1995, at which time several underground chambers were discovered, which still lay open in the cutting at the side of the road. The artifacts found within are now in the possession of the Antalya Museum.

Just beyond Gelemiş, the signed main road reaches an admission gate that serves for both the ruins and the beach beyond ($3—ticket good for seven days; 8:30 a.m. to 5 p.m., 7:30 in summer).

The first indication of the former city is in evidence at **Kısık Boğazı**, the cleft in the high rock walls as you enter Patara. This was once walled and fortified, giving way to a small valley. In Patara's heyday the bay reached up deep into the valley, probably as far as the city center where the road to the western beach turns off. The majority of the Patara ruins skirted the eastern side of the bay, generally along the course of the main Patara road. The road was widened in 1995, at which time several **underground chambers** were discovered, which still lay open in the cutting at the side of the road. There is discussion of displaying the artifacts found within at a museum.

The first significant ruin is, appropriately, the **ceremonial gateway** just beyond the ticket booth. Close inspection is not possible, as the gateway is fenced off, but there are inscriptions concerning Mettius Modestus and identifying statues of his family that are no longer there. It wasn't this particular Modestus that gave us the term modest, apparently. Immediately beyond the arch is a hill of special interest to archaeologists, where new discoveries have led some to hope the Temple of Apollo may be located. The hill stands just above the former bay, whose opposite shore corresponded to the long low granary building to the west. The granary is the counterpart to the granary at Andriake, built during Hadrian's reign (117-138 A.D.).

Fields cover much of the terrain between here and the other acropolis hill at the beachside, but a collection of tombs and walls winds to the highlight of the ruins, the half-sunk Patara **theater**. Above the theater is the most likely true **acropolis**, topped by the foundation of a smallish temple of Athena. There is also a deep cylindrical hole, possibly a cistern, that has puzzled archaeologists. Scan the hills above you to the east; an old Byzantine fortress is secreted there. If you have the time and inclination, a trail originating at Patara climbs to the west in the direction of Delikkemer. This trail, part of the Lycian Way, skirts astounding sections of the ancient Patara aqueduct for several kilometers. You can reach the same area by car by taking the south turn at Yeşilköy three kilometers.

Sports & Recreation

Patara Beach

The beach at Patara is spectacular, stretching 14 kilometers from end to end. The entire length of the beach, and hundreds of meters of foreshore dunes, are covered in fine white sand.

The beach is accessed via Gelemiş/Patara town; follow the signed main road due south to an admission gate ($3—ticket good for seven days; 8:30 a.m. to 5 p.m., 7:30 in summer). From there, skirt the ruins to your right and continue two kilometers to a parking area behind the beach. There are few amenities at the site; two refreshment stands and some beach umbrella and sunbed vendors ($2 apiece for the day). The area immediately around this entrance to the beach can be crowded in the summer, but venturing west you'll find all the room in the world. The one trick is that you need to bring sandals—the sun-blasted beach will scorch your soles.

Xanthos

Xanthos ($2, 8:30 a.m. to 5:30 p.m.) was the dominant city throughout most of the Lycian League's history, a powerful inland city populated by strong-willed, determined people. Today the city's sprawling ruin is in the heights above the modern town of Kınık, on a steep bluff above a bend in the River Xanthus (Esen Çayı).

History

Xanthos' history is epic. Sarpedon, one of the heroes of the Trojan War, was a King of Lycia from Xanthos; he was the grandson of Bellerophon, slayer of the Chimaera, and the son of Zeus besides, according to Homer. "Godlike Sarpedon" was a good warrior and the leader of the Lycians who fought with Troy, eventually falling to Patroklos. The reality of this man and this war is probably less important than the great reputation of Lycia synonymous with Xanthos, so often referred to as the "rich country of Lycia" and "bountiful Lycia."

It was perhaps with this legendary wealth in mind that the Persian General Harpagus was dispatched to subdue Lycia in 545 B.C., seeking to complete Persian domination of Asia Minor. Harpagus arrived with a great Persian army after clearing the western coast of opposition.

What happened then, according to Herodotus' *History* (The University of Chicago Press, 1987) was this: *The Lycians, when Harpagus drove his army into the plain of Xanthus, came out against him and fought; they were few against many, but they performed great deeds of bravery. Still, they were defeated, and, being driven into the city, they gathered their wives, children, property and servants into the citadel and then set fire to the entire citadel, to burn it all. Having done so, and sworn mighty oaths to one another, they issued forth and died in battle, all the men of Xanthus.*

The city rose from the ashes relatively quickly, when the few families that had been outside the walls at the time of the siege returned and the Persians settled others here as well. It is surprising to note that just 60 years later the Lycians marched and sailed against Greece with the Persian King Xerxes, wearing, Herodotus notes a little jarringly, "feathered caps on their heads." Alexander the Great was greeted warmly, freeing the Lycians from the constant threat of Persian domination, and Xanthos (called Arna in the Lycians' own tongue) regained its former importance, earning the maximum number of votes in the Lycian League.

But the shadow of the ancient massacre was long. In 42 B.C. two of Julius Caesar's assassins, **Crassus and Brutus**, descended on Lycia, seeking to finance their civil war against Marc Antony. Once again the Xanthians were outnumbered and overwhelmed, and once again, rather than surrender to the invader they rounded up their citizens and massacred the entire population.

Xanthos recovered yet again, but the city's strength was largely spent. Roman rule proved to have its advantages, and this section of Lycia was at peace for centuries. Xanthus was later the site of a Byzantine cathedral.

Arrivals & Departures

Xanthos is located on a bluff above the Esen river, just alongside the old highway in Kınık. Today, the route is well-signed from the main highway (which now loops through the plains to the north). Dolmu ş serveKınık from both directions, Kalkan in the east and Fethiye in the west.

Seeing the Sights

Xanthos is bisected by a modern road curving between the theater and the ruins of the main city in the heights above. The ruin lacks the dynamic nature of the cities high in the mountains, such as Tlos, but its convenience and importance makes it a staple on most tours. Xanthos also has two classic pillar tombs, a sizable necropolis, and one stunning spot on the hill behind the theater.

Upon entering the site you pass the site of the Nereid Monument, which once stood here and does no longer, having been crated up and shipped to London 150 years ago. The **Nereid Monument** is one of English antiquity thief Charles Fellows' great prizes, now reassembled in the British Museum in London. The monument was cast down when Fellows arrived, and its reconstruction was a puzzle for over a century. The museum believes it has finally got it right, but that does the visitor to Xanthos a fat lot of good. The Nereids for whom the monument was named were twelve water nymphs, but they've since been identified as Aurae, wind nymphs. All of which is academic, since only the platform at the base remains. The monument may have been a memorial to the tragic defeat to Harpagus, a small temple, or an elaborate tomb.

The Nereid Monument was just within the ring of walls erected in the third century, walls that extended around the tops of both hills and off a considerable distance to the east. The city was refortified by the Romans and Byzantines and intermittently sacked, which resulted in much destruction and recycling of buildings; it is therefore much less comprehensible than cities that fell into disuse earlier.

Ascending the hill to the right, you arrive at the site of a great Byzantine church whose mosaic floors have recently been uncovered. Continuing around the base of the hill you pass some deep tomb openings and arrive at the picturesque **necropolis**, the site of several square cut rock tombs and a soaring pillar tomb of a kind particular to Lycia; this sight is a fixture of local hotel brochures and personal slideshows. The tombs here are some of the only structures in this section of Xanthos that pre-date the Roman period, hailing from the fourth century. The hilltop above the necropolis is the site of the acropolis in the Roman era, a much more sprawling version of the city that in earlier times had been centered on the hill above the theater. The chief feature of the hilltop today is a Byzantine basilica and the Roman walls, which continue until they are redundant in the heights above the modern road.

Descending now to the road you come to the area of Lycian Xanthus. Notable here is the **Xanthos Obelisk**, whose long inscription tells of a great Xanthian leader from the end of the fifth century. This man, the son of Harpagus, but not the aforementioned Harpagus, is credited with slaying seven men in a day and other great feats of virility and derring-do. His various exploits were commemorated in reliefs now found in the İstanbul Archaeological Museum, and included leading the Xanthians against the Athenians in one of the battles that helped Sparta to victory in the Peloponnesian War.

The **Harpy Tomb** is also here in the vicinity of the theater, opposite the open space that formed Xanthos' marketplace. The reliefs atop this tomb have been copied and returned to Xanthus (the originals are in

London), and depict small flying bird women. As with the Nereid Monument, the Harpy Tomb now seems hastily named; the Harpies may in fact be Sirens hauling spirits of the dead to Hades, one of their various duties. The tomb was built for an unknown man in the third century B.C., and was the combined work of Lycian and Greek artists.

Ascending above the theater you find a great hodgepodge of buildings from various eras. Structures dating to ancient and Hellenistic Lycia are no longer recognizable. Complete your tour at the tip of land jutting out above the river, the likely site of a former temple or defensive tower. While here consider that the account of the siege under Brutus mentions Roman soldiers trying to break through the Xanthos defenses by swimming, a method that would seem to leave them at the base of this sheer acropolis hill, stones raining down on their dripping wet heads. Anyway, the swimmers were foiled and entangled by nets dropped in the river, and the city was eventually taken by a standard storming of the walls. The remaining citizens, having retreated to this high point, engulfed their acropolis and themselves in flames, and acrid black smoke rose over the valley for the second time.

Letoon

Letoon is a bookend to the huge beach of Patara, with the Patara ruins at the eastern end. The Xanthos valley was home to many temples and oracular shrines, and of these Letoon was the greatest. This was at no time a fortified city, only a temple precinct of Xanthos; the grand, half-sunk ruins that remain occupy a limited area.

History

Letoon's history begins with a legend. **Leto** was special among Zeus' many conquests in that the King of the Gods evidently felt real affection for her, which was a threat to Hera. Hera banished the pregnant Leto, who gave birth to both Apollo and Artemis on the Greek island of Delos, then made her way to Lycia in order to wash the children in the waters of the Xanthos River. As the story goes, Leto was turned away from the river by shepherds, perhaps fearing the wrath of Hera. With the assistance of a wolf pack she made her way to the river, drinking from it and bathing her children in its good water. Not content to let the shepherds get away with their lack of chivalry, she returned, godlings tucked under one arm, and turned the foolish men into frogs.

Leto's spirit continued to inhabit the place, and frogs still do. It was Leto who changed the Lycian's name from the Termilae, out of respect for the wolves (lycos), and, more subtly, perhaps lent the Lycians their name for woman, lada (perhaps a root of "lady"). Herodotus, it should be noted, has an altogether different conception of the origin of "Lycian," claiming it comes from a certain Lycus, a son of Pandion and a citizen of Athens. Letoon has a great sanctuary to Leto, as well as somewhat lesser sanctuaries to Apollo and Artemis. The layout of the city, one temple immediately beside the other, underscores its religious focus. The Lycian League held its gatherings here, and Letoon's high priest was considered the high priest of all Lycia.

Letoon was a holy place, not a military fortification, and it was seemingly left in relative peace by invaders. One account of Mithradites VI's siege of Patara notes that the king destroyed not Letoon's buildings, but its trees in the manufacture of siege engines. Even in this he was discouraged by a dream, and abruptly stopped; the damage may have been done, as Mithradites' warfare against Rome came to naught, and he lost his home, his empire, and, in 69 B.C., his life. Roman rule was beneficial throughout Lycia, but Letoon ceased to thrive after Theodosius I's edict against pagan worship–not even a Christian basilica on the site saved the temple precinct. Letoon was finally destroyed in the seventh century during Arab incursions.

Arrivals & Departures

A new highway opens up soon after reaching Kınık, and two kilometers along is a signed turning for Letoon. This road takes you back to the old highway, 1/2 kilometer along, then on to Letoon, four kilometers south. If you're using public transportation, take a dolmuş from Kınık or Fethiye to Kumlova—Letoon is just 500 meters beyond.

Seeing the Sights

The road to the site terminates at the theatre, a grand building dating from the Hellenistic heyday of Letoon. Great arched entrances pierce the outer walls; the north entrance once displayed 16 faces in relief, including that of Dionysius. The size of this theatre was out of proportion to the modest size of Letoon; it was used to host pan-Lycian councils.

The entrance to the ruins ($1.50, 8:30 a.m.-6 p.m.) is adjacent to the theatre; you'll find a refreshment stand here in the high season. Ahead, the three temples were once the centerpiece of Letoon, and remain so now. En route, you pass the ruins of stoas dating from Roman and Hellenistic times. These covered halls were presumably the residence of temple priests, and archaeologists have made several interesting discoveries here. Among these, excavations have uncovered evidence of older temples and the votive offerings buried with them.

Continuing to the main temples, you'll find the lay side by side; the Temple of Leto, the largest of the three, is located to the west. In the center is a smaller, far older temple to Cybele/Artemis. The third temple is that of Artemis and Apollo. A sacred spring was at the heart of these precincts. That spring has flourished, if not the temples themselves; the water table is now high enough to flood the foundations of the agora. All excavation here is accompanied by constant pumping to keep the pits from flooding.

The Temple of Leto, 95 feet by 45 feet and once adorned with Ionic columns, was completed in the third century B.C. Worship had been underway here for far longer—as evidenced by the discovery of votive figurines dating to at least 600 B.C. found on the site. The Temple of Artemis—as it is now thought to be—is smaller than its fellows, and older. Archaeologists date this building to the fifth century B.C., and they puzzle over the presence of a stone outcrop within the structure—it is presumed that this was somehow central to worship here. Finally, the Temple of Artemis and Apollo is next, its ruins heaped upon an intact 85 foot by 45 foot stylobyte. The temple draws its name from a mosaic that remains in situ (covered for its own protection with sand and sheetmetal); the mosaic depicts the lyre of Apollo on one side, the bow and quiver of Artemis on the other.

Just to the south is the flooded nymphaeum, site of ongoing excavation. The elaborate semicircular building was an ornamental fountain; these are common in Hellenistic cities and temple precincts, but rarely on this grand scale. The distinctive ruins of a Byzantine church are located on the higher ground.

Pinara

Pınara is a beautiful site, and its endless wealth of cliff tombs boggles the mind. As you approach this somewhat remote site, 5 kilometers from the highway, high cliff walls honeycombed with tombs rise before you, defying all good sense. The site is rarely visited, and is the better for it. The town of **Minare** ('minaret') offers the Pınara café at the crossroads to Pınara—it is only open in summer. (What about Minare's minaret, you wonder? Standard, tipped with blue.)

History

Pınara was probably a settlement of Xanthos, and grew to be of such importance that, like Xanthos and the greatest of the cities in the Lycian League it was allowed the maximum votes in League affairs. Pınara shared the fate of its fellows in the League, falling to Harpagus, surrendering peacefully to Alexander, and enjoying a period of prosperity under Roman rule. The original city was located atop the stone, tomb-pocked acropolis—inaccessible today for anyone without days to spare. The later settlement was located on the steep, terraced slope where most ruins are now found. Earthquakes badly damaged the city in the second and third centuries, but the site remained important into the Middle Ages before fading.

Arrivals & Departures

By Bus

Pınara is not easy to reach using public transportation. Dolmuş serve Minare—2.5 kilometers below the ruins—from the town of Esen on the main highway. This service is rare—only two or three dolmuş make the trip daily. From Minare, hiking the final distance to the ruins is certainly possible, but the hike is steep and shares the dirt road with the occasional minibus. Taxis are a possibility—particularly now that the road is decent—but that will cost you $30 or more from Esen, including two hours to explore. Consider a tour trip, available from Fethiye or Kalkan, with lunch, at prices of $25 per person or so.

By Car

Four kilometers north of Esen take the Pınara/Minareköy exit. Minareköy is three kilometers along, from which there is a steep, but recently regraded, 2.5 kilometer road to the site.

Seeing the Sights

Upon arriving at Pınara you'll be greeted by a caretaker; since 1984 that caretaker was the weathered, helpful Fethi Bey, but he was set to retire at the end of 2001. With any luck, his replacement will be as quietly helpful as Fethi was. You can find your way around the site yourself, but a guide can be quite helpful.

Before setting out (particularly if you've just hiked up the road!) buy a soft drink at one of the small booths open in summer, pay the $1.50 admission, and take stock of the site. Pınara spills over the sides of a small valley high in the mountains above the Xanthian plain. The best way to see the ruins is to follow a clockwise course beginning just beyond the makeshift ticket booth—the beginning of the route is crudely signed with red arrows.

Picking your way along the path, you climb into a narrow draw lush with oak trees. Re-emerging on the far side, the trail climbs along the base of a cliff. Here you'll find a set of tombs, several of them beautifully carved. The finest of these is the Royal Tomb, marked with a sign saying "Rock Tombs/Roman Period." This tomb has more than a beautiful façade; the walls to either side of the entrance are decorated in reliefs. Upon discovering these in 1839, British archaeologist Charles Fellows recognized how unusual they were and made plaster casts of them. The in situ reliefs have deteriorated, but remain quite recognizable as a fortified city in profile, together with a family. The identity of the tomb's former occupant is unknown; the moniker "Royal Tomb" is sheer supposition.

Descending slightly, then jogging left under the ridge, you begin ascending again into the ancient city proper, past piles of worked stone and column drums. Continuing a few minutes around the hillside with the theatre off to the distance to your right, you arrive at three landmark tombs. These three are all at ground level; the center tomb, decorated with horns and uniquely arch-shaped, is the aptly named Ox Tomb. You'll find these tombs, like most others, bear ample, ancient soot from their new role as shelters for the goatherds and shepherds.

Just above these tombs, the trail opens into an open set of terraces littered with Hellenistic and Roman stone. This is an ideal site for a picnic. You have by now broken a sweat hiking to this point, so it is with some astonishment that you see in the heights above so many hundreds of tombs, cut into the stone pinnacle at great labor. The tombs were carved by workers lowered from above; they have never been catalogued. The walls would offer some wonderful challenges for historically-minded rock climbers.

At the edge of the terrace to the north, under a thick layer of pine needles, is a temple of Artemis. Its site overlooking the theatre below suggests some importance, but few clues remain. Above, level after level of stone-walled terraces ascend to the foot of the cliff above, with clusters of standing columns here, a tumbled building there. Cobbled Byzantine walls surmount massive irregular archaic walls with paper-thin seams. In the spring, when the carpet of grass is a vivid green, this is an enchanting place. Only turtles and goatherds remain resident here.

Returning to the floor of the small valley, cross the road and continue past a field being sown by hand, cleared of stone with astounding patience and ringed with brush to keep goats at bay. The theatre is in excellent shape, and on most visits you'll have it, and the view of the fallen city above, all to yourself.

Tlos

Tlos is credited with having the most commanding view of any Lycian city, a great boast and a probably a fair one. A visit here should be combined with the gorge at **Saklikent**, less than six kilometers away.

History

Tlos' history has spanned more than 3,000 years, from Hittite times to an 18th century feudal baron who resided at the site. Discoveries at Tlos date occupation here to the Hittite era, which corresponds to mentions of a Dalawa in 13th century Hittite texts (akin to the Lycian name for Tlos, Tlawa). The inhabitants of this towering city probably enjoyed great success in the toll trade, owing to their proximity to the routes into and out of the Xanthos plain.

Tlos and Pınara were sister cities, sharing the mountainous high ground. Both rose and fell with the Lycian League, bearing the brunt of land invasions that entered Lycia from the northwest. Tlos' own history mirrored that of its fellows, and it was one of the Lycian League's leading members, but there seems to be no records of the battles that surely occurred here. The one anomaly on Tlos' record is its relatively recent use by a brigand during the late Ottoman Empire. Kanlı ("Bloody") Ali Ağa retired to this castle after a brush with Ottoman law, allegedly after killing a man. Rehabilitating the castle, Kanlı Ali Ağa went on to set up a remote feudal system amid the debris of a badly overextended Ottoman Empire.

Arrivals & Departures

By Bus

Tours to Saklikent are increasingly popular, usually bundled with a side trip to Tlos. These originate as far away as Kalkan, but are most common (and inexpensive) from Fethiye (7 hour round trip, $15).

You can get a dolmuş bound for Saklikent from Fethiye in the high season (hourly, $2), and there are also high-season Saklikent-Tlos package trips (daily, $5). Both dolmuş depart from the main dolmuş station in Fethiye.

By Car

Tlos is easy to spot off to the north of the main highway, but it's a bit difficult to reach. If you take the road from Kinik straight back through the Xanthos ruins and up the Esen Cayı, the river that issues from Saklikent, you can bear left and get to Tlos and Saklikent. Far better is to return from this direction and, on the way in to Tlos and Saklikent, follow the sign from the main Fethiye intersection.

Tlos is located alongside the village of Yaka, four kilometers south of Guneşli village. The easiest way to Guneşli is via the Fethiye-Korkuteli road. Turn right off of the Fethiye-Korkuteli (350) road at the Tlos/Saklikent sign and 8 kilometers along you'll see the sign to Tlos, 4 kilometers away. You can keep an eye on Tlos itself, as well.

From this intersection, continuing a further 12 kilometers brings you to Saklikent. You'll certainly want to spend some time here. If you're continuing east, cross the bridge and go straight ahead 12 kilometers, climbing away from the river after a while and passing through two small villages. Take the first major right turn, in a pine forest, and the road will take you south and west, eventually passing through Xanthos and arriving at the main highway.

Seeing the Sights

Tlos is built around a stony outcrop, which is now topped by the ruin of the remarkably recent **fortress** of Kanlı Ali Ağa. Arriving at the village of **Yaka**, you are near the center of the smallish city, the theater off to your left, the fortress above a tangle of old walls and buildings to your right. The fortress is built on the obvious site of the former acropolis, which has a spectacular view of the valley below, reminiscent of Karpu Kale on the Black Sea. Yaka is alongside a long set of ruined foundations, probably of Tlos' marketplace. A church was built on the site, this just past the curve in the road bearing off toward the theater. The **theater** has several friezes, but is thickly overgrown and far less gratifying than the **acropolis** area with its tombs and fortress.

You've already glimpsed the best of Tlos' tombs on your way up to Yaka, and these are reached via several paths, according to your agility. The easiest approach is from below, following the stream, dry in the high season, and climbing up to have a look around. The most remarkable tomb in Tlos is far and away the **tomb of Bellerophon**, so called not because Bellerophon was interred here but, like Alexander's sarcophagus in İstanbul, the named individual is depicted on the tomb. In this case Bellerophon is in midflight, about to choke the Chimera with his leaden spear. This is to the left, but other decorative carvings are also found in the large open area at the mouth of the rooms. There are tombs to the left and right, with resting places for the deceased.

One of the reasons this site was chosen for a citadel is the abundance of fresh water, filtering down from the Akdağ Mountains and welling up here. **Yaka Park**, near Tlos, is thick with springs and even some pools. They are what the English might call "bracing." The **castle** atop the acropolis has aged poorly, considering its recent use, but it's still a fine destination. This was the site of the ancient settlement, later used for the citadel of Hellenistic Tlos. For a quick education in wall construction, have a look at the walls along the east side of the acropolis, facing the town. These have been built and rebuilt over the course of more than 2,000 years. If you're in a hurry, accept the nearly certain offer of a local kid; he'll be able to whisk you through the most interesting of the area's sights.

Saklikent

You turned off the road leading to Saklikent on the way to Tlos. Consider retracing your steps and continuing on to this beautiful gorge. In addition to the now plentiful signs there is a thick trail of köfte and gözleme restaurants along the correct route.

Saklikent is a wonderful place to spend a couple of hours. The road leads to a collection of parking lots at the mouth of the gorge, and you can dip your burned body in the chill, clear water that percolates out of the mountain and emerges here. You can grab fish, mezes, or a drink at one of the many covered wooden platforms built atop the river; the quality's the same at all of them, and they're impossible to tell apart.

For $2.50 you can head into the gorge along a boardwalk. You can peer into the gorge for nothing, and it gives you a pretty good sense of how marvelous Saklikent is; you'll need to spend the $2.50 to journey the 500 feet back into the gorge on the boardwalk. The gorge walk is worth the $2.50, and if you don't agree you can discuss our poor advice over a meal at a restaurant on a platform within the gorge.

Fethiye

Fethiye is a hub for visiting the ruins and beaches in the vicinity, but it lacks the appeal of Dalyan to the west and Patara, Kalkan, and Kaş to the east. The city is home to the ruins of ancient Telmessus, and is improved by the booming growth in Ölüdeniz, which has left Fethiye a little quieter and more relaxing. The once-great attraction of Ölüdeniz Beach remains a marvelous beach, but the town is a thickly overdeveloped mess. Hisarönü and Ovaçk squat in the heights above, growing exponentially.

History

There has been a settlement on this excellent harbor since at least 1500 B.C. The ruins undergirding Fethiye are of **Telmessus**, the Lycian League's westernmost outpost. The city's name echoes the name of the original Lycian name for Lycia, Termilae, which is odd considering that Telmessus was not considered part of Lycia proper until Pericles welcomed the city to his new Lycian League in the campaign against the Persian satrapy at Helicarnas/Bodrum. Telmessus' bay was known as the Bay of Glaukos after one of the Lycian heroes of the Trojan War.

The city shared the fate of its neighbors in Lycia, opening its gates to Alexander, chafing under Rhodian rule in the second century B.C., and suffering badly under Arab attacks in the seventh century. The Crusaders probably left a garrison at the hilltop fortress here in the 15th century, and the Crusaders certainly staked a claim to the islands dotting the Fethiye Bay, where they have left evidence of their occupation.

Fethiye's modern name derives from **Fethi Bey**, a Turkish military pilot who crashed and died here in 1913. The former name of the city was Makri.

Note: the curious broad stripes cut into the bare hillsides approaching Fethiye are firebreaks.

Arrivals & Departures

By Bus
The otogar is inconveniently distant from the town center, about two kilometers. Dolmuş run into town from the road you enter town on, Atatürk Caddesi, and major bus lines offer service buses into town. Driving times from Dalaman Airport (see Dalyan, Chapter 20) have been cut dramatically by a new highway opened in 1999.

By Car
The main road into Fethiye becomes the town's main street. After passing a left turning leading to Ovacık, Hisarönü, and Ölüdeniz, the road continues directly to the marina and tourism information office, then winds around the marina and waterfront—this is where our recommended accommodations in town are located.

Orientation
Between the town's new name and devastating earthquakes, Fethiye has few traces of its former self. The sole remnants of ancient Telmessus are at the theater, near the tourism information center at the town center, and in the scattering of tombs at the base of the steep hill directly above town. A Crusader-era castle stands on the acropolis, surely fashioned from - and covering over - ruins of Telmessus' temples or fortifications.

Fethiye's **tourism information** office is located just inland of the marina on İskele Karşısı, *Tel/Fax 252 614-1527*. The town is a regional hub, and it has everything you need; a hospital (on the main road into town, Atatürk Caddesi, *Tel. 252 614-4017*), ATM machines, banks, and post offices.

Where to Stay
Fethiye is useful as a base for embarking on a Blue Cruise, but it has little of interest for most visitors. That said, Fethiye hotels compares favorably to the uniformly poor hotels in the Ölüdeniz area, so Fethiye makes a good base for day trips to Ölüdeniz beach and Kayaköy. Several good hotels in the hills above Ölüdeniz and Fethiye are listed.

VILLA DAFFODIL, *Ikinci Karagözler, Fevzi Çakmak Cad. No. 115, Fethiye. Tel. (252) 614-9595; Fax (252) 612-2223; Email: oteldaffodil@superonline.com; Web: www.villadaffodil.com. Rooms: 27. Credit cards accepted. Open year-round. Double: $45.*
The Villa Daffodil is the best small hotel in Fethiye. Opened in 1995, the Daffodil has nice pine trim, pleasant rooms, and a nice pool and small garden featuring walnut, pear, olive, fig, and pomegranate trees. Rooms are small and clean; the suite room, 301, is spacious. When booking, request a view room—they cost $5-10 more than the opposite side. The hotel restaurant, opened in 2000, offers a good fixed-menu dinner. Villa Daffodil is located on the main shore road, one kilometer beyond the marina.

YACHT HOTEL, *Birinci Karagözler Cad., Yat Limanı Karşisı, Fethiye. Tel. (252) 614-1530; Fax (252) 612-5354; Email: none; Web: none. Credit cards accepted. Open year-round. Rooms: 45. Double: $30.*
The Yacht is a great, inexpensive option in Fethiye, located directly above the marina on the water. Rooms are simple, but quite nice; the 15 sea view rooms—with balconies—are a steal at this price. The convenience of this hotel to the city center and marina are, again, surprising given the $30 room price. At our last visit, in 2001, the carpet and paint were new, and everything was just so. The Yacht Hotel has a pool and rooms with television (no foreign channels, but we're told they're coming). The **Yeni Yacht Hotel**, just 100 yards further around the bend from the marina, is another pleasant surprise (*Tel. (252) 612-5067; Fax (252) 612-5068; Email: info@yachtplazahotel.com; Web: www.yachtplazahotel.com; Double: $35*).

IDEAL PENSION, *1 Karagözler, Zafer Cad. No. 1, Fethiye. Tel. (252) 614-1981; Fax (252) 614-1981; Email: idealpension@hotmail.com. Rooms: 18. Credit cards not accepted. Open year-round. Double: $17.*
In the heights above the sea road, Ideal Pension is one of the best budget accommodations in Fethiye. Catering to backpackers, the Ideal Pension has the full range of perks backpackers have come to expect; laundry, video room, book exchange, and Internet access. To get there, turn inland at Yıldırım Pension. The **Irem Pansiyon**, in the same neighborhood, is another clean budget option (*Tel. 252 614-3985*).

Near Ölüdeniz
OCAKKÖY, *Ovacık, Fethiye. Tel. (252) 616-6157; Fax (252) 616-6158; Email: ocakkoy@superonline.com; Web: www.ocakkoy.com. Cottages: 35. Credit cards accepted. Open April-October. Double: $50.*
Ocakköy is a set of small cottages in the countryside above Hisarönü. Each cabin is like a Turkish country house; whitewashed walls two feet thick, wooden screens, ceilings held aloft with long pine beams, kilims,

wood floors, a south-facing front porch, and a fireplace—often two. On cool evenings, you'll have firewood delivered. The setting is lovely, on a pristine hillside at the end of a half-kilometer dirt track. Just beyond are abandoned Greek buildings dating to the exchange of populations in 1923—hors d'ouevres for the Kayaköy settlement seven kilometers to the southwest. There is a pool and a restaurant on the premises—your room has a kitchenette if you prefer to cook for yourself. This is a place where people spend weeks on end; you'll wish you had more time yourself.

To get there: if you have your own transportation, look for a signed right turning just before entering Hisarönü. If not, call Ocakköy for a transfer.

Selected one of our favorite small hotels.

MONTANA PINE HOTEL, *Ovacık Köyü, Fethiye. Tel. (252) 616-6252; Fax (252) 616-6451. Rooms: 154. Credit cards accepted. Open April-October. Double: $85.*

Set in the pine trees 1,200 feet above Ölüdeniz beach, the Montana Pine Hotel is built in the image of a mountain village. Rooms are scattered among various pine-trim cottage buildings, the overall plan owing to an architect whose traditional plans have earned him an architectual award from the Aga Khan. The craftsmanship is not quite on par with the plan, and rooms are a bit stolid, but the Montana Pine is deservedly popular with tour groups.

The hotel has an unusual and wonderfully conceived set of public areas, long patios and arched interior spaces with traditionally decorated couches and tables, ideal for unwinding after a long day. The hotel is perched above forest, through which you can just glimpse the sea. Half-board accommodations are recommended here; dolmuş travel to Ölüdeniz and back on the road one kilometer below the hotel.

OTEL MERI, *Ölüdeniz, Fethiye. Tel. (252) 616-6060; Fax (252) 616-6456. Rooms: 83. Credit cards accepted. Open March-October. Double: $115 (half-board).*

Otel Meri is an overpriced fixture on the inner bay at Ölüdeniz; we recommend it only because we feel we must recommend something in Ölüdeniz, and it is the best option. The dramatic growth of the area has now engulfed the hotel—located out at the end of the road to the inner bay—but it remains protected by the mountains behind and the end of the beach beyond. You may access the new units in the heights above the old hotel via a small escalator car. For budget accommodation in Ölüdeniz, try the **Oba Hotel** *(Tel. (252) 617-0470; Fax (252) 617-0470; Email: obamotel@superonline.com; Double: $28)* 200 meters inland of the waterfront in the center of town.

Kayaköy
LES JARDINS DE LEVISSI, *PK 195 Kayaköy, Fethiye. Tel. (252) 618-0188; Fax (252) 618-0240. Rooms: 4. Credit cards not accepted. Open May-November. Double: $50 (breakfast included).*

Set behind a heavy iron gate at the foot of the Kayaköy ruins are the four rooms of Les Jardins de Levissi. The stone houses adhere to the vernacular of the ghost town above, and share their peace. Owners Figen and Michel Tesson, former owners of a creperie, cook meals for customers most evenings; if you prefer, you can use the kitchenette in your room. The rooms are spacious, with high ceilings and skylights. A budget alternative 300 yards closer to the entrance to Kayaköy is the clean, eight-room **Selcuk Pansiyon** *(Tel. (252) 618-0148; Double: $14).*

Where to Eat
Fethiye has a few dining options that have stood the test of time; not so Hisarönü and Ölüdeniz. Most of the restaurants we recommend have their own restaurants or kitchenettes—that's fortunate.

Fethiye
MEĞRİ RESTAURANT, *Eski Cami Geçidi, Likya Sok. No. 8, Fethiye. Tel. (252) 610-4046. Moderate.*

Meğri has for ten years been the favored restaurant in Fethiye; consequently it has grown to encompass a virtual complex around a small square in central Fethiye. Fortunately, prices remain quite reasonable; mezes are $1 apiece, entrees are $3-5 (a bit more for fish), and bills add up correctly. Be aware that they have some touts who are an annoyance if you're not going there; but you are going there. 2001 saw the opening of a new Meğri Ice Cream stand on the corner, as well.

The Meğri is located just inland of the Yapı Kredi bank on the main waterfront road.

Ovacık & Ölüdeniz
We've combed through Hisarönü and Ovacık in search of some redeeming spots amid the places catering to U.K. package visitors. There aren't many, and those there are have a half-life of months.

ŞAHİN TEPESİ, *Ölüdeniz Yolu, Hisarönü, Fethiye. Tel. (252) 616-7074.*
This is a diamond in the rough. The Şahin Tepesi is a large, open restaurant in the heights above Ölüdeniz on the main Fethiye-Ölüdeniz road. The walls of this large, open wood space are all windows, and they are flung open in summer. It is as close to a local secret as we have been able to find, with big, flaky pide reminiscent of Nan (called lavaş), and well made mezes and grills.

Şahin Tepesi (Falcon Hill) is located on the Fethiye-Ölüdeniz road, just as you descend from Hisarönü before the turnoff to the Montana Pine hotel. The staff is accommodating, but they struggle with English.
BEYAZ YUNUS, *Ölüdeniz, Fethiye. Tel. (252) 616-6799. Moderate-Expensive.*

In a town where restaurants disappear very, very quickly, the Beyaz Yunus on the eastern end of town has been in place for years. Beyaz Yunus (White Dolphin) has earned its reputation for good seafood—and for slightly expensive prices. As an inexpensive alternative, dine at the Oba restaurant (see hotel listings, above).

Seeing the Sights

The castle and acropolis above Fethiye is reached after a hike up the road behind the theater or up Kale Caddesi from the east, and is signed in both directions. The **Knights of St. John** probably built the fortress in the 15th century, fortifying the mainland ports opposite Rhodes as protection against attack from Asia Minor and to better command shipping. The castle is bare, but it is worth a visit simply for the view.

The **rock tombs** at Fethiye constitute the city's most interesting ruins. The cluster of tombs in the eastern part of the city, above the dolmuş station in the direction of the city center, has Telmessus' finest remaining relic, the **Tomb of Amyntas**. The tomb has been dated to the middle of the fifth century, but about Amyntas not much is known. The necropolis is meager compared with areas such as Pınara, but the set of tombs here is lovely at sundown.

The **museum** has one very important piece, the **Letoon Trilingual** that helped scholars untangle the Lycian language, but the museum is not particularly instructive.

Tuesday is Fethiye's **market day**, an excellent opportunity to browse, watch people, and perhaps even pick up some irresistible vegetables or souvenir.

Sports & Recreation

Beaches

Ölüdeniz beach is one of the most beautiful and overcrowded stretches of sand in the world. Dolmuş travel back and forth between Fethiye and Ölüdeniz half-hourly in the summer. The beach is served by a great variety of restaurants and cafes, and shops sell everything from sunglasses and Ölüdeniz T-shirts to paragliding from Babadağ mountain high above. There's a $1 entry fee.

Ölüdeniz is also the jumping-off point for boat rides to Butterfly Valley, a favorite spot among backpackers.

From Fethiye you can secure cruises to **Haghia Nikola Island**, a small, pretty spot with Byzantine ruins and a good beach. From Fethiye you can visit **Çaliş Beach**, on weekdays less crowded (but less pretty) than Ölüdeniz beach.

Rafting/Canyoning

Several companies arrange trips on the **Dalaman River** west of Fethiye, and canyoning trips are also available into **Saklikent**. Never been canyoning? Hell, no one else has either. **Alternatif Turizm**, based in Marmaris but with a base camp on the Dalaman River, is recommended. Contact them at: Şirinyer Mah. Çamlık Sok. No. 10, Marmaris, *Tel. 252 413-5994, Fax 252 413-3208.* Their Ölüdeniz agent is **Aventura Turizm**, Belcekız Tatil Köyü, Ölüdeniz, *Tel. 252 616-6427.*

Excursions & Day Trips

By all means spend a day on a **12 Island Cruise** around Fethiye Bay. Prices vary with the season and the number of people along for the trip - the cost rises if you insist on a semi-private cruise. As a baseline, the standard trip lasts for 8 hours and costs $12 with lunch.

Cruises depart from the Fethiye Harbor every morning, spending the day visiting various islands and selling you drinks. As mentioned, lunch is included, as are opportunities to swim from the boat or, if it is the will of the boat, from beaches on various islands. Your hotel can set you up with a specific company, which is ordinarily easier than hunting down a boat on your own.

The other popular boat trip from Fethiye (and from Ölüdeniz) is to **Butterfly Valley**. This cruise heads east to Butterfly Valley, a backpacker idyll, stopping at good swimming holes en route. Although it can be a day trip ($12 return), many budget travelers will disembark and stay in the valley. There are some treehouses here, similar to those in Olympos. Why treehouses? They permit the pension owner not to build on the land, thus, technically, not to violate the National Park laws. Of particular repute is the **George House** in Feralya village (a mildly harrowing hike above the beach, *Tel. 252 642-1102*). You'd need a sleeping bag to stay here, but the cost of your entire day, food and accommodation, would be about $10 per person.

KAYAKÖY

This once-bustling town in the mountains above Fethiye was emptied in the trade of Greek and Turkish populations in 1923. The Turks relegated to this area proved unwilling and unable to assume the role of their Greek predecessors, and the city was eventually abandoned. The ghost town is animated today by a few inhabitants on the main road, but the overall effect is a powerfully sad testament to a powerfully sad event. Several small shops are located here to outfit you with a picnic, two good hotels are also available (see accommodations). Admission is $1.50.

The stone city sprawls up and over the ridge behind, and included in the wreck are small chapels and two large churches, the interiors of which remain decorated with paintings. You can hike through the narrow pedestrian lanes and ascend to the ridgeline, where you'll wind through a strange set of gulches en route to the small chapels atop the hill. The wind usually whips over this hill from the seaside (that's Ölüdeniz far below), and it's certainly worth the hike to the top.

The route to Kayaköy is signed. Tours visit the town, but guides have little to say that the town doesn't say itself. In high season you can get a dolmuş from Fethiye to Kayaköy several times daily.

CADYANDA

This ancient ruin is located in a thick pine forest in the hills above Fethiye to the northeast. Signs direct you from the main Muğla/Marmaris road, and **Cadyanda** is near Üzümlu, a total of thirty kilometers from Fethiye. Archaeologists from the Fethiye Museum are at work here, giving some order to what has always been a confusing muddle of old stone foundations. The highlights of a visit to Cadyanda, aside from the view, are the sarcophagi cut from within boulders.

Gocek

The town of Göcek is home to a marina all out of proportion to Göcek's small size. The town caters to people on Blue Cruise and private yacht trips; as a result there are several fine hotels, restaurants, and cafes. Göcek offers easy access to the islands of Fethiye Bay, but is not historically significant. Göcek Yachting Service, headquartered here, is recommended in our Blue Cruise section.

Arrivals & Departures

Göcek is entirely oriented toward its marina. The main road into town runs parallel to the waterfront behind a row of buildings. Most shops and restaurants are near the center of town. Olympos Internet Café is located on the main road, several doors west of Deniz Hotel.

Where to Stay & Eat

YONCA RESORT, *Cumhüriet Mah., Göcek, Fethiye. Tel. (252) 645-2255; Fax (252) 645-2275; Email: yoncaresort@superonline.come. Rooms: 8. Credit cards accepted. Open April-October. Double: $50 (breakfast included).*

This pretty little hotel is located 200 meters inland of the marina, and is frequented by people who want to spend a few nights on dry land. The Yonca offers fine attention to detail; lovely period furniture, a pleasant sitting room, thick curtains, and rooms with balconies and shower. The Yonca has a private boat that is ideal for a day trip; the owner rents it out to as many as six people for $90. There is a small pool. The Yonca is located behind the Nirvana Hotel.

A&B HOTEL, *Turgut Özal Cad., Göcek, Fethiye. Tel. (252) 645-1820; Fax (252) 645-1843; Email: birkanc@superonline.come. Rooms: 11. Credit cards accepted. Open year-round. Double: $45 (breakfast included).*

Like the Yonca, the A&B caters to the yachting clientele, as well as to discerning Turks from Istanbul and elsewhere. The appearance of the A&B is nondescript, but the clean, carefully-maintained rooms and pleasant public areas belie the exterior. The hotel is located on your left hand as you enter town. If full, consider the Deniz Hotel (Tel. (252) 645-1902) at the upper end, or Dim Pansiyon (Tel. (252) 645-1294) at the budget end.

DR. JAZZ, *Iskele, Göcek. Tel. (252) 645-1729; Fax (252) 614-1732. Moderate.*

Dr. Jazz, next to Göcek Yachting Service, is resplendent in photos of Miles Davis and Chet Baker and has a fine jazz collection to go with them. This is a great little place to while away an afternoon; a great bar, chessboard, food, and company.

AYRAN CAFÉ & RESTAURANT, *Iskele Mah. Çarşı Içi, Göcek. Tel. (252) 645-1178. Inexpensive.*

The Ayran is a local favorite for pide; this is a great place for an inexpensive meal. Pelin Restaurant, 50 meters up the street toward the highway, is also recommended.

Chapter 20

This section of coast was once home to the cities of **Caria**. Today, it is far more heavily developed than the Lycian Coast to the east, but there are still plenty of secluded spots, fine hotels, and impressive ruins. **Marmaris** and **Bodrum**, which have two of Turkey's largest marinas, are located here, busy throughout summer with yachts and Turkey's traditional double-masted wooden gulets. **Caunos** and **Cnidos** are two of the best preserved and interesting ancient cities in Turkey, and there are dozens of other, less impressive ruins along the lush coast.

The dividing line between the Mediterranean and the Aegean is off the tip of the Cnidos Peninsula. This region is staked out by the Dalaman Airport in the south and the Bodrum Airport at Güllük in the north.

Dalyan (Caunos)

Dalyan has a charm all its own. The small town hugs the eastern side of the **Koyçeğiz delta**, a pleasant and abundantly fertile place that pulses with birds, turtles, and fish, with the bray of frogs and, unfortunately, the whine of mosquitoes. Shallow draught boats ply the channels back and forth between the four-mile long sand beach and the town three miles inland, passing the outstanding ruins of Caunos on the way. The boats continue puttering upstream to mud baths, sulfur springs, and, finally, **Koyçeğiz Lake**. The entire course of the river is unbridged, choking off develop-

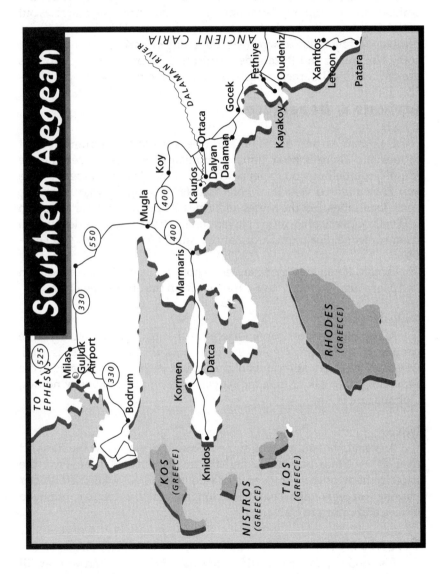

ment of the western shore and ensuring that boat travel remains the main means of transportation.

Dalyan boasts one of the most remarkable ancient cities in the Mediterranean in **Caunos**, a short distance downstream. The endless city walls enclose two spurs of a mountain and a towering crag that rises out of the river and commands the entrance to the delta. This sheer spire was once topped by Caunos' acropolis, but today offers only the remains of some Hellenistic and Byzantine fortifications. Upriver of the acropolis are 4th century B.C. rock cut tombs overlooking the town.

Arrivals & Departures
By Air
Dalaman Airport opens up Turkey's western Mediterranean coast to tourism. There is no dolmuş or municipal bus system serving the airport, compelling you to get a taxi ($4) to the Dalaman otogar unless you have a rented vehicle or hotel transfer waiting. Havaşbuses serve some local cities, but the routes and times change, so look for the green and yellow livery of a waiting Havaş bus and try to wrest the destination from someone. For more information, call **Turkish Air**, *Tel. (252) 692-5499.*

Finally, if you are staying at a good hotel in the strip between Kalkan and Marmaris you may have a transfer from the airport awaiting.

By Bus
Major bus services serve Ortaca on the main road, and if you're coming from Dalaman you'll need to pass through Ortaca as well. Ortaca's main bus station and dolmuş/minibus station are located in the same otogar, so ask or look for Dalyan signs in the minibus windows. Dolmuş fare is 75¢.

By Car
As usual, the route is well signed. From the east follow the signs off the E400 at Ortaca, passing through the small town of Okcular. From the E400 in the west there is a shortcut via a road about 4 kilometers after passing Köyçeğiz Lake—but it is no longer signed. Better to continue to Ortaca and return to Dalyan.

Orientation
It's good to plan on spending a few days in Dalyan, and you can fill a week with day excursions and side trips. The Dalyan Tourism information office is located by the river, near the river taxi cooperative and mosque *(Tel. 252 262-4703)*. Foreign newspapers and magazines can be

found at Nokta Market, in the streets inland of the main road behind Ali's Restaurant.

To do anything in Dalyan, you need some mastery of the initially puzzling river taxi system. A fleet of shallow draft boats are moored along Dalyan's waterfront, and they are grouped according to their purpose. Beginning upstream, the boats that tie up in front of Melody Restaurant are owned primarily by hotels and restaurants. A bit downstream is a pier for private boats, followed by a collection of boats making the trip to the beach and back (departing between 10 a.m. and 3 p.m. and returning from 1 p.m. to 7 p.m.; $3 round trip).

Downstream still further, in front of the tourism office, are the boats belonging to the cooperative. Touts are eager to sing the praises of their five hour, $6 trips that include a token look at Caunos, a stop at the mud baths and the hot springs, and a final stop at the beach. In truth, these trips are a good time and we recommend joining in on your first full day in town to better understand how Dalyan is pieced together.

River taxis, freelance boats willing to take you anywhere along the river, are parked a little further downstream (If you pay more than $2 per person for a trip to Caunos and back you're not haggling very well).

At the bottom of the boating food chain are the rowboats, located furthest downstream at the end of a gravel path. These small boats leave from behind the health clinic and Caria Hotel, crossing to the small town of Çandir on the opposite shore. Once across you can find your own way to the tombs, upstream, or the ruins, downstream. You can rent rowboats for less than $15 per day, finding your own little pool amid the reeds and swimming, or exploring the coastline.

Dalyan is an excellent place to relax and fall off the ruin-a-day pace; confine yourself to exploring a town with ruins and rock cut tombs, interesting cafes, shops, and a great beach.

Where to Stay

Dalyan's popularity has grown through the years, but the terrain - and some careful restrictions on development - has dictated that growth be limited. At a distance of three miles from the beach, Dalyan is prohibitively far for genuine "beach resort" status. That is the town's saving grace, since it is otherwise an idyllic vacation spot—and, anyway, shallow-draft boats travel to beautiful Iztuzu Beach throughout the day. Most hotels in the area are closed during winter.

Because the town is built up against the Dalyan River it is easy to figure out once you get oriented. Most hotels have done a careful job of posting signs along the main road into town.

HAPPY CARETTA, *Maraş Mah., Dalyan. Tel. (252) 284-2109; Fax (252) 284-3295. Rooms: 18. Credit cards not accepted. Open year-round. Double: $30 (breakfast included).*

Clean and simple, this hotel has a pretty waterfront location made all the better by a painstakingly tended lawn and garden. Like most of the hotels in the south end of Dalyan, the Happy Caretta has a grill in the back on the river, perfect for cooking your own meal in the evening. You're welcome to sip drinks amid the roses and bougainvillea, watch the boats putter past, or swim from the dock. Owners Ilknur and Münir Idrisoğlu are helpful, and can call upriver to the boat cooperative to have you picked up on the way to Iztuzu Beach. This is a good place to choose in winter, with in-floor heating and a cozy upstairs lounge.

The Happy Caretta is located 800 meters south of the center of Dalyan; follow the main road south and look for a right turn signed for the Happy Caretta.

Selected one of our favorite budget hotels.

LINDOS PANSİ YON, *Maraş Mah. No. 24, Dalyan. Tel. (252) 284-2005; Fax (252) 284-4460. Rooms: 9. Credit cards not accepted. Open year-round. Double: $22.*

Just down the street from the Happy Caretta is a hotel that maintains a similar standard. Rooms are small, clean, and simple, and have no air conditioning, but do have screens on the windows. You can swim in the river from the dock. Every afternoon at 5:00 p.m. they serve beşte çay — five o'clock tea — for their guests.

HOTEL DALYAN, *Maraş Mah., Yah Sok., Dalyan. Tel. (252) 284-2239; Fax (252) 284-2240; Email: info@dalyanhotel.com; Web: www.dalyanhotel.com. Rooms: 20. Credit cards accepted. Closed November-April. Double: $65 (including breakfast).*

The Hotel Dalyan (not the Dalyan Motel) is located on a spur of land jutting out into the river. Rooms are linked by a series of pleasing arched arcades, and each has a patio that looks out onto the pool and the tombs beyond. Original pastels hang on the walls, and rooms are equipped with air conditioning. Books and magazines left by previous guests are available in the lobby for swapping. The Hotel Dalyan has a barbeque for guests on Saturday evenings; open buffet dinner costs $11 per night every evening.

The Hotel Dalyan is located south of the town center; the route is well signed, just beyond Dipdağ Otel.

OTTOMAN RETREAT APARTS *(Osmanlı Hanı Apartları), Gülpı nar Mah., Dalyan. Tel. (252) 284-4498; Fax (252) 284-4751; Email: info@ottomanretreat.com; Web: www.ottomanretreat.com. Rooms: 14. Credit cards accepted. Open April-October.*

Dalyan has several hotels with en suite kitchens ("aparts"), and this is the best of the lot. Several stone-clad buildings with overhanging eaves—modern recreations of traditional Ottoman buildings--surround a large pool. The grounds are screened behind palms. The design of the rooms, the setting, the arrangement of the cottages, all of it is well done. This hotel caters to travelers visiting for a week or so. The rooms are sharp, the view of the cliff tombs outstanding, and the lawn and pool that is the centerpiece of the Ottoman Retreat is brightly lit through the day. Group tours book here for days at a time, and you can probably get in on some of their activies in the area. The Ottoman Retreat is located north of town alongside the new **Alla Turca**—also recommended *(Tel. (252) 284-4616; Fax (252) 284-4387; Email: info@cluballaturca.com; Web: www.cluballaturca.com.* Double: $70.)

DERVIŞ HAN, *Gulpınar Cad., Dalyan. Tel. (252) 284-2479; Fax (252) 284-3539. Rooms: 9. Credit cards not accepted. Closed November-March. Double: $35 (breakfast included).*

The Derviş is off the beaten track on the north end of town in the neighborhood of the Denizatı, the Sultan Palas, and Dalyan's new soccer field. If you take the trouble to find it and sort out language difficulties with owner Hüseyin Kural (Turkish and German) you'll find a stunning garden looking up at the sheer slopes beneath Caunos. Rooms are tidy and practical, but the garden is wonderful and backs up to the river – you can swim or pick up a ferry here.

On the west side of Dalyan River

SULTAN PALAS HOTEL, *Dalyan. Tel. (252) 284-2103; Fax (252) 284-2106; Email: sultanpalasotel@superonline.com. Rooms: 26. Credit cards accepted. Closed October 30 to April 1. Double: $70 (half board).*

The Sultan Palas is tucked away on the "other side" of the Dalyan River, alone in a small valley at the base of the sprawling Caunos ruins. The hotel's centerpiece is the stone tower that serves as a late evening bar, although some might claim that the generously sized pool is the crucial bit. Rooms are practical and have their own balconies, but the real fun is in lounging at the poolside or joining in on one of the many day trips. The Sultan Palas caters to vacationers who are in the area for several days or a week, and is typically booked through an agency in the U.K. The hotel has its own boat service between the hotel dock and town.

If you're coming on your own in a car, head directly to Denizkızı Restaurant and park at the end of the dirt road by the river (see Where to Eat section below). You can have the staff at the Denizkızı call a ferry taxi from just across the river. If you're coming in by public transportation, the scheduled Sultan Palas servis boat leaves the Dalyan docks Monday-Saturday at 10:30am, 12:30pm, 2:30, 4:30, and 6:00pm.

Köyceğiz
TANGO PENSION, *Ali Ihsan Kalmaz Caddesi, Köyceğiz. Tel. (252) 262-2501; Fax (252) 262-2501; Email: tangopension@superonline.com; Web: www.tangopension.com. Rooms: 15. Credit cards not accepted. Open year-round. Double: $17.*

Thousands of backpackers can certainly be wrong, but they aren't about this place. Tango is located in Köyceğiz, directly on the main road between Marmaris and Fethiye. This town is on a lake that drains past Dalyan to Iztuzu Beach, so it is linked by boat to everything that Dalyan is, and it's quieter than Dalyan. This a great place from which to arrange boat and hiking tours. The hotel itself looks out over the lake and is usually packed with budget travelers.

IBEROTEL SARIGERME PARK, *Ortaca Postanesi PK 1, Ortaca. Tel. (252) 286-8031; Fax (252) 286-8043; Email: sarigerme@superonline.com; Web: www.iberotel.com.tr. Rooms: 372. Double: $160, Half board.*

One of the best holiday villages in Turkey is located a short drive - or a one hour pair of dolmuş - east of Dalyan. In a land filled with hotels that are less than the sum of their parts, the Sarigerme Park is a bewitching exception. The Sarigerme Park is precisely what most of the large beachfront hotels intend to be, a full-service retreat with horse riding, volleyball, and a whole range of beachside diversions. Nightfall even brings the noisy "animations," Turkey's ubiquitous and typically unsuccessful humor and dance numbers, and here they work. Here everything works.

You get a pot of coffee in the morning, not a tiny cup; you get good potatoes and eggs if the standard bread, jam, cheese and tomato diet is wearing thin. Most rooms have a balcony bedecked with flowers, and air-conditioning and CNN/NBC is standard. The hotel has a swimming pool, of course.

The Iberotel benefits from the great size of its property - it is on more than 14,000 square meters - and from the happy coincidence that the property is on the grounds of ancient Pisilus. The bulk of the ruins are off the path to the beach to the right. Here you can clamber up a hill and poke around the acropolis, trampling through the thick undergrowth to investigate tumbled Roman structures and the large ring of 6-foot wide city walls. The necropolis is built on the buttress just above the beach, with other ruins scattered around the hotel grounds. Amateur archaeologist Heinz-Otto Lamprecht has identified many of the Pisilus ruins, and the hotel staff leads occasional tours of what amounts to its own ruins.

Where to Eat

Fish thrive in reedy Köyceğiz lake, and fish restaurants thrive by its shores. Your hotel is likely to have a meal plan of its own—you can't go wrong with grilled fish at your hotel.

RIVERSIDE RESTAURANT, *Maraş Mah. No. 90, Dalyan. Tel. (252) 284-5269. Moderate.*

People in the area are fond of this restaurant on account of its setting on the river and its excellent food. The cost is on par with restaurants in the town center, and the food is superior. The Riverside has a covered patio on the river, the perfect place from which to dine on eclectic dishes such as a delicious chicken stir fry with onion, peppers, and mushrooms ($3). The nearby Beyaz Gül is also a reasonable option.

DENIZATI, *Çarşı İçI Kordon Boyu, Dalyan. Tel. (252) 284-2129. Moderate.*

The Denizatı ("sea horse") is located next to the boat cooperative in the center of town. Of the town center hotels, this and the nearby **Golden Crab** *(Tel. 252 284-4941)* are the best. Cold mezes cost $1, hot mezes $1.75, and specialized entrees such as Bombay chicken and Chicken Curry cost $4. The stock in trade of the restaurants located along the waterfront is seafood; seasonal fish dishes cost $6-$7.

DENIZKIZI, *Çamur Banyosu Karşısı, Dalyan, Muğla. Tel. (252) 284-2129; Fax (252) 284-2635. Moderate-Expensive.*

The Denizkızı (formerly the Denizati) is a Dalyan institution, offering a menu with a full assortment of fresh seafood. The restaurant is a mile north of Dalyan on the east bank of the Dalyan River, across from the Sultan Palas dock - a $4 cab fare. Better still, take a ferry from town—inquire at the landing. The slight inconvenience of getting here from Dalyan is worthwhile; the mezes (appetizers), in particular, are expertly prepared. Prices are comparable to those in town (meze are $1.30, beer $1.00, entrees $4-8). Celebrity footnote: Mick Jagger ate here in July, 1998.

THE MEDITERANEAN FRUIT BAR, *Dalyan. Inexpensive.*

Near the center of town, the employees here squeeze a wondrous assortment of fruit into icy cold shakes and smoothies. Just the thing after, well, anything at all.

Seeing the Sights

The ruins of **Caunos,** just across the river from Dalyan, are sprawling and, like the greater Dalyan area, can be explored for days.

You get to Caunos via Dalyan, unless you arrive from the sea. Tours to Caunos put in at the harbor on the seaside, two kilometers downstream of Dalyan. If you catch a boat to Caunos independently you will be dropped off at the end of a long dirt track at the base of the Acropolis hill. Forge your way inland along the road and around the peak and after ten minutes you arrive at one of the ticket booths. The main entrance to Caunos is at the end of a long boardwalk downstream of the acropolis.

History

It is unclear who initially settled the site of Caunos, and historians agree it was probably not the Greeks. It may have been a native settlement or a colony of Rhodes, but whoever settled the area left it with odd customs and language. The early tongue of Caunos, like Carian, remains uncracked by scholars. Herodotus commented on the oddity of the Caunians: *"In their customs they are different from the Carians, and, indeed, from the rest of mankind. The finest thing for them is to keep company together, men, women, and children, in groups according to age and friendship - for drinking."* Evidently they were like the British.

As often happens in history, the first news about Caunos is bad. Like the Lycian cities to the east it resisted the Persian general Harpagus and was badly defeated, although apparently not with the drama of Xanthos' self-immolation. Harpagus was seeking to tame the whole of Asia Minor, and probably valued the harbor at Caunos. The harbor, which extended to the foot of the city, has long since silted up. The harbor was the key to the prosperity of Caunos for almost 1,000 years.

The advantages of the well-protected and easily defensible harbor were somewhat offset by the problems of living on the delta. Mosquitoes in the area were probably malarial in ancient times, and anopheles took its toll on the local inhabitants. Neighboring cities enjoyed making jokes at the expense of the Caunians: One unkind wit said that the greenish pallor of the Caunians gave meaning to Homer's phrase "the generations of men are like the leaves of trees." At the time the blame for the citizens' ill health fell on fruit.

Given the popular opinion of the city, no one was especially interested in moving here. The Persian satrap Mausolus (377-353 BC) had his own ideas, however, and extended and reinforced the city walls until they formed an immense ring around the city. This work went on during his campaign against Lycia, when Caunos was very near the front lines.

Despite Mausolus' optimistic building program, Caunos' appeal does not appear to have grown much, and it certainly never occupied the grand space within its walls. The cycle of deterioration was relentless: the Dalyan River silted up the harbor and the rest of the delta, mosquitoes increased, trade fell off, and, in time, the city died behind its magnificent walls.

Visiting Caunos

First, you need to get across the river. Rowboat ferries are recommended, although the considerably more expensive river taxi service bring you around to the main entrance on Sülüklü. Either way, you'll be asked to pay $1.50 at a booth.

Most of the space within Caunos' impressive circuit of walls is empty. The bulk of ruins are located at the inland foot of the acropolis, near the theatre. The summit of the acropolis itself is mostly bare, excepting a few defensive walls, but its dominant position above the **Dalyan River** makes it an enjoyable twenty-minute climb. To reach the acropolis, follow the paths from behind the theater. The theater is substantial, looking out in the direction of **Sülüklü Lake**, the site of the former harbor.

Inland of the theater are market areas and a small church. Slightly downhill are several inscribed stones and the foundations of a temple to an unknown deity. A collection of buildings descends toward Sülüklü Lake, where old harbor buildings border the water. The lake's unappealing name, literally "Leech Lake," surely refers to the leeches once found here. English traders once imported medicinal leeches from east of this area. Don't let the name put you off swimming in the Dalyan River – there are no leeches lurking in the deep green water, and swimming the river is a joy.

Caunos' **baths**, auxiliary to those at Sultaniye on Koyçeğiz Lake, were built in the higher ground above the church and behind the ticket booth. Another temple is located above the baths complex.

By the downstream boardwalk entrance there is a small restaurant and some tombs on the southern hill.

The lower end of the city's great ring of walls begins on the ridge to the west - seaside - of the city, on the opposite side of the lake from the theater. The walls continue in a great circuit along the steep ridge high above town and end on a cliff top above a bend in the river. The ashlar walls were an awesome engineering project using an immense wealth of great stone blocks, but the millennia of disuse have carpeted them with pine needles and soil. (Ashlar walls are walls built with precisely cut rectangular blocks of stone, unlike the cobbled together Roman walls that followed them or the giant oddly shaped Cyclopean walls that predated them.)

If you spend the morning ascending along uncertain trails to the top of the walls, you may want to return to town via the dirt road on the far side of the ridge. This road terminates at the Dalyan River at a small dock just across from the Denizati Restaurant, two hundred feet upstream of the mud baths. There's always boat traffic from the mud baths.

Dalyan's most distinctive features are the Caunian **rock-cut tombs** carved out of the cliffs on the western bank of the river. These tombs date from Mausolus' time, the mid-fourth century B.C. A few tombs hug the bottom of the cliff, and you can spend an intrepid few hours nosing around them, but the reward is inevitably your own sense of adventure; the interior of the tombs are uniformly square and uniformly bare, except for goats or garbage. Somehow the most interesting of the tombs to marvel at is the unfinished tomb, which is easy to spot amid a cluster somewhat downstream. The tomb began in an ambitious fashion, but work was inexplicably cut short after workers had completed the upper half of the tomb. The 2,300 year-old work-in-progress offers a glimpse of how these tombs were created.

Sports & Recreation
Mud Baths
Dalyan's mud baths are less than one kilometer upstream on the far bank of the river. The best mud is toward the back of the mud hole, and you should dig deep for the freshest and healthiest mud. So we are told. For the full beauty and health benefits, cover yourself well, with particular care for areas troubled by mosquito bites, and wait in the sun for the mud to dry before washing yourself off in the river. Keep your eye peeled for the large Nile turtles who bask in the sun just downstream of the mud baths.

Hot Springs
Sultaniye has best sulfur springs, but plan on a dip and an extended mud bath afterward. The sulfur at these springs is potent stuff, liable to cling to you for an evening. The springs are located on **Koyçeğiz Lake** to the west of the entrance to Dalyan River. The springs were turned into a spa by the citizens of Caunos, and the Byzantines established their own hot springs here. The ruins of the old bath buildings have been partially swamped by a water table that has risen as the delta silted up. You can conceivably spend your day shuttling back and forth between the mud hole and the sulfur springs, with dips in the river in between.

Beaches
Dalyan's **Iztuzu Beach** is more than four kilometers long, a clean, sandy spit of beach extending almost across the mouth of the delta. The northern tip of beach has small refreshment stands, but the beach is otherwise bare, and the central reaches are usually empty. Most people wind through the reeds to this beach on boats from Dalyan, which shuttle back and forth between 10 a.m. and 3 p.m., every half-hour, returning between 1 p.m. and 7 p.m. for $2.50. (If you insist, you can also reach the beach by road, heading for Gökbel at the southern edge. Dolmuş serve Gökbel periodically throughout the day, departing from Dalyan's otogar, but the river ferries are far the better option.)
The beach is excellent all through the day, although the sand cooks in late afternoon. There is no cover here, other than in the specific areas where umbrellas are permitted. In general, beach umbrellas are strongly discouraged owing to the **turtle** eggs beneath the sand. The eggs belong

to Caretta Caretta, an increasingly rare turtle native to this long spit of beach.

The turtles bury their eggs by night and the eggs incubate beneath the sand, which remains at a cozy temperature, neither too hot nor too cold. In September the young turtles hatch and scurry for the sea, a race against birds and other predatory wildlife that is wise to the rhythms of turtle hatching. The beach is closed at night to protect the turtles and allow them to breed unimpeded.

If you should inexplicably want a change of scene from Iztuzu Beach, consider **Ekincik beach** to the west. The beach is accessible by road, but only after circumnavigating Koyçeğiz Lake and following the signs to Hamitköy, then taking a winding 14 kilometer road to Ekincik. Most people arrive here by boat, which is much easier.

Birding

Dalyan's delta is a musical stew of peeping and chirping during the spring and fall. Birders should contact Nil at the Sultan Palas Hotel for further information about the bird watching season.

Shopping

The weekly Dalyan bazaar happens on Saturdays across from the PTT.

Marmaris

Marmaris is a popular yacht harbor and package vacation spot, with large hotels and large foreigners making neat rows along the thin strip of sand northwest of the marina. Marmaris' waterfront—particularly Barlar Sok.—is lively from dawn 'til dawn, a go-go pace that is suited to some. Bodrum provides the same things Marmaris does with an equivalent marina, better ambiance, a far superior fortress, and better hotels. The peninsula's most interesting ruin, **Cnidos**, is best seen by boat from Datça.

History

Marmaris is the site of ancient **Physcos**, a surprisingly small town given the impressive nature of the Marmaris bay. The fortress above the harbor probably stands atop some older ruins, but the Physcos ruins are located in the mountains at the northern end of town.

The modern fortress is the work of the Ottomans, built one year in advance of their use of this bay for the invasion of Rhodes in 1522. After a failed attack under Sultan Mehmet II, conqueror of Constantinople, Süleyman the Magnificent amassed a huge force of ships here to ferry an army of 100,000 men across to Rhodes, where fewer than 3,000 Knights of St. John fought for eight months before accepting terms and abandoning their fortress. The small Marmaris fortress could easily have been built on the foundations of a structure once used by the knights themselves, for whom the extremely convenient Marmaris Bay would have been important.

Arrivals & Departures

By Bus

Because of its distance from the main sea road, Marmaris can require patience if you do not have a car. Most dolmuş and buses pass the turnoff by, leaving you at a small service station across the road from the turnoff. In this event cross the road and wait for a dolmuş to make the turn toward Marmaris, although they often seem to come tightly packed. The bus station is in the flats behind the Netsel Marina at the east end of town. The dolmuş station is inland of the Atatürk statue on the main road out of town, Ulusal Egemenlik Bulvari.

Kamil Koç bus schedules: İzmir, hourly, 5 a.m. to 2 a.m. $8; İstanbul, five times, 8:30 a.m. to 9 p.m., 9 p.m. $20; Ankara, three times; 9:30 a.m. to 10 p.m., $16; Antalya, four times; 1 a.m., 9:30 a.m., 3:30 p.m., 8:00 p.m. $15

By Car

Marmaris is 30 kilometers south of the main Muğla-Fethiye road, less than 100 kilometers west of the airport at Dalaman.

Orientation

Marmaris is a wonderland of leather, carpets, gold, yacht cruises and discotheques. The city has a long strip of sand beach, backed by Marmaris' sea road, itself beneath a long row of cookie-cutter hotels. The beach can be fun, but there's no elbow room, and the smell of slowly cooking human flesh wafts inland.

Where to Stay

Marmaris is popular for package holiday visitors from Germany and England, and most hotels cater to that clientele. Without a package booking, you'll find most hotels here overpriced and unappealing; to be quite honest, there's little other than a large marina (for setting out on a Blue Cruise) and a robust nightlife to recommend the town. Marmaris closes down in the off season.

MARINA HOTEL & RESTAURANT, *Barbaros Cad. No. 37 Yat Limani, Marmaris. Tel. (252) 412-6598; Fax (252) 412-6598; Email:*

m_yatmanes@yahoo.com; Web: www.turkuaz-guide.net/marina. Rooms: 11. Credit cards accepted. Open April 1-Nov. 15. Double: $33 (half-board $48).
At last there is a small Marmaris hotel deserving of a strong recommendation. Owner Murat Yatmaneş thoroughly remodeled this rambling older building on the Marmaris waterfront in 2001, and each of the rooms is cheerfully distinctive. Credit for that peculiarity is due the way the building is built back up against the stone spur beneath the Marmaris fortress; in some rooms, the walls are living stone. Most rooms are small, but they are clean and (a blessing in Marmaris) quiet.

The Marina has a restaurant upstairs, with a fine terrace overlooking the sea, and we recommend it; a meal of soup, a few mezes, Içli köfte (spiced meatballs), and beer will cost $13.

HOTEL LIDYA, *Siteler Mahallesi No. 131, Marmaris. Tel. (252) 417-3350; Fax (252) 417-3355; Email: liyahotels@superonline.com. Rooms: 349. Credit cards accepted. Open year-round. Double: $75 (40% discount in off-season).*

The Lidya is a fixture of the Marmaris waterfront, and continues to be superior to its more recent rivals. The date palms lining the beach catch a pleasant breeze throughout summer, as do the seaview rooms. The beach and lush grounds make this our choice among Marmaris' larger hotels; some details of the rooms leave something to be desired, but they are perfectly adequate and offer a full list of 4-star amenities. The Solaris cinema is located in an adjoining building. To get there: follow the waterfront road west two kilometers outside of the Marmaris city center. If the Lidya is full, consider the five-star **Grand Azur**—*Tel. (252) 417-4050; Fax (252) 417-4060; Email: info@hotelgrandazur.com; Web: www.hotelgrandazur.com. Double: $130 half-board.)*

INTERYOUTH HOSTEL, *Tepe Mah., 42 Sok. No. 45, Marmaris. Tel. (252) 412-3687, Fax (252) 412-7823; E-mail: interyouth@turk.net. Rooms: 12. Double: $12.*

An accredited youth hostel in the best tradition, clean, simple, and honest, with lots of extras. The hostel, within the bazaar behind the bus ticket offices and AkBank, has common kitchens and a terrace. It's a hostel, so you can't hear a pin drop, but you'll find lots of insight into upcoming destinations. In the tradition of good hostels throughout the country, you'll find movies on DVD, laundry service, Internet access, and free spaghetti dinners in the high season. Take the hostel up on its offer of a transfer from the bus station or port, highly recommended given the hostel's location within the bazaar labyrinth. Finally, the Marmaris Hostel offers the least expensive gulet cruise in Turkey (see Blue Cruise section).

HOTEL BEGONYA, *Kısayalı Hacı Mustafa Sok. No. 101, Marmaris. Tel. (252) 412-4095; Fax (252) 412-1518. Rooms: 24. Credit cards accepted. Open April-October. Double: $40.*

The Begonya has the nicest rooms and ambience in Marmaris; alas, it is located in the center of Marmaris' bar district (on the aptly named Barlar Sokak). Rooms have double-glazed windows, and earplugs are available, but the throb of the bars just yards away still boggles the mind. If you plan to indulge in Marmaris nightlife, this may be a good choice; otherwise, the lush patio garden, pleasant rooms, and air conditioning are all beside the point.

Bozburun

SABRINA'S HAUS HOTEL, *48710 Bozburun. Tel. (252) 456-2045; Fax (252) 456-2470; Email: sabrinashaus@superonline.com; Web: www.sabrinashaus.com. Rooms: 20. Credit cards accepted. Open April-December. Double: $45.*

Sabrina's is only worth considering if you want to take a break for a few days; it's 1.5 hours away from Marmaris, accessible from Bozburun only on foot or by launch. Consider it a land-bound gulet cruise.

This getaway was built in 1986, and is managed today by Tobias and Aynur Knörle (Sabrina returned to Germany in 2000; Tobias looks remarkably like Sting). With great swimming, hiking, and good food, Sabrina's Haus has built a strong reputation with German clientele— English-speakers are welcome, too. Rooms are distinctive, some with balconies, some with little libraries, but in every case the rooms are clean and tasteful. Families are in the habit of staying for weeks at a time. Transfers are available from the Dalaman airport or elsewhere.

Where to Eat

The city's best restaurants cater to the yacht clientele in the immediate neighborhood of the Netsel Marina; including Antik, La Campana, and Fellini Restaurant. Marina Restaurant, above the Marina Hotel, is included in the hotel listings.

SOFRA, *Tepe Mah. 36 Sok. Mustafa Yaylalı Işhanı No. 23, Marmaris. Tel. (252) 413-2631. Inexpensive.*

The Sofra is a hugely popular dining spot for people in search of good, decent Turkish food. This no-nonsense restaurant has white tile interior and inexpensive food--Iskender Kebap or mixed grills cost $2. The Sofra is located two blocks behind Barlar Sokak, inland of the PTT.

TÜRKAY RESTAURANT, *Barlar Sok. No. 107, Marmaris. Tel. (252) 412-0741. Very Expensive.*

Traditional Turkish fare with a French flair. Its location on Barlar Sokak puts it in the center of late evening bar-hopping frenzy.

BIRTAT RESTAURANT, *Barbaros Cad. No. 19, Marmaris. Tel. (252) 413-2343. Moderate-Expensive.*
The Birtat is our favorite of the restaurants clustered along the marina in front of Barlar Sok. You can expect to pay for the view—a beer costs $3, an entrée costs $9.

Seeing the Sights

The city's lone classic feature, the small hilltop **fortress**, is somewhat obscured by development nearby. It is not a particularly impressive fortress, and no less discerning a connoisseur of fortresses than the man who commissioned it says so. Süleyman the Magnificent, in his displeasure at the small, badly designed fortress is reported as saying *"Mimarı as,"* "Hang the architect." Some say that Marmaris' name derives from this very term. Today the fortress houses a pretty but uninspired **museum**.

The peninsulas west of Marmaris have several ruins, most of them along the seaside. Boat trips are available past the ruins from Bozburun, Datça, Selimiye, and Marmaris proper. These often-remote ruins give gulet cruises through the area much of their charm, but the most significant of the ancient foundations, other than Cnidos and Cedrae, mentioned below, is at **Loryma**, accessible from Bozburun. The ruins remain in forbidding shape above tiny Bozukkale.

Sports & Recreation

The long sand beach west of the Atatürk statue in city center is very popular, and many people swim here. For cleaner water, consider swimming as part of a boat trip. Many take a dolmuş to the beaches at İçmeler, departing from the waterfront road just inland of the Atatürk statue.

As home to the largest marina in Turkey, it is no wonder that **Marmaris** is a popular base for daily boat trips. Daily boat trips leaving from Marmaris include a trip ($14 per person) to **Paradise Island** at the opening of the bay; **Ciftlik Beach**, a phosphorous cave; and other islands just outside of Marmaris Bay. The stops are interesting, but are mostly a pretext to lounge on the boat and swim every time the boat drops anchor.

Be wary of "boat trips" that actually involve a long bus shuttle, such as that to Dalyan and Iztuzu beach: if you want a day-long boat trip the bus component may be unwelcome. One exception enjoyable trip to **Cleopatra Island** (Sedir Adası), located on the northern side of the peninsula, costing about $14. This requires a short bus ride across the peninsula, with a boat to the island.

An entertaining bit of folklore suggests that the white sand along Cleopatra Island was shipped in specially from Egypt prior to the famous queen's stop here on her romantic voyage with Marc Antony. Geologists can disabuse you of this notion. The ruins of **Cedrea** are located on the east side of the island. This city's one brush with history was grim; as punishment for its opposition, the Spartans sold the inhabitants as slaves in 450 B.C.

Small towns dot the coasts of Bozborun and Datça peninsulas, but precious few remain without large hotels marring the landscape. You can reach some of these towns by boat from Marmaris, including the popular hourly boat to **Turunc** departing from near the Atatürk Statue. Turunc is hardly unspoiled, but it offers more room than Marmaris and the boat trip helps you get your bearings. Other towns are accessible by dolmus or minibus from the small station located two blocks inland of the waterfront Atatürk statue on Ulusal Egemenlik Caddesi.

Ferries
Flying dolphin hydrofoil ferries to Rhodes depart daily at 9 a.m., leaving Rhodes at 4:30 p.m. The cost is $40 for a single day round trip, with the price rising in accordance with visa fees if you choose to stay in Rhodes. The Interyouth Hostel occasionally has even cheaper tickets. Always check visa information with the tourism information bureau, as arrangements change in accordance with Turkish/Greek diplomacy. Ferries depart from the far eastern side of town, beyond Netsel Marina on the way toward Günlucek National Park.

Ferries depart from Körmen, opposite Datça, for Bodrum daily at 9 a.m. and 5 p.m. in the summer (no ferries between late October and April). The trip from Bodrum to Datça takes about two hours and follows a winding mountain road; the cost is $25 one way for a car and driver, $6 for each additional passenger. The crossing takes about 1 1/2 hours. Automobile reservations are usually important; contact the **Bodrum marina**, *Tel. 252 316 0882*, where an English-language speaker is usually available.

Ferries depart Marmaris for Venice at noon on Wednesdays, arriving on Tuesday at 2 p.m.

Gulet Cruises
There are many companies selling gulet cruises out of Marmaris. See the Bodrum section for details. **Bozburun**, south of Marmaris, is one of the centers for construction of gulets.

Shopping
Marmaris' **bazaar**, inland of the Atatürk statue and winding in the

direction of the hilltop fortress, offers leathers, kilim (including wool rugs from nearby Milas), jewelry, and endless souvenirs, including the popular local honies. For specialized shopping, say the accessories for fashionable yachting, try the Polo, Vakko, and Beymen outlets in the Netsel marina.

If you are in need of detailed charts or other nautical supplies, check in at **Taka Bookstore**, *33 Sok. No. 20/4, Tel. 252 412 2242*, just across the waterway from the bus terminal, inland of the yacht harbor.

Practical Information

There are several cinemas in Marmaris. One is the small outdoor **Netsel Cinema** in the Netsel marina, just across the bridge from Barlar Sokak. **Solaris Theatre** is located in a building adjoining the Hotel Lidya near the eastern end of the waterfront.

The favored hamam is the state-of-the-art **Armutalan Turkish Bath** (8 a.m. to 10:30 p.m.), located two kilometers northwest of the town center. The interior is a peculiar mix of white marble floors and black and blue marble columns; the baths themselves are standard cream marble. $15 buys you a sauna, hamam, scrub (kese), massage, and jacuzzi. (If the scrub or massage are too strong, say "lütfen, ümüshak"—please, soft). Buses run to Armutalan every 15 minutes from the main street (Ulusal Egemenlik Cad.)—it is located directly behind the Devlet Hastanesi (State Hospital).

Marina Laundry *(Tel. 252 413-0845)* is located just across from the marina on Hacı Mustafa Sokak; $6 per load, open til 11 p.m.

Cnidos

Cnidos has a truly romantic setting, surrounded by the waters of the Mediterranean. Contributing to Cnidos' romance was the presence of the greatest shrine to Aphrodite, Goddess of Love, on the southern Turkish coast. History says that ships anchored here to wait out the meltem, the north wind, but it would be a wonder if sailors weren't also encouraged to stay by a city that worshipped the Goddess of Love.

History

Cnidos' history began at modern **Datça**, 30 kilometers east. On that location Cnidos was an extremely successful Greek colony, master of the local seas as well as an active settler of far off lands, including Sicily. Trade and good fortune helped Cnidos grow in wealth and power, all of which seemed liable to come crashing to an end in 540 B.C., in a tale related by Herodotus. The Persian Harpagus, charged with subduing the

Not Just Any Port in a Storm

Cnidos had more than shelter for a weary sailor. In what may have been an early example of clever marketing, the new city of Cnidos was built around a Temple of Aphrodite of Fair Voyages. Here sailors could view the legendary statue of Aphrodite by Praxiteles, a scandalous work of art, but one that four centuries later Pliny the Younger considered the finest statue in the world. Sailors, always eager to learn more about fine art, were enthusiastic to stop at Cnidos, view the statue and visit the temple 'priestesses.' Cnidos was not only a necessary anchorage, but a much anticipated one.

entire coast of Asia Minor for his King, Cyrus, was crushing all resistance and appeared certain to march on wealthy Cnidos.

Trusting to their proven naval skills, the citizens of Cnidos set to work at the narrowest point of the peninsula inland of their city and began digging away at the land in the hopes of isolating the peninsula from the rest of Asia Minor.

In the midst of this frenzied activity a suspiciously large number of workers were injured by bits of stone in their eyes and the Cnidans, nonplused, sought advice from the Oracle at Delphi. The Oracle returned a blunt answer: if Zeus had wanted the peninsula to be an island, he would have made it an island. The Cnidans are reported to have quit their work and returned home, surrendering to Harpagus on his arrival.

In the middle of the fourth century Cnidos, now under the control of the Persian satrapy in Helicarnas/Bodrum, moved. This traumatic undertaking - the new site had very little fresh water and vegetation - seems to have been brought on by financial concerns. In its new position at the head of the peninsula, Cnidos could offer a safe harbor to ships unable to round the tricky cape during bad weather. The large southern harbor is still discernible, having been built to shelter northbound ships during the cape's strong, steady northerlies. As if difficult weather and the illicit charms of the new port city weren't enough (see sidebar), Cnidos also had a reputation for producing good wines.

With all of this inspiration, several luminous figures hailed from Cnidos, most notably **Sostratus**, the designer of the Pharos Lighthouse in the third century, one of the Seven Wonders of the World. The sculptor Praxiteles was not from Cnidos, but from Athens.

Alas, Cnidos' glory ebbed under the Romans, perhaps in direct proportion to Christian assaults on the rampant vice of **Aphrodite's**

Temple. As its sea power faded, its position at the tip of the peninsula turned from a strength to a weakness, and Cnidos was probably preyed on by successive waves of invaders.

Evidence of Aphrodite Temples are rare, and no evidence of them remains on Turkey's southern coast. There may have been no way to identify the Temple of Aphrodite at Cnidos if it hadn't been so famous that archaeologists were searching specifically for it. An American archaeologist, improbably named Iris Love, located pieces of what appears to be the statue's pedestal amid a collection of broken stone. Temples of Aphrodite were probably stamped out with especial enthusiasm when Christianity supplanted the traditional forms of worship, and the Cnidos' Temple of Aphrodite was clearly broken up almost stone by stone. The statue's fate is unknown, but the Metropolitan Museum in New York has a possible replica, as does, ironically, the Vatican Museum.

Arrivals & Departures

The best way to see Cnidos is on a cruise from Datça, departing daily in the high season at 9 a.m. The best way to get to Datça is either by dolmuş from Marmaris or by ferry from Bodrum (the latter is less harrowing, more beautiful).

Remember that Cnidos' entire wealth was based on tricky weather at the furiously boiling point of the peninsula, something that forced ships to seek harbor here and await more favorable conditions. You may get a little of this yourself in the interest of historical flavor.

Public transport does not serve the remote ruin, but with a car you can reach Cnidos by ignoring the Datça turn and continuing straight along what becomes a dirt road, staying to the left at unsigned intersections. There are cafes at the site, but no accommodation. The roads are winding, narrow, and pot-holed; proceed with caution.

Seeing the Sights

The **Cnidos ruin** tumbles along for about two kilometers at the end of the peninsula. Few ruins give a sense of what their inhabitants must have been like so well as Cnidos, whose distance from the mainland on this long, sparsely vegetated spit of land has an isolated, desolate feel. The location is unique in the style of mountaintop cities that controlled trade routes, but without the reassurance of much water or arable land.

The central feature of the city is the **isthmus**, formerly a bridge. This connected the two sections of Cnidos and divided its two harbors into the commercial harbor on the south (left as you look out from the mainland), and the military harbor to the north. Sunken sections of the breakwaters and wharves are visible beneath the sea. The northern harbor has the smaller mouth, which is fortified with a tower.

The **acropolis** is on the mainland, as are most of the temples and other public buildings. Climb the steep hill behind the north harbor to reach the site of the former Temple of Aphrodite. This was built on a circular foundation, surrounded by columns and centered on the Praxiteles statue. Another temple, that of Demeter and Kore, is located nearby, and itself involved some risque traditions (see Priene). The statue of Demeter was located here and transported to the British Museum. The city walls are another staggering example of ashlar construction, a circuit of great cut blocks running along the spine of the peninsula. The fact that the city was planned deliberately allowed the use of central planning, so streets are designed on a grid system akin to that at Priene.

If you arrive by sea you will have a chance to see the ruined **Lion Monument**, a trophy of an Athenian victory over Sparta here in the years before the new Cnidos was built. The lion from which the monument draws its name is also in the British Museum. The monument is located at a section of shoreline inaccessible by land. The necropolis is at the inland end of Cnidos by the road, scattered along a hill.

From Marmaris to Bodrum

Marmaris and Bodrum are just 70 kilometers apart as the crow flies, but making the trip requires a big loop out of the way inland, or a harrowing ride out to Körmen near Datça, then a car ferry (see Bodrum section for details).

The route inland follows the main road through plane trees back to the highway, then follows the main coast highway up a series of switchbacks above Gökova and on to the provincial capital of Muğla. The road is in good condition, continuing a flat course as far Yatağan, at which point you follow the Milas/Bodrum signs west. Yatağan is home to several massive power plants, and one of the most dispiriting ruins in the country is located just beyond at Stratonikea. The highway continues west past tables crammed with preserves and honey sold by local farmers, then drops dramatically out of the heights to make a final descent into Milas. The highway forks at Milas, heading southwest to Bodrum and the Gulluk airport, and northwest toward Ephesus and Izmir beyond. The beautiful ruins of Labranda and the small, pretty temple at Euromos are located a short distance from Milas along the northwest fork.

STRATONIKEA

The ruins of Stratonikea are just one-half kilometer off the main highway, scattered around the mortar and stone houses of a dead

Turkish village. The ruins and Eskihisar village are literally in the shadow of a 60-foot high mountain of spoil from an astoundingly huge lignite quarry just to the north; it is this quarry that drove out the villagers; mining seems to have stopped.

The ruins here are less interesting for most visitors than the nearly perfect preservation of Eskihisar. The houses, cobbled of small, flat stones, roofed with tile and always shuttered, stand abandoned. Occasionally you will see some evidence of local life—including a small refreshment stand in the summer—but Eskihisar is truly abandoned. One can scarce imagine the dirt and dust disgorged by the massive open pit mining operation as it drew closer to the town.

Upon arriving at the fork in the road at the entrance to town, the right turning takes you into the narrow cobbled lanes of the town, the left turning takes you under the wall of mining spoil to the north gate of the ancient city, whose pylons still stand. The arch of the gate is broken and cast down. Just within the gate stands a great column, its partner on the far side toppled.

LABRANDA

Labranda was the sacred precinct of Caria, a holy place long before the construction of its principal ruin, the Temple of Zeus. This is a beautiful site, well-worth a side trip from the transit hub of Milas 14 kilometers to the west. A sacred way has always linked the temple precinct with Milas in the valley below, but this road has been in awful shape for years. It was regraded in 2000 and is now accessible to people even without four-wheel drive vehicles—marked every couple of kilometers by "Labranda 14 km." signs, of which there seems to have been some overproduction.

You will share the road with hulking Mercedes "Fatih" trucks filled with stone, winding past the lovely, exceedingly poor village of Kargacık. After 14 kilometers, you cross a small bridge and arrive at the site. You will find a small car park and café. The ruins are arrayed on the slope above, mostly out of sight. You may enter through a sliding gate just above the café. If you continue to the end of the asphalt a few hundred feet further, you'll find an entrance through a gate with massive courses of stone. Yellow metal signs at the site offer faded maps of the site.

Climbing from the road, the site teems with cicadas, turtles, and bees. In many places, shelters and tombs have been carved into the face of boulders. On one of the upper terraces is the 4th century B.C. Temple of Zeus, formerly the centerpiece of Labranda. Today, it is in a poor state of preservation, less so, even, than the sanctuary structures just to the west (to the left as you look uphill). The temple terrace is cleared and pieces of columns suggest the outline of the former colonnade.

Some of the most interesting ruins are in the heights just above. Barbed wire fences criss-cross the ruins, particularly as you ascend above the temple. If you close gates behind you, nobody minds. The path climbs past a small stream and uphill beneath a great stone buttress, the upper section of which is pocked with carved tombs. As you climb, you pass through a gate in massive stone walls, courses of which are 30-feet long. The walls are built into the face of the stone buttress, into which elaborate tombs have been carved.

EUROMOS

Euromos, located just 200 meters off the main highway north of Milas, is the site of a Temple of Zeus that remains in unusually good condition. Because of its convenience to the main coastal highway, this site is frequented by tour buses—there is a $1.50 entrance fee.

There are two principal sites at Euromos, the temple directly behind the entrance booth, and the seldom-visited small theatre on the hillside to the north. The temple is on a more modest scale than those at Didyma or Sardis, but significant portions of the temple are intact; 16 of the columns still stand, supporting an incribed architrave. Kilns built alongside the temple were in use as recently as the 18th century, incinerating the marble to produce lime to fertilize their fields.

The temple was located outside the walls of Euromos, and bastions of the fallen walls can be seen atop the low hill to the north. Following a path behind the restrooms to the hilltop ruins, then continuing north 150 meters brings you to the theatre. This small, 2,000-person theatre is a pleasant getaway on a hot summer day, and a fine place for a picnic.

Bodrum

Like Marmaris, **Bodrum** has been discovered and developed in the course of the past decade. Unlike Marmaris, Bodrum has retained a lot of its original charm, owing, perhaps, to the lack of beaches immediately along the waterfront. You'll find a selection of excellent accommodations in and around the Bodrum peninsula and a great variety of ways to entertain yourself while here, although the number of legitimate historic sights falls off dramatically after the attractions in Bodrum itself.

History

The fine, defensible anchorage at **Helicarnassus** made this site one of the first settled by the waves of Greek colonists, perhaps as early as 1200 B.C. There were probably people here earlier than that, but the evidence is buried beneath the daunting Castle of St. Peter on the isthmus.

Helicarnassus was a member of the **Dorian Hexapolis**, a union of six cities with ties to the Peloponnese that also included Cnidos and four cities in modern Greece. These ties were broken after Cyrus' Persian Army swept Asia Minor, seizing Helicarnassus; thereafter the city, together with Milas inland, was often the seat of Persian power in the region. **Artemesia I**, Helicarnassus' ruler, sailed for Greece with Xerxes' invasion force in 480 B.C. During the battle of Salamis, with Xerxes watching from his throne on shore, Artemesia distinguished herself on a day when the Persian navy suffered a grave defeat. **Xerxes** commented sourly that his men were fighting like women, his women like men. This cemented Xerxes' lousy reputation in modern eyes as both environmentally insensitive (he whipped and shackled the Hellespont) and a misogynist.

The Artemesia account is of particular interest because it was written by Herodotus, a citizen of Helicarnassus only slightly younger than Artemesia herself. His account of the period from 560 B.C. to Xerxes' failed invasion less than a century later earned Herodotus the title "father of history."

Shortly after Xerxes' defeat, Helicarnassus slipped away from Persian control, but it was returned to the Persian fold early in the fourth century. The Persian satrap Mausolus (377-353) made Helicarnassus the provincial capital, undertaking an ambitious building program. The city was completed during Mausolus' rule and adorned with Mausolus' own massive funerary monument, later considered one of the Seven Wonders of the World.

During this time, two major cities under Mausolus' command, Caunos and Cnidos, were rebuilt on a massive scale - Cnidos was moved to an entirely new location - while Mausolus prosecuted a war against the Lycians to the southeast.

Thus it was with the city in a state of prosperity, secure behind high new walls, that Alexander the Great arrived just twenty years after Mausolus' death. Alexander met heavy resistance here, as a large Persian garrison had been left to challenge him, commanded by Memnon of Rhodes. A prolonged siege finally succeeded in breaching the walls, but once within the city Alexander was met with the prospect of another long siege against the inner citadel - on the site of the Castle of St. Peter. For this he had no time, and Arrian reports that he "razed the town to the ground;" but with the mausoleum still standing Helicarnassus could hardly be considered "razed." Leaving the Persians within the small harbor citadel, Alexander passed control of Caria to Ada, Mausolus' sister, and continued south.

Helicarnassus was put in order during the busy, confusing period following Alexander's death. The rivals for Alexander's empire refortified the town in order to defend themselves from one another, and when it passed to Rome in the second century B.C. it was in good condition.

The city declined under the Byzantines, who were unable to protect their provinces from the ravages of Arab and other corsairs and invaders. The Knights of St. John seized the city in the chaos following Tamurlane's invasion in 1402 - the burgeoning Ottoman empire was smashed and the Knights' own fortress at İzmir was destroyed. After establishing themselves here, the Knights remained secure until the great Crusader fortress at Rhodes capitulated to Süleyman the Magnificent (1520-1566), at which point they sailed away. The Ottomans occupied the fortress, but with the eastern Mediterranean secure and the interior under control, the fortress was irrelevant to the empire's defense.

Arrivals & Departures
By Air
The **Bodrum-Milas Airport** at **Güllük**, north of Bodrum by about 30 minutes, began operations in 1997, and is able to serve 4 million passengers annually. The **Turkish Airlines** office in Bodrum is on the waterfront road at Neyzen Tevfik Cad., No. 208, *Tel. 252 313 3172*. You can contact them directly about arranging transportation, or you can check with your hotel.

By Bus
Buses are available between Bodrum and most sites in western Turkey. Buses depart for Milas and Selçuk (passing Didyma, Miletus and Soke) on the half-hour. Bodrum's otogar is several blocks inland of the city center. Follow Cevat Sakir Sokak slightly downhill and you arrive at the tourism information office on the isthmus below the Castle of St. Peter. Dolmuş are centered at the same place, serving the surrounding towns on the half hour, including Bitez, Yalıkavak, Turgutreis, and Türkbükü.

By Car
Bodrum is just over an hour's drive from Milas on the main 330-525 coast road, and is one-half hour from the airport at Güllük.

Orientation
Bodrum is a major city, with all of the amenities you could want. The tourism information office is located at the Fortress of St. Peter, not far from the wharf where ferries arrive. The address is 48 Barış Meydanı, *Tel. 252 316 1091*, but it's easier to find it by locating the fortress. The office is open until 7:30 p.m. in summer, 5 p.m. between November and March.

The Public Hospital is located at the entry to town, on Kıbrıs Sehitleri Caddesi, *Tel. 252 313 1421.*

You'll find banks, ATMs, and laundromats aplenty – Can Çamasır laundry is just opposite Buğday restaurant and charges $2.50 per load.

Where to Stay

ANTIK THEATRE HOTEL, *Kıbrıs Sehitleri Caddesi, 243, Bodrum 48400. Tel. (252) 316-6053; Fax (252) 316-0825; Email: theatrehot@superonline.com; Web: www.pathcom.com/~antique. Rooms: 20. Credit cards accepted. Open year-round. Double: $140 (15% discount between November and April)—add $50 for half board.*

Once acclaimed as the "best small hotel in Turkey" by The New York Times, the Antik Theatre Hotel is no great secret; it just feels that way. This is a quiet, comfortable place that happens to be a beautiful hotel.

The hotel's architect, Cengiz Bektaş, built the terraced hotel for owners Zafer and Selmin Başak—Mrs. Başak was a design school colleague of the architect's and has done all the interior design and decorating herself. Every room looks out on the picturesque Castle of St. Peter through shuttered door and windows. Every terrace has its own small patio with a deliberate jumble of gravel and stepping stones and greenery sprouting by the rail, with bougainvillea crawling up wooden frames and old terracotta pots tucked in corners. On the bottom tier is a deep swimming pool, recalling in shape the curved seats of the ancient theatre. Guests gather here on summer nights, toasting the magnificent castle and bay below.

The decoration is simple whites and marble, with spare blonde wood furnishings. You'll find a candle and an old framed nautical chart or boat diagram for decoration, and take especial note of the bedspreads; the thick linen fabric comes from a weaver on the Black Sea who uses an old hand loom, and the lace is handmade as well. The corner bathrooms are particularly cleverly designed. The aesthetics and attention to detail are helped along generously by a good staff that, far from aloof, is engaging and friendly. The owners spend a fair bit of time enjoying the hotel themselves.

After all of this, it comes as no surprise that chef Arif Çenerli turns out fine cuisine every evening, putting to good use the four weeks he spends training in France every year. The patios are ideal for late evening dining, the castle illuminated and the harbor alive with lights.

The Antik Theatre is directly across Kıbrıs Sehitleri Caddesi from the real antique theatre, on the westbound side of the main "Cevre Yolu," or ring road.

Selected one of our favorite small hotels.

MUNAHAN, *Kumbahçe Mah. Akçabük Sok., Bodrum. Tel. (252) 313-6482; Fax (252) 313-6485; Email: info@munahan.com; Web: www.munahan.com. Rooms: 9. Credit cards accepted. Open year-round. Double: $150 (20% off-season discount).*

The Munahan, in the hills above the eastern Bodrum bay, is a beautiful small hotel. The hotel has clean lines, beautiful woodwork, and a quiet elegance. The Munahan is all whites and wood hues and greens, a pleasant exercise in the whitewashed cubes that typify Bodrum architecture. It has, too, the painstaking woodwork and simplicity of design of a ship.

The courtyard below the rooms has a pool and dining area, and a rooftop bar offers is a lovely place for a drink, offering views in all directions.

MERVE PARK SUITES HOTEL, *Atatürk Cad. No. 73, Bodrum. Tel. (252) 316-1546; Fax (252) 316-1278; Email: mpark@efes.net.tr; Web: www.mervepark.com. Rooms: 19. Credit cards accepted. Open year-round. Double: $100 (40% discount in off-season).*

The entrance to the Merve Park, with the look and feel of a small, spartan gallery (the genuine ancient artifacts behind glass add to the effect), gives way to a network of elegantly-appointed rooms that continue along the antique theme. The rooms are painted a cheerful yellow, have impressive marble and glass bathrooms, wooden armoires, air-conditioning, and satellite televisions. Some rooms have a view of the courtyard, whose mature palm trees shade wrought iron tables and chairs. Others look out over the pool, sea, and fortress below. The antiques scattered throughout — ranging from anchors to millstones to amphorae — are registered with the Bodrum underwater archaeological museum. Suites come with working fireplaces and kitchenettes, and during the summer months the terrace is home to a restaurant and bar. There may be some traffic noise, as the Merve Park is at a busy intersection.

BAÇ PANSIYON, *Cumhuriet Caddesi No. 18, Bodrum. Tel. (252) 316-1602; Fax (252) 316-7917. Rooms: 18. Credit cards accepted. Open year-round. Double: $60.*

The Baç is an extremely comfortable small hotel located along the seaside in Bodrum's city center. The hotel is a good bargain, with carefully detailed interiors, pretty balconies, nice wood furniture, and TVs. The rooms have air conditioning and, on the waterfront, small balconies. The terrace has a cool interior bar and a nice patio for keeping an eye on the bustle of boats in the harbor. The Belediye otopark (municipal parking lot) is located 300 kilometers away near the police station—call ahead for instructions if you're driving a rental car.

USLU PANSIYON, *Cumhuriet Cad. No. 35, Bodrum. Tel. (252) 313-6848; Fax none. Rooms: 10. Credit cards not accepted. Closed November-February. Double: $16.*
This is a wonderful, cheap little pension right in the middle of Bodrum's busiest area. The Uslu is just beyond the Baç Pansiyon, and it opens into a narrow, whitewashed courtyard crisscrossed with stairs, landings, and clothes lines. The interior is cool and lined with plants, and everything is painstakingly clean. There are no frills; shared bathrooms and a no-nonsense hostess.

EMIKO PENSION, *Atatürk Cad. Uslu Sokak No. 11, Bodrum. Phone/Fax (252) 316-5560; Email: emiko@turk.net. Roooms: 8. Credit cards not accepted. Closed in winter. Double: $15.*
Our biggest concern about the Emiko Pension is that the owner may be returning to Japan in 2002. If she does not, this remains a marvelous budget option in an old whitewashed Bodrum building, a building complete with three-foot-thick walls. Cool in summer, warm in winter, the Emiko Pension is a hospitable home away from home. The outdoor grill is available for guests' use. The Emiko is located just east and one block inland of the Uslu Pension, beyond the Akgün Hotel; from the otogar, walk toward the sea on Cevat Şakir Cad., take a left on Atatürk Caddesi, and look for a sign directing you right to Emikio. If full (or closed), consider the nearby **Aşkin Pansiyon**, a short distance east (*Tel. (232) 313-3167*).
Selected one of our favorite budget hotels.

Around Bodrum—Türkbüku
ADA HOTEL, *Cataldibi Mevkii, Tepecik Cad. No. 44, Türkbükü. Tel. (216) 378-6440; Fax (216) 378-1433; Email: info@adahotel.com; Web: www.adahotel.com. Rooms: 14. Credit cards accepted. Open year-round. Double: $250-$475 ($195-$375 between October and May).*
The Ada Hotel in Türkbükü is the most refined and exacting hotel in the whole of Turkey, and one of the most expensive. This is one of only two hotels in Turkey listed by Relais & Chateau, and with good reason: it is audacious and inspired, in every way the perfect retreat.
The Ada has a humble exterior, but within it takes the breath away. The stone-walled Ada has a sprawling collection of public spaces, reading rooms, and gardens; they unfold for you peacefully, hour by hour. Take the Mahzen Restaurant, downstairs; the stone walls are softened by white drapes and tables have with crimson tablecloths to create a feeling is part Ottoman fortress, part Scottish Highlands palace. And so it is throughout, solid, beautiful, and in a place somewhere almost out of time.

Rooms are as you would expect. The suites are stunning, and even the standard "deluxe" rooms are marvelous; expect stone walls, wood trim, rich textiles, beautiful lighting, a full set of amenities, and a fruit basket upon arrival.

The Mahzen Restaurant is a marvelous indulgence; consider a reservation. A meal and a bottle of wine for two will cost roughly $75.

Selected one of our favorite small hotels.

Torba

QUEEN ADA HOTEL, *Kilise Mevkii No. 28, Torba, Bodrum. Tel. (252) 367-1598; Fax (252) 367-1614; Email: queenad@ibm.net; Web: www.queenada.com.tr. Rooms: 22. Credit cards accepted. Open year-round. Double: $190 (50% discount between November and March).*

The Queen Ada is related to the Ada Hotel in name and beauty alone. If the Ada Hotel has the more elegant interiors, the Queen Ada has the better location, on the waterfront and backed up against an unspoiled hill. And, make no mistake, the rooms, pool, and dining areas at the Queen Ada are among the best in the country. The hotel has its own pier and stretch of beach, and the pool is artfully build up against the stone walls of some old buildings. Torba is overdeveloped, but the Queen Ada is isolated from that development.

Where to Eat

Bodrum has some exceptional dining. Note that the Antik Theatre Hotel and the Ada Hotel, listed above, have two of the finest chefs in the region.

EPSILON RESTAURANT, *Türkkuyusu Mah., Keleş Çıkmazı No. 5, Bodrum. Tel. (252) 313-2964. Moderate-Expensive.*

"I think you could say 'almost refined'," laughs owner Lon Briet, trying to describe her restaurant. And that sounds about right; this restaurant, tucked away in an alley east of the Mausoleum, has fine food, great service, and a relaxed atmosphere that's much more enjoyable than it is refined. The Epsilon offers several dining rooms, as well as a brick-paved courtyard with a massive palm tree as the centerpiece.

The meal begins with an array of mezes, from which you can select what you like. Entrees include jumbo prawns from Mersin ($9), lamb kebap atop a bed of pureed eggplant ($6), and Köfte Daruzziyafe—lamb, veal, chicken, an pistachio rolled in philodough and grilled ($6). For dessert? Indulge in the Shadow of Cheops. A meal for two will cost about $35.

To get here: The Epsilon is located on the same road as the Mausoleum, Turgut Reis Sokak.

SECRET GARDEN RESTAURANT, *Eskiçeşme Mah. Danach Sok. No. 20, Bodrum. Tel. (252) 313-4479. Moderate-Expensive.*

On our last visit we interrupted the chef and owner in the midst of a cooking course she was offering some local chefs. One can hope that the lessons stick, and that, like her, chefs throughout Bodrum will soon be offering whole crab with garlic butter ($7), scallop and prawn gratin ($8), stuffed quail ($9), and fillet steak with roasted tomatoes ($9.50). Until that happens, the fine selection of food and wine at the Secret Garden should be on your evening dining itinerary. You can dine in the garden in hot weather, or in the quirky, simple dining room in cooler weather, huddling around a fireplace.

The Secret Garden is located in the streets behind Marina Vista Hotel (and Sutte on the corner), at the west end of the Bodrum waterfront road.

SÜNGER RESTAURANT, *Alim Bey Cad. No. 218, Bodrum. Tel. (252) 316-5286. Inexpensive-Moderate.*

This is a great choice for a quick bite at lunch. Ask anyone in town for the best three reasonably-priced restaurants, and they'll include Sünger in that list somewhere. Surprising, then, how unassuming this restaurant is; you'll find a few patio tables on the road directly behind the marina (the view has been cut off by construction of some new shops). The menu is reasonably priced; $3 buys you a generous plate of beef, garlic, and minced onion stewed in tomato sauce, together with a basket of fresh bread. The Sünger is located near the west side of the waterfront road, just beyond the Tepecik Mosque.

LIMAN KÖFTECESI, *Neyzen Tevfik Cad. No. 74, Bodrum. Tel. (252) 316-1516. Moderate.*

The Liman is the best of the restaurants located just inland of the Castle of St. Peter. Prices are a bit higher than they are further inland, but the waterfront view and decent service make this a tempting option. It's a good place to get some lentil soup (mercemek çorbasi), meatballs (köfte), shepherd's salad (çoban salatasi) and rice pilav. Lunch for two, with water, costs about $8.

PALMİYE INTERNET CAFÉ, *Neyzen Tevfik Cad. No: 196, Bodrum. Tel. (252) 313-9184; Email: palmiye1@hotmail.com. Web: www.sailturkey.com/internetcafe.*

In addition to checking your email ($3.50/hour for Internet access), you can get a nice cup of espresso and something sweet while you surf.

Seeing the Sights

Bodrum has two significant historical sites, the **Castle of St. Peter** and the **Mausoleum at Helicarnassus**, and we highly recommend both despite the latter's sad decline. Most of the city's significant ruins, including the once mighty Temple of Mars erected under the Romans, have disappeared. The 10,000 seat theater was the site of gladitorial contests and combat against wild animals, although the lower seats no longer seem quite insulated from the floor of the theater.

The Castle of St. Peter

The city's centerpiece is the castle separating Bodrum's harbors. This remarkable fortress was constructed atop the site of the archaic acropolis, which was itself replaced with Mausolus' fortified palace. The archaic acropolis was on an island once known as Zephyrion, now the isthmus of the **Castle of St. Peter**. The Knights of St. John set to work on the castle in 1402, taking advantage of Tamurlane's crushing defeat of the Sultan Beyazid I at the Battle of Ankara and the near collapse of the young Ottoman Empire. The new castle was intended to extend the Rhodes-based Knights' naval power, and by the time the Ottoman Empire had recovered its strength the Castle was complete and the Knights were harassing Moslem shipping.

The castle was a thorn in the Ottomans' side, but it did not prove an insuperable obstacle to Ottoman armies and navies, who avoided the area as they swarmed on to Egypt and the Holy Land and extended their power. Still, the consistent shipping losses to the Knights demanded action. When the Ottomans finally sought to dislodge the Knights they headed directly for Rhodes via a safe harbor in Marmaris, again bypassing Bodrum. Sultan Mehmet II Fatih encountered a rare setback at Rhodes, failing to take the city in 1479. Forty-three years later Süleyman the Magnificent, too, thought better of besieging the Castle of St. Peter as a preamble to an attack on Rhodes, his ultimate goal. He attacked Rhodes directly, and after a six month siege forced the Knights of St. John to surrender on Christmas Day, 1522. The Knights at the Castle of St. Peter surrendered only after installation of the high-gigawatt speakers at the Helicarnas Disco across the water, although history would have us believe that the Knights sailed away without a fight in January 1523 as a condition of the peace at Rhodes.

The castle was alternately a fortress and a prison, and is today one of the most imaginative and informative museums in Turkey. The **Museum of Underwater Archaeology** is among the attractions here. One building houses a complete recreation of an 11th century shipwreck, as discovered and moved by Texas A&M. The contents of the wreck are also on display, as is the cargo from fourth and seventh century wrecks.

The **Carian Princess Hall** exhibits the contents of a burial chamber found in 1989. The tomb chamber of a Carian princess - probably Queen Ada, Alexander the Great's ally – was intact, and forensic scientists have used the bones to recreate the features of its occupant. This is the woman who Plutarch reports would send Alexander "dainty dishes and sweetmeats and at last presented him with pastry cooks and bakers who were considered to be very expert." The young conqueror, who felt much fondness for Ada, would nevertheless reject her entreaties; his strict tutor Leonidas had taught him to prefer "for breakfast a night's march, and for dinner a scanty breakfast."

The **English Tower**, the dominant fortification at the back corner of the fortress, is filled with battle standards and wooden tables that look out on the Aegean; wine is served by men and women in page costumes and knight grafitti is etched into the walls. The exterior's west wall has an archaic lion relief, evidence of past occupation of the site and the source of the name **Lion Tower**. In the castle's front court there is even a **Medieval Grocery**, offering an odd selection of herbs and peculiar medicinals. The sole discordant note is at the **German Tower** on the inland wall, where the **Torture Chamber** is witlessly animated by flashing lights and a Halloween tape. The bits of reality, including the inscription above the entry - "*Inde Deus Abest*," "the place without God" - are all that's necessary here. Finally, near the contemporary public toilets (impressively clean, about twenty-five cents), you'll come along the "Ottoman toilets," which are sure to get a giggle from Turkish school kids.

At the entrance to the fortress is a pleasant tea garden, as well as a Dösim shop, one of the state-run stores that sells Turkish handicrafts at fixed prices. Most of the exhibits in the museum are open from 8 a.m. to noon, and from 1:30 p.m. to 5:30 p.m., closed Mondays. Although the fortress itself is open on Sundays, many of the museums inside are not. If you go on a Sunday, keep your ticket and you should be allowed back in on the following Tuesday to see what you missed.

The Mausoleum of Helicarnassus

In the center of town, on Turgut Reis Caddesi directly between the theater and the Castle of St. Peter, is the site of the **Mausoleum at Helicarnassus**. The greatest highlight in the city tumbled in an earthquake and was picked apart by Crusaders preparing for a battle that never took place. This mausoleum was one of the Seven Wonders of the World, and like the Temple of Artemis at Ephesus and six of the seven wonders, it is now gone.

This structure, like the Cheops Pyramid - the only Wonder still standing - was built to honor a dead ruler. The ruler in this case was **Mausolus**, not even a king but a particularly powerful and autonomous satrap of the Persian Empire. Mausolus' rule was distinguished by several military campaigns and the establishment of the regional capital in Bodrum. His solid but unspectacular rule may not merit such a monument, but the playwright Diogenes has the satrap justify it thus: "I am handsome and tall and mighty in war." Professor Kristian Jeppeson, the Danish archaeologist who has driven the research at the site since 1966, offers a different explanation: "Architecture has always been a symbol of power," he says. "Any potentate who wants to be remembered by posterity will make efforts to leave some outstanding monumental building."

This Mausolus certainly did. A 300 yard by 100 yard area was set aside as grounds for Mausolus' tomb complex, and work on the monument within this complex was started during Mausolus' reign. The mausoleum itself measured 130 feet square at the base, rising to a height of 150 feet. With the exception of the small burial chamber under an arched space in the foundations, the monument was constructed entirely of dressed stone, fitted one to another with metal pins. To this solid, sheer stone mountain were added beautiful works of artistry. The four greatest sculptors of the day were brought in and set to work at the site, each responsible for the work on one side of the monument. The competing artists sheathed the mausoleum in marble, then added row after row of statues and columns. Reliefs and sculpture of Mausolus' exploits ringed the building at several levels.

Alas, Mausolus died too soon, and his resting place was incomplete, but Mausolus' devoted wife and sister Artemesia II proved a devoted widow as well. (The practice of sibling marriages was commonplace among the Hecatomnid royals, and, sure enough, the quality of the gene pool seems to have withered rapidly.) She pressed forward with the construction, aided by the desire of the four principal artists - Scopas, Bryaxis, Timotheus, and Leochares - to leave the temple as their legacy.

During Artemesia's brief reign, the Mausoleum was completed, and Mausoleus' remains secured in the tomb. The satrap was burned on a pyre, and his bones were bathed in wine and collected in an ornate gold sarcophagus. After interring a farmload of slaughtered animals to feed the dead ruler in the netherworld, workers slid a massive stone "plug" into the entrance, and it was fixed in position by a set of cylindrical dowels that clicked into place. The grand mausoleum was basically intact as late as the 1100s, according to accounts.

When the Knights of St. John arrived they found the monument ruined, probably toppled by a great quake in 1304. The Knights began work on the Castle of St. Peter in 1402, and they are likely to have made a habit of using cut stone from the mausoleum's huge pile just across the harbor. They were certainly using cut stone from the Mausoleum at the time they refortified the castle in 1494.

A Crusader named Claude Guichard describes his colleagues' appreciation of the ruins: "*Having at first admired these works and entertained their fancy with the singularity of the sculptures, they pulled it to pieces and broke up the whole of it."* Guichard has long been thought to have told the next chapter in the tale, telling a picturesque story of Crusaders discovering a tomb beneath the mountain of stone, but having time only for a cursory look before being recalled to the castle for the night. In the morning, he writes, thieves had broken into the tomb, removed the lid from the sarcophagus, and run off with the treasure.

The Danish archaeological expedition has found evidence that the Crusader-era thieves came far too late. Stymied by the plug stone - which remains scarred by efforts to dislodge it - and stopped cold by the thick courses of lava stone on all sides, earlier thieves apparently burrowed through the softer tufa rock beneath the mausoleum and thus entered the tomb chamber. A few small gold buttons and pins were found in the tunnel outside of the chamber, indicating their success. None of the other, more magnificent valuables from Mausolus tomb have ever come to light.

A small **museum** within the Mausoleum compound explains the archaeology at the sight and offers several possible recreations of the original building. The grounds themselves are unimpressive unless you take the time to look them over carefully. A large indentation indicates where the tomb was located, with its original access opposite the museum. The greenish plug stone is still in its place, too heavy and unwieldly for use in the Castle of St. Peter.

A series of irrigation channels radiate from the lowered tomb area, and there are two other interesting features in the stone beneath the mausoleum.

The first is the stairway and set of chambers skirting the southern end of the mausoleum site, opposite the museum entrance. This is a tomb which predated the Mausoleum, a tomb whose complexity has led some to wonder whether it belonged to Artemesia I.

The second thing to notice is the shallow indentation along the southern side of the burial chamber in the Mausoleum. This is thought to be evidence of the tomb-robbers tunneling, first overshooting the mark, then returning and knocking loose a block of stone to gain entry.

The Tomb in the Supermarket

On your way to picnic on the western shores of the Bodrum peninsula, pick up some bottled water, bread, and cheese at the **GİMA** supermarket west of the theater ruins (along the north side of the Kıbrıs Şehitleri highway). There you'll find a testament to the undiscovered history of the region, an in-situ Roman tomb in the northeast corner near the meat department. It could happen elsewhere; archaeological discoveries are made on building sites the world over. But this example is somehow fitting for modern Turkey, a present that fills in around the rubble of the past. Philosophizing aside, how often do you get your archaeology fix while grocery shopping? Go see it — it's just plain fun. Note that the Tomb in the Supermarket is much more impressive than the **Myndos Gate** located a few blocks south. A dig is under way at the gate, but there's precious little to see beyond a lot of dirt and rocks piled around some high stone walls.

Touring By Ferry

Consider using Bodrum's ferries for seeing some of the Aegean's most important ruins. The Bodrum-Körmen/Datça ferry, *M/F Fahri Kaptan 2*, is excellent for continuing on to **Cnidos**, with departures at 9 a.m. and 5 p.m. in both directions. The two-hour trip (round trip, one day) costs $9 per person, $28 with a car and driver. Automobile reservations are necessary. Dolmuş are usually on hand at Körmen to shuttle people on to Datça, whence you can get on a cruise to Cnidos. It's often easier to simply share a taxi.

The May-November ferry from Torba, a short dolmuş ride north of Bodrum, to Altınkum is ideal for seeing **Didyma** (it is locally called the Didim ferry). Once there it's easy to continue on to **Miletus** or **Priene** and loop back in time for the return trip. This ferry departs both ways at 9 a.m. and 5 p.m. on Mondays, Wednesdays, and Saturdays, with a same day, single person round trip for $13 and a one way trip for $8. Cars can travel on this ferry for the same rate as the Körmen fairy, but automobile reservations are a good idea.

Another car ferry departs Bodrum for the Greek island of Coş.

All ferries from Bodrum proper launch from the marina jutting out from the Castle of St. Peter, departing at 9 a.m., returning at 5 p.m. Contact the main office of the **Bodrum Ferryboat Guild**, Kale Cad. No. 12, *Tel. (252) 316-0882, Fax (252) 313-0205*, located near the marina on the waterfront road.

Nightlife & Entertainment

HADİ GARİ, *Cumhuriyet Caddesi, Tel. 252 313 1960/9087.*

This nightclub, located just opposite the moat of the Fortress of St. Peter on the eastern side, is slick and stylish, with exhaustive exterior spaces overlooking the water and building done up in glass, stone, and metal. Original art adorns the walls inside, as does extensive stereo equipment; jazz is played until midnight or so, at which point the music shifts to techno. Stop in for a drink after visiting the Fortress of St. Peter.

HELİKARNAS DISCO, *Cumhüriyet Cad. No. 128, Bodrum, Tel. 252 316 8000, Fax 252 316 1237. Expensive.*

There is dining here, but dining isn't why you come. Helikarnas booms into the early morning throughout the summer, with DJs from

London, whirring laser lights, hordes of people and a $10 cover. Lest you be concerned, uncool people are filtered out. Just so you know, Sundays are Ladies Night, Mondays are half-price, and Tuesdays offer free beer. A boat for Helikarnas departs from the center of the west dock.

Sports & Recreation

Beaches
Bodrum's own waterfront is neither sandy nor clean, so plan on swimming elsewhere. Beginning in mid-May, regular boats begin shuttling visitors to the best beach sites in the area, including **Bitez, Bağla,** and sand beaches at **Ortakent Yalısı** and **Akyarlar.** Dolmuş also serve **Karaincir** and **Akyarlar,** as well as places farther afield such as **Turgutreis.**

Boat Trips
In addition to the boats between Bodrum and the nearby beaches, there are day trips to **Kara Ada,** Black Island, beneath which is a cave with orange mud that is said to beautify the skin. A hot springs also issues from the cave into the sea. This is one of several stops on a day tour, the others varying according to the boat company.

Türkbükü is as close as Bodrum's peninsula comes to a charming hideaway. Türkbükü does not have its own beach, but offers small family pensions, swimming piers, and has regular minibuses to the beach at Turgutreis. The ruins of Karyanda are nearby.

You may want to spin out past old windmills to **Gümüşlük,** where you'll find the site of **Myndos** and a small, decent beach. Like Türkbükü, Gümüşlük has many small cottages that have mostly been snapped up by a London firm called Simply Turkey (*E-mail: turkey@simply-travel.com*), which has given them names such as "Jasmine Cottage" and "Villa Magnolia." Several restaurants line the shore, and you can wade out over a broken causeway to an island in the bay.

Other interesting peninsula towns include **Turgutreis,** with the peninsula's best beach, stuffed with tourists in the high season. Directly across the peninsula from Bodrum, the active seaport of **Torba** serves local islands and even the ruins of **Didyma** far across Güllük Bay.

Chapter 21

Owing to the **Ephesus** ruins, this is probably the most popular section of the Turkish coast. The sprawling beauty of this ancient city earns its place on any but the most cramped itinerary, despite thick summer crowds. Ephesus is the best recognized, but the ancient cities of **Priene**, **Miletus**, **Didyma**, and **Heracleia** hug the coast as well, while three of the greatest ruins in the interior – **Sardis**, **Aphrodısıas**, and **Pamukkale** – are just to the east. Between visits to ruins you can while away your time at excellent beaches.

In addition, there are dozens of virtually unvisited sites barely even mentioned on maps. This region has excellent public transportation and getting around is generally easy. The metropolis and air hub of **İzmir** is in the north, and Bodrum's new Güllük Airport provides quicker access to the south.

Beginning in Bodrum, the three principal sites south of Ephesus can be visited in a day, ending at Kuşadası or Selcuk. Didyma offers a slightly eerie glimpse into the maw of an oracle, Miletus is a landlocked wreck of stone, and Priene is a towering, column-strewn beauty. From Bodrum you can begin by taking the seasonal ferry to Altınkum and working your way north from Didyma. By this route you can even go to Didyma in the evening and check in at one of the pensions by the oracle, continuing on to Miletus and Priene the next day.

From the north consider the reverse: see Priene and Miletus, then make it to Didyma where you can sleep in the shadow of the oracle and visit in the morning.

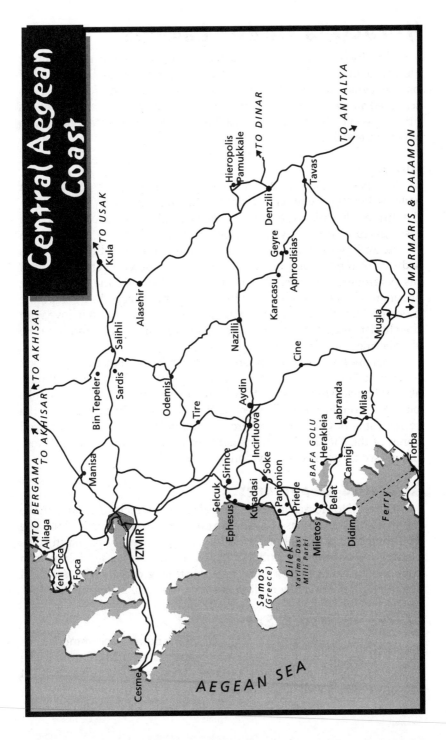

Heracleia Under Latmus

This city is one of the most potent examples of siltation in Asia Minor; Heracleia ad (under) Latmus was located on a great bay that extended past Miletus. Now the bay is an inland lake, and the former city is scattered along the shore and onto the mountain above. Heracleia offers little to people visiting for part of a day, but has a lot to offer hikers who stay for a few days.

History

The port at Heracleia was always secondary to the great port of Miletus, but the city remained viable into Byzantine times. The siltation that turned this inland sea into an lake was a deathblow to the city; as a result, its ruins are a fairly pure reflection of the Hellenistic city at this site.

According to mythology, a young shepherd named Endymion was seduced by numerous gods, as shepherds often were. When Zeus, one of his paramours, discovered that Hera had also paid the busy young shepherd a visit he put the boy into a perpetual sleep. As he slept, the moon goddess Selene happened upon him and she, too, fell in love with the charismatic shepherd. She descended to him nightly and bore the slumbering young man 50 daughters.

This myth was of great interest to anchorites and monks, who took to the quiet hillside caves of Mt. Latmos in great numbers. The mountain above Heracleia remains full of their small caves and chapels. The monks put a gloss on the tale by suggesting that Endymion had discovered the secret name of God, and gathered annually to listen to the supposed bones of the shepherd hum the name of God. We simply report these things, we do not necessarily understand them.

Arrivals & Departures

The road to Heracleia (the principal ruins of which are located in the town of Kapıkırı) begins at Bafa town on the south side of Lake Bafa. The 10 kilometre road is flat and winding, and was freshly paved in 2001. Getting to Heracleia by public transportation is not easy; dolmuş run back and forth only twice a day. If you plan to stay, contact your hotel and request a ride—for a few million lira your host will be happy to help.

Where to Stay & Eat

Kapıkırı, on the site of Heracleia, has some humble accommodations suited to people with an interest in hiking around Mt. Latmus. The village is riddled with huge boulders. There are no banks or ATM machines; this is well off the beaten path.

AGORA PENSION, *Kapıkırı Köyü, Milas. Tel. (252) 543-5445; Fax (252) 543-5567; Email: agora@urlaubstrip.de. Rooms: 14. Credit cards not accepted. Open year-round. Double: $30 (half-board).*

Established in 1994 by a local guide, the Agora is the best hotel in Kapıkırı, a small town in the shadow of Mt. Latmus. The Agora has eleven standard rooms, plus three more in small bungalows; all are decent and simple, with nice lace curtains, reading lights, and pine furniture. The hotel is arranged around a nice garden, and meals are served. A critical mass of good hiking guides and maps makes this a smart choice. If full, consider the **Pelikan Pension** *(Tel/Fax 252 543-5158)*.

CLUB NATURA OLIVA, *Kocaorman Mah. No. 10, Pınarcık Köyü, Milas. Tel. (252) 519-1072; Fax (252) 519-1015; Email: info@clubnatura.de; Web: www.clubnatura.de. Rooms: 38. Credit cards accepted. Open year-round. Double: $55 (full board).*

The Club Natura is located below the main Izmir-Milas highway, across the lake from the ruins at Heracleia. The Natura has been in operation for 15 years, and is located in a richly overgrown former quarry that was the source of marble for Didyma 2,300 years ago. The sprawl of little cabins and communal dining areas is particularly popular among Germans, with daily classes in yoga, astrology, and Tai Chi. Mercifully, perhaps, these classes are not available in English. In addition, there are daily trips across the lake to Heracleia for hiking or swimming, and kayaks available for day use. Many European guests stay for a week or more, but you're welcome to stay for only a night or two.

Seeing the Sights

The ruins of Heracleia are scattered over several acres, and it is difficult to make sense of them. An hour or two of walking will bring you to the Temple of Athena perched above Kapıkırı, the theatre up a road behind town, and along the massive, square-cut city walls that were erected during the reign of Lysimachus, soon after the death of Alexander the Great. The other significant ruins are located along the waterfront; there are Byzantine-era fortresses on two points of land jutting into the lake, and between them is the Sanctuary of Endymion. This is the sanctuary where monks once gathered to hear the hum of Endymion's bones.

In addition to the somewhat uninspiring set of ruins, Heracleia is an excellent base for hiking and swimming. For the latter, the best spot, bar none, is Ikiz Ada (twin islands). You can make your way there by foot in 1.5 hours, by kayak or canoe, or rent a motorboat (expect to pay $20-$30 for a day). Ikiz Ada features a small fortress on one island, a monastery on the other. The fortress is now connected to the mainland by a sandy isthmus.

It is no wonder that hiking is so popular here. If accompanied by a guide, you will be rewarded with the discovery of cave churches and dwellings. These are decorated with paintings and frescoes created by Christian anchorites, and in some cases the cave drawings date back to the Paleolithic era. You can arrange for hiking guides at the recommended hotels: rates for a three hour hike to the Paleolithic caves are a negotiable $25 with lunch; rates for a five hour hike to the cave church at Yediler are $40 with lunch.

Didyma

Herodotus lists eight sacred oracles in the ancient world, and **Didyma**, or Branchidae, was one of the greatest of these. In Hellenistic times it was housed in one of the world's largest buildings. There is no mention of how the oracles were selected, but at Didyma we know that the small spring and grove of olive trees were venerated even before the arrival of the Greeks. There's really not much to see at Didyma beyond the single, fascinating building.

History

This was a mystical place before the arrival of the Greeks, and some say it has remained mystical long after. The source of the mysticism is a fissure in the earth, at which priests labored, undertaking to glimpse the future. There is debate about whether oracles were originally Anatolian or Greek, but this one, at least, appears to have predated the Greeks. This is especially odd given that the Oracle at Delphi was already in use, and underscores the peculiarity of such a belief crossing cultural lines; we are told the Greeks and the Anatolian natives both revered oracles, as did the Anatolian-based Lydians. Only the Persians were skeptical, and Herodotus reports that they got theirs when the Oracle of Apollo at Delphi mowed down part of Xerxes' army with lightning and stones.

Didyma was a temple, not a town. Its inhabitants were the temple priests, whom Herodotus refers to as **Branchidae**. The name was a reference to their descent from Branchus, an oracular priest from Delphi who in his younger years was one of the many wandering shepherds seduced by a god, in his case Apollo. It was Branchus who founded the Temple of Apollo in the tenth century B.C., soon after Herodotus reports Athenian settlers to have seized Miletus and put the entire male population to the sword. Apollo, by the way, had led the settlers to Miletus in the form of a dolphin, and the Delphinium sanctuary at Miletus commemorates that (Delphi being the root of "dolphin," and the Delphi Oracle thus, too, related to the dolphin.)

The Oracular Temple at Didyma was not a city in its own right, but the property of **Miletus**, to which it was connected by a 20 kilometer road called the **Sacred Way** (basically the same as today's Highway 09-55). The oracle attracted pilgrims from throughout Asia Minor intent on glimpsing the future, each bringing a suitable gift. The Lydian King **Croesus** was a particularly generous donor. Despite favoring the Oracle of Apollo at Delphi (see Oracle sidebar), Herodotus reports that the king made sacrifices at Didyma "equal in weight and alike to those at Delphi." On one occasion alone Croesus offered 117 gold bricks, each two feet long, one foot wide and four inches high - in all more than 250 talents-weight - and donated a lion made of refined gold.

This wealth was tempting to the Milesians when they rose up against Persia in 499 B.C., but they refused to use the treasure at the Oracle to fund their war. Unfortunately, four years later King Darius destroyed Miletus, then looted and burned the oracle and its sacred grove. The great wealth was used to send a massive fleet against Athens, but this effort failed at the Battle of Marathon in 490.

The Oracle

That the oracles delivered judgments and forecasts of the future we know, but did it work? The Lydian King Croesus wondered the same thing in 555 B.C. and set about finding out. The King needed the best possible mystic intelligence before mounting a campaign against the Persians in the east, and he tested the oracles to find which was most accurate. He arranged for messengers to seek the answer to a single question from each of the world's oracles at the same time on the same day. On that day he secreted himself in the kitchen and set about an unguessable task, boiling diced tortoise and lamb in a bronze cauldron.

As the weeks passed his messengers returned with various answers that disappointed the king. Finally, the messenger returned from Delphi with the answer "A smell steals over my senses, the smell of a hard-shelled tortoise, seethed in bronze with the meat of lambs, mingled together." Croesus, impressed, did business almost exclusively with the Delphic oracle thereafter, flooding Delphi with golden gifts and pestering the oracle with repeated questions about the campaign he was considering. As related in the story of the campaign on Sardis, Croesus fatally misinterpreted the oracle's answers and was crushed by the Persians.

The Oracle lapsed into disuse, but, according to one of his chroniclers, with the appearance of Alexander the Great the Oracle's fortunes were restored. The water of the sacred spring suddenly flowed anew at his approach, and the Oracle anticipated that Alexander would be victorious in an upcoming battle. Alexander was duly impressed by this and helped fund the reconstruction of the temple. The temple's association with Miletus continued, and under the Roman Emperor **Trajan** (98-117) the sacred way between the city and the oracle was paved with stone. There were repeated upgrades to the structure, but it is largely the one designed soon after Alexander's time.

The Persians, Celts (285 B.C.), and Goths (237 A.D.) all managed to severely damage the temple, but it took the Christians to wreck it for good. Under the staunchly Christian Theodosius the Great (378-395) the temple had to be abandoned. The rise of Christianity, combined with the steep decline of Miletus, resulted in the abandonment and neglect of Didyma.

Arrivals & Departures

By Bus
Dolmuş from Milas and Söke go to Didyma (Didim), continuing on to the beach at Altinkum. Dolmuş between Akköy and Didyma are frequent, but reaching Akköy from Miletus on public transportation takes time. It's a good time to spring for a cab. See the Miletus section for further information.

In the summer season a ferryboat plies back and forth between Altınkum and Torba on the Bodrum peninsula, departing Altınkum in the morning and returning in the evening. The cost is $5 per person. Service is canceled in the stormy and tourist-less winter months.

Packaged, unguided dolmuş trips to Didyma, Miletus, and Priene typically cost about $16 per person for one or two hours at each site. It isn't a bad option, but it dramatically restricts your ability to see the ruins, particularly at Priene and Miletus. These tours can be arranged through your hotel or the local dolmuş station in Selcuk, Kuşadası, Didim, Söke, or even at Didyma. Larger groups can bargain the price down.

By Car
The direct route to Didyma is from the main coast road, 525, via Akköy. A smaller road runs parallel to 525, connecting Didyma (Didim/Yenihısar) with Miletus and Priene. See information about the car ferry below.

By Ferry
A ferry serves Altınkum from Torba, just a few kilometers from Bodrum on the Bodrum peninsula. Service is limited to Monday, Wednes-

day and Saturday between May and November. Ferries depart in both directions at 9 a.m. and 5 p.m., and the one way, one person cost is $8. The cost for a car and driver is $28; car reservations should be booked with the Bodrum office, *Tel. 252 316 0882.*

Where to Stay & Eat

ORACLE PANSİYON, *Didim. Tel. (256) 811-0270; Fax (256) 811-0105. Rooms: 18. Credit cards not accepted. Open year-round. Double: $20.*

The Oracle Pension is not particularly sophisticated. There is no Internet access, no DVD player. Rooms are spartan, featuring a bed, a window, and a shower. We know of nowhere else with a setting so breathtaking.

The Oracle is perched above the excavated ruin of the Oracle at Didyma, whose great walls and columns soar high above. The large, enclosed patio looks out over this, as do the second floor rooms. The patio offers a grand fireplace, low Turkish couches, plants, and the considerable low-key hospitality of owner Mahmut Gönül, a schoolteacher. The evening wind blows in over the ruins, keeping the non-air conditioned rooms reasonably cool even in the dog days.

Selected one of our favorite budget hotels.

MEDUSA HOUSE, *Didim. Tel. (256) 813-4491; Fax none; Email: kirasus@aol.com. Rooms: 14. Credit cards accepted. Closed in winter. Double: $24.*

The Medusa is located behind the Oracle Pension. It's a lovely building clad in stone, but it hasn't the immediacy to the Temple that the Oracle does, and we have had complaints that it's not particularly clean.

AŞIK RESTAURANT, *Didim. Tel. (256) 811-0031. Credit cards not accepted. Inexpensive.*

The Aşık is located opposite the Oracle Pansiyon, also facing the Oracle ruins. Food is cheap and plentiful, all you can eat for $5.

Seeing the Sights

The **Temple of Apollo at Didyma**, which may have never been completed, was conceived to be as grand as the Temple of Artemis at Ephesus, and is far more intact than that vanished structure. The Oracle's massive temple had 122 columns, a forest of stone. Today the forest is felled, the columns broken. A colonnade two columns deep surrounds the central area, and the entrance is five columns deep. Climbing the stair and entering into the interior you wind toward the small antechamber, where two standing columns give way to a door; this was the spot where visitors would ask the oracle their questions. A staircase leads down to the open central area, the site of the sacred spring and an olive tree, or possibly an interior grove. A statue of Apollo was housed here. Adjacent to the entrance small staircases once led down to the fissure beneath the temple.

The structure at Didyma now is basically the same one begun soon after Alexander's arrival, and on which work was done for centuries. The temple is Ionic, quite traditional and quite Greek, and it relied on the great height of its columns, rather than its location, to impress the visitor. The exterior had a band of friezes above the columns, one of which, the Medusa head, is near the entrance. For the proper perspective, duck down and look up at the face the way it was designed to be seen, from below. The relief is much improved. The marble work throughout is of high quality, much of it coincident with the most skilled work at Aphrodisias and possibly supplied by that inland city.

Two roads of note began here. The first, lined with statues, descended to the sea. The statues were stolen in the name of British archaeology in the early 19th century. The second, the paved **Sacred Way** leading to Miletus, is being excavated across the present-day street from the temple.

Miletus

Miletus, the most powerful of the three cities, is today the least impressive. If you are at Priene with the intention of visiting Didyma (or vice versa), then by all means visit. Like so many ruins, Miletus benefits from time spent wandering around.

History

Miletus' former situation was ideal for a settlement, a long isthmus into one of the Aegean's finest bays topped by a hill. It requires a Cray II supercomputer mind to recreate today, but Miletus was both beautiful and prosperous.

Homer mentions a Carian contingent among the Trojan allies, referring to Miletus in the same breath, but this suffers from Homer's having written his centuries-old account at least 400 years after the fact. In any event, Homer was not impressed with the leader of the Carians, a man named Nastes who "came like a girl to the fighting, in golden raiment." Nastes was duly slain by Achilles, who paraded around with his foppish armor.

Despite fighting on the side of the Trojans, Miletus made some of the most concrete gains as a result of Troy's defeat. With Troy out of the way, the furiously colonizing Milesians were able to establish towns at Cyzicus on the Sea of Marmara and at Sinop on the Black Sea; but then these Milesians were probably Greeks, and no longer Carians at all. Miletus' fortunes improved, not those of its Carian population. This is dramatically supported by Herodotus, who says that the Greeks massacred every male in the city and took the women as their wives; and that, as a result, the women of Miletus would neither eat nor sit with their own husbands.

Miletus was the principal maritime city along the Aegean coast when the Persian King Cyrus wrested control of the area from Lydian King Croesus, and it was always a source of unrest. The Milesians, almost always in close contact with the cities of Greece, eventually stoked the Ionian revolt against Darius. One of the key moments in the ill-fated uprising concerned Miletus' relationship with its Oracle at Didyma.

Great wealth was stored at Didyma, including Croesus' spectacular gifts and other prizes from as far away as Egypt. In 499 B.C., the Milesians were sorely tempted to seize the treasure and build a great navy. With such a navy, some argued, the coastal cities considering revolt against Persian rule could establish mastery of the sea. The people of Miletus, however, feared the wrath of the Oracle more than the possibility of defeat. Within five years the revolt had ended in disaster, with King Darius himself on hand for the naval defeat of Miletus and the comprehensive annihilation of the city. The population was massacred and enslaved, and for good measure Darius looted and destroyed the Oracle at Didyma. The priests of the temple willingly handed over their treasures, and were thus branded traitors and forced to flee into Persia in later years.

Miletus was rebuilt and repopulated, and it slipped Persian control after Darius' army was beaten at Marathon. For a full century Miletus struggled to regain its former status, and had made great strides when the King's Peace of 387 B.C. returned the city to Persian control. Perhaps Miletus had reformed its rebellious ways, or perhaps a large Persian garrison left no option, but during Alexander the Great's campaign 54 years later Miletus chose to contest his passage in concert with a powerful naval force. With Alexander encamped by the city the Milesians wavered, offering Miletus as a neutral port, but that wasn't good enough; the next morning Alexander's armies stormed the walls and took the city. For once the population of men was not systematically massacred.

Alexander continued quickly south, while Miletus set once more to putting itself in order. After the dissolution of the Kingdom of Pergamon, Miletus passed under Roman control in 133 B.C. Shortly afterwards, Miletus finally picked a winner, backing Rome against Mithradites VI in the Pontic Wars while neighbors like Ephesus backed Pontus. Rome was grateful for the support, and Roman rule was good to Miletus. It was during the Roman period that most of the current structures were built. It was also at this time that St. Paul passed through Miletus and spoke to the Ephesians.

Miletus' final undoing was much less cruel than those at the hands of Darius and the Greeks before him, it was simply siltation. The only thing that isn't difficult to conceive of about Miletus is its harbor's relentless recession to the west. Following the loss of Miletus' harbor it faded from historical view. George Ostrogorsky's definitive Byzantine history mentions the city only once, and then indirectly, as a site near a minor Byzantine principality following the fall of Constantinople in 1204. That Miletus remained mildly important is certain; there is a Byzantine fortress atop the acropolis as evidence, and the fortress, Kastrion, was apparently occupied into the 13th century, but it may have been vacated before the Turks occupied the region.

Arrivals & Departures
By Bus
Miletus is the weak link for cheap transportation. Dolmuş serve Miletus from Söke and from Priene/Güllübahçe in the north, hanging a Balat or Milet sign in their window. Once in Miletus, however, continuing southward to Didyma is tricky since you must wait to get to Balat a few kilometers south, then wait again for the next dolmuş to Akköy, then wait yet again for a dolmuş to Didyma, whether Didim- or Altınkum-bound.

One solution is to spring for a taxi from Miletus to Akköy, about 10 kilometers south. Akköy has relatively frequent service to Didyma, or to Söke if you've had it and you want to go home.

By Car
From Priene, continue toward the sea, away from Güllübahçe. A few minutes after passing Atburgazı a road signed "Milet" and "Balat" forks off to the left, across the plains. About 15 kilometers along another signed road directs you the remaining few kilometers to Miletus.

Seeing the Sights
On your way to Miletus from Priene you pass the island of Lade, the site of two historical naval battles. The "island," however, is now a nondescript knoll, helping set the tone for Miletus. Miletus was not only left high and dry, but, like so many coastal ruins, picked over by early archaeologists on behalf of their native countries.

Near the car park get your bearings by the map and the great open face of the theater. The **theater** is immediately compelling, but with its sea view stolen it's slightly forlorn. Begin by ascending the theater to the fortress, after which you have a long, clockwise descent. The theater had a capacity as great as the theater at Ephesus and was clad entirely in marble. It was successively rebuilt and improved over the course of 600 years, with the final changes in the fourth century A.D.

The **fortress** is just a shell, offering a good opportunity to understand Miletus' layout. The military harbor was located opposite the theater, with two great lion statues at each side of the harbor mouth. A raised road now cuts across the mouth of the harbor. Beyond the harbor the ground rises, but the sea once encircled this, too. The neck of the isthmus was located to the south, in the direction of Balat and Didyma. Walls encircled the entire isthmus, and they are still in evidence along most of their course. The main section of the city lay in the low area at the head of the former military harbor, continuing around toward the car park.

From the fortress, head down the slope opposite the theater to the raised road crossing the mouth of the harbor. Just after you begin crossing the road look to your right for the top of one of the two lion statues, both of which have started dramatically settling. The second is almost covered in mud, the top of its head poking out just after leaving the road and turning right. If you have plenty of time you can double back from the statue and follow the peninsula around the long way, returning on the opposite side. Otherwise skirt the edge of the former bay past a Byzantine church toward the mass of ruins at the center of the former town. Here, during most of the year you will find the former marketplace flooded, the ironic twist for a city left stranded by siltation: the water is land, the land, water.

The **gymnasium** is the first well-preserved building you come to, followed by the **nymphaeum**, or fountain. Signs give some hints about your whereabouts. The area is difficult to navigate but its tumbled ruins are appealing. The finest monument in the city, the market gate, once stood to the southeast of these buildings, facing the open area from the side and marking the beginning of the processional to Didyma. Picking your way back to dry land, the **baths of Faustina** are a particular highlight of Miletus, a remarkably large baths complex built on behalf of the wife of Marcus Aurelius. Within the bath is a statue of a lion and of the local river god, Meander; given the city's sorry state, the river god was not appeased. The **Delphinium** is alongside the bath, a sanctuary for Apollo who, in the form of a dolphin, led the colonists here.

Other highlights include the nearby **Ilyas Bey Mosque**, at the end of a winding path from the baths, away from the theater. This abandoned building has some excellent stonework and is cool in the summer heat. Also worth finding is the **Temple of Athena**, across the road on the far side of the museum. This is on the site of the original Mycenean settlement. If you continue to the walls, or get out as you drive by them in the direction of Balat, you will be rewarded with a view of foundations of the six-foot thick walls that Alexander stormed during his siege.

Priene

Priene is well worth the trip out of your way. This Hellenistic fortress city is a picturesque gem, perched on a steep bluff beneath a towering 1,217 foot crag.

History

The city clearly owed its existence to maritime trade, having little room to spare for agriculture in the immediate vicinity. The bay that it once served, however, was well and truly silted up by the time Strabo happened by at the end of the first century B.C. Though the silting destroyed the town's fortunes, it saved the Hellenistic ruins for posterity; neither the Romans nor anyone else took much interest in building atop the original ruins once Priene's usefulness as a port ended.

Priene's still-evident beauty was attended by its citizens' reputation for intelligence. Foremost among them was Bias, one of the Seven Sages (see the *Bias Toward Shrewdness* sidebar). Priene was responsible for administering the **Panionium**, a congress of coastal Greek cities that gathered on the opposite side of Mt. Mycale. On a clear day one of the other principal members of the Panionium, Miletus, is visible across the valley floor.

Priene and Miletus had an often adversarial relationship as they battled for commerce. Miletus was a huge, economically dominant city, however, and when Priene wasn't directly under Miletus' thumb Priene still usually had the worst of it. Priene's military history is punctuated by its affable surrender to Alexander the Great, who graciously supplied enough funds to Priene's new Temple of Athena that the structure was dedicated to him. After his welcome in the city in 334 B.C., having secured his flank, Alexander marched around the bay and, to the delight of the citizens of Priene, besieged the stubbornly pro-Persian Miletus. The distant land-sea battle must have been a fine spectacle from atop Priene's acropolis. Alexander, incidentally, won.

When Alexander arrived, Priene was in the act of building the city at its current site. The original site is probably buried in the alluvial plain below and farther inland, and the new city was probably, like Ephesus to the north, chasing after a receding sea. The rebuilding occurred at roughly the same time of rebuilding at Cnidos and Helicarnassus in the south, and, like Cnidos, was done on a grid pattern. Although silting eventually left even the new city commercially and strategically bankrupt, it left its charm intact. Priene is thick with crafted marble and stone, including a playground of column drums by the Temple of Athena. The adventurous can spend hours wandering around the forested upper slopes of the bluff, and even take a winding stair up the right side of the crag to the dizzying acropolis.

Arrivals & Departures

By Bus

Dolmuş run regularly from the well-signed dolmuş stop in nearby Söke, and Söke can be reached from anywhere in the region. Don't mistake one of the small dolmuş stops for the main transit hub, a large municipal parking lot with dolmuş arranged by destination.

By Car

From the north, take the main (525) road south from Söke toward Savulca/Bodrum. Three miles after passing through tiny Savulca, take a right turn on the Güllübahçe road and drive ten kilometers to the other side of Güllübahçe, where the familiar yellow signs direct you up the hill to Priene. If you are quite adventurous, you can try the mountain road from Güzelçamlı on the other side of the mountain range at the entrance to the Dilek Yarımadası Milli Parki. According to maps, it passes the ruins of the Panionium on the north slope and descends to Atburgazı, where it meets the Priene road three kilometers west of Priene.

Where to Stay & Eat

The most inviting spot for a bite to eat is **Şelale Restaurant** at the base of the hill. In the dog days you may be unable to resist the cascade of water and greenery and the shaded patio here. The Şelale has good food, but it isn't a bad idea to visit one of the small local shops for some bread, fruit, water and a bottle of Villa Doluca wine and pack it along with you to the lightly forested upper slopes of the ruin.

The pensions in Güllübahçe, at the base of Priene's hill, are good only in a pinch.

Seeing the Sights

After entering Priene through a gap in the battered old walls near the East Gate, the main path takes you to a signed intersection. Turn left and descend one block to the **bouleterion**, a small theater, on your right. This building was the meeting place of the city council, erected around 170 B.C. and holding about 500 people. The intimate space opening out on the valley and sea below is typical of the aesthetically pleasing structures in the city. The small theater structure was covered with a wooden roof, which would have been an unfortunate addition on clear days when the view of the cliff face above is as appealing as the land and seascape below.

As you may have gathered on the walk in, the city is laid out on a perfect grid pattern despite the difficulties of the sloped site. Hippodamus of Miletus is responsible for this contribution to civic planning. The small ruins to the left of the bouleuterion, the way you entered, is the **prytaneion**, or city administrative office. The city's sacred flame was located here, and members of the city council would dine by its light. Directly in front of the bouleuterion and across the street is the Ionic **Temple of Zeus**. This temple was partially demolished when a small Byzantine fort was erected that overlapped its east side. German archaeologists did further damage, seeking to out-plunder the British in the European's bizarre antiquity race. The altar remains.

Ahead and out of sight against the lower city walls are the **gymnasium** and the **stadium**. If you aren't on a tight schedule the steep walk down to these buildings is worthwhile, though less so than the hike to the summit. The two old structures formed the academic and athletic heart of the city. The gymnasium was both an athletic training facility and an institution of higher learning. While in this building, note various inscriptions etched into the interior walls of the gymnasium - they are roughly equivalent to "Phileas Son of Pausanius was here." The 600 foot long stadium was the site of all sorts of athletic contests, ranging from boxing and javelin hurling to running and the pancration - a no holds barred wrestling/kickboxing match.

About 750 feet west (seaward) along the road in front of the bouleuterion is the **House of Alexander**. This building was clearly venerated, but there is argument as to whether it was out of respect for Alexander's brief stay here or because this was a shrine to gods of the underworld. The underworld adherents use the small fissure in the floor of the building as exhibit A of their Chthonic argument - supporters of the thesis that this house was associated with some form of underworld worship cite the small fissure in the floor as evidence.

A hundred feet uphill of this on a flat open space northwest of the Bouleuterion is the **Temple of Athena**, a good place to sit on a fallen column drum and rest. The Temple of Athena is the city's centerpiece, a large complex with a splendid view. A handful of the tumbled column drums have been collected and set up to reproduce five columns, but the original temple boasted 61 more, in six rows of eleven. The 120 foot long temple was designed by Pytheos, and Priene's city fathers were probably impressed that he had one face of the Mausoleum at Helicarnassus - one of the Seven Wonders of the World - on his resume. Unlike the mausoleum, this was a classic Ionic temple. City fathers dedicated the temple in Alexander's name, thankful for his financial assistance in its construction, but the inscription is now in the British Museum in London. Just below the temple is the footprint of a thinner, longer Doric colonnade whose thick column drums are mixed in with the Ionic pieces.

If you head through the scrub and pine trees directly uphill from the Temple of Athena you will arrive at the **temple of Demeter and Kore**. The two goddesses were linked with the prosperity of crops, and the sanctuary here has a pretty situation but is otherwise enigmatic. Herodotus singles out the rites of Demeter as particularly secret, and the Egyptians called the acts of Demeter - or Isis - worship of the "Mysteries." A contemporary historian, W. Berkert, reports that the sea god Poseidon assumed the form of a horse and mated with Demeter, and rituals may have celebrated this unlikely union. All the uncharacteristically tight-lipped Herodotus will say is that the ritual was "an exhibition of the gods' sufferings."

Rounding the hill and ascending to the east you arrive at the area where the eastern defensive walls meet the cliff face. There is a defensive tower here alongside settling basins that purified water entering the city by aquaduct. A path follows a mildly harrowing route to the small acropolis, which is also walled.

Looking up at the crag from below, note the squared section slightly recessed into the natural rock; this was probably the site of a statue or monument, the ancient equivalent of a big letter "P" in the local high school's colors.

Bias Toward Shrewdness

Priene's most famous son was **Bias**, considered one of the wisest men of ancient times. Herodotus passes along accounts of his wisdom in **The History**, including this exchange with the powerful Lydian King, Croesus:

"After defeating the cities along the Aegean coast, the Lydian King Croesus returned to the inland capital of Sardis and began contemplating a campaign against the island kingdoms of Greece. Upon hearing that Croesus was preparing to create a navy, Bias approached him and said "Sir, the islanders are buying up ten thousand horses, as they have in mind to make a campaign on Sardis and yourself." Croesus imagined he spoke seriously and said "Would that the gods would put this idea into their heads; that islanders should come against the sons of the Lydians with horses." Bias answered "Sir, you seem to me to pray very earnestly that you might catch the islanders riding horses on the mainland, and your hope in this is very reasonable. But do you believe that the islanders have any other matter for prayer than that they will catch the Lydians at sea and so take vengeance on yourself?" Croesus was extraordinarily pleased with this answer and gave up his ship-building."

After descending you'll find Priene's main theater is slightly lower than the temple of Demeter and Kore, around the ridge toward the entrance. This fine old building is surrounded by small trees and is a good place for a rest. Five chairs are still arranged around the floor of the building for VIPs, a status symbol as well as a dubious perk - no napping during drawn-out speeches - and they seem to establish beyond a doubt that the Romans' violent forms of circus entertainment were not on display here. Behind the stage is another Byzantine addition to the city, a small church that constituted the local Bishopric.

Kusadasi

"Make your spending a memorable experience," chirps the Kuşadası tourist bureau's brochure, which is your first clue to the nature of this bustling port. We recommend you don't make your spending a memorable experience here, as the prices are inflated. If you aren't foolish enough to pay $75 for a standard ceramic plate, someone from one of the luxury cruise liners is and - poof! - there goes the shopowners' incentive to haggle.

Frankly, aside from being home to the Kismet Hotel, we don't like Kuşadası much. Selçuk is better in every regard but nightlife. Still, if you would like to use Kuşadası as a base, it's not bad.

History

Kuşadası's history is relatively short, having been ushered in by the siltation at Ephesus. Upon conceding the uselessness of Ephesus' receding port the Byzantines began settling here, referring to the city as Scala Nova, or New Ephesus. The fortress was probably constructed by the Byzantines, but it was modified and improved by the Venetians and, later, the Ottomans.

In recent history, Kuşadası was a pit stop on the great hippie trail of Western backpackers. The very qualities that made it so popular have been, alas, overrun by development.

Arrivals & Departures

Kuşadası is less convenient than Selcuk, and arriving from the north or east you will pass through Selcuk on your way here. The strip of hotels along the coast between Selcuk and Kuşadası offers holiday and tour group accommodation, and if you plan to stay put awhile they can be a good option; otherwise, don't pay for amenities you won't use.

Where to Stay

Kuşadası has long since surrendered its former "sedate" status for "rambunctious." We prefer Selcuk for its proximity to Ephesus and its smaller size. Within Kuşadası, the anachronistically peaceful Kismet is an eddy of calm.

KISMET HOTEL, *Akyar Mevkii, Yacht Marina, Kuşadası. Tel. (256) 614-2005; Fax (256) 614-4914; Email: kismet@efes.net.tr; Web: www.kismet.com.tr. Rooms: 102. Credit cards accepted. Open April-October. Double: $110. Half-board available. Restaurant.*

The Kismet is one of the country's best hotels. The 35 year-old Kismet is the grand old institution of Kuşadası, a sparkling relic of old world calm and decorum that has seen guests such as Jimmy Carter and Queen Elizabeth II. A daughter of the last Ottoman sultan opened this hotel with her husband, and it remains in the family.

In a region where three-year-old hotels appear tattered, the Kismet is natty, with marvelously manicured grounds and a charm like San Simeon. The rooms are attractive and peaceful, with shutters that open and allow the sea breezes to blow through. It is isolated on a hill overlooking the Kusadası Marina, and it is the ideal English colonial location for an afternoon gin and tonic under the trees.

The Kismet has undergone a mild change, adding an elegant new swimming pool compound just below the parking lot. The tennis court is one of the most beautiful anywhere, but a mis-hit backhand will float to Egypt. Open April-October.

Selected as one of our favorite small hotels.

CLUB CARAVANSERAIL, *Atatürk Bulvarı No.2 09400, Kuşadası. Tel. (256) 614-4115; Fax (256) 614-2423. Rooms:40. Credit cards accepted. Double: $85. Restaurant.*

Built during the heyday of the Ottoman Empire, the building is a sturdy old fixture on the Kuşadası waterfront. The wagonloads of traders have given way to busloads of tourists, but if you're so inclined, this is the place to indulge in a late night belly-dancing experience, which is part of the extra $30 price for an open buffet in the courtyard garden. They will cram fun down your throat here until late, and your nicely furnished room will shudder and throb until midnight. Best not to be in it.

DERİCİ HOTEL, *Türkmen Mah. Atatürk Bulv. No. 40, Kuşadası, Tel. 256 614 8222, Fax 256 614 8226. Rooms: 90. Double: $50. Restaurant.*

The Derici is the best of the standard hotels in Kuşadası, with clean, pleasant rooms and a view out over Kuşadası's waterfront.

HOTEL ROSE, *Aslanlar Cad., Aydınlık Sok. No. 7, Tel. 256 614 1111. Double: $12.*

Given Kuşadası's backpacking legacy you'd expect more budget hotels to have figured out how to do it right; unfortunately this is one of the few. It has the slew of comforts that you just don't find in expensive places; laundry, English movies on the VCR, discounts on long distance bus trips, and cooking by the proprietor's mom. The Rose is just up the hill behind the tourism information office. The Hotel Park, just up the street, is another decent budget spot.

Slightly more expensive, with an excellent view, is the **HAZGÜL PANSİYON**, *Tel. 256 614 3641*, up the hill to the south. Hazgül is closed in the off season.

Where to Eat

Most hotels offer dinner as part of a half-board price, and many of the buffet extravaganzas are excellent (the Kismet distinguishes itself). The reasons to eat out are to dine at one of the fish restaurants, enjoy some entertainment like that at the Caravanserail, or to get something cheap. You'll find many of the latter in the disorienting streets of Kuşadası's bazaar.

KAZIM USTA, *Liman Cad., Kuşadası, Tel. 256 614 1725. Moderate-Expensive.*

Asked where the best restaurant is, most locals will reverentially point toward one of the restaurants on the waterfront by the harbor master's office. This is one of these, and a veteran of the fish restaurant trade. You should find the food delicious and the service very good. Agree on what you're paying up front, although the Kazım Usta usually makes prices fairly clear. To find out what's in season ask *"Mevsimlık ne var?"* **ALİ BABA**, nearby, also has a good reputation.

ADA RESTAURANT, *Güvercin Island, Kuşadası, Tel. 256 614 1725. Moderate.*

You'll want to walk out to the island anyway, so you might as well take the opportunity to eat here. The island has had a thorough going over by the municipality with paths and tea gardens, but it remains a pretty spot, benefiting from the charm of the old harbor fortress. The food is at least as good as the food in town, and no more expensive. There are several good, cheap restaurants tucked in elsewhere on the small island.

Seeing the Sights

The three cities of Priene, Miletus and Didyma constitute a full day trip from Kuşadası. The thin layer of ruins at Panionia is discussed below, as is the source of Kuşadası's rise to prominence, Ephesus.

Pigeon Fortress, the small castle at the southern end of Kuşadası's harbor, is a Byzantine fortification, now given over to a collection of small çay bahçesi (tea gardens) and restaurants (including the Ada Restaurant, reviewed above). The main keep is kept locked tight, but the fortress remains relatively intact, including, even, the pigeons.

In the summer, ferries depart to **Samos Island** in Greece at 8:30 a.m. and 5 p.m., with a two hour travel time. Departures from Samos are on the same schedule. Ferries may not depart between November 1 and 31 March due to weather or lack of bookings, but there tends to be one ferry daily.

Contact one of the travel agencies to find out if a departure is planned. One way trips cost $30, with $35 for same day returns and $50 for open ended returns. A visa is required. Contact any of the following: **Azim Travel**, Liman Cad. Yayla Pasaj, *Tel. 256 614 1553*; **Diana Travel**, Kıbrıs Cad. No. 4, *Tel. 256 614 1399*; or **Scalanova Travel**, Yalı Cad. No. 17, *Tel. 256 614 3268.*

Nightlife & Entertainment

If you are staying in Kuşadası you should take advantage of the bar scene. Even the fairy tale fortress just offshore on tiny **Pigeon Island** throbs with dance music late at night.

One convenient pub crawl opportunity is on **Eski Pazar Cad.**, inexplicably a shamrock-spangled Irish wonderland. The gauntlet of bars includes Molly Malone's, The Green House, Shamrock Steak House, The Irish Watering Hole, Murphy's, The Asgard Irish Pub, and the Log Cabin Irish Bar. You walk in one way and lurch out the other.

Sports & Recreation

Kustur Plaj to the north of town is a popular beach, as is the slightly better beach to the south, **Kadınlar Plaj**. Both are below a row of hotels. The best beaches are at the national park (see below). Dolmuş serve both beaches, with trips to Kadınlar every half hour in the summer.

You can combine a day at a relatively isolated swimming area on the coast with a visit to an obscure ruin. The national park at **Dilek Yarımdası Milli Parki** is 26 kilometers south of Kuşadası and accessible by dolmuş. The town of **Güzelcamlı**, located just outside the park, is on the slope below the ruins of **Panionia**. Panionia was the meeting place of the **Ionian League**, and, like Letoon in Lycia, the spiritual capital. The area is dense with foliage, and has not been picked over by archaeologists. There was temple to Poseidon, he of the seas and the earthshaking, at the city. The north slope of the 4,000 foot Samsun Dağı also has the remnants of fortifications that once stood watch over the straits of Samos.

If you have a rented vehicle, you can hazard the route that is supposed to exist past Panionia, over the hill and down to Priene on the far side. The park, with its numerous coves and small beaches, shares Panionia's lush plant life. The sand beaches further along are, predictably, more secluded, but the whole lot is a step up from the strips of sand beneath the new hotels.

On weekends the national park is packed. If you are with a group of four, consider shelling out $40 for a full-day taxi to the park. Dolmuş usually serve Güzelcamlı and turn back, except in the high season. Some dolmuş will post "Güzelcamlı/Milli Park" signs, indicating they shuttle you directly to the beach.

Shopping

As noted, the literature advises us to make our spending a memorable experience, so let's start there. Kuşadası is thick with bars, nightclubs, and shops. Cruise ships and bus tours dump people here just long enough to pick up food, meerschaum pipes, leather goods and Turkish rugs. It is, for many who arrive by cruise ship, the only exposure to Turkey's goods and price structure, and the shopowners have discovered that they can charge a lot. "You will enjoy the fun of bargaining with smiling salesmen," wheedles the Kuşadası tourism bureau, but they're smiling a little too broadly. Unless you're in Turkey for a day and that day is spent in Kuşadası, consider waiting to make that big purchase.

The **Doluca Şarap Fabrikası** (wine plant) is located just outside of town to the south. If you stop in during business hours and boldly ask around, they'll happily let you taste some of the local stuff.

Selcuk, Sirince, & the Ephesus Ruins

Selcuk *is* **Ephesus**, located at the site of the original Ephesus settlement. Ephesus is now located little more than two kilometers away, as kings kept scooting it in the direction of the receding harbor. They didn't scoot it fast enough, unfortunately, and the city died. In addition to the Ephesus ruins just down the road there are several wonderful things to see within Selcuk itself.

Today, the Byzantine Ayasoluk Castle commands the crest of the main hill, not far above the nicely restored ruins of the Basilica of St. John, which is itself just above the İsa Bey Mosque. Together with the town's outstanding Ephesus Museum, you might enjoy Selcuk as much as the famous Ephesus.

The mass of historical sites has generated a powerful tourist gravity, drawing hundreds of thousands of people annually. As a result, Selcuk has its share of aggressive lads selling carpets, hotel rooms, meals, and guided tours to vacationing Westerners. They are a persistent nuisance in town, but it's pretty peaceful outside of the town center.

If it's peace you want, you may wish to head up a winding 8 km road from Selçuk past the remains of an aqueduct and groves of olive, fig, and orange trees to the formerly Greek hillside village of Şirince. Accommodations there have recently blossomed as money has come in from tourists seeking out the locally produced wines. Tour buses disgorge people there for day trips and they leave a few hours later; you can spend the night.

Arrivals & Departures

By Bus

The main bus station in Selcuk doubles as the dolmuş/minibus stop for most routes. (Şirince is an exception, with dolmuş leaving from the railway station. The last dolmuş from Şirince back to Selcuk is 8p.m. in the summer, 5 p.m. in the off-season.) The bus station is at the northeast corner of the town's main intersection; here in the city that had so much to do with civilization's birth, the intersection is decorated with a dramatically inappropriate monument to Fulda tires.

Selcuk is a good place to catch buses in every direction, since it is at the junction of the main highway and the southbound coastal roads. Fares: Izmir $2, Bodrum $6.50, Marmaris $8, Fethiye $8.50, Antalya $10, Cappadocia $17, İstanbul $15.

By Car

Selcuk is on the main İzmir-Aydın road, just 50 miles south of İzmir and 55 miles west of Aydın. Selcuk is essentially the end of the line on this main road; hereafter it dives inland to Denizli, then cuts through the interior to Antalya.

To get to Şirince from Selcuk, head north out of town on the road to İzmir, and follow the signs that will take you east. The quality of roads along the coast to the south falls off slightly, but is not bad; Kuşadası is 21 kilometers, Bodrum 163 kilometers, and Marmaris 230 kilometers.

Orientation

Selcuk's sites are mostly clustered around the hill in the center of town. The tourist office is across the main road from the bus station in the direction of "Efes/Artemesion," *Tel. (232) 892-6945*. The Selcuk Devlet Hastanesi, which has a new emergency room: *Tel. (232) 892-0736*.

Where to Stay

Tourists flock to this area, and the coast from Selçuk to the far side of Kuşadası is littered with big hotels. With rare exceptions, the quality of these big hotels is poor—we recommend the small, marvelous lodging options in and around Selcuk.

HOTEL NİLYA, *Atatürk Mah, 1051 Sok. No. 7, Selcuk. Tel. (232) 892-9081; Fax (232) 892-9080; Email: nilya_ephesus@hotmail.come. Rooms: 12. Credit cards accepted. Open March-October. Double: $45 (breakfast included). Open year-round.*

The Nilya, opened in 1997, was a welcome addition to Selcuk. Nilgun Kaytancı has created a fine, relaxing inn on the back side of the Selcuk hill looking west. The rooms are clean and cool (the upstairs rooms have fans, the downstairs rooms do not need them) in the summer, featuring comforter covers, iron bedsteads, lace tablecloths, and old oil lamps. The hotel is unpretentious, but there are nice touches everywhere. For reading or relaxing the sitting room is ideal, a jumble of Turkish textiles cover the couches and tables, and you'll find wrought iron lamps and metal and wooden knick-knacks in every corner. In many ways, it feels like you're staying with a friend—you'll be offered a glass of wine and invited to relax. Breakfast, with orange slices, strawberries or other seasonal fruit, pastriy, cucumber and tomato slices, cheese, toasted bread, olives, orange juice and coffee, is wonderful.

To get there: from the Izmir direction, take the first right after passing the Basilica of St. Jean (St. Jean Caddesi). Atop the hill, follow the Nilya signs left, right, and immediately left again.

Selected one of our favorite small hotels.

HOTEL KALEHAN, *Atatürk Cad. No. 49, Selcuk. Tel. (232) 892-6154; Fax (232) 892-2169; Email: ergirh@superonline.com; Web: www.kalehan.com. Rooms: 52. Credit cards accepted. Open March-October. Double: $55 (breakfast included). Restaurant.*

Tucked between two massive palms behind a whitewashed wall right at the entrance to Selcuk, the Hotel Kalehan is the grand dame of area inns. Once the centerpiece of a large cotton and fig plantation, the inn has been the centerpiece of Selcuk lodging since 1981. The original building has been joined by two modern wings, as well as a small Ottoman-style guest house and a swimming pool. On warm afternoons, guests lounge in the garden; on cool evenings, guests gather around the hearth in the main hall. The staff is carefully attentive, and the rooms simple and pleasant.

The atmosphere, while nice, is a bit staid, with shut doors at 11 p.m. The owner, Erol Ergir, grew up here after his family was transferred from Crete in 1920. This, by the way, is where George B. Quatman of the George B. Quatman Foundation of Lima, Ohio used to stay (see Basilica of St. John the Apostle under *Seeing the Sights*, below).

Selected one of our favorite small hotels.

BARIM PENSION, *Müze Arkasi Sokak, Selcuk. Tel. (232) 892-6923. Rooms: 12. Credit cards not accepted. Open year-round. Double: $14.*

The Barim Pension is an inexpensive little gem located immediately behind the Ephesus Museum—distinguished by its stork-topped chimney. The owners, Adnan and Ayşe Barim, live here with their family and have taken great care in the restoration of this 140 year-old whitewashed house, a house that has been in the family since the early 1920s. Adnan is a metalsmith, and lovely wrought iron is on display everywhere; candlesticks, mirror frames, and bedsteads. The old house has a lush courtyard garden in the back, a terrace, and innumerable nooks and crannies, including a new sitting room.

Like the Nilya, this is a great place for women traveling alone. To get there, circle behind the museum; you'll see signs with a stork on them leading the way.

Selected one of our favorite budget hotels.

AUSTRALIA NEW ZEALAND PENSION, *1064 Sok. No. 12, Selcuk. Tel. (232) 892-6050; Fax (232) 891-8594; Email: oznzpension@superonline.com; Web: www.anzturkishguesthouse.com. Rooms: 24. Credit cards not accepted. Open year-round. Double: $18 (half board).*

Selcuk is thick with backpacking hotels, and this is far and away the best of them. Family-run since 1986, the Australia New Zealand Pension has everything you would expect of a great backpacking hotel: DVDs in a rooftop lounge, clean rooms, friendly staff, reams of information about local sites, cheap meals, ongoing travel tickets, and a book exchange. The OZNZ is slightly upscale of other backpacker hotels in the area, and well worth the extra dollar or two. There is an additional charge for heaters in the offseason.

The carpet-bedecked rooftop lounge has an appropriately nomadic air, and is an excellent place to convene and discuss ongoing travel plans. The best part is, as good as this pension is, it improves from year to year; room remodels one year, a new covered patio the next. Anyone is welcome to stop in for an inexpensive, filling meal and puzzle over a staggering array of in-house bar tricks. If full, consider the nearby Ak Hotel.

Selected one of our favorite budget hotels.

NAZHAN PENSION & CAFÉ, *Saint Jean Cad., 1044 Sok. No. 2, Selcuk. Tel. (232) 892-8731; Fax (232) 891-4011; Email: nazhan@superonline.come. Rooms: 5. Credit cards not accepted. Open year-round (occasional closures in winter). Double: $30 (breakfast included).*

Across the street from the Basilica of St. John is a tiny, intimate hotel opened in 1997 that has taken some cues from the Hotel Kalehan. Knock on the wooden door, and you'll be ushered into a tiny courtyard dominated by an old, fruit-bearing lemon tree. The owners, Nazan and Kemal Erdoğan, are a retired librarian and accountant, respectively. They moved from İstanbul, restored this small house, and decorated it tastefully with nostalgic photos, trinkets, and local textiles. Breakfast and dinner are served on the covered terrace in the summer. One man's intimate is another man's cramped—some readers have found the Nazhan a bit small for comfort, particularly the bathrooms.

Şirince

If you have only a little time available—particularly if you're without your own transportation—staying here, 7 kilometers from Selcuk/ Ephesus, can be inconvenient. If you have a few days, consider it.

NIŞANYAN EVLERI, *Şirince, Selcuk. Tel. (232) 898-3209; Fax (232) 898-3117; Email: nisanyan@nisanyan.com; Web: www.nisanyan.com. Rooms: 7. Credit cards accepted. Open year-round. Double (20% discount in low seasons): $85 (hotel rates: $60).*

We don't believe it's possible to set your expectations too high; the Nişanyan Evleri (Nişanyan Houses) are magnificent. Perhaps this helps explain: during our visit in 2001, owner Sevan Nişanyan was nearing completion with a small four-room inn to augment his three impeccable individual houses. Sevan was disappointed; time constraints had forced him to forgo a second layer of frescoes on the walls of the inn; this layer he had planned to subsequently smash to expose bits of the first layer underneath.

Such is the almost preposterous attention to detail found here in the mountains above Selcuk. The houses have a few things in common: hardwood floors, high ceilings, tasteful Turkish textiles, wood furniture, CD players, and kitchens. They also have peculiarites; the recessed marble shower in one, the second floor nooks in another, the sitting room in another. Each comfortably suits five people—they're ideal for two couples—and as Sevan says "you can spend three days and still keep discovering things." A breakfast hamper is delivered each morning with coffee, eggs, bread, jams, cheese, and other seasonal groceries.

As noted above, a new four-room hotel is due to open a stone's throw from the houses, and it promises the same level of care. A few nights in Nişanyan Evleri is a marvelous tonic if you want to get away from it all. The houses are located in the heights of Şirince, and you'll need to do some steep hiking on foot. In the evening, Sevan expects to make dining available at the inn; dining is also available at restaurants such as **Dereli** *(Tel. 232 893-1206)* in Şirince.

Selected one of our favorite small hotels.

ŞIRINCE EVLERI, *Sirince. Tel/Fax (232) 898-3099; Email: sirince@sirince_evleri.com, Web: www.sirince_evleri.com. Rooms: 5. Credit cards accepted. Open year-round. Double: $60 (breakfast included).*

The Şirince Evleri are two restored nineteenth-century Greek houses owned and operated by Ahmet Kocak. Each room is lovingly detailed with original built-in cabinetry, wooden ceilings, colored glass lamps, traditional quilts and textiles, and brass beds. Some rooms even have working fireplaces. Eat your breakfast on the garden terrace overlooking the village.

Where to Eat

Selcuk is by no means packed with excellent dining options, but there are some very good restaurants. Note that readers report the **Great Hong Kong Chinese Restaurant** (*Tel. (232) 892-9310*), near the museum, is quite good as well.

ESKI EV, *Atatürk Mah., 1005 Sok. No. 1A, Selcuk. Tel. (232) 892-9357. Moderate.*

The Eski Ev (Old House) is fairly considered the best dining option in Selcuk. With dining inside and out, and a nice location just behind the PTT, this is an excellent choice for a meal. A meal of patlican salatasi (a marvelous mix of eggplant, tomatoes, parsley, and peppers) and tender grilled chicken will cost $8.

EJDER, *1047 Sok. No. 6, Muse yani, Selcuk. Tel. (232) 892-3296. Credit cards accepted. Inexpensive.*

This is an excellent little hole-in-the wall restaurant located up a cobbled side street directly next to the museum. The specialty of the house is the Urfa kebap.

SEÇKİN BİZİM EV, *Şirince Yolu, Selcuk. Tel. (232) 892-9066. Inexpensive-Moderate.*

This restaurant, whose byline is "with a woman's hands," was once located in the city center, and is now located outside of town on the Şirince road. Hatice Mercan owns the place with her husband İsmet, and although the whole family pitches in, Hatice does most of the cooking herself. A meal of outstanding green beans (taze fasulye), stuffed peppers, eggplant salad and a grill such as Adana kebap will cost $8. Bizim Ev (our house) is located two kilometers outside of Selcuk on a small farm teeming with ducks, sheeps, and chickens; if you don't have your own vehicle, you can take a Şirince dolmuş or a taxi there and count on a ride home from the staff.

HOTEL KALEHAN, *Atatürk Cad. No. 49, Selçuk. Tel/Fax (232) 892-6154. Moderate-Expensive.*

The Kalehan offers some of the better dining in Selcuk, featuring a fixed menu each night. The restaurant at the Hotel Kalehan has an intimate, greenhouse-like setting, but the prices are higher for the same quality you'll get elsewhere. It's also slightly out of the way if you're not staying actually there.

TADIM LOKUM, *Atatürk Cad., 1008 Sok. No. 1, Selcuk. Tel. (232) 892-3998; Fax (232) 892-4492; Email: mr_lokum@hotmail.com. Inexpensive.*

This isn't really a restaurant, it's a place to get Turkish Delight. It's all here—pistachio, rose, apple, raspberry, chocolate, walmut, honey, ha-zelnut... 2.2 pound boxes cost $7. The owner, Hikmet, is likely to play a tune on the seven-stringed saz as you consider the alternatives. Great for gifts.

Şirince

Dereli, mentioned in accommodations, above, is the best choice for dinner if you're staying here. If you're visiting for the day, consider the landmark Artemis Şirince.

ARTEMİS ŞIRINCE, *Şirince. Tel. (232) 898-3201; Fax (232) 898-3204. Inexpensive-Moderate. Credit cards accepted.*

You can't miss this place as you come into the village. The Artemis Şirince is situated in the restored building and grounds of an old stone school. The grounds are quite nice, with wrought iron and wood tables that overlook the wonderfully serene view of the village and its vine-yards. In the airy first floor of the building you'll find a long dining hall reserved for tour groups, a gift shop, and a traditional Turkish coffee salon where one can also smoke a narghile ($2.50). Below, the basement restaurant is dark, cavernous, and comfortable. The original stone foun-dations are exposed and decorated with strings of dried eggplant and colorful textiles. You can feed yourself on traditional Turkish fare (appe-tizers are $1.50, entrees $2-$6) and purchase their strawberry, cherry, or grape wines or apple cider by the glass or bottle. At a mere $2-$3 a bottle and tasting available, it's hard not to walk away with a couple of bottles.

Seeing the Sights

The **Basilica of St. John the Apostle** is well worth a look, a pleasantly situated ruin that has seen some faithful restoration by, of all things, the George B. Quatman Foundation of Lima, Ohio. The basilica was erected in the 6th century directly above the tomb of St. John. Owing to the standard confusion that swaddles the apostles, St. John either died a natural death, was boiled in oil, or disappeared and will appear in Ephesus on Judgment Day. Adherents of the first story built a small church at the site of his supposed tomb. The Byzantine Emperor Justinian chose to massively renovate the church, sparing the taxpayers no ex-pense and creating a cathedral that was one of the largest in the world at the time (even today it would have been the seventh largest).

The grand cathedral proved, in the words of Procopius, to be one of Justinian's many "crazy building schemes." Ephesus' problems with the silting bay were already serious, and this was compounded by the deteriorating fortunes of the Byzantine Empire. Ephesus was in foreign hands within 150 years, together with its stunning cathedral, and was thereafter an afterthought in a chaotic theater of war. The ill-fated structure was pressed into service as a mosque and a bazaar and damaged by earthquakes, yet it continued to command enough respect that in the 14th century Selcuk architects erected the minaret of the İsa Bey Mosque on a line with the Basilica entrance, like a punctuation mark at the base of a crucifix. Check out the beautiful inscriptions on many of the pillars, and the crude but effective relief maps of the area just inside of the southern entrance.

On the hill above the cathedral is the citadel of the **Ayasoluk fortress**, rebuilt, like the basilica, during Justinian's reign as part of a massive overhaul of the Byzantine Empire's defenses. The citadel was at the northern end of the original fortress, an immense walled city that enclosed the Basilica. Today only a suggestion of the original walls remains. Impressive as the fortress was, it did not help the Byzantines stop repeated invasions of the area by Persians, Arabs, Crusaders, Selcuks and, finally, Ottomans. The citadel's last serious occupation was by Selcuks, and it has been partially restored in recent years. Today the citadel is a nice backdrop to the town, but relatively dull inside - there is a converted chapel, a mosque, broken ground where storehouses and cisterns have caved in, and crumbling ramparts. The name Ayasoluk derives from the Greek name for the Church of St. John. The fortress is almost always closed, but it is almost always easy to climb into, as the locals often do. You aren't supposed to, technically.

The **İsa Bey Mosque** is directly to the west of and below the basilica. It was built in the 14th century by one of the Turkish tribes who scattered throughout Anatolia in the wake of the Mongol invasions. Like the basilica, the mosque took advantage of the dressed marble scattered on the grounds of the temple of Artemis (perhaps also the city walls and basilica). The long building has a beautiful western entrance, clean lines, and an attractive forecourt on the northern side. Just above this, between the mosque and the Basilica of St. John, is a large sloping pasture littered with marble. Take a break here and have a look out over the area's sites.

The aqueduct running through the center of Selcuk was one of three major lines that supplied Ephesus at its zenith. Water was rerouted from 10, 12, and 25 miles away to supply Ephesus with 1,600 gallons of water per minute. The aqueduct in Selcuk carried water from a valley below nearby Şirince.

Before venturing to Ephesus, stop in at the **Ephesus Archaeology Museum**, Kuşadası Caddesi, behind the tourism information office, *Tel. 232 892 6010*; open 9 a.m. to 5 p.m. daily, where your $2 and one hour is well spent. The Ephesus museum is just to the northwest of the town's main intersection, and its collection breathes life into Ephesus, which has been picked over for many of its best pieces. Our favorite item is the massive marble slab with 63 paragraphs of Roman customs laws for Asia;

and you can't miss the gargantuan statue of Emperor Domitian - if St. John the Apostle was boiled in oil, Domitian is the one who boiled him. Try to miss the adjoining museum of modern art, with pieces for sale that are likely to double or triple in value in the next 3,000 years.

There was some confusion as to the whereabouts of the Virgin Mary's resting place, but the Holy See put an end to that in 1950. Based partly on the vision of Katharina Emmerich (1774-1824), a Bavarian nun, the Catholic Church ruled that Mary's resting-place was on a small hill near Ephesus. After her son Jesus entrusted her to the care of St. John, she followed John here and lived out her final days. The current chapel, the **House of the Virgin Mary**, is located on the site of a small Byzantine church, and the church appears to have been associated with a monastery. Catholics often make a pilgrimage to the site, and typically give the restorative water from the fountains here a try. Pope John Paul II visited here in 1979 so if you're Catholic you have to go; otherwise drop by if you have a car and some extra time. Some visitors claim to have been relieved of maladies. To get there follow the road from the upper Ephesus gate. Taxis from the Selcuk otogar will shuttle you back and forth with one half hour to see the site for $10.

The town of Şirince is in the mountains above Selcuk, an old Greek village that was emptied in the population exchange. Two Greek Orthodox churches are located here, one of them in mid-remodel thanks to the ever-busy George B. Quatman Foundation of Lima, Ohio. The villagers sell lace, cheap red and apple wine and even olive oil—they sell enough of it that the pacific lanes of Şirince have become a bit choked with local vendors. Still, this is a beautiful side trip; dolmuş depart throughout the day from the main otogar between 8 a.m. and 7 p.m. There are several pensions—including one of the best in the whole of Turkey—in Şirince, providing a relentlessly peaceful option to life in Selcuk once most of the visitors depart at 4 p.m. Tuesday is market day, although most days are market day in the tourist season. Consider giving Şirince a miss on weekends.

Nightlife & Entertainment

Selcuk hosts two dramatically different festivals. In the third week of January camel wrestling fans congregate here for, yes, Selcuk's acclaimed **Camel Wrestling Festival**. In May, the **International Music and Folk Dancing** festival arrives, and the Great Theatre at Ephesus has been used for performances.

The crowds for the two festivals are alike only in that they make lodging difficult. Information is available at the tourism information office, *Tel. 232 892 6550*.

Excursions & Day Trips
NEARBY RUINS

On your way to or from Selcuk, consider stopping at **Belevi Mauso-leum** (signed, 12 kilometers northeast of Ephesus) near where the road branches to Tire. If you pass through the roadside village and follow signs to Belevi you'll skirt the new freeway, then pass beneath it and see the mausoleum emerge on your right.

This is a burial mound and the remains of a huge structure that archaeologists suspect was akin to Mausolus' tomb at Helicarnassus. A great block of stone was clad in courses of ashlar. These concealed that one side of the stone circuit (opposite the freeway) was open. Tunnels shot in several directions beneath the structure, including a 65-foot passageway that led to the center, where a sarcophagus was located. The tunnel, originating on the lower side of the hill, is now obstructed by the spoil of persistent treasure hunters. The sarcophagus is on display at the Ephesus Museum in Selcuk. The **Goat Fort** (Keçi Kalesi) is located atop a bluff to the west.

The three ruins of Priene, Miletus, and Didyma are a good day trip from Selcuk, and you can make it to Aphrodisias or Pamukkale in the interior and back in one long day. Trips depart almost daily in the high season from the otogar.

THE TEMPLE OF ARTEMIS

The most significant ruin at Selcuk is the **Temple of Artemis**, which we recommend stopping by en route to Ephesus, on foot. If you like your history straight, the Temple of Artemis is the place for you; a big muddy field, a column, and fascinating history. This was one of the Seven Ancient Wonders of the World, ranked by one Spartan as the best of the lot. Unfortunately, in the words of an Australian friend, today "Ya look and ya wondah."

Leaving Selcuk for Ephesus, you pass the Temple of Artemis at Ephesus on your right. The site is just adjacent to Selcuk to the west, a short walk from the otogar. The road from Kuşadası in the south cuts across the mountains and arrives from the west.

In its heyday, the temple was three times larger than the Parthenon in Athens, and, if long dead observers are to be believed, far more ornate and glorious. Doric temples, like the Parthenon and the Temple of Athena at Assos, were relatively squat structures that crowned hills. Ionic temples were built with tall, slender columns, and the Temple of Artemis was the most massive of the world's Ionic temples, with 127 columns 60 feet tall covering the area of a football field.

Artemis-worship was not restricted to Ephesus, but it flourished here like nowhere else. Upon arrival in 1000 B.C. the seafaring Greeks grafted their goddess of chastity, Artemis, with the native Anatolian fertility goddess Cybele. The result was the many-breasted deity that adorns postcards and statues throughout Selcuk. The priests and followers of Artemis had a set of rituals as elaborate as their temple, mostly revolving around agriculture and procreation. If you want a root cause for confusion about sexuality, look no further: ceremonies at the fertility/chastity temple included orgies and great spectacles of self-abuse that evidently included self-castration. Eunuchs were responsible for affairs at the temple, and perhaps castration was the hazing ritual for the administrative good life.

There were several versions of the temple, which was old when Herodotus wrote about it. In 560 B.C., the Ephesians attempted to save their city from King Croesus of Lydia by stringing a cord between the temple and the city wall, thus currying Artemis' favor. Herodotus does not tell us how Croesus overcame this obstacle; presumably he sent a Lydian soldier shinnying up a column with a pair of scissors. At any rate the Ephesians' ploy failed, and Croesus' army sacked the city. Croesus, a great believer in the mystical, helped fund restoration of the temple, helpfully contributing several golden cows.

The temple again came to harm in 356, when an arsonist allegedly burned it down. Legends recount that on the day of the fire the goddess Artemis had left the temple to be on hand at the birth of Alexander in Macedon. When the precocious 22 year old arrived in 334 B.C. he was evidently apologetic, allowing the Ephesians to devote their tax money to renovating the structure. The ensuing temple, even more incredible than earlier versions, was the structure deemed one of the Seven Wonders of the World. Worship at the temple continued under the Romans, who knew Artemis by the name of her Roman equivalent, Diana.

Christianity began to erode Artemis-worship. St. John may have settled here in the company of his adoptive mother, Mary, the mother of Christ, and organized the spread of Christianity from this Roman capital of Asia. By the time his colleague St. Paul arrived, the local silver smiths at Ephesus were becoming concerned about Christianity's affect on their trade in Artemis/Diana figurines. St. Paul's evangelizing about the evils of their icons was the last straw, and they rioted, storming around and declaring "Great is Diana of Ephesus." St. Paul, sensing that Christ was not fully in their hearts, did verily split. Eventually, however, the ingenious city fathers (see *Economics of Religion* sidebar below) built a thriving tourism industry around Christian pilgrimage to the site of the Virgin Mary's death, and the silversmiths beat their Diana figurines into crucifixes.

The combined forces of Christianity, a receding sea, and a good, sound sacking by Goths in 237 A.D. finally put an end to worship at the temple. Thereafter the temple site was plundered for its vast wealth of dressed stone and picked over for its best statues and artifacts. Principally, Justinian looted the ruins during the construction of the Basilica of St. John - although the temple columns do not appear to have been shuttled to İstanbul to construct the Haghia Sophia, as is often claimed. What remained was buried by the silting of the Cayster River until it was unearthed and hauled off in the 19th century. Many of the best artifacts from the temple now reside in the British Museum in London and the Kunsthistorische Museum in Vienna.

There is little left to see at the temple. A token column has been assembled from spare drums, but the foundation is gone and what hasn't been carted off has been buried. The only thing of note is on the side of the temple distant from Selcuk, where the remains of the temple altar have been found. This was, like most major temples, by the side of a spring or fissure, although no trace remains. What was sacrificed at the altar is not known.

Did They Have a Santa Bunny?

Worshippers of the fertility goddess Cybele had an oddly familiar celebration each spring to mark the beginning of the growing season and to bring themselves luck. A pine tree was decorated with a garland of flowers and became the focus of a three day period of mourning for Cybele's lover Attis, the god of flora. After three days the mourning would end with a festival to celebrate Attis having arisen from the dead, and the coming of spring.

EPHESUS

Ephesus is the most marvelous Hellenistic ruin in the Aegean, and, some say, the world.

Once upon a time, everything about Ephesus was impressive. This was the capital of the Roman province of Asia and the most bustling metropolis in the world, with a population of 250,000. Ephesus had streetlights and running water, a grand stadium, a theater, avenues paved with marble, and one of the wonders of the world just cubits away at the Temple of Artemis. It was a nerve center for the world's commerce, joining the western end of the Royal Road to Babylon with Mediterranean sea trade.

Even a plague of 19th century archaeologist/looters have not managed to destroy Ephesus' charm. Sites from Assos to Xanthos have been emptied by the battleship load, but museums have not floated the fleet that could strip Ephesus bare. True, some of the ancient city's masterpieces have been hauled off to Europe, but long dead builders and artists seem to have stocked Ephesus well against just such a possibility. There remains a remarkable sprawl of engraved marble and cunningly wrought sculpture, great columns and capitals, mosaics and theaters and wide streets.

Ephesus' great fault is that it numbs you, a drudgery of ornate marble. Advice: Ignore guided tours to the site and see it on your own, lingering over what you enjoy. There is always a covey of guides waiting to help, for a small fee, at both gates.

Getting to Ephesus

Many Selcuk hotels will provide transportation to Ephesus. The two kilometer distance from Selcuk to Ephesus begins along a wide tree-lined pedestrian path alongside the five kilometer Selcuk coast road. At the sign you bear left and follow the road to the site. The road is well-signed. A slightly longer route takes you to the Magnesia Gate at the upper end of the city, but that route is less pleasant by virtue of the highway's short shoulder. The main parking lot is at the bottom gate, where knick-knacks and snack food are on sale.

Taxis between Ephesus and Selcuk cost $3, and there's no need to let the taxi wait for your return since there are ordinarily plenty here anyway. From Kuşadası a round trip with three hours at the site is $30.

History

The ruins of Ephesus are from one distinct phase in the wandering city's past. Alexander seized early Ephesus without a fight in 334 B.C., but after his death 11 years later possession of the city was hotly disputed among his squabbling generals. Around 300 B.C. one of the Diadochi (squabbling generals), Lysimachos, took control of the city. He brought a fresh perspective to the problem of Ephesus' increasing distance from the sea, abruptly ordering everyone to build an entirely new city at the present site. The Greeks were the founders of democracy, but not these particular Greeks, and everyone reluctantly did as they were told.

The move put the new harbor flush with the sea and fixed Ephesus' place in maritime commerce for the next thousand years. The city was massive, with walls completely encircling **Mt. Pion** (the hill behind the theater) and marching along the ridge far above the slope houses. Within 500 years continued deposits of silt had forced Roman emperors to order massive dredging operations, none of which delayed the inevitable. The

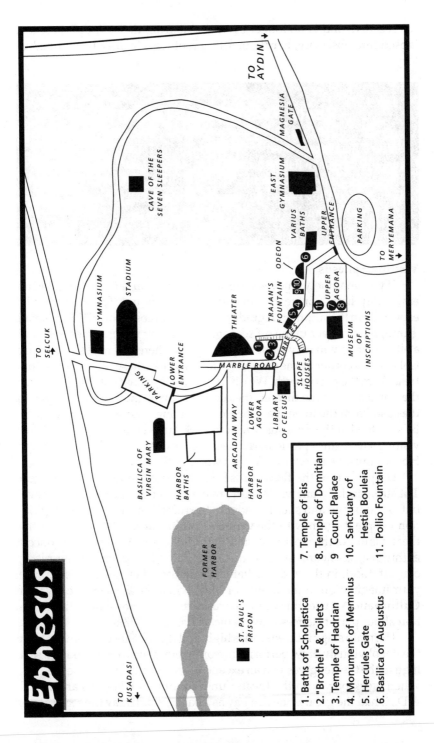

Ephesus

TO AYDIN →

MAGNESIA GATE

TO SELCUK ↑

TO KUSADASI ↓

TO MERYEMANA →

CAVE OF THE SEVEN SLEEPERS

GYMNASIUM

STADIUM

EAST GYMNASIUM

VARIUS BATHS

ODEON

UPPER ENTRANCE

PARKING

THEATER

TRAJAN'S FOUNTAIN

CURETES

UPPER AGORA

MUSEUM OF INSCRIPTIONS

MARBLE ROAD

LOWER ENTRANCE

PARKING

SLOPE HOUSES

LOWER AGORA

LIBRARY OF CELSUS

ARCADIAN WAY

HARBOR GATE

HARBOR BATHS

BASILICA OF VIRGIN MARY

FORMER HARBOR

ST. PAUL'S PRISON

1. Baths of Scholastica
2. "Brothel" & Toilets
3. Temple of Hadrian
4. Monument of Memnius
5. Hercules Gate
6. Basilica of Augustus
7. Temple of Isis
8. Temple of Domitian
9. Council Palace
10. Sanctuary of Hestia Bouleia
11. Pollio Fountain

sea receded, and is no longer even visible from the city. Ephesus, too, lapsed into obscurity, hardly meriting footnotes in later Byzantine history.

Reply Hazy, Ask Again Later

According to a myth shrouded in legend, the Greeks who settled here first consulted the Oracle at Delphi. The oracular insight was that a fish and a boar would reveal the site of their new home. Sure enough, the settlers found a few fish and wild boar near Ephesus - as they would have at any site within 2,000 miles. A low point for the Oracle.

Visiting Ephesus

If you genuinely enjoy wandering in ruins, you can plan to spend an entire day here - or years. Several hours is enough for most people, especially in the summer. A guide at the site will cost about $13 for a small group, much lower in the off season. Bring along water, sunscreen, and a bite to eat, as you may want to spend a while here and refreshments are isolated in a corner by the entrance. The sun cooks these ruins and visitors fresh from the pasty north. We divide Ephesus' ruins into three sections: the north area by the theater, the center of town, and the upper town to the east. From the lower gate, begin by making your way to the theater. Be sure to visit the Ephesus Museum in Selcuk - better before than after visiting the ruins, particularly because tickets to the Ephesus Slope Houses must be purchased at the museum.

Despairing of the florid prose that has tried to animate the **Great Theatre**, Mark Twain wrote: "One may read the Scriptures and believe, but he cannot go and stand yonder in the ruined theater and in imagination people it again with the vanished multitudes." He's right, but the theater is one of the most accessible parts of the city. Any sports or concert enthusiast has heard the roar that once filled this place during plays, concerts, and, in the end, gladiatorial combat. There's less need to use your imagination in the month of May, when the **Ephesus Festival of Culture and Art** uses this venue for concerts and performances (information about performances is available at *Tel. (232) 892-6550*).

The main stage is three stories high, and the 25,000-seat, 100 foot high theater obviously drew performers from around the world. Taking a seat high in the theater gives you an excellent perspective on the ancient city. When work began on the theater under Emperor Claudius around 50 A.D., it had the great Ephesian bay as a backdrop. Today the sea is gone, having receded behind the spur of Mt. Koressos on the left, and the great colonnaded road that once served the shipyards ends abruptly near the great heap of the harbor gates.

The building on the distant hill a little to your left is known as **St. Paul's Prison**, hearkening back to the evangelizing Paul's troubles with the Ephesians. It's unlikely he was ever anywhere near the place, since it was a military outpost and fortified lookout tower, but the name persists.

To the left, across the avenue in front of the theater, is the **lower marketplace**, a vast space still delineated by standing columns that once supported extensive galleries. To the right of the Agora (marketplace) a road heads directly away from the theater toward the former harbor. This road was extended under the Emperor Arcadius in the late fourth century, and is thus called the **Arcadian Way**. The harbor road was always a place of great pomp, and one of the spectacles that occurred here was the procession of Cleopatra and Mark Antony down the avenue to their pleasure barge. The lower section of the road is occasionally closed, but that's not a great loss.

The most interesting structures in the waterfront section of the city are the **Harbor Baths**, whose black marble was reused in the İsa Bey Mosque in Selcuk, and the ruinous gates themselves.

Running parallel with the Arcadian Way on the right hand side are the ruins of the **Basilica of the Virgin Mary**. This was far too grand a structure to be the one mentioned in The Book of Revelation, but it may be located on the same site. The gist of St. John's message in Revelation was that the cosmopolitan Ephesian Christians were not passionate enough in their belief. The basilica was the site of the Third Ecumenical Council (see sidebar below), and Popes continue to drop by occasionally.

The **Marble Road** in front of the theater continues past the **Library of Celsus** to the left and, to the right, once continued around Mt. Pion, past the **Stadium** (built in Emperor Nero's era), and on to the Temple of Artemis. The huge ruins of the stadium are scattered along the ridge above the main Selcuk road, the only section of Ephesus visible from Selcuk today. Contests, gladitorial combat, and races too unruly for the Great Theatre were held here. From the theater, continue up the Marble Way toward the city center to the left.

From the Theatre

The centerpiece of Ephesus is the **Library of Celsus**, the grand structure at the juncture of Curettes Street and the Marble Way. The reconstruction is the work of a team of Viennese archaeologists, and if the library didn't quite look like this in antiquity, well, it should have. The building dates back to 117 A.D., when the governor at the time built it for a hero of the Empire, his father Gaius Julius Celsus Polemaeanus. The

The Economics of Religion

In 428, Nestorius of Antioch became the patriarch of Constantinople, bringing with him the belief that Jesus Christ was a mortal man forced to come to terms with his divinity. Other religious thinkers maintained that Christ had a wholly united divine spirit, a single perfect God, Man, and Holy Spirit. This fairly obscure theological debate became the pretext for persecution and unrest throughout the empire. Finally, in 431, Emperor Theodosius II summoned members of the clergy to Ephesus to settle the matter, convening the Third Ecumenical Council.

It was a fortunate choice for the city fathers of Ephesus, who had a vested interest in the outcome. They reviled Nestorius' rationalist idea that Christ had the spirit of a mortal man, since that meant, too, that the holy status of Mary would be undermined. In short, the patriarch Nestorius' theology threatened to kill Ephesus' revenues as the site of Mary's tomb and a place of holy veneration and pilgrimage–this, on the heels of their loss of Artemis pilgrimage.

During the council, Nestorius was outmaneuvered by the Alexandrian patriarch Cyril, who, playing before the sympathetic Ephesian crowd, managed to not only have Nestorius' theology denounced, but get Nestorius condemned as a heretic and exiled to Egypt. The Ephesian city fathers were surely much relieved.

Lest you think this all an unlikely subject for such great debate, the world-altering Great Schism between the eastern Orthodox and Roman Catholic was rooted in nothing greater.

academics and wise men of the age would collect here to pore over a great collection of papyrus scrolls, or, alternately, duck through a secret tunnel that led to the brothel across the street. The library was one of the world's great repositories of writing, with all of the scrolls administered by an early librarian. The Library and its works suffered badly during the sack of the Goths, no great lovers of books.

To the left as you near the end of the Marble Road are the **Baths of Scholastica**, once a vast three story spa complex of swimming pools, baths, libraries, and private rooms. Some suspect it was associated with a **brothel** here at the city's main intersection, but this may just as well be the prurient fantasizing of archaeologists digging in the sun too long. It is based largely on the discovery of the small but distinctive Priapus statue (now in the Selcuk museum and featured extensively on local postcards). An inscription of a woman, a heart, and a foot on the main street is said to suggest that if a man's foot is not of that size he isn't old enough to be welcome.

In any event, the sprawling baths complex, accessed from higher on Curettes Street, underwent its last great renovation in the fourth century under its namesake, and offers an interesting warren of rooms, heating tunnels, and statuary (some pilfered from the Temple of Hestia Boulea). One of the great matter-of-fact places of antiquity is located in the collection of buildings just beyond the baths. A long L-shaped marble bench with forty-six holes cut in the seats once served as a restroom, and waste was carried away by running water in the pit below. This elegant system surrounded a large, columned pool.

The facilities were apparently reserved for the upper classes and rumor has it that during winter wealthy cityfolk would send their slaves ahead of them to warm a seat. No word on where, or if, the poor were able to go to the bathroom. This section of buildings has several interesting mosaics that are worth hunting for, and the multi-layered flooring is ideal for kids to clamber through.

The **Temple of Hadrian** is to the left of Curettes Street, its back to the Baths of Scholastica. This is one of the city's great sites, part of the great wave of construction that swept every site in Asia Minor, even Petra in Jordan, when Emperor Hadrian (118-138 AD) went on his grand tour of the provinces. The ornate building has a detailed frieze that relates the legend of the city's founding. The front arch has the face of Tyche, the Goddess of Fortune, and the interior arch has Medusa, whose role was to protect the temple by turning vandals and miscreants to stone.

To the right as you ascend you'll see some fine mosaics, more of which are contained in the modern buildings on the slope above the library. These buildings preserve the Slope Houses. At the time of this writing, admission to the Slope Houses was only possible by getting a ticket at the Ephesus Museum in advance ($4).

For centuries this section of town was Ephesus' toniest neighborhood, and archaeologists continue to unearth a wealth of artifacts and architectural curiosities. The mosaics, frescoes, statues, and central heating system inside will help dispel any lingering 21th century misconceptions about the engineering and artistic cunning of our Ephesian forebears. The Slope Houses are a powerful part of the city's story, featuring gorgeous in situ mosaics. Recommended.

After viewing the slope houses, take a left up the sloping road just above the baths (the road that originates across from the tree with the "no smoking" sign). Ascending this road gives you a good overview of this part of the city and, with luck, gets you away from the crowds. The road once ran to the top of **Panayir Dağı** (Mt. Pion), meeting the top of the great theater.

Continuing on up the Street of Curettes (so-called because that was the name of the city council), you pass through the columns of the **Horcules Gate**, built relatively late in the city's history with statues and reliefs recycled from elsewhere in the city. The **Fountain of Trajan** celebrates the emperor (98-117) who replaced the out-of-control Domitian. You have to piece together the emperor's appearance based on a hunk of his chest and his two feet.

As you continue to ascend, you'll see a relief of Nike, the winged goddess of victory. Nike sits by the side of the road near the **Monument of Memnius**. Memnius was a local hero, and the grandson of Sulla, emperor during much of Julius Caesar's rise to power.

Directly ahead as you ascend is the Temple of Domitian, and within its former precincts the museum of inscriptions. Off the left is the great, naked arch of the Tomb of Pollio. This is a heavily refinished recreation of the Pollio Fountain's main arch, whose cast of fourth century characters from *The Odyssey* now resides in the Selcuk museum.

If you continue to the museum of inscriptions you'll find that entrance is free, but it's probably not open. Never is. The area is littered with inscribed stones that you can try to make out as best you can. The structure itself, the Temple of Domitian, honored Domitian, an emperor from 81-96 A.D. His immense likeness, bulbous forehead and all, once adorned the temple, but is now kept in the Ephesus Museum in Selcuk. The temple itself was ransacked by the Ephesians themselves after the welcome end of Domitian's reign. At this point, return to the Nike relief and continue on up the path to the Odeon and climb to the top.

At the Odeon

First of all, understand that the entire hill at your back was once populated and surrounded by a defensive wall. The wall ran up the slope far ahead of you, at about the point where the road to Maryemana circles right, and along the top toward the distant hill away to your right. This city was vast.

This theater was Ephesus' junior version of the main theater in the city below. It was built in the 2nd century B.C. by the local philanthropist Vedius and seated about 1,500 people. The **Odeon** was covered with a wooden roof, and was used for slightly more bourgeois purposes than the main theater; city council meetings, conferences, and sophisticated drama. When work began at the site this building had almost disappeared into the hillside, but it has been excavated and repaired.

The building to the left of the Odeon is the **Basilica of Augustus**, which served as a sort of early stock exchange and financial institution. The capitals atop this ancient stock exchange's columns were adorned with, optimistically, bull's heads. Beyond the Basilica is a substantial structure built into the hillside, which at one time served as the public baths. These **Varius Baths** were, like most things in this neighborhood, Roman era.

The colonnaded **Curettes Street** that you have ascended was one of Ephesus' three main roads. It extends from the Magnesia Gate to your left into central Ephesus. The road's name derives from the city fathers' Council of Curettes, not to the coincidental discoveries pointing to Ephesus' early importance in surgery and medicine - the curette of Diokles, the earliest device found to remove arrowheads, was located here. Like the other major streets in Ephesus, the road ran atop a water and sewage system. Beyond the road is the wreck of the **Upper Agora**, strewn with marble. Agoras were market areas, sometimes used for political and religious meetings. The foundation of the **Temple of Isis** is sunk in the earth ahead and to the right. The temple was sacked in the third century, like the Temple of Artemis.

Directly to your right are two structures, the **Council Palace** (Prutaneion) and, beyond it, the **Sanctuary of Hestia Bouleia**. The Council Palace is your standard wreck, dating back to the city's initial construction in 300 B.C. by Lysimachos. The Sanctuary was built at the same time, and was the site of the city's eternal flame, long since snuffed out. The Sanctuary was the town's heart and soul for hundreds of years, but after the comprehensive ravages of the Goths in 263 A.D. it became a source of building material.

Exiting the Magnesian Gate you can usually find a taxi ($9 for one half hour) to shuttle you the five kilometers to the **House of Mary**, or you can descend to the main parking lot, having one more lingering look at the city. The **Cave of the Seven Sleepers**, located on the opposite slope of Mt. Pion, has nothing much to see and a tepid story about seven boys who fall asleep and wake up hundreds of years later, like the story of Rumplestiltskin but more tiresome. In short, seven persecuted Ephesian Christians hid within the cave, dropped off to a two century sleep, and wandered back into Ephesus to find that Christianity was now the favored religion.

If you want to get the most for your admission fee, strap on a daypack and haul some water along with you along the two hills flanking Ephesus. The hill behind the theater has a scattering of ruins, and the course of the Lysimachos-era walls are intact along the great ridge to the south that heads out toward the former sea. Most of Ephesus' best pieces have been removed to the local museums, but there are still buildings - and excellent views - atop Mt. Pion and Mt. Panayir.

Aphrodisias

The inland trade routes from Ephesus have been important for many thousands of years, and vital, thriving cities have emerged at the inland passes and mountaintops. One of the cities enjoys fame for its white mineral pools, Pamukkale, while the other, **Aphrodisias**, would find itself on the cover of Archaeology Magazine's "Hot" issue. If they had such a thing. Which they don't.

There were always hints that Aphrodisias might be an important ruin, and recent excavations have borne that out in dramatic fashion. Aphrodisias was not as large as Ephesus, but it was an important religious site with a population of skilled craftsmen and artists. Aphrodisias is worth taking the trouble to visit, and can be given as much time as Ephesus. Many people make it an adjunct to a visit at Pamukkale, which makes good sense. If you're traveling with a sketch pad, this is a place you must visit.

History

Aphrodisias' history dates back to the distant past, when there was a Bronze age trading center on the site, but the first evidence of its mystical importance appears in its name during the middle of the second millennium B.C., Ninoe, from Nin, an Anatolian goddess of love and war. Nin was probably a precursor to Ishtar, who was later adapted into Aphrodite.

But Aphrodite was a goddess of love without war. In *The Iliad* she appears on the battlefield to retrieve a stricken Aeneas, but in the midst of her rescue the Greek warrior Diomedes recognizes her as "a god without warcraft" and takes the opportunity to strike her with his bronze sword. Athena would surely have wiped up the battlefield with him then and there, but Aphrodite tumbles to the ground wounded and drops Aeneas, who is spirited away by Apollo. Aeneas, according to the legend, went on to found Rome. It is fitting that the city of the goddess of love was unwalled in Roman times, trusting to its status as a shrine of art and peace.

A temple to Aphrodite was built in or before the third century B.C., but before the city passed into Roman hands in the second century B.C. it was rarely mentioned in historical records (then as Megalopolis and Plarasa). The citizens of Aphrodisias (as the city gradually came to be known) found security under Roman rule, and during the Pontic Wars of Mithradites VI (120-63) against Rome, while Mithradites was ranging from his base on the Black Sea as far south as Lycia, Aphrodisias remained loyal to the empire. Rome was grateful for the contribution of fighting men and support, and this gratitude was to prove extremely valuable to the city.

It was under Rome that the city blossomed. Not only did the shrine of Aphrodite, with its celebration of loves both sacred and profitably profane, attract visitors and wealth, but the great success of the Roman Empire provided a ready market for the city's great export, **marble**. With the quarrying of marble came an expertise in working the stone, and one of the world's foremost schools of sculpture developed here. The works of Aphrodisian sculptors are scattered throughout the Mediterranean basin, many in Rome itself. Roman Emperors, not forgetting the city's service during the Pontic Wars, extended special allowances and privileges to Aphrodisias. These began under Julius Caesar and continued for well over a century. Trajan (98-117 A.D.) pronounced that Aphrodisias' ambassadors would have places of honor in Rome.

The city's prosperity continued until Christianity began asserting its hold. Since the Bronze Age a kernel of love goddess-worship had survived all the changes at Aphrodisias, but Christianity brought the practice to an end; Christians occupied the temple and converted it to a basilica. As at Cnidos, Aphrodite seems to have posed a particular threat to the more puritanical Christians, and, as at Cnidos, the church endeavored to supplant her.

The city of Aphrodisias, so ornate and beautiful, began a long decline. Some of the damage was self-mutilation caused by the construction of city walls. Perhaps the city was under pressure to get the walls up quickly; in any case workers dismantled nearby buildings to provide stone. Under the Byzantine Empire Aphrodisias became **Stavropolis**, the City of the Cross. The traffic of Aphrodite's pilgrims died, and without a vigorous empire to serve, the market for marble, let alone sculpture, died with it.

The city's economy a shambles, the new walls were no help. Invaders from the east repeatedly ravaged the city, and soon after the coming of the Selcuks Stavropolis was abandoned. The city of **Geyre** (perhaps deriving from the ancient place-name Caria), now beside the ruin, was located directly atop the city when archaeologists began work.

Arrivals & Departures

By Bus

Nazilli is the public transportation hub for Geyre town and Aphrodisias. Trains and buses serve Nazilli, and Nazilli has several minibuses daily to Geyre. In the slower season they depart only on the morning and evening. You can also get a dolmuş as far as Karacasu, 10 kilometers shy of Aphrodisias, every half hour or so. From Karacasu you should be able to catch a dolmuş once an hour, bound for Aphrodisias/ Geyre and beyond. This is the weak link, and you may have a wait.

As an alternative, Kamil Koç offers morning minibuses from Pamukkale in the high season, charging $12 and staying three hours at the ruins. This offers the appealing option of arriving at Pamukkale in the morning and spending the day there, booking a trip to Aphrodisias for the next morning and your ongoing journey the next evening. You can also get to Aphrodisias on a package tour from Selcuk, which makes things simpler but, like the Pamukkale trip, may rush you through the site. Aphrodisias is an excellent place to have time.

By Car

Aphrodisias was never convenient, and is not now; traveling to the site and back from the Aegean coast near Selcuk requires a full day and an early start by car. Better to plan on a night here or at Pamukkale afterwards. Aphrodisias is by the town of Geyre, 35 kilometers south of the main Aydın-Antalya road by Kuyucak and 50 kilometers west of the same E 87 road at Kazıkbeli. This secondary 585 road that serves the site is in decent condition.

Orientation

The walled city of Aphrodisias is about 1.5 kilometers in diameter. The parking lot is located alongside a breach in the east wall by a necropolis. A man at the ticket booth at the site will charge $3, open 8:30 a.m. to 7:30 p.m. in the summer, until 5:30 p.m. in the winter. There is an outstanding museum here open during the same hours (separate admission fee).

Where to Stay & Eat

If, as mentioned above, you will not be staying in Pamukkale, there is limited lodging at Karacasu and Nazilli, as well as the following options near Aphrodisias. We favor the Chez Mestan within walking distance of the ruins. There are several trout (alabalık) restaurants along the roadside nearby.

CHEZ MESTAN, *Afrodisias, Karacasu, Aydın. Tel. (256) 448-8046; Fax (256) 448-8132. Rooms: 28. Credit cards not accepted. Open year-round. Double: $15.*

This convenient hotel is just shy of the ruins on the Karacasu road. The Mestan is a large house converted into a hotel, offering decent rooms and a large patio for dining. If there is no room here they will send you down the road to their other, more hotel-shaped hotel, the **Aphrodisias Hotel-Restaurant** (*Tel. 256 448-8132, Fax 256 448-8422*). The Mestan serves breakfast and dinner, and it's good, filling food (dinner will cost about $7 per person). There are also several tour bus restaurants with perfectly decent food on the road near Aphrodisias. This is one of our favorite spots; you feel more interesting by simply spending a night. Several buses daily pass through here bound to and from Nazilli and Aydın.

Aydın
   TURTAY HOTEL, *Aydın, Muğla Karayolu, Tel. 256 213 3003, Fax 256 213 0351. Rooms: 72. Double: $57.*
   If being near the sea is not a particular imperative for you, consider this hotel in Aydın, ancient Tralles, with its convenience to Pamukkale and Aphrodisias to the east, Ephesus, Priene, and Didyma to the west, and the ruins of Nysa, Alinda, and many other cities nearby. The hotel has four stars from the tourism bureau, a pool, satellite television, and air conditioning.

Seeing the Sights

   The **museum,** just inside the wall, is mostly a collection of statuary (probably the elite 20 percent of the vast discoveries here). It's both educational and impressive, and can be visited for $2.
   The centerpiece of the city was the **Sebasteion,** down the street from the museum. This colonnaded way celebrated Roman Emperors and gods together, and may never have seen completion. The lower level of this three story structure was decorated with Doric columns, topped by Ionic columns, while the upper course had Corinthian columns. Statues and reliefs celebrated the successes of the gods and the emperors, and provided some of the lucrative flattery that helped Aphrodisias thrive. Many of the statues from this building were destroyed by Christian zealots, but some have survived and are on display at the museum. The Sebasteion opened onto a temple to the east, on the side where the walls are located. Part of this temple may have found its way into the walls.
   The Sebasteion's entrance is on the city's central marketplace, to the south of the acropolis. The **acropolis,** the site of the early city and the final refuge of the dying city, has an excellent theater opening onto an extensive bath. The theater was restored under Marcus Aurelius at the same time work was underway at Aspendus. Another bath is located to the north, this bath at least as extensive and dedicated to the emperor Hadrian. These baths were built at the time of Hadrian's tour of the provinces, and were surely a welcome relief from the arches he was honored with almost everywhere else he went.
   The **Odeon,** buried at the time work at the site began, has been cleared of soil. This pristine little meeting area was used by the city's leaders. The Odeon backs up to a small area that is believed to have been the city's sculpting workshop. In the same area is a building whimsically

referred to as the **Bishop's Palace** due to the number of Christian artifacts found here.

The Bishop's Palace is, suitably, beside the city's great basilica. The layout of this building, with an apse and two side aisles, is conspicuously Christian, but it was built on the foundation of the **Temple of Aphrodite** in the fifth century. Aphrodite's temple was on the site of an earlier shrine to Ishtar, but that shift was probably less traumatic than the move to Christianity. In addition to dramatically altering the building's structure to suit their needs, Christian reformers were required to change the nature of the worship; Aphrodite's priestesses prostituted themselves, as did the temple slaves. Romans offered marvelous treasures to the temple, seeking surcease from amatory woes or in thanks to the city.

The world's best-preserved Roman **stadium** is north of the temple. The stadium, initially used for races and similar athletic events, seems to have been bisected with a wall in the seventh century to provide the city, now firmly Christian, with a better venue for gladiator games.

The **propylon**, the ceremonial entrance to the Temple of Aphrodite, seems to have stood at the crossroads of a road running south past the entrance to the Sebasteion. This building has been completely reconstructed. The man responsible for the research and reconstruction at Aphrodisias between 1961 and 1990, Kenan Erım, is buried nearby.

Pamukkale

You have seen pictures of **Pamukkale** ("Cotton Castle"). This is a fixture of tourist brochures and slideshows, with good reason. With its snow white travertine pools descending in picturesque terraces from the tumbled ruins of **Hierapolis**, the appearance of Pamukkale is more confection than geology. Pamukkale is an oddity of mineral and geothermal activity on a baffling scale.

Time was, hotels were scattered among the upper pools at Pamukkale, each with its own mineral baths. Diversion of the mineral water began to take a toll some twenty years ago—the travertines began to darken and the lustre of the pools began to fade. Spurred into action by declining tourism, Turkish authorities closed down and dismantled the clifftop hotels, one by one. Today, nothing remains but their foundations; accommodation is now located in Pamukkale town at the base of the pools, and up the road a few kilometers near Karahayıt.

Pamukkale is a two-and-one-half hour trip inland from the Selcuk area, via Denizli. The Selcuk-Denizli route follows the E-87 highway past the Aphrodisias turnoff, and continues south all the way to **Antalya.**

Pamukkale merits a day on your itinerary, and can be rewarding for a few nights that include a day trip to Aphrodisias.

History

A peculiar chemical phenomenon is responsible for the travertines at Pamukkale, and has been at work for far longer than humans have resided here. As water emerges from beneath the earth, it is rich with calcium bicarbonate. Reacting with oxygen, this breaks down to carbon dioxide, water, and calcium carbonate. The latter of these leaves deposits that collect over time—at the rate of several inches per year. As the deposits have grown, the water has fanned out, spreading the deposits over more than one and one-half miles.

Humans have surely been speculating about origin of the pools since they chanced upon them untold thousands of years ago, and in a less scientific age the explanations were simpler and more colorful. In one version, the moon goddess Selene descended to earth by night to seduce the handsome shepherd Endymion. Endymion, much distracted, neglected his flocks, whose milk spilled out in a torrent down the side of the hill. In another version, the travertines are huge sheafs of wool left to dry by giants.

The waters of Pamukkale are thought to be good for rheumatism, high blood pressure, heart trouble, nervous disorders, urinary problems, and even ugliness (see sidebar below under *Seeing the Sights*). Today we know that the waters have iron, magnesium, and sodium chloride, perhaps accounting for some beneficial effects. Residents of the area have long made use of these waters, both for their curative and beautifying properties and more practical things; according to Vitruvius, area farmers would make an annual harvest of the newly formed limestone, stripping it from the walls of their irrigation channels. This limestone they would use as field markers.

At the beginning of the second century B.C. Eumenes II of Pergamon founded Hierapolis, probably naming it after Hiera, the wife of the dynasty's founder. The city of Hieropolis enjoyed both the water's marvelous properties and some strategic importance. Hierapolis straddles trade routes in four directions, and it was a center of mining and wool production.

The ruins of Hierapolis are impressive, but otherwise the city has left little for the historic record. There is much evidence that quakes plagued the area, this despite extensive supplication to Poseidon the Earth Shaker. Several Roman Emperors visited, including Valens and the eponymous Hadrian, attracted by word of the medicinal waters. As the Byzantine empire waned, so too did Hieropolis; the city was ravaged by Arab and Turkish invaders, then abandoned.

Arrivals & Departures

By Bus & Train

Virtually all bus service is based out of Denizli, 18 kilometers south of Pamukkale. Minibuses make trips back and forth between Denizli and Pamukkale on the half-hour through most of the year ($1). In addition, most hotels are so wary of competing touts that they will gladly provide a ride.

Several bus companies—including the Pamukkale company—have offices in Pamukkale town, and you can make all ongoing arrangements from there. In the high season you can secure bus service—directly or via Denizli—to İstanbul (10 hours, $13, 8:30 a.m. to 11 p.m.), Ankara (6 hours, $6, round-the-clock), Antalya (4.5 hours, $6, round-the-clock), Dalyan (4.5 hours, $4.50, two times daily), Selcuk (3 hours, $4, three times daily), Bodrum (5 hours, $6, four times daily), and many other destinations. In Pamukkale buses and dolmuş leave you in the center of town below the travertine cliffs.

Note: if you have an ongoing reservation, bus companies in Denizli will hold your luggage while you head off to see Pamukkale. Outside of high season, be aware that minibuses from Pamukkale to Denizli are not frequent—you may need to take a taxi ($10).

A sleeper train travels back and forth between İstanbul and Denizli. This is one of the few train services that we recommend; trains depart Haydarpaşa station in İstanbul at 5:35 p.m. daily, arriving Denizli at 8:34 a.m. Return trains depart Denizli at 17:05, arriving Haydarpaşa station at 8:343 a.m. Sleeper cabins cost $20 per person.

By Car

Pamukkale is 18 kilometers north of Denizli. The highway between Izmir and Antalya is heavily-used and in excellent shape; the two lane road to Pamukkale is also in good condition.

Orientation

An excellent tourism information office is located in the bowels of the Denizli otogar, Atatürk Cad. Ufuk Apt. No. 8, *Tel. (258) 264-3971*. Another small tourism information office is located atop the Pamukkale pools in the high season; this is a useless location for anyone in search of information about accommodations.

Where to Stay & Eat

With the closure of the hotels atop the upper travertines, accommodations are now limited to those in Pamukkale town and in Karahayıt nearby. The tourism infrastructure in Pamukkale town swelled in the

1980s and 1990s, well beyond the pace of tourism itself; the contraction has been unpleasant, and competition is fierce. We recommend dining at your hotel.

KORAY HOTEL, *No. 27 Fevzi Çakmak Cad., Pamukkale. Tel. (258) 272-2300; Fax (258) 272-2095; Email: korayotel@hotmail.com; Web: www.korayotel.com. Rooms: 45. Credit cards accepted. Open year-round. Double: $22 (half-board $28).*

The Koray, run by some half-dozen sons of patriarch Rifat Durmuş, offers spare, tidy, conscientiously-maintained rooms. "Clean, hot water, food, smile," says youngest son Nevzat, and that litany rings true. In addition, you'll find a courtyard pool fed by the springs and a dining room with one real vanity, an enclosed freestanding terrace used for bellydancing shows in high season. This is a solid, friendly choice in Pamukkale, and you'll find lots of information about local sights and Internet access. The Koray Hotel is located about one half kilometer from town center, south of the main road at the Aspawa Hotel.

YÖRÜK MOTEL, *Atatürk Caddesi, Pamukkale. Tel. (258) 272-2073; Fax (258) 272-2073. Rooms: 58. Credit cards accepted. Open year-round. Double: $30 (breakfast included).*

The Yoruk, located just 100 paces downhill from the center of town, is a long-time fixture in Pamukkale. The standard of accommodation is good, with pleasant rooms surrounding a large courtyard with a garden and pool. Details are amiss, but everything works and the staff is helpful.

MELTEM MOTEL, *Kuzey Sok. No. 9, Pamukkale. Tel. (258) 272-2413; Fax (258) 272-2414; Email: meltemmotel@superonline.com; Web: none. Rooms: 19. Credit cards not accepted. Open year-round. Double: $14.*

This is the finest budget/backpacker hotel in Pamukkale, offering a marvelous combination of clean, simple rooms and a great (albeit smoky) sitting room. You'll find Internet access, a DVD player with a huge selection of American films, snacks, laundry, book exchange, and note-books full of information about the local sites. Evenings in high season see bellydancing shows. The Meltem is located a couple of blocks west of upper Pamukkale town. Ownership was in the process of opening the Meltem II during our last visit; it looks likely to be a fine option in Pamukkale, offering air conditioning, a small pool, and bright rooms at $30 for a double.

Karahayıt

HIERAPOLIS THERMAL HOTEL, *Karahayıt, Pamukkale. Tel. (258) 271-4105; Fax (258) 262-4816; Email: hierapolis@superonline.com; Web: www.clubhierapolis.com.tr. Rooms: 179. Credit cards accepted. Open year-round. Double: $55 (half-board).*

Karahayıt is home to several upscale hotels, but few of them match their ambition. The Hierapolis is by far the most comfortable and pretty of the lot, offering spring-fed pools and thermal springs. Mosaics, busts, and reliefs pepper the interiors; they are not poorly done. You'll find tennis courts and pools in the large garden area, as well as a sizeable population of French and German tour groups.

Seeing the Sights

Pamukkale town is built up against the base of the white travertine baths. The route to the top is along a path that climbs the face of the cliff; the path follows the course of a road closed in 1994, and is entirely overrun with calcium pools. Streams of warm water sluice down the path, and are great for soothing tired feet.

The Pamukkale Travertine Baths

For most people, the first order of business upon arrival is—and should be—a walk up along the pools. Wear shorts and bring sandals if you have them; if not, bare feet work fine. If you prefer, get transportation to the upper pools and Hierapolis ruins and walk down the path, instead.

Access to the travertines is directly above Pamukkale town, along the road that passes by a ticket kiosk ($2, open dawn-dusk). A hundred yards beyond the ticket booth, you'll be wading ankle-deep in water. Most people begin at the top and hike down a short distance; the higher you climb, the more people you will see wading and swimming in the pools. At the time of this writing, the pools along the path (and the sacred pool, above) are the only places open for the public.

One kilometer above, where the path reaches the top, you'll find the blasted foundations of the hotels that once stood here. Around to the left, jutting out over the valley floor, is a point of high ground punctuated with a ruined Selcuk fortress. The large building just uphill from the upper entrance to the travertine path is **Pamukkale Museum** ($1, 9 a.m. to noon, 1-5:30 p.m.), featuring rooms full of statues, sarcophagi, and grave goods from Hierapolis.

Just beyond the museum is the centerpiece of the travertines, the sacred pools. These crystal clear pools, five kilometers deep in places and roughly 100 degrees Fahrenheit, are littered with marble columns and other detritus of their Roman heyday. The cost--$5 per person—is steep, and the pools are ringed with café tables. These pools were once on the grounds of the Pamukkale Hotel, but that hotel is among those closed.

The sacred pools mark the upper end of the springs area, and the bottom of the Hierapolis ruins. The upper entrance to the travertine path,

Forget Evian

Once upon a time, a young woman of marrying age grew despondent as years passed and no suitors came forth to ask for her hand in marriage. Finally, poor and homely, she gave up hope and pitched herself off of a cliff at Pamukkale, only to land in a large pool. A young lord came upon the girl, unconscious and injured by the fall, and tended to her. Upon her recovery, the young woman, transformed suddenly into an ethereal beauty by her immersion in the water, was asked to marry by the lord.

the museum, the sacred pools, and the ruins are all accessible by vehicle via roads that loop far around the travertines.

The Ruins of Hierapolis

Hierapolis catches many visitors off guard; they come for the bright white travertines and discover the impressive ruined city in the heights above. The ruins sprawl along the top of the cliffs, and seeing the principal sights without your own transportation entails a considerable amount of hiking.

There are several entrances to ruins; one to the east of the ruins, one to the west, and another immediately above the travertine path, alongside the sacred pools. The principal ruins run along an northwest-southeast axis with the **Arch of Domitian** to the northwest and a monstrous modern carpark canopy outside the Roman city gates in the southeast. If you're visiting by car, we advise entering from the northwest (the direction of Karahayıt)--$2, open 8:30-5:30 p.m. The main clusters of sites are by the Domitian Gate to the northwest, by the Temple of Apollo in the center of the city, and, in the heights above, the Martyrion of St. Philip.

Working your way in from the northwest you pass through the northern necropolis. One of several necropoles outside the city walls, the northern section has the most impressive set of tombs. Hieropolis proved a crossroads even in death, as the citizens of the city chose to be buried in various ways according to different traditions. There are several interesting circular tombs, hearkening back to a tradition more Lydian (6th century B.C.) than Roman. Several of the tombs are adorned with warding inscriptions. The massive arches of a broken building stand further along the main road; this was by turns a baths complex and in latter years a Byzantine basilica.

The agora, or marketplace field, uphill of the main road, sprawls behind the basilica, some three football fields in size. The back of the agora is dug into the hillside and surmounted with a line of columns. This area has been of great interest to the Italian archaeological team working at the site, as centuries of flash flooding have buried many things of note; you'll see evidence of their excavations here. The grassy agora plain is a fine place to picnic, with a fine view of Babadağ mountain above. The web of calcified streamlets that fans out over the plain is fascinating.

The modern road and the ancient road through the city part at the triple arched Domitian Gate. Continuing by foot you can follow the road directly into the heart of Hierapolis along the colonnaded main way, or hike uphill to the Martyrion of St. Philip; if you continue by road, you'll arrive at the car park by the museum and the sacred pools.

The **Martyrion of St. Philip**, perched above the ruins of Hierapolis outside the gates, is an architecturally unusual building without known precedent in Asia Minor. In original appearance somewhat like a small version of the Dome of the Rock in Jerusalem, the Martyrion was built to honor the apostle Philip, murdered while evangelizing here. The Martyrion was a site of pilgrimage, and chambers of the unique octagonal foundation were set aside for resting pilgrims. The construction of the building dates to the 5th century. If you're traveling by foot, the hike is fairly rewarding—but be aware that the hike is a long one.

Descending again into the center, you pass through the ruined city walls before reaching the **Roman Theatre** off to the left. This monumental theatre is spectacularly well-preserved, with a surprising amount of statuary and reliefs still in place. If you are fortunate enough to arrive in late June, you may have an opportunity to view a performance during the International Pamukkale Festival. Note the small details; the bottom 11 rows of seats have carved lions feet to honor the city's best citizens, and, likewise, several rows are pierced with holes for the planting of an umbrella. There are many extravagant marble details, but the Athena and Apollo reliefs on the façade of the stage buildings are the centerpiece. The Apollo reliefs, to the left, depict Apollo's birth, continuing on the battle with the Titans, then Apollo victory over Marsyas, then the Muses dancing to Apollo's tune, and conclude with a relief of the goddess Tyche—much honored for protection of walled cities. The Athena/ Artemis reliefs, to the right, are more extensive still, featuring depictions of her hunting prowess and bits of myth.

Continuing downhill from the theatre you arrive at the ruined **Temple of Apollo**. Apollo was the central deity of Hierapolis, having supplanted Cybele, and the jumble of ruins offers little today. Most interesting by far, is the nearby **Plutonium**, a cave to the south of the temple that ws in the care of its priests. Lethal gases collect in the cave, and the priests established their holiness through demonstrations of their immunity. By some forgotten trick—surely more deceptive than holding their breath—the priests would enter the cave. The deadly gas was associated with Hades, both venerated and feared. The temple is gone, but the gas remains deadly; the opening being gated off from those more curious than sensible.

Below the Plutonium is a baths complex, then the ancient way that originated at the Domitian Gate. A ruined basilica stands just below the road, hard by the sacred pools.

Izmir

The main road north from Selcuk joins a stretch of six lane toll freeway at Belevi, whipping you through the flats toward İzmir. Should you turn south toward Pamukkale, the freeway passes within 200 yards of the stone ruin of the Belevi tomb within a mile of the freeway access.

İzmir is, and long has been, Turkey's principal city of commerce along the Aegean, having taken up the mantle Ephesus dropped so long ago. It is a bustling sea port and a city of three million people, almost entirely rebuilt since the raging fires that swept the city at the end of the Turkish War of Independence, the Greek army taking to the sea in flight. For all its 3,000 years of history, İzmir retains precious few historical sites; there is little to reward a seeker of ruins. That said, İzmir is a cosmopolitan city, a transit and commerce hub, and home to a NATO headquarters. You can get anywhere from Izmir, and indulge in some night life, dining, and bazaar hunting while here.

History

There were native Anatolian settlements at İzmir (ancient **Smyrna**) throughout the second millennia B.C., possibly including the Hittites. This has never been established as a certainty, and would shed an interesting light on the Hittite's dealings with Troy. Some legends suggest that the area was an early Amazonian settlement, unlikely because of the distance from the Amazon's native Black Sea region. The area may have simply been ruled by a matriarchy.

Greek settlers made a habit of mistreating local populations, and Herodotus reports they were true to form here. Ninth century B.C. Greek settlers arrived and were welcomed by natives of mixed Greek blood from an 11th century wave of settlement; while the hosts held a festival outside the city walls, the Greek newcomers seized the empty city.

Smyrna is honored as the birthplace of Homer, though there is really very little to indicate the claim is true. Homer is probably from somewhere in Asia Minor, but nowhere in *The Iliad's* innumerable references does he mention the Smyrnaeans or make other allusion to the region. It seems likely that the great poet would have made mention of the natives of his own city, and this he probably did, but Smyrna was not that city.

Smyrna dropped out of sight for hundreds of years after the Lydian King Alyattes decimated it in the early sixth century B.C. The great bay was still served by a minor town when Alexander the Great arrived in 334 B.C., and he spurred his generals to found a new city on the site. Ever obedient, they built a formidable trading center. Smyrna emerged from the post-Alexander wars intact, shifting peacefully to the Kingdom of Pergamon, then Rome. The Roman peace was relatively uneventful, punctuated by the contributions of Marcus Aurelius to the city after a severe earthquake.

Smyrna was the site of one of the seven churches of Revelation. In Revelation 2:9-11, St. John reassured Smyrna's congregation that the persecution it was enduring would be rewarded: "Only be faithful until death and I will give you the crown of life. He who is victorious cannot be harmed by the second death." The site of the church may have been at Tepekule, inland of Turgut Özal Parkı in the northeast of town, but this early settlement had been largely abandoned after the foundation of a new town by Mt. Pagus.

The Byzantine peace did not last as long. The city fell to the Arabs in 672, and the Muslim hold on the city proved fairly tight. In 1090. the Emir of Smyrna contributed to a siege of Constantinople that seemed likely to breach the walls, but was eventually stopped by the diplomatic maneuvering of the Byzantines. A mere seven years later the First Crusade swept through Asia Minor, and the Byzantines took the opportunity to seize Smyrna back from its Muslim occupiers. The Byzantine grip on the area became even more sure when, in 1204, the Fourth Crusade seized Constantinople; Byzantine rulers fanned out into the region and established strong, short-lived kingdoms, though İzmir was left for the Latin Knights of St. John to seize after the Byzantines retook Constantinople.

Even the Knights of St. John, however, stood no chance against the sudden storm that came in 1402, when **Tamurlane** emerged from the east and shattered the Ottoman army. The conqueror next set his heart on Smyrna, which he took after a ferocious battle, building a great pile of heads in the aftermath. After Tamurlane's return to the east, one of the first acts of Mehmet I's reign was to occupy Smyrna, which remained in Ottoman control thereafter.

At this point the history of most cities fades. Not so Smyrna. Smyrna was given to the Greeks as part of the partition of Turkey following WW

I. It was from here that the Greeks, spurred on by Prime Minster Lloyd George of England, invaded the heart of Turkey to seize further territory. This proved a fatal mistake. The Turks, demoralized and spent after the collapse of the long-suffering Ottoman Empire, were roused at last by the invasion and intelligently marshalled by Mustafa Kemal (Atatürk). Under Kemal, a Turkish Nationalist movement blossomed. When the Greeks drove toward the nationalist capital at Ankara, Kemal checked them, defeated them, and on September 9, 1922 drove them back across Anatolia and out, often literally, into the sea. During this battle a fire began that raged through the northern end of the city; Turks and Greeks still blame one another for the damage.

As a result of that fire, İzmir began with a clean slate, and, as at Ankara, the result is admirable. For all its gruesome history, İzmir is an eminently liveable city.

Arrivals & Departures

By Air

İzmir's **Adnan Menderes Airport** has flights to Ankara and İstanbul, as well as international connections. As usual, Havaş buses run between the airport and the Turkish Airlines office (THY) in the Alsancak district. The THY office is located below the Büyük Efes Otel inland of Cumhuriet Meydanı and the Atatürk statue (Gaziosmanpasa Bulvarı No: 1/F, Büyük Efes Oteli Altı. *Tel. (232) 425-8280*). Havaş buses run throughout the day, leaving from in front of the Grand Efes Hotel and Tourism Information office ($2); a taxi from downtown will cost $15.

By Bus

All roads lead to Izmir, and the new otogar on the ring road east of town is busy day and night. Upon arrival, your bus company will provide ongoing minibus service to downtown. In addition, minibuses marked "Efes" ply the 5 kilometer route between the otogar and the Grand Efes Hotel in the center of downtown every half-hour ($1.25). Taxis are always available as well; better to take the minibus to downtown Izmir and continue by cab from there.

Leaving Izmir via bus, make reservations with one of the larger bus companies (Varan and Kamil Koç, for instance); they will provide service to the otogar. Bus information: İstanbul, 9 hours, $11; Ankara, 9 hours, $9; Marmaris, 6 hours, $6; Selcuk, one hour, $2; Antalya, 8 hours, $10; Çanakkale, 5 hours, $7; Bursa, 5 hours, $5; Fethiye, 7 hours, $7; Bodrum, 6 hours, $6.

By Car

İzmir is the hub for traffic along the coast north and south, and also

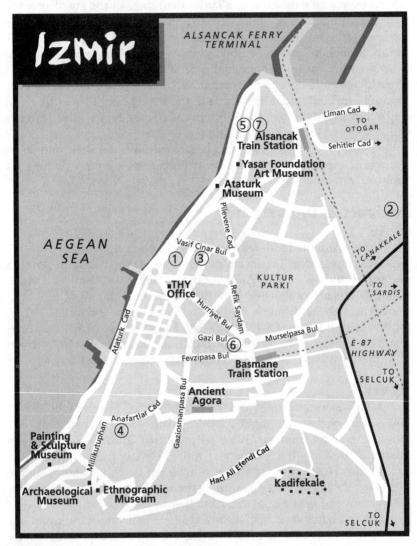

Izmir

ALSANCAK FERRY TERMINAL

Liman Cad →
TO OTOGAR

Sehitler Cad →

⑤ ⑦ **Alsancak Train Station**

②

TO CANAKKALE

■ **Yasar Foundation Art Museum**

■ **Ataturk Museum**

Pilevene Cad

AEGEAN SEA

Vasif Cinar Bul

① ③

KULTUR PARKI

TO SARDIS

■**THY Office**

Hurriyet Bul

Refik Saydam

Ataturk Cad

Gazi Bul

⑥

Murselpasa Bul

E-87 HIGHWAY

Fevzipasa Bul

TO SELCUK

Basmane Train Station

Gaziosmanpasa Bul

Ancient Agora

Anafartlar Cad

Millikutuphan

④

Painting & Sculpture Museum ■

Haci Ali Efendi Cad

Kadifekale

Archaeological Museum ■ ■**Ethnographic Museum**

TO SELCUK

HOTELS

1. Kismet
2. Anba Hotel
3. Karaca Hotel
4. Hotel Antikhan
5. Turkevi Pansiyon
6. Hisar Hotel
7. Deniz Pansiyon

for traffic to Çeşme and İstanbul via Manısa. If traveling to Istanbul, strongly consider driving as far as Bandirma and catching an ongoing ferry (six daily, $39 for car and driver, $8 per passenger).

Because of incessant road construction in all parts of the city, major arterials are often diverted to other roads or highways, and they can be poorly signed, if at all. Stay alert (and make sure you pick up the Turkey country map and an İzmir city map at a tourist information office).

By Ferry & Private Boat

Turkish Maritime Lines cruises depart from İzmir for Venice, Italy once a week between April and early September (see Chapter 6, Planning Your Trip). The trip to Venice takes 2 and one-half days and leaves on Wednesdays at 4 p.m. (subject to change); the ferry leaves Venice at 9 p.m. on Saturdays. One way rates for two range from $200-$500 in high season, from $150-$400 in low season. The Turkish Maritime Lines İzmir office is located on the waterfront at Deniz Yolları Acen., Yeni Liman. *Tel. (232) 421-1484; Fax (232) 421-1481*—the tourism inforamtion office below the Grand Efes Hotel can be of great assistance. Ferries from Çeşme, west of İzmir, travel to Brindisi, Italy

Direct ferry service to İstanbul leaves Izmir on Saturday was discontinued as of 2000. İzmir's main private marina is located far on the south of town at Levent Marina, *Tel. (232) 277-1111; Fax (232) 259-9049*.

By Train

Train travel compares unfavorably with bus travel in Turkey, but the Izmir-Ankara route is worth considering.

The İzmir-Ankara sleeper train, Ankara Mavı Tren, departs at 8:00 p.m. and arrives at 9:30 a.m. A sleeping compartment for two costs $60, dinner $10. Trains depart the Basmane train station (İzmir is listed as "Basmane" on schedules). Information is available at the Turkish Railways office in the Basmane station, *Tel. (232) 484-8638*.

Orientation

The bulk of good hotels are located in two clusters. The first is in the area of Cumhüriet Meydanı, the roundabout at the center of Izmir's waterfront; the landmark Hilton hotel stands here. The second neighborhood with good lodging is located slightly inland, near Basmane and the bazaar.

There are two other neighborhoods of note, less for their accommodations than their restaurants and nightlife.

Alsancak, north of Cumhüriet Meydanı in the direction of the Alsancak Ferry Terminal, has wide pedestrian lanes and many shops and restaurants. Ferries ply the waters back and forth to the Karşiyaka district, as well; you'll find plentiful music, bars, and fish restaurant.

The Tourism Information office, located below the Grand Efes Hotel in Cumhüriet Meydanı, is one of the most helpful in the country— Güzfent Dilemre and her colleagues can find whatever information you need. (No. 1D Gaziosmanpaşa Bulvari, *Tel. (232) 484-2147, Fax (232) 489-9278.*) There is a second Tourism Information office at Adnan Menderes International Airport, *Tel. (232) 251-5480, Fax (232) 251-1950.*

Where to Stay

Most foreign travelers have little reason to stay in İzmir, but for those who do the city has a good assortment of high-end and affordable hotels. Budget accomodations tend to be clustered around the Basmane train station.

GRAND EFES HOTEL, *Gaziosmanpaşa Bul. No. 1, İzmir. Tel. (232) 484-4300; Fax (232) 441-5695; Email: efesotel@superonline.com; Web: www.grandhotelefes.com. Rooms: 446. Open year-round. Credit cards accepted. Double (40% on-and-off season discounts available): $170.*

The Grand Efes is every bit as much a fixture in İzmir as the neighboring Hilton, and it is better regarded. The huge gardens are one attraction; another is the standard of the rooms, which offer balconies, new carpet, thick cotton bedspreads, and satellite television. The Grand Efes offers two pools; better, you can expect to receive friendly, attentive service.

İZMİR HILTON, *Gaziosmanpaşa Bul. No. 7, İzmir. Tel. (232) 441-6060; Fax (232) 441-2277. Rooms: 381. Credit cards accepted. Open year-round. Double: $130.*

If you have a terrible sense of direction, this may be the hotel for you- -the İzmir Hilton towers above the city and is visible for miles. The hotel has all of the comforts you would expect of a Hilton, including satellite television, swimming pool, a squash court, a no-smoking floor, and a, uhm, heliport.

OTEL KISMET, *1377 Sok. No. 9, Alsancak, İzmir. Tel. (232) 463-3850; Fax (232) 421-4856; Email: kismet@efes.net.tr; Web: http://www.kismet.com.tr. Rooms: 62. Open year-round. Credit cards accepted. Double (20% off-season discount available): $65, breakfast included.*

Like its sister hotel in Kuşadası, the Kismet is a three-star hotel that pays attention to the little things. The interiors are bright, clean and freshly painted, bathrooms offer marble basins, and rooms are quiet and offer satellite television and nice touches such as prints of architectural cross-sections. The location—just inland of Cumhüriet Meydanı on Sehit Nevresbey Bulvari and left on 1377 Sokak—is convenient, and stands alongside the American Hospital.

OTEL KILIM, *Atatürk Bulvarı, İzmir. Tel. (232) 484-5340; Fax (232) 489-5070; Email: kilim@kilimotel.com.tr; Web: www.kilimotel.com.tr. Rooms:*

70. *Open year-round. Credit cards accepted. Double (50% off-season discount available): $60.*

The Kilim offers clean, reasonable accommodation just a stone's throw south from Cumhüriet Meydanı. The Kilim offers air conditioning, hairdryers, and tidily off-kilter bathrooms. Twenty-eight of the Kilim's 70 rooms offer sea views for a premium of $5-$10 dollars, depending on the season—request a "deniz manzara odasi, lutfen."

OTEL MARLA, *Kazım Dirik Cad. No. 7, Pasaport, İzmir. Tel. (232) 441-4000; Fax (232) 441-1150. Rooms: 68. Open year-round. Credit cards accepted. Double: $55, breakfast included.*

The Marla is a clean, decent choice just inland of the Otel Kilim. The interiors are white with gray trim, and you'll find generous use of marble. We prefer the Kilim Hotel with its waterfront location, but the two are quite similar.

HOTEL ANTİK HAN, *Anafartlar Cad No. 600, Çankaya, İzmir. Tel. (232) 483-5925; Fax (232) 483-5925; Email: antikhan@turkport.net; Web: www.hotelguide.com.tr. Rooms: 30. Open year-round. Credit cards accepted. Double: $35.*

The Antik Han is our value choice in İzmir, a surprisingly good value in the Çankaya district, near the outskirts of the bazaar. The hotel is located in a gutted and remodeled 150-year old building, with some rooms in a modern extension. Rooms offer air conditioning and satellite television; our favorites are the two-story rooms surrounding the courtyard, each with a small desk. The courtyard, whose centerpiece is a lemon tree, is used for serving meals. Note: the Çağdas Kebap Salon across the street offers good, inexpensive meals.

DENİZ PANSİYON, *Kıbrıs Şehitler Cad., 1469 Sok. No. 122, Alsancak, İzmir. Tel. (232) 421-0187; Fax (232) 422-0343. Rooms: 9. Open year-round. Credit cards not accepted. Double: $9.*

This is strictly a budget option, but it is one of which we're fond. Young Murat Veral rents out rooms here, many of them to young Turkish students, and usually has some rooms left for travelers. It is not fastidiously clean or quiet, but there's a great tone to the place and it will afford you a great chance to get acquainted with some of the students who stay here. Bathrooms are shared, and a dinner of rice, köfte, and fries costs $1. To get there: Deniz Pansiyon is located in Alsancak near Alsancak station, just beyond where the highway ends and the ring road around the waterfront begins; look for the Akinin Yeri sign on 1469 Sok.

Çeşme

ÇEŞME KERVANSARAY OTEL, *Çeşme Kalesi yanı, Çeşme, İzmir. Tel. (232) 712-7177; Fax (232) 712-6491. Rooms: 44. Open year-round. Credit cards accepted. Double: $70.*

A charming old restored kervansaray, formerly a halfway house for traders and military people traveling along the coast. The trip to Çeşme is worth it for the sake of Çeşme's fortress and restaurants alone, but the Kervansaray offers another reason to take a spin out to the end of the peninsula. The Kervansaray is relatively expensive and can be noisy, but these venerable old buildings are always an interesting experience. The plumbing in the building has come a long way in the past five centuries, by the way: the hotel has in-room showers. The Kervansaray is closed in winter.

Where to Eat

İzmir has great fish restaurants, and you'll find most international fare represented.

DENIZ RESTAURANT, *Atatürk Cad. No. 188, Kordon, İzmir. Tel. (232) 422-0601. Moderate-Expensive.*

The Deniz Restaurant, just north of Cumhüriyet Meydanı, is considered one of the best fish restaurants in the region. A meal of soup, well-prepared cold mezes, and köfte will cost you $8; a bottle of raki for the table is another $4.50. Fish prices vary according to what is in season—the fish of the month should cost no more than $4.50. "Mevşimlik ne var?" is how to enquire after seasonal fish. Outdoor dining is available when the weather is good, with an unobstructed view over the waterfront road toward the sea. The Cordon Bleu, a few doors closer to Cumhüriyet Meydanı, is a fine choice, as well.

ALTIN KAPI, *1444 Sok. No. 9, 14 & 16, Alsancak, İzmir. Tel. (232) 422-2648. Moderate.*

1444 Sokak is home to three different Altın Kapı restaurants sharing the same ownership. Izmir residents heap praise on their doner and grills, and for good reason. The Iskender kebap, for instance, comes with thick yogurt, light pide, thin strips of lamb, and liberal doses of butter and tomato sauce poured at the table. The cost? $3. Also recommended are the Inegol köfte and spicy Adana kebap. The Altın Kapı restaurants are located just off of the Kibris Şehitler pedestrian lane, across from a Burger King and past the similarly distinguished Sofra restaurant.

VEJETARYAN RESTAURANT, *1375 Sok. No. 11, İzmir. Tel. (232) 421-7558. Moderate.*

The Vejetaryan seems to be holding its own in a world of meat-eaters and NATO warriors, making the most of traditional meatless mezes. The restaurant is operated by the İzmir Vegetarian Foundation, and is located on 1375 Sokak, by the American Hospital and the Kismet Hotel.

CENEVIZ RESTAURANT, *Asansör Teras, İzmir. Tel. (232) 443-2344.
Expensive.*
The most extravagant restaurant option in İzmir offers patio dining atop the landmark Asansör Terrace. The menu is Italian; the views of the wide crescent of lights surrounding İzmir bay are romantic.
WINDOWS ON THE BAY, *31st floor, Hilton Hotel, Gaziosmanpaşa Bul. No. 7, İzmir. Tel. (232) 441-6060. Expensive.*
Windows, high atop the Hilton hotel, is an excellent choice for an evening out. The view of the bay and the surrounding city is unparalleled, and the dining is quite good.

Karşıyaka
Things change in the hip, cobbled lanes of this district; best to enquire about which restaurant is now in favor. To get to Karşıyaka take a regular ferry from Alsancak Iskele or Konak Iskele.
HANIM AĞA, *Yalı Caddesi No. 424, Ağa, Karşıyaka, İzmir. Tel. (232) 323-5395. Moderate.*
This restaurant does great things with some of the staples of Turkish cuisine such as mantı and gözleme.

Seeing the Sights

The clock tower in the center of town beside Konak Square, was a gift from Abdül Hamid in 1901, and it displays the same elaborate flair as other late Byzantine structures. Just south of the clock tower is a cluster of public buildings, including the Fine Arts Museum and the Atatürk Cultural Center.

Inland and uphill of these, behind Turgutreis Parkı, is İzmir's **Archaeological Museum** (8:30 a.m. to 5:30 p.m., closed Mondays, $1.50). The museum has a solid collection of pieces from the ruins in the area, as well as some fine statuary from Smyrna itself. The **Ethnographic Museum** next door has a collection of furniture, textiles, and crafts that is not especially compelling.

Returning to the clock tower you can dive into the city's bazaar inland and north. The **bazaar** is closed on Sundays, otherwise it is as chaotic and interesting as that in İstanbul. We strongly recommend against a visit to the agora; an agora (marketplace square) is by nature flat and dull, and should never be a sight unto itself. There is an altar of Zeus in Smyrna's agora, which does little to invigorate the site.

The **Kadifekale**, atop Mt. Pagus, is much more interesting, and accessible by dolmuş from back at the Konak Square. This is the latest iteration of the fortresses that were built and rebuilt here. It is difficult to determine which of the many armies that occupied Smyrna were responsible for which sections of the fortress.

Today the fortress is filled with residences and birahanes (beer houses). There is no charge to enter the fortress. Note that this is one of the few sites on which the theater, once below the fortress and facing the harbor, is gone, erased by time and stone bandits. From atop Kadifekale you have an excellent overview of the city and out into the Bay of İzmir. While atop Mt. Pagus make a mental note of the green Kültürpark just beyond the Basmane railway station, particularly if you have children along; there is an amusement park there.

The peninsula is dotted with historical sites, enough to keep the intrepid ruin seeker very busy for days on end. None of the ruins are especially spectacular, but there are several worth a visit, including Teos, Colophon, and those near Çeşme.

Nightlife & Entertainment

İzmir has several cinemas featuring English-language films with Turkish subtitles. Two theatres are a short walk from Cumhüriyet Meydanı--**İzmir Sineması**, is adjacent to the Deniz Restaurant, just north of Cumhüriyet Meydanı, and **Karaca Sinemasi** is on the pedestrian lane near the Hilton (Sevgi Yolu). Tickets cost $3; less for matinees.

Magazine and bookshops with English-language news and books are plentiful. Two such: **D&R Music and Books** is on Cumhüriyet Caddesi north of the roundabout, kittycorner from McDonalds; and **Dunya Bookshop**, down the street from Deniz Restaurant on the waterfront.

İzmir's **International Festival**, an annual June/July event, is the opportunity to see concerts at ancient theaters in the vicinity, including performances at the Great Theatre at Ephesus. You can find information about the sheduled performances for the coming year by contacting the **İzmir Culture Foundation** in Alsancak (*Tel. (232) 463-0300; Fax (232) 463-0077*).

Options for nightlife abound, with the best being in the Alsancak area. During our last visit, the Outside (Şehitler Caddesi, by Alsancak Stadium east of Alsancak) was the best option for house music; Club 33 (1469 Sok. No. 40, just west of the highway offramp, a block in from Atatürk Caddesi) offers dance music well into the night.

Practical Information

The **United States Consular Agent**: Amerikan Kültür Derneği, Kazim Dirik Cad. No. 13, eighth floor, Pasaport, İzmir. *Tel. (232) 421-3643.*

The **U.K. Consulate**: 1442 Sokak, No. 49, Alsancak, Izmir. *Tel. (232) 463-5151.*

Excursions & Day Trips
SARDIS

The ancient Royal Road that wound 2,000 miles from the Mediterranean to Susa in Persia officially began in Sardis, three days march from İzmir. Today, the journey to **Sardis** takes all of two hours and follows a four-lane highway along the course first engineered thousands of years ago.

Sardis is slightly isolated from the great ruins of the coast, and is seldom overrun with visitors. So much the better; the remains of the Temple of Artemis and an impressively restored set of Roman ruins justify the 90 kilometer side trip from İzmir. If you must stay in the area, continue east to Salihli; the **Hotel Akgül**, immediately behind the Belediye building by the Otogar, is the best of your limited choices, charging $24 for a double with breakfast (*Tel/Fax (236) 713-3787*).

History

Homer counts the Maeonians, the original name of people from Sardis, among those who fought with Troy, but it was Herodotus, writing in the fifth century B.C., who ushered the city into the historical record.

The Lydian Kingdom arose in the sixth century B.C., growing in power and extending its reach from one generation to the next. The kings of this land made their capital at Sardis, a city whose own influence waxed as its coffers filled with gold mined from the nearby Paktolos River. It was here that the world's first system of coinage was developed, and the martial success of the Lydians was founded in this abundance of wealth.

The city reached its zenith under King Croesus (560-546 B.C.), from whom the fading term "rich as Croesus" remains 2,547 years after his death. Herodotus concerns himself at length with Croesus, and it is possible that some of Herodotus' information came from Aesop, a teller of fables who lived in the area at the time.

Croesus' reign was punctuated by a further succession of victories that allowed the Lydians to secure domination over the cities of the Aegean. Croesus, prospering in his great city, his armies riding roughshod, wealth pouring into the state coffers, once asked one of the Seven Sages who was the world's most fortunate man. The answer, to Croesus' surprise, was not himself but a man long dead, and the sage explained that Croesus' life, perfect in every regard, was not yet over.

The wisdom of this was soon evident. Croesus began to concern himself with the Persians, whose campaigns had pressed ever further west along the Royal Road until they now were at the Lydian frontier.

Croesus' preoccupation with oracles (see Didyma) compelled him to seek advice on whether he should go to war with the Persians. The oracle answered famously that If he went to war with the Persians he would destroy a great empire. Croesus, unfamiliar with the inscrutable ways of the oracle, assumed that the oracle was talking about the Persian Empire and unleashed a massive army, which was summarily beaten in central Anatolia. The Persians pursued Croesus' army back to Sardis, where they invested his city and took it after several Persian soldiers scaled the steep southern wall of the fortress.

Sardis fared well under the Persians, basically continuing its dominance over Asia Minor as a Persian satrapy rather than a Lydian capital. The trade routes passing the city were rendered new permanence under the Persians, who built the 2,000 mile Royal Road to Babylon and Susa. This route was appointed with inns, forts, and border crossings along its entire course, and was one of the great civil engineering feats of the age.

During the 499 B.C. revolt of the Greek coastal cities Sardis was sacked, an act that roused the Persians and ended with the leading city of the revolt, Miletus, destroyed, and its population enslaved. There was still a Persian garrison here when Alexander arrived, but the Persians chose the better part of valor and opened the city gates. Alexander found a good deal of treasure here with which to pay his troops and fund the next steps in his campaign. Nor did he forget the local population, commissioning a great Temple of Zeus. While considering where to locate the temple, Arrian reports, an isolated electrical storm occurred at one of the proposed sites, and Alexander located the temple accordingly.

Alexander's conquest went smoothly, but the consistency of the Persian peace was sorely missed during the relentless campaigns of Alexander's generals after his death. Sardis eventually fell to the Kingdom of Pergamon, and Attalus III bequeathed it to the Romans in 133 B.C.

Roman rule meant a long spell of peace here as elsewhere, although Mithradites VI's campaigns caused a bloody interruption at beginning of the first century B.C. Christianity found a receptive audience at an early date, and one of the Seven Churches of Revelation was located here. John's mention of the Sardis congregation is fairly critical. He scolded Sardis' Christians for an appearance of piety not borne out in their acts: "I have not found any work of yours completed in the eyes of God," he explained.

The city fell to the Arabs, but was back in Byzantine control in 743, when it was the site of a major battle between rival Byzantine Emperors. The iconoclast Constantine V defeated a defender of icons named Artabastus here, clearing the way for the iconoclast's march on Constantinople and an important victory for those who believed that representations of living things were anathema to God. Their political and religious eminence within the Byzantine Empire lasted a full century; it was during this period that mosaics and frescoes within churches throughout Asia Minor—including the Hagia Sophia in Constantinople—were destroyed or covered over.

Turkish tribes did not seize Sardis until the 14th century. Their control of the region slipped away in the face of Tamurlane's invasion in 1402, and the fortress at the site was sacked and badly damaged. Following Tamurlane's withdrawal into the east, Turks resettled the area without restoring the fortress.

Getting to Sardis

The highway from İzmir climbs away from the Aegean through Belkahve Pass, where an immense statue of Atatürk commemorates the closing act of the Turkish War of Independence, when the Turkish forces swept down from this pass to drive the Greek army into the sea at İzmir. Further along, entire mountainsides to the north are rent with the open scars of marble mining.

Sardis is 93 kilometers east of Izmir, on the Uşak/Ankara highway. At the time of this writing, work on the final segments of four-lane highway near the town of Sart and the Sardis ruins was being completed; the two eastbound lanes will follow the route of the old road directly past the main cluster of Sardis ruins. The westbound lanes are located one-half kilometer north of these ruins; the turning should be signed by the time you read this.

Buses and minibuses pass through Sardis from İzmir constantly, making their way inland toward Salihli, Uşak, and Ankara well beyond. Transportation each way should cost about $5; on return, take a minibus as far as Turgutlu, and another on to İzmir. The main cluster of ruins is located directly alongside the highway; the Artemis temple is located one kilometer south of town along the Sart Çay (the ancient Pactolus).

Seeing the Ruins

The ruins of Sardis are scattered for miles in all direction of the central bluff, but the principal sites are in two clusters.

Arriving from the west, you'll see the signed turnoff for the Temple of Artemis to the north. The road passes through the outskirts of Sart town, skirting broken city walls and the ruins of several old buildings. Some of the foundations along the east bank of the river were used for the heating and separating of gold. There is a small fairground with old carnival rides further along.

Set just above the stream, the Temple of Artemis is one of the most ambitious in the ancient world. Like the oracular temple at Didyma, this temple was never entirely completed. Also like the Didyma temple, its proportions are gargantuan; some column drums are more than 8 feet in diameter. The footprint of the structure is intact, starkly beautiful with its thick, broken columns—two of which still stand—against the mountainous backdrop. Worship at the site predated the Lydians, but the first record of a temple at the site was during the reign of Croesus; the sacred site was honored under the Persians, as well.

Construction of the great temple whose remains you see today began in the fourth century. Funds were probably forthcoming from Alexander (his biographer Arrian reports that Alexander, instead, bankrolled a Temple of Zeus). Work proceeded in fits and starts, and was not wholly completed 800 years later. At that time, the temple was converted to a church. The temple altar is located to the west of the temple, closest to the river. A Byzantine church is located to the south.

The hilltop just above the temple is a marvelous setting for a picnic. Returning back toward Sart town past the excavation houses, you will see a signed path for the Pyramid Tomb. The trail is difficult to follow along the terraced slope, and the tomb itself is of little interest; only its foundation peeks from beneath a tumbled earth. It is said to have been the resting place of a Persian satrap under King Cyrus.

Return to the main highway and continue a short distance east past roadside restaurants. To the north side of the road are the ruins of the Sardis Gymnasium and Synagogue (9 a.m.-6 p.m.; $1.50). This Roman section of Sardis has undergone significant restoration efforts under direction of American archaeologists from Harvard University. The centerpiece of their effort is the 50-foot high façade of the gymnasium complex, constructed in 211 A.D. The pools and chambers of the complex offer little of interest.

The synagogue building, however, is of particular interest; very few such Jewish temples have been restored to this degree in Asia Minor. Construction of the synagogue appears to have been funded by the Roman Emperor Verus (161-169 A.D.), and there is evidence that Jews settled here while it was the capital of Lydia under Croesus' predecessors. Little remains of the mosaics that once adorned the floor of the synagogue, but you will find gorgeous stretches of exposed mosaic scattered throughout the complex.

Away south, in the hills above the road, is the badly ruined theatre; far above it, inaccessible, remnants of the acropolis. To the northeast are the huge, ruined piers of the former aqueduct and the foundations of a basilica. None of these ruins are of much interest, and they are difficult to access. Bin Tepe (1,000 Hills) is an interesting site, visible in the distance to the north. This is the Royal Necropolis of Sardis, resting place of all of the Lydian Kings, most impressively that of King Alyattes. Alyattes was interred in a gigantic circular monument; it is mentioned by

Herodotus. This tumulus, which contains the father of Croesus and thus the last man to die ruler of Lydia, is more than 300 yards in diameter - three football fields - and ascends to a height of more than 160 feet. The tumulus was penetrated by a trench long ago, and Alyattes has long since surrendered his grave goods.

Chapter 22

Jason and the Argonauts and Odysseus once sailed in these waters, where the swirl of legend, myth, and fact is more intense than anywhere in the world. This forgiving landscape of cypress, olive groves and cultivated land has been the site of epic battles recorded first at **Troy** and last at **Gallipoli**.

The two battlegrounds are located less than 30 kilometers apart in the north of the Troad, separated by the Dardanelle Straits.

The road north from Izmir skirts inland, passing within 7 kilometers of the great ruins at Pergamon—now the modern city of Bergama. En route, the seaside towns of Foça and Ayvacık—somewhat overdeveloped Turkish holiday areas—afford some decent lodgings in their old towns.

At the head of Edremit Bay, the two-lane highway veers west into the Troad past another overdeveloped resort area at Akçay. Further along, where the Troad begins to reach out in the direction of the isle of Lesbos, is Assos. Many of the finest small hotels in the whole of Turkey are located in this region, built up around a gem of Hellenistic ruins.

North of Assos are the sleepy transit hubs of Ayvacık and Ezine, which offer access to peaceful Bozcaada island offshore, adorned with a magnificent Genoese fortress. Following the road north you come within five kilometers of Troy before curving inward along the Dardanelle Straits to Çanakkale, where ferries ply back and forth throughout the day and night.

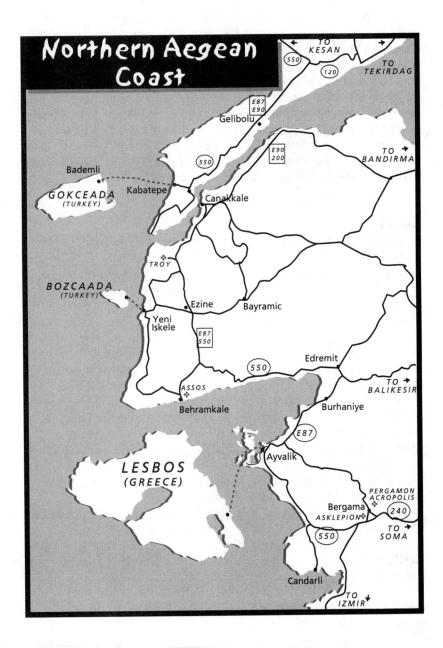

Northern Aegean Coast

TO KESAN

TO TEKIRDAG

550

120

E87
E90

Gelibolu

E90
200

TO BANDIRMA

550

Bademli

GOKCEADA
(TURKEY)

Kabatepe

Canakkale

TROY

BOZCAADA
(TURKEY)

Ezine

Bayramic

Yeni
Iskele

E87
550

Edremit

550

TO BALIKESIR

ASSOS

Behramkale

Burhaniye

E87

Ayvalik

LESBOS
(GREECE)

PERGAMON
ACROPOLIS

Bergama
ASKLEPION

240

TO SOMA

550

Candarli

TO IZMIR

Foca

As you head north from İzmir, a subtle change comes over the landscape; the soil becomes redder, the olive trees thicker. Foça, a short distance from the İzmir-Çanakkale (E 87) highway, is one of the most beatific little towns along this stretch of Aegean coast. The town's small bay is lined with rowboats, old stone houses, and waterfront restaurants.

Foça is a cozy alternative to İzmir, and is a good place to stay overnight on you way either to or from Bergama/Pergamon (although getting from Foça to Bergama and back will take some time if you aren't in a rental car). Even if you don't stay here, it's a nice place to stop in for lunch or dinner. Foça is 65 kilometers north of İzmir, and hugs the sea as it did in its day as Phocaea when its seafaring citizens settled Marseilles in the 8th century B.C.

History

The **Phocaeans**, Greek settlers themselves, never seemed to get the wanderlust out of their blood. Greeks settled the area in the ninth century B.C., although they may have replaced or mixed with an existing population. The excellent, protected harbor served the Phocaeans well, and they carried on heavy sea trade and made great voyages through the Mediterranean and the Black Sea.

Marseilles is among the cities the Phocaeans are credited with founding, and others have been located as far away as Spain. The city had an advantage in such long haul voyages, in the form of unusually massive oared ships.

The city was relegated to lesser status when the great harbors to the south began exerting themselves. The autonomous city probably fell to the Lydians during their campaign through the northern Aegean under Croesus around 555 B.C., and was subsequently taken by the Persians upon their defeat of Croesus in 546. Sometime after 190 B.C., Foça was sacked by the Romans and the Kingdom of Pergamon after those two succeeded in driving off Foça's ally, the Seleucids.

Its later history was relatively uneventful, and Foça devolved into a small fishing village. The area remained strategic, as evidenced by the Genoese walls surrounding the city. An Ottoman castle (the **Outer Castle**, or Diş Kale), built later, stands guard over the bay. The Ottomans forced the Genoese out soon after taking Constantinople.

Arrivals & Departures

By Bus

Buses travel between Eski Foça and İzmir's otogar every half hour between 6 a.m. and 9:30 p.m. in the summer. The last bus leaves İzmir at

9 p.m. There are no buses or dolmuş to Bergama or Ayvalık; bus out to Menemen and pick up an ongoing bus there.

By Car
A Yeni Foça has sprung up, literally "new Foça," but Eski Foça has the best accommodations and the nicest atmosphere. Yeni Foça is basically made up of vacation house developments (*sites*), with few facilities to serve a walk-up traveler. The road between Yeni Foça and Eski (old) Foça hugs the coast, with wonderful views of the Greek islands to the west, and plenty of militarized zone signs to match. Eski Foça, or simply Foça, is directly on the west end of the peninsula at the end of Highway 250, which leaves the main coast 550 highway 10 kilometers north of Menemen.

Orientation
The **tourism information** office is opposite the PTT at the center of town, Atatürk Bulvari No. 1, *Tel/Fax (232) 812-1222.*

Where to Stay & Eat
The hotels in Foça are generally clean, simple, and pleasant, fitting this seaside town. You probably won't fall in live with any lodgings here, but they're perfectly fine for spending a night or two.

VILLA DEDEM, *Sahil Cad. No. 66, Foça, Tel. (232) 812-1215, Fax (232) 812-2838. Rooms: 18. Double: $40.*

The Dedem is another friendly spot on the waterfront. Unlike the Amphora and Karaçam, it isn't a special class hotel, but it's just as charming.

KARAÇAM OTEL, *Sahil Cad. No. 70, Foça, Tel. (232) 812-1416, Fax (232) 812-2042. Rooms: 21. Double: $44.*

Nearby, also on the waterfront, the Karaçam is a classic whitewashed stone building looking out over the bay. Rooms are stark but pleasing. The rooms in the front half of the hotel have some of the building's old charm; the back half is a functional addition. If you have a strong reaction to mildew, this may not be the best hotel for you; the hallways have a definite mildewed taint, although the rooms themselves seemed to be fine.

ALİ BABA RESTAURANT, *Büyükdeniz Sahil Cad., Foça, Tel. (232) 812-1173. Moderate-Expensive.*

One of Foça's deservedly popular restaurants. Like all of the restaurants in town it has a good selection of fish, but more alternatives than many of the others. Be sure to ask fish prices before ordering in any of the waterfront restaurants.

CELEP RESTAURANT, *Küçükdeniz Sahil Cad., Foça, Tel. (232) 812-1495. Moderate-Expensive.*

The Celep's waterfront location makes it a beautiful place to relax in the early evening and watch the sun set. The restaurant offers fish dishes and grills.

BALIKÇI BAR, *Küçükdeniz Sahil Cad. No. 52 E, Foça, Tel. (232) 812-6270. Moderate.*

A 3-year old stylish waterfront bar that features live music, often jazz, every weekend. A beer will set you back about $2.

Yeni Foça

CLUB MEDITERANEE FOÇA HOLIDAY VILLAGE, *Yeni Foça, Tel. (232) 812-3691, Fax (232) 812-2175. Rooms: 350. Double: $90.*

This is the best of the holiday villages in the north Aegean, offering open buffet meals, pools, and a good many diversions.

Seeing the Sights

At the northern tip of the Foça harbor is a little waterfront sanctuary to Kybele that was uncovered in 1993, and a new stone path has been put up around it. There are several pretty beaches near Foça, including some at the rocks offshore. These are known as the **Siren Rocks**, so named for the whine of the breeze passing through them, and like the Sirens in *The Odyssey* they sing when the breeze stiffens. There are a smattering of ruins around town, including some restored city walls and mosaics - check in at the tourism information office for more information. The **Outer Castle** (Diş Kale), the Siren Rocks, and beaches can be visited by daily boat tours that originate in the Foça harbor. Look for the boat tour company signs.

One of the most interesting things at Foça is the **Taş Evi**, or stone house, seven kilometers east of Foça on the main road. This 8th century B.C. stone cut tomb dates almost to the arrival of colonists here and has a melange of ornamental styles reflecting native influence, such as a typically Persian stepped base. The tomb is unique, although its various elements can be found at other sites. There is no evidence of who was interred here.

Pergamon

Pergamon is one of the greatest sites in Turkey. Like Ephesus, it belongs on your itinerary if you approach the northern Aegean. Pergamon is a site that can keep you busy for days, but it is usually squeezed between a departure from İzmir or Selcuk and an arrival elsewhere. Budget at least five hours to see the major sites by car, a full day without. The ruins are located near the modern town of **Bergama**, seven kilometers off the main north-south highway. The cobbled, narrow back streets of Bergama's old quarter (clustered around the Kızıl Avlu river at the north end of town) affords great opportunities for photographers.

History

Pergamon emerged from obscurity when one of the Diadochi, the old general **Lysimachos**, stashed his hoard here during a campaign. He entrusted his vast treasure to his lieutenant, **Philetarus**, then marched out against the Seleucids, where he was defeated and killed in 281 B.C. Philetarus, much aggrieved, solaced himself by going on a great shopping spree for new city monuments and setting himself up as king in Lysimachos' stead. Philetarus (281-263 B.C.) proved a competent leader, and left the kingdom to his nephew, Eumenes. Eumenes I (263-241 B.C.) was tested almost immediately, forced to take the field against the old king Antiochus I. Eumenes won the day at the Battle of Sardis, holding off the Anatolian threat, and won the budding kingdom breathing space.

Pergamon had a wealth of arable land, and the town excelled at cultivating valuable crops and promoting trade. Both Eumenes and his successor, Attalus I, fended off a new threat from a settlement of Gauls along their eastern border. The Gauls had been hired by the Kingdom of Bithnia to serve as mercenaries, but they proved terrible neighbors to the Bithnians and the rest of Asia Minor, and Attalus I determined to put an end to their truculent, ceaseless warfare. Contriving to imprint a message saying "Victory for the King" on the innards of a sacrificial animal, Attalus inspired his army to believe that Zeus had made his judgment, and, awash with confidence, the Pergamene soldiers defeated the Gauls. Subsequent rulers began cultivating a relationship with Rome that paid off handsomely when, under Eumenes II (197-160 B.C.), the Kingdom of Pergamum and Rome combined to defeat the troublesome Seleucids, again, at the Battle of Magnesia. Pergamum reached its zenith in the years that followed, extending its reach into the interior and establishing Attaleia (modern Antalya) on the southern coast. It was under Eumenes II that the library was built and the **Asklepion** achieved fame as a place of medicine.

Pergamon's fall from greatness was extremely unusual. Attalus III (138-133 B.C.) was an oddball, busying himself with designing and testing poisons on prisoners and trifling with sculpture. None of his hobbies seem to have endeared him to his subjects, and upon his death Attalus III, with no heir, left his kingdom to Pergamon's former ally,

Rome. Many smelled a rat, and there was serious opposition to Roman occupation, which the Romans dealt with in their typically forthright fashion, posting a garrison and executing the opposition. The shift to Roman rule was unusual, but relatively smooth, and the city became a favorite of the Empire. Pergamon became the administrative capital under the Romans.

Pergamon is the site of one of the Seven Churches of Revelation, and John the Apostle was later honored by the dedication of the **Red Basilica**. The end of Roman rule and the deterioration of the Byzantines left Pergamon to be ravaged throughout the middle ages by the Arabs, the Crusaders, and a host of others as well. The city fell to the Ottomans in 1336, and they regained their grip on the city following Tamurlane's 1402-1403 invasion of the area.

Arrivals & Departures
By Bus
Bergama is located east of the main highway, and many buses passing this way unload Bergama-bound passengers at the junction. This is not ordinarily a problem, since dolmuş await by day and taxis by night, but occasionally people find themselves alone at the junction like something out of a Beckett play, and may want to try hitching the five kilometers to town. A taxi will come, eventually. Within town there is no public transportation to the acropolis, making the taxi drivers happy and $5.50 wealthier with your fare.

There are two bus stations in Bergama. The old otogar (*eski otogar*) is just south of the Kızıl Avlu river, and just east of the red basilica. Buses depart from this station to İstanbul, İzmir, Ankara, Bursa, and Soma. The new otogar (*yeni otogar*), on the main north-south street running through town across from the Çamlı Park, has buses leaving for the same destinations, plus minibuses to Ayvalık. Only two buses per day leave for İstanbul, but buses to İzmir leave every 30 minutes; it's easy to go to İzmir and then find yourself an İstanbul-bound bus from there.

By Car
Pergamon is located at Bergama, 93 kilometers north of İzmir and five kilometers off of the coast road. Pergamon is an especially fine place to bring a car, as the distances within the ruin are so unwieldy otherwise. Parking in town is easy to find.

Orientation
Modern Bergama is superimposed atop sections of the former city, but the greatest ruins stand revealed (albeit some in Berlin). Pergamon's

acropolis (to the north after going through town) and the Asklepion on the plain just west of town are the major sights, although the looming Red Basilica in the northeast quarter near the road that leads up to the acropolis shouldn't be missed. The archaeological museum is a worthwhile visit because it has a model of the Zeus alter that now lives in Berlin, but otherwise is not one of Turkey's best.

The tourism information office, *Tel. (232) 633-1862 Fax (232) 633-1862*, newly renovated, is located on Atatürk Meydanı in the center of town next to the archaeological museum.

Where to Stay & Eat

Most travelers spend one night in Bergama, a town with a serviceable range of accommodations.

Near the base of Pergamon

PENSION ATHENA, *Barbaros Mah., İmam Çıkmazı No. 9, Bergama. Tel/Fax (232) 633-3420; Email: aydinathena@hotmail.com; Web: www.athenapension.8m.com. Open year-round. Credit cards not accepted. Rooms: 8. Double: $20 (breakfast included).*

Owner Aydın Şengül has created the finest budget accommodation, and arguably the best accommodation period, in Bergama. True to its catchphrase "We are not the best, but trying to get there," Pension Athena is a humble, friendly place. The hotel is housed in a 160 year-old building near the river, and the rooms within are worn, but fine. Kitchen facilities, laundry, and Internet access are available. Aydın's boast that he offers "one of the best breakfasts in Turkey" is on the mark; he'll also prepare a picnic lunch for people who will be climbing to the Pergamon acropolis. To get there: Follow signs through town toward the Acropolis. As the road jogs right, you'll see a posted left turn toward "Kozak;" take it. One block along, where a stone bridge crosses the river, head one block left.

NİKE PENSION, *Talatpaşa Mah., Tabak Köprü Çıkmazı No. 2, Bergama. Tel. (232) 633-3901. Rooms: 5. Double: $18. Breakfast $2, dinner available.*

A lush courtyard with hundreds of carefully-tended plants (74 different flowers, according to the business card) gives way to a small set of individual and dormitory rooms. The owners, friends of the owner of the Athena Pension, are warm and helpful; they offer photocopied, hand-drawn Bergama maps that are better than the ones from the tourism information office. At our visit in 2001, the Nike Pension was being renovated. To get there: from the neighborhood of the Pension Athena, cross the old stone bridge, climb one block, turn left, and hook back right to the front door.

Near the Center
BÖBLINGEN PENSION, *Zafer Mah., Asklepion Cad. No. 2, Bergama. Tel. (232) 633-2153. Rooms: 13. Credit cards not accepted. Open year-round. Double: $20 (breakfast included).*

The Böblingen, run by the family of Hacer Altın, is a clean, quiet hotel to the west of the city center near the Asklepion. The simple, spartan rooms are available with en suite bathrooms and without. The friendly owner and his family will be happy to give you suggestions for things to see and places to eat. This is an "aile pansiyon," or "family pension", in the best sense.

ANIL HOTEL, *Hatuniye Cad. No. 4, Müze Karşısı, Bergama. Tel. (232) 631-1830; Fax (232) 6323-1615; Email: anilhotel@usa.net; Web: none. Rooms: 12. Credit cards not accepted. Open year-round. Double (30% off-season discount available): $50 (breakfast included).*

Directly across the street from the museum, the Anıl Hotel is the most comfortable accommodation in Bergama. Some of the decorative touches gave us pause--the walls are pink, the bedsteads teal—but the Anıl is new, clean, and central. Satellite television and in-room air conditioning provided.

ACROTERİA PENSİON, *Bankalar Cad., Eski Hamam Yanı No. 11, Bergama. Tel. (232) 633-2469; Fax (232) 633-1720. Rooms: 16. Double: $18. Breakfast $2. Open year-round.*

This budget pension, tucked in a side street next to the old hamam, is a three story structure surrounding a bare courtyard. Rooms are decent, but not particularly well-kept or clean. The friendly, conscientious people who operate the Acroteria try their best to make up for the shortcomings, however. Water is solar heated.

PERGAMON PENSION & RESTAURANT, *Bankalar Caddesi No. 10, Bergama. Tel. (232) 632-3492. Rooms: 6. Closed in winter. Credit cards not accepted. Double: $15 (breakfast not included).*

This budget pension is housed in a 150 year-old mansion, and feels it. In better days, Atatürk stayed in a second floor room here. Today, the hotel is dark and unclean, with a single restroom downstairs through the courtyard dining area. In a pinch, you can find it on the road to the Acropolis.

Seeing the Sights
The Acropolis
The **Acropolis** (8:30 a.m.-5:30 p.m.; $2.50), above town to the north, has the main concentration of Pergamene ruins. A narrow road of dueling tour buses winds its way to the top, where you pay $1.50 for parking and a $2.50 entrance fee. The German archaeology team responsible for the excavation of Pergamon has posted explanatory signs

among the ruins. The **Altar of Zeus**, above the agora, was built to commemorate the Pergamene victory over the Gauls under Eumenes II. The altar was decorated with statues and a frieze of giants doing battle with the gods and was perhaps the most stunning monument in the city; it is now located in Berlin's Pergamon Museum. This altar may have been what John the Apostle referred to as "the Throne of Satan" in the Book of Revelations - although John may have been referring to Pergamon's role as Roman provincial capital.

The terraced palaces along the rim of the Acropolis were occupied by various kings of Pergamon, including Eumenes II, nearest the parking lot. Heading toward the summit, you arrive at the **Library** once adjacent to the **Temple of Athena**. At the top of the hill are a set of buildings for storing food and arms against the possibility of a siege.

Backtracking to the lower levels on the theater side, the emerging form of the **Temple of Trajan** is of particular interest. Archaeologists have been piecing together bits of rubble, now strewn across the ground at the temple, trying to recreate the building. If they have continued success, this may become another Turkish photographic cliche, like the Library of Celsus at Ephesus. Even in its badly damaged state it shines like a beacon across the valley floor. The building originally had 54 columns and was dedicated to both the Emperor Trajan (98-117) and his heir, Hadrian (117-138).

Descending steeply below the acropolis is the **theater**, a peculiarly high and narrow structure owing to the cramped space. There is a stair from the Temple of Athena to the theater, which has 80 rows. Around to the side of the theater is the lower section of the city, including the **Temple of Demeter**, goddess of the harvest, and gymnasium and bath buildings. If you continue to the foot of the acropolis you arrive at the **Acropolis Gate**, a partially intact Hellenistic fortification.

Bringing water up to the Acropolis, which has no natural springs, was done by aquedect. You can see the course along a ridgeline in the hills north of the acropolis. The 3-channel terracotta pipeline, made up of 240,000 sections, ran from Madra Dağ a stunning 45 kilometers to the north, and the lead pipe that brought it up to the acropolis was capable of handling 20 atmospheres of pressure.

The Asklepion

The **Asklepion**, (8:30 a.m.-5:30 p.m.; $2.50), on the valley floor across the river, is partially in a military zone and thus you have to be careful what you do with your camera. This was a medical center, one of the leading medical institutions of the Roman age. The Asklepion functioned like a spa, with springs, water therapy, and dream analysis. Roman Emperor Caracalla (211-217 B.C.) was among the patients, and the

The Library of Pergamon

Under Eumenes II (197-160 B.C.) the **Library at Pergamon** had 200,000 books and scrolls, and the extent of the institution was considered a direct challenge to the status of Alexandria's famous library. Accordingly, the Egyptians refused to sell papyrus to their rivals, thinking that would bring to a halt the expanding collection at Pergamon. In response Pergamon created its own alternative, thin sheets of specially treated goat hide that came to be known as Pergamon-paper, and emerged in modern English as **parchment**. The shift away from papyrus, in turn, forced the Pergamenes to shift from scrolls to pages, the first step in the evolution of books as we now know them.

The great collection continued to grow even after Pergamon came under Roman control, attracting scholars from around the world. In the end the destruction of the Library at Alexandria proved the destruction of Pergamon's library as well. Marc Antony, seeking to comfort Cleopatra after the Library burned down during the Roman civil war, gave her the contents of Pergamon's Library. A new library at Alexandria used the Pergamon volumes as the core of its new collection. The loss would have been Pergamon's alone, except that after Alexandria's fall to the Arabs in 642, Caliph Omar ordered the contents of the library destroyed, eliminating in a single blow the accumulated knowledge of millennia.

presence of a library and theater on the site suggests that convalescence was fairly luxurious.

A colonnaded **Sacred Way** connected the Asklepion with the main city. In the Asklepion's forecourt you'll see the first of many snakes in relief; snakes were, then as now, a symbol of the medical profession. The significance of snakes as icons is allegedly that snakes could regenerate, but it seems likely that the early doctors would have known better. Here, as on the Acropolis, there was a library. Archaeologists are uncertain about an underground passage from the main court to a round chamber just off the premises; it may be a temple of Telesphorus, a god of healing, but it was probably related to a course of medicine. One entertaining theory is that patients were told to walk through the tunnel while doctors dropped snakes through the gaps in the ceiling as shock therapy.

The great **Red Basilica** (entrance fee $1.50), towards the northeast of town just south of the river, provides an arresting sight, a vast stone wreck looming above an otherwise typical-looking Turkish city. The basilica is built atop the **Selinus River**, with arched passageways in the foundation for the river to pass through. The peculiar situation of the basilica owes to the fact that it was not built as a basilica at all, but as a great temple, probably to the Egyptian god **Serapis**.

The building was clearly built as a center for worship, and the river's course underground was probably integral. The round towers alongside the main building served related religious functions and had pools within. The Pergamenes completed the complex, originally clad in marble, in the second century A.D. under Emperor Hadrian. Serapis worship flared up in the second and third centuries, only to be extinguished by Christianity. Christianity staked its claim to the site after the Edict of Theodosius in 392, and a church was built here. Today there is a mosque on the site.

The Doomed Baths at Allianoi

Not for the first time in Turkey, plans are afoot to erect a dam that will flood an ancient site. This time, the site is Allianoi, an elaborate Roman bath complex. The complex is being hastily explored, but its fate is in jeopardy; if the site remains open, it constitutes a very interesting half-day trip using your own transportation from Bergama. Huseyin Sengül (*Tel. (232) 659-1496*), host at the modern baths complex, can serve as guide.

The site is just across a stone Selcuk bridge on Ilie Çay, and most of the ruins have been covered by meters of siltation. As exploration continues, researchers have discovered several remarkable statues—including the statue of Aphrodite holding a basin now on display in the Bergama museum. The scale of the baths is also surprising—one arched chamber buried near the café is 65 meters long. Across the river, the extensive ruins of the Roman retreat are sprinkled with mosaics.

An extremely spartan bath complex remains in operation today, with modern pool chambers and access to some of the ancient bath structures. Turks take these waters in the summer season, citing their benefits for kidney ailments and rheumatism; outside of summer season and weekends, you're unlikely to find anyone on hand.

To get there: turn south at the Kinik/Akhisar sign next to Hotel Serapion west of Bergama. At Göcbeyli turn left at the Irindi sign; 5 kilometers along, in Irindi, take the turning 4 kilometers toward Paşaköy; Allianoi is just beyond Paşaköy.

The **Pergamon Archaeology Museum** has an admirable collection of ruins, but they are not arranged to inform. The museum has inscriptions, altars, and statues galore inside the building and on the grounds, and the pieces succeed in breathing some life into the ruin. Of particular value are depictions of great pieces looted by the Germans. There is also a statue of Nike, pre-swoosh. At the time this book went to press, the museum was still closed for restoration; it is slated for a spring 1999 re-opening.

Feeling grimy? The 600 year-old **Çarşı Hamamı** (Bankalar Cad. No. 32, *Tel. (232) 632-1075)* is the place to have it scrubbed off. Men and women have separate sections. A scrub and massage will cost you $8; it's less than $4 if you clean yourself.

Ayvalik

From Bergama, the highway slips in and out of view of the sea, following a flat course that winds around the Gulf of Edremit. You will often see the storied Greek island of Lesbos on the horizon in the west; the island is accessible from **Ayvalık**, a settlement that was once heavily populated by Greeks. Today, Ayvalık is a passable pit-stop on your journey, but offers very little to hold your attention; we recommend moving on to Assos or Yeşilyurt to the north or to Bergama in the south.

History

Although there are scattered traces of ancient communities around the Ayvalık peninsula, there is nothing of historic interest here beyond the remains of the houses and churches built by the town's formerly Greek residents. Most of the Greek residents of Ayvalık were forced to leave as part of the exchange of Greek and Turkish populations in the 1920s.

Arrivals & Departures

By Bus

It is possible to get direct buses to the Ayvalık otogar north of town, but only those that specify "Ayvalık otogar" really go there; the rest pass by on the main highway 5 kilometers east of town. The surest connection from Ayvalık is to Edremit, and all ongoing buses pass through Edremit, whether en route for Çanakkale ($7, three hours), İstanbul ($13, seven hours), Bursa ($7, five hours), or points south such as İzmir ($5, three hours). Within town, municipal (belediye) buses run from the otogar south through the center of town and on to Sarımsaklı beach.

By Ferry

One of the principal reasons for a visit to Ayvalık is to travel to Lesbos, but this is both expensive and unreliable. According to the official schedule, departures are at 9 a.m. on Tuesday, Thursday, and Saturday; plan to be in Ayvalık a day early to have your paperwork done. The cost? $50 per person one way, $70 return. To make arrangements, contact **Jale Turizm** (*Tel. (266) 312-2740, Fax (266) 312-2470*). Inquire about port tax assessed on the Greek side, as well; this varies with relations between the countries.

Orientation

The Tourism information office is located just south of the marina along the main highway. This is an inconvenient spot if you're without your own transportation, but the staff assembled by Ayşe Aksoy is extremely helpful. During the summer months a satellite tourism office opens along the waterfront in the town square. Note that the yacht marina is served by a massive Migros grocery store. Outside of central Ayvalık you'll find a long row of monstrous hotels along Sarımsaklı beach to the south, and a more sedate collection of smaller hotels on the peninsula to the west.

Where to Stay & Eat

Ayvalık boasts a few good pensions, and there is a pleasant retreat at the end of Alıbey Adası. We cannot recommend any of the hotels along Sarımsaklı beach in the south, but readers have given the small **Varol hotel** (*Tel. (266) 324-0999*) their recommendation.

TAKSIYARIS PENSION, *İsmetpaşa Mah., Maresal Çakmak Cad. No. 71, Ayvalık. Tel/Fax (266) 312-1494. Rooms: 15. Credit cards not accepted. Double: $16 (breakfast not included).*

This is one of Ayvalık's little gems, housed in a building adjacent to the Taksiyarhis Church in the narrow lanes of Ayvalık's old town.

CHEZ BELIZ, *Fethiye Mah., Maresal Çakmak Cad. No. 28, Ayvalık. Tel. (266) 312-4897; Fax (266) 229-7764. Rooms: 8. Credit cards accepted. Double: $18 (breakfast not included).*

Quite a bit further inland, Chez Beliz is a fine refuge from the hustle and bustle of Ayvalık's streets, with a friendly tone set by its hostess, Beliz Soysal. She manages, offers suggestions, and cooks dinner with equal aplomb.

YALI PANSIYON, *PTT Arkası No. 25, Ayvalık. Tel. (266) 312-2423; Fax (266) 312-3819. Rooms: 8. Credit cards not accepted. Double: $20 (breakfast not included)*

Yalı, located on the waterfront just west of the PTT, is an extraordinary 160-year-old Greek house still inhabited by its owner, Çetin Akkoç.

He rents out the upper rooms, but maintains the ground floor as his own house, complete with Turkish Republican décor. Rooms do not have bathrooms and have seen little maintenance over the years, but each room does have a soaring ceiling and marvelous built in cabinets; the balcony rooms in the back offer fine views out over the bay. You can swim from the small dock in the tree-shaded backyard.

DAYIM OCAKBAŞI, *Inonu Caddesi, PTT Yani, Ayvalık. Credit cards not accepted. Prices: Inexpensive.*

Dayım, alongside the PTT, has the advantage of being easy to find, and of offering good soup and grilled food. Alas, restaurant quality is notoriously changeable, so check with your host before heading out—and if your host is Beliz at Chez Beliz, eat in.

On Alibey Adası

ORTUNÇ, *Alibey Adası, Ayvalık. Tel. (266) 327-1120; Fax (266) 327-2082. Rooms: 22. Closed October-May. Credit cards accepted. Double: $42 (breakfast not included).*

If you are seeking a retreat, consider making your way 8 kilometers west along the newly paved road past Alibey to the tip of the peninsula. Here, a secluded set of adjoining cabins open onto a bay. A broad lawn is dotted with amphorae and with palm, fig, and olive trees, and in quieter times all you hear is the sound of the waves and the wind in the trees. The coarse sand beach opens onto one of the cleanest beaches in Turkey, as attested by its Blue Flag designation. A restaurant at the site serves fine meals. Getting to Ortunç requires your own transportation or a $15 taxi ride from Ayvalık.

Seeing the Sights

Within Ayvalık, the best thing to do is to meander through the bazaars and gawk at the fine old Greek buildings that dot the landscape. Chief among these buildings is **Taksiyarhis Church**, a former cathedral that is no longer used. If the caretaker is on hand, you can have a look around the 130-year-old building, taking in the remaining frescoes as you do.

A boat trip to the islands near Ayvalık is the best way to while away an afternoon or evening. Inquire with boats along the main square; prices hover between $9 and $11, and should include a meal.

Seytan Sofrası (Devil's Table), located about 10 kilometers west of Ayvalık, offers a nice view of sunset. If you don't have your own transportation, you'll find trips advertised as you wander along the waterfront. Atop the mesa is a recess in the stone that stories say is the footprint of the devil.

Local municipal buses and minibuses travel south from Ayvalık to Sarımsaklı Beach throughout the day ($1).

Behramkale (Assos) & Yesilyurt

From Ayvalık, the highway continues its low course along the eastern shore of Edremit Bay, passing the holiday town of Ören and the industrial city of Edremit. At Edremit the highway veers left, following the coast past the holiday town of Akkum. At Küçükuyu the the main highway begins a long climb, passing beneath Yeşilyurt and winding up towards Ayvalık on on to Çanakkale. A left turn near the outskirts of Küçükuyu takes you on a lower road through olive groves, skirting the coast for 24 kilometers to **Assos/Behramkale**.

The ruins of Assos (and, not far from here, Troy) provide the historic underpinning for spending time in this area. The ruins, the charming accommodations, the sparkling sea, and renowned air quality owing to upwelling from the deep, crystal clear waters of the Aegean make this an excellent candidate for a four day stay.

Arrivals & Departures

By Bus

Ayvalık is the regional transportation hub on the main E87 road from İzmir to Çanakkale, and Behramkale is 18 kilometers south. Dolmuş bound for Behramkale leave hourly in summer. In the off season private drivers heading into Ayvalık will take you for the going dolmuş fare. Upon arrival in Behramkale, most dolmuş go no further than the main intersection; if your hotel is in the upper city, great. If your hotel is at the Iskele, call to your hotel, find a taxi, or take a hike the steep 2 kilometer descent.

Dolmuş serve the beaches to the east and the towns to the west, stopping at the town's main intersection as they head out along the coast road. Küçükkuyu, 24 kilometers east on the E87 route, also serves Behramkale by dolmuş in the high season.

Yeşilyurt: Disembark at Küçükkuyu and find a taxi to take you to your destination in Yeşilyurt ($4).

By Car

From Küçükkuyu, follow the signed turning left 24 kilometers along the sea to Behramkale/Assos. The main highway ascends from Küçükkuyu past the Yeşilyurt turnoff, then continues a mildly harrowing road to Ayvalık. At Ayvalık one road heads 18 kilometers south to Behramkale/Assos, and the main highway continues north to Troy and

Çanakkale beyond. Should you be stuck in Ayvalık, stay at the Hotel Belediye (Municipal Hotel), also on Assos Caddesi. The Küçükkuyu-Ayvalık road and Ayvalık-Assos road are both at once picturesque and perilous–lay on the horn in those blind turns.

Orientation

The modern town of Behramkale is divided in two parts – the town, clustered around the Assos acropolis atop a hill, and the Iskele, cramped along the bottom of the steep cliff face. A sharply winding two-kilometer road connects the two. The upper section of town is an interesting warren of houses and shops built with stones that people have been recycling from the Assos ruins for thousands of years, and cobbled with more of the same. The stone town climbs toward the acropolis, where it is built up against great boulders jutting out of the hillside. The soaring acropolis, topped by the Doric Temple of Athena, was considered classic in the classic age, and remains beautiful even in its fallen state.

The town's lower section, the Iskele, is also constructed out of recycled stone, and is almost entirely given over to a handful of guest houses and restaurants. A few ships continue to fish out of the small harbor (this is not the same harbor used in ancient times - the original harbor was further around the bluff to the east).

The setting of the ruins is marvelous, with a fine view of Lesbos six miles offshore.

Where to Stay

This area has far more than its fair share of good hotels. Time was the best accommodations at Behramkale were those at the foot of the hillside at the Behramkale Iskele. The accommodations there are certainly pleasant, but they are also clustered close to one another and subject to noise til all hours. Today, the most charming, peaceful, and beautifully-constructed small stone hotels are now located in upper Behramkale by the Assos acropolis.

Reservations are necessary at any of these hotels in summer.

In upper Behramkale

THE OLD BRIDGE HOUSE, *Behramkale-Ayvacık Yol, PK2, Assos. Tel. (286) 721-7426; Fax (286) 721-7427; Email: oldbridgehouse@yahoo.com; Web: www.assos.de/oldbridgehouse. Rooms: 5, including bunk house. Credit cards accepted. Open year-round. Double (discounts in off-season): $50 (includes breakfast).*

The marvelous Old Bridge House inn derives its name from a 14th century Turkish bridge over the Tuzla River, a bridge located just 75 paces north of the front door. The setting, as elsewhere in Behramkale, is lovely, with a backyard that meanders endlessly back into the stone-strewn hills and quarries of the local countryside. People come for serenity, and find it; the sounds you hear are rain pattering on windows, the bells of sheep ambling past.

Owners Cem and Diana are massage therapists, and they embarked on building this as a labor of love. The love—and the creativity—shows. The public areas are spacious, with a cunning custom-designed stove for heat and a winding bridge to the computer niche that is an exercise in both sheetmetal and architectural philosophy.

The rooms are marvelous, both cozy and clever. Old wooden doors give way to carefully appointed rooms with white tile floors and big, comfortable beds. Radiators on each side of the bed help take the edge off the cool evenings. Budget travelers can take advantage of a bunkhouse, as well. Breakfast is delicious, and it's served 'til 3 p.m.

Selected one of our favorite small hotels.

ERİŞ PANSIYON, *No. 6, Behramkale Köyü , Kadırga Çıkışı. Tel. (286) 721-7080; Email: erispansiyon@yahoo.com; Web: www.assos.de/eris. Rooms: 4. Credit cards not accepted. Open year-round. Double (15% off-season discount available): $35 (includes breakfast).*

You enter the Eriş Pansiyon through a small courtyard bordered with roses and paved in stone. The terrace looks out over the valley below, with its back to the stone buttress below the Assos acropolis. The rooms have been carefully shaped by the American owner, a retired academic, offering double-paned windows, wood furniture, central heating, Moroccan rugs, lovely cotton bedspreads, and paintings by Rothko. Things here are just so, in a marvelous way.

Selected one of our favorite small hotels.

TIMUR'S PLACE, *PK 1 Behramkale, Ayvacık, Çanakkale. Tel/Fax (286) 721-7449; Email: timurpansiyon@yahoo.com. Rooms: 4. Two rooms open year-round. Credit cards not accepted. Double: $30(includes breakfast).*

Timur's Place is perched above Behramkale, located at the root of a great cylindrical tower that climbs to the acropolis. The view over the blue Aegean in the direction of Lesbos is mesmerizing, and it's a fine place to sip coffee in a stiff evening breeze. The rooms are less refined than others in town, but in some ways they are the more charming for it. The owner has installed false wood floors, en suite bathrooms, and other nice touches, but the roots of the old houses remain unchanged, with wood stoves and old lace curtains.

ASSOS KONUK EVI, *Behramkale, Assos. Tel. (286) 721-7081. Rooms: 4. Credit cards not accepted. Open year-round. Double: $25.*

The Konuk Evi is a sprawling place built atop a spur of the hill above Behramkale. It offers a huge garden, shockingly large stone rooms with en suite kitchens, and a sense of "Eureka." Most rooms include fireplaces, shuttered windows, and lovely views out over Behramkale; each is kept immaculate and features lots of local touches—old samovars, rugs, and pictures are tucked into every corner. You're welcome to use the grill on the expansive patio, or have the owners cook for you. The owners, Cevat and Aytaç Göner, speak little English, but they're accustomed to foreign visitors.

DOLUNAY PANSIYON, *Behramkale, Assos. Tel. (286) 721-7172. Rooms: 6. Credit cards not accepted. Open year-round. Double: $30 (includes breakfast).*

Another gorgeous offering in the upper city, set on the hillside and crafted of stone blocks culled from the ruins of Assos. The centerpiece is a large stone courtyard outfitted with vases, old wooden chairs, and growing herbs. Rooms are simple and pleasant, and painstaking clean.

Behramkale Iskele

The Iskele is located at the base of a sheer red cliff face below the ruins of Assos. The iskele has a picturesque set of old stone warehouses—now converted to hotels—and looks out over the sparkling blue water of the Aegean. By day the sounds are of lapping water, the chatter of fishermen, and birds wheeling in the breeze; by night, alas, things stay noisy til late.

BEHRAM HOTEL, *İskele Mevkii, Behramkale (Assos). Tel. (286) 721-7016; Fax (286) 721-7044; Email: behramassos@yahoo.com; Web: www.behramotel.com. Rooms: 17. Double (off-season discounts available): $55, half board. Restaurant.*

The Behram, one of the smaller hotels along the Iskele waterfront, is the most well-run of the bunch. The public spaces are heavily decorated with plants and oversized art, and the rooms are cozy. There are eight waterfront rooms, with the upper level (rooms 302-305) in nice attic spaces, so long as you don't mind low ceilings. Unlike the other hotels, the Behram does not have a central public court—which keeps it quieter. The Behram Hotel has a good patio restaurant and the exceptionally friendly and helpful Ayhan Aykanat at the front desk.

NAZLİHAN HOTEL, *İskele Mevkii, Behramkale (Assos). Tel. (286) 721-7064; Fax (286) 721-7387; Email: assos.eden@garanti.net.tr; Web: www.assosedengroup.com. Rooms: 35. Double (with view, high season): $75, half board. Restaurant.*

The Nazlıhan occupies a solidly constructed stone storehouse originally built in the 1890s. Rooms are arrayed around spacious courtyard filled with greenery and sparrows. The best rooms here have a sea view, of course, and some offer fireplaces and spacious balconies. Rooms in the back are pleasant, and are more quiet; beware those rooms facing the Fenerlihan bar to the west. Another good hotel in Behramkale's iskele area is the **Hotel Assos Kervansaray** (*Tel. (286) 721-7093; Fax (286) 721-7200*).

Near Küçükkuyu

The Çetmi Han opened its doors in Yeşilyurt in 1995, and has since been joined by three other fine hotels. We list the best of the recent additions below—if full, you will be referred to good alternatives, the four-room **Hanedan** (*Tel. (286) 752-5427*) or the sprawling Cengiz Bektaş-designed natural **Öngen Country Hotel** (*Tel. (286) 752-2434; Email: ongencountry@hotmail.com*).

ÇETMİ HAN, *Yeşilyurt Köyü, Küçükkuyu. Tel. (286) 752-6169; Fax (286) 752-6488; Email: fahir@cetmi.com; Web: www.cetmi.com. Rooms: 16. Credit cards accepted. Open year-round. Double: $60, half board. Restaurant.*

Well-run Turkish inns have a lot in common with ranch-style inns in the American west—the rooms are comfortable and spare, the service is attentive, and the food is plentiful. Canadians and Americans fond of that atmosphere, and of long evenings in the public area by a fire, will love the Çetmi Han. You can't retire to your room to flip back and forth pointlessly between CNN and MTV - the only TV is in the small bar downstairs.

This pretty hillside hotel is built with blocks of pudding stone carved square with torches. The building is not a restoration, but a faithful rendering of traditional buildings true to owner Fahir İskit's imagination; simple and traditional, with wine nooks along the wall. İskit bought the land perched high above the Aegean in 1990 and, retiring from a career with companies ranging from Sheraton to Citibank, commenced building in 1993. The hotel opened in 1995, introducing a new pit stop for those who appreciate Prokofiev over breakfast and true isolation. The Han has a section of waterfront on the seaside below.

Selected one of our favorite small hotels.

MANICI KASRI, *Yeşilyurt Köyü, Küçükkuyu. Tel. (286) 752-1731; Fax (286) 752-1734; Email: info@manicikasri.com; Web: www.manicikasri.com. Rooms: 7. Credit cards accepted. Open year-round. Double: $100 (suites $120), breakfast included. Restaurant.*

The newly-opened Manici Kasrı is sumptuous, a carefully appointed hotel for elite vacationers from Istanbul. Opened by a scion of the Ulusoy family, the Manici Kasrı offers tasteful tile, sprawling kilims, bold green walls, heavy drapes, and dark wood furniture. The interior spaces and broad patios share views out over the green valley below. Rooms offer recessed windows, old armchairs, vaulted ceilings, velvet bedding and grand paintings. Elegant Turkish dining is offered; a meal and a bottle of wine cost $25. To get there: in the center of Yeşilyurt, follow the cobbled lane left down to the end.

Selected one of our favorite small hotels.

Where to Eat

All of the recommended hotels offer excellent dining, excepting Timur's Pension. For an alternative, consider the fish restaurants along the Iskele waterfront—particularly the Behram. The docks are lined with their tables in the summer.

Upper Behramkale

CAFÉ LEMBAS, *Assos-Behramkale Köyü PK 7. Tel/Fax (286) 721-7391. Email: café_lembas@yahoo.com. Hours: 9:30 a.m. to midnight. Moderate.*

Just below the Dolunay Pansiyon in upper Behramkale, Café Lembas is set behind low stone walls and has an enclosed patio for cool evenings. The interior is simple and comfortable, with couches, armchairs, a stone hearth, and books and games. You'll want to adopt this as your home away from home while staying in Behramkale, enjoying deliciously prepared dishes that range from strawberries and cream to grilled green beans and washing them down with gin and tonic or Turkish coffee. Just ask to see what's available—it will look delicious. Mezes cost $1.50 apiece.

Behramkale Iskele

FENERLI HAN, *Iskele Mevkii, Behramkale, Ayvacık. Tel. (286) 721 7385.*

On the western side of the Iskele, big wood doors with black metal hinges open into the interior of a beautifully restored stone building. The long wood bar, heavily beamed wooden roof, and the small tables ringing the open upper level are all classic. The setting is magnificent, and the food is decent—shrimp stew, a salad and a bottle of rakı cost $15. Or, buy a $2.50 beer and watch the sun set from here. The Fenerli Han stays open til 3 a.m. on summer nights, but tries to muffle the noise – with varying degrees of success—after midnight.

Seeing the Sights

The Ruins of Assos

Behramkale's obvious site is **Assos**, a former Aeolian city with a glorious setting. This was the occasional home of Aristotle, who, later in life, would judge that a smallish, cosmopolitan city like Assos is ideal.

Assos was settled by colonists from Lesbos in 1000 B.C., chosen for its position atop a 900 foot granite bluff that rises abruptly out of the Aegean. In the ensuing centuries the settlement developed some permanent characteristics with a walled acropolis atop the peak and an artificial harbor in the sea below. Commerce thrived as the city began attracting regional trade, probably trade that had once been funneled through Troy, now in serious decline since the catastrophe of the Trojan War.

Assos' success caught the Lydian King Croesus' eye during his successful campaigns along the Aegean coast, and Croesus seized Assos by 555 B.C. The Lydian Empire was defeated by the Persians under King Cyrus just ten years later, and the Persians went on to gain control of most mainland Aegean cities, Assos included. It was during these confused times that the **Temple of Athena** was founded (signs at the site say 530 B.C., but that's a little specific). When the Persian Emperor Xerxes' army and navy were defeated in Greece (479 B.C.), Assos was among the cities that broke free and joined the Athenian Sea League.

Assos' golden age dawned in the fourth century B.C. under **King Hermias**, a student of Plato. Hermias had studied alongside Aristotle and, realizing his friend's gifts, invited the great philosopher to Assos. **Aristotle** founded his first school of philosophy in Assos in 348 B.C., a school that continued to thrive for centuries and established Assos as a place of higher learning. Soon after, Alexander the Great, Aristotle's pupil, passed unhindered through the region (334 B.C.) after giving the Persian army its first thorough beating at the River Granicus to the northeast. The Kingdom of Pergamon annexed the city toward the end of the third century B.C., and in 133 B.C. the Pergamene King bequeathed his kingdom to the Romans upon his death.

As the Romans tended to do, they brought a period of stability to Assos. St. Paul and St. Luke passed this way during their ecclesiastic journeys, and Assos became a center of Christianity as Roman power shifted to Constantinople. Alas, it was the wrong kind of Christianity for Byzantine Emperor Theodosius I, an ardent foe of "heretical" Christian sects. His edict resulted in the destruction of the town's principal temples around 382 A.D., just one of many scorched earth measures that led his Christian allies to bestow upon him the honorific "The Great." It was the same Theodosius who ended the Olympics and caused the destruction of temples throughout Asia Minor. Assos was thereafter a relatively minor city, passing back and forth between various kingdoms until annexation by the Ottomans in 1330.

The ruins at Assos are not well signed and no longer offer anything unique (to witness the wonders of the Temple of Athena you will have to visit museums in Boston, Paris, Berlin, and the Archaeological Museum in İstanbul). Still, Assos is filled with still-mighty old walls and tumbled buildings that are fun to spend a morning wandering in, and restoration work on the theater facing the sea is well underway.

The site of the **Temple of Athena** atop the hill is well marked, and has an exceptional setting. Some genuine capitals and column sections remain, but a lame restoration effort has left the temple littered with large concrete cylinders intended as faux-marble columns. The lions that once adorned the temple have been shuttled off to the aforementioned museums, along with long, beautiful reliefs and the rest of the most interesting things.

Near the upper entrance, the large stone buildings above the mosque are Byzantine towers, built on the foundations of earlier Greek structures, and the base of a Byzantine wall makes a circuit of the entire hilltop. Lower, near the road to the iskele, are the old marketplace and gymnasium, confined within a line of walls that run down toward the iskele and date back to Assos' thriving Roman period. Sections of this huge circuit of walls remain in very good condition. Note: local picture book guides to Assos are uniquely worthless.

On the way to the ruins you pass the Murat Hudavendigar Cami. This mosque, a bit boxlike, is interesting mostly as a typical example of mosque architecture in the century before the Ottomans captured Istanbul and made the quantum leaps afforded by ready access to monuments such as the Hagia Sophia. Sultan Murat I (1359-1389) was the second proper Ottoman sultan; his 30 year reign brought great tracts of land under Ottoman sway.

Near Küçükkuyu

Near the east side of Küçükkuyu is a signed turnoff for the **Zeus Altar**. The paved road winds through the ubiquitous olive groves and uphill toward the attractive Greek town of Adatepe; just before descending to Adatepe, at the three kilometer mark, a gated road leads 1.5 kilometers to the Zeus Altar. The altar is little-visited, carved into a stone buttress that juts south toward the Aegean like the prow of a ship. The views are stunning, and the carved burial niches and barrel-vaulted altar cut into the rock are interesting. The pieces of cloth tied to nearby foliage represent wishes or prayers; on weekends you may find yourself in the company of picnicking Turks, but on weekdays you'll probably be all alone. Adatepe, the town just beyond the turnoff to the Zeus Altar, offers fine accommodation at the **Hunnap Han** (*Tel. (286) 752-6581; Email: hunnaphan@mynet.com*).

Also near Küçükkuyu is the **Ethnography Museum**, located in Tahtakuşar village one mile off of the E87 highway east of Küçükkuyu. The museum has a collection of artifacts from the eastern nomadic tribes that came west and eventually formed the Ottoman Empire, and the collection is all the more intriguing with its odd similarities to Native American art and tools. Another diversion near Küçükkuyu is at the curative waters of the Kestanbolu springs.

Sports & Recreation
Beaches

There is a small beach to the east side of the Iskele. For a proper beach, however, follow the road east from Behramkale to **Kadirga beach**. Dolmuş and share-taxis run from the Iskele and Behramkale to the nearby beaches during the high season, neglecting them in winter and in the off-season. Hotels in Yeşilyurt can arrange trips to their own sections of beach.

Shopping

Piramid Gümüş (Pyramid Silver) is located in Behramkale just up the lane from the Dolunay Pansiyon. Owners Hilal and Levent Durakçay create lovely, imaginative pendants, bracelets, and rings, and they're priced quite reasonably. Recommended.

Bozcaada

Bozcaada Island is a little-known gem tucked just southwest of the mouth of the Dardanelles. Because it scarcely makes its way onto maps and into guidebooks, it is not famed for its beaches, wine, sandy cleanliness, soaring Venetian fortress, or atmosphere of relaxed calm. It should be. The hot summer season is relatively short, from June to late September, but the island's quiet times have their advantages.

History

If the wine and beaches are not enough for you, if you need some historic underpinning to justify spending a few nights on the vineyard-covered island, Bozcaada has that as well. Bozcaada, once known as **Tenedos**, was where the Greeks retired during the Trojan War to lull the Trojans into thinking the war was over. It is also home to a magnificent fortress that was occupied by the Byzantine empire, the rival Venetian and Genoese mercantile navies, and the Ottomans.

The name Tenedos comes from the island's first king, Thenes. Thenes' father, King Kynikus of Kolonus, was turned against the boy by Thenes' wicked stepmother. As seemed to be the habit at that time, Kynikus put the boy in a chest and cast him into the sea. Sure enough, Thenes washed up on a small island and became a mighty king in his own right. Years later, when his father learned of his wife's deceit he sailed out to find his son and beg his forgiveness. Alas, Thenes saw the old man approach and rushed to the docks, bitterly slashing his mooring lines. The end; the moral is wrapped up in there somewhere.

The best time to visit is between May and September, and the island is at its most beautiful toward the end of this period when the vineyards that cover the island are nearing harvest.

Arrivals & Departures

By Ferry

A ferry runs from Geyikli's Yeni Iskele to Bozcaada four times daily in summer, at 10 a.m., and 2, 7, and 9 p.m., and at midnight on Saturdays and Sundays. Leaving Bozcaada you can catch a boat at 7:30 a.m., noon, 5:30 and 8 p.m., and 11 p.m. on Saturdays and Sundays. You can stay overnight on Bozcaada, get the morning ferry, visit Troy, and make a leisurely way back to Geyikli even using public transportation. To get to Geyikli from the north, leave the main highway at Taştepe, a few miles after the Troy entrance, and follow the signs. From the south, turn off of the main highway at Ezine and continue to Geyikli. Once in Geyikli follow the signs to "Bozcaada" or "Yeni Iskele."

While waiting at the docks on the way to Bozcaada, stop off in the small restaurant just down the shore, Geyikli Sehayat Dinlenme Tesisleri, and get a bite to eat (go ahead and try the "tost," a compressed half-loaf of bread with ketchup and pastrami). Note that transporting a car across on summer weekends (especially Fridays and Sundays) can be a distinct problem as people pour in from İstanbul.

Where to Stay

Accommodations are basic, clean and usually quite appealing. The waterfront is lined with good fish restaurants.

GÜRKOL PANSİYON, *Bozcaada, Tel. (286) 697-8011. Rooms: 22. Double: $29.*

In a town packed with small pensions, the Gürkol pensions stand out. Amenities vary from room to room; the best rooms have their own stoves, allowing you to pick up some fresh seafood on the docks and cook for yourself. The owner, Halit, is one of the island's few English speakers, ever helpful and knowledgeable.

EMİROĞLU PANSIYON, *Bozcaada. Tel/Fax (286) 697-8882. Rooms: 11. Double: $32.*

The Emiroğlu is a nice choice on the northern bay, featuring a small garden for breakfast. From the ferry, bear right behind the fortress and down toward the bay on the far side.

THENES OTEL, *Bozcaada, Tel. (286) 697-8888, Fax: Tel. 286 697 8367. Rooms: 35. Double: $45. Restaurant.*

Simple, spacious, and in a cove to the south of town, the Thenes is Bozcaada's most ambitious hotel, but not in such a way as to mar the landscape or disrupt Bozcaada's peace. The Thenes has wonderful sea views and a small cove almost to itself. The hotel's biggest drawback is its inconvenience to Bozcaada town, but transportation options abound.

GÜMÜŞ HOTEL, *Kale Arkası, Bozcaada. Tel. (286) 697-8252; Fax (286) 697-0052. Credit cards not accepted. Rooms: 8. Double: $28.*
The Gümüş, located just inland of the ferry terminal, is located in an old house. Rooms in the old house are nice, with wood floors and high ceilings; rooms in the new section are not as charming, but have bathrooms en suite.

Budget Pensions
There are many small house pensions in Bozcaada as well, and you will probably be met at or even on the ferry by someone interested in taking you to their pension. Almost 100 percent certainly a good idea to have a look if you need accommodation, just don't be afraid to say no if you want to say no.

Where to Eat
ZORBA RESTAURANT, *Bozcaada. Tel. (286) 697-8616. Moderate.*
Quality seafood and other Turkish staples in a friendly atmosphere. Seasonal fish costs about $5.
YAKAMOZ BALIK RESTAURANT, *Bozcaada, Tel.* **(286) 697-8616.** *Moderate.*
Hectic, but good food. The terrace bar upstairs is excellent on a hot afternoon.

Seeing the Sights
The **Venetian fortress** is the first thing that will seize your attention upon arrival. The giant structure commands the Bozcaada harbor, and was always valued for its strategic location just across from the mouth of the Dardanelles. The Phoenicians and Greeks occupied the area, but the original fortress was Byzantine era. During the Byzantine Empire's decline the fortress became increasingly important to the great mercantile navies of the Venetians and Genoese, and the two fought and negotiated bitterly to control the island, eventually bringing the matter to arbitration in 1382, where it was decided to raze the fortress entirely. This the Venetians, who occupied the fortress, were loathe to do, and did slowly.

Still, by the time the island was ceded to the Ottomans in 1480, the fortress was a great ruin and the island virtually deserted. Under Sultan Mehmet II the Conqueror, the fortress was rebuilt, and settlers on the island were offered years of freedom from taxes. Later improvements were undertaken by Süleyman the Magnificent and Mahmud II, and, most recently, the Ministry of Culture and Tourism restored the site in 1970.

In the end, the fortress was almost too indomitable. No great battles were fought here because it was such a dominating fortification, although the Venetian and Genoese mercantile empires fought over it elsewhere. The fortress is ringed by a 30-foot wide moat and is entered from the land side by a single bridge spanning the moat - which today is used as a parking lot. The large enclosed area is fairly hilly, rising in the west to take advantage of the natural cliff face, and on the exterior grounds you find ammunition depots and wells. Within the middle ring of defenses are several structures; from north to south are the barracks and toilets, the gate house for the central keep, a mosque, an infirmary, and, on the lowest level, a garden.

Entering the keep, there is an arsenal to your right, the main storehouse in the center and, straight ahead, the commander's tower. This place is a sprawling marvel that children, photographers, and immature adults will love.

Sports & Recreation

Beaches

The best beaches on the island are in the south, conveniently shielded from the summertime north winds. The southern beaches are all about four miles away over low rolling hills, and you can get there by dolmuş, share taxis, car, or rental bikes. For bike rentals, camping information, or most other needs, contact **Ada Turism**, *Tel. (286) 697-8795*, near the city center.

Ayazma is the most popular beach, with a few small cafes along the bottom of the ridge behind it and an old Greek Orthodox monastery higher up. **Sulubahçe** and **Habbele**, further west, are also good beaches, but less isolated than Ayazma. None of these beaches are likely to be crowded in the Antalya sense, however, and the company is generally much more pleasant. If you want a section of coastline all to yourself, head to the northern side of the island and take one of the many small roads that jog one-quarter mile down to the water.

Shopping

There is a sole Yapı Kredi Bankası ATM machine on Bozcaada, and it can be fussy with foreign ATM cards. The PTT changes money for a fee attached, and they also cash traveler's checks.

Wine

The island's three major wineries offer a variety of different table wines, all of them quite cheap and sassy. None of these wines are likely to put France out of business, but there are some decent ones in the bunch. Those who claim to know say the whites are especially good.

For the price of a few $2 bottles of wine you can make the rounds of all of the wineries and try sample glassfuls at each place. There's none of the studied elegance of wineries in North America; you'll often be served directly from the pumping hose in the warehouse.

The wineries are packed close to one another; **Talay** is behind and to the left of the Belediye (Municipality) building, while **Rağbet** is a few blocks deeper in that direction. **Ataol Fabrikasi** is closer to the sea, also over on the south side of the harbor.

Wines Available at Talay Fabrikasi

The following is an example of one of the winery's offerings:

Ada Yildızı	Red/white	2 years	$1
Trova	Red/white	3 years	$1
Halikarnas	Rose	2 years	70¢
Assos	Red/white	5 years	$1
Talay	Red/white	2 years	50¢
Tenedos	Red/white	8 years	$2.50
Talay Üzümlu	Red	5 years	$1

Canakkale

Çanakkale is practical, but it is not especially alluring. If you plan to spend more than one night in this area (or if you have your own transportation), strongly consider staying at Behramkale/Assos or Bozcaada.

Çanakkale is situated between Troy and Gallipoli in the northwest corner of Turkey, on the Asian side of the Dardanelles' main ferry crossing. Whether coming from İstanbul at the beginning of a loop out to the Aegean or heading back at the end of a trip, most travellers spend a night in the region.

The declaration on the hill opposite Çanakkale on the northern side of the Dardanelles commemorates the Ottoman victory at Gallipoli and reads: "Stop ye passersby! The land you stand on is where an era sank. Listen! Put your ear to the ground. There beats the heart of a nation."

History

Two of Turkey's most famed sites are located in the Dardanelles. The **Gallipoli** war memorial, a place of pilgrimage for Australians and New Zealanders on the European shore, is fascinating and touching. An altogether different sort of fascination transfixed the world in 1871, when Heinrich Schliemann announced that he had discovered the site of ancient Troy at the mouth of the Dardanelles. Thirteen distinct towns have been unearthed by archaeologists at Troy since Schliemann made his discovery, layered one on top of the other. And as Schliemann theorized, the ancient Troy, the Troy of Priam and Hector that passed into legend, is, indeed, in this cake of cities.

While wandering through the stark landscape of Gallipoli and hunting through Troy, you will appreciate the beauty of the **Dardanelles** - or **Hellespont** - as a backdrop. The Gallipoli peninsula and the Hellespont have been a beautiful lure for thousands of years, and skeptics say it was the control of these straits, not Helen, that the Greeks coveted in the 13th century B.C. Whatever the truth, myth and reality are wonderfully intertwined in this region.

The name "Hellespont" derived from the mythical princess Helle who, with her brother, was kept imprisoned by her stepmother. Fortunately, a winged ram came along and rescued them, but, alas, young Helle fell from the soaring ram, drowning in the straits. Her brother, Phrixus, wisely waited until landing, then slew the flying ram and put the ram's golden fleece in a tree protected by a dragon, where it hung until its discovery by Jason and the Argonauts. The strait's current name, the Dardanelles, refers to Dardanos, the second king of Troy (and, they say, one of Zeus' many bastard sons).

A last, fairly pointless piece of guidebook mythology is the story of **Hero and Leander**. Leander, a native of Abydos on the Asian side of the strait, fell deeply in love with the beautiful Hero, a priestess at the Temple of Aphrodite on the European side. Every night he would brave the Hellespont and swim to her, returning in the morning. One stormy night the young Hero waited in vain; Leander never came. Knowing him drowned, Hero leapt into the sea and drowned herself. An interesting note: experts say that the only way to swim the strait is from Sestos to Abydos, not in reverse. Lord Byron swam the straits in 1810 as an experiment, concluding that the young Leander could have made the crossing, but that he would have been too exhausted by the ordeal to consider romance.

Not everyone here was mythical; real people populated the area, too. With the help of hundreds of ships, **Xerxes** bridged the section of the Dardanelles near Çanakkale. His engineers used braided cords of papyrus and flax strung from shore to shore and twisted taut with wooden windlasses. Dirt, logs, and brushwood were laid over this. The effort failed initially, but was eventually successful. Xerxes mighty army - not as mighty as Herodotus' estimate of 5 million men - passed over the straits, but was stalled by the Spartans and eventually defeated at sea at the Battle of Salamis and on land at the Battle of Plataea by the united Greeks. The Persians fled back over the strait piecemeal. Note that the Serpent Column in the Hippodrome in Sultanahmet, İstanbul, was built in Greece to commemorate the Greek land victory at Plataea in 479 B.C.

Some 150 years later, Alexander the Great bridged the strait in reverse, crossed into Asia, and within two years shattered the Persian Empire. Mastery of the straits assured control of the heavy commerce between Europe and Asia, and was critical to the later success of the Romans, Byzantines, and Ottomans.

Persian Managerial Techniques

Herodotus tells of Xerxes' famous crossing in 480 B.C. As a prelude to his invasion of Greece, the Persian King assembled hundreds of ships to draw cables across the sea and form bridges for his vast army.

"But when the strait had been bridged there came a great storm upon it and smashed it and broke it all to pieces. On learning this Xerxes was furious and bade his men lay three hundred lashes on the Hellespont and lower into the sea a yoke of fetters. Indeed, I have heard that he sent also branders to brand the Hellespont. He told those who laid on the lashes to say these words, of violent arrogance, worthy of a barbarian: "You bitter water, our master lays this punishment on you because you have wronged him, though he never did you any wrong. King Xerxes will cross you, whether you will or not; it is with justice that no one sacrifices to you, who are a muddy and briny river." So he commanded that the sea be punished, and he ordered the beheading of the supervisors of the building of the bridge."

In *The Innocents Abroad*, Mark Twain mulled over this last detail: "The King, thinking that to publicly rebuke the contractors might have a good effect on the next set, called them out before the army and had them beheaded. In the next ten minutes he let a new contract on the bridge. It has been observed by ancient writers that the second bridge was a very good bridge. If our government today would rebuke some of our shoddy contractors occasionally, it might work much good."

Arrivals & Departures

By Bus

Bus travel is easy in all directions, with its hub at the otogar on

Atatürk Caddesi several blocks inland of the ferry terminal. Buses that use the Eceabat-bound ferry will drop you off and pick you up at the ferry terminal.

If you are traveling lightly and heading south you may want to pack your things along with you to Troy and afterwards get a ride to the main highway where you can grab one of the frequent southbound dolmuş (Ezine or Ayvacık) on the highway and travel onward to Assos/ Behramkale or Yükyeli Iskele/Bozcaada. Çanakkale buses to both İstanbul and İzmir cost $10 and take 5 hours.

By Car
Çanakkale is at the intersection of two major highways: the E-90 heading out to Bursa via Bandirma, and the E-87, the north-south road that runs along the entire Aegean coast, crosses from Çanakkale to Eceabat by ferry and continues up the Gallipoli peninsula to Edirne. The northern, E87, route has the better roads, but both are two lane highways in good condition.

Ferries run hourly from Eceabat on the European shore to Çanakkale according to the schedule below.

By Ferry
The ferries that call at Çanakkale are the aforementioned Eceabat ferry, a Kilitbahir ferry, and a daily ferry to Gökçeada island. The cross-Dardanelles ferry from Çanakkale to Eceabat leaves hourly between 6 a.m. and midnight and costs $3 per car plus $1 per person. The trip takes 30 minutes. The Kilitbahir ferry departs from the marina just 50 meters west of the main ferry dock, a short crossing (15 minutes), $3 per car plus $.50 per person. The Gökçeada ferry leaves Çanakkale daily at 2 p.m. in winter, 5 p.m. in summer. Other ferries of interest:

Bandirma-Istanbul. Departs for Istanbul several times daily (see İstanbul chapter for details) from Bandirma, 168 kilometers east of Çanakkale, frequent bus service.

Geyikli/Yükyeri Iskele-Bozcaada: Departs for Bozcaada island several times daily (see Bozcaada section). Located 49 kilometers south of Çanakkale.

Orientation
The main east-west road passes through the city center just a few blocks south of the ferry terminal (located on Cumhüriet Meydanı). The **tourist information office** (*Tel. (286) 217-1187*), bank machines, ferry tickets, and bus tickets, are all located at the main ferry dock in the square at the end of Cumhüriet Meydanı.

Where to Stay

Çanakkale has an undistinguished selection of hotels, but some fiercely competitive pensions. If you have your own transportation, consider staying at the gates to Troy in Tevfikiye (25 km west of Çanakkale) or in the pine forest west of Güzelyalı (10 km west of Çanakkale). If you intend to spend more than one night in the region, consider the excellent accommodations 95 kilometers south at Behramkale/Assos.

In Çanakkale, the top-end hotels are tattered, decent mid-range options are few, and two pensions are quite good (and fiercely competitive). The two best options in the area are 10 km west of town in Güzelyalı. Note: If you arrive in this area in the third week of April, you will run headlong into the week-long commemoration of Gallipoli — reservations are imperative.

Güzelyalı

TUSAN HOTEL, *17001 Güzelyalı, Çanakkale. Phone: (286) 232-8746; Fax: (286) 232-8226; E-mail: info@tusanhotel.com; Web: www.tusanhotel.com. Rooms: 64. Credit cards accepted. Open May to November. Restaurant on premises. Double (no off-season discounts): $70 (includes breakfast).*

The Tusan is at the western end of Güzelyalı, far removed from Çanakkale for better and worse—mostly better. Rooms are set back into a ridge looking out in the direction of the Dardanelles through a screen of pines. Each room has a balcony, television and the standard conveniences, and the hotel offers access to its own beach just 200 meters away. Its location 10 km west of Çanakkale and two kilometers off the main Çanakkale-Troy road makes having your own transportation essential (the hotel does not offer transfers from Çanakkale—a taxi costs $15). A typical dinner (a la carte) costs $10.

IRIS HOTEL, *Mola Caddesi No. 48, Güzelyalı, Çanakkale. Tel. (286) 232-8628; Fax (286) 232-8028; E-mail: ergentur@ttnet.net.tr; Web: www.irishotel.com. Rooms: 74. Credit cards accepted. Open year-round. Restaurant on premises. Double (45% off-season discount): $72 (includes breakfast).*

The Iris, near the center of Güzelyalı 10 km west of Çanakkale, has simple rooms with phone/tv/minibar—type conveniences, arranged around a pool. The hotel abuts the straits, and has its own stretch of beach. The garden is sprinkled with marble capitals and statuary—you're greeted by a bust of Homer. Transfers from Çanakkale available. Open buffet dinner: $10.

Çanakkale

HOTEL ANAFARTLAR, *Iskele Meydanı, Çanakkale. Tel. (286) 217-4454; Fax (286) 217-4457. Rooms: 70. Credit cards accepted. Open year-round. Restaurant on premises. Double (25% off-season discount): $35 (includes breakfast).*

The Anafartlar, located directly alongside the ferry terminal, is the best of Çanakkale's three-star options. The lobby is a bit dark and smoky, rooms are worn but clean, and the views out over the Dardanelles (in those rooms that have them) are quite good. You'll also find satellite TV and an in-house guiding company, Sudular.

OTEL BAKIR, *Iskele Meydanı, Çanakkale. Tel. (286) 217-2908; Fax (286) 217-4090. Rooms: 35. Credit cards accepted. Open year-round. Double (25% off-season discount): $25 (includes breakfast).*

A fine choice 100 meters to your right as you disembark from the ferry, just past the waterfront cafes. The Bakir stands directly above the Kilitbahir ferry marina and commands wonderful views at no great price. Freshly painted in 2001, the Bakir is worn but less ragged than the "best" hotels in Çanakkale. Get a sea-view room on an upper floor.

YELLOW ROSE PENSION, *Yeni Sokak No. 5, Çanakkale. Tel/Fax (286) 217-3343; E-mail: yellowrose1@mailexcite.com; Website: www.yellowrose.4mg.com. Rooms: 16. Credit cards accepted. Open year-round. Kitchen on premises. Double (25% off-season discount): $14 (no breakfast).*

Young Australians come to Çanakkale in droves on their way to Gallipoli, fostering booming business. Both the Yellow Rose and the Anzac House (below) are perennial, and deserving, favorites. Hot water, TV and movies, internet access, good travel information, a patio, and nightly screenings of the Gallipoli film. The best rooms in the Yellow Rose are in the old house, on the second floor—quieter, cooler in summer, and smoke from the lobby can't get up here. Easy access to TJ's Tours information. To get there: from the ferry dock, head a 20 meters inland, continue right to the clock tower, then take a left for another 20 meters—you'll see the signs.

ANZAC HOUSE, *Cumhüriet Meydanı No. 61 17100, Çanakkale. Tel. (286) 213-5969; Fax (286) 217-2906; E-mail: hasslefree@anzachouse.com; Website: www.anzachouse.com. Rooms: 25. Credit cards accepted. Open year-round. Double (25% off-season discount): $14 (no breakfast).*

The Anzac House offers the same perks and popularity available at the Yellow Rose, in a somewhat slicker manner. Its location directly on the main road from the ferry terminal helps it poach the most backpackers, so it's a bit noisier than the Yellow Rose. Clean, freshly painted in 2001, new tile, and sporting a renovated lobby and Gallipoli viewing area.

Tevfikiye
HOTEL HISARLIK, *Tevfikiye Köyü 17120, Çanakkale. Tel. (286) 283-0026; Fax (286) 283-0087; E-mail: thetroyguide@hotmail.come. Rooms: 11. Credit cards accepted. Open year-round. Restaurant on premises. Double (25% off-season discount): $30 (breakfast included); $40 half-board.*

Run by Mustafa Aşkın, the top Troy guide in the area, the Hotel Hisarlık is hard by the gates to Troy in the tiny village of Tevfikiye. The hotel offers a fine, quiet alternative to Çanakkale, complete with good Turkish food in the restaurant, balconies with sweeping views of the Aegean and Tenedos Island, bare, decent rooms with pine furniture, a gift shop, and a PTT office just paces away. If you have your own transportation, just follow signs to Troy. If you don't, you can pick up a direct Troy minibus at Çanakkale or simply ask to be dropped at the Troy intersection on the Çanakkale-Ezine road, where you'll await a minibus to haul you the five kilometers to Troy. Note: Mustafa suggests that, in a pinch, you knock on the door of the mechanic across the road from the Troy turnoff—he can offer a lift or call in to the hotel.

Eceabat:
TJ'S HOSTEL, *Kemalpaşa Mah., Cumhüriet Cad. No.5/A, Eceabat, Çanakkale. Phone: (286) 814-2940; Fax (286) 814-2941; E-mail: tjs_tours@excite.come. Rooms: 22. Credit cards accepted. Open year-round. Double (25% off-season discount): $14 (no breakfast).*

TJ's Hostel, whose owner runs TJ's Tours (for both Troy and Gallipoli), is the place to stay if you're particularly interested in the Gallipoli site, since it's on the European side of the straits opposite Çanakkale. The quality of TJ's is similar to the caliber of the Yellow Rose and Anzac House, with similar amenites, but the rooms are bare.

Where to Eat
You'll find several café restaurants on the marina (left as you disembark from the ferry).

LIMAN YALOVA RESTAURANT, *Gümrük Sok. No. 7, Çanakkale. Tel. (286) 217-1045; Fax (286) 217-6360; Email: yalovarest@hotmail.com. Credit cards accepted.*

Our favorite for fish, with a great view over the strait. Seasonal fish usually costs about $4—but you need to know what's seasonal around here. Here's a tip sheet: May through August: Uskumru, Sinorit, Mercan, Tekir, Barbun. September through December: Lüfer, Palamut, Karagöz, Mercan, Cıpra. To get there: bypass the waterfront cafes (Rıthım, Keyif, Yeni Intellektual, etc.) and head to the building at the end of the waterfront and up the steps.

DOYUM RESTAURANT, *Cumhüriet Meydanı No. 13, Çanakkale. Tel. (286) 217-4810.*

This is a local favorite for pide and all variety of kebaps—including Urfa (non-spicy) and Adana kebaps (spicy). The clean, popular restaurant is located directly inland of the ferry docks, four blocks in on the right hand side. Most entrees cost $3.

TRUVA 2001, *Saat Kulesi Meydanı No. 9, Çanakkale. Tel. (286) 213-3281.*

A solid choice for a relatively inexpensive meal just inland of the ferry port and clock tower. A filling meal of rice, kofte and potatoes, and stuffed zucchini costs $3.

Seeing the Sights

If you have some spare time, you should have a look around Çanakkale's **Military Museum** (closed Monday and Wednesday, closed lunch, 60¢). You can't miss it; it's housed alongside the old Çimenlik fortress on the shore. The fortress was one of two built at this section of the strait by the industrious Sultan Mehmet II, in preparation for his conquest of İstanbul. Together with the Kilitbahir ("Lock of the Sea") fortress on the European side, Çimenlik (whose name translates into the less menacing "Meadow Plain") formed the tightest bottleneck in a long gauntlet of Dardanelles fortresses.

The **Çimenlik fortress** houses a smattering of old artillery pieces and the Piri Reis Gallery of maps and books within the arsenal. Piri Reis (1470-1551) was a Gelibolu native, the foremost sailor among a people famed for their skill at sea: Gelibolu's children natives "grow up in water like alligators, their cradles are the boats, they are rocked to sleep with the lullaby of the sea" wrote one Ottoman historian. Reis demonstrated just such an affinity for sailing, and combined it with cartographic genius to create navigation books, current atlases, and even two ambitious maps of the world relying only on scattered charts and accounts.

Reis had the good fortune to be a sailor in the Ottoman fleet at its zenith under Barbarrosa, and rose to the rank of admiral of Ottoman naval forces in Egypt. His luck ran out, however, when Sultan Süleyman sent him against the Portuguese in the Gulf of Oman. After several initial successes, Reis was unable to dislodge the Portuguese from their key fortress on the Straits of Hormuz and lost his fleet in the Persian Gulf. The elderly Reis escaped, but upon his return to Cairo he was beheaded for his failure.

The maps, weapons, and munitions at Çimenlik are all interesting, but the highlights may be the two gargantuan holes poked in the fortress by the *HMS Queen Elizabeth*, one of which penetrated a deeply buried magazine. Incredibly, both shells were fired 15 miles over the Gelibolu peninsula from the open sea.

Inside the house near the entrance is a collection of models, photos, and paraphernalia that helps explain the campaign, and an entire floor devoted to pleasant charcoals and watercolors of the various battlefields by Mehmet Ali Ağa, a soldier at the time. The ship in front of the castle is a recreation of the Nusrat, a mine layer that helped doom the Allied naval assault.

The **Archaeology Museum** (closed Mondays, 75¢) in the west of town has a large collection of inscriptions, pottery, and reliefs. It is quite convenient, beside the road to Troy on your way out of town. Many of the Iron and Bronze Age pieces are from the Frank Calvert Collection, named after a U.S. Consulate officer who did some digging of his own at Hisarlık and helped draw Schliemann's attention to the area. There are some magnficient sarcophagi in the garden outside.

Across the straits is the picturesque **Kilitbahir Fortress** ($1). Together with Çimenlik, Sultan Mehmet II built Kilitbahir to prevent assistance from reaching Constantinople during his siege, and, likewise, to challenge anyone seeking to evacuate. Kilitbahir has little of interest within, but is certainly worth your time if you find yourself here.

Nightlife & Entertainment

The best place to spend an evening is **TNT Bar**, across from the clock tower. Çanakkale offers the **Tarihi Yali Hamamı** two blocks inland of the waterfront near Çimenlik fortress, on Çarşı Caddesi, and the **Büyük Hamam**, further inland at Namik Kemal Mahallesi No. 31, across from the Kurşunlu Mosque. Both are open from 6:30 to midnight ($4 for hamam, massage and rub additional $5). The modern Ferhat Hamam— 800 meters west of the ferry port, across the bridge and left on Havalani Yolu—is now the best hamam option in town ($5 for hamam, massage and rub additional $5).

Excursions & Day Trips

You've probably come out to the northeastern tip of Turkey to see Troy, perhaps Gallipoli as well. Both are well-signed, but neither is easily accessible without your own transportation or a guided tour. Excursions to both sites are addressed in detail below, and are treated differently than other excursions in this book. Note that snorkeling trips to the landing craft offshore of Gallipoli are available—inquire.

Troy

The ragged appearance of **Troy** (open 8 a.m. to 5 p.m. daily, $3.50 per person) belies its incredible past. The fall of Ilium recounted by Homer was not the final chapter in the history of this city, but it was certainly its zenith of power.

The past 3,200 years have not been kind to Ilium. Trade routes shifted and the strength and influence of its rivals grew, and even the appreciation of Romans like Julius Caesar—for whom Troy represented the home of Aeneas, the founder of Rome--did little to stall the deterioration of the city. The town was eventually abandoned in the 1300s as the Ottoman Empire began consolidating power in the region. More than a century of digging has done much to uncover sections of the city and lend coherence to the city, but with its nine layers and multiple sublayers, the city can be quite confusing. In short, Troy does not have the sheer sprawling mass or postcard horsepower of other of Turkey's ruins.

What distinguishes Troy is its marvelous history. Heroes walked the earth here, Hector and Achilles, Paris and Ajax. There is something defiantly magical about this place of myth and childhood fairy tales.

History

One of the keystone narratives of western civilization is the legend of the Trojan War. The tale of the Trojan War was scrabbled together from the accounts of Greek soldiers and lords—and the precious few Trojan survivors—who survived a long, successful siege on at the mouth of the Dardanelle straits.

This tale, passed from generation to generation as oral history, assumed different variations and new dramatic elements through the centuries. By the time Homer committed *The Iliad* to writing, the story had acquired sea serpents, a magical apple, and a cast of meddlesome gods.

By the 19th century, 3,100 years after the actual battle, most good historians were extremely skeptical of the tale, and believed the Trojan War to be little more than an idle tale. Archaeologists made some desultory attempts to locate Troy, which had long since fallen off the map, but most efforts were concentrated near Ballidağ south of the actual site. In 1870, an eccentric tycoon named Heinrich Schliemann showed up at a mound known as Hisarlık, convinced that the experts were wrong. Troy was here, he said, it had to be.

Schliemann relied on the pioneering work of Frank Calvert, an American living in the area who had become convinced that Hisarlık hid the ruins of ancient Troy. Together, using *The Iliad* as their guide, the two men set to work. The tale was very clear in some of its particulars: Troy was a close march from the sea; Troy was near two springs; the city was small enough, and the terrain smooth enough, that Hector could race around it, and later be dragged around it by Achilles' horse. Using these and other clues, the men hunted through the region, finally concluding that Troy was at Hisarlık. Years of sifting through the increasingly ancient layers proved Schliemann correct.

Just how accurate is Homer's *Iliad*? What really happened at this place? Read on.

Arrivals & Departures

By Public Transportation

Troy is located five kilometers west of the main Çanakkale/Ezine/Ayvacık highway. Major bus lines will drop you at the intersection, from which you must get to Troy on your own. During daylight hours in summer, this is not difficult—dolmuş from Çanakkale travel back and forth between Çanakkale and Tevfikiye/Hisarlık every hour or so, and you can hitch, as well.

Worst case scenario: If you find yourself waiting at the intersection with night falling, don't hesitate to walk 100 meters south to the mechanic's shop and he'll give you a ride for a few dollars or call the the Hisarlık Hotel to pick you up (*Tel. 283-0026*).

To play it safe, you can get a direct dolmuş from Çanakkale to the north or Ezine to the south. From Çanakkale, these depart frequently (almost hourly, as they fill up) from the dolmuş area alongside the bridge. From the ferry terminal, check with the Tourism Information folks to be sure no dolmuş are running from there, then go straight inland from the ferry terminal on Demircioğlu Caddesi, turn right on the main İzmir-Bandırma road (Atatürk Caddesi), and go three blocks until you are about to cross the bridge. The dolmuş stop is below on your right. To get to the dolmuş area from the central otogar, simply walk four blocks west along Atatürk Caddesi.

By Car

From Çanakkale in the east take the Çanakkale-Ezine road past Intepe, staying on E87-D550 by turning staying left at the Kumkale-Taştepe fork. The Troy turnoff is five kilometers along on the right hand side, posted with the brown "ruins" road signs, and the ruins are five kilometers further on, just 200 meters past Tevfikiye.

From the south, the main coast road takes you north past Ayvacık and Ezine. The Tevfikiye/Troy turnoff is to the left about 8 kilometers after Taştepe.

By Tour

A guided tour is quite helpful at Troy. This book should serve as a good substitute, but, like Cliff Notes, it should probably supplement a real guide. It is easy to lose your bearings among the layers and the confused terrain. The Çanakkale-area guiding services—**Hassle Free** (Çanakkale, *Tel. (286) 213-5969, Email: hasslefree@anzachouse.com*) and **TJ's Tours** (Eceabat, *Tel. (286) 814-2950, Email: tjs_tours@excite.com*)—have both have stood the test of time, get started early in the morning, and charge roughly $15 per person.

Another good option is to go straight to the master--**Mustafa Aşkın**, the man all guides at Troy consider 'hoca' (teacher) or 'habi' (uncle). Aşkın runs the Hisarlık Hotel at the gates of Troy and is tapped to show groups around the ruins several times each day, charging about $30 for a thorough private tour (*Tel. (542) 243-9359, Email: thetroyguide@hotmail.com*). His enthusiasm is endless, as is his patience with everything except guidebooks that suggest people skip Troy, for whose authors he reserves special contempt. He has, literally, written the book on Troy based on his years of guiding and investigating the sites alongside archaeologists who descend on the site each summer, including teams from the University of Cincinnati and Bryn Mawr.

THE ILIAD

The **Trojan War** began innocently enough, with a wedding. The goddess of discord, not invited, chose to liven up the proceedings by lobbing a golden apple into the crowd labeled "To the Fairest." The goddesses Hera, Athena, and Aphrodite all claimed the apple as their own, and called upon Zeus, in his infinite wisdom, to decide. Zeus, truly wise, wanted nothing to do with such a decision and passed the decision along to the naive young Trojan prince **Paris**, instead.

Each goddess tempted Paris in her way. Hera offered wealth and dominion over Asia; Athena enticed him with wisdom and martial success; Aphrodite promised the most beautiful woman in the world for his bride. It was Aphrodite's offer that stole the heart of the prince-he gave her the apple and won the beautiful Helen as his prize. And, in so doing, won the eternal enmity of Hera and Athena.

The most beautiful woman in the world was, alas, married to **Menelaus**, king of Sparta. When Paris sailed off with his bride the enraged Menelaus formed a league against Troy with the help of his brother, the great king Agamemnon. After long preparation, a force of 1,184 ships from throughout the Mediterranean set sail against Troy, seeking to force Helen's return. The attackers drew their ships up on the shore of Troy and encircled Ilium (ancient Troy) with siege walls. Powerful as they were, they were overmatched by the great wall of the city and could do nothing to seize the city. The siege continued for nine bloody years, with pitched battles fought on the plains of Troy.

The Iliad is an account of the last months of the long siege. The Greek camp is in disarray owing to the unwillingness of its champion, **Achilles**, to fight. Achilles and his soldiers remain at the rear of the Greek camp throughout the siege, embittered by an insult from Agamemnon. Determined to put an end to the long standoff, and emboldened by Achilles' absence, the Trojans begin increasing their pressure on the Greek army. With losses mounting, the Greeks beg Achilles to return to battle. He refuses, even when the Trojan champion **Hector** leads an attack that leaves Greek ships burning. The fortunes of the Greeks continue to deteriorate. Desperate, Achilles' closest companion, Patroclos, arms himself in Achilles armor and marches into battle.

Terrified at the advance of the man they believe to be Achilles, the Trojans retreat in disarray. Finally, driven across the plain to the city walls, Hector finds the courage to challenge the Greek champion. Fighting desperately, without hope of victory, Hector delivers a blow that knocks his opponent's helmet to the ground. Realizing that it is not Achilles he faces, hope returns and Hector slays Patroclos and takes the armor as his own. The Greek army flees the field, and the Trojans win the day.

This victory is the Trojans' undoing. When Achilles hears of his friend's death he is tormented and enraged, and at last vows to return to battle. As day breaks, Achilles leads the Greeks into battle and drives the Trojans into their city. For the second time, Hector stands forth as the Trojan champion, challenging Achilles outside the city walls. This time, the Trojan champion is overcome by terror and flees at Achilles' approach.

Unable to elude Achilles, Hector resigns himself to his fate, turning to fight. He overpowered by the Greek champion and killed on the spot. Achilles drags Hector's lifeless body around the besieged city on horseback, repaying the Trojans for his grief over the loss of Patroclos. In time he returns Hector's body to his father the King, and The Iliad ends with Hector burning on a funeral pyre.

As told elsewhere, Achilles died soon after, struck in the heel - his only vulnerable spot - by Paris' arrow. The Greeks, at last exhausted, resolve to make one last attempt on the city. Abandoning the field and setting sail, the Greeks leave behind a great wooden horse. The Trojans, finding their enemy of 10 years decamped, interrogate a lone Greek they find on their shores, a man who claims to have escaped becoming a human sacrifice. The man, an agent of the Greeks, explains that the horse is an offering to Athena, and that if the Trojans wheel the horse into their city the blessings of Athena will be theirs. The Trojans bring the horse within the walls and celebrate the end to their long ordeal. In the dead of night, Greek soldiers secreted in the horse steal forth and open the gates of Troy, outside of which the Greek army has hidden under cover of darkness.

In the ensuing carnage, the Greeks slaughter and enslave the entire population (excepting a precious few, including Aeneas, whose family escapes to found Rome). Troy is looted, burned, and destroyed.

THE HISTORIANS

There is indeed evidence to suggest the Trojan War occurred. A likely scenario is this: Troy had accumulated immense wealth because of its location at the mouth of the Dardanelles. Merchants, unwilling or unable to battle the great north wind that blows down the Hellespont nine months of the year, stopped at the mouth of the strait and did business in the marketplaces of Troy. The Trojans encouraged this with a naval force that could close the strait or demand payment for safe passage. Thus Troy profited from all of the trade between east and west and became the marketplace of interior Asia and Europe. Centuries of such commerce made the city prosperous.

Troy's success was coming at the expense of Greek colonists and merchants, however. The Greeks wanted unrestricted access to the interior markets and were tired of paying the Trojan duties and taxes. Compounding this, Herodotus reports that the Trojans had invaded Europe and seized a great expanse of lands extending toward Greece. The threat and the market restrictions were probably at the heart of the real conflict, although the kidnapping of Helen could certainly have been used as a pretext. The Greeks, under Mycenean control, assembled an army and landed at Troy - perhaps to the west at Beşik Cove - investing the city with siege walls rather than attacking it. Housing within Troy VIIa, the level thought to correspond with the Trojan War, is extremely cramped, and storage containers for food and water suddenly appear in this period, which would make sense if the Trojans and their goods were forced within the city walls for security reasons.

In the end, the city was defeated, looted, and burned in the 13th century B.C. How that was accomplished is unknown, but one theory is that the earthquake that struck Troy in this period coincided with the siege, and the Greeks poured through the breaches. In the aftermath, the

Greeks erected a horse as a tribute to the gods. The earthquake could have predated the siege, however, and the Trojans may have been defeated by sheer force of arms - or trickery.

Defeat finally befell the Trojans, and at least one historian puts an ironic twist on the ten-year war. No less an authority than Herodotus writes that Helen was never in Troy, having been seized, along with Menelaus' loot, in Memphis by the Pharoah Proteus. Proteus was appalled to learn that Paris had abducted Helen from her husband and stolen his treasure, and held Helen and the treasure until the wronged Greek Menelaus should come to claim them.

Herodotus says that Helen fit too tidily in Homer's epic poem to discard merely because she wasn't really there.

THE LAYERS OF TROY

I. Prior to 2500 B.C.

The first Troy was a standard town of the early Bronze Age, a collection of crude brick huts with roofs of wood and earth. As time went on houses began to assume more sophisticated designs, and defensive walls appeared around the entire citadel. Troy I was abruptly destroyed.

II. 2500-2280 B.C.

This is the level that Schliemann picked as the Troy of legend, and "Priam's Treasure," largely collected here, demonstrated that it was a time of great wealth. The Trojans repeatedly expanded their city walls to accommodate an increasing population. Troy II was destroyed by fire.

III, IV, and V. 2280-1800 B.C.

Schliemann's dig did the most damage to these layers, and he left inadequate records to reconstruct this period. The culture was unchanged from Troy II, and archaeologists believe that the town continued to prosper.

VI. 1800-1270 B.C.

Evidence appears of a new culture, probably Greek, and pottery and art establish a link with the empire at Mycenae. The city walls rise to a new height, 12 feet wide at the base and 15 feet high. There is a distinct city plan, suggesting strong authority. An earthquake ravaged Troy VI.

VII. 1270-1190 B.C.

Troy was rebuilt and its walls further strengthened, the period of wealth apparently continuing. However dwellings within the walls grew increasingly cramped, and a cataclysm befell the city around 1250 B.C. Fire raged through Troy, and there is evidence of slaughter - both of which suggest that this was indeed the unfortunate Troy of legend. As the period came to an end, people were rebuilding amid the ruins.

VIIb-2. 1190-1100 B.C.

Troy is occupied by unknown people with relatively primitive artistic skills. The city is sacked at the end of the period, and is left unoccupied.

VIII. and IX. 700 B.C.-330 A.D.

The Greeks appear again at Troy, this time establishing their own city, Ilium. The Iliad was already a famous piece of legend, and travelers came from afar to visit the city. Ilium never had the commercial success of ancient Troy, however, and in 85 B.C. the Roman general Gaius Flavius Fimbria sacked and burned the city, afterwards declaring that he had done in 11 days what it took the Greeks 10 years to do.

The city was again rebuilt, and it proved popular with the Romans, whose legendary ancestor Aeneas was supposed to have been an escaped Trojan warrior. Its success was so great that in 321 A.D. Constantine seriously considered founding his new Roman capitol here - laborers had started erecting great gates at the ancient city when a dream convinced Constantine to build at Byzantium instead. That fateful decision shifted the focus of trade to the east and into Europe, and Troy's fortunes declined steadily thereafter.

Seeing the Sights

The site ($4 per person, $2 for parking) is open between 8 a.m. to 8 p.m. in summer, 8 a.m. to 5 p.m. during the winter, with the museum, The Excavation House, maintaining the same hours. The museum is to the right of the gravel path into the Troy, and offers a valuable overview. Daimler Benz AG has spent 3.5 million DM on excavations at Troy since 1988, and some of that money has been spent on new signs.

We suggest skipping the postcard shop on your way in—make your way directly to the ruins on the gravel path between the flags. The first of the excellent new informational signs, The "Troia Logo" and "The Wind Brings Wealth to Troy", are to your left. The full circuit is a little more than one kilometer of (generally) smooth paths.

As you approach the site, the first sign is "1b. The Discovery and Excavation of Troy." (Sign "1a." was out of commission at the time of this writing.) The sign provides some background about the site.

Next is "2. The East Wall", located up the path to your right. This vantage point gives you an excellent overview of Trojan War-era Cyclopean walls—so named because later generations thought the massive pieces of stone used in their construction could only have been moved by a mythical Cyclops. The walls are at the cutting edge of the period's engineering, and would have topped by a breastwork built of baked clay bricks. Even the tower that juts out from the walls, built using dressed, iron-cut stones, was Trojan War-era. The ground at the base of this length of walls was the real ground level at the time of the Trojan War.

Descending from sign two, follow the gravel path along the foot of the walls, then left around a sharp bend and up into the city. This bend is a trick of Hittite military engineering that was employed by their Trojan contemporaries—proof against battering rams. As you ascend into the open area, bear right up a set of stairs to a flat hilltop area that looks northward toward the plains of Troy and the Dardanelle Straits.

Here, find sign "3. The Northeast Bastion." Read it, then, if nobody seems to mind, hop the line and take a look down through the grill just below—it protects a trench that extends all the way to the foot of the Troy VII city walls, far, far below.

From sign 3, descend back toward sign "IX, VIII" and continue a short distance up a small hill to "4. Athena Temple". This temple was similar to the one later built at Assos (a temple whose foundation is intact). Alexander the Great, Julius Caesar, and even the Persian King Xerxes made offerings at this site, although offerings here did the Trojans precious little good—Athena, angry with Troy on account of Paris' decision with the apple, sided with the Greek armies.

At the time of this writing, scholars were building walls of red mud-brick, testing their theories about the composition of the battlements that topped the walls of Priam's Troy VII.

From sign 4, return to the "IX, VIII" sign and descend to your left past great pieces of worked marble and column drums and continue to "5. Fortification Wall." It is a wall of this kind that would have been surmounted by the mud brick walls currently being tested.

From sign 5, continue toward sign II, then to sign "6. Aristocrat's Residence." This spot offers an excellent view of the mouth of the Dardanelles, on the horizon. At the time of the Trojan War, the Greek ships were drawn up at the coast in the direction of Kumkale, but possibly quite a bit nearer—the sea was much closer to the city walls 3,000 years ago.

A little further on sign "7. The Schliemann Trench" gives you a glimpse of the great historic cake that the German archaeologist struggled to make sense of. Still further along a wooden platform, sign "D." offers an excellent illustration of the levels of Troy, with each period clearly identified. Continue down wooden stairs past a cistern—on your left—and you find yourself at the quite unmistakable Great Ramp. The sign for this area is ahead and to the right.

Sign "8. The Ramp" marks one of the most distinctive sites at Troy. The ramp post-dates the Iliad-era Troy, but it was near here, in 1873, that Schliemann discovered "Priam's Treasure." The treasure – thousands of pieces of gold, ceramics, and ornaments – was actually cobbled together piecemeal through years of digging. The bulk of this treasure is now housed in the Pushkin Museum.

Looping back around to Sign "9. Palace House," consider for a moment that the ground you stand on is at least 30 feet above ground level at the time of the Trojan War. From there, continue down a slope past a collection of tagged marble pieces to "10. Sanctuary," then uphill past a picturesque temple to "11. Odeon & Bouleterion." These structures were fixtures of civic life in the Hellenistic world.

The final sign, on the path back toward the entrance –"12. South Gate" — stands beside what remains of the great Scian Gate, the gates at which Hector fought Patroclos and was slain by Achilles. Atop the tower here King Priam and his wife Hekabe witnessed the death of their son, and the cruel ride of Achilles with Hector's lifeless body dragged behind his horses: *"His mother tore out her hair, and threw the shining veil far from her and raised a great wail as she looked upon her son; and his father beloved groaned pitifully."*

Driving Around The Ruins

The plain surrounding Troy is dotted with tumuli—none are particularly gratifying for anyone other than experts. If you're interested in seeing the Ajax or Achilles tumuli, get directions from Mustafa Aşkın at Hisarlık Hotel in Tesvikiye. Caesars and kings have paid their (occasionally unusual) respects to the fallen heroes here: According to Plutarch, Alexander the Great carried a single book with him on his campaigns, a copy of The Iliad with corrections by his tutor, Aristotle. He considered this the definitive guide to military strategy, and himself, as Achilles' descendent, the man to continue the epic deeds of the book. Upon arriving on the Asian shore he emulated the Greeks, sinking a spear into the earth and claiming it as his own, and, finding Achilles' tomb he sprinkled it with oil, stripped naked, and ran around it tossing flowers.

Schliemann's Dream

Heinrich Schliemann was captivated by *The Iliad* as a boy, and vowed to his father that he would one day find Troy. In young adulthood, he demonstrated a unique gift for languages, and could read, write, and speak a language after only six weeks of intense shouting and ranting in the new tongue that drove his neighbors berserk. He also proved a cunning businessman: he had made a fortune by his thirtieth birthday exporting olive oil to Russia, multiplied his wealth by trading goods in the gold fields of Northern California, and eventually built a small trading empire. Then, with characteristic single-mindedness, Schliemann suddenly freed himself of his business responsibilities and dedicated his resources to pursuit of his childhood dream. He at last acquired the Greek language, which he had waited to learn lest he be seduced too early by the search for Troy. He set out on some preliminary digs at Mycenae - where he concluded that the site was, as suspected, the home of the Greek overlord Agamemnon.

Next Schliemann began his search for Troy. He limited his search to the northwest corner of Turkey, where conventional wisdom suggested sites at Alexandria Troas and Pinarbaşı. Because of his faith in literal validity of The Iliad, he employed such simple expedients as trying to run around the sites in the manner of Hector. Finding Hector's run impossible, and precious little else to support the claims of these sites, he turned elsewhere.

Based largely on the pioneering work of Frank Calvert, a British resident of the Çanakkale area – Schliemann concluded that Troy was located at a small town called Hisarlık near the mouth of the Dardanelles. At Hisarlık, he dug deep trenches through the layers and was able to amass an impressive collection–8,700 pieces of gold that included rings, earrings, images, dishes, and a golden goblet weighing 600 grams. Schliemann smuggled the wealth out of the Ottoman Empire and home to Germany, stunning the world with "proof" that he had discovered Troy.

In addition to a gift for tongues, Schliemann had a knack for melodrama and carnival theatrics - he claimed that the wealth from the years of digging was all from King Priam's treasury, and he adorned his wife Sophia with a diadem and, famously, whispered "Helen!" Photos tell us that even in regal jewelry Sophia's face might only have launched a solidly built rowboat or two, but Schliemann captured the world's imagination.

Schliemann fabricated parts of his story and was wrong about which level was the Troy of The Iliad - his Troy II predated Homer's Troy by almost 1,000 years - but he was right about the site. Unfortunately, in his excavations of Troy II, Schliemann destroyed much of the evidence from the shallower levels, including Troy VIIa, which long study and increasingly precise dating has determined must be the Troy of legend. Furthermore, the treasure Schliemann unearthed at the site was scattered during World War II, disappearing in the wreck of Nazi Germany. In 1996, the treasure reappeared at Moscow's Pushkin Museum.

Gallipoli

A spare peninsula juts into the sea on the northern side of the Dardanelles, and it is here that the Allies in World War I felt certain they could claim the high ground and force the famous straits. They failed, and the bloody campaign marked a startling change in nations around the world. This site is particularly moving for the British, French, Australians, New Zealanders and, of course, Turks, whose people died here, but there is plenty of sadness to go around.

History

World War I had settled into a stalemate in the west, when a maverick British First Lord of the Admiralty named Winston Churchill helped conceive an attack that promised to bring the war to a sudden end. The British and French resolved to punch their way through the Dardanelles and assault İstanbul. In a single stroke this would cripple one of Germany's allies, threaten Germany's flank, and open the supply route between the allies and the tottering Russian monarchy. At a time when both sides were tired of "sending men to chew barbed wire" in Europe's trenches, the plan had appeal.

A mighty French and British fleet was ostentatiously assembled in the Aegean. Eighteen British and French battleships and a collection of support vessels steamed into the Dardanelles on March 18, 1915, ran afoul of several mines, plowed into the shelling crossfire between the gauntlet of Turkish fortresses, and sailed right back out again. The fleet commander, British Admiral Draybeck, lost his nerve when six battleships were knocked out - the Bouvet, Ocean, and Irresistible sank outright - even before reaching Çanakkale. Unknown to the allied fleet, the Ottoman defenses were exhausted and out of ammunition and the ships would have fared better had they continued up the straits.

The British did not know this, however, and became determined to clear a path through the straits with a land operation. One month after the naval setback, troops from British Commonwealth nations, including, famously, the ANZACs (Australian and New Zealand Army Corps), landed on the northern side of the long Gallipoli peninsula. The plan was for the forces to dig in, seize the high ground, then descend on the Dardanelles fortresses from behind. There was every reason to expect that the battle would end quickly. The British armada had control of the Aegean and offered protection to its troops along the coast, and the Ottoman military - routed in the 1912-1913 Balkan conflicts by Greek, Bulgarian, and Serbian armies - was expected to fold up in the face of a determined attack.

Ironically, the attackers were bedeviled by failures in the vaunted British officer corps. The British landed their troops at some of the steepest points in the Ottoman defensive line, relying on surprise and speed. However, when the ANZACs poured up the ridges on the first day they were left unsupported and the early opportunities provided by the colonial army were squandered - in some cases the ANZACs deepest penetration of the coming nine months was on the first day. The Ottoman Turks were soundly led by the German Marshall **Liman Von Sanders** and, critically, by an intelligent and courageous Lieutenant Colonel **Mustafa Kemal (Atatürk)**. Kemal, the pivotal figure in contemporary Turkish history, had an uncanny ability to anticipate Allied strategy. From the eve of the battle, when Kemal exceeded his orders by reinforcing the highlands near Anzac Cove, his forces were dug in and prepared every time the ANZACs came flooding over a ridge.

Kemal led the resistance despite being racked with malaria and other illness. He was famously unconcerned for his own well-being, and in the early stages he coolly barked orders and surveyed the battle from atop ridges where the ANZACs could get off pot shots at him. On one fateful occasion his pocket watch stopped a piece of shrapnel from piercing his heart. He was also pitiless with his own troops, most of whom did not have pocket watches in the right places.

On the first day of the Allied attack, determined to control the critical ridge below Çunuk Bair, he barked this famous order: *"I am not ordering you to attack; I am ordering you to die. In the time it takes us to die, other troops and commanders will arrive to take our places. I cannot believe that there is anyone in the troops I command who would not rather die than suffer again the disgrace that fell on us in the Balkans."* The men of the regiment did, indeed, die, but they held out long enough for reinforcements to arrive.

Kemal lends a heroic element to what is otherwise a sad tale of mutual butchery. As was happening in Europe, military tactics had not caught up with technology, and neither entrenched side could sustain an attack against withering machine gun fire and high explosives. Both sides fought with great resolve, hurling themselves into almost certain death. The British commanders (and the ranking ANZACs eager to prove their countrymen's mettle) refused to relent, even after the situation was clearly hopeless, and continued upping the ante with mostly colonial ANZAC troops. By the time the British recognized the futility of further attacks and pulled out in January 1916, there were a total of 500,000 casualties and 100,000 dead, evenly divided between the attackers and defenders.

Almost 20 years later Atatürk, who reluctantly engineered so much of the Gallipoli bloodshed, returned to Anzac Cove and wrote a brief speech that cast the struggle in an appropriate light:

" Those heroes that shed their blood and lost their lives are now lying in the soil of a friendly country, therefore rest in peace. There is no difference between the Johnnies and the Mehmets to us where they lie side by side here in this country of ours. You, the mothers who sent your sons from far away countries wipe away your tears. Your sons are now lying in our bosom and are in peace. After having lost their lives on this land they have become our sons as well."

Arrivals & Departures

By Taxi
Short of using your own car, taxis offer the only way to see the sights on your own. Rates for four hours vary greatly, but hover around $40. The major battle sites feature signs posted by the British War Graves commission.

By Tour
There are some time-tested, professional guiding services that specialize in Gallipoli tours. The guides have good tales to tell, provide transportation, and offer lunch. Both **Hassle Free tours** (based in Çanakkale out of the Anzac House hotel—*Tel. (286) 213-5969, Fax (286) 217-2906, Web: www.anzachouse.com, Email: hasslefree@anzachouse.com*) and **TJ's Tours** (based in Eceabat out of TJ's Place hotel—*Tel. (286) 814-2940, Fax (286) 814-2941, Email: tjs_tours@excite.com*) have five-hour tours departing in the late morning, $18. Both tours are a bit Anzac-centric, neglecting the southern end of the peninsula where the French and British died in droves.

Seeing the Sights
The greatest concentration of memorials begins about six miles from Eceabat - two miles north there is a well-signed road that cuts across the peninsula past the Kabatape Museum and arrives at Brighton Beach, just south of the Allied landing site. The ANZACs landed in the shadow of the steeper ridges just north of here, and if you drive along the coast you arrive at **Anzac Cove** and numerous cemeteries. Like military cemeteries at Normandy or elsewhere the uniformity of the grave markers, like the uniformity of the dead men's youth and fear, leave even the most boisterous visitors hushed.

Backtrack a little to the ridge road and turn inland. As you ascend you pass further cemeteries and monuments. The **Lone Pine monument** commanding a ridge marks, vaguely, the ANZACs side of the battlefield, and all of the terrain between here and Çunuk Bair was hotly contested. There remains a warren of trenches and even the mouths of tunnels - an ambitious idea that was never used with great success - on the ridgeline above Lone Pine. Shrapnel and bones still turn up among the pine needles.

The road winds along the ridge past more monuments, including a new Turkish monument to the 57th Infantry Regiment who received the order to attack and die. Further along is a spur of road that goes a short distance in the direction of the Aegean. This is **The Nek**, a piece of land that the ANZACs tried in vain to take in one of the campaign's decisive battles, and, incidentally, the area immortalized in the *Gallipoli* film. There is another cemetery here, and yet another atop the next hill, **Çunuk Bair**. In the height of summer the ANZACs scaled the surrounding hills despite steady fire and got a foothold here. The Turks mounted an attack of their own and pressed them back, and when the ANZACs effort was finally exhausted almost 30,000 men lay dead here, filling the trenches and soaking the earth. There is a massive Turkish memorial here, and a statue of Atatürk near where his pocketwatch stopped the shrapnel, as well as a collection of restored trenches winding through the pines.

Descend the direction you came from Çunuk Bair to the **Kabatepe Museum** (all days, 50¢). The museum is not particularly edifying, but it further emphasizes the awfulness of the whole affair. You'll find a collection of weapons, shell casings, ribbons, letters, and even some skulls from the battle.

If you head down the peninsula instead of back toward Eceabat, you arrive at another cluster of cemeteries and monuments on the southern tip of the peninsula. This is where the bulk of the French and British troops came ashore, with the expectation that the ANZACs assault in the center of the peninsula would cut the peninsula in two and trap the Ottoman defenders between the two forces. The troops here at **V Beach** and **Cape Hellas** were stopped and pinned down just like the ANZACs inland, however, and their progress was measured only in meters.

This region is dominated by the commanding **Martyrs' Memorial**, Çanakkale Şehitleri Abidesi, at **Morto Bay**. The 150 foot tall structure was erected in gratitude to the Turkish men who gave their lives here, in effect saving İstanbul from the guns of Allied warships and, ultimately, saving Turkey from collapse.

Sports & Recreation

There are swimming beaches at **Kum Koyu**, **Morto Bay**, and just south of **Kabatepe**. Car ferries depart Kabatepe four times daily in summer for Gökçaada, a pleasant, seldom-visited island just outside the Dardanelle Straits.

o t h e r   p l a c e s   o f   i n t e r e s t

Chapter 23

We have presumed to lead you through our favorite spots in Turkey, but Turkey is far too big to fit in any single guidebook. Should you set out in another direction, here is some information that will help.

Afyon

Western Anatolia

Cappadocia doesn't have a monopoly on stone oddities; near **Afyon** you'll find several Phrygian rock cut tombs with impressive facades - echoes of the strangeness at Ünye. Afyon is Turkey's opium capital, but this is good opium, harvested before it turns narcotic.

Other things of interest are the delicious pans of cream that arrive each morning and **Afyonkarahisar**, the Black Fortress of Opium above town. The **ORUÇOĞLU HOTEL**, Bankalar Cad. No. 3, Afyon, *Tel. (272) 212-0120, Fax: (272) 213-1313*, offers decent accommodation.

Ayancik

Black Sea

The accommodations in this small Black Sea town include the **BELEDIYE TESISLERI**, *Tel. (368) 613-1003*, and the **Apart Hotel** (contact Adem Tahtacı, Sinop, *Tel. (368) 261-7900*).

Bolu

Between İstanbul & Ankara
KORU HOTEL, Ömerler Köyü, Bakirli Mevkii P.K. No. 10, Bolu, *Tel. (374) 215-2528, Fax (374) 215-3850*, is on Bolu's old main road (since the building of the new superhighway). This is an appropriately alpine/ Stratford on Avon looking hotel, excellent for spending a few days hiking in the forests and lakes nearby.

Cavdarhisar/Aizanoi

Western Anatolia
Few people make it to **Aizanoi**, where one of the best preserved temples in Asia Minor still stands. The Temple of Zeus here is as complete an Ionic Temple as you are likely to find. It is built above an underground shrine, which was appropriated by Zeus when the temple was built in the second century A.D. Cybele was originally worshipped here.

Kütahya is the nearest major town, 60 kilometers northeast, and if you get a dolmuş to the **Çavdarhisar intersection** the ruins are just a short hike. Dolmuş pass back and forth between Kütahya and Uşak occasionally throughout the day.

Erzurum

Eastern Anatolia
Erzurum has to be considered the official crossroads of east and west, the fortified site where western empires have fought off invasions and launched their own. Erzurum's elevation (6,300 feet) and location in the center of the Anatolian plain subject it to extreme cold in winter, but the town is a fascinating mishmash of beautiful mosques and old fortifications - especially impressive is the **Çifte Minare Medresse**.

Most lodging is near the train station. The **ORAL HOTEL**, Terminal Caddesi No. 3, Erzurum, *Tel. (442) 218-9740, Fax (442) 218-9749*, is a reliable three star hotel, and the area's best is the wintertime **PALANDÖKEN DEDEMAN**, Palandöken Dagı PK 115, Erzurum, *Tel. (442) 316-2414, Fax (442) 316-3607*, 15 kilometers out of town at the country's best ski mountain, **Palandöken**. The most reliable budget option is the **HOTEL POLAT**, Kazım Karabekir Cad. No. 4, *Tel. (442) 218-1623*.

Gerze

Near Sinop

Our notes remark that Gerze would be a "nice place to hide." Some good beaches, particularly the one on the west side of town. The **ERMİŞ OTEL**, *Tel. (368) 718-1540,* in the middle of town is spacious and peaceful, with a largely Turkish crowd taking advantage of the local beaches.

Kastamonu

Interior Black Sea region

If you want to see how a man famed for sacking fortresses built them himself, you should take the time to look around Tamurlane's **Kastamonu fortress** (1403). Tamurlane razed the original structure (and slew those inside) and had a new structure built.

Mersin

Eastern Mediterranean

People come to **Mersin** to make the crossing to The Turkish Republic of Northern Cyprus; you didn't fly from North America to stay here. If you do, however, the best hotel in town is the **MERSIN HILTON SA**, Adnan Menderes Bulv., Mersin, *Tel. (324) 326-5000, Fax (324) 326-5050,* and a good, fairly cheap hotel is the **HOTEL GÖKHAN**, Mersin, *Tel. (324) 231-6256.*

The **tourism information** office is in the city center, Ismet Inönü Bulv. No. 5/2, Liman Girişi, *Tel. (324) 238-3270.* Ferries depart for Northern Cyprus at 10 p.m. on Mondays, Wednesdays and Fridays.

Milas

Near Bodrum

Milas was long the capital of the Caria, but its ruins are in poor condition. The most interesting site is the atop the original settlement, at **Peçin Kale** (Beçin), visible from the road just south of Milas. Peçin Kale is a flat topped mesa that was populated in archaic times owing to its natural defenses. In Herodotus' day there was a substantial Temple of Zeus located here - and he should know, having come from Helicarnas just on the coast.

As Milas grew it shifted onto the valley floor, but Turkish tribes resettling the area again saw the advantages of Peçin Kale, building a fortress there. The mesa is reached from Milas, following the road toward Ören and the Ceramos ruins 48 kilometers distant on the Gökova Bay. Peçin Kale is just five kilometers from Milas.

Ordu

Near Black Sea

The **BELDE HOTEL**, Kirazlimanı Mah., Ordu, *Tel. (452) 214-3987, Fax (452) 214-9338*, Rooms: 64. Double: $50, is one of the best full-service hotels on the Black Sea coast. Ordu is convenient to several beaches (**Çaka** and **Efirli**), but it is not especially close to any historical sights. The ancient name of the settlement is Cotyra, and one the city's distinctive feature is the beautifully restored Greek Orthodox cathedral just to the west of the town center. Xenophon's 10,000 considered stopping here and founding a city, they were so fond of the area. Ordu's Golden Hazelnut Festival each July is good fun.

Sagalassus

Near Egirdir

Alexander passed through **Sagalassus**, too, welcomed by the warlike Pisidians as an ally against the Persians. Excavations by the Catholic University of Louvain have turned up some excellent mosaics and temples on the terraces of Sagalassus. This is one of Turkey's most beautiful ruins.

Samsun

Black Sea

An unappealing transit hub on the Black Sea. This fairly large industrial center has several large hotels, including the four star **BÜYÜK SAMSUN OTEL**, Atatürk Bulvarı No. 629, Samsun, *Tel. (362) 435-8018, Fax (362) 431-0740*, and the cheaper **YAFEYA OTEL**, Cumhuriet Meydanı, *Tel. (362) 431-1531, Fax (362) 431-1135*. The otogar is to the east of town.

If you must spend time here, stop in at the museum. For more on Samsun, contact the **tourism information**, *Tel. (362) 435-2887*.

Side

Near Antalya

Side's impressive ruins add a little cachet to what is otherwise an overburdened holiday town. The town winds out along the former citadel peninsula, and its residents have created a big open air market. In town you'll find good inexpensive accommodations at **PETTINO PANSİYON** just off the main road in town.

Side's **tourism office**, *Tel. (242) 753-1265*, is ridiculously far outside town and occasionally beset by an incredible stench, but you can always call them.

Terme

Black Sea

Presumably near the ancient city of Themistikos on the Thermodon River. **Terme** has a single hotel just a block from the otogar, and is rarely visited. The city's greatest claim to fame is its association with the legendary city of the Amazons, of which there is today no trace. The **Thermodon** (now Terme Çayı) has completely choked the former site of Themistikos with soil, creating a beautiful, lush plain and several small lakes. Beneath the surface of one of these shallow lakes, Akgöl, local residents say buildings have been spotted.

Yalova

Sea of Marmara

The healing powers of **Yalova/Termal's hot springs** are explained thusly in one of the hotel brochures "with its radioactivity, semi-dead cells are reactivated." If you can bear up to that, Termal is a fairly quick ferry ride from İstanbul, and a 15 kilometers dolmuş ride from the Yalova ferry stop.

The **TURBAN YALOVA HOTEL**, Yalova, *Tel. (226) 675-7400, Fax (226) 675-7413*; Double: $58, is recommended, an old standby at the area, just uphill from the extensive, reactivating thermal bath.

Chapter 24

If you're interested in Turkey's history and the many ruins dotting the landscape, you'll probably be interested in some of these books. This bibliography is supplemental to various books we've mentioned throughout the text.

Gibbon, Edward, *The Decline and Fall of the Roman Empire*. London, 1910

Gibbons, Herbert Adams, *The Foundation of the Ottoman Empire*. Oxford, 1916

Plutarch, *Selected Lives and Other Essays*. Roslyn, N.Y., 1951

Guillaume, Alfred, *Islam*. New York, 1967

Procopius, *The Secret History* (trans. G.A. Williamson). London, 1966

Joinville & Villehardouin, Chronicles *of the Crusades*. Baltimore, 1963

Sewell, Brian, *South From Ephesus*. London, 1988

Ostrogorsky, George, *History of the Byzantine State*. New Brunswick, New Jersey, 1969

Miller, John, (Ed.), İstanbul, *Tales of the City*. San Francisco, 1995

Vasiliev, A. A, *History of the Byzantine Empire* (two volumes). Madison, Wisconsin, 1952; Madison, Wisconsin, 1958

Melville, Herman, *A Visit to Europe and the Levant*. New York, 1857

Arrian, *The Campaigns of Alexander* (trans. Aubrey de Selincourt). Middlesex, 1958

Sumner-Boyd, Hilary, and Freely, John, *Strolling Through İstanbul, A Guide to the City*. London, 1972

recommended reading

Harrel, Betsy, *Mini Tours, Book II*. İstanbul, 1978
Durant, Will, *The Story of Civilization*. New York, 1935
Appollonius, *The Voyage of Argo* (trans. E.V. Rieu). Middlesex, 1971
Akurgal, Ekrem, *Ancient Civilizations and Ruins of Turkey*. Ankara, 1983
Stoneman, Richard, *A Traveler's History of Turkey*. New York, 1993
Şen, Ömer, *Sümela: Monastery in the Clouds*. Trabzon, 1994
Freely, John, *The Bosphorous*. İstanbul, 1993
Yazici, Nuri, *Terme Tarihi*. Samsun, 1982
Kranzler, Jerry and Kranzler, Carolyn, *On the Trail of Ulysses*. İstanbul, 1989
Erim, Kenan, *Aphrodisias, City of Venus Aphrodite*. London, 1986
Freely, John, *Classical Turkey*. London, 1990
Sunay, Melisa, *Executives Handbook Turkey Almanac 1996*. İstanbul, 1995
Straube, Hanne, *Türkei*. Hamburg, 1990
Bulutoğlu, Halim, *Hotel Guide 1996*. İstanbul, 1995
Spiro Kostof, *Caves of God*. Oxford Press
Guillaume de Jerphanion, *Une Nouvelle Province de l'Art Byzantin*.

Turkey Guide

index

Things Change!

Phone numbers, prices, addresses, quality of food, etc, all change. If you come across any new information, we'd appreciate hearing from you. No item is too small! Drop us an email note at: Jopenroad@aol.com, or write us at:

Turkey Guide
Open Road Publishing, P.O. Box 284
Cold Spring Harbor, NY 11724

travel notes

travel notes

travel notes

travel notes

travel notes

Open Road Publishing
Catalog of Titles

U.S.
America's Cheap Sleeps, $17.95
America's Most Charming Towns & Villages, $17.95
Arizona Guide, $16.95
Boston Guide, $13.95
California Wine Country Guide, $12.95
California's Best B&Bs, $14.95
Colorado Guide, $17.95
Florida Guide, $16.95
Hawaii Guide, $18.95
Las Vegas Guide, $14.95
New Mexico Guide, $16.95
San Francisco Guide, $16.95
Southern California Guide, $18.95
Spa Guide, $14.95
Texas Guide, $16.95
Utah Guide, $16.95
Vermont Guide, $16.95

Family Travel Guides
Caribbean with Kids, $14.95
Disneyworld with Kids, $14.95
Italy with Kids, $14.95
L.A. with Kids, $14.95
Las Vegas with Kids, $12.95
National Parks with Kids, $14.95
Washington DC with Kids, $14.95

Eating & Drinking on the Open Road
Eating & Drinking in Paris, $9.95
Eating & Drinking in Italy, $9.95
Eating & Drinking in Spain, $9.95
Eating & Drinking in Latin America, $9.95

Middle East/Africa
Egypt Guide, $17.95
Kenya Guide, $18.95

Latin America & Caribbean
Bahamas Guide, $13.95
Belize Guide, $16.95
Bermuda Guide, $14.95
Caribbean Guide, $21.95
Chile Guide, $18.95
Costa Rica Guide, $17.95
Ecuador & Galapagos Islands Guide, $17.95
Guatemala Guide, $18.95
Honduras Guide, $16.95

Europe
Czech & Slovak Republics Guide, $18.95
Greek Islands Guide, $16.95
Holland Guide, $17.95
Ireland Guide, $17.95
Italy Guide, $19.95

To order, send us a check or money order for the price of the book(s) plus $3.00 shipping and handling for domestic orders, to:
Open Road Publishing
PO Box 284
Cold Spring Harbor, NY 11724

London Guide, $14.95
Moscow Guide, $16.95
Paris Guide, $13.95
Prague Guide, $14.95
Rome Guide, $14.95
Scotland Guide, $17.95
Spain Guide, $18.95
Turkey Guide, $19.95

Asia
China Guide, $21.95
Japan Guide, $21.95
Philippines Guide, $18.95
Tahiti & French Polynesia Guide, $18.95
Tokyo Guide, $14.95
Thailand Guide, $18.95